BIHAR PEASANT LIFE

BIHAR PEASANT LIFE,

BEING

A DISCURSIVE CATALOGUE

OF THE

SURROUNDINGS OF THE PEOPLE OF THAT PROVINCE

GEORGE A. GRIERSON, B.C.S., M.A.S.B., M.R.A.S.

GYAN

Published by

Gyan Publishing House
5, Ansari Road
Daryaganj, New Delhi-110002
Phone: 011-47034999, 9811692060
E-mail: books@gyanbooks.com

Distribution Network
gyanbooks.com
India, USA, Canada, UK, Australia, France

ISBN: 978-81-212-8913-9 (PB)
First Published, 1885

2nd Impression 2023

Printed at: Gyan Press, Delhi.

BIHAR PEASANT LIFE

AUTHOR: GEORGE A. GRIERSON

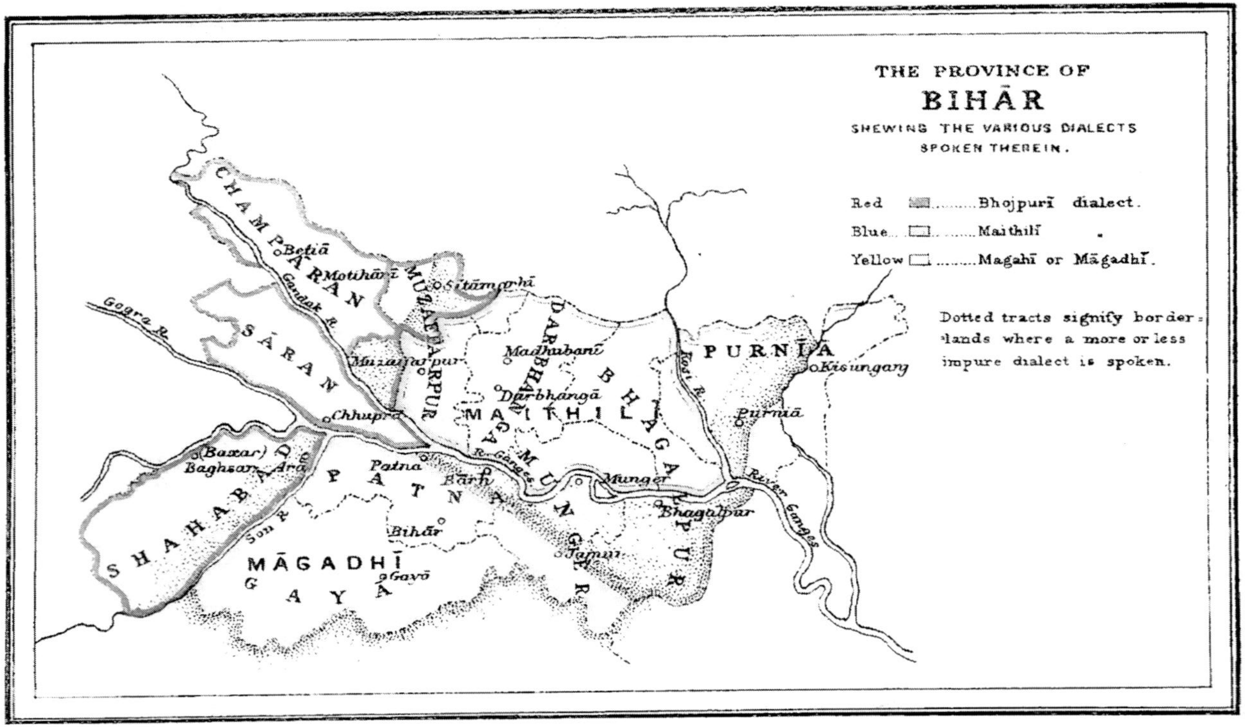
THE PROVINCE OF
BIHĀR
SHEWING THE VARIOUS DIALECTS
SPOKEN THEREIN.
Red ....Bhojpurī dialect.
Blue ....Maithilī
Yellow ....Magahī or Māgadhī.
Dotted tracts signify border-lands where a more or less impure dialect is spoken.
CHAMPARAN
Betiā
Motihārī
Gandak R.
Gogra R.
SĀRAN
Chhuprā
MUZAFFARPUR
Muzaffarpur
Sītāmarhī
DARBHANGA
Madhubanī
Darbhangā
MAITHILĪ
BHAGALPUR
Bhagalpur
PURNIĀ
Kosi R.
Purniā
Kisungang
River Ganges
R. Ganges
Munger
MUNGER
Jamui
PATNA
Patna
Barh
Bihār
MAGAHĪ
MĀGADHĪ
GAYĀ
Gayā
SHAHABAD
(Baxar)
Baghsar
Ārā
Son R.

BIHĀR PEASANT LIFE,

BEING

A DISCURSIVE CATALOGUE

OF THE

SURROUNDINGS OF THE PEOPLE OF THAT PROVINCE,

WITH MANY ILLUSTRATIONS FROM PHOTOGRAPHS TAKEN
BY THE AUTHOR.

Prepared, under Orders of the Government of Bengal,

BY

GEORGE A. GRIERSON, B.C.S., M.A.S.B., M.R.A.S.,

FELLOW OF THE UNIVERSITY OF CALCUTTA: FORMERLY SANSKRIT AND HINDUSTANI
EXHIBITIONER, TRINITY COLLEGE, DUBLIN.

Calcutta:

THE BENGAL SECRETARIAT PRESS.

LONDON: TRÜBNER & Co., 57 & 59, LUDGATE HILL.

1885.

TO

Sir Augustus Rivers Thompson,

K.C.S.I., C.I.E.

IN GRATEFUL ACKNOWLEDGMENT

OF THAT COUNTENANCE AND ASSISTANCE WITHOUT WHICH IT WOULD

NEVER HAVE BEEN WRITTEN,

THIS BOOK

IS DEDICATED

BY

THE AUTHOR.

Bankipore, 4th April 1885.

INTRODUCTION.

WHILE this work professes to be a catalogue of the names used by the Bihār peasant for the things surrounding him in his daily life, yet, in order to relieve the dryness which such a mere list would possess, the writer has attempted to give a description, more or less complete, of that life and of its character and incidents. The book is in fact a discursive catalogue, and it is hoped that it may serve as a solid foundation for more elaborate disquisitions on the Bihār *raiyat* and his surroundings.

Such a work as this is nothing if not accurate, and no ordinary pains have been spared to compass the greatest accuracy possible. Existing treatises on Indian rural life are not always trustworthy; and as it is impossible to tell what is and what is not correct in them, the writer has avoided taking them as the groundwork of his compilation. Every word in this book has been collected from the mouths of the people, and noted on the spot where it was spoken, either by the writer himself or by one of his assistants. When the work began to assume shape, it was carefully compared with every available book of reference, and where discrepancies occurred, they were either reconciled or explained. Finally the proof-sheets have been circulated to all the Bihār districts, and have been again checked on the spot by competent observers, different from the original persons who collected the materials on which the book was founded.*

So far, therefore, as its contents go, this book may claim to be entirely original, and the writer hopes, to a certain degree, accurate. No originality can, however, be claimed for its general system and arrangement. This is closely modelled on Mr. Crooke's "Materials for a Rural and Agricultural Glossary of the North-Western Provinces

* The writer would here tender his thanks to the various district officers of Bihār, who have spared no trouble in having this local checking performed in a satisfactory manner. The amount of new information gained, and of mistakes and misprints corrected through their help, has been very considerable.

and Oudh."* The writer has followed him very closely in the arrangement of his matter, and in many cases has not scrupled to use his very words when they were the most suitable that could be adopted. The vernacular words embodied in this book have in fact been brought together from two sources, viz. the writer's own private researches during the past seven years, checked and supplemented by actual translations of the words given by Mr. Crooke's work made by the writer's assistants once and sometimes twice over in every district of Bihār. It will thus be seen how much the writer is indebted to the latter gentleman. Mr. Crooke's book differed from the present work in being to some extent a compilation from existing dictionaries; and as these were not all of them as accurate as could be wished, it was impossible that it should not contain some mistakes. But as one who has probably worked through it with more minute attention than most people, the writer gladly bears witness to its general accuracy. This may be considered as really wonderful, when the extremely slovenly scholarship of some of the books on which Mr. Crooke had to depend is taken into account.

In the present work every native word is written twice over—once with accuracy in the native character for those who are able to read it, and once in the English character for those who are not acquainted with the Indian vernaculars. This transliteration does not pretend to be scientifically accurate. Such a transliteration with its diacritical dots and dashes would only puzzle those for whom it is intended, viz. those who are ignorant of the language. All that has been attempted for them is to give them a general idea of the correct pronunciation of the words, without professing to tell them the exact pronunciation, which they hardly require, and which would be difficult to do. For these persons all that is necessary is that they should pronounce the vowels as in Italian, and the consonants as in English, and they will then approach sufficiently near to the way in which the natives themselves pronounce the words.† For those who are acquainted with the

---

* Allahabad, 1879. Printed at the North-Western Provinces and Oudh Government Press. The writer would take this opportunity of acknowledging his indebtedness to Mr. Crooke for this really admirable work. Without it the present book could never have been written without an expenditure of labour which few district officials like the writer would have been able to bestow.

† The system of transliteration adopted may be briefly described as the Jonesian system, with every possible diacritical mark omitted. In pursuance of this the cerebral letters are given no dots, and, as nearly every final vowel is long, the long mark has been omitted from final vowels.

vernacular languages, no instructions for pronouncing the words in their vernacular dress are necessary.

In quoting Arabic and Persian words in the Nāgri character, the dots, which are sometimes used to indicate an original z, &c., are omitted, for the reason that the words are given as they are pronounced in Bihār, and that all the dots in the world will not make a Bihāri pronounce a z as other than *j*, or a *ṣād* as other than *s*.

In order to understand the meaning of the words which the writer has used to express locality, it is necessary to explain that, under the name Tirhut, he has included the whole tract which lies between the river Gandak on the west and the river Kosi on the east, and which is bounded on the north by the Nepāl frontier and on the south by the Ganges. He, therefore, indicates under this term not only the districts of Muzaffarpur and Darbhanga, but also North Bhagalpur and North Munger (Monghyr). This was rendered necessary by the language of these latter tracts being practically the same as that of Darbhanga. By North-West Tirhut he means the Sitāmarhi and Sadr subdivisions of Muzaffarpur; by South-West Tirhut, the subdivision of Hājīpur; by North-East Tirhut, the Sadr and Madhubani subdivisions of Darbhanga and the Supaul subdivision of North Bhagalpur; and by South-East Tirhut, the Tājpur subdivision of Darbhanga, North Munger, and the Madaipūra subdivision of North Bhagalpur. By North Bihār he means all Bihār north of the Ganges, and by South Bihār all Bihār south of it. When he speaks of the east or the west, the north-east or the north-west, he means, of course, the east, west, north-east, and north-west respectively of Bihār.

One more word of warning regarding these localities. When the writer says that a word is used in a certain place, he does not mean by implication that it is not used anywhere else. He means simply that the word has been noted by him in such and such a place, and not elsewhere. That it may be used elsewhere is very possible, and any notes on this or kindred topics addressed to the writer, care of the Secretary to the Bengal Government, Revenue and General Departments,* will be gladly welcomed.

Regarding the illustrations, they are all (with one or two small exceptions) lithographed or cut on wood from photographs taken by

---

* The writer would also suggest, as an excellent field for the discussion of the various points noted in this book, a magazine called *Punjāb Notes and Queries*, edited by Captain Temple, Cantonment Magistrate, Amritsar. Although published in and taking its title from the Panjāb, this useful little work deals with the whole of Northern India.

the writer, who is glad to be able to thank Mr. Schaumburg and the students of the Government School of Art, Calcutta, for the excellent pictures they have produced out of what, he must confess, were too often very indifferent photographs. The difficulties experienced by the writer in taking some of these pictures were great. The most ludicrous reports spread through the city concerning his work. The camera of course was looked upon as a fearful engine of destruction, and sometimes half an hour has been wasted in futile diplomacy to persuade an old lady to allow the lens to be pointed at her. Under these circumstances photographs had almost always to be taken by the instantaneous process, which, however certain it may be in the hands of the professional, frequently disappoints the mere amateur. The last photograph the writer took—that of a native house—was spoilt because the grandmother of the family refused to allow any of the children to appear in the picture, her reason being that the Government was building the bridge across the Gandak and wanted children to bury under its foundations. Just, however, as the plate was exposed, one of the little boys determined to immortalize himself, and leaped in front of the lens to the dismay of the female members of his family. He had his wish in appearing in the picture, but he was so near the lens that he covered half of it with his shoulders. On other occasions the writer was believed to be collecting carts and boats for the Egyptian war, or to be counting the wells in the country, because he knew a famine was approaching, and so on *ad infinitum*. However, the pictures were finally taken, and, such as they are, are certainly accurate representations of the originals.

In conclusion the writer has to draw attention to the thoroughness and accuracy with which his assistants, Munshi Dilāwar Ali and Munshi Moti Lāl have done their portion of the work The former has, the writer much regrets to say, died since the above was first written. The latter has been his assistant to the last, and the writer begs to record his high sense of his industry and intelligence, and to recommend his services to the favourable notice of Government.

ADDENDA ET CORRIGENDA.

A good many types have broken in the process of printing. Advantage is taken of this list of errata to add information obtained after the sheets went to press.

These *addenda* and *corrigenda* are printed on one side of the paper only, and can be cut up and pasted in the appropriate places in the book.

Page.	Line.	Section.	For	Read.
3	5	……	समधर … …	सभऽधर.
5	……	27	फह्वोड़ा, फह्वोरा …	फह्वोड़ा, फह्वोरा.
10	16	……	ढकौया … …	ढकिया.
13	……	63	फड़ग्रा … …	फड़ुग्रा.
17	4	……	खान्ना … …	खन्ना.
21	4	……	चावक … …	चाबुक.
22	……	113	वागऽडोर *bāgdor* …	बाग डोर *bāg dor*.
23	7 from bottom.	……	चखबँधऽना … …	चखऽवँधऽना.
24	3	……	बँतऽड़ी … …	बँतऽड़ी.
25	Last line of foot-note.	……	देखे … …	देखे.
26	……	137	थपऽड़ी … …	थपऽरी.
27	2	……	नदोद्द … …	नदोद्द.
34	2	……	खूँटिहऽरो … …	खुँटिहऽरो.
42	……	230	पटॅली … …	पटेली.
44	……	238	सूतै, सुतैऽवनियाँ …	सूतैं, सुतैंऽवनियाँ.
52	5	……	ढँकुहा … …	ढँकुहा.
58	……	317	चबतऽरा … …	चबुतऽरा.
63	5	……	upper screw … …	upper roller.
63	Title of illustration.		CHARKI … …	CHARKHI.

Page.	Line.	Section.	For	Read.
78	15	......	*बक्-स्*	बक-सा.
85	......	404	जवहूरा	जन्हूरा.
87	17	......	झुरस-ा	झुर-सा.
,,	29	......	गरीव	गरीब.
95	1	......	वमाकुबाला	तमाकुवाला.
,,	2	......	तमाकुल-वाला	तमाकुब-वाला.
,,	Last ...	......	*dornsa*	*dorassa.*
96	18	......	*nariyal*	*nariyāl.*
97	Last ...	......	चल-ट	चल-टी.
102	......	510	धौक-नौ	धौक-नी.
103	......	516	सेंहूना	सेंहुना.
105	......	538	चकर सान *chakar sān* ...	चकर-सान *chakarsān.*
108	......	558	*thatherar*	*thathera.*
109	......	567	छुँटा, छुँटी	चूँटा, चूँटी.
110	......	570	नरि	नरी.
111	......	572	निचन्त	निचिन्त.
,,	......	,,	*kumhaïn*	*kumhaiïn.*
,,	......	575	पिँढरौ	पिँढुरी.
112	......	584	अ-रथा	अथ-रा.
113	14	......	झरँ	झरं.
114	......	586	काग-जो	काग-जी.
117	1	......	कोल-सूप *kolsūp* ...	कोल-सुप *kolsup.*
128	......	660	विर-हरा *birhara* ...	बिरह-रा *birahra.*
134	......	713	चढैया	चढ़ैया.
141	......	715	कात्रछल	काँवछल.
145	......	732	चमा *jama*	जामा *jāma.*
152	......	759	घुँघ्र, घुँघ-रु	घुङ्गुर, घुँघ-रू.
153	7	......	डवर-ना	लतर-ना.
154	......	766	*sari*	*sāri.*

Page.	Line.	Section.	For	Read.
154	3 from bottom.	......	बिछलि	बिछली.
155	......	771	किँकिनि, घुघरु, घुँघरु ...	किँकिनी, घुघरू, घुँघरू.
157	2 from bottom.	......	उषड़	उघड़.
159	......	784*a*	*Add*—'A homestead is also called डीँड़ा *dĩnra* or डीँड़ो *dĩnro* in South Bhagalpur.'	
161	......	786	*After* '*goriatta,*' *add*—'or in South Bhagalpur गोरन्टी *goranti.*'	
164	12	......	*For* 'तरि' *read* 'तरी.'	
"	......	794	*Add*—'Soil mixed with coarse gravel is also कँकरोटिया *kankrotiya,* and hard rocky soil पथरौटी *pathrauti* in South Bhagalpur.'	
165	......	797	*Before* 'खिलकट,' *insert* 'कुराव *kurāo*;' and *before* 'and पोह,' *add*—'कनिल *kanil* in South Bhagalpur.'	
166	1	......	*After* '*chānch,*' *add*—'or पह परती *pah parti.*'	
"	......	801	*After* '*melani,*' *add*—'or छिट्टा *chitta,*' and also *add*—'Irrigation from wells is कुँड़िया चास *kunriya chās* in South Bhagalpur.'	
168	......	808	*For* 'होवन्ती *hewti*' *read* 'हेँवन्ती *heñwti.*'	
"	......	812	*For* 'धन कियारी *dhan kiyāri*' *read* 'धनकियारी *dhankiyāri.*'	
"	......	814	*After* 'बीटो *bīto,*' *add*—'or बेरो *bero.*'	
169	......	"	*After* '*laugāchhi,*' *add*—'or नौगाछी *naugāchhi.*'	
"	......	815	*Add*,—'Land producing brushwood is झाँटी *jhānti* in South Bhagalpur.'	
171	......	818	*After* '*phāran,*' *add*—'and in South Bhagalpur हर समौध *har samaudh.*'	
173	......	827	*After* '*dahina,*' *add*—'and in South Bhagalpur, उखड़ हाल *ukhar hāl.*'	
...	......	828	*For* '*bhaunrīya*' *read* '*bhaunriya,*' and *add*—'in South Bhagalpur मण्डो जोत *mando jot* or चौमण्डी *chaumandi.*' *For* 'ऊनाडेढ़ी' *read* 'ऊना डेढ़ी,' and *after* 'other names current are,' *add*—'लमन्ती *lamti* in South Bhagalpur.'	

Page.	Line.	Section.	
174	......	830	*For* 'हँगाप्रब' *read* 'हेँगाप्रब.'
„	Last ...	......	*For* 'झरन्की वाला' *read* 'झरन्की बाला.'
176	......	837	*For* 'साँझ ले' *read* 'साँझले,' and *for* 'हँझिया' *read* 'सँझिया.'
177	2	......	*After* '*somāta,*' *add*—'or हर समौध *har samaudh.*'
„	......	842	*Add*—'A ploughman who works for advancces is साम्रोँख *saonkh* in South Bhagalpur.'
179	......	848	*Add*—'Manure is also called हूरा *hūra* in South Bhagalpur.'
180	......	850	*Add*—'Heavily-manured land is also said to bc पटाएल *patāēl* north of the Ganges.'
182	......	856	*Add*—'Barren seeds are called कुब्बी *kubbi* in South Bhagalpur.'
183	3	......	*For* 'बावर' *read* 'बावग.'
„	......	859	*After* '*barua,*' *add*—'and in South Bhagalpur कुब्बी *kubbi.*'
184	......	862	*After* '*benga,*' *add*—'and in South Bhagalpur बिचरा *bichra* or बिहन्तर *bihantar*.
			For 'बीहन्नार' *read* 'बिहन्नार.'
„	......	864	*Add*—'The bamboo on which the seedlings are carried is called धरङ्गी *dharangi* in South Bhagalpur.'
185	......	866	*Add*—'Hoeing is called केलौनी *kelauni* or कमौनी *kamauni* in South Bhagalpur.'
„	......	867	*After* '*kelauni,*' *add*—'or कमौनी *kamauni.*'
186	......	871	*For* 'चकन्लेदा' *read* 'चकन्लेदार.'
187	......	873	*Add*—'Cane-cutting is पतौर पारब *pataur pārab* in South Bhagalpur.'
„	......	875	*After* '*agra,*' *add*—'or अलगा *alga.*'
188	1	......	*For* '*jhārjharāēl*' *read* '*jharjharāēl.*'
192	......	887	*Add*—'Treading grain is दमाही *damāhi* in South Bhagalpur.'

Page.	Line.	Section.	
192	......	888	*Add*—'The first treading out of the grain is also called खूआ *khūa* or खोआ *khoa*, and the second treading तरझार *tarjhār* in South Bhagalpur.'
,,	3 from bottom.	......	*For* 'दोगहा *dogha*' *read* 'दोगहा *dogaha*.'
193	......	891	*After* 'खूआ *khūa*,' *add*—'or खोआ *khoa* or पौर *paur*.'
194	......	894	*Add*—'Loose straw that has been threshed is मीड़ा *mīra* in South Bhagalpur.' *After* '*newāri*,' *add*—'or in South Bhagalpur गभौरी *gabhauri*.'
,,	......	895	*Add*—'घोरान *ghoran* is also used in South Bhagalpur.'
195	......	896	*After* '*thathero*,' *add*—'When applied to *janera* (*holcus sorghum*).'
196	......	902	*After* '*kurtāli*,' *add*—'when between tenant and subtenant.'
198	......	911	*For* 'खूद काश्त *khūd kāsht*' *read* 'खुद्‌काश्त *khudkāsht*.'
201	......	915	*Add*—'A man irrigating is in South Bhagalpur लरवाहा *larwāha*.'
203	......	918	*After* '*dhurka*,' *add*—'or उपटा *upta*.'
204	......	922	*Add*—'The spring is in South Bhagalpur also भूर *bhūr* or सोआ *soa*.'
208	......	939	*Add*—The 'wooden framework is called जलाला *jalāla* in South Bhagalpur.'
214	5	......	*For* 'सुआल' *read* 'सुआ.'
,,	......	958	*For* 'टूंड़ा' *read* 'टूँड़ा.'
224	14	......	*For* 'खौँरचा' *read* 'खोरचा.'
226	8 from bottom.	......	*For* 'मल' *read* 'मेब.'
228	4	......	*For* 'रहरेंठा' *read* 'रहरेठा.'
,,	6	......	*For* 'ढेंढी' *read* 'ढेँढी.'
230	......	1001	*For* 'पटाएब' *read* 'पटाएब.'
247	10	......	*For* '1464' *read* '1458.'

Page.	Line.	Section.	
248	......	1050	*For* 'भीट *bhīt*' *read* 'भीठ *bhīth*.'
253	5 from bottom.	......	*For* 'गलन्हयट्टा' *read* 'गोलन्हयट्टा.'
273	......	......	In last column, *for* 'असन्नी' *read* 'पसन्नी.'
274	10 from bottom.	......	*For* 'अवाव' *read* 'आवव.'
280	16 from bottom.	......	*For* 'बरसे' *read* 'बरसै.'
"	4 from bottom.	......	*For* 'आमवास' *read* 'अमावस.'
281	3	......	*For* 'neede' *read* 'need.'
290	......	1110	*For* 'ढेर' *read* 'छेर.'
292	......	1117	*For* 'रन्ककट' *read* 'करन्कट.'
299	......	1147	*For* 'चद्ङ्गर' *read* 'उदङ्गर.'
300	......	1151	*After* '*kās charāï*,' *add*—'काह चराइ *kāh charāï*.'
310	13	......	*For* 'मड़भाटी' *read* 'मड़ुभाटी.'
"	15	......	*For* 'यसैन' *read* 'सैयन.'
"	17	......	*For* 'चोरा' *read* 'चारो.'
316	10 from bottom.	......	*For* 'टकही *takahi*' *read* 'टकन्ही *takhi*.'
318	12 from bottom.	......	*For* 'कोयाली *keyāli*' *read* 'कोआली *keāli*.'
322	......	1209*b*	*After* 'rent-free,' *add*—'or revenue-free.'
323	8 from bottom.	......	*For* '1487' *read* '1482.'
330	2	......	*For* 'money rents are always assessed,' *read* 'extra money rents are assessed.'
333	8 from bottom.	......	*For* 'क्काउनी' *read* 'क्काउनि.'
337	7	......	*For* 'लोदूया' *read* 'लोड़या.'
357	4 from bottom.	......	*For* 'मेंहराग्ह' *read* 'मेंहन्राह.'
359	......	1285	*For* 'बरेखि' *read* 'बरेखी.'
360	......	1288	*For* 'क्का' *read* 'कँका.'

Page	Line.	Section.	
366	......	1323	*Add at end of section*—'and in West Tirhut लठङ्गर *lathangar*.'
369	......	1338	*Add at end of section*—'and in West Tirhut खिरखियौनी *khirkhiyauni*.'
372	......	1349	*Add*—'The ceremony of cutting the nails is called in West Tirhut नौह छिल्ली *nauh chhilli*.'
389	4 from bottom.	......	*For* 'दोनी *doni*' *read* 'दौँनी *donni*.'
391	3 from bottom.	......	*For* '*nagra*' *read* '*nagar*.'
412	......	1461	*For* 'धारनिक' *read* 'धारनिक.'
	APPENDIX.		
2	......	No. 2	*For* 'खसरा' *read* 'खसरा.'
,,	......	No. 2*a*	*For* 'गफअञ्जूद' *read* 'गञ्ज अफञ्जूद.'
14	......	14	*For* '*am*' *read* '*ām*.'
		15	*For* 'बद्दा' *read* 'बद्दा.'

CONTENTS.

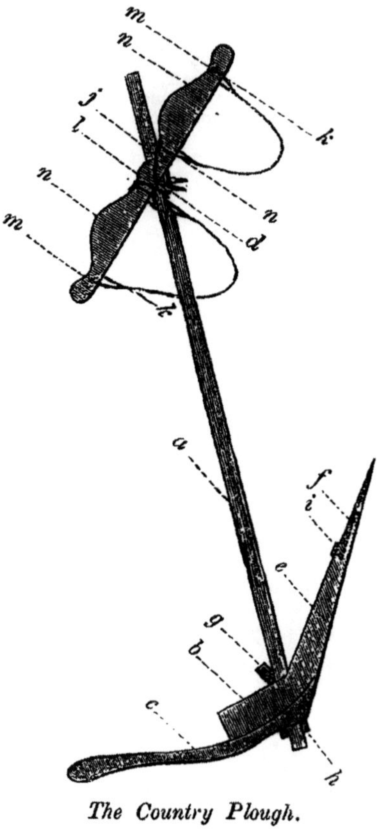

The Country Plough.

(NOTE.—The front portion of the body is given in section, so as to show the position of the share.)

DIVISION I.

IMPLEMENTS AND APPLIANCES

USED IN

AGRICULTURE AND RURAL MANUFACTURES.

SUBDIVISION I.

IMPLEMENTS USED IN PREPARING LAND FOR CULTIVATION.

CHAPTER I.—THE PLOUGH.

1. The ordinary country plough is generally known as हर *har.* Sometimes the Hindi form of the word, हल *hal,* is used. In Gaya the word लाँगल *lāngal* is also used.

2. खिनौरी *khinauri* is used for an old or worn plough. In the South-East and in North-West Tirhut this is ठेँठी *thenthi,* and generally over North-East and South Tirhut ठेँठा *thentha.* In Shahabad it is खुटहन्रा *khutahra.* A new plough is नवꣵठा *nawtha* or नौठा *nautha* to the west, नवꣵघर *nawghar* in Champāran, and लवꣵठा *lawtha* generally over North-East and South Tirhut.

3. In West Bihār and South Bhagalpur साँगठ *sānga,* and in South Munger साँगह *sāngah,* mean the plough and all its appurtenances, as in the sentence साँगठ (or हर साँगठ) लेने आव बहियार *sānga* (or *har sānga*) *lene āw bahiyār,*—bring the plough, &c., to the field.

4. The various parts of the common plough are as follows :—

5. *The beam* (*a*).—North of the Ganges this is हरिस *haris,* and so also in Shahabad. In East Tirhut it is also called हरसी *harīs.* In Patna, Gaya, and South Munger it is साँढ़ *sānrh.* In South Bhagalpur it is ईस *īs.* हरिस *haris* is, however, understood more or less everywhere.

6. *The body* (*b*).—This is everywhere हर *har*.

7. *The handle or stilt* (*c*).—In Shahabad and north of the Ganges this is परिहथ *parihath;* in the eastern portion of the latter tract it is also लागन *lāgan*. लगन्ना *lagnā* is used in South Munger, Patna, and Gaya, and नाँगन्नो *nāngno* in South Bhagalpur. In South-Western Shahabad परिहत *parihat* is used. The knob at the end of the body near the handle is in Patna चँदन्वा *chandwa*, in Gaya चाँन्दी *chāndi*, north of the Ganges and in Shahabad मूठ *mūth* (or in the south-west of the district चँदुली *chanduli*), and in the south-east मुठिया *muthiya*. In South Bhagalpur मकन्री *makri* is a piece used for mending it when broken. The first, second, and fourth names are only used if it is a separate piece of wood.

8. *The notches on the beam* (*d*), by which the share is raised or lowered.—In Sāran खेढ़ा *kherha*, in Gaya खेँढ़ी *khenrhi*, and in Shahabad खेढ़ी *kherhi*. In Patna they are खेहा *kheha*, in Champāran खाता *khāta*, and throughout Tirhut खाढ़ी *khārhi*. In South-East Tirhut it is also खड़न्हा *kharha*, and in South-East Bihār खोँढ़ा *khonrha* or काढ़ *kārh*.

9. *The sole* (*e*), in which the share is fixed.—

In West Bihār it is टोर *tor* or टोरा *tōra*. In East Bihār it is नास *nās* or नासा *nāsa*.

North of the Ganges the thicker end of the sole is called माँथ *mānth* or माँथा *māntha*.

10. *The share* (*f*).—Everywhere फार *phār*. In North-East Tirhut also फारा *phāra* or फाला *phāla*, and in South-East Tirhut also लोहामा *lohāma*.

11. *The wedge fixing the beam to the body* (*g*).—North of the Ganges and in Shahabad and South Munger this is पाट *pāt*. Variants are पट्टा *patta* (Gaya), पाटा *pāta* (South Tirhut and Patna), and पाटो *pāto* (South Bhagalpur).

A second wedge is sometimes added, which is known as चैली *chaili* everywhere north of the Ganges and in Gaya and the south-west, and also as चेलन्खी *chelkhi* in South-East Tirhut. In East Tirhut it is also called चेरी *cheri*. Another name is पाचड़ *pāchar* (in North-East Tirhut and Shahabad), or पचन्ड़ी *pachri* everywhere south of the Ganges. In South Bhagalpur it is called उपर पाटो *upar pāto*.

12. *The peg* (*h*) passing through the shaft at the end, to prevent the body coming off.—This is बराइन *barāin* generally, or बरैन *barain*

in Champāran and Tirhut; the latter is also used in South Munger. Other forms are बरेन *baren* in North-East Tirhut, बरऽहन *barhan* in Sāran, बरैनी *baraini* in Patna, and बरन *baran* in Shahabad. Other names are सभ धरिया *sabh dhariya*, सत धरिया *sat dhariya*, in Patna, and सभधर *sabhdhar* in Gaya, because it holds the whole plough together. Also तरैलऽ *taraila* in South Bhagalpur, तरैली *taraili* in South-West Shahabad, and हुमऽना *humna* in Patna.*

13. *The iron clamp* (*i*) for preventing the share falling off.—करुआर *karuār* or करुआरा *karuāra* everywhere to the west. A variant is करुआरी *karuāri* (Patna, Champāran, and West Tirhut). In South-West Shahabad it is also called खूरा *khūra*. In Patna it is also called जोँका *jonka*, and the same name is current all over Bihār. जोँकी *jonki* and चोभी *chobhi* are also used in South-East Tirhut. In North-East Tirhut a wedge is also used for the same purpose, and is called गासी *gāsi*.

14. *The yoke.*—North of the Ganges always पालो *pālo*; so also in Patna, Gaya, and South Munger, with a variant पालऽ *pāla* in South Bhagalpur. In Shahabad and Gaya the word is generally जुआठ *juāth*, which is also sometimes used in Sāran and the east. Sometimes it is made up of two bars. The upper bar then is considered the yoke proper, and is hence usually called the जुआठ *juāth*. The lower bar is generally तरऽसैला *tarsaila*.

This double-bar arrangement is not commonly found in the plough yoke. It is more usually met with in the yoke for well irrigation (मोट *mot*); so also the two following pins. As a general rule पालो *pālo* or जुआठ *juāth* (according to locality) may be safely used for the single-bar plough-yoke and for the double-bar irrigation yoke, and जूआ *jūa* for the single-bar cart-yoke. See § 938.

15. *The outer pins,* which join the two bars of the yoke, are सैला *saila* or समैल *samail* to the west and कनैल *kanail* to the east. They are also कनऽकिल्ली *kankilli* in South Bhagalpur.

16. *The inner pins* are समैल *samail* or (Patna and the south-east) समैला *samaila* and (Gaya) समैया *samaiya*.

17. *The leather thongs* (*j*), which attach the yoke to the beam of the plough.—These are from Patna to the east of the South Gangetic tract, and in Champāran, नारन *nāran*, with a variant लरऽनी *larni* in

---

* About हुमऽना *humna* there is a story of a Jolha (the proverbial fool of Bihār stories) who found a *humna* on the road and cried out in his foolishness पाओँ हर के हुमऽना, खेतीकरब बनाय *pāon har ke humna, kheti karab banāy*,—I have found the rear peg of a plough, I'll turn a farmer at once.

North-West and South-East Tirhut, and optionally लारन *lāran* in South-East Bihār. नाधा *nādha* and नरैली *naraili* are used in Shahabad, and variants of the former word occur in लदन्धा *ladha* (South-East Tirhut), लैधा *laidha* or लाधा *lādha* (North-East Tirhut), and हर लधी *har ladhi* or हर नाधा *har nādha* over South Tirhut generally. नाधा *nādha* is also used in Gaya. हर ना धा *har nādha* in Sāran is only used when they are of string. When they are of leather, in that district they are called दुआली *duāli*. South Bhagalpur has डोँड़ा *donra* or लेधा *ledha*.

18. *The ropes* (*k*) which go round the bullocks' necks.—These are everywhere except in the extreme west जोती *jōti*. In the extreme west (Sāran, Champāran, and Western Shahabad) the masculine form, जोता *jōta*, is the usual one. In North-East Tirhut they are also समेल *samel* or समैल *samail*, and in South Bhagalpur फाँसा *phānsa*.

19. *The projecting knob* (*l*) in the middle of the upper part of the yoke.—Round this the thongs which fasten the yoke to the beam are fixed. This is everywhere महादेवा *mahādewa*. Variants are महादेओ *mahādeo* (Patna and Gaya) and महन्दवा *mahdawa* (South Munger). In South Bhagalpur it is मँझवारा *manjhwāra*.

20. *The notches* (*m*) near each end of the yoke.—To these the ropes which go round the bullocks' necks are fixed. These are खाँड़ी *khānri* in Patna, with variants खाढ़ी *khārhi* in South-East Tirhut and खेढ़ी *kherhi* to the west. South-West Shahabad has खड्ढी *khaddhi*. In Gaya the word used is कनौसी *kanausi*, and in South Bhagalpur खाता *khāta*, while सिमल *simal* or नकटी *nakti* are optional names in South-East Tirhut.

21. *The leaf of the yoke* (*n*).—This is पत्ता *patta*, पल्ला *palla*, or (in South Munger) पलई *palaī* and (in Sāran) पाता *pāta*.

22. *The trough* in which the share lies when fixed in the body is खोल *khol*, or in South Bhagalpur खोली *kholi*.

23. *The bamboo whip* with which the bullocks are driven is पैना *paina*, and its *lash* is छिटि *chhiti* in North-East Tirhut. Other names will be found in § 98 and ff.

24. *A drill plough.*—This is generally टार *tār*, with variants in South-East Tirhut टाँड़ी *tānri* and टोर *tor* in South Munger. The share is टरसूई *tarsūī*. खिल्ला *khilla* is the nail which fastens the share to the body. The bamboo pipe is in West Bihār बाँसा *bānsa*, also sometimes बन्सा *bansa* in Shahabad. In East Bihār this is generally चोँगा *chonga*, except in South Munger, where it is हर चाँड़ी *har chānri*.

The cup at the top, into which the grain is poured, is in West Bihār माला *māla* or मलन्वा *malwa.* In East Bihār it is पैला *paila* (sometimes spelt पइला *païla* or पएला *paëla*) or माली *māli.* In South Munger it is also उखन्री *ukhri*, and in Patna अकन्री *akri.*

25. ***The sharpening of a ploughshare*** is called as follows in the various districts:—

Shahabad: धार पिटावल *dhār pitāwal*; or in the south west of the district धार फरन्गावल *dhār phargāwal.*

Patna: धार असन्राएब *dhār asräëb.*

Gaya: असार *asār.*

South Munger and South Bhagalpur: धार पजाव *dhār pajāw* or असार *asār.*

North of the Ganges generally: धार पिटावल *dhār pitāwal.*

Also, North-West Tirhut and Sāran: धार पिजावल *dhār pijāwal.*

North-East Tirhut: धार बनाएब *dhār banäëb.*

South-East Tirhut: फार करा लाएब *phār korā läëb.*

26. When a man wishes to ***plough deep*** he harnesses the yoke higher up the beam in the notches (*d*). This is called in West Bihār औगार *augār.* In North-West Tirhut it is called लगार *lagār*, and in the rest of Tirhut तरख *tarakh.* In South-West Shahabad it is called अवाए *awäë*, in South Munger ठाढ़ा *thārha*, and in South Bhagalpur ठाढ़ *thārh.* Light ploughing is done in the converse way, and is known everywhere as सेव *sev*, or in North-East Tirhut सेब *seb.*

CHAPTER II.—MATTOCKS AND SPADES.

27. A large mattock is in West Bihār and Gaya फौरा *phaura.* Variants are फहोड़ा *phahora* (Patna and Gaya), फहोरा *phahora* (South Munger), फओरा *phaöra* (Patna and Gaya), and फउरा *phahura* or फरुहा *pharuha* in Shahabad. In South-West Shahabad it is फरन्सा *pharsa.* In Tirhut it is कुदार *kudār*, and in South Bhagalpur and South Mungēr कोदार *kodār.* Another name current in Gaya is झाम *jhām* or झामा *jhāma.* In the same district आभी *ābhi* is a heavy kind of wooden spade tipped with iron for hard soils, and खुरन्नी *khurni* or खुदन्नी *khudni* is a kind of spade.

28. A mattock with a narrower blade is कुदारी *kudāri*, कोदारि *kodāri*, or कोदारी *kodārī.* South of the Ganges it is also कुदाली *kudāli.*

कुदाल *kudāl* and कुदार *kudār* are often used to signify also the smaller variety. In South Bhagalpur it is ठेँठी कोदार *thenthi kodār*.

29. The handle is बेँट *bent*, and the upper end of it, which projects beyond the socket, हूरा *hūra* or हूर *hūr*, or (in South-West Tirhut) मूठा *mūtha*. Other names for this end are एड़ा *era* or आड़ानी *ārāni*, and in South Bhagalpur पाटऽ *pāta*. The ring or socket in the blade, to which the handle is fixed, is पास *pās* or पासा *pāsa* (or in South Bhagalpur पासो *pāso*). In South-West Shahabad it is पँवाँरी *pamwānri*, and in South Munger (optionally) पसाटा *pasāta*. The curved part of the blade is in Sāran and Patna फरी *phari*. Elsewhere, north of the Ganges and in South Munger, फरकी *pharki*. In Patna and South Munger it is also called फल *phal*, in South Bhagalpur फरो *pharo*, and in Gaya फारी *phāri*. In Shahabad it is धार *dhār*, and in the south-west of the district डम्फ *damph*. The place where the ring and the blade meet is कण्ठी *kanthi* in Patna and Gaya, नहीं *nahīn* in Shahabad, सन *san* or कण्ठ *kanth* in South Bhagalpur, and सुन *sun* in South Munger. In Sāran the part of the handle which is grasped is मूठ *mūth*, and the corners काना *kāna*. A new mattock is नवघर *naughar*, and a worn one ठेँठी *thenthi*.

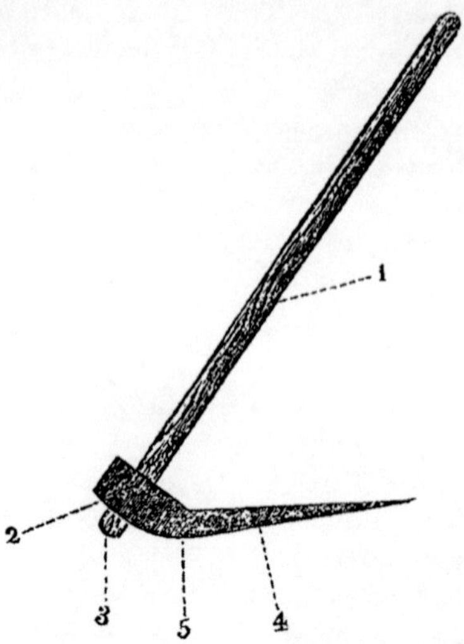

1. *Bent* (handle).
2. *Pāsa* (socket).
3. *Hūra*.
4. *Phari* (blade).
5. *Kanthi* (neck).

The Mattock (*Phaura or Kodār*).

CHAPTER III.—THE HARROW.

30. This is usually the *flat plank*, with (in the east) a grove along the underside. It is dragged along the ground to break the clods after ploughing, while a man stands on it to give weight. In West Bihār and in South-East Tirhut it is called हेँगा *henga*, and in East Bihār more usually चौँकी *chaunki* or चौकी *chauki*. In Patna it is also called सिलवे *silwe*, पटवे *patwe*, or लगावरी *lagāwri*.

31. When drawn by one pair of oxen—one ox at each end—it is called हेँगी *hengi* in Champāran, दुगोड़ी *dugoṛi* in Tirhut, एक हरा *ek hara* in South Bhagalpur, and दोबरदा *dobarda* elsewhere. When drawn by two pair of oxen—one pair at each end—it is called in North-East Tirhut चौगोड़ा *chaugora*, in the rest of Tirhut चरगोरी *chargori*, दो हरा *do hara* in South Bhagalpur, and elsewhere चौबरदा *chaubarda*.

32. The pegs to which the hauling ropes are fastened are generally खूँटी *khūnti*. In Shahabad they are also called सँडु *sanrusa*, and in the south-west of the district गुल्ली *gulli*. In Gaya they are बौँखा *baunkha*, in Patna and South Munger बहखा *bahkha*, and in South Bhagalpur अंकोरा *ankora*.

33. The hauling ropes are, north of the Ganges generally, and in West Shahabad, बरही *barhi*. North of the Ganges they are also हेँगही *hengahi*. In Shahabad chains used for the purpose are सीँकर *sīnkar*, and in Patna and Gaya सीकर *sīkar* when used with four bullocks abreast. These words are also used in North Tirhut. In Patna they are also चौक नारन *chauk nāran* when of rope. In South-East Tirhut they are also called मरिखर *marikhar*, and in South Bhagalpur जगडोरी *jagdori*. In South Munger they are सीकर *sīkar* when made of chain, and मरिखर *marikhar* when made of rope, and मझौतर *majhautar* is the rope or leather strap joining the two yokes when four bullocks are used. So also in Patna and Gaya. The last word is मझोतर *majhotar* in East Tirhut. In East Tirhut, when made of leather they are called मैरन *mairan* or मेढ़न *merhan*, and when made of rope बरहा *barha* or बरही *barhi*. Sometimes long strips of bamboo are made to serve as hauling ropes. They are then called in South Munger कुडण्डी *kudandi*, in South Bhagalpur बसजोती *bansjoti*, and elsewhere अरौआ *araua*.

34. The channel in the lower part of the plank to break the clods is in South Bhagalpur घघरी *ghaghri* or घाई *ghāï*, in South Munger खढ़ा *khadha*, and elsewhere खड्डा *khaddha*. The channel is generally the hollow of the stem of the talipot palm, the harrow being composed of the split half of a log of that tree.

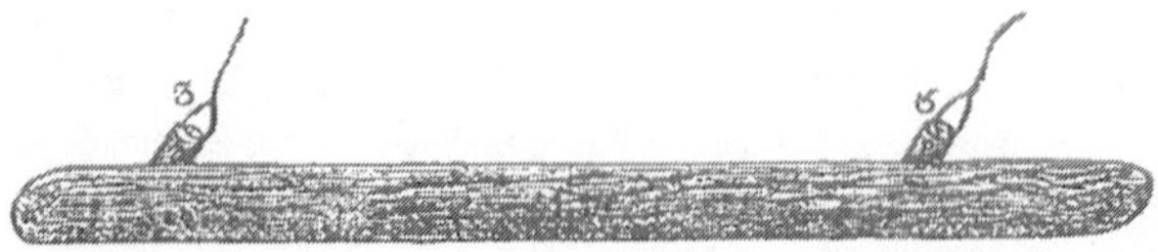

1. *Henga* (harrow). 2. *Khūnti* (pegs). 3. *Barhi* (ropes).

The Harrow (*Henga or Chauki*).

35. The *cylindrical roller* is rarely used in the field. It is called everywhere by a corruption of its English name, viz. रोल *rol.* The block itself is called पल्ला *palla* (Patna), कड़ी *kari* (Gaya), एकठा *ektha* in Shahabad, and लकड़ी *lakri* in South-West Shahabad. Elsewhere it is simply चौँकी *chaunki* or चौकी *chauki.*

36. Sometimes the harrow is made of two parallel planks joined together. This is called हेँगा *henga* or चौकी *chauki,* &c., as above.

CHAPTER IV.—RAKES USED IN FIELD WORK.

37. Rakes are seldom used. Sometimes a bundle of thorns is dragged over a field to soften the surface when it has been baked hard by the sun after rain or irrigation. This has no special name. In parts of Tirhut the कण्टा *kanta* or खखोर्नी *khakhorni* is a sort of rake or harrow worked by oxen to loosen the soil and extricate weeds from a crop of young rice. A पचफरिया *pachphariya* or (in Sāran) गेल्ह्नी *gelhni* is a kind of plough with five shares used in indigo factories.

CHAPTER V.—PICKAXES, PITCHFORKS, &c.

38. *A pickaxe.*—North of the Ganges this is गैँता *gainta,* south of the Ganges it is गैँता *gainta* or गैँती *gainti.* In South Bhagalpur it is गैँचा *gaincha,* and in South Munger गाता *gāta.*

39. The *dredger,* used in well-sinking, has various names. In Shahabad, Sāran, and South Tirhut it is चल्ना *chalna,* and in Champāran

A Collection of Baskets.

1. Chhainta.	made of	split bamboo.
2. Ditto	,,	ditto, woven up with tāl fibre.
3. Oriya	,,	split bamboo.
4. Daura	,,	ditto
5. Dauri	,,	ditto, strengthened with tāl leaves.
6. Two ditto	,,	split bamboo.
7. Dagra		ditto, edge sewn with rattan.
8. Dagri.	made of	split bamboo, edge sewn with tāl leaves.
9. Dāla	,,	split bamboo.
10. Tokri	,,	tāl slips and bamboo.
11. Tāp	,,	bamboo slips.
12. Sikshuti	,,	munj grass.
13. Phuldāli	,,	flower-basket.

Printed by Abdool Rohim Gost, School of Art Calcutta.

तरच्छी *tarchhi.* In North-East Tirhut it is छीटी *chhīti,* कठुली *kathuli,* or पथिया *pathiya.* छीटी *chhīti* is also used in South-East Tirhut, where also occur कठ्वत *kathwat* and (also in Shahabad) तगाड़ी *tagāri.* Elsewhere south of the Ganges it is गैंता *gainta* or खन्ती *khanti,* and in South Munger छीटा *chhīta.*

40. The ***pointed iron spear*** for tapping the well-spring also has various names, viz. खुण्टा *khunta* north of the Ganges generally, गजाड़ा *gajāra* in Sāran, and गोभनी *gobhni* in South-West Tirhut. In Gaya it is खोभना *khobhna,* and in Shahabad खोभन *khobhan,* but in the south-west of the latter district it is लरहा *larha.* In South Munger it is देभन *debhan,* and in South Bhagalpur it is गजाड़ा *gajāra* or खन्ती *khanti.*

41. The ***hooked stick*** for pulling down fruit from trees is generally लग्गा *lagga* or लग्गी *laggi.* The hook of this is अँकुसी *ankusi* or (in South Bhagalpur) कानी *kāni.* The long pole with a small net at the end to catch the fruit as it falls is झोला *jhola,* खोंची *khonchi,* or (in Sāran) झोरा *jhora.* Another optional name in South Munger is जलखरी *jalkhari.*

The short stick thrown up into fruit-trees to bring down fruit is झटठा *jhatha,* and also (in Sāran) लगूसी *lagūsi.*

SUBDIVISION II.

IMPLEMENTS USED IN SOWING, WEEDING, AND IRRIGATION.

CHAPTER I.—BASKETS.

42. Baskets are generally woven of bamboo slips or twigs. Unless otherwise stated, this may be assumed of all the following.

43. Baskets used specially by the sower are called generally ओड़ा *ora,* ओड़ी *ori,* or ओड़िया *oriya* (sometimes made partly with the fibre of the leaves of the tāl palm); also we meet, to the west, छैंटी *chhainti,* and to the east छीटा *chhīta* (a large one), छीटी *chhītī* (a small one), or दौरी *dauri.* South of the Ganges they are also called in Patna बट्टा *battā,* (also in Shahabad) दौरा *daura,* or दौरी *dauri* (sometimes made of the culm of the *sik* grass, *andropogon muricatum*), in Gaya (also in North-

East Tirhut) पथिया *pathiya* (also used for feeding cattle), and in South Munger खँचिया *khanchiya*. The only difference amongst all these is that in the case of the दौरा *daura* and दौरी *dauri* the bottom is woven of bamboo slips, like a mat.

44. There are likewise several other kinds of baskets, used indiscriminately for this and other domestic and agricultural purposes. Thus, small straw grain-baskets are चँगेली *changeli* or चँगेरी *changeri*, and sometimes डाली *dāli* or डलिया *daliya*, especially towards the east. In Patna and South Munger they are called बटरी *batri*. Another very similar basket (but still smaller) is called very generally मौनी *maunni* or मौनिया *mauniya*, also बट्टा *batta* in Patna, Gaya, and South Munger, and फुलुकी *phuluki* in East Tirhut. A large open basket made of split twigs of bamboo generally woven up with the fibre of the leaves of the tāl palm is called टोकड़ा *tokra*, ढाका *dhākā*, ढाकी *dhāki*, ओड़ा *ora*, or छैंटा *chainta*. A smaller variety is called गाँजा *gānja*, टोकड़ी *tokri*, ढकीया *dhakiya*. When the bottom is very finely woven, so as even to hold water, it is called ओड़ैसा *oraisa*. The धामा *dhāma* is an open basket made of rattan. The खैंचा *khaincha* or खाँचा *khāncha* is a large coarse basket made of twigs of *cytisus cajan* (*rahar*) or tamarisk (*jhāü*). South of the Ganges we also find डेली *deli*. A smaller basket of the same kind is known as खाँची *khānchi* (also खाँझी *khānjhi* in North-East Tirhut), खँचिया *khanchiya*, खचोली *khacholi*, पथुली *pathuli* (Gaya), नोनीहारी *nonīhāri* (Patna), or (South Bhagalpur) दमहरिया *damhariya*. The डगरा *dagra*, डगरी *dagrī*, also called south of the Ganges दौरा *daura*, दौरी *dauri*, or (in South Bhagalpur) डाला *dāla*, is a large shallow basket. These are all made of either bamboo twigs or slips, except the दौरा *daura* or दौरी *dauri* (see above). In Shahabad करुइ *karuï* or डोकी *doki*, and north of the Ganges सिकहुती *sikahuti* or सिकौती *sikauti*, is a little basket made of the stalks of the *mūnj* grass.

45. A broken basket is छितनी *chhitni*, or in Gaya छतना *chhatna*, or in South Bhagalpur छितना *chhitna*.* The झाँपी *jhampi* or झँपिया *jhampiya* is a little basket with a lid. It is also called पौती *pauti* or पौतिया *pautiya* (being then generally made of *mūnj* grass) and पेटारी *petari* (made of bamboo or rattan). A larger kind is called झाँपा *jhāmpa*. The lid of all these is called पेहानी *pehāni* or झाँप *jhāmp*. ठैचा *thaicha* or चँगोर *changor*, or in Shahabad ठैंचा *thaincha* or ठींचा *thīncha*, is a kind of large open basket. फुलडाली *phuldālī* is a flower-basket.

* A common curse amongst Gaya women is छितनी बढ़नी लागौ *chhitni barhni lāgau*,—may your wealth be swept away.

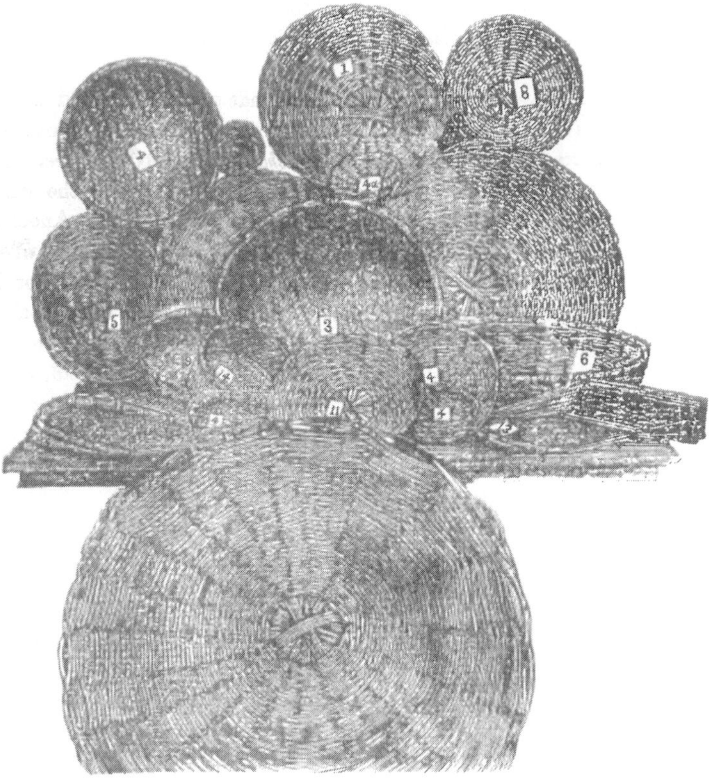

From a photograph.

A Collection of Baskets and of Other Articles of Basket-work.

1. Oriya.
2. Chhaintas of various sizes.
3. Daura.
4 & 4*a*. Dauris of various sizes.
5. Deli.
6. Khaincha.
7. Tāp.
8. Tokri.
9. Dagri.
10. Dagra.
11. Tarāju (scale-pan).
12. Kolsup. } (Winnowing sieves).
13. Sūp. }
14. Chalni (sifting sieves).

MATERIALS.

Nos. 1 and 8 are made of split bamboo twigs, woven up with the fibre of the leaves of the tāl palm.

4*a*, of the culm of the ***sīk*** grass (*andropogon muricatum*).

5 & 6, of tamarisk (jhāū).

7, of ***rahar*** (*cytisus cajan*).

11, of bamboo twigs.

13, of ***sirki*** (the upper joint of *saccharum procerum*).

The rest are of bamboo slips.

साजी *sāji* is one with a handle. In North-East Tirhut मटोर *mator* is a basket used by betel-growers (बरई *baraī*).

46. डेली *deli* is the basket employed by coolies when working on roads. In the North-Western Provinces the same word is used for a basket in which wild fowl, fish, or young pigs are kept.

47. A winnowing-basket or sieve is कोलसुप *kolsup*, or in North-West Tirhut डगरा *dagra*. A basket for sifting grains of various sizes is सूप *sūp*. A scale-pan is तराजू *tarāju* or तरजुई *tarjūi*.

48. There are several kinds of baskets used for catching fish, viz. टाप *tāp*, टापा *tāpa*, टापी *tāpi*; गाँज *gānj* or गाँजा *gānja*; सरैला *saraila* (Tirhut); अनटा *anta* in East Tirhut; परवे *parwe* or आरसी *ārsi* in Patna; अरसी *arsi*, पेरवा *perwa*, or सैरा *saira* in South Bhagalpur; and छोपा *chhopa* in Shahabad. The last is also worn over the head and down the back in the rainy season to keep the wearer dry, and is called in Sāran छोपी *chhopi*.

49. South of the Ganges भौंकी *bhaunkī* is a large basket with a narrow mouth. तरौना *tarauna* in Gaya is a basket made of tamarisk for carrying refuse, and in Patna बोगिया *bogiya* is a small basket for cowdung. In South-East Tirhut चाँग *chāng* is a large basket equal to four टोकड़ी *tokri* for carrying chaff. टँगौर *tangaur* is a similar kind, but made of *rahar*, and rougher.

50. In Sāran तरछा *tarchha* is a basket used in weeding poppies. टाप *tāp*, टापा *tāpa*, or टापी *tāpi*, or (in South-East Tirhut) खोंप *khomp*, and in Sāran झाँप *jhāmp*, is a basket under which chickens are kept. These are generally made of *rahar* (*cytisus cajan*).

51. बत्ती *batti* or बाती *bāti* are the twigs used for weaving baskets.

CHAPTER II.—BROOMS.

52. These are used for various agricultural and domestic purposes.

53. The ordinary sweeper's broom is झाड़ू *jhāru* and झाँड़ुआ *jhārua* or झड़ुआ *jharua*. In South-West Shahabad it is also called सेथन *sethan*, and near Ara कूँचा *kūncha*. South of the Ganges, to the east, it is called बोढ़न *borhan* or बोढ़नी *borhni*.

54. The broom used by women in sweeping out the house and also by sweepers is बढ़नी *barhni*, or in North-East Tirhut also बाढ़न *bārhan* or बाढ़नि *bārhani*. According to Crooke it is so called because the family is supposed to prosper (*barhnā*). It is also called towards the west कूँची *kūnchi*.

55. The broom used for sweeping up the grain on the threshing-floor has various names. North of the Ganges, in Sāran, it is सिरहथ

sirhath, and in North-West Tirhut सर॰हथ *sarhath*. In Champāran it is खर॰हरा *kharhara*, and in the rest of Tirhut खर्रा *kharra*. South of the Ganges it is, in Gaya and South Munger, कुच्चा *kuchcha*, in Shahabad कूँचा *kūncha*, and in the south-west of the district कुच्ची *kunchi* or सेथन *sethan*. In South Bhagalpur it is झटई *jhataī* or खर॰हरा *kharhara*.

56. The broom used by grain-parchers for turning the grain which is being parched is झारु *jhāru* in Patna and Gaya, बढ़॰नी *barhni* in the south and east generally, लर॰ना *larna* in North-East Tirhut, छिप॰नी *chhipni* iu South-East Tirhut, चलौनी *chalauni* to the west of the North Gangetic tract, and in South-East Bihār भुँजा॰नाठी *bhunjnāthi*.

57. The long twig broom used for sweeping up leaves and rubbish is north of the Ganges, to the west, खर॰हरा *kharhara*, and to the east खर्रा *kharra*. South of the Ganges, in South Bhagalpur, it is खर॰हरो *kharharo* ; but in Patna झाँटा *jhānta*, in Gaya झाड़ू *jhāru*, in Shahabad सिर॰हत *sirhat* or झाँखी *jhānkhi*, in the south-west of the same district झर॰ना *jharna*, and in South Munger झाँटा *jhānia* or झटैनी *jhataini*.

58. To sweep is in Patna and Gaya बोहारब *bohārab* or बाढ़ब *bārhab* ; the former is also used in the south-east. To the west it is बहारल *bahāral*, and in Tirhut बाढ़ब *bārheb*, झारब *jhārab*, or झारि झुरि देब *jhāri jhuri deb*.

CHAPTER III.—IMPLEMENTS USED IN WEEDING, &c.

59. The खुर॰पा *khurpa* is a sort of hoe used for loosening the earth round young plants or in weeding.

60. Of this the iron blade is खुर॰पा *khurpa*, or in North-East Tirhut पासङ्ग *pāsang*. The handle is बेंट *bent*. The iron ring-fastening in the blade is साम *sām* or सामी *sāmi*, and also in Shahabad चुरिया *churiya*, and in the south-west of the district मुँद॰री *mundri*. The spike of the blade which goes into the handle is north of the Ganges नार *nār*, and south of it नार *nār* or डण्टी *danti* or (South-West Shahabad) डाँड़ी *dānri*. Towards the east we find, north of the Ganges, an optional variant लार *lār*, and in South Bhagalpur लारु *lāru*.

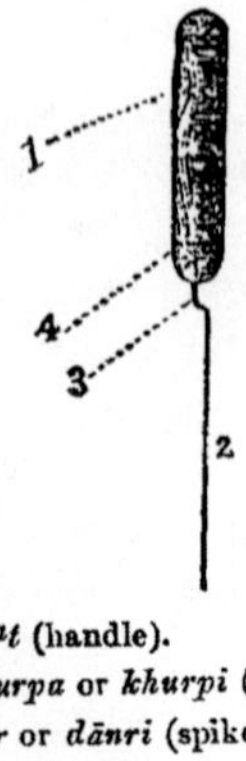

1. *Bent* (handle).
2. *Khurpa* or *khurpi* (blade).
3. *Nār* or *dānri* (spike).
4. *Sām* (ferule).

The Hoe (*Khurpa or Khurpi*).

61. A smaller instrument for scraping grass or weeding is called,

when the blade is curved, खुरपी *khurpi*, and (south of the Ganges) when it is straight पसनी *pasni*. An optional name for the curved variety in Gaya is बँकुआ *bankua*.

CHAPTER IV.—IMPLEMENTS USED IN CONNECTION WITH IRRIGATION.

62. The beds formed in a field for irrigation are called कियारी *kiyāri*. In South Bhagalpur they are called केआरी *keāri*. In South Munger गँड़ारी *ganrāri* are smaller sized beds for the same purpose.

63. These are made with an implement with a handle and board fixed at the bottom, like a rake without teeth. This is worked by a single man, much as a rake is used. In the North-Western Provinces it is usually pulled with a rope, but not so usually in Bihār. It is called generally to the south of the Ganges फरुही *pharuhi*, and in East Tirhut फरुहा *pharuha*. North of the Ganges, to the west, it is called फहुरी *phahuri*. In South Bhagalpur it is called फड़ुआ *pharua*, and in South Munger फड़ही *pharhi*. In Gaya it is called पँड़नी *penrni*.

64. A wooden shovel used in distributing the water in a field is called हथा *hatha* or हत्था *hattha*. South of the Ganges it is also called आभा *ābha*, in South Bhagalpur छिट्टा *chhitta*, and in South Munger कठौआ *kathaua*.

65. Other appliances used in connection with irrigation from wells, tanks, or streams will be found in the chapter on irrigation.

SUBDIVISION III.

APPLIANCES USED IN FIELD WATCHING.

CHAPTER I.—THE SLING.

66. This is generally ढेलमास *dhelmās* or ढेलवाँस *dhelwāns*. In Patna, Gaya, and (optionally) Shahabad it is also called ढेंकवाँस *dhenkwāns*. Another name current in Shahabad is ढेकुआस *dhekuās*.

In South-East Tirhut it is also called ढेलौरी *dhelauri.* In South Munger and South Bhagalpur it is डिँड़ोर *dinror.* गुरऽदेल *gurdel* or, to the east, गुलेती *guleti* is a pellet-bow.

CHAPTER II.—THE SCARECROW.

67. This is generally धूह *dhūh*, धूहा *dhūha*, or धुआ *dhua.* In Patna it is पुतऽला *putla*, and in Gaya ढही *dhahi.*

68. A scarecrow pulled by a string and hung on a tree is north of the Ganges ढबऽढबऽवा *dhabdhabwa*, ठकऽरा *thakra* to the west, ढकऽढकिया *dhakdhakiya* in South-West Tirhut, अकासी *akāsi* in South-East Tirhut, and elsewhere तारक छजा *tārak chhaja* or धुआ *dhuā.* South of the Ganges it is in South-West Shahabad डमऽहौआ *damhaua*, elsewhere in the district डमऽको *damko.* In Patna it is डमऽकौला *damkaula*, and in Gaya ढलऽकौआ *dhalkaua.* In South Bhagalpur and South Munger it is हरऽका or हड़ऽका *harka.*

69. Cultivators also usually put an old black earthen pot in a field to keep off the evil eye, which is called in Tirhut टोटऽका *totka*, or in North-East Tirhut तौला *taula.* South of the Ganges we find also टोटऽका *totka*, with variants टोटऽमा *totma* (Gaya) and टोटवाँ *totwān* (South Bhagalpur). In Shahabad it is called टोना *tona* or नजर गोजर *najar gojar*, and in South Munger नजर गुजर *najar gujar.* Another general name is करिखाइ हाँड़ी *karikhāï hānri* or करऽखाहि हँड़िया *karkhāhi hanriya*, from करिखा *karikha* or करऽखा *karkha*, 'soot.' Local variants of this last word are करऽखी *karkhi* (Shahabad), कारिख *kārikh* (Gaya), and करऽखो *karkho* (South Bhagalpur). Generally this pot is marked with lime (चूना *chūna*). Thus, a man of Ara would say हँड़िया मेँ करिखा लगा के चुन्ना के टीक दे के खेत मेँ धै आवल जाला *hanriya men karikha laga ke chunna ke tīk de ke khet men dhai āwal jālā*,—he has come back after setting up in the field the pot on which he has laid soot and marks of lime.

CHAPTER III.—THE WATCHMAN'S PLATFORM.

70. This is known as मचान *machán*, with an optional variant माँच *mánch* in the west.

71. The shed over the platform has various names, viz. north of the Ganges झाँपड़ी *jhompri* and खोँपड़ी *khompri* generally, छपड़ी *chhapri* (North-West Tirhut), छाही *chhāhi* (North-East Tirhut), and लगौरी *lagauri* (South-East Tirhut). South of the Ganges we have छपड़ा *chhapra* to the west and मरुका *maruka* and छपड़ी *chhapri* to the east.

72. मड़ई *maraī* and also (in East Tirhut) मर्रा *marra*, गोहिया *gohiya* (South-West Tirhut) and पलानी *palāni*, is a shed on the ground without any platform.

SUBDIVISION IV.

IMPLEMENTS USED IN HARVESTING.

CHAPTER I.—THE SICKLE OR REAPING-HOOK.

These are either toothed or with a sharp cutting edge.

73. (*a*) *With a sharp cutting edge.*—These are everywhere हँसुआ *hansua*. A kind with a heavier blade is called पघरिया *paghariya* or पघरुआ *pagharua*, or बधड़ा *badhra*, बधड़ी *badhri*, बधरिया *badhariya*, or बधारू *badhāru*. It is also called in East Tirhut सँगिया *sangiya*, in South Bhagalpur डाबठ *dāba*, and in Gaya चिलोही *chilohi*.

(*b*) *With teeth.*—These are called दँतुला *dantula*, from दाँत *dānt*, 'a tooth.' They are also called कैँचिया *kainchiya*, of which कचिया *kachiya* is a variant in South-East Bihār.

74. हँसुली *hansuli* is a small sickle without teeth, principally used by girls for cutting spinach (साग *sāg*), and by toddy-sellers (पासी *pāsi*) for cutting palm-trees. The पहसुल *pahsul* is a fixed upright sickle, which is kept in position by the foot resting on the wooden base in which it is fixed, and is used for cutting spinach and other vegetables. In Patna and Gaya, कत्ता *katta* is an instrument used by Doms for cutting bamboos, and क्योँचा *kyoncha* is an instrument for barking wood.

75. The above names are also used for the curved part of the blade. The straight part of the blade is called नार *nār* or (to the east)

लार *lār*. Other names are डाँड़ी *dānri* (South-West Shahabad), नरिया *nariya* (Gaya), and नाब *nāb* (Patna). The handle is बेंट *bent.*

The ordinary Sickle (hansua), and that of the Toddy-seller (hansuli).

CHAPTER II.—RAKES USED ON THE THRESHING-FLOOR.

76. This is अखैना *akhaina.* It is a kind of hooked stick used for pushing the sheaves under the bullocks' feet while the grain is being trodden out. This word is only used south of the Ganges. Local variants are खेना *khena* and अखेना *akhena* (Patna, Gaya, and South Munger), अखैन *akhain* in South-West Shahabad, and उखैनो *ukhaino* in South Bhagalpur. When it has five prongs, it is called पचक्खा *pachkha* north of the Ganges, in South Munger, and in Shahabad, and पाँचा *pāncha* also in the last district. This is also called in South Munger पाँचख *pānchakh.*

CHAPTER III.—GRANARIES.

77. These are of four kinds—

1st.—A structure of straw or brushwood in the open air.—These are बखार *bakhār*, बखारी *bakhāri*, or कोठी *kothi.* Local names are बेढ़ी *berhi* north of the Ganges generally, ठेक *thek* in South Bhagalpur, and बदारी *badāri* (also in South Bhagalpur) or मुनहर *munhar* in South-East Tirhut. In Tirhut a गोली *goli* is a round कोठी *kothi ;* जबरा *jabra* in Gaya is a small granary.

2nd.—Underground pits for storing grain.—These are everywhere खाद *khād,* and also (south of the Ganges) खाता *khatta* or खाता *khāta.* Local names are चौर *chaur* in South-East Tirhut, माट *māt* in Gaya, and खाध *khādh* or खधा *khadha* in South Bhagalpur.

3rd.—Granaries inside the house.—In Sāran डेहरी *dehri* is a small circular closet for holding grain, and is generally made of wattle and mud. The कोठी *kothi,* कोठिला *kothila,* or कोठिली *kothili* is everywhere generally made of sun-baked mud, and is larger.

4th.—A space surrounded by mats for holding grain is ठेक *thek.* A granary made of straw only is in South Bhagalpur खोँचरी *khonchri,* and in South Munger बाँध *bāndh.*

78. The *support* of the granary is गोड़ा *gora* generally. Local optional names are बेसना *besna* (South-East Tirhut), बैसक *baisak* (East Tirhut and South Munger), खूरा *khūra* (Patna), and ओटा *ota* (Shahabad).

79. The *cover* of a कोठी *kothi* is everywhere except in South-East Bihār पेहान *pehān* or पेहना *pehna.* In Sāran and Gaya it also means the plug or stopper (see § 81). Local names are झपना *jhapna* (South Tirhut and South Munger), ढपना *dhapna* (East Tirhut and South Bhagalpur), and चाक *chāk* (Patna, Gaya, and South Munger). The opening covered by it is मुँहखड़ *munhkhar* in Sāran. In the same district the cover of a बखारी *bakhāri* is खोँप *khomp.*

80. The *bottom* is called everywhere पेँद *pend,* पेँदा *penda,* पेँदी *pendi,* or पेनी *peni.* The South Bhagalpur form is, however, पेँदो *pendo.*

81. The *hole* through which the grain is removed is generally आन *ān* or आना *ānā,* local names being आएन *āēn* or मोहखा *mohkhā* in East Tirhut and Patna, and मुँह *munh* north of the Ganges. The plug for filling the hole is दबकन *dabkan,* or in the south-east मूँदन *mūndan.* In Sāran and Gaya it is also पेहान *pehān* (see § 79), and in South Bhagalpur ठेपी *thepi.*

82. A heap of grain is ढेरी *dheri* or रास *rās.* In Gaya it is also सिल्ली *silli.* In South Munger a smaller heap is called कुड्डी *kuddi.*

83. Various earthen vessels are used for holding grain. These are north of the Ganges generally कूँड़ा *kūnra,* माट *māt,* घैला *ghaila,* or हँड़िया *hanriya.* मटुका *matuka,* छोँढ़ *chhonrh,* चेरुइ *cheruï* are also used, but principally to the west. South of the Ganges we have चरुआ *charua,*

खुम *khum*, खोरा *khora*, and मटकी *matki* in Patna, Gaya, and South Munger (the last two also in Tirhut); छौंड़ *chhonr* in Shahabad, and कूँड़ी *kūnrī* in South Bhagalpur.

84. The covers of these are the same as those mentioned above; the local names are ढकना *dhakna* (Shahabad), झकना *jhakna* (East Tirhut and Gaya), and मुन्दन *mundan* (East Tirhut and South Bhagalpur).

85. An earthen cupboard similar in shape to the कोठिली *kothili*, but used for keeping cooking-pots and curd-dishes, &c., is called जबरा *jabra*.

SUBDIVISION V.

IMPLEMENTS AND APPLIANCES USED IN CONNECTION WITH CATTLE.

CHAPTER I.—THE FODDER-CUTTER AND TROUGH.

86. This is गँड़ास *ganrās*, गड़ाँस *garāns*, गँड़ासा *ganrāsa*, or गँड़ासी *ganrāsi*. Local variants are गँड़सी *ganrsi* in North-West Tirhut and गड़ाँसा *garānsa* in South Tirhut. The word गँड़ासी *ganrāsi* is the usual one. It has a short heavy handle. Other similar implements are दाव *dāw*, टँगाड़ी *tangāri* (Tirhut), and (in Patna, Gaya, and South Munger) काकुट *kākut* or काँकुट *kānkut*. The गँड़ास *ganrās* and गँड़ासा *ganrāsā* are properly heavy implements at the end of a long handle, four or five feet long. They are weapons rather than fodder-cutters.

87. The heavy *wooden part* immediately over the blade of the fodder-cutter is called जाली *jāli*, जलिया *jaliya*, or मुँगरी *mungri*. Sometimes, especially to the east, it is simply called बेँट *bent*.

88. The *blade* is गँड़ासी *ganrāsi*, &c., as above. The handle is north of the Ganges मूठ *mūth* or मूठी *mūtki*, and south of it बेँट *bent*.

89. The *knob* at the end of the handle has various names, viz. एड़ा *era* north of the Ganges generally, हूर *hūr* in North-East Tirhut, ठेकवा *thekwa* in South-West Tirhut and in Shahabad, and आरहक *ārhak* in South-West Shahabad. Elsewhere no special name has been noted, unless we include मूठ *mūth* and मुठिया *muthiya* in South-East Bihār.

90. The *spiked part of the blade*, which goes into the handle, is खुरा *khura* or खुरी *khuri* to the west generally. Also, north of the Ganges, to the west, गोड़ा *gora*, and in North-East Tirhut चोभी *chobhi*.

A very general name is नार *nār* (East Tirhut, Patna, Shahabad, and South Munger), नारी *nāri* (Gaya), or लार *lār* to the east generally.

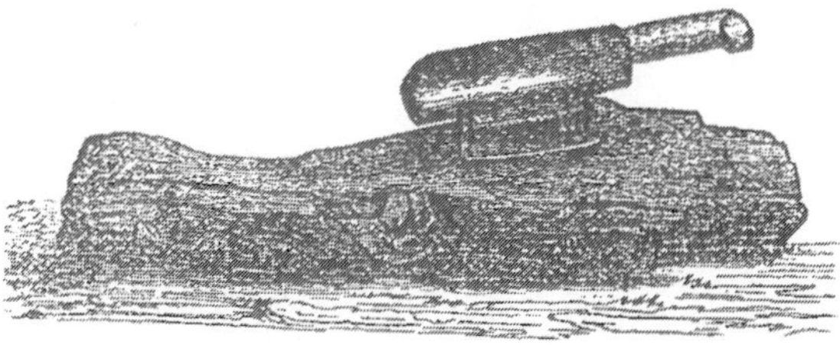

Fodder-cutter *(ganrāsi)* and block *(theha)*.

91. The *block on which the fodder is cut.*—This is north of the Ganges and in Shahabad ठेहा *theha.* Another name is परिकठ *parikath* (Shahabad and North-East Tirhut), or परिअठ *pariath* (South-East Tirhut and Gaya), परकट्ठो *parkattho* or परैठा *paraitha* (South Bhagalpur), and परहटा *parhata* (South Munger). Other local names are कुटकटना *kutkatna* (Shahabad) and निसुहा *nisuha* (South-West Shahabad).

92. The *feeding-trough*—When made of earthenware this is नाद *nād* or नाँद *nānd* generally, a local variant being लाद *lād* or लाएद *lāëd* towards the east.

93. In Champāran and North-East Tirhut पथिया *pathiya* is a basket used for the same purpose; elsewhere it is ओड़ैसा *oraisa.* In the same tract a wooden trough for feeding cattle is called नाव *nāw,* a general name for the same being कठरा *kathra.* In Shahabad चरन *charan* or चरनी *charni,* in Gaya गौरी *gauri,* and in South Munger गोँड़ी *gonri,* mean a long feeding-trough of sun-dried mud.

CHAPTER II.—THE MUZZLE AND BLINKERS.

94. The *net cattle-muzzle,* which is put on them when treading corn and at other times, is जाब *jāb ;* local variants being जाबा *jāba* (Gaya) and जाबी *jābi* (East Tirhut, Patna, and South Bhagalpur). North of the Ganges (to the west) जाबी *jābi* means a smaller muzzle, put on calves to prevent them eating earth. Instead of जाब *jāb,* जाली *jāli* is used in South Munger. मोहरी *mohri* in Shahabad is a rope attached to the head-rope of an animal to prevent it opening its mouth too wide.

95. The *conical wooden frame* put on a calf to prevent it sucking its mother is डील *dīl,* with for local variants डीला *dīla* (Shahabad and the east) and डीलो *dilo* in South Bhagalpur. In South Bhagalpur another name is कँटेलो *kantelo.*

96. In Patna ढाठा *dhātha* is a piece of wood tied round a bullock's mouth to prevent it eating. Elsewhere strings are used, and are called in Tirhut बेरुआ *berua* (west), कजई *kajaī* or लगामी *lagāmi* (south-east), टेमा *tema,* (north-east), and जूना *jūna* (east generally).

97. *Blinkers* for cattle are in Sāran and Champāran अनपट *anpat,* and in Tirhut and the south-east खोलसा *kholsa.* To the east generally they are also खोल *khol* or खोला *khola.* In Shahabad they are छोपनी *chhopni* or नोकता *nokta,* in Patna अँधियारी *andhiyāri,* and in Gaya अँधेली *andheli.* In Patna टोकनी *tokni* or खोला *khola* are the blinkers used in oil-presses or sugar-mills. The cloth tied over the blinkers is अँखमुँदनी *ankhmundni.*

CHAPTER III.—THE WHIP AND GOAD.

98. The *whip* used in driving *bullocks* is पेना *pena* or पैना *paina.* The latter is sometimes spelt पएना *paēna.*

99. Its *lash* is generally चाबुक *chābhuk,* with a variant चबुकी *chabhuki* in the north-west. In North-East Tirhut it is छिटि *chhiti.* साँटा *sānta* is found in South Bhagalpur, and local variants of this are साटा *sātā* in Sāran and South Tirhut and सटका *satkā* in Shahabad. छरकी *chharki* is used in Patna and Gaya, and झिट्टी *jhitti* in South Munger.

100. The *thong* at the end of the lash is झब्बू *jhabbū* in North-West Bihār, गिरह (the *knot*) in North-East Bihār, फुन्ना *phunna* in Gaya, फिक *phik* or फुदना *phudna* in South Bhagalpur, and फुँदना *phundna* in Shahabad.

101. The *spike* at the end of the stick is अरई *araī,* of which अरौआ *arauā* is a local variation in Patna and South Munger and आर *ār* or अरुआ *arua* in South Bhagalpur.

102. An *elephant-goad* is अङ्कुस *ankus* or आँकुस *ānkus.* A *spear* for driving elephants is भाला *bhālā,* बरछा *barchhā,* बरछी *barchhi,* or (in Shahabad and East Tirhut) बल्लम *ballam.* Another name is गजबाक *gajbāk* or (Patna and Gaya) गजबाग *gajbāg.* The *wooden club* studded with iron spikes, with which an elephant is beaten over the tail, is simply मुगदर *mugdar.* The अकुरी *akuri* is a *wooden goad* for young elephants, and when made of bamboo it is called (in South-West Tirhut) कनार *kanār.*

103. डाँग *dāng* (East Tirhut and Patna), डेंग *deng* (Gaya), and सोँटा *sontā,* are short *sticks* which may be used for driving cattle.

छाकुन *chhākun,* छकुनी *chhakuni,* or (South-West Shahabad) छिटःकन *chhitkan* and (Gaya) पिटौर *pitaur,* are twig whips used for the same purpose.

104. A *horse-whip* is कोरा or कोड़ा *korā* or चाबक *chābuk,* and a spur काँटा *kāntā.*

CHAPTER IV.—HOBBLES FOR CATTLE.

105. These are छान *chhān* or छाँद *chhānd.** Other local words are पैड़ *pairh* or पैड़ा *pairhā* or (in East Tirhut) पैकर *paikar* or पैंकर *painkar* and (in South Bhagalpur) गोड़ानी *gorāni.*

106. A piece of wood tied to the neck of a vicious or runaway animal is ठेकर *thekar* or (to the west) ठकर *thakar.* In South-West Tirhut it is ठोकर *thokar,* and in North-West Tirhut ठोकरा *thokra.* In Patna it is ठेकरा *thekrā,* and in South Munger ठेकुर *thekur.* North of the Ganges we often find मुँगरा *mungra* or मुँगरी *mungri,* and other local names are डगरन *dagran* (Gaya) and गरहर *garhar* or गड़हड़ो *garharo* in South Bhagalpur.

107. A cattle chain is सिक्कर *sikkar,* सीकर *sīkar,* सिकरा *sikra* or सिकरी *sikrī.* Sometimes these are spelt with a dotted *ṛ*: thus सिक्कड़ *sikkaṛ,* &c.

CHAPTER V.—ROPES.

108. *A. Those used for cattle.*—The rope for tethering cattle is everywhere पगहा *pagha,* and also in South Bhagalpur जोर *jor* or गेंठा *gentha.* In Sāran and Gaya it is also तगही *taghi.* The knots or loops by which they are tied are जोर *jor* or ठेका *theka.*

109. In Gaya and the south-east सेली *seli* is a hair string tied from the neck to the feet of a calf when milking a cow. In Gaya it is also called सेल *sel.*

110. A tethering-rope, by which cattle are tied to a peg, is छान *chhān* generally, or (locally) गूड़ा *gūrha* (North-West Tirhut, Gaya, and Shahabad), गोड़ाँव *gorānw* (South-West Shahabad), गोड़ार *gorār* (Patna and Gaya), गोड़ावन *gorāwan* (Gaya and South Munger), डेढ़ौराजोर *derhaurājor* (Gaya and North-West Tirhut), मलौ *malau* (South-East Tirhut), जोर *jor* (Champāran and North-East Tirhut), and जोरो *joro* or गोड़ानी *gorāni* (South Bhagalpur). Most of these

* As in the proverb गदहा गेलाह सरग, छान लगले गेलैन्हि *gadha gelāh sarag, chhān lagle gelainhi,*—the donkey went to heaven and took his hobble with him; *i.e.,* vices follow one to a future life.

refer rather to the kind of knot or loop with which they are tied than to the rope itself.

111. A double tether for wild cattle, held by two men round the animal's neck, is north of the Ganges दोबग्गी *dobaggi*, or in South-East Tirhut दोगहा *dogahā*, in North-East Tirhut दोबगल्ली *dobagli*, in North Bhagalpur दोबागी *dobāgi*, and in Sāran दुबगल्ली *dubagli*. South of the Ganges छरकी *chharki* is used in Gaya and Munger in the sense of this method of attaching ropes. It is also used for the mode in which a log is attached to an animal's neck.

112. नाथ *nāth* is a head-rope for cattle, passing through the animal's nose.

113. अगाड़ (or अगार) *agār* or अगाड़ी (or अगारी) *agāri* is a head-rope for horses, a local name being गलखोर *galkhor* in Gaya and Shahabad. पिछाड़ी (or पिछारी) *pichhāri* is the heel-rope, which is also called (north of the Ganges) पछाड़ *pachhār*. बागडोर *bāgdor* or बगडोर *bagdor* is a rope for tying horses. ताँत *tānt* or मोजम्मा *mojamma* is the thin leather rope tied round the horse's hooks. The halter tied round a horse's neck is गरौंधन *garaundhan* or गरदाँव *gardānw*, or (in Shahabad) गर औंधा *gar aundha*, and (in North-East Tirhut) गरदम *gardam*.

114. To the west and north पैकर *paikar*, पैँकर *painkar*, or पैँकरा *painkra* is a heel-chain for a camel, while to the south-east it is used for elephants. It is also used by travelling merchants for cattle. नकैल *nakail*, नकेल *nakel*, or in Sāran नकलोल *naklol*, is the nose-rope of a camel.

115. *B. Ordinary ropes.*—An ordinary rope is रस्सी *rassi*, रसरी *rasri*, डोर *dor*, डोरी *dori*, or जेँवर *jemwar*. जोर *jor* is also used, and (in Tirhut, Patna, and Gaya) जौरी *jauri*.* रस्सा *rassa* is a cable. A ship's cable is लहासी *lahāsi*, or in Sāran लहास *lahās*; and a tow-rope, गून *gūn* or (in Gaya and the south-west) गोन *gon*. गैँता *gainta* in Gaya is a rope for carrying beams. A coil of rope in the same district and in Champāran is घुरचीला *ghurchīla*. For the ropes used by a पासी *pāsi* or toddy-seller, see § 375. The string used in drawing water from a well with a brass vessel (लोटा *lota*, &c.) is called डोरी *dori*; while the general name with other vessels is उबहन *ubhan*, उबहनी *ubahni*, or (in South Bhagalpur) उबहैन *ubhain*, and in North-East Tirhut उघेन *ughen*. The knot round the neck of the vessel is north of the Ganges and in Shahabad अरवन *arwan*, and in Patna, South Munger, and South-East

---

* As in the proverb जौरी जरि गेल, ऐँठन ठामे *jauri jari gel, ainthan thāme*,—the rope may be burnt, but the strands remain (even though reduced to ashes); *i.e.*, a rich man come down in the world retains his pride.

Tirhut रौना *rauna.* Other local names are फनःकी *phanki* (North-East Tirhut), फँद्ःनी *phandni* (Gaya), फाँस *phāns* (East Tirhut and South Bhagalpur), and फँसर्ःगाली *phansargāli* in Gaya and South Munger. A small piece of rope attached to the vessel and then tied on to the regular well-rope is generally पनःछोर *panchhor.* A local name is छोरी *chhori* (Champāran and South-East Tirhut). Its knot is मुनःधी *mundhi* in Tirhut and the north-west, and मुद्धी *muddhi* in Shahabad. A thick well-rope is रस्सा *rassa* or बर्ःहा *barha.*

116. The rope which is used in working the irrigation lever (लाठा *lātha,* &c.) is बर्ःहा *barha,* with an optional variant बरह *barah* in South Munger. Other names are हथबर्ःही *hathbarhi,* and in Champāran and North-East Tirhut उबहनि *ubahani.* The short rope joining it and the bucket by a slip-knot is पनःछोर *panchhor* or छोरी *chhori* everywhere, with the following local names:—छोर *chhor* (South-West Shahabad), जोता *jota* (Sāran, Patna, and Gaya and the south-east), जोती *joti* (Shahabad and South Munger), नाधा *nādha* (optionally in Gaya), नधान *nadhān* (optionally in Sāran), and बगःहा *bagha* (South Bhagalpur).

117. The strings used in working the irrigation swing baskets (चाँड़ *chānr,* &c.) are known as डोर *dor* or डोरी *dori.* In Sāran they are जोती *joti.*

118. The ropes used for dragging a harrow are north of the Ganges generally हेँगही *hengahi* or बर्ःही *barhi,* &c., as described in § 33.

119. To the west मोजर *mojar* or मोजःरी *mojri* is a rope put round the roots of young trees to hold up the earth as they are being transplanted, other names (in South-West Tirhut) being गेरुआ *gerua* or (also in Champāran) बन्हःना *banhna.* In West Shahabad and Gaya it is गुढ़ी *gurhi,* and in South Bhagalpur जड़ःबँधःना *jarbandhna.*

120. The generic term for a grass rope is जुन्ना *junna* or जूना *jūna,* and in Patna and Gaya also जौरी *jauri,* and in Champāran पतःहर *pathar.* It is used for tying up bundles and for cleaning vessels. Another name in Tirhut is सर्ःपत *sarpat.* गतान *gatān,* or in Shahabad गात *gāt,* is a straw rope for tying up bundles. Ropes for tying up bundles of sugar-cane are जोती *joti,* उखबँधन्ना *ukhbāndhna,* गतौरा *gataura* (South-West Shahabad), and पँगार *pangār* (North-East Tirhut) or पगःड़ा *pagra* (made of sugar-cane leaves in South Bhagalpur). गुर्ःही *gurhi* in Shahabad and north of the Ganges, to the east generally कचःरा *kachra,* and in East Tirhut ओदार *odār,* is a loosely-twisted hemp rope (but गुर्ःही *gurhi* may be either straw or hemp) for tying up bundles of crops.

121. A rope made of the stems of the *cytisus cajan* (*rahar*) and similar plants for tying up bundles is called बैंती *benti* in Patna, Gaya, and South Munger, and बैंतड़ी *bentri* in South Bhagalpur. In Gaya it is also called बँधेरी *bandheri*. जुनेरी *juneri* (Gaya) is a similar rope made of *kus* grass. Ropes made of thatching-grass are called north of the Ganges झलास *jhalās* or झलसी *jhalsi*. Bundles of *mūnj* grass twisted up for cleaning vessels are लूँड़ा *lūnra* or नूँड़ा *nūnra*. A thick hemp rope is बरहा *barha*, बरही *barhi*, or (in Gaya and South Munger) बरता *barta* or बरती *barti*.

122. For most of the above the word जूना *junā* or (when the rope is made of straw) गतान *gatān* may be used, or a periphrasis may be used, *e.g.* कुसक रसरी *kusak rasri* for जुनेरी *juneri*.

123. सूत *sūt*, सूता *sūta*, or तागा *tāga*, is ordinary thread for sewing and weaving. सुतरी *sutrī* or (rarely and only in the extreme west) सुतली *sutli* is twine. This in South Bhagalpur is called सुथरी *suthri*. Twisted string is south of the Ganges ठर्रा *tharra*. North of the Ganges and in South Munger बाँटल रस्सी *bāntal rassi*, ऐंठल रस्सी *ainthal rassi*, or (to the west) बरल रस्सी *baral rassi*, is used.

124. To the west चोप *chop* is string made of the bark of the *butea frondosa* (परास *parās*) or of the palm-tree. In Gaya it is called चोंप *chomp*.

CHAPTER VI.—PADS FOR CATTLE.

125. These are known generally as गद्दी *gaddi* or पलान *palān*. In Patna, Gaya, and Shahabad बखरा *bakhra* is a leather sheet which goes over this. A खरहिया *kharahiya*, or in Sāran खरैया *kharaiya*, is a pad stuffed with खर *khar*, and under it is placed the कन्हेली *kanheli*. पेटार *petār* is in South-West Shahabad a belt for tying them, and पछोली *pachholi* a rope fastened to the animal's tail for the same purpose.

126. The pad for an ass is लेवा *lewa*, local names being पिठिया *pithiya* (Tirhut) and सुरका *surka* (also in East Tirhut) or तरछी *tarchhī* (Shahabad). In North-East Tirhut and Gaya छलौनी *chhalauni* is the cover of the pad. That of a bullock is (besides गद्दी *gaddi* and पलान *palān*) north of the Ganges and in South Munger कन्हेली *kanheli*, and south of it, to the west, छल्लाबखरा *chhallābakhra*, and to the east छल्ला *chhalla*.

127. An elephant's pad is गद्दी *gaddī*, and in Shahabad also गद्दा *gadda*. Underneath is placed a softer one called गदेला *gadela*.

A COUNTRY CART (CHHAKRA) SHOWING THE USE OF THE BODY-CLOTH (JHOLI).

CHAPTER VII.—GRAIN-BAGS AND PANIERS FOR LOADED CATTLE.

128. These are आखा *ākha*, आँखा *ānkha*, or टङ्गी *tangi;** south of the Ganges they are also गेठिया *gethiya* or पट्टा *patta*. In Shahabad, however, they are जोरा *jora* or गोन *gon.** A large grain-bag carried on a bullock's back is in Sāran लदौरी *ladauri*, or (also in North-West Tirhut) लगौरी *lagauri*. In Gaya this latter word means the cord by which the bag is fastened on the animal's back.

129. खुरजी *khurji* is a gunny (टाट *tāt*) bag borne by asses and used by potters for bringing clay from earthpits (मटिखान *matikhān*), and by others for carrying bricks, &c.

130. A rice-sack is बोरा *bora* or टङ्गी *tangi*.

131. In South Bhagalpur a bag borne by the bullock, in which the drivers put their luggage, is कटारी *katāri*, and in South Munger it is हँड़वाय *hanrwāy*. In Sāran it is खास *khās*.

CHAPTER VIII.—CANVAS, LEATHER, OR TARPAULIN COVERS.

132. These are तिरपाल *tirpāl* or (when made of छाल *chhāl*, leather) छल्ला *challā*.

133. झूल *jhūl* or झोली *jholi* is a body-cloth put over bullocks in cold weather. In Gaya it is also झोला *jhola*, and in Sāran ओढ़ना *orhna*. झूल *jhūl* also means an embroidered cloth spread over an elephant's pad.

CHAPTER IX.—VESSELS FROM WHICH ANIMALS ARE FED.

134. The bag from which cattle are fed is झोली *jholi*, or in Champāran झोला *jhola*. A horse's grain-bag is तोबड़ा *tobra*. In Patna कपाई *kapāi* is a fodder bag for cattle.

135. Feeding-troughs are described in §§ 92, 93.

CHAPTER X.—DAIRY UTENSILS.

136. *The milkpail.*—This has various names, according to locality. North of the Ganges generally they are झब्बी *jhabhi* or दुद्ही

* As in the proverb बैल न कूदे, कूदे टङ्गी *bail na kūde, kūde tangi*,—a bullock does not leap, but his load does, of which the Shahabad version is बैल न कूदे कूदे गोन, ई तमासा देखे कोन *bail na kūde, kūde gon, ī tāmāsa dekhe kon.*

कँठिया *dudahi kantiya*; but they are also भाँड़ा *bhānra* in Champāran, घुर॰ला *ghurla* in the North-West generally, and चपई *chapaī* in North-East Tirhut. South of the Ganges we have टह॰री *tahri* or पूरा *pūra* in South-West Shahabad, and कँठिया *kantiya* in the rest of the district and East Bihār; चाँपी *chāmpi*, टेह॰री *tehri*, or पत॰ला *patla* in Patna and Gaya; दुह॰नी *duhni*, चुक्की *chukki*, कठिया *katiya*, मेंटिया *metiya*, कठ॰ली *kathli*, or कठई *kathaī* in South Bhagalpur; and चुक॰ड़ी *chukri* or चुक्का *chukka* in East Tirhut and South Munger.

137. डाबा *dāba*, डब॰ही *dabhi* (also in Champāran), पाथा *pātha*, राइस *rāis*, or रासि *rāsi*, are large milkpails used in North Tirhut, and थप॰ड़ी *thapri* is a smaller one. काँड़ी *kānri* or कठई *kathaī*, also in North-East Tirhut कट्ठा *kattha*, are in Tirhut wooden milkpails. In South Munger रास *rās* is used instead of राइस *rāis*.

138. *Vessels used in making and keeping clarified butter* (घूा *ghyū*, &c.) *and curds* (दही *dahi*, &c.).—This also has various names, viz. north of the Ganges दहियाही हाँड़ी *dahiyāhi hānri* or कड़ाही *karāhi*. A local name is कर॰ना *karna* (Champāran and Tirhut) or कौर॰ना *kaurna* in North-East Tirhut. South of the Ganges we meet भाँड़ा *bhānra* generally, with a variant भाँड़ठ *bhānra* in South Bhagalpur and दहेंड़ी *dahenri* to the west. In Patna and Gaya we have चम्पा *champa*, महाड़ा *mahāra*, and नदिया *nadiya*. The last is also used north of the Ganges and in South Munger. In South Bhagalpur other names are कँम॰री *kantri* and छाँछ *chhānchh*.

139. There are sometimes special names for special sizes. Thus while हाँड़ी *hanri* or हँड़िया *hanriya* is everywhere used for the larger size, the next smaller size is in Tirhut कोहा *koha* or करुना *karuna*. कोहा *koha* is also used in South Munger, and पतिला *patila* or पतुकी *patuki* is used with the same meaning in Sāran. The next smaller size is कोही *kohi* or कह॰तरी *kahtari*. A still smaller size is छाँछी *chhānchhi*, ट॰मकुरी *matkuri* (of earth always) or मट॰कूही *matkūhi* (North-West Tirhut), and the smallest size of all is छँछिया *chhanchhiya* or नदिया *nadiya*.

140. The vessel for holding clarified butter is घिवही भाँड़ा *ghiwahi bhānra*, कँठिया *kantiya*, कोही *kohi*, राइस *rāis* (large), चुक्का *chukka* (small), &c. Other names in North-East Tirhut are घिवक कड़॰हा *ghiwak karha* (large) or घिवक कड़॰ही *ghiwak karhi* (small). In Patna, Gaya, and South Munger चम्पा *champa* or चाँपी *chāmpi* are used, and रसोली *rasoli* (large) and फेरुआ *pherua* (small) are met in South Bhagalpur.

141. The leather vessel in which it is exported is कुप्पा *kuppa* or कुप्पी *kuppi*. The latter is smaller than the former, and is also used for

holding oil. In North-East Tirhut it is also called चमन्ड़ी *chamri* or चौकन्ठी *chaukthi*. नदोइ *nadoï* is used in Gaya, and गेल्हा *gelha* is a similar smaller vessel.

142. *The churn.*—To churn is महल *mahal* to the west and महब *mahab* to the south and east. The act of churning is महाइ *mahāï* or मथाइ *mathāï*; local variants being मही *mahi* in Champāran and South Bhagalpur, and मथई *mathai* or महन *mahan* there and in Gaya and South Munger.

143. A churn is north of the Ganges, to the west, मटमहनी *matmahni*. In Tirhut and Gaya it is कूँड़ा *kūnra* or (south-east and also in Gaya and Champāran) कुण्डा *kunda*, and (north-east) खोर *khor*. South of the Ganges it is कमारी *kamāri* in South-West Shahabad, तौला *taula* in the rest of the district (also in East Tirhut), घोरमाहा *ghormāha* north of the Ganges and in Patna and Gaya, and महाँड़ा *mahānra* in South Munger.

144. The stirrer or stick moved in the churn is रही *rahi* generally, and also महनी *mahni* to the west and in Tirhut. The latter has local variants, viz. मथनी *mathni* (Tirhut and the West), महान *mahān* (West), and महोंनी *mahonni* (Gaya). Local names are गजन्ही *gajhi* (South-East Tirhut), छोर्ही *chhorhi* (South-West Shahabad and East Tirhut), and घोराठी *ghorāthi* (Patna, Gaya, and South Munger).

145. The rope with which it is twisted is generally रसरी *rasri* or डोरी *dori*; but more specific names are नेत *net* (generally), with local variants नेवत *newat* or नेवन्ता *newta* (east) and नेतो *neto* (South Bhagalpur). In Patna it is खिँचनी *khinchni*, and in South Munger दम *dam*. Another name in South Bhagalpur is जोती *joti*.

146. *Various vessels.*—In South Bhagalpur काइँ *kāīn* is a small vessel containing a quarter of a *ser* of milk. A पाथा *pātha* contains one *ser*, and a चूका *chūka* four *ser*. In Sāran a चुक्का *chukka* contains a quarter of a *ser*.

SUBDIVISION VI.

APPLIANCES USED IN THE CONVEYANCE OF GOODS OR PASSENGERS.

CHAPTER I.—THE COUNTRY CART.

147. The ordinary cart is called everywhere गाड़ी *gāri*, but in Saran it is more usually गड़ी *gari*. The छकन्ड़ा *chhakra* or

गाड़ा *gāra* is the large complete full-sized cart, with long bamboo poles projecting from each side in front. In North-East Tirhut it is sometimes called चघूस गाड़ी *chaghūs gāri*. The सग्गड़ *saggar* or सागड़ *sāgar* is a lighter and rougher kind of cart for carrying country produce. In Gaya and Shahabad it is also called लड़न्हिया *larhiya*.

148. For carrying passengers the रथ *rath* or रन्थ *ranth* is a light four-wheeled cart used by rich people. A similar two-wheeled cart is called साँवन्गी गाड़ी *sāmwgi,gāri* or (in Gaya) सौंगी गाड़ी *saungi gāri*. It is also called मँझोली *manjholi* in Tirhut and Gaya and बहल *bahal* generally, with variants बहेली *baheli* (Patna and Gaya) and बहल्ली *bahli* (Gaya). The एक्का *ekka* is a two-wheeled light trap, generally drawn by a pony. In Sāran it is also called घोड़ बहल *ghor bahal*. The किराँची *kirānchi* is a covered cart something like an omnibus on two wheels.

149. A cart drawn by a single pair of bullocks is दोबरन्दा *dobarda* or दोकन्ड़ा *dokra*. One drawn by two pairs is चौबरन्दा *chaubarda* (but this hardly ever occurs). In a team of three bullocks the wheelers are called धूरी *dhūri* or धुरिया *dhuriya* to the west and जोड़ी *jori* to the east, and the leader बीँड़ *bīnr* or बिँड़िया *binriya* to the west and झिट्टी *jhitti* (also in Sāran) or नाटा *nāta* to the east.

CHAPTER II.—THE LARGE COMPLETE COUNTRY CART.

150. This is छकन्ड़ा *chhakra*, गाड़ा *gāra*, or चघूस गाड़ी *chaghūs gāri* (see Chapter I). Its parts are as follows:—

151. *The wheel.*—This is everywhere पहिया *pahiya*. To the west, and also in Gaya and South-East Tirhut, it is also called चक्का *chakka*.

152. The *felloe* is called मङ्गर *mangar*, except in Gaya, where it is जमोट *jamot*. It is made of six segments of *sisu* wood, called each पुट्ठी *putthi*.

153. The *nave* is called नाह *nāh*. In Gaya it is also नह *nah*, and in Sāran नाहा *nāha*. Through this the spokes run completely through and through, each spoke terminating at each end in the felloe, each thus forming in reality two spokes. There are six of these double spokes altogether, making three pairs of two parallel spokes each (see illustration). These three pairs are of varying thickness. The first pair driven in is thicker and stronger than the second pair,

a = projecting end of the axle.
b = end of tekāni.
c = end of āk.
d = the tulāwas.
e = the painjani.
f = the jants.
g = the karis.
h = the amerhi.
i = the kulangra.
j = the pirhiya.
k = the tij.
l = the khuntri.
m = the balla.
n = the bilaiya.
o = the sagūn.
p = the munhthopra.
q = the utra.
r = the lappa.
s = the jhatka.

Lith. by Bepin Behary Das, Student Govt. School of Art Calcutta.

A full-sized Bullock-cart (Chhakra), side view

Cornwallis Press Calcutta.

and the second pair than the third pair. In crossing each other in the nave, the second pair runs through the first pair, and the third pair through the second and first. These pairs have names, viz.—

154. *The spokes.*—1.—The first pair is called **आरा** *āra.* This is the thickest and strongest pair of spokes in the wheel.

2.—The second thickest and second strongest pair of spokes is called **निमारा** *nimāra*, other names being **बेलि** or **बेली** *beli* (Tirhut and South Bhagalpur), **नीम धूरी** *nīm dhūri* or **नेबारा** *nebāra* (South-East Tirhut), and **लेवारा** *lewāra* (Shahabad).

3.—The weakest and thinnest pair of spokes in a wheel is called **गज** *gaj.*

To the west and in Gaya, both the second and third pairs are called **गज** *gaj.* The spokes are collectively called **डँड़िया** *danriya*, and to the west also **आरागज** *ārāgaj.*

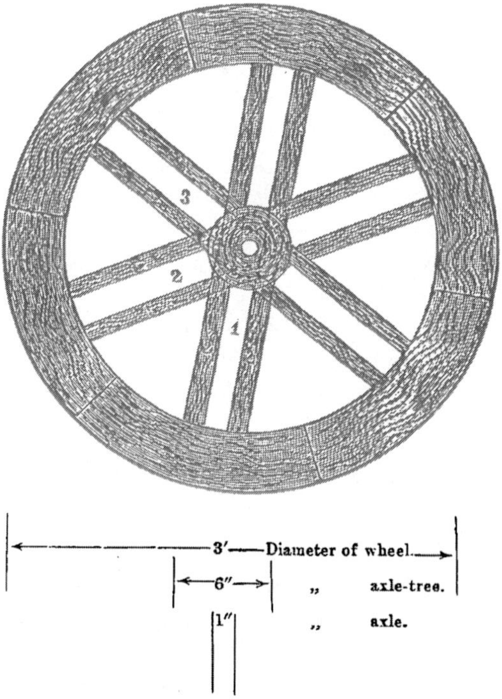

1. *Āra.*
2. *Nimāra.*
3. *Gaj.*

Scale 1 inch to a foot

155. The six segments of the felloe are fastened together by a wedge of wood called चूर *chūr* or, in Gaya, चूल *chūl*, fitting tightly into two mortices, one in each of the two contiguous ends of the segment. This wedge is also called चोन्ही *chonhi* generally, also जोन्ही *jonhi* or जोन्हिया *jonhiya* to the west of the North Gangetic tract and गरब खिल्ला *garab khilla* in Shahabad, Gaya, and South-East Tirhut. In Shahabad it is also called चौंटी *chonti* or चेंघी *chenghi*, and in Patna चूल *chūl*.

156. The mortice in the end of each segment of the felloe is called छेद *chhed* or भूर *bhūr*, or in Sāran खोल *khol*. The end of the wedge is called डांकन्नी *dākni*.

157. A wedge driven through the segment of the felloe from outside to tighten the spokes in their places is called पच्चर or पच्चड़ *pachchar*, or in Sāran पच्ची *pachchi*.

158. The *iron hoop* round the nave to prevent it from splitting is called बन्द *band* or बन *ban*.

159. Inside the nave is sometimes tightly fastened an iron tube to receive the axle. This is called the मोहनन्री *mohanri*, and in Gaya also मोहनन्दी *mohandi*.

160. The *iron axle-box* passing through the centre of the nave inside the मोहनन्री *mohanri*, when there is one, is called आवन *āwan*, and also (in Champāran, North Tirhut, and South Munger) आओन *āon*.

161. When the outside edge of the felloe is bevelled to prevent wearing, it is called north of the Ganges and in Shahabad टाल *tāl*, with variants टलुआ *talua* (East Tirhut, Patna, and Gaya), टलन्हा *talha* in West Tirhut, and टलाह *talāh* in South-East Tirhut. To the east it is also called मङ्गर *mangar*, मँगन्रा *mangra*, or मैगर *moigar*, with a variant मेघन्रा *meghra* in North-East Tirhut. In South Munger it is called कोरन्मार *kormār*.

162. When the outside of the felloe is flat it is called पाथर *pāthar*, but this rarely occurs.

163. *The tire.*—When the wheel is tired, the tire is called हाल *hāl*.

164. The *linch-pin* is generally धुरन्किल्ली *dhurkilli*, local optional names being रनन्किल्ली *rankilli* (Gaya and South-East Tirhut) and कील *kīl* in Shahabad. In East Tirhut, Gaya, and South Bhagalpur it is पचड़ *pachchar*. The peg inside the wheel is फरन्किल्ली *pharkilli*, or in Sāran फरन्किल्ला *pharkilla*. In a छकन्ड़ा *chhakra* there is generally only one linch-pin, on the inside end of the axle.

FULL SIZED BULLOCK CART (CHHAKRA)—BACK VIEW.

165. The outside washer of hemp (सन *san*) is चेनी *cheni*, चँद्री *chendi*, or (in Sāran) चेन्ही *chenhi*. That inside the wheel is खानन *khānan*, with variants खनन *khanan* (Sāran), खनन्हन *khanhan* (South-East Tirhut), खाँगन *khāngan* (South-West Shahabad), and खाँदन *khāndan* (South Munger, Patna, and Gaya).

166. *The axle.*—Each wheel has an axle of its own, each supported entirely by struts descending on each side of the wheel from the side of the cart to which the wheel belongs. The axle is धूरा *dhūra* or धूरी *dhūri*. Sometimes a distinction is made, धूरा *dhūra* being used when the axle is of wood and धूरी *dhūri* when it is of iron; but this is by no means universal.

167. *The outside supports of the axle.*—The supports outside the wheel are two pieces of wood meeting outside the wheel in front of the nave, where, at the point of crossing, they receive the axle. The upper end of one fits into one end of the front crossbar of the frame of the body of the cart (टेकानी *tekāni*, &c.), and that of the other into one end of the rear crossbar of the frame of the body of the cart (आक *āk*, &c.) (see illustration). These supports are called तुलावा *tulāwa*. They are fastened to the body of the cart by chains or ropes, called बान *bān* or बन्द *band*.

168. The *curved branch* of *sisu* wood which passes under the point of the axle, where it projects from the तुलावा *tulāwa*, and thus further supports the axle, is called पैँजनी *painjani*, wtih variants पँजनी *panjani* (Shahabad optionally) and पैँगनी *pengni* (North-East Tirhut). In Gaya it is called दाब *dāb*. It is pulled tightly up against the axle by three ties, two in front and one behind.

169. The front ties fastened to the fore end of the पैँजनी *painjani* are called जन्त *jant*. The other end of each of these ropes is fastened to a hook, called कड़ी *kari*. One of these hooks is fastened to the टेकानी *tekani*, and the other to the bottom of the cart, farther on in front, to one of the कड़न्हड़ी *karhari* (*vide post*). The जन्त *jant* are tightened by a stick called अमेढ़ी *amerhi*, or in Sāran सलैया *saluiya*, which passes between them and twists them together to the requisite degree of tightness.

170. The rear tie of the पैँजनी *painjani* is called कुलँगन्ड़ा *kulangra*, or in Sāran तुलँगन्ड़ा *tulangra*. It generally consists of one iron chain. Two rings (खड़न्खड़िया *kharkhariya*) hang in two staples (कोँड़ा *konrha*) to the underside (पड़ाक *parāk*) of the rear bar (आक *āk*) of the cart. One of these rings hangs near the centre of the आक *āk*, and the other

at the end near the wheel. The chain is fastened to one, then passes round the end of the पैंजनी *painjani*, and the other end is fastened to the other ring. In this way the पैंजनी *painjani* is held in its place. The accompanying sketch will make this clear.

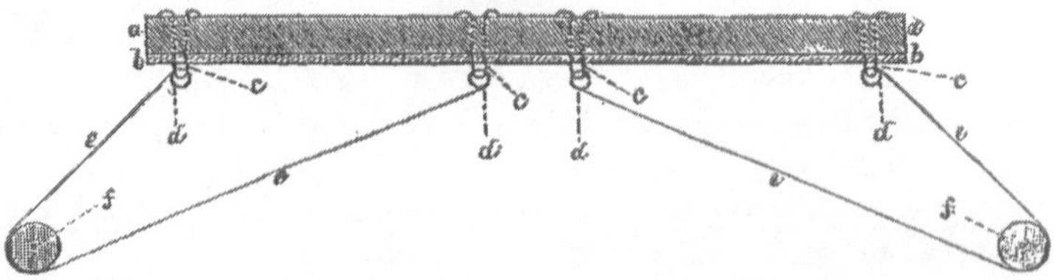

a—a	=	the *āk.*	d	=	the *kharkhariya.*
b—b	=	the *parāk.*	e	=	the *kulangra.*
c	=	the *konrha.*	f	=	the rear end of the *painjani.*

171. The ***body of the cart*** may roughly be described as a long triangle strongly built, lying on one surface, and arched so that its convex side is uppermost. Viewed from the side it resembles a shallow arch, and from above a triangle. Across the back a strong square or oblong frame is laid. This serves as the foundation for the carrying portion of the cart. The annexed illustration is a plan of a cart taken from above.

172. The आक *āk* or आग *āg* is the ***main beam in the rear*** of the cart. It is made of *sisu*. In Shahabad this is called आँख *ānkh*. Another and lighter piece of wood going underneath the आक *āk* to strengthen it, and also made of *sisu*, is called पड़ाक *parāk*. A slip of bamboo tied on behind the आक *āk* and forming the tail of the cart is known as पछलकड़ा *pachhlakra*, with local variants, viz. पँचलकड़ा *panchlakra* in West Tirhut, पिछलकड़ा *pichhalkara* in Patna and Gaya, and पिछलकड़ा *pichhlakra* or कड़ा *kara* in Shahabad. In South Bhagalpur it is अँकोरा *ankora* or पछेड़ना *pachherna*.

173. The ***front bar*** of the square portion of the cart is known as टेकानी *tekāni*. In South Munger it is तेकानी *tekāni* with a dental *t*.

174. The ***sides*** of the square part of the body, going over the wheels and joined at one end to the आक *āk* and at the other end fitting on to the top of the टेकानी *tekāni*, are called धुरौटी *dhurauti*.

175. The piece of wood fitting over the end of each of the धुरौटी *dhurauti*, where it joins the टेकानी *tekāni*, and holding the former in its place, is called बिलैया *bilaiya*.

a—a = the *āk*.
b—b = the *pachhlakra*.
c = the *tekāni*.
d, d = the *dhurauti*.
e, e = the *bilaiya*.
f = the *pirhiya*.
g = the *sagūn*.

h = the *phar*.
i, i, i = the *karhari*.
j, j, j = the 13 *batti*.
k = the *pachhua*.
l—l = the *tīj*.
m, m = the tops of the two *khuntri*.
n = the *munhthapra*.

Plan of a Cart (chhakra) from above.

FULL SIZED BULLOCK CART (CHHAKRA)—FRONT VIEW.

W. Newman & Co., Limited, Calcutta.-Imp

176. The short stout *cross-bar* of *sisu* wood crossing the triangular body of the cart between the टेकानी *tekāni* and the apex of the triangle, in front of the driver's seat, is called पिढ़िया *pirhiya.*

177. The *point* which is the front of the cart, and which forms the apex of the triangle, is called सगून *sagūn*, or in Patna and Gaya सगुनी *saguni.* The lower portion of this is called in Sāran थोप *thop.*

178. The two long *sides* of the cart, forming the sides of the triangle, starting one from each end of the आक *āk* and meeting in the सगून *sagūn*, are known as फर or फड़ *phar*, a local variant being फेड़ *phair* (North-East Tirhut). They are also called ताँगा *tānga* south of the Ganges and हरसा *harsa* in Sāran and Champaran. They are sometimes strengthened with a band of iron, called पत्तर *pattar*, बन *ban*, or बन्द *band.*

179. The whole *bottom* of the cart is called छज्जा *chhajja.* It is composed of the फर *phar*, the आक *āk*, the टेकानी *tekāni*, and the पिढ़िया *pirhiya*, and has in addition three long strips running the length of the cart, called कड़हड़ी *karhari*, and thirteen cross-pieces called बत्ती *batti*, or in Sāran बत्ता *batta*, and in Gaya also चाली *chāli.* The कड़हड़ी *karhari* are also called फरी *phari* in Patna and the south-west and चपोट *chapot* in Shahabad. North of the Ganges they are also called मन्झा *manjha*, माँझा *mānjha*, or भरानी *bharāni.* They are fastened in their places by pegs, called फरकिल्ला *pharkilla*, कठकिल्ली *kathkilli*, or किल्ली *killi*, पच्चर *pachchar* (&c.), or काँटी *kānti.* Of the thirteen बत्ती *batti* or cross-pieces, there are three between the आक *āk* and the टेकानी *tekāni*, four between the टेकानी *tekāni* and the पिढ़िया *pirhiya*, and six between the पिढ़िया *pirhiya* and the सगून *sagūn.*

180. This completes the description of the main frame of the cart.

We now come to the various contrivances for retaining goods in the cart. These are the following, but they are not all used in one cart:—

181. At the rear of the cart, just in front of the आक *āk*, is tied a thick bough of wood. This is called the पछुआ *pachhua.* It prevents goods falling out behind.

182. Over the पिढ़िया *pirhiya*, and of equal length to the टेकानी *tekāni*, runs a bamboo called the तीज *tij*, supported by two stout pillars about a foot high, each standing on one end of the पिढ़िया *pirhiya.* These pillars are called the खुंटरी *khuntri* or खुंटरा *khuntra*, local variant being खुंटहन्री *khuntahri* (Sāran and South Tirhut) and खुंटेहन्री *khuntehri* or खूंटिहन्री *khuntihri* in Shahabad. In Gaya similar posts are called माँची *mānchi*.

183. Two very long bamboos now form *sides*, each resting on one end of the आक *āk*, on a बिलैया *bilaiya*, and on one end of the तीज *tīj*. Each projects behind the आक *āk* and a long way in front of the तीज *tīj*, and is called बल्ला *balla*. Other names are बाँस *bāns*, बँसबल्ली *bansballi*, बँसौरा *bansaura* (Shahabad), or चँदवा *chandwa* (Patna).

184. Sometimes bamboos run from end to end. These are called चीप *chīp* when they commence at the टेकानी *tekāni* and run close under and fastened to the फर *phar*, up to the सगून *sagūn*. They serve to strengthen the फर *phar*. When they run the whole length of the cart, from the आक *āk* to the सगून *sagūn*, and form as it were the string of the bow formed by the body of the cart, running close to and parallel with the झटका *jhatka* (*vide post*), they are called लप्पा *lappa* or (in Tirhut) लप्पू *lappu*. They are fastened to the body of the cart by ties, known as दाँगली *dāngli* in Sāran, दौंगड़ी *daungri* in East Tirhut, बाधी *bādhi* in Shahabad, जौंढ़ा *jaunrha* in Gaya, and सौंठ *sonth* in South Bhagalpur. Elsewhere they are simply रस्सा *rassa*, &c.

185. Sometimes the बल्ला *ballā* is raised behind by a pillar (खुंटन्री *khuntri*) at each end of the आक *āk*, and the space between it and the body of the cart filled up with a *rope siding*. This rope siding is then called हँथवासा *hanthwāsa*, or in Patna फड़का *pharka*, and in Sāran एड़ा *era*.

186. The flat board forming the *driver's seat* is called मोहरा *mohra*, or in South Bhagalpur मोढ़ा *morha* and in Shahabad मुँहड़ा *munhra*.

187. *The parts underneath the cart supporting the inner end of the axle-tree.*—There are two supports inside each wheel, like the तुलावा *tulāwā* outside. They cross each other opposite the inner end of the axle which passes through the intersection. As each wheel has a separate short axle, there are therefore two independent pairs of these, one inside each wheel.

188. The rear one of each of these pairs is called गुड़िया *guriya* or गोड़िया *goriya*, or (in Patna) खजाना *khajāna*. Like the rear तुलावा *tulāwa*, its upper end is fastened into the आक *āk*. It is strengthened in its place in the आक *āk* by a strut, called मेहराब *mehrāb*, and the two गुड़िया *guriya* are further strengthened by a cross-piece called हँड़री

danrheri, joining the two, which thus prevents them approaching each other. The annexed illustration will make this clear.

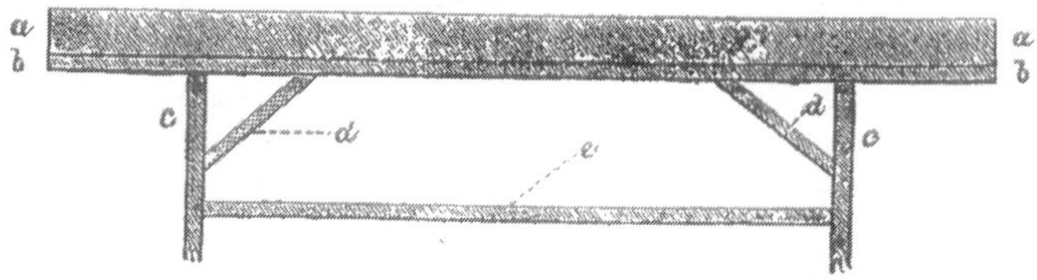

a—a = the *āk*.
b—b = the *parāk*.
c, c = the two *goriya*.
d, d = the two *mehrāb*.
e = the *danrheri*.

189. The front supports of these pairs are each called थोभ *thobh* or थोप *thop*. The upper ends of these are fixed in the टेकानी *tekāni*.

190. *The apparatus for keeping the body of the cart curved.*—This consists of a set of strings called झटका *jhatka*, which passes right under the cart from end to end, one end being fastened to the आक *āk* and the other to the सगून *sagūn*. This is kept tight, so that it keeps the whole cart bent exactly like a bow.

The following illustration shows the arrangement :—

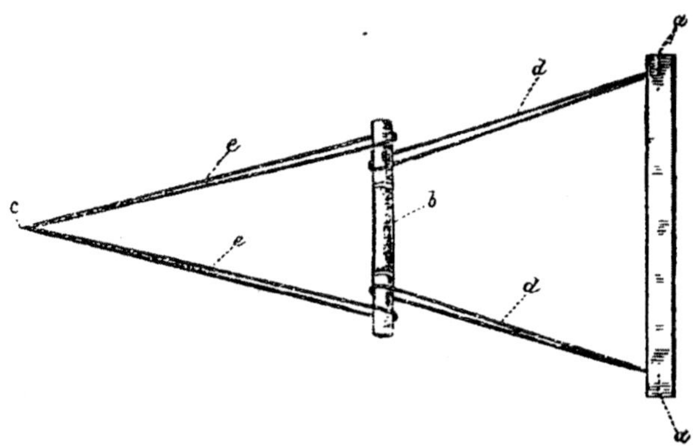

a—a = the *āk*.
b = the *danta*.
c = the *sagūn*.
d = strings fastened to the *āk*, passing round the *danta* and back to the *āk*.
e = strings fastened to the *sagūn*, passing round the *danta* and back to the *sagūn*.

191. The डण्टा *danta*, or in south Bhagulpur अमेड़ी *ameri*, in the above figure is a stout piece of bamboo. It will be evident from the figure that it affords increased leverage, and offers a ready means for tightening the झटक्का *jhatka* when necessary. Sometimes bamboos run parallel to the झटक्का *jhatka* from the सगून *sagūn* to each end of the आक *āk* as further strengtheners. These are called लप्पा *lappa* or (in Tirhut) लप्पू *lappū*.

192. The छतिया *chhatiya* is a slip of wood fastened across and under the body of the cart from थोभ *thobh* to थोभ *thobh*, which serves to hang baskets, &c., from.

193. The point which is the front of the cart, and which forms the apex of the triangle, is, as already stated, the सगून *sagūn* or सगुनी *sagun*. It is here that the yoke is fastened. Underneath it, to prevent the point resting on the ground, is fixed a stout peg, called उटरा *utra*. On the top of the सगून *sagūn*, to afford a boss for fastening the yoke to, is fixed the मुँहथोपड़ा *munhthopra*, मुँहथपड़ा *munhthapra*, or (south of the Ganges) मोथांपड़ा *mothāpra*. In Champāran it is called मोहड़ा *mohra*.

194. The *yoke* is जूआ *jūa*, and also in Shahabad जूअड़ *jūar*, as distinct from पालो *pālo* or जुआठ *juāth*, a plough yoke (see § 14). The pegs passing through the ends of the yoke, outside the bullocks' necks, to prevent them shirking their work, are made either of wood or iron. The name समैल *samail* is generally applied to them when of wood, and सेमल *semal*, सम्मल *sammal*, or सिम्मल *simmal* when of iron; but this distinction is not always observed. To the east they are called कनैल *kanail*. The inner pegs towards the middle of the yoke, on the inside of each bullock's neck, are called (in East Tirhut) चिरैया *chiraiya*. They may be of either iron or wood.

195. *Props.*—When the bullocks are unyoked, the front of the cart is supported at the सगून *sagūn*, to prevent it falling forward, by the सिपावा *sipāwa* or (in North-East Tirhut) सिरपाया *sirpāya* and (in Sāran) सिपवा *sipwa*. The top of this is called in Gaya मांझा *mānjha*. The prop to prevent the cart falling back is एड़ा *era*, उलरुआ *ularua*, सिधवाइ *sidhwāï*, or (in Patna) लरुआ *larua*.

196. The *ropes* which go round the bullocks' necks are जोता *jota*, जोती *joti*, or गलजोती *galjoti*. When three bullocks are yoked, the rope which goes over the leader's neck is to the west बिँड़िया *binriya* or बिरिया *biriya*, and in Sāran and the east झिट्टी *jhitti*. The rope (रस्सी *rassi*, &c.) by which the yoke is kept in its place is called बिछुआ *bichhua*, or in North-East Tirhut झोंक *jhonk*.

197. The *mat* put in the bottom of the cart to prevent grain from falling out is चटाए *chatāi* generally, but it is हरियार *hariyār* in Patna and भँडारी *bhandāri* in South Bhagalpur. The last is also used optionally in Gaya and East Tirhut. In Sāran a canvas mat used in the same way is called ढाला *dhāla*.

198. The *iron chain* for tying up the bullocks at night is generally सीकर *sīkar* or जनज्जीर *janjīr*. Local names are पाही *pāhi* or डाँड़र *dānrar* in Champāran and Tirhut, बेल *bel* in Gaya, and पैकल *paikal*, (also in Gaya) पैकर *paikar*, or पैँकड़ *paiṅkar* in Shahabad. The portion round the bullock's neck is called गरदनी *gardani*.

199. The above is the description, except where otherwise stated, of a very complete छकड़ा *chhakra*, which is itself the most complete kind of cart. Few carts are as complete as this; but they differ merely in being less complete, and in no other way.

200. As regards size, the cart of which the above is a description had the following measurements, a cubit being taken as equivalent to 1½ feet:—

		Cubits.
Length from आक *āk* to टेकानी *tekāni*	...	1½
,, टेकानी *tekāni* to पिढ़िया *pirhiya*	...	1½
,, पिढ़िया *pirhiya* to सगून *sagūn*	...	3
Total length	...	6 cubits,
		= 9 feet.

The आक *āk*, टेकानी *tekāni*, and तीज *tīj*, were each three cubits long.

The बल्ला *ballā* were each six cubits long, and the खुँटरी *khuntri* one foot. The wheel was two cubits across.

The greatest height of the arch was at the पिढ़िया *pirhiya*, where it was one cubit.

The height of the सगून *sagūn* from the ground when supported by the सिपावा *sipāwa* was 2½ cubits, and that of the आक *āk*, at the same time, 1½ cubits.

CHAPTER III.—THE LIGHT COUNTRY CART.

201. This is सग्गड़ *saggar*, सागड़ *sāgar*, or लड़हिया *larhiya* (see § 147). In Sāran it is called गाड़ा *gāra*.

This cart is rougher, lighter, and cheaper than the छकड़ा *chhakra*.

202. The *wheel* is the same as in the छकड़ा *chhakra*.

203. *The axle.*—There is only one axle (धूरा *dhūra*), which goes right across under the cart, and on which both wheels run. It runs through a block of wood which runs across from wheel to wheel, and out of each end of which the ends of the axle project. This block is called मँड़रा *mandra.* The projecting ends of the axle receive the wheels, which are held in their places by outside *linch-pins* (धुरकिल्ली *dhurkilli*, &c. (see § 164). Sometimes the wheels of the सग्गड़ *saggar* are protected by a board outside, one end being fastened to the आक *āk* and the other to the टेकानी *tekāni* (see §§ 172, 173). Through this the end of the axle projects, and is made secure by the linch-pin. This board is called पैंजनी *painjani*, पंजनी *panjani* (Shahabad optionally), or (North-East Tirhut) पैंगनी *pengni*, and must be distinguished from the different wheel support bearing the same name in the छकड़ा *chhakra.*

204. The body of the सग्गड़ *saggar* is not arched, as in the छकड़ा *chhakra.* It is simply a flat triangle of wood, principally bamboo. The two long sides of the body, commencing at each end of the आक *āk* and ending together at the सगून *sagūn*, are called, as in the छकड़ा *chhakra*, फड़ *phar*, &c. As the सग्गड़ *saggar* has no तुलावा *tulāwa*, थोभ *thobh*, or गुड़िया *guriya*, the body rests directly on the axle, being supported by two blocks of wood, called तेतला *tetla*, तेतलिया *tetaliya*, or in Sāran तेंतुला *tentula*, each of which rests on one end of the मँड़रा *mandra*, and on which, on the other hand, the corresponding फर *phar* rests. Along the फर *phar*, and underneath it, is tied a bamboo to strengthen it. This is called बाँगर *bāngar*.

205. In other respects a सग्गड़ *saggar* differs little from a छकड़ा *chhakra*, except that it is built lighter and almost entirely of bamboo. As the body is not arched, the former has of course no झटका *jhatka*, &c.

CHAPTER IV.—THE BULLOCK CARRIAGE.

206. When it has four wheels, it is called रथ *rath* or रन्थ *ranth*. This is rare in Bihār.

207. When it has two wheels, it is called बहल *bahal*, with variants बहेली *baheli* (Patna) and बहली *bahli* (Shahabad and Gaya).

208. This cart is almost exactly the same in principle as the छकड़ा *chhakra*, except that it is generally built lighter. On the square portion at the back is reared a kind of canopied seat, called साँवगी *sāmwgi* or सौंगी *saungi*; hence the cart is also called a साँवगी गाड़ी *sāmwgi gāri*.

The light Country Cart (Saggar)

Lith by Babu Prosunno Mukerjee Student Govt. School of Art Calcutta. Printed by [illegible] Govt. School of Art Calcutta.

THE BULLOCK CARRIAGE (SAUNGI GĀRI).

Printed by Abdul Rahim Govt. School of Art Calcutta

209. Its parts are as follows:—

The wheel.—As in a cart (see § 151 and ff.).

The leather washer is called चकन्ती or चकन्टी *chakti*, गद्दा *gadda*, or बिठई *bithaī*.

210. *The axle.*—As in a cart (see § 166).

211. *The supports of the wheels and axles.*—These are the same as in a छकन्ड़ा *chhakra* (see § 167 and ff., § 187 and ff.).

212. *The body of the vehicle.*—The lower part is like a छकन्ड़ा *chhakra*. Over it is placed the following, the whole of which is called साँवन्गी *sāmwgi* or सौंगी *sāungi*.

213. The frame of the seat is पट्टी *patti*, local variants being पट्टा *patta* (East Tirhut and Patna), पटिया *patiya* (East Tirhut and the west), and बौडण्डी *baudandi* (Gaya). Its supports are खूँटा *khūnta* or खुण्टा *khunta*. On these are ornamental brass knobs, called फुलिया *phuliya*. The posts supporting the awning are डण्डा *danda* or डण्टा *danta* (East Tirhut and the west). The top of the awning is छतन्री *chhatri* or (in Shahabad and Gaya) ठटन्री *thatri*, and the stuffed cover to keep off the sun is गद्दा *gadda* or गद्देला *gadela*. In South Munger it is गद्दी *gaddi*. The net forming the bottom of the seat is साँवन्गी *sāmwgi* or सौंगी *saungi*, and the leather guard of the body inside the wheels is धमाका *dhamāka*.

214. The two long sides are called फड़ *phar*, &c., or ताँगा *tānga*, as in the छकन्ड़ा *chhakra*. Between them are placed narrow planks, called माँझा *mānjha*.

215. The supports of the body behind are ढरुआ *dharua* or ढँरुआ *dhanrua*, and similar smaller ones inside are बावन्ली *bāwli*.

216. The दँतुआ *dantua*, or in Sāran ढाला *dhāla*, is the back seat for carrying luggage, and it is also called अड़ानी *arāni* in South-East Tirhut and Champāran. डोरी *dori* are the strings forming the side of the awning, and परन्दा *parda* is the side awning, which may be raised or let down as required. In Sāran it is also called ओहार *ohār*.

217. The rails on each side of the driver's seat are बल्ली *balli*.

218. In other respects the bullock carriage is the same as the छकन्ड़ा *chhakra* (see Chapter II).

CHAPTER V.—THE PONY CARRIAGE.

219. This is nearly the same as the bullock cart, on a smaller scale, except in the following particulars :—

220. The *wheel* is the same as in the bullock carriage (see § 151 and ff.).

221. The *axle* is धूरा *dhūra* or धूरी *dhūri,* which is strengthened inside by a short metal tube, साँमा *sāmma*, सामा *sāma*, or सामी *sāmi*. In North-East Tirhut the latter is also called साम *sām*. There is one of these inside each wheel, and they act as a kind of washer. There is only one axle (धूरी *dhūri*), on which both wheels run. Outside each wheel are a pair of तुलावा *tulāwa*, but inside there are no थोभ *thobh* or गुड़िया *guriya*, as in the bullock cart (see § 187 and ff.). Round the ends of the टेकानी *tekāni*, the आक *āk*, and the axle, forming a triangle outside the wheel, is tightly tied a rope called the जन्त *jant*, and just above the lowest angle of this triangle (*i.e.*, just above the point of axle), is tied to it a short stick serving as a footstep, called सलाइ *salāi* or सलैया *salaiya*.

222. The तुलावा *tulāwa* are fastened to the आक *āk* and the टेकानी *tekāni* (see §§ 167, 172, and 173) by iron hooks, called अँकुरी *ankuri* or (Champāran, South Tirhut, and South Munger) अँकुरा *ankura*. South of the Ganges they are also called in Shahabad and South Bhagalpur तुलाइ *tulāi*. हाल *hāl* is the tire of the wheel. The leather splashboard over the wheel is तखन्ता *takhta* or तखन्ती *takhti*. In South-West Shahabad it is called पटन्रा *patra*.

223. The props of the *body* are डण्डा *danda* (west), डण्टा *danta* (east and Champāran), or खूँटा *khūnta*. The top of the awning is छतन्री *chhatri*, and the roof of it is छत *chhat* or (in Gaya) तड़क *tarak ;* गदेला *gadela* or (in South-East Tirhut and South Munger) गद्दी *gaddi* is a cushion at the top to keep off the sun. The awning at the sides is परन्दा *parda*, or in Sāran घटा टोप *ghata top*, which is fastened by iron rings, कड़ी *kari* or (in Gaya) खोली *kholi*. The ropes which support the awning poles are हथन्वाँसा *hathwānsa*, and the rope trellis between the two rear awning poles चौक *chauk*. This last serves as a back to lean against.

224. The खूँटा *khūnta* or खुँटन्रा *khuntra* are posts which support the body in front on the axle. ढरुआ *dharua*, ढाँरुआ *dhārua*, or (in South Bhagalpur) ढाँलुआँ *dhāluān*, are the posts which support the body on the axle behind the खूँटा *khūnta*. बावन्ली *bāwli* or बौली

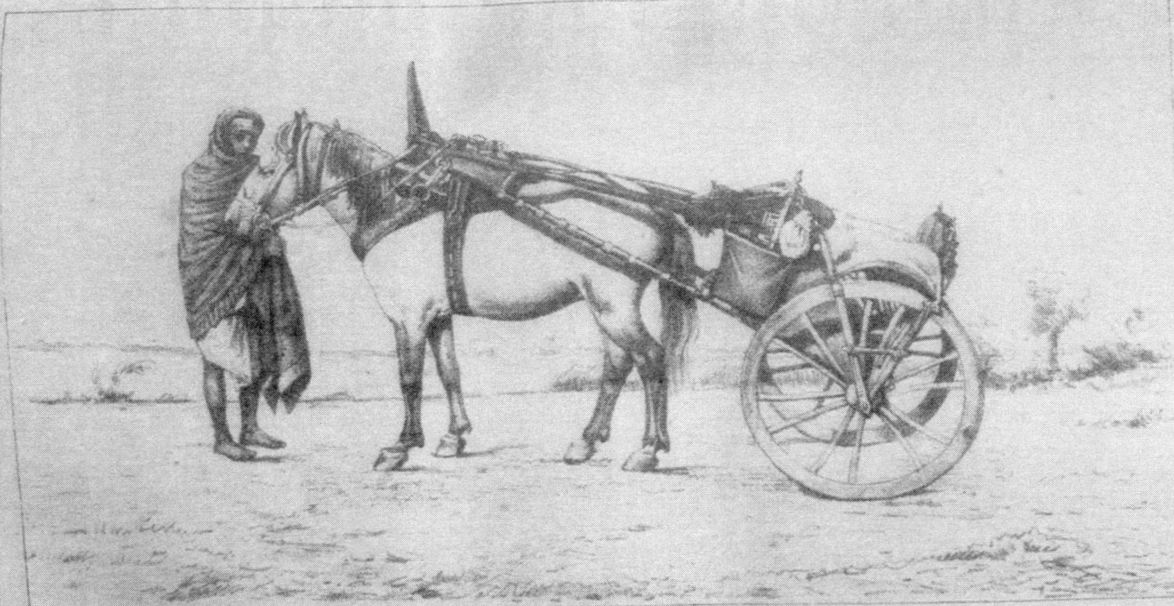

PONY CARRIAGE (*EKKA*), WITHOUT CANOPY.

Lith. by Hem Chunder Dutt, Student, Govt. School of Art, Calcutta.

Printed by Abdool Rohim Govt. School of Art Calcutta.

AN EKKA WITH CANOPY

Printed by Abdool Rahim Govt. School of Art Calcutta.

bauli are similar posts behind the खूँटा *khūnta*, but in front of the धरुआ *dharua*. They are quite inside the body of the cart. To the west of the North Gangetic tract they are also called गञ्ज *ganj*. The पोँछिया *ponchhiya* or (to the west) पिछुआ *pichhua* are the pointed ends of the lower shafts behind. In South Bhagalpur they are called दगल्ली *dagli*. तान *tān* are the four iron bars which support the body on the axle. Two of them are called खुँटातान *khuntātān* or (in South-West Shahabad) गजबाग *gajbāg*. माँझा *mānjha* are similar wooden supports. The साँवग्गी *sāmugi* or सौँगी *saungi* is the twine net under the seat, and the straps which keep it up are the सौँगी के नारी *saungi ke nāri*. The गोड़िया *goriya* are side ropes which fasten the splash-board to the axle, and the धमाका *dhamāka* is the leather siding inside the wheels. The four curved bamboo shafts are ताँगा *tānga* or (in Patna) टाँगा *tānga*. The छाती के नारी *chhāti ke nāri* is a strap inside, fastening the body to the axle in front of the सौँगी के नारी *saungi ke nāri*. The लदाव *ladāw* are cross-pieces of bamboo from shaft to shaft, forming the body of the cart. In North-East Tirhut they are called फठी *phathi*, and in South Bhagalpur बत्ता *battā*. The net at the bottom is जाला *jāla*, and the झटका *jhatka* is a strong rope behind and below, fastening the cross-pieces of the body.

225. The *driver's seat* is करतली *kartali*. The pieces of bamboo which run underneath from shaft to shaft, on which the driver rests his feet, are लतखोरा *latkhora* generally north of the Ganges, or डड़ेँड़ी *darenri* in Sāran and डँड़ेड़ा *danrera* in South-East Tirhut. In Shahabad they are लतेड़ा *latera*, in Patna and Gaya डड़िया *danriya*, and तरेरा *tarera* in South Bhagalpur. The गोड़िया *goriya* or (in South-East Tirhut) घोड़िया *ghoriya* are pieces of wood which join the upper and lower shafts. पङ्खी *pankhi* are pieces of leather joining the upper and lower shafts near the yoke. These shafts are also fastened by a leather rope called, north of the Ganges, मुठरा *muthra*, and to the south of it मोठड़ा के नाड़ी *mothra ke nāri*, or in Shahabad मुँहड़ा के नारी *munhra ke nāri*. In Patna and Gaya it is called छड़ा *chhara*. The मोथपड़ा *mothapra* is a brass cap fitting on to the ends of the two shafts.

226. *Harness*.—The pointed part of the saddle is खोगीर *khogīr*, or in Shahabad and East Bhagalpur खगूर *khagūr*. The pad is गदी *gadi* or गद्दी *gaddi*. The wooden block is कठरा *kathra* or (in South-West Shahabad) कठला *kathla*. The rings through which the reins pass are कड़ा *kara* or रास कड़ी *rās kari*. The leather surcingle going over the saddle, round the horse's shoulders and across his chest, is पुश्तङ्ग *pushtang* or पुस्तङ्ग

pustang. Another name is जोत *jot*. The leather belly-band is तङ्ग *tang*. रास *rās* means the reins; तावा *tāwa* or (in South Bhagalpur) तवक *tawak*, the leather cover of the saddle; नांगला *nāgla*, नगला *nagla*, or तस्मा *tasma*, the straps which fasten the shafts to the saddle; and कैंची *kainchi*, the wooden side supports of the saddle. Other names for this last are कैंचिया *kainchiya* (Champāran and Tirhut), गोड़िया *goriya* (South Tirhut, Patna, and Gaya), टिकठी के लकड़ी *tikthi ke lakri* in South-West Shahabad, and टेटखी *tetkhi* in South Bhagalpur. दुमची *dumchi* or दुमकजा *dumkaja** is the crupper. The bridle is पूँजीपट्टा *pūnji patta*, and the iron bit लगाम *lagām*. The martingale is जेरबन्द *jerband*, the cloth over the eyes which serves as blinkers अँधारी *andhāri*, the neck-ornament कण्ठा *kantha*, and the brass moon on the horse's forehead चाँद *chānd*.

227. गँजिया *ganjiga* or तोबड़ा *tobra* is the bag hung on either side for holding the passenger's shoes, &c.

228. The above is a description of an एक्का *ekka* when the canopy is attached. When this is taken down, a back railing is added, कटहरा *katahra*, instead of the rear posts, and instead of the two front posts two shorter ones are set up, one on each side of the driver's seat, called निमडण्डा *nimdanda*.

CHAPTER VI.—THE COUNTRY BOAT.

229. Boats are of various kinds. The following may be noted :—

The general term for a boat is नाव *nāw*, and to the west also नैया *naiya*.

230. The larger kinds of boats are उलाँक *ulānk* (which has a long narrow bow overhanging the water in front), मेल्हनी *melhni* (which has a broad bluff bow), पटेली *pateli* or पटैली *pataili*, also called in Sāran कतरा *katra* (on which the boards forming the sides overlap and are not joined edge to edge), कच्छा *kachchha* (which is shaped like a square shallow box, without proper bow or stern, and is steered with two rudders. It takes great burdens, and will go in very shallow water), and the सरङ्गा *saranga*, or in Shahabad सलीना *salīna*, and in Tirhut सरिन्ना *sarinna* (which has a round bottom for shallow water).

231. Smaller varieties are डोहट *dohat* or in Shahabad डोएट *doët* (which has a flattish bottom for shallow water, and has its bow and

---

* The fate of the *ekka* pony is well shown in the proverb दाना न घास दुनु साँझ दुमकजा *dāna na ghās, dunu sānjh dumkaja*,—no grain or grass, and the crupper on night and morning.

PALWĀR. SARANGA.

Lith. by H. C. Ghosal Student Govt. School of Art Calcutta. Printed by A. Kohim Govt. School of Art Calcutta.

A GROUP OF MELHNIS

J. Schaumburg, Lith.[s] Printed by Abdool Rohim, Govt. School of Art Calcutta.

Stern of a Melhni. Dohat. Pansùhi. Bow of a Dengi Machhua.

BOATS USED IN BIHAR.

SARINGA. PATAILIS.

PATAILI. ULĀNK.

J. Schaumburg, Lith.

Printed by Abdool Rohim Govt. School of Art Calcutta

stern portions cut out of solid wood), and पनसुही *pansūhi* (which has a round bottom, but goes in shallow water).

232. The smallest kinds are पलवार *palwār* or skiff and एकठा *ekthā* or dug-out. The latter is also called बँगड़ा *bangra*. Also the खोलनैया *kholnaiya*, with both ends rising like a gondola well out of the water, and which cannot sink. Another similar boat is called the डेंगी मछुआ *dengi machhua*, or dingy. घरनई *gharnaī* (South Bihār) is a temporary raft made of water-jars (घड़ा *ghara*) and bamboos tied together.

233. The *parts of a boat* are as follows:—The thwarts are गूढ़ा *gūrha* and the ribs बाता *bāta* or (in Champāran) ठड़बाता *tharbāta*, ठढ़िया *tharhiya* (in Champāran and North-West Tirhut), गोछा *gochha* (in Sāran and South-West Tirhut), गुच्छा *guchchha* (in North-East Tirhut), and काछ *kāchh* (in South-East Tirhut). Smaller transverse ribs are बाँक *bānk*. The outer planking is हार *hār* or (in South Munger) बाकल *bākal*, (in Champāran and West Tirhut) बगल *bagal*, and (in North-East Tirhut) काछक पाटी *kāchhak pāti*. In Gaya it is जलमहार *jalamhār*. In Shahabad the planks which run from end to end in the length of the boat are अहार *ahār*, and देवाल *dewal* is also used to mean the "wall" or side planks. The flooring inside the boat is पाटन *pātan* or पटवटन *patwatan*, or in Sāran पटौरी *patauri*. A long plank running over this is in Shahabad अपती *apti*. The grating above the bottom of the boat is चाली *chāli* or (in South-West Tirhut) उड़हा *urhrha*, and (in North-East Tirhut) पटाइ *patāi*. In a पटैली *pataili* the planks at the bottom which run from end to end are लेवा *lewa*, and in other kinds of boats मरिया *mariya* or (in North-East Tirhut) मरेया *mareya*, and in Sāran मोरिया *moriya*. The platform on which the rower sits is पटौरी *patauri* or बिटन *bitan*. When on the roof of a large boat, it is बीट *bīt* or पटाइ *patāi*, or in Shahabad हलमचानी *halmachāni* or मचान *machān*. The deck planks in the middle are पाटना *pātna*. चचार *chachār* is brushwood put in the bottom to stand on. कड़वा *karwa* or कँड़वा *kanrwa* are the posts which support the thwarts. जोँका *jonka* are iron rings to which the roof of the boat is fastened by ropes. In North-East Tirhut and South Munger they are called कड़ी *kari*.

234. When a boat is calked with the bark of the पराස *parās* tree (*butea frondosa*) the calking is called रसवत *raswat*, and when with hemp it is गहनी *gahni*. अटार *atār* (in Champāran and North-West Tirhut) is string used for calking.

235. The keel, which is the first plank laid in making a boat, is सिक्का *sikka*. In Champāran it is सहन *sahan*, and पतैन *patain* or डण्डा *danda* in South-East Tirhut. It runs the whole length of the boat, and hence

सिक्का *sikka* is also used to mean the two ends of the boat. The length of the boat is दवर *dawar*, and the stern post गलही *galhi*. The prow is मलङ्ग *malang*, माँगि *māngi*,* or माँग *māng*.

236. The rudder is पतवार *patwār* or (in North Tirhut) पतियार *patiyār*. In Gaya it is पटवार *patwār*. This is properly the lower piece. The rudder post is गोल *gol*, (in Shahabad, North-East Tirhut and, optionally, South Munger) खम्हा *khamha*, or in Gaya गौला *gaula*, and it is fastened to the thwart by a rope called नथिया *nathiya*. The tiller is सैला *saila* or (in South Munger and North-East Tirhut) डण्टा *danta*, and the socket in which it works बनरा *banra* or (in North-West Tirhut) ठेल *thel*, and (in North-East Tirhut) ठेहरी *thehri*. One rope, by which the rudder is fastened to the boat, is गँड़कस्सा *ganrkassa*, and another, by which it is held up, is अँकवरिया *ankwariya*. The steersman is माँझी *mānjhi*.

237. सेवता *sewta* or (in South-East Tirhut) सोता *sota* is the wooden vessel used for baling out water. An oar is डाँड़ *dānr*, a paddle करुआर *karuār*, केरुआर *keruār*, or in Sāran करुआरी *karuāri*, and the blade of it पाता *pāta*. A punting pole is लग्गी *laggi* or लग्गा *lagga*.

238. The mast is गुरखा *gurkha* or मस्तूल *mastūl*, or in Shahabad गुनरखा *gunarkha*, and the yard is मोरनी *morni*. The mast is raised on a post to which it is spliced. This is दरसूधा *darsūdha* or जसोधा *jasodha* in South Munger and Tirhut, जरसुधा *jarsudha* in Champāran, and जवसधा *jawsadha* there and in North-West Tirhut. The socket in the bottom, in which the post is stepped, is दरसूधा के मलिया *darsūdha ke maliya* or मलवा *malwa*. The सतवनियाँ *satwaniyān* is the thwart to which the post is tied. It is called in South-East Tirhut सूत *sūt*. The pulleys are घिरनी *ghirni*, and the sail is पाल *pāl*, and in Shahabad सूर्त *sūrt* or सुर्तवनियाँ *surtwaniyān*.

239. The tow-rope is गून *gūn* or (in Gaya and the south-west) गोन *gon*, which is tied to pieces of bamboo called बेरुआ *berua* or खूँटा *khūnta*, or in Shahabad बरुआ *barua*, which the boatmen press against their shoulders when hauling a boat up stream. The man who tows is गुनवाह *gunwāh*. लहासी *lahāsi* is a cable, and लङ्गर *langar* or गिराबी *girābi* the anchor. A large iron anchor is लोहलङ्गर *lohlangar* or गिरामी *girāmi*.

240. To draw water (of a boat) is पानि तोड़ब *pāni torab* to the east and पानि तूरल *pāni tūral* to the west, *e.g.* ई कच्छा बहुत कम पानि तूरल

---

* The most comfortable seat is in the bow. Hence the proverb जनिका खेवा नहिँ से अगिला माँगि सवार *janikā khewa nahin, se agila māngi sawār*,—the fellow who hasn't money to pay his fare takes the bow seat.

THE ORDINARY COUNTRY LITTER (DOLI).

बा *i kachchha bahut kam pāni tūrat bā*,—this *kachchha* draws very little water. To be aground is ठोकब *tikab.*

CHAPTER VII.—THE LITTER.

241. The litter is खटोली *khatoli,* डोली *doli,* or (in North-East Tirhut) खोटली *khotli.* डोली *doli* is also used for the ornamented litter used at marriages, which is also called in South Bhagalpur चनडोल *chandol* or तड़तड़वाँ *tartarwān.* The last word is said by natives to be a corruption of the Persian تخت روان *takht rawān,* or moving throne. In the west it is also called नांलकी *nālki* or बियहुती पांलकी *biyahuti pālki.*

242. The bamboo pole is बाँस *bāns,* and from it the litter is suspended.

243. The litter itself is खटोली *khatoli,* and is a kind of small bed (चरपाय *charpāy*) with a bottom made of rough twine (सुतरी *sutri*). The sides and ends of the bed are पाटी *pāti.* In South Bhagalpur the sides are called पट्टी *patti* and the ends सिरवा *sirwa.* At each end two pieces of split bamboo run up from each corner, meeting about 3 feet above the bed, and thus forming a triangle. These bamboos are called सिपावा *sipāwa,* or in South Munger सिपाहा *sipāha,* and in Sāran सिपवा *sipwa,* and they are fastened to the corners of the bed, and, at the apex of the triangle, to the pole by a string called बरकस *barkas.* This string is also twisted round the सिपावा *sipāwa* to strengthen them. A bamboo stick passes through the pole just behind the rear सिपावा *sipāwa,* and, descending perpendicularly, is braced to them by strings. This is called टेँड़ुआ *tenrua* or टेरुआ *terua.* It prevents the pole slipping round. The illustration shows a litter as carried by four persons, but this kind is more usually borne by two.

244. The feet of the bed are called पौआ *paua,* and the strings for tightening the bottom of the bed are ओरचन *orchan,* and also in Shahabad ओरदावन *ordāwan.*

245. Fastened to the pole over the bed, and in a plane parallel to it, is an oblong framework of bamboo slips for supporting the canopy. This is called ठटरी *thatri,* and in South Bhagalpur also छतनी *chhatni* or छतरी *chhatri;* and the string braces descending from its four corners to the four corners of the bed, to keep this awning steady, are called तान *tān.*

246. The illustration shows a litter without the curtains. When a woman travels in it, the whole is enclosed in a set of curtains like a bell-mouthed bag, called ओहार *ohār* or परदा *pardā.*

247. A superior kind of litter, used by richer women, is मेआना *meãna*, मँआना *meñāna*, महप्पा *mahappha*, डाँड़ी *dānri*, or डँड़िया *danriya*. It has a domed roof, called ठठ्री *thatri*, supported on eight pillars (four at each side), called डण्टा *danta*. The side-boards of the body are called दीवाल *diwāl*, or in Shahabad दिल्हा *dilhā*, and the doorway दुहारी *duhāri*, or in South Munger दुआरी *duāri*. The rest is like the डोली *dōli*.

248. The बर्दरी *bardari*, or in Shahabad बरह्दरी *barahdari*, also called in Sāran खर्खरिया *kharkhariya*, is the corresponding litter used by wealthy men. It is the native form of the Europeanized palankeen. In this the side-pieces at the bottom are called पाटी *pāti* or पटिया *patiya*, the net bottom बिनावट *bināwat*, the legs पौआ *paua*, the side-boards पटरी *patri*, the four pillars at each side सिपौआ *sipaua*, the doorway दुहारी *duhāri*, and the roof छत *chhat*. The shelf inside at the feet end of the litter is दराज *darāj*.

249. The poles are called बाँस *bāns*, and the curved end of the front pole थोप *thop*. The four iron struts at each end are called तान *tān*, and they meet in a ring (चुकिया *chukiya* or in South Bhagalpur सामी *sami*), which goes round the pole. The inner end of the pole rests in a socket in the end of the litter, which is also called चुकिया *chukiya*, and also in South Munger सामी *sāmi* or खुबिया *khubiya*. The rope network filling up the space between the two lower struts at each end is called कसावट *kasāwat*, or in South Bhagalpur कसन *kasan*.

SUBDIVISION VII.

APPLIANCES USED IN RURAL MANUFACTURE.

CHAPTER I.—APPLIANCES USED IN THE MANUFACTURE OF OIL.

250. The oil-mill is known as कोल्ह *kolh* or कोल्हू *kolhu* throughout the province. In Gaya it is also केल्हू *kelhu*. It closely resembles the sugar-mill, as described in the next section, and a detailed description is not necessary. Nevertheless, owing to the circumstances stated therein, it has been found inconvenient to give an illustration of a sugar-mill, and accordingly the following description of a Patna oil-mill is here given in order to explain the accompanying sketches. To these reference can be made in reading the section on the sugar-mill, in which the few points of difference are noted. A well-known proverb

THE LITTER USED BY RICH WOMEN (MEYĀNA).

Lith: by Nritya Kali Mookerjee Student Govt. School of Art Calcutta. Printed by Abdool Rohim Govt. School of Art Calcutta.

BARDARI (COUNTRY PALANKEEN).

An oil-mill, showing the manner of yoking and blindfolding the bullock.

An oil-mill (kolhu)

Cornwallis Press Calcutta

about the oil-mill is देल खरी खाय नहिँ, कोल्ह चाटै जाय *del khari khāy nahiñ, kolh chātai jāy,*—(the bullock) won't eat oil-cake when it is given to him, and yet it goes to lick the oil-press; *i.e.*, stolen goods are sweet.

251. *The hollow wooden block forming the bed of the mill.*—This is कोल्ह *kolh* or कोल्हू *kolhu*, and in Gaya also केल्हू *kelhu*. In this the cavity in which the oil-seeds to be crushed are placed is known as पेट *pet* or हण्डा *handa*, or in North-East Tirhut कूँड़ *kūnrh* and in Shahabad खान *khān*. In the oil-mill this cavity is shaped like an inverted cone, the apex reaching to about midway down the block. There it is about two inches wide, and thence it widens again like an hour-glass till it leads into the back of the top of the निरोह *niroh*. The lower half of this hour-glass cavity is known as अथन्री *athri*. The lower end (मूँड़ी *mūnri*) of the pestle (महन *mahan*) is just wide enough to fit tightly into the narrow part of the cavity at the waist. The upper half of the cavity is that in which the oil-seeds are placed. It has a lining of a series of longitudinal pieces of hard wood, wider at the top and tapering to the bottom, which are very tightly wedged together. These are called पाचर *pāchar*. Sometimes, when these get worn away by the constant working of the pestle, a fresh lining is put inside them. In this case the old lining is called ठरपचन्रा *tharpachra*, or in North-East Tirhut तरपचन्रा *tarpachra*, and the new inner lining पेटपचन्रा *petpachra*.

252. The block is buried very deeply in the ground to steady it. The part below ground is called जङ्घा *jangha*. Round the base a circular mound of earth is fitted, called भौँटा *bhaunta*, or in South Bhagalpur भौँठो *bhauntho*, in North-East Tirhut भट्टा *bhatta*, and in Sāran मँझौटा *manjhauta*; and in this, below the exit for oil, a space is dug out for the vessel (छन्ना *chhanna*) receiving the oil.

253. The exit for oil is the triangular hole at the bottom of the block over the above-mentioned cavity. It communicates at its upper end with the अथन्री *athri*. This oil exit, together with the cavity for holding the vessel, are together called निरोह *niroh*, and in Sāran and Tirhut also नरोह *naroh*.

254. The flat top of the block is called पारा *pāra*.

255. *The horizontal board to which the bullocks are attached.*—This is called कतन्री *katri*. On it the oilman (तेली *teli*) sits, and while he drives the bullocks he at the same time keeps pressing down the seeds into the cavity with his left hand.

256. *The upright beam, or pestle, which moves in the hollow of the mill and crushes the seeds.*—This is मोहन *mohan* or महन *mahan.* To the west it is also called जाठ *jāth,* or in Shahabad मोँहन *monhan,* and in North-East Tirhut मोहैन *mohain.* The ball at the end of this beam, which fits into the narrowest part of the hollow of the block, is मूँड़ी *mūnri.* The ferrule round this is मुड़वारी *murwāri.* The notch above this is कान्ह *kānh* or कन्धा *kandha.* The upper end of the pestle rounded off is चूर *chūr* or पूँछी *pūnchhi,* and the curved piece of wood joined to this is ढेँका *dhenka,* or in North-East Tirhut ढेँकुआ *dhenkua.* This curved block of wood connects the pestle with the upright post which is fixed in the horizontal driving-beam: thus—

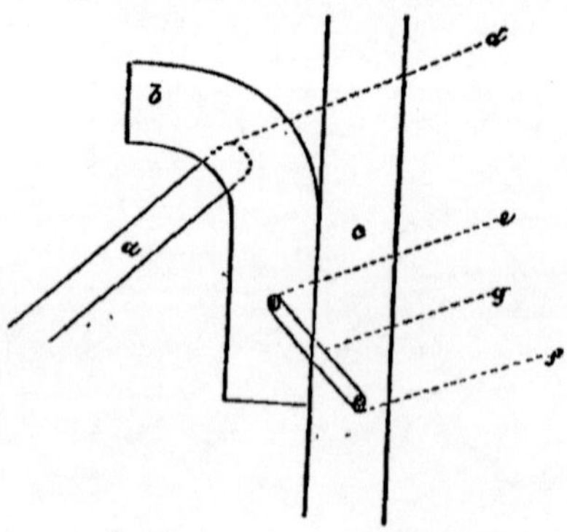

257. In the above sketch *b* is the ढेँका *dhenka, a* is the top of the मोहन *mohan* fitting into it up to the point marked *d.* The upright post is *c,* which is fastened to *b* by a string *g* passing round the two pegs *e* and *f.*

258. The upright post is called मरथम्ह *marthamh,* or in Sāran मलिक थम *malik tham,* the pegs *e* and *f* खूँटी *khūnti,* and the string *g* नाधन *nādhan,* or in East Tirhut लाध *lādh* and South Bhagalpur लेधा *ledha.* The string is generally made of straw. The upright post is fastened to the horizontal board, कतरी *katri,* by a wedge, गड़किल्ली *garkilli,* which goes through the former and under the latter.

259. The horizontal board revolves round the main block of the machine; at the end of the board nearest the block is fastened a thick lump of wood called फेँटा *phenta,* or in Sāran फेटा *pheta,* which acts as a kind of washer between the end of the board and the block, and which also rests against the latter, revolving in a horizontal groove (called माँदर *māndar*) out in the latter's exterior surface. A bamboo strut runs up from the inner portion of the horizontal board to meet the upright post, so as to strengthen the joint. It is called खरन्चाली *khar-chāli*, or in North-East Tirhut खँड़न्चारी *khanrchāri*, and in Gaya and Shahabad खँड़न्चर *khanrchar*.

260. *The arrangement for stirring up the oil-seeds.*—This is called रेवन्टी *rewti*, or in South Bhagalpur भरन्नाठी *bharnāthi* or उटन्कनी *utkani*, and does not exist in the sugar-mill. It consists of a peg, खूँटी *khūnti*, standing up in the cavity amidst the oil-seeds, alongside the peste; to its top is fixed a horizontal pole or handle, the other end of which is fastened to the upright post, मरन्थम्ह *marthamh*, by another peg, खूँटी *khūnti*. The whole therefore revolves with the pestle, the first peg moving amongst the seeds concentrically with it and stirring them up. At the same time the stirring is rendered more effective by the peg being perpendicular and the pestle on a slant.

261. *The yoking apparatus.*—The rope which is fastend to a peg in the end of the horizontal beam, passed round the hump of the bullock and back again to the beam, where it is tied into a hole, is called काढ़ा *kārha*, and the rope passing under the bullock's chest, joining the two traces thus made, is पेटी *peti*. The canvas pad on the bullock's hump is काँधी *kāndhi*, and the cloth or wicker basket by which he is blindfolded is टोकन्नी *tokni* or खोला *khola*, or to the east खोलन्सा *kholsa*. The rope from the bullock's neck up to the curved block or ढेंका *dhenka* is पगन्हा *pagha*, and the iron link fastened to this close to the bullock's neck is भौंर कली *bhaunr kali*. The rope round his neck, connected to the पगन्हा *pagha* by this link, is गरन्दवानी *gardawāni*, or in North-East Tirhut गरन्दामी *gardāmi* and in Champāran गरन्दानी *gardāni*, and that going through the bullock's nose is नाथ *nath*. A bullock employed in an oil or sugar-cane press is called a नाटा बैल *nāta bail*.

262. *Miscellaneous.*—The circle in which the bullocks move is called पौर *paur* or पौरी *pauri*, and in South Bhagalpur also भर *bhar*.

263. The pot into which the oil drops is called छन्ना *chhanna*. As much oil-seed as can go into the press at one time is called घानी *ghāni*. The oil-cake which remains after the oil has been expressed is called खल्ली *khalli*, or in Sāran खर्री *kharri*, except the oil-cake of poppy seeds (पोसन्ता *posta*), which is called पीना खल्ली *pīna khalli*, or simply पीना *pīna*.

264. To work the mill is पेरब or पेड़ब *perab*.

CHAPTER II.—APPLIANCES USED IN THE MANUFACTURE OF SUGAR.

A.—THE CANE-MILL.

265. The cane-mill is known as कोल्ह *kolh* or कोल्हू *kolhu* throughout the province. Patent mills introduced by European firms are known as कल *kal.*

266. It is apprehended that the following description of a country sugar-mill will be of little else than antiquarian interest, for such mills are fast disappearing from Bihār, being superseded by the English-made iron crushing-mill made at Bihia. To such an extent has the use of country mills died out, that the writer found it impossible to find a single one in the sadr subdivision of the Patna district which was in a fit state for a photograph to be taken of it. They had all been broken up for firewood, only a few dismantled ones being available. For a general idea as to its appearance, the reader is referred to the illustrations of an oil-mill in the last chapter.

267. The following are the principal points of difference :—

(1) The hollow in the block has perpendicular and not sloping sides, and it is hence cylindrical, and not conical, in shape.

(2) The sugar-mill has no रेवटी *rewti.*

(3) In a sugar-mill the pestle and its appurtenances are on a much larger scale. The मोहन *mohan* is six or seven cubits long, while in an oil-mill it is seldom more than three and a half cubits, the rest in both cases being in proportion.

(4) The names of the parts differ.

268. *The hollowed wooden block forming the bed of the mill.*—This is generally known as कोल्ह *kolh* or कोल्हू *kolhu.* The cavity in this, in which the pieces of cane to be crushed are placed, is known north of the Ganges, to the west, as खान *khān*, or in Champāran घर *ghar ;* and to the east, कुण्ड *kund* or कूँड़ *kūnr.* In Shahabad it is known as हण्डा *handa* or हँड़ोलन्वा *hanrolwa.* In South Munger it is हाँड़ा *hānra*, and elsewhere south of the Ganges हण्ढा *handha* or हण्डा *handa.* Round the edge, at the top of this, a rim of mud is sometimes placed to prevent the pieces of cane falling off. This is called पीँड़ *pīnr.* An iron ring fastened round the block to strengthen it and prevent it from splitting is बन *ban*, and in Tirhut also पत्तर *pattar*, and in South Bhagalpur मड़न्रो *marro.*

269. An iron ring is sometimes fixed under the block to prevent it being worn away by the crushing-pestle. This is generally मोरन्वार

morwār, with variants मोरवाह *morwāh* (North-East Tirhut), मुड़वार *murwār* (Shahabad and Patna), मूड़ *mur* (Gaya), मुरेरा *murera* or मुड़वारी *murwāri* in South Munger, and चनवा *chanwa* in Sāran. The पाचड़ or पाचर *pāchar* is a round piece of wood placed in the bottom of the cavity, and on which the crushing-pestle moves. रोड़ा or रोरा *rora* is used for the smaller wedges of wood placed in the cavity above this to help in crushing the juice. These are also called चँड़िया *chandiya* in Champāran and North-East Tirhut, and खोंच *khonch* to the east. In Sāran and Champāran रौन *raun* is a canal cut on the surface of the block through which any juice thrown up may flow back into the cavity. In North-West Tirhut this is called रैन *rain*, in North-East Tirhut रसपैन *raspain*, and in South-East Tirhut खाता *khāta*.

270. The drain for the juice cut in the bottom of the block is to the north नरदोह *nardoh;* also in Tirhut नरोह *naroh*, in North-East Tirhut नरोही *narohi*, and in South-East Tirhut रसेड़ *raser;* in South-West Shahabad it is गुजुरुआ *gujurua*, and in the rest of the district जोहा *joha* or रसहा *rasha;* in Patna it is रसघारा *rasghāra* or निरोह *niroh;* in Gaya it is छोनी *chhoni;* in South Munger, चोना *chona;* and in South Bhagalpur, लरलो *larlo*.

271. The wooden spout through which the juice drops is पतनारी *patnāri*. In the body of the block a channel is cut in which the block, फेंटा *phenta*, of the driving gear works. This is called घररा *gharra* in Shahabad and माँदर *māndar* in Patna.

272. *The horizontal board to which the bullocks are attached.*—This is कतरी *katri*, with a variant, कातरि *kātari* or कातर *kātar*, in Shahabad, South-East Tirhut, and South Bhagalpur.

273. *The upright beam or pestle which moves in the hollow of the mill and crushes the cane.*—For this three names are current, viz. मोहन *mohan* (Tirhut, except the north-west, Champāran, Patna, and South Munger), with variants, महन *mahan*, in Gaya and North-West Tirhut, and मोँहन *monhan* in Shahabad, लाठ *lāth* (Tirhut and Champāran), and जाठ *jāth* (Tirhut and Shahabad). The last word is used in Sāran only in reference to the oil-mill, and not to the cane-mill.

274. The ball at the end of this beam, which fits with the hollow of the block, is मूँड़ *mūnr*, मूँड़ा *mūnra*, मूँड़ी *mūnri*. The notch above this is north of the Ganges and in Patna कान्ह *kānh* or कन्धा *kandha*. In North-West Tirhut it is कन्हिया *kanhiya*, and in South-East Tirhut पञ्जा *panja*. In Shahabad it is कान *kān* or लँगरा *langra*. In Gaya it is

मोहनन्थम्भा *mohanthambha*, and in South Munger ढेंका *dhenka*. The upper end rounded off is चूर *chūr* or चुरिया *churiya*, or (in North-East Tirhut) मूँड़ *mūnr*; and the curved block of wood joined to this is ढेंका *dhenka* or (in North Tirhut, Shahabad, and South Bhagalpur) ढेंकुआ *dhenkua*, and in Sāran ढेंकुहा *dhenkuha*. This curved block of wood connects the pestle with the upright post which is fixed in the horizontal driving-board.

275. This upright post is north of the Ganges, to the west, हरसा *harsa* or हरिसा *harisa*, and to the east (and in South Bhagalpur) मनिकथम *manikthам* or मानिक थम *mānik tham*. In Shahabad it is मनखम *mankham*, in Patna and Gaya खूँटा *khūnta* or मरथम्ह *marthamh*, and मानिखम *mānikham* in South Munger. The pieces of wood which keep the beam of the driving gear in the channel at the base of the block are जीभा *jībha* or जिभिया *jibhiya*, or in Sāran the front one is called फेंटा *phenta*, and the back one कनैल *kanail* or (south of the Ganges) कन्हेली *kanheli*, and in Sāran कनैली *kanaili*. In North-East Tirhut they are called जिबिया *jibiya*.

276. A rope of straw supporting the pestle by fastening it to the upright beam is north of the Ganges, to the west, नाधन *nādhan*, in Champāran नधना *nadhna*, in Tirhut नधान *nadhān*, but in East Tirhut लाध *lādh*. In Shahabad it is टँड़ना *tanrna*, in Gaya नाध बरता *nādh barta*, in Patna नाधन *nādhan*, in South Munger नाध *nādh* or बरह *barah*, and in South Bhagalpur सारंगी *sārangi* or लेधा *ledha*.

277. The bamboo strut attached to the horizontal driving-board, and running up obliquely to meet the upright post, is called north of the Ganges खरचाँड़ी *kharchānri*, or south of it कमोरा *kamora* (Shahabad), खँड़चर *khanrchar* (also in Shahabad), खड़चर *kharchar* or खरचाली *kharchāli* (Patna and Gaya), कुदँड़िया *kudanriya* in South Munger, and खँरचारो *khanrchāro* in South Bhagalpur. This is fastened to the driving-beam by a rope, called नारन *nāran* or नाधा *nādha*, or in East Tirhut लारन *lāran*.

278. The part of the horizontal beam on which the driver sits is कातरि *kātari*, कातर *kātar*, or कतरी *katri* as above.

279. The leather thong by which this horizontal beam is connected with the yoke is नाधा *nādha* or (in Sāran) कन्हेली *kanheli*, (in Gaya) नाधा बरता *nādha barta*, and in Patna माँझा *mānjha*. काढ़ *kārh* or (in North-East Tirhut and Shahabad) काढ़ा *kārha* is a rope which is tied to a peg in the end of the horizontal board, passed round the hump of the bullock and back again to the board, where it is tied into a hole;

and the rope passing under the bullock's chest, joining the two traces thus made, is पेटी *peti*.

280. *Miscellaneous.*—The circle in which the bullocks move has various names, viz. गोरऽपौर *gorpaur* (Sāran), पौदर *paudar* (Champāran and Shahabad), पौर *paur* or पौरी *pauri* elsewhere north of the Ganges, in Patna, Gaya, and South Bhagalpur, बही *bahi* also in Patna, and बड़ऽहरा *barhara* in South Munger.

281. The receptacle for the cane before it is cut (generally a hole in the ground) is गँड़ियारी *genriyāri* generally, and गेड़ियार *geriyār* to the west. The receptacle for cane ready cut is टोनियारी *toniyāri*, with variants टोनियाठी *toniyāthi* (Sāran, Champāran, and South-West Tirhut), टोनियासी *toniyāsi* (North-West Tirhut), and टोनऽखाद *tonkhād* (South Bhagalpur). In Shahabad it is called अँगरऽवार *angarwār*.

282. A wooden mallet is used for pressing the cane under the crusher. This is थापी *thāpi*; also in North-East Tirhut मिलिट *milit*.

283. The cane as it is crushed is stirred up by hand, and the man who does this is called मोरऽवाह *morwāh* or मोँरऽवाह *monrwāh*, or in South Bhagalpur घनऽवाहा *ghanwāha*. This man sometimes drives the bullocks also, and when he does so he is still called by this name.

284. The pot into which the juice drops is called generally खोरा *khora* or (in South-East Tirhut) खोर *khor*, other local names being नाद *nād* (Shahabad) and कुण्डा *kunda* (Shahabad, West Tirhut, and Patna), or (generally) छन्ना *chhanna*. Over this is often placed a basket or earthen pot with the bottom pierced like a sieve. This is called generally छन्ना *chhanna*, रसऽछन्ना *raschhanna*, or छेनी *chheni*. Local names for this are तरौड़ी *tarauri* (Sāran and Champāran), छिट्टा *chhitta* (also in East Tirhut), or छिरऽहिरा *chhirhira* (Shahabad), and डलिया *daliya* (South Munger). An earthen vessel for holding the juice is in Gaya हथैला *hathaila*.

285. From these vessels the juice is removed to the boiler in a pot called कराह or कड़ाह *karāh*, or sometimes कराहा *karāhā*.

286. The blocks on which the cane is cut are north of the Ganges and in Shahabad निसुहा *nisuha*, a variant being निसुआ *nisua* in South Bhagalpur. Other names are ठेहा *theha* (North-West Tirhut), परियेठा *pariyetha* (Gaya), कुकाठ *kukāth* (Patna), परऽकठ *parkath* (South Bhagalpur), and टोनऽकट्टा *tonkatta* or टोनऽकट *tonkat* in South-East Tirhut and Munger.

287. The hollow in the mill is in Bihār cleaned by hand while the crusher is turning: hence there is no apparatus in existence for raising the latter, as there is in Gorakhpur and Āzamgarh.

288. The basket from which the mill is fed is चैँटी *chainti* north of the Ganges, with a variant, छीटी *chhīti*, in North-East Tirhut. In Shahabad it is ओड़ी *ori* (also in East Tirhut) or खैँची *khainchi*, and in South Bhagalpur ओड़िया *oriya*. In Patna it is बट्टा *batta*, and in Gaya पथिया *pathiya*. The pieces of cane cut up ready for the mill are गेँड़ी *genri* to the west and optionally in East Tirhut, and टोनी *toni* in Patna, Gaya, and to the east. In South-West Shahabad they are अँगारी *angāri*.

289. As much chopped cane as can go into the press at one time is घानी *ghāni*, and as much juice as can be boiled at one time ताव *tāw*. The latter is also खेपान *khepān* in South-East Tirhut, पाक *pāk* in Patna, and रान *rān* or रान्ह *rānh* in South Munger and South Bhagalpur.

290. The cane after the juice is expressed is called खोइया *khoïya*, with local variants खोहिया *khohiya* (Patna, Gaya, and the east) and खोइहा *khoïha* in South Bhagalpur. In Shahabad it is also चेफुआ *chephua*.

291. To work the mill is पेरब or पेड़ब *perab*, and when several cultivators take it in turns, each turn is called भाँज *bhānj*, पारी *pāri*, or (Gaya) पलऽटी *palti*. When men work it turn by turn they are said to do it भाँजा सिरे *bhānja sire* north of the Ganges, फेरा फारी *phera phāri* in Tirhut, and elsewhere पारा पारी *pāra pāri*. Sometimes a mill is owned by co-sharers, and then their taking it in turns is भँजऽहरिया *bhanjhariya*, सझियैती *sajhiyaiti*, or (Tirhut) सबऽठैती *sabthaiti*, and also in North-East Tirhut सझिया *sajhiya*. In South Munger ढेँक *dhenk* is the working of a mill by cultivators for a week in turn, one after the other, till the turn of the first comes again.

292. *The men engaged on the mill* are as follows:—

(1) *The man who cuts the standing cane.*—This man is अँगेड़ीहा *angerīha* to the west generally, गेँड़ऽवहिया *genrwahiya* in the north-west, पजऽवाहा *pajwāha* and पगरऽवाह *pagarwāh* or पँगरऽवाह *pangarwāh* in Tirhut. In Shahabad he is also गेँड़ऽछीला *genrchhīla*, or in the south-west of the district छोलऽवा *chholwa*; in Patna and Gaya he is केतरऽपारा *ketarpāra* (from केतारी *ketāri*, sugar-cane), परऽताहर *partāhar*, or परऽनिहार *parnihār*, and in South Munger कतरऽपारा *katarpāra* or पतरऽपारा *patarpāra*. In South Bhagalpur he is घुरऽकट्टा *ghurkatta* or कटनिया *kataniya*.

In Sāran and Champāran these men do their work without wages in money, their pay being the leaves of the cane which they cut, which they take home and use for cattle fodder.

293. (2) *The man who cuts the cane into lengths for the mill* is कानू *kānu* in South Tirhut and Sāran. In Champāran he is पकवाह *pakwāh,* and to the west he is गँड़िकाटा *genrikāta* or अँगरवाह *angarwāh.* Elsewhere he is टोनकट्टा *tonkatta,* with a variant, टोनिकट्टा *tonikatta,* in South-East Tirhut. In North-West Tirhut he is simply called मजूरा *majūra,* and in North-East Tirhut sometimes जन *jān.* In Sāran and Champāran the same person cuts the cane and boils the juice, hence his name.

294. (3) *The driver of the mill* is कतरवाह *katarwāh,* with variants कतरिवाह *katariwāh* or कतरवाहा *katarwāha,* and in South Bhagalpur कतरबहा *katarbaha.* In South-West Shahabad and in Tirhut he is called हँकवा *hankwa.*

295. (4) *The man who feeds the mill.*—He is मोँरवाह *monrwāh* or मोरवाह *morwāh* generally. In Patna and Gaya he is घनवाहा *ghanwāha* or (in South Bhagalpur and South Munger) घनबहा *ghanbaha.*

296. (5) *The man who removes the crushed cane.*—He is हलुआइ *haluāi* in North Tirhut; elsewhere this is done by the man who feeds.

297. *The buildings.*—The whole manufactory, including both cane-mill and boiling-house, is called कोल्हुआर *kolhuār,* or in South-West Shahabad गोलौर *golaur.* In Patna, Gaya, and the east it is called कोलसार *kolsār.*

298. The house in which the cane is cut into slips for the mill is called गँड़ियार *genriyār,* or गँड़ियारी *genriyāri* to the west and टोनियारी *toniyari* to the east. Local varieties of this last are टोनियासी *toniyāsi* in North-West Tirhut and टोनखाद *tonkhād* in South Bhagalpur.

299. *Folklore on the subject.*—Near the place where the cane is cut into slips the men make a round idol of a deity called मकार बीर *makār bīr,* or in Shahabad महकार बीर *mahkār bīr,* and in North-East Tirhut महकार *mahkār.* He is said to have been originally a Dom, who once came to a sugar manufactory in the olden time and asked for juice, which the people refused to give to him. Thereupon he jumped into the boiler and was boiled to death. His spirit became deified, and is now worshipped by the workmen. The worship consists in pouring a little water on the

image when the cane is brought into the manufactory from the field, so that he may wash himself. Then five canes are put before him. They are then cut up and put first into the mill. The first juice that comes out is also poured over him, and then the rest may go into the boiler. In South Bhagalpur the deity worshipped is बिसकर्मा *biswakarma.*

B.—THE BOILING-HOUSE.

300. This is in Sāran गुड़ौर *guraur*, and in Shahabad गोलौर *golaur*; elsewhere it is simply कोल्हुआर *kolhuār* or कोलसार *kolsār* as above.

301. The fireplace is चूल्हा *chūlha*, or in South Munger गमहेर *gamher*. The hole through which the fire is fed with fuel is generally मुह *muh* or मुँह *munh*, but in Patna and Gaya it is मोक्खा *mohkha*. The hole through which the fire is raked is साँसी *sānsi* generally north of the Ganges, नँगड़ा *nangra* in North-East Tirhut, लँगड़ा *langra* in Shahabad, and उधान *udhān* in South-East Tirhut. Elsewhere it has no special name. In Sāran लँगड़ा *langra* is a receptacle for the juice when removed from the boiling-pan.

302. The outlet for smoke is धुआँकस *dhuānkas* north of the Ganges and in Shahabad. In South-West Shahabad it is धुँधुका *dhundhuka*, in Gaya it is हिक्का *hikka*, in Patna हींक *hink*, and नेंगड़ा *nengra* in South Bhagalpur and South Munger.

303. The stick used as a poker is खोरनी *khorni*, or in Patna खोरना *khorna*. Local names are खोदौना *khodauna* (South-West Shahabad), लहुआइ *lahuāi* (Shahabad), and अँचना *anchna* (to the east). In Shahabad फरुही *pharuhi*, or in the west generally फहुरी *phahuri*, is a piece of wood used for raking out ashes. The man who stokes the fire is called कानू *kānu* north of the Ganges and in South Bhagalpur and Shahabad. Local names are धुरकमिया *dhurkamiya* (South-East Tirhut), चुलझोंका *chuljhonka* (East Tirhut and Shahabad), चुल्हाँचा *chulhancha* (East Tirhut and Gaya), अँचवाहा *anchwāha* (Patna), and अँचताहर *anchtāhar* (South Munger).

304. The vessel in which the juice is collected before boiling is नाद *nād* or नादी *nādi*, or (in Gaya) चट्टी *chatti*, (North-East Tirhut) गगरी *gagri* or घैला *ghaila*. Generally, however, it is kept in the छन्ना *chhanna* (see above), of which there may be several in use at one time.

305. The spoon for taking the juice out of the boiler is north of the Ganges, to the west, कठही *kathahi* or कठखुरपी *kathkhurpi*, and to the east (also in Shahabad) सैक *saik* or सैका *saika*. Elsewhere south of the Ganges it is सफई *saphai* or सफैया *saphaiya*. In South-West Shahabad it is, however, डोहरा *dohra*, and in South Bhagalpur it is डपन्टी *dapti* or डब्बू *dabbu*.

306. The scraper to prevent the sugar resting on the bottom of the boiler is खुरपी *khurpi* generally. In Sāran and Champāran it is खुरपा *khurpa*, and in North-East Tirhut कठखुरपी *kathkhurpi*, the meaning of which here is different from that in Sāran, Champāran, and West Tirhut. In Patna it is पेड़नी *perni*, and डपटन *daptan* in South Bhagalpur.

307. The iron ladle used as a skimmer पौना is *pauna*, or (North Tirhut) मैलछन्ना *mailchhanna*, (South-West Shahabad and South Bhagalpur) थापी *thāpi* (also made of wood), and झँझरा *jhanjhra* in Patna, Gaya, and South Munger. Sometimes it is not necessarily of iron, and then it is खुरपा *khurpa* in South-West Shahabad, हथा *hatha* or हत्था *hattha* (of earthenware) in Patna, Gaya, and South Munger, and छनौटा *chhanauta* in Sāran and South Bhagalpur.

308. The boiling-pan is called कराह, कड़ाह *karāh* or कराही *karāhi*. The earthen vessel used for removing the cooked juice from the boiler is north of the Ganges सैक *saik* or सका *saika*, and in Shahabad it is पँगौरा *pangaura*; in Sāran it is पौँड़ा *paunra*. The pot in which the boiled syrup is placed is called मटुकी *matuki* south of the Ganges, also (South-West Shahabad) ओड़ी *ori*, (Gaya) नदुआ *naduа*, खोरा *khora* in the South-East, and कूँड़ी *kūnri* in South Bhagalpur.

309. नाद *nād* is a hole in the ground dug for receiving the coarse sugar. North of the Ganges it is also पौँढ़ा *paunrha* or पौँढ़ी *paunrhi*. The sugar is collected and thrown into this with a bamboo fitted at one end with a roller, which is called गुरदम *gurdam* or (in South-West Shahabad) गुरदन *gurdan*. In Tirhut it is also called दबकन *dabkan*, and in South-East Tirhut सपई *sapai*.

310. In North-East Tirhut माट *māt* or कोठी *kothi* is the large vessel in which the juice is finally coagulated. These are in Tirhut गुरपौर *gurpaur*, and in Champāran (made of sun-baked earth) डेहरी *dehri*.

311. राब *rāb* is undrained raw sugar, and गूर *gūr* is *rāb* boiled down for a longer time. Further particulars concerning these and the other products will be found in the chapter relating to sugar-cane (§§ 1014, 1015).

C.—THE SUGAR REFINERY.

312. A sugar refinery is known as चीनी के करखाना *chīni ke karkhāna* or चीनी के गोदाम *chīni ke godām.* South of the Ganges the word खँड़सार *khanrsār* or खँड़सारी *khanrsāri* is also used. The house in which the sugar is refined is called चूल्हा के घर *chūlha ke ghar* or कराह के घर *karāh ke ghar.* In South Bhagalpur it is भट्ठा *bhattha.*

313. In making coarse sugar (काँची चीनी *kānchi chīni*), a vat, a drain, a reservoir, and a treading-floor are used.

314. The *vat* is in Shahabad हौद *haud* or हौदी *haudi*, in Gaya चहबच्चा *chahbachcha*, in Patna खँड़गरना *khanrgarnà*, and in South Bhagalpur गुरहंडी *gurhandi.* North of the Ganges and in Gaya it is नाद *nād* or नाँद *nānd.*

315. The *drain* is नाली *nāli* or नारी *nāri*, or in South Bhagalpur करहा *karha.* In Sāran it is also called खाता *khāta.*

316. The *reservoir* is north of the Ganges, and optionally in Shahabad, नाद *nād* or नाँद *nānd.* In Shahabad it is डोभा *dobha*, in Patna हौद *haud* or चरुआ *charua*, and elsewhere south of the Ganges चहबच्चा *chahbachcha.*

317. The *treading-floor* is पट्टा *patta* north of the Ganges. South of it, it is in Shahabad पाटा *pāta*, in Patna and Gaya चबूतरा *chabutra*, and to the east चट्टी *chaṭṭi.*

318. In making regular sugar or सक्कर *sakkar*, the drain and the reservoir are used as before. The bundles (मोटरी *motri*, or in Patna नारगी *nārgi*, in Gaya थैया *thaiya*, and in South Bhagalpur गाजा *gāja*) of sugar are tied up in cloths [लोथा *lotha* or (in Patna and Gaya) छलना *chhalna*], placed on a bamboo framework and pressed with weights of stone or sun-dried clay. The framework is called north of the Ganges खाँच *khānch* or खाँचा *khāncha*, or (in Champāran and East Tirhut) छैंटा *chhainta.* In Shahabad it is ठटरी *thatri* or टिकठी *tikthi*, in Patna and Gaya टेकठी *tekthi*, and in South Bhagalpur चाँचरी *chānchri.* The weights are चाँपा *chāmpa*, or, when made of stone, पत्थल *pathal*, or in Saran थापी *thāpi.*

319. The following *utensils* are used in the boiling-house :—

(*a*) An iron boiler, कराह *karāh*, कराहा *karāha*, or कराही *karāhi.* When an earthen boiler is used, it is called खपड़ा *khapra* or खपड़ी *khapri*, or in South-West Shahabad and East Tirhut अथरी *athri.*

(*b*) An iron ladle for removing the scum. This is छनौटा *chhanauta* or पौना *pauna*, also in Patna and Gaya झँझरा *jhanjhra*.

(*c*) An earthen pot with holes in it, used as a filter, नाद *nād* or नाँद *nānd*. In South-West Shahabad it is ठेंठिवाल नाद *thenthiwāl nād*.

(*d*) A filter of river grass, known as सेँवार *semwār* or सेवार *sewār*, or in North-East Tirhut सेमार *semār*.

(*e*) A scraper for removing the layer of clean sugar. When made of shell it is called सितुआ *situa*, or in South-West Shahabad सितुहा *situha* or सुतुहा *sutuha*. A curved knife used for the same purpose is सिहोरनी *sihorni* in Sāran and Champāran, सेहोरना *sehorna* in Shahabad, and सोहरना *soharna* in North-East Tirhut.

(*f*) The filtering-basket for cleaning the same is खाँचा *khāncha* or खाँची *khānchi*. In Gaya it is डलवा *dalwa*, and in the east also डेली *deli*.

(*g*) The wooden or iron ladle for cooling the boiling syrup is north of the Ganges ताँमिया *tāmiya* or (in Sārān and North-East Tirhut) तमिया *tamiya*. South of the Ganges it is डब्बू *dabbu*, (in Shahabad) गुरदन *gurdan*, or in South Bhagalpur झँझरा *jhanjhra*.

(*h*) The iron stirring ladle used for taking syrup from the boiler and larger than the last is तामा *tāma* north of the Ganges; in Shahabad it is खुरचनी *khurchani* or डोहरा *dohra*; in Patna and Gaya it is छोलनी *chholni*; and in South Bhagalpur डोहला *dohla*.

(*i*) The earthenware jug for pouring the syrup into the boiler is सैका *saika*, also हत्था *hattha* in Patna and Gaya, and पँचनी *panchni* in South Bhagalpur. A larger jug of the same kind is निमड़ा *nimra* north of the Ganges, and निबड़ा *nibra* or परछा *parchha* south of it; also तौला *taula* in the east.

(*j*) The wooden supports of the filter are north of the Ganges खाता *khāta*, or खूँटा बल्ला *khūnta balla* south of the Ganges. They are in Shahabad सिढ़ी *sirhi* (also in South Munger) or तिरपाई *tirpāī*, and टेपाई *tepāī* in South Bhagalpur. In Patna and Gaya they are made of earth or brick, and are called गोड़ी *gori*.

(*k*) The shovel for stoking the fire is फरुही *pharuhi* or फहुरा *phahura* in Sāran and Champāran, and फरुहा *pharuha* or कोदारी *kodāri* in East Tirhut. In Shahabad it is खड़्मा *khorma*, or in the south-west of the district फरसा *pharsa*. In Gaya it is कढ़नी *karhni*, in Patna अगकढ़ना *agkarhna*, and in the east करछुल *karchhul*.

(*l*) The ladle for stirring the hot syrup in the cooling pan is तमियाँ *tamiyān* north of the Ganges and तँबिया *tambiya* in Shahabad. In South-West Shahabad it is डब्बू *dabbu*, in Patna and Gaya घटना *ghatna*, and in the east also दाबा *dāba*.

(*m*) The piece of matting or cloth in which the sugar is dried in the sun is पाल *pāl*, also in South-West Shahabad पाटा *pāta*, in Gaya टप्पर *tappar*, in Patna टाट *tāt*, and in South Bhagalpur चट्टी *chatti*.

(*n*) The flat wooden pans for cooling the syrup are कठौता *kathauta* or कठौती *kathauti*, also in the east कठौत *kathaut*, and in Sāran कठवत *kathwat*. In Sāran and Champāran they are नाद *nād* or ओसौनी *osauni*.

(*o*) The vessel into which the juice drops as it is filtered is परछा *parchha* or (North-East Tirhut and Shahabad) तौला *taula*.

CHAPTER III.—APPLIANCES USED IN THE MANUFACTURE OF INDIGO.

320. Indigo manufacture is confined almost entirely to North-Gangetic Bihār.*

321. The indigo beating-vat is महाइ के हौज (or हौद) *mahāi ke hauj* (or *haud*), and also in North-East Tirhut महनिया हौद *mahaniya haud*. The water reservoir is खजाना *khajāna*. The upper or steeping-vat is बोझाइ के हौद *bojhāi ke haud*, or in East Tirhut बोझनिया हौद *bojhaniya haud*. The rake for agitating the fermented liquor is फहुरी *phahuri* in Sāran and फरुहा *pharuha* elsewhere. In North-East Tirhut it is also फरमा *pharma*.

---

* The author is indebted to W. B. Hudson, Esq., for much of the information contained in this chapter. The system of manufacture described is the old style, now only used by natives. In European factories the use of steam power has made considerable changes.

322. The beams of wood for pressing the plant are दबौटा *dabauta* in Sāran and Champāran, सहतीर *sahtir* in Tirhut and Sāran, दाब *dāb* or धरन *dharan* in North-East Tirhut, and बीम *bīm* in South-East Tirhut. These are supported on projections in the walls of the vat, called मजुसी *majusi*, or in Champāran तान *tān*. In East Tirhut they are called सिरपाहा *sirpāha*. Under these pressing-beams are placed, बल्ला *ballal*, or in Sāran कैंच *kainch*, which are bamboos laid immediately on the top of the plant.

323. The हौदरी *haudri* (Sāran and South Tirhut) or माल झड़ी *māl jhari* (Champāran and North Tirhut) is the small reservoir where the indigo juice collects to be taken to the boiler. The drain is नाली *nāli* or नारी *nāri*, or in Sāran मोरी *mori*, and the छेकन *chhekan* is the door by which it is closed. The strainer is छन्ना *chhanna*, or in South-West Tirhut चद्दर *chaddar*.

324. The boiling-room is कराह घर *karāh ghar*. The मेज *mej* is the wooden or masonry straining table in which the indigo is put after being boiled. This is the name in Sāran, Champāran, and West Tirhut; to the east it is बालू मेज *bālu mej* or (in South-East Tirhut) माल मेज *māl mej*.

325. The पीरिच *pīrich* or पीरिस *pīris* is a corruption of the English word "press," in which the boiled liquor is placed in a cloth and the water pressed out. In Sāran डाला *dāla*, and elsewhere चलना *chalna*, are the perforated boards placed above and below the indigo in the press. The screw of the press is पेंच *pench*. The square boss or nut on it is ढिबरी *dhibri*. The मोरनी *morni* is the spanner or apparatus for turning the screw. In South-East Tirhut it is also ममोरनी *mamorni* or पेचकस *pechkas*. The large wooden beam through which the screw passes is ठेहा *theha* in Sāran, and elsewhere दबौटा *dabauta* or दाब *dāb*; when it is made of iron it is called in South Tirhut बाँक *bānk*. The कुटका *kutka* are small pieces of wood placed below and above the डाला *dāla* or चलना *chalna*.

326. The machine for cutting cakes is फरमा *pharma*, and the wires with which they are cut तार *tār*.

327. The cakes of indigo are गोटी *goti*, and they are dried in a drying-house, गोटी घर *goti ghar*, on shelves, called in East Tirhut मचान *machān*, and elsewhere चाली *chāli*.

328. The following are among the implements used in indigo agriculture:—

(1) The धरम लग्गी *dharm laggi*, a wheel for measuring land, each revolution of which covers one लग्गी *laggi*.

(2) The कुदार *kudār* or कुदारि *kudāri*, a mattock for digging.

(3) The हर *har* or plough, which is of two kinds—

(*a*) बिलाएती *bilāëti*, or English plough.

(*b*) देसी *desi* or कठौर *kathaur*, the country plough.

(4) टाँड़ी *tānri*, the drill plough.

(5) कान्टा *kanta* or खखोरनी *khakhorni*, the rake or harrow.

(6) खुरपी *khurpi*, the spud for weeding.

(7) हाँसू *hānsu* or हँसुआ *hansua*, the sickle for cutting the plant.

CHAPTER IV.—THE SPINNING-WHEEL.

329. The following diary shows the process of spinning thread and making cloth in the subdivision of Madhubani, in North-East Tirhut, in the year 1879:—

On the 20th September the writer bought 24 *sers* of cotton, being a day's plucking on a sunny day from about a bigha and a half of cotton field. The cotton बाँगा *bānga* (see § 1016 for the various names and varieties) was of the kind called कोकटी *kokti*, which ripens in the month of *Bhādon* (August–September). It was pulled out of the husks from the tree.

20*th*—26*th September*.—During this time the cotton has been drying in the sun, and now (26th) two old women are employed to clean it, picking out the dirty and immature cotton, called करकुट *karkut*. This is principally composed of seeds which have come to nothing and been worm-eaten. This cleaning is done by hand. It lasted to the 30th September.

1*st October*.—Commenced to separate the seeds, बँगौर *bangaur*, from the बाँगा *bānga*. This is done by a machine called चरखी *charkhi*, which consists of two rollers, about an inch thick, of hard wood tightly wedged one above the

THE SPINNING-WHEEL (CHARKHA).

...th by Bepin Behary Dass Student Govt. School of Art Calcutta.

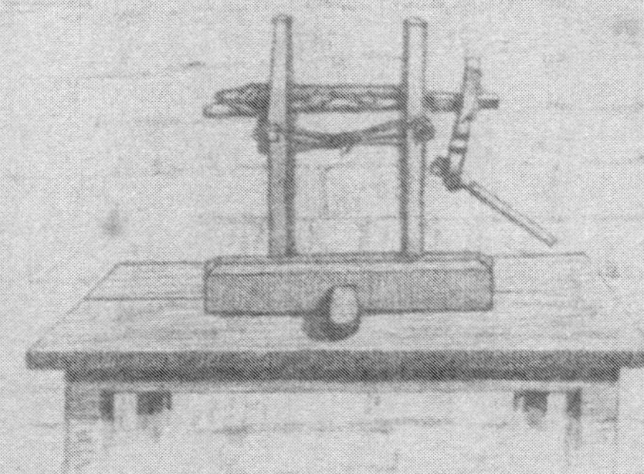

MACHINE FOR CLEANING RAW COTTON (CHARKI)

Printed by Abdool Rohim Govt. School of Art Calcutta.

other; both rollers are supported in uprights, the ends passing through. At one end the lower roller is turned by a handle, and has at the other end, where it projects from the upright, a screw cut in it. The same end of the upper screw has a reversed screw cut in it, and these two screws fitting into each other act like cog-wheels; but when the lower roller is turned, the upper roller turns in the direction reverse to that of the lower one, so that they act as a pair of feeders tightly wedged together. The बाँगा *bānga* or uncleaned cotton is then applied to the feeding side of the two rollers, and on the handle being turned the cotton is pulled forcibly through by their revolution, while the seeds remain behind and fall down to the ground.

330. The two upright standards are called खूँटा *khūnta*, and each of the rollers जाठि *jāthi*, or in Sāran सँड़ारी *sanrāri*. Underneath the rollers is a cross-bar, called कल *kal*, joining the two uprights and holding the machine together. The खूँटी *khūnti* is a wedge going through each upright from front to back, under the cross-bar and holding it and the roller in their places.

331. The पचरी *pachri* are the wedges running sideways through each upright and tightening the two rollers together. The crank which turns the lower roller is called मकरी *makri*, and it is held to it by the किल्ली *killi* or linch-pin. The handle at the other end of the crank, which is held in the hand, and by which the machine is turned, is called लागनि *lāgani*, or in Sāran चलौनी *chalauni* and in Gaya हथौरी *hathauri*.

332. The base of the machine in which the uprights rest si called पीढ़ा *pīrha*, or to the west पिढ़िया *pirhiya*, and out of this projects behind, along the ground, the मझवा *majhwa*, on which the foot of the operator is placed to keep the machine steady.

333. The cotton, when cleaned from the seeds by this machine, is called रू *rū*, रूई *rūi*, or तूर *tūr*,—the last by women of the upper Hindu castes, and the two first by Musalmāns and low-caste Hindus. रूआ *rūa* is used in Shahabad.

334. The above lasted three days. It was then again cleaned (तूनब *tūnab*, तूँनब *tūnnab*, or (in Shahabad) तूमब *tūmab*, to clean), the few remaining pieces of husk, &c., being picked out by hand.

21*st October.*—The cotton was to-day put out in the sun preparatory to being carded (धूनब *dhūnab,* to card).

22*nd October.*—To-day two cotton-carders (धुनिया *dhuniya*) came to card the cotton. Each brought with him a machine, called a धुनन्की *dhunki*, or to the west धनुही *dhanuhi.* In Gaya it is धुनेठी *dhunethi,* in South Munger and South-East Tirhut धुनैठ *dhunaith,* and in South Bhagalpur धुनन्हठ *dhunhath.*

335. It is composed of the following parts :—

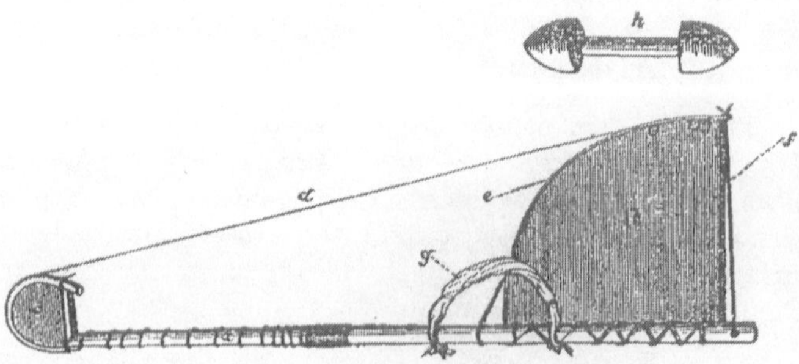

(*a*) The flexible piece of wood acting as a bow, called डण्टी *danti* or डण्टा *danta* to the east and डाँड़ी *dānri* to the west.

(*b*) A broad wooden board, called फरेहा *phareha* in North-East Tirhut. In South-West Tirhut it is फरौटा *pharauta,* in South Bhagalpur फरुहा *pharuha,* and elsewhere as फरन्हा *pharha.*

(*c*) The bridge over which the string is passed, माँगी *māngi.* In Shahabad and also optionally in East Tirhut it is माथा *mātha,* in South Bhagalpur मथन्वा *mathwa,* and in South Munger मगन्वासी *magwāsi.*

(*d*) A leather string, called ताँत *tānt.* In Patna and Gaya it is also called रोदा *roda.*

(*e*) A leather strip acting as a sounding board, lying along the round edge of the फरेहा *phareha,* on which the string rebounds, called पुछेट *puchhet* or पुछेटा *puchheta* generally,

A Cotton-carder (*Dhuniya*) at Work

Lith. by Ram Chunder Ghosal, Student Govt. School of Art Calcutta. Cornwallis Press Calcutta.

पछौटा *pachhauta* in Tirhut, and काँकर *kānkar* in Sāran and Champāran. In North-East Tirhut it is पुश्तैल *pushtail,* and an optional name in Shahabad is पुछौटा *puchhauta.*

(*f*) A stout leather string along the outer side of the फरेहा *phareha,* to one end of which the ताँत *tānt* is attached, while the other end is fastened to the डण्टी *danti.* It is used to tighten the ताँत *tānt,* and is called घिरची *ghirchi* or घुरची *ghurchi.* When pegs are used for tightening this, they are called बीरी *bīri* or बिरिया *biriya.*

(*g*) The हथहर *hathhar,* हथगर *hathgar,* or हथकर *hathkar,* is a loop of string under which the left hand is passed to hold the machine steady. The above is the name current in North-East Tirhut. South of the Ganges it is also called हथकर *hathkar,* with variants हथकड़ *hathkar* or हथकड़ा *hathkara* in Shahabad. In North-West Tirhut it is हथरा *hathra,* in South-West Tirhut and Sāran हथा *hathā,* and in Sāran and Champāran मुठवारा *muthwāra.*

(*h*) The mallet for twanging the bow, of wood, shaped like a dumb-bell. It is held in the right hand, and the ताँत *tānt* is struck and twanged with it. It is called जिस्ता *jista,* and also (in Tirhut and South Bhagalpur) दिस्ता *dista.* In Patna it is called दस्ता *dasta,* and in South Munger दिस्था *distha.*

336. In using this instrument it is held by the left hand under the हथकर *hathkar,* which passes over the wrist, and the ताँत *tānt* twanged in the midst of the cotton by the जिस्ता *jista,* which is held in the right hand. This process loosens the texture of the cotton, and causes all the dust and dirt to fly out of it. The धुनकी *dhunki* is not allowed to rest on the ground, but is supported in the air by the हथकर *hathkar* passing over the wrist, and it springs up and down as the ताँत *tānt* is twanged.

337. The whole pile of cleaned cotton was called गोठी *gothi.* While this was going on, two old women were called in to make little hollow rolls of cotton to be made into thread. They are called to the east पीनी *pīni,* and to the west पिउनी *piuni* or पेवनी *pewni.* A local name in East Tirhut is पीर *pīr.* These are about four inches long and a quarter of an inch thick. A lump of clean cotton, the size of a walnut, is put round a thin skewer, called पिंढ़सरि *pinrhsari,* and is then rolled on a board, called पिढ़िया *pirhiya,* with the palm of the hand. These are then tied up in bundles of about ten each, called मुट्ठी *mutthi.*

338. These पीनी *pīni* are now ready for being made into thread in the spinning-wheel.

339. The spinning-wheel is चरखा *charkha*, but in South-West Shahabad it is रहटा *rahta*, and in the south-east जरखा *jarkha*.

340. Its parts are as follows :—

The foundation.—This is in the shape of a double letter T : thus—

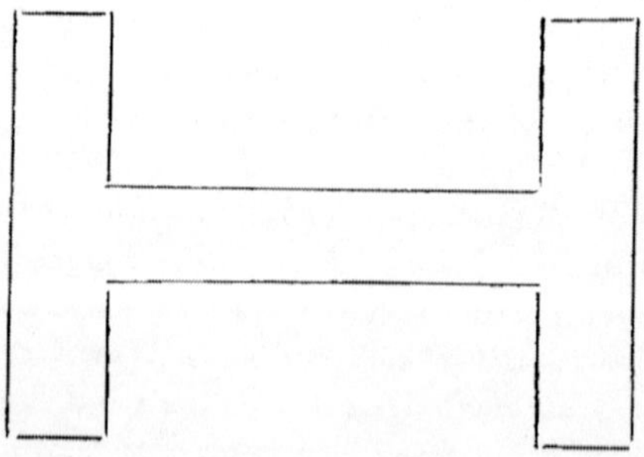

341. On one of the cross-pieces the driving-wheel stands, and on the other the spinning apparatus. This foundation is called पीढ़ा *pīrha* or पिढ़िया *pirhiya* to the east, and पिढ़ई *pirhaī* to the west. The connecting bar between the two cross-pieces is मँझवा *manjhwa* or माँझा *mānjha*, in Patna and Gaya it is लतखोरा *latkhora*, and in South Bhagalpur मनझाई *manjhāī*.

342. *The driving-wheel.*—The supports of the driving-wheel are called खूँटा *khūnta*. The wheel itself is composed of two parts,—

(*a*) The central boss or nave, and

(*b*) The four spokes on each side of the nave.

343. The nave is called मूँड़ी *mūnri* or मूड़ी *mūri* south of the Ganges, and मूँड़ी *mūnri* or मुँड़िया *munriya* north of it; in East Tirhut it is also तामा *tāma*, and in South Bhagalpur and South Munger पैला *paila*. It is about 5 inches long and 4 inches thick.

344. There are four spokes lying across each end of the nave from one circumference to the other; there are therefore eight radii on each side, and they are so arranged that the radii on each side are not opposite each other, but alternate. Each of these cross spokes is called पुत्ती *putti* or पूती *pūti*, or in South-West Shahabad कमरी *kamri*; sometimes they are also called खूँटा *khūnta* or खूँटी *khūnti*.

345. These spokes are held in their places by a string, called अवाल *awāl* to the west, अँवाल *amwāl* in Patna and Gaya, and अमाल *amāl* or अमाल्ह *amālh* to the east. In South Munger it is अम्हाल *amhāl.* This string goes round the extremities of each radius of each side alternately: thus—

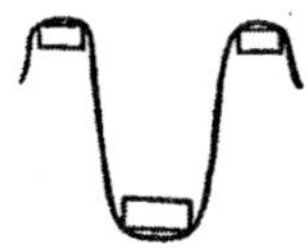

It forms therefore a kind of edge or rim of a broad wheel, something like a paddle-wheel, and over it passes the driving-band which turns the spinning apparatus. This paddle-wheel is about a foot in diameter and five inches thick.

346. The central axle of the driving-wheel is called लाठ *lāth* generally north of the Ganges and in South Bhagalpur. In Tirhut it is called जाठ *jāth*, and in North-East Tirhut also लाइठ *lāïth* or जाइठ *jāïth.* South of the Ganges it is generally बेलना *belna.* It is caused to revolve by a crank end called मकरी *makri,* or in Shahabad and West Tirhut नाक *nāk.* It is दाढ़ी *dārhi* or दढ़िया *darhiya* elsewhere south of the Ganges, except South Bhagalpur, where it is again मकरी *makri.* To this is attached a handle, called to the west and in Gaya चलौना *chalauna*, and to the east लरना *larna* or लारनि *lārani* In South-West Shahabad it is called भौंती *bhaunti* or भाँवत *bhāmwat*, and in Sāran optionally चलौनी *chalauni.*

347. *The driving-band* is called माल *māl* or माल्ह *mālh.* It is rubbed with rosin (धूमन *dhūman*) and oil (तेल *tel*), and is then blackened with charcoal (कोइला *koela*). The driving-band goes twice round the driving-wheel and the spinning-axle, once passing through the मलकाठी *malkāthi* (*vide post*), and once not.

348. *The spinning apparatus.*—We now come to the spinning apparatus. There are three perpendicular uprights. The two outside ones are called खूँटी *khūnti*, and the middle one is called मलकाठी *malkāthi.* In Patna these three uprights are called together पचकठिया *pachkathiya*, and in South-West Shahabad खुँटिपुत्ती *khuntiputti.* The two outside ones support the bearings of the spinning-axle, and the centre one has in its length, facing the driving-wheel and going right through its thickness, a long slot cut. One of the strings of the driving-band passes through this slot, and the other passes outside it, so that the double turn round the spinning-axle can never get jammed up together, and so entangled.

349. On the two outside uprights, on the side furthest from the driving-wheel, project two stiff pieces of leather, called चमरख *chamrakh.* These form the bearings of the spinning-axle, which passes through them.

350. *The spinning-axle.*—This is called टकुआ *takua,* and also to the west टेकुआ *tekua.* It is an iron skewer about 8 inches long and an eighth of an inch thick at the thickest part. It projects a distance of three inches beyond its bearing on the same side as the handle of the driving-wheel. This bearing has on each side two little pieces of wood fitting on to the spinning-axle, which act as washers, and are called छुच्छी *chhuchchhi.* Outside the outer washer on the spinning-axle is a flat disc called फिरकी *phirki,* and two and a half inches of the axle project beyond it.

351. The driving-band, after passing twice round the driving-wheel, passes through the मलकाठी *malkāthi,* then twice round the spinning-axle, and then back to the driving-wheel outside the मलकाठी *malkāthi;* and it is evident that even the slow turning of the driving-wheel will make the spinning-axle revolve at a very high speed indeed.

352. In spinning, the projecting point of the spinning-axle has a short length of thread attached to it, and then, while the handle of the driving-wheel is turned with the right hand, a roll of cotton (पीनी *pīnī*) is held in the left hand between the finger and thumb, and the cotton, being quickly caught up by the length of thread, is drawn off in the shape of thread on to the quickly revolving spinning-axle.

353. When the projecting point of the spinning-axle is filled with thread, the whole is called a कुकरी *kukri,* or in Sāran कुकुड़ी *kukurhi,* and is wound off on a winder, called परता *parta* or परेता *pareta.* It is also called in South-West Tirhut नटवा *natwa,* and in East Tirhut लटवा *latwa* or नटवा *natwa.* In South Bhagalpur it is called नटई *nataī.* This is like an ordinary silk-winder. The handle (चलौना *chalauna*) of the driving-wheel is taken out of its socket in the crank (मकरी *makri*), and in its place is placed one end of the axle of the winder. The other end is held in the right hand, and is revolved between the finger and thumb. The winder is conical in shape, and does not need further description. It will hold half a quarter of a *ser* of thread at a time. When it is filled, the thread is taken off and tied in hanks. These are generally पोला *pola*, पोली *poli*, or पोलिया *poliya*. Local names are नत्ती *natti* (North-East Tirhut), लत्ती *latti* (Patna and Gaya), and करन्ची *karchi* in South-West Shahabad.

354. The diary breaks off here temporarily, as the spinning of this particular cotton was not done in the writer's presence. He wished the thread to be spun as fine as possible, and as this could only be done by Brāhmani women, who would not come to a strange house, this part of the work was done by them at home.

CHAPTER V.—THE WEAVER'S LOOM.

355. The following is a continuation of the same diary.

18*th January* 1880.—The skeins of fine thread were brought to me to-day, and were put in water to soak for eight days. This strengthens it.

27*th January*.—After they had soaked this period I sent for a weaver. A Muhammadan weaver is जोलन्हा *jolha* or मोमिन *momin*, and a Hindu weaver is तँतन्वा *tantwa* or ताँती *tānti*, or, in Shahabad ताँतो *tānto*. Sometimes the Hindi word जोलाहा *jolāha* is used instead of जोलन्हा *jolha*.

356. The Musalmān weaver or जोलन्हा *jolha* is the proverbial fool of Hindu stories and proverbs. He swims in the moonlight across fields of flowering linseed, thinking the blue colour to be caused by water. He hears his family priest reading the *Qurān*, and bursts into tears to the gratification of the reader. When pressed to tell what part affected him most, he says it was not that, but the wagging beard of the old gentleman so much reminded him of a pet goat which had died. When forming one of a company of twelve he tries to count them, and finding himself missing wants to perform his own funeral obsequies. He finds the rear peg of a plough, and wants to set up farming on the strength of it. He gets into a boat at night, and forgets to pull up the anchor. After rowing till dawn he finds himself where he started, and concludes that the only explanation is that his native village could not bear to lose him, and had followed him. If there are eight weavers and nine *hukkas*, they fight for the odd one. Once on a time a crow carried off to the roof of the house some bread which a weaver had given his child. Before giving the child any more he took the precaution of removing the ladder. Like the English fool, he always gets unmerited blows. For instance, he once went to see a ram fight and got butted himself, as the saying runs:—

करिगह छाड़ तमाशा जाय
नाहक चोट जोलाहा खाय.
Karigah chhār tamāsa jāy,
Nāhak chot jolāha khāy.

—'He left his loom to see the fun, and for no reason got a bruising.' Another story (told by Fallon) is, that being told by a soothsayer that it was written in his fate that his nose would be cut off with an axe, the weaver was incredulous, and taking up an axe kept flourishing it, saying यों करबा तऽ गोड़ काटबों, यों करबा तऽ हाथ काटबों, और यों करबा तह ना-, *yon karba ta gor kātbon, yon karba ta hāth kātbon, aur yon karba tah nā-*, —if I do *so* I cut my leg, and if I do *so* I cut my hand; but unless I do *so* my no—, and his nose *was* off. A proverb जोलहा जानथि जौ काटै *jolha jānathi jau kātai*,—does a weaver know how to cut barley,—refers to a story (in Fallon) that a weaver, unable to pay his debt, was set to cut barley by his creditor, who thought to repay himself in this way. But instead of reaping, the stupid fellow kept trying to untwist the tangled barley stems. Other proverbs at his expense are कौआ चलल बास कें, जोलहा चलल घास कें *kaua chalal bās ken, jolha chalal ghās ken,*—the weaver went out to cut grass (at sunset), when even the crows were going home; जोलहा भुतिऐलाह तीसी खेत *jolha bhutiaitāh tīsi khet*,—the weaver lost his way in the linseed-field, an allusion to the swimming exploit already recorded. His wife bears an equally bad character, as in the proverb बहसलि जोलहिनि बापक दाँढ़ी नोचे *bahsali jolhini bāpak dānrhi noche*,—a wilful weaver's wife will pull her own father's beard.

357. The weaver proceeded to set up in the ground seventeen pairs of sticks in two lines, at a distance between each pair of about one and a quarter cubits, and between the lines of about two cubits. At each end of each line a stout bamboo post is fixed, and close to each of those at one end another smaller staff. Round these sticks the thread is twisted as follows :—

A, A, A, A, are the tops of the bamboo posts, and the dots are the tops of the smaller sticks.

358. This operation of setting the warp is called तानी करब *tāni-karab*, or in Shahabad ताना करब *tāna karab*. The bamboo posts are called खूँटी *khūnti*, and each stick, सर *sar*. These last are called in Sāran, Champāran, and North-West Tirhut सर॰का *sarka*.

359. The sticks immediately in front of the bamboo posts are called to the west छिटुआ *chhitua*, in Shahabad छिप॰की *chhipki*, and to the east छिट॰की *chhitki*, also in North-East Tirhut डोरीक सर *dorīk sar*. The whole apparatus is called तानी *tāni*, or in Shahabad ताना *tāna*, and the thread to be stretched is put on a kind of pyramidal reel called चर॰खी *charkhi*. It spins on a spindle, called दग॰नी *dagni*, or in Shahabad डाँगी *dāngi*, and in the inside of the apex of the cone is a cup called थोड़ी *thori*, or in Shahabad थोल॰री *tholri*, in South Munger थोड़॰ली *thorli*, and in South Bhagalpur टोई *toï*, which rests on, and revolves on the point of, the spindle : thus—

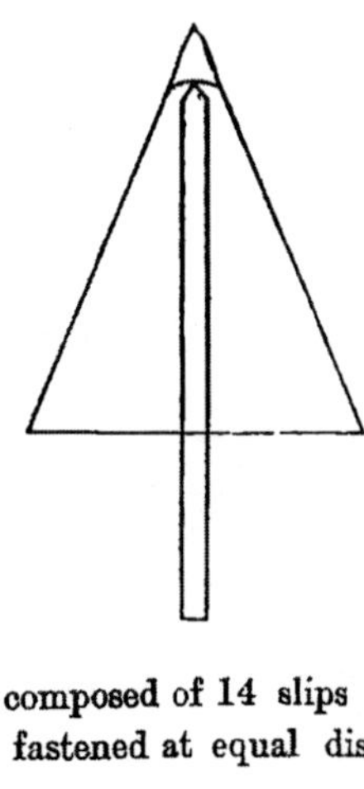

360. The spool is composed of 14 slips of bamboo, forming the framework of the cone, fastened at equal distances round the circum-

ference (चक्कर *chakkar*) of the base of the cone, and converging to a point at the top.

361. The spindle of the spool is held in the left hand, and the weaver walks up and down between the two lines of thread, directing the thread by a hook called खूँड़ी *khūnri* or खोँड़ी *khonri*, or in South-West Shahabad खुण्डा *khunda*, in South Munger खुण्डी *khundi*, and in North-East Tirhut and Shahabad खूँड़ा *khūnra*, and shaped as follows :—

The hook at the top is made of iron.

362. *5th February* 1880.—The warp having now been all set upon the sticks (सर *sar*), they were, with the खूँटी *khūnti*, pulled up, rolled up, and put by till to-day. To-day they were unrolled and laid out in a long line on the grass. The खूँटी *khūnti* were then carefully drawn out, and a bamboo staff, called सिरार *sirār* (or सिरारि *sirāri*), put in the place of each. It will be remembered that the सर *sar* were in pairs, and that at each pair the thread crossed thus 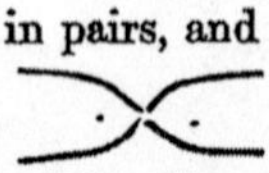 Another kind of सर *sar* is now taken, made like a long shallow bow, except that the string is made of a thin strip of bamboo. This bow is called सुतरी *sutri*, or in Tirhut बन्हका *banhka*. The arch of the bow is also made of bamboo. The bamboo string is called डोरी *dori*. The arch of the bow is now passed through the threads where one of the old सर *sar* was, and the bamboo string through where the other सर *sar* of the pair was, so that the cross of the threads is still preserved. The bow and string are then fastened to each other at each end. The arches of the various bows all face one way. The warp is then laid out on the ground, and the threads neatly spread out upon the bows in parallel lines, to the width of the future piece of cloth.

362A. *9th February.*—The thread thus arranged was rolled up, dipped into, and well wet with cold rice-water (माँड़ *mānr*), to which some मड़ुआ *marua* seeds had been added to stiffen it. It was then unrolled and stretched out horizontally at a height of three feet from the ground and brushed with a large brush, called कूँच *kūnch*, dipped in mustard oil and water, which smooths the threads and takes away any knots or inequalities in the thread. This brush is also called मज्ना *majna* in West Tirhut, माँजा *mānja* in South Bhagalpur, and माँजन *mānjan* in South-West Shahabad. The cross sticks on which the thread rests are called माँझा *mānjha*, and the cross bamboos at each end are ठेँघ्नी *thenghni* or लाठी डोर *lāthī dor* to the west, गोड़ा *gora* to the east, खस्रैया *khasraiya* in North-West Tirhut, ढट्ठा *dhattha* also in North-East Tirhut, ढाँठा *dhāntha* in South Bhagalpur, and लाठी *lāthi* also in South-East Tirhut. This brushing is hard work, and takes eight men to do it properly. The brushing is along the threads, and not across them. The bristles of the brush are made of खस्खस *khaskhas*, called also in Sāran कत्रा के जड़ *katra ke jar*, such as is used for tatties, and are about two and a half inches long. The brush itself is about a foot long and two inches wide. The brushing went on for three days, and is called पाइ करब *pāi karab*, and also in East Tirhut तासन करब *tāsan karab*. The phrase आइ पाइ *āi pāi* means the brushing and other preparations, and there is a proverb, जोल्हा के आइ पाइ, चम्रा के बिहान *jolha ke āi pāi, chamra ke bihān*,—when a weaver says the cloth will be soon ready, as he is now brushing it, don't believe him, any more than you believe a shoemaker who says 'the boots will be ready to-morrow.'

363. When this was concluded, the threads were put into the loom and woven at the rate of a yard a day. The *loom* is little different from that used in England. It is called करिगह *karigah* to the west and करगह *kargah* to the east. It consists of the following parts :—

(1) The *shuttle*.—This is ढरकी *dharki* in Gaya and to the west, and कपरबिन्नी *kaparbinni* or कपरबीनी *kaparbīni* to the east. In North-East Tirhut it is also called कपरनी *kaparni*.

(2) The *needle* inside the shuttle, on which the thread is wound, is तिरी *tiri*, and the tube which revolves on this छुछी *chhuchchhi*, or in Shahabad छुंछी *chhunchhi*. When thread is wound on this tube the whole is called नरी *narī*, also in East Tirhut लरी *lari*. This is held in its place in the hollow of the shuttle by a pin made of a feather. This is called पखनरी *pakhnari* to the west and in South-East Tirhut, बीर *bīr* in South Bhagalpur, and पखबीर *pakhbīr* or पखेआरी *pakheāri* to the east. A weaver estimates his work by the number of नरी *nari* which he uses up, as in the proverb in which he is supposed to address a man who has seized him to carry a load, टँगबह त टाँगह, नहिँ त नौ नरीक हरकति होएत *tangbah ta tāngah, nahiñ ta nau narīk harkati hoet*,—if you must load me, load me quickly, otherwise the time of nine shuttles will be wasted.

(3) The *wooden frame* suspended from the roof, which after the shuttle passes is pulled forward by the weaver and drives the thread home. This is हथा *hathā* or हत्था *hattha* in West Shahabad, Patna, and West Tirhut, कमँहड़ *kamhanr* in the west generally, कमहर *kamhar*, in the north-west, and कमहंडा *kamhanda* in Gaya. In North-East Tirhut it is ताना *tāna*, and in South-East Tirhut तानी *tāni* In South Bhagalpur it is तनकर *tankar*.

(4) The *comb* of reeds or bamboo in this bar, which keeps the threads of the warp apart, is called राछ *rāchh*.

(5) The *heddles*, which alternately raise or depress the threads of the warp, are बए *bae* or बै *bai*.

(6) The set of three *reeds* which is placed in front of the heddles to keep the two sets of the threads of the warp apart is

The Country Loom (Karigah).

1. *Hatha.*
2. *Rāchh (comb).*
3, 3. *Bai (heddles).*
4, 4, 4. *Sar.*
5. *Chaupat (roller).*
6. *Jibhela.*
7. *Bamwāri.*
8. *Kharkhaut.*
9. *Kanaili.*
10. *Agela.*
11. *Dorbandha.*
12, 12. *Nachni (heddle-levers).*
13. *Kar (upper beam)*
14. *Pāi (woof).*
15. *Sirāra.*
16. *Tangni.*

अतरावन *atrāwan* north of the Ganges generally and in Shahabad, and तरावन *tarāwan* elsewhere south of the Ganges. Another set of three reeds also used is called भँजनी *bhanjni* in Champāran, North Tirhut, Gaya, and South Munger, and the two sets together are called in North-East Tirhut अतरावन भाँज *atrāwan bhānj*. In Patna and the south-east the reeds are also called सर *sar*.

(7) The elastic *bow* which keeps the woven cloth stretched in front of the weaver is पन्निक *pannik* south of the Ganges; north of the Ganges it is पन्निख *pannikh*, and also पन्नी *panni* in East Tirhut.

(8) The wooden *roller* behind which the weaver sits, and on which the cloth is wound up as fast as it is made, is in the north-west, in West Shahabad, and in South Munger लपेटन *lapetan;* elsewhere it is चौपत *chaupat.*

(9) This is supported by *posts* called खूँटा *khūnta;* also the right and left ones have different names, viz. the right-hand one, which passes through the roller and prevents it turning round, is जिभेला *jibhela* everywhere, in North-East Tirhut also जिहला *jihla*, and in South-East Tirhut also जिहेला *jihela*. In South Bhagalpur it is गाली खूँटा *gāli khūnta*. The left-hand one, against which the roller rests, is बँघेला *banghela* north of the Ganges everywhere. Also, in East Tirhut, as also to the west and Gaya, it is बँवारी *bamwāri* or बँवरिया *bamwariya*, in Shahabad it is also पछेला *pachhela*, and in South-West Tirhut कँधेला *kandhela*. In South-East Tirhut it is also called बमैला *bamaila*. In South Bhagulpur it is simply खुट्टा *khutta*.

(10) The woof is supported at the end opposite the weaver by a piece of wood called खरकौट *kharkaut* to the west and खरकौटी *kharkauti* to the east or खरकूटी *kharkūti* in South Bhagalpur, which is held up by pillars called कनैली *kanaili* to the north and west, खूँटा *khūnta* in East Tirhut, थूम *thūm* in Patna, थुम्भी *thumbhi* in Gaya, and थुम्भा *thumbha* in the east, and also खरको खूँटा *kharko khūnta* in South Bhagalpur.

(11) The woof is held tight by a string, which is fastened to its end and passes round a peg at the extreme end of the loom and back again up to the weaver, where it is fastened within his reach to another peg. He is thus able to slacken the woof as necessary. The first peg is called अगेला के खूँटा *agela ke khūnta*, or in Tirhut सरकौनी के खूँटी *sarkauni ke khūnti;* the second peg is called डोरबन्धा के खूँटा *dorbandha ke khūnta*, or in South Bhagalpur कनकिल्ली *kankilli.*

(12) The *treadle,* which the weaver moves with his foot, is पौँसार *paunsār* or पौसार *pausār* generally, and in East Tirhut पसार *pasār*. The knob on this, held between the weaver's toes, is पौतान *pautān.*

(13) The *upper levers,* to which the heddles are attached, are नचनी *nachni* generally. In East Tirhut they are लोचनी *lochni*, and in South Munger लचनी *lachni.*

(14) These levers are fastened to an *upper beam,* which has various names, viz. अभेर *abher* to the west, भितभेरा *bhitbhera* in Sāran and Champāran, धचाना *dhachāna* in South-West Tirhut, धचान *dhachān* or अकासी *akāsi* in North-East Tirhut, उपरकर *uparkar* in South-East Tirhut, करबार *korbār* in Gaya, and कर *kar* in Patna and South Munger.

364. The loose end of the woof (पाइ *pāī*) is called सिरारा *sirāra*, and it is wound up on a टंगनी *tangni*, which is hung up out of the way.

CHAPTER VI.—THE SALTPETRE MANUFACTURER.

365. He is called नोनियाँ *noniyān.* The round vat in which he dissolves the saltpetre from the saline earth is कोठी *kothi* north of the Ganges, and south of it अहरी *ahri.* The mother liquid thus produced flows out through a drain called पनार *panār* in Tirhut and to the east, and पौनार *paunār* to the west; also in Sāran मोहान *mohān*, and in South-West Shahabad परनौहा *parnauha.* It flows into an earthen vessel fixed in the ground, called नदहा *nadha*, नाद *nād*, or नादा *nāda*, also परछा *parchha* in Tirhut and towards the west, and गड़नी *garni* in South-East Tirhut.

366. The mother liquid is called रस *ras*, or in South-West Shahabad अगरस *agras.* After the saltpetre has been deposited, the refuse liquid from which salt can be educed is called पछाड़ी *pachhāri*, or in South-West Shahabad काही *kāhi*. In Sāran काही *kāhi* means the liquor from which salt is educed, and पछाड़ी *pachhāri* the refuse which is thrown away.

367. Over the round vat are placed bamboo rafters, which are called कोरई *koraī* to the west, कोरो *koro* in North-East Tirhut, and पटवटन *patwatan* in South-East Tirhut. These are supported on bricks, ईंटा *īnta*, and over them is spread straw, called छाजा *chhāja*, छिट्टी *chhitti*, or खर *khar*.

368. The mother liquor is boiled in a large iron pan called कराह *karah*, or (to the east) तौला *taula*. When made of earth it is called कुण्डा *kunda*, or in Sāran खोर *khor*. The fireplace is called चुल्हा *chūlha*. The pot for cooling the boiled liquid is हँड़िया *hanriya*, or to the east तौला *taula*.

369. The iron curved spud by which the saline earth is scraped from the ground or wall is खुरपा *khurpa*, and the mattock for digging is फहुरा *phahura* to the west, कोदार *kodār* in Tirhut, and कुदारी *kudāri* in Sāran. The basket for carrying the saline earth is टोकड़ी *tokri*, and that for carrying the saltpetre छैंटी *chhainti*

370. In South-West Shahabad—

(*a*) जरुआ सोरा *jarua sora* is saltpetre prepared by boiling ;

(*b*) आबी सोरा *abi sora* is saltpetre prepared by evaporation by the sun's rays ; and

(*c*) कलमी सोरा *kalmi sora* is refined saltpetre.

CHAPTER VII.—A DISTILLERY OF COUNTRY-LIQUOR.

371. भट्ठीदार *bhatthidār* or आबकार *ābkār* is a distiller. In Sāran he is also called राँकी *rānki*. कलाल *kalāl* is a Muhammadan who sells country-wine ; कलवार *kalwār* is a Hindu who does this. कलाल *kalāl* and राँकी *rānki* are caste names. When a man of another caste sells liquor, either on his own account or as a servant, he is called गद्दीवान *gaddiwān*. भट्ठी *bhatthi* is a distillery. कलाली *kalāli* or गद्दी *gaddi* is a place where country-spirits are sold.

372. The still is called भट्ठी *bhatthi*, and consists of the following parts :—

(1) देग *deg* or डेग *deg*, the boiler.—This has a baked earthen cover called अधकार *adhkār*, or in Sāran अधकर *adhkar*.

(2) Over this is inverted a wide-mouthed globular copper vessel; this is called तम्मी *tāmmi*, or in Sāran तमिया *tamiya*. It serves as a condensing-vessel. The spirit rises into it, and over its outside surface runs continually a supply of cold water.

(3) The water reservoir is नाद *nād*. The water flows from this through a pipe called पौनल्ली *paunalli*, or in South Bhagalpur पन्नाली *pannāli*, and in Sāran also ढोंगा *dhonga*, on to the top of the condensing-vessel.

(4) The spirit thus condensed flows out through a pipe called मधनरी *madhnari*.

(5) The spirit is collected in an earthen jar called टाँक *tānk* or मटुका *matuka*, and in this it is carried to the place of sale.

(6) The refuse left in the boiler is रस *ras*; also, in Gaya, बकसा *baksa*, and in South Bhagalpur also गोरा *gora*.

(7) साजन *sājan* or छाबन *chhāban* is water used for diluting spirit, so as to increase the quantity for sale.

(8) The liquid for distillation is made as follows. Liquid (रस *ras*) and sweet preparations (मीठा *mītha*) are mixed and buried in the ground. This mixture is called कसौंजी *kasaunji*. When it is ripe महुआ *mahua* is poured into it. This act of mixing is called भरती *bharti*. When the mixture is sufficiently fermented for distillation it is called बोझाइ *bojhāi*. The constituents of the रस *ras* and of the मीठा *mītha* vary, and are not detailed here.

(9) Earthen cups for drinking country-spirit are चुकड़ *chukkar*, गुड़की *gurki*, or पिटौआ *pitaua*.

(10) Pots for keeping the spirit in the shop are called माट *māt*, कोरेना *korena*, or in Shahabad कौरेना *kaurena* and बुइयाम *buiyām*. In Sāran another name is कराबा *karāba*.

373. Ordinary weak country-spirit is दोकानी *dokāni*, and also in Sāran खसिया *khasiya*; the next strongest (when made of गूर *gūr* only) is कन्दी *kandi* or (when made of other materials) दोबारा *dobāra*; the next strongest is सौंफी *saumphi*, or in South-East Tirhut सेबारा *sebāra*; and the strongest of all, महरन्दार *mahardār*.

SUBDIVISION VIII.

APPLIANCES USED BY MISCELLANEOUS VILLAGE TRADERS AND PROFESSIONALS.

CHAPTER I.—THE PALM-JUICE SELLER.

374. The palm-juice seller is पासी *pāsi.*

375. In climbing up the palm-tree he uses a heel-rope, which ties his feet close together. At the same time he has a stout rope passing round the tree and his body. He leans back against this rope, and presses the soles of his feet, thus tied together, against the tree. He then climbs up the tree by a series of hitches or jerks of his back and his feet alternately. The heel-rope is called मक॰री *makri*, or to the west पकुसी *pakusi.* In Shahabad it is पक॰सी *paksi*, and in Tirhut and Patna फँदिया *phandiya.* The body-rope is generally डँड़॰वाँस *danrwāns.* In the east it is also रस्सा *rassa*, and in South Munger बार॰ता *bārta.*

376. The longish earthen pot in which the juice is collected is called लब॰नी *labni*, or to the east उड़ह *urharh.* Round its neck is tied a string, called to the west अर॰वन *arwan* and to the east फन्नी *phanni* or फन॰की *phanki*, or in South-East Tirhut रौना *rauna* . This string is hooked on to a hook, अँकुरा *ankura*, or in Sāran अँकुड़ा *ankurha*, in Shahabad अँकुसी *ankusi*, and in South Bhagalpur अँकोरा *ankora*, which is tied to the man's waist by a rope, लेवार *lewār*, or in Sāran डँर॰कस *danrkas*, in Champāran डाँड़ा *dānra*, and in South Bhagalpur पेटार *petār*.

377. The sickle used for cutting the palm-tree is हँसुली *hansuli* to the west and हँसुआ *hansua* to the east. It is sharpened on a piece of wood called लौठा *lautha*, and also, to the east सोंटा *sonta*, or बलुअठ *baluath* in South Bhagalpur and बलेठा *baletha* in South Munger.

378. A हथौना *hathauna* or तर॰कट्टी *tarkatti*, or in Sāran लब॰ना *labna*, is a large longish earthen pot for holding toddy (ताड़ी *tāri*). In South Bhagalpur तौला *taula* or कुण्डा *kunda* is an ordinary vessel for holding it. नापा *nāpa*, or in Sāran नप॰ही *naphi*, is a small earthen pot used for measuring it, and जोर॰वा *jorwa*, बररिया *barariya*, and गोल॰वाँ *golwān* are in South Bhagalpur earthen vessels in which toddy is sold.

379. A toddy palm-tree is तार or ताड़ *tār*, and the juice is तारी or ताड़ी *tāri.* There are two kinds of this tree—the female one, which bears fruit and is called फल॰तार *phaltār*, or in South Bhagalpur फल्ला *phalla*, and the male one, which produces hairy flowers and is called बलतार *baltār* or फुलतार *phultār*, or in North-East Tirhut फुलदो *phuldo*, and in Sāran बलिहा *baliha*. A खँगरा *khangra*, खगरा *khagra*, or खगरी *khagri* is a young palm-tree. A कोढ़ी *korhi* (North-East Tirhut) or a बहिरा *bahira* (South-East Tirhut), बाँझी सिसवा *bānjhi siswa* or अनाथु *anāthu* (South-West Tirhut), is a palm-tree which does not produce juice; a बसन्ती *basanti* is a tree which produces juice in spring, and जेठुआ *jethua*, or in Sāran साल *sāl*, one which does so in summer, while घौद *ghaud* is one which does so all the year round. In the east घौर *ghaur* is a tree which produces juice in the rainy season.

380. To cut a palm-tree for the juice is छेवब *chhewab*.

CHAPTER II.—THE BIRD-CATCHER.

381. The bird-catcher or मिरसिकार *mirsikār*, or in Shahabad बहेलिया *baheliya*, uses a number of नल *nal* or नर *nar*, which are long shafts of bamboo tied together like a fishing rod, of which the top one is called कम्पा *kampa*, or in South Bhagalpur खोंचा *khoncha*. On this last is applied bird-lime (लासा *lāsa*), and the bird-catcher cautiously approaches the bird, concealing himself behind a टट्टी *tatti* or screen of leaves and branches. When the bird is within distance it is struck with the limed कम्पा *kampa*, and thus caught. The चोंगा *chonga* is the bamboo tube for keeping the bird-lime.

382. The फाँद *phānd* or फाँदा *phānda* and चौगोड़ा *chaugora* are two kinds of nooses. बटियारी *batiyari* is a net used in the day-time, and चातर *chātar*, one used at night for catching birds.

CHAPTER III.—THE BARBER.

383. The barber is हजाम *hajām*, ठाकुर *thākur*, नाइ *nāi*, नाउ *nāu*, or नौआ *naua*. In North East Tirhut he is also नहेरि *naheri*, and in Sāran sometimes ओस्ता *osta*. He has his लोखर *lokhar* or किसमत *kismat*, किसबत *kisbat*, or किसबद *kisbad*, which is his instrument-bag. Also he has a चमौटा *chamauta* or चमौटी *chamauti*, or piece of thick leather used as a strop, a मोचना *mochna* or tweezers, and a छूरा *chhūra* or अस्तूरा *astūra*, or to the east खुर *khūr*, or razor. His nail-parers are नहरनी *naharni*, but in Champāran they are नहरन *nahran*, and लहरनी *laharni* in East

Tirhut. His whetstone is सिल्ला *silla* or सिल्ली *silli.* कैंची *kainchi* is his scissors, कटोरी *katori* his brass cup for water, दरपन *darpan* his looking-glass, and लुङ्गी *lungi* the cloth which he spreads in front of the person he is shaving, and on which the hairs fall.

CHAPTER IV.—THE COUNTRY SURGEON.

384. The country surgeon is जर्राह *jarrāh*, जराह *jarāh*, or हजाम *hajām.*

385. Among his instruments are जमूरा *jamūra*, a tooth-extractor, चोभा *chobha* or नस्तर *nastar*, a lancet for the arm, and ठुनका *thunka*, a lancet for the head.

386. For circumcision (सुन्नत *sunnat* or खतना *khatnā*) he has जन्त्री *jantri*, घोड़ी *ghori*, or in South Bhagalpur चूँटा *chūnta*, which are nippers of bamboo, and सलाइ *salāï*, which is a bamboo needle for holding up the foreskin.

CHAPTER V.—THE FARRIER.

387. The farrier or नालबन्द *nālband* has the following appliances.

388. A मेखारी *mekhāri* or किसबत *kisbat*, which is the bag in which his tools are carried, a छूरी *chhūri* or curved knife, a सुमतरास *sumtarās* or large curved knife, a जम्बूर *jambūr* or pincers, a रेत *ret* or file, a बलखा *balkha* or मार्तौल *mārtaul* or small but long hammer, a दोआली *doāli*, or in South Bhagalpur बलखा *balkha*, which is a leather for holding up the horse's hoof, a पुजमाल *pujmāl* or hair string for tying the ear of a refractory horse, a हलखा *halkha* or iron ring, and a सुमकट्टी *sumkatti* or chisel for cutting the horse's hoof.

CHAPTER VI.—THE WASHERMAN.

389. The धोबी *dhobi* or washerman uses a पटहा *patha* or *pāt*, which is the washing-board, of which the support is in Shahabad ठेहुआ *thehua* or नेवनाथ *newnath.* In South-West Tirhut it is

called चौकी *chauki,* and, when made of stone, पथल *pathal.* His iron is इस्तिरी *istiri* or (in North-East Tirhut) मिस्तिरी *mistiri.* His ironing cloth is बेठन *bethan,* and his starch कलप *kalap* or कलफ *kalaph.*

390. When the article to be washed is too heavy for him to lift up and dash upon the washing-board, he beats it with a mallet, called मुँगरा *mungra* or मुँगरी *mungri,* or (in Sāran) डाँसन *dānsan,* (in North-East Tirhut) सोँटा *sonta,* and in South-East Tirhut लाठी *lāthi.* In South-West Shahabad it is called कठका *kathka,* and in South Bhagalpur धोबडाँग *dhobdāng.* The clothes-line or drying-frame is तनाव *tanāw.* His bundle of clothes is बकुचा *bakucha.*

391. The act of beating the clothes is कुन्दी *kundi,* and to beat the clothes is पीटब *pītab,* or धोएल *dhoël* north of the Ganges, बिछरब *bichharab* (in Patna), निछरब *nichharab* (in Gaya), निखारल *nikhāral* (in Shahabad), खींचब *khīnchab* (in South Bhagalpur), and छाँटब *chhāntab* or फींचब *phīnchab* (in South Munger and Shahabad).

392. South of the Ganges clothes which are well washed are निमाड़ *nimār,* or in South Bhagalpur गोबर झार *gobar jhār.* In Champāran they are निखार *nikchār.* The half-washing given to new clothes is खमसो *khamso,* or in South Bhagalpur खाँमसो *khāmso.* In Gaya the washing of a cloth after it has had patterns printed on it is बिछरनी *bichharni.*

393. The honesty of the washerman and his tenderness for the clothes committed to his care are not considered of much account in Bihār, and there are numerous proverbs coined at his expense, *e.g.* धोबी पर धोबी बसे, तब कपड़ा पर साबुन पड़े *dhobi par dhobi base, tab kapra par sābun pare,* —no soap ever touches clothes unless many washermen live together (when owing to competition they wash well). Again, धोबिक बाप केर किछु नहिँ फाट *dhobik bāp ker kichhu nahiñ phāt,*—nothing belonging to a washerman's father is ever torn by him (*i.e.* those are the only clothes about which he is careful). It is also a wise precaution, which according to Bihār ideas should universally be adopted, to disbelieve a washerman when he says the clothes are 'nearly' ready. A washerman's donkey is a bye-word, as in the proverb गदहा केँ नञ दोसर गोसैंयाँ, धोबिया केँ नञ दोसर परोहन, *gadha ken na dosar gosainyān, dhobiya ken na dosar parohan,* —an ass has only one master (a washerman), and the washerman has only one steed (a donkey). Again धोबी नाउ दरजी, ई तीनू अलगरजी *dhobi, nāū, darji, i tīnu algarji,*—there are three careless people, the washerman, the barber, and the tailor.

SUBDIVISION IX.

TOOLS AND APPLIANCES USED BY COUNTRY ARTIZANS.

CHAPTER I.—THE CARPENTER AND TURNER.

394. The carpenter is बड़ही *barhi*, or in East Bihār optionally कमार *kamār*. In South Bhagalpur he is also called मड़ैया *maraiya*. His workshop is कमरसायर *kamarsāyar* or बड़ही खाना *barhi khāna*. A proverb about him is ई बुरिबक गाम कमैताह जनिका रुखान नऽ बसुला *i buribak gām kamaitāh, janika rukhān na basula*,—this fool (of a carpenter) would serve the village when he has neither chisel nor adze; said of one who undertakes to do a thing without possessing the means. He uses the following tools:—

395. The *adze*.—बसूला *basūla* or, especially in South and West Bihār and South Bhagalpur, बसुला *basula*. In South Munger it is बसिला *basila*. A similar tool is टङ्गा *tanga*, टाँगा *tānga*, टाँगी *tāngi*, or टँगारी *tangāri*. In North and East Bihār it is also called कुल्हारी *kulhāri*. This is a larger adze, and is used chiefly by sawyers (अरकसिया *arkasiya* or आराकस *ārākas*) in squaring logs, and by carpenters for rough work or for cutting down trees.

396. The large *saw*.—आरा *āra*, and south of the Ganges also अर्रा *arra*. The small saw.—आरी *āri*.

397. The large *hammer*.—हथौरा *hathaura*, or in South Bhagalpur लिहावर *lihāwar*. The small hammer.—हथौरी *hathauri*, मारतौल *mārtaul*, and in West Tirhut and south of the Ganges also घन *ghan*. In South Bhagalpur it is called मरिया *mariya*.

398. The बरमा *barma* or बरमाँ *barmān* is a *revolving awl or drill*, worked with a bow and string, and used as a gimlet or centre-bit. The bow used with it is कमानी *kamāni*, or in South-West Shahabad कमानक *kamānak*. The handle round which the string goes is गुलफी *gulphi* or गुल्ली *gulli*. In South and East Tirhut the word is कुलफी *kulphi*. In Gaya it is मूठ *mūth*. The cap at the top, on which the palm of the hand rests to press the awl, is टोपी *topi*, पैला *paila*, दबनी *dabni*, or दबौटा *dabauta*. The awl itself is बरमा *barma* or बरमाँ *barmān*. The string is north of the Ganges दोआली *doāli*, and south of it डोरी *dori* or जोती *joti*, or in South-West Shahabad जेंवर *jemwar*.

399. The following are various kinds of *chisels* :—

(*a*) The कच्चक *kachchak* north of the Ganges, and the बटारी *batāri* or बटाली *batāli* south of the Ganges, is broad at the base and narrow at the point. In South Bhagalpur it is called कज्जक *kajjak*.

(*b*) The रम्भा *ramba* is a long chisel for making mortice holes.

(*c*) The चौरसा *chaursa* is broad and straight; another name in Gaya and Shahabad is बतासी *batāsi*.

(*d*) The रुखान *rukhān* or रुखानी *rukhāni* is like the *kachchak*, but is larger and thicker, and is used for coarse work. It is also a generic term for all chisels.

(*e*) A small chisel with a rounded edge for making lines on wood is north of the Ganges गोलक बुरुज खाब *golak buruj khāb*. South of the Ganges and in Sāran it is गिरदा *girda* or गोरदार रन्दा *gordār randa*. In South Bhagalpur it is also खोलिया *kholiya*.

400. *Gouges* are गोलक *golak*, गोलख *golakh* (Gaya), गोला रुखानी *gola rukhāni*, or गोरदार रुखानी *gordār rukhāni* ; other names are गौच *gauch* (South West Tirhut) and गिरमिट *girmit* (? gimlet), North-West Tirhut. A large gouge for heavy work, such as hollowing out rice-mortars, is बाँक रुखानी *bānk rukhāni*. A square gouge is कच्चक रुखानी *kachchak rukhāni*.

401. The common *plane* is रन्दा *randa*, of which the blade is फल्ली *phalli*, or in Shahabad फलसा *phalsa*, and the body कुन्दा *kunda*. The wedge for holding the blade has various names, viz. north of the Ganges खूँटी *khūnti*, ठेकी *theki*, or चैली *chaili*. South of the Ganges it is in Shahabad खूँटी *khunti* or ठेपी *thepi*, and to the east पच्ची *pachchi*, पंचड़ी *pachri*, or पच्चड़ *pachchar*. When the blade has a coarse edge for rough work, it is झरना रन्दा *jharna randa* ; also दाँत रन्दा *dānt randa* in South-West Shahabad. A plane with a fine blade is साफी रन्दा *sāphi randa*. The दराज *darāj* is a narrow plane for squaring the edges of boards.

402. *Grooving-planes*.—There are—

(*a*) The plane for cutting square grooves.—बुरुज खाब *buruj khāb*, or (South of the Ganges) बुरुज (*or* गुरुज) खाप *buruj* (or *guruj*) *khāp*.

(*b*) The गलता *galta* is for cutting round grooves. In West Bihār and South Munger it is also called खिरची *khirchi* or खिलती *khilti*.

TURNER (KHARĀDI) AT WORK.

Lith. by Hem Chunder Ghosal, Student, Govt. School of Art Calcutta. Printed by Abdool Rahim, Govt. School of Art Calcutta.

(*c*) The झारी के रन्दा *jhāri ke randa* or (north of the Ganges) पलाउँ *palāun* is a plane for making grooves for panelling.

403. The following are *files* :—

(*a*) रेती *reti* is the common file.

(*b*) The file for sharpening saws is generally कतरा *katra*. Local names are कतरि *katari* in North-West Tirhut, कतरोही *katrohi* in East Tirhut, तेफल *tephal* in Gaya and Shahabad, तेफल्ला *tephalla* in Sāran, and कनासी *kanāsi* in West Shahabad.

(*c*) सोहन *sohan*, or in East Tirhut सोहेन *sohen*, is a coarse rasp.

(*d*) The चोरसा *chorsa*, or to the west चौरसा *chaursa*, is a broad file.

(*e*) The निमगीरिद *nimgīrid* is a half-round polishing file. In South Bhagalpur it is मैगिरी *maigiri*.

(*f*) The चौरस रेति *chauras reti*, or in South Bhagalpur चौपहल रेती *chaupahal reti*, is a square file.

404. The *square*, or gnomon, is बटाम *batām*, गुनियाँ *guniyān*, or चलता बटाम *chalta batām*. The *compasses* are परकाल *parkāl*. A *blunt point* for drawing lines is खतकस *khatkas*, or in South Bhagalpur कोरसूत *korsūt*. *Sand-paper* is सरेस कन्ना *sares kanna*, सरेस कागज *sares kāgaj*, or सरेस पत्ता *sares pattā*. In South Bhagalpur it is साफी *sāphi*. The *pincers* for drawing nails are जम्हूरा *jamhūra*, जमूरा *jamūra*, or सँड़सी *sanrsī*. *Glue* is सरेस *sares*. पत्थल *patthal*, पथल *pathal*, or सिल *sil*, is the *grindstone*. The *block* on which the man works is ठीहा *thīha*, ठेहा *theha*, or in South Bhagalpur ठिया *thiya*, ठिहा *thiha*, or परकट्ठो *parkattho*. In Gaya and Champaran it is called परियाठा *pariyātha*.

405. The English *auger* is also used, and is called अवगर *awgar*, or in Tirhut गिरमिट *girmit* (? = gimlet).

406. A *lathe* is खराद *kharād*, and the man who works it is खरादी *kharādi*, a turner.

CHAPTER II.—THE BLACKSMITH.

407. The blacksmith is लोहार *lohār* generally, and in South-East Tirhut he is also ठाकुर *thākur* or कमार *kamār*. His smithy is कमरसायर *kamarsāyār*. In Sāran it is also लोहसारी *lohsāri*, and in South Bhagalpur it is कमरसारी *kamarsāri* or मड़ई *maraī*.

408. His *anvil* is निहाइ *nihāï* or नेहाइ *nehāï;* but in South-East Tirhut it is लेहाइ *lehāï*, and in South Bhagalpur लिहाइ *lihāï*. This is fixed in a block called ठेहा *theha* north of the Ganges, ठीहा *thīha* in Shahabad, and in South Bhagalpur ठिया *thiya*, परकठ *parkath*, or गड़ियास *gariyās*. In Patna and South Munger it is परेठा *paretha* or परहट्ठा *parhattha*, and in Gaya परियाठा *pariyātha*. In South-West Shahabad it is आँकुठ *ānkuth*. A well-known proverb about an anvil is सुन्न चोट नेहाइक माँथा *sunn chot nehāik māntha*,—if the anvil has nothing on it, the blow falls on its head.

409. The घनमुधी *ghanmudhi* is the *swage block* or *perforated anvil* on which iron is placed when being pierced with holes, and बीरी *bīri* or बीर *bīr* (east generally, Patna, and Gaya) or हन्ना *hanna* (South Bhagalpur) is the round block of iron placed on this, also pierced with a hole. This latter is also used for making heads of nails, and another name for it is चपरावन *chaprāwan*, चपरौना *chaprauna*, or चपरौनी *chaprauni*.

410. The large *hammer* for welding is घन *ghan ;* smaller than this is the हथौर *hathaur* or हथौरा *hathaura ;* and smaller still the हथौरी *hathauri* or मरिया *mariya*.

411. The जम्हूरा *jamhūra* or जमूरा *jamūra* is a pair of *pincers* or *tongs* round at the tips; other names are गहुआ *gahua* (Champāran, West Tirhut, and Patna), सँड़सी *sanrsi* (Shahabad and South Bhagalpur), and बँगुरी *banguri* (South-West Shahabad). Everywhere सँड़सी *sanrsi* is used for a pincer adapted for taking a hot piece of iron out of the fire, tightening nuts, &c. To the west the सुगही *sugahi* is a pair of horn or wooden pincers.

412. The iron *poker* for stirring the fire is north of the Ganges अँकुड़ा *ankurha ;* in Gaya and Shahabad it is अँकुरा *ankura* or अँकुरी *ankuri ;* and in South Bhagalpur अँकोरा *ankora* or ओँकड़ा *onkra*. North of the Ganges, to the west, it is also कुलतारा *kultāra ;* while in Patna, Gaya, and South Munger it is कोलटारा *koltāra*.

413. The *cold chisel* is छेनी *chheni*, and the chisel for making holes in iron is टोपन *topan*, with a variant टोपना *topna* in Patna and Gaya; another name is सुम्भा *sumbha* south of the Ganges or सुम्मा *summa* or सुम्मी *summi* north of the Ganges.

414. The fixed *bellows* is भाथी *bhāthi*, and also (south of the Ganges) भाँथी *bhānthi*. The hand-bellows is दुहन्थी *duhanthi* when worked with both hands, एकहन्थी *ekhanthi* when worked with one hand, and हपौआ

supaua in South-West Shahabad. In the south-east it is also काठ भाँथी *kath bhānthi*. The end of the bellows pipe which goes into the fire is मूड़ा *mūra*, मूड़ी *mūri*, or मुड़िया *muriya*. In Sāran it is अँकुड़ा *ankurha*; in South Bhagalpur, मूढ़ी *mūrhi* or सालक *sālak*; in Patna, मोहखा *mohkha*; and in South Munger, मोखड़ी *mokhri*. The pipe itself is फूँक *phūnk*; also north of the Ganges and to the west छूँछी *chhūnchhi* or छुच्छी *chhuchchhi*; and in Patna, Gaya, Sāran, and East Tirhut चोँगा *chonga*, or in South Tirhut चोँगी *chongi*. The clay pipe over this is आरन *āran* or अरनी *arni*, or in South-East Tirhut आर *ār*. In East Tirhut it is also मटिहम *matiham*, and in South-East Tirhut मेटुम *metum*. The wooden sides of the bellows are तखता *takhta*; also in Patna, Gaya, and South-West Shahabad पटरा *patra*. The leather sides are चमड़ा *chamra*; also चाम *chām* (optionally south of the Ganges) and खाल *khāl* in Champāran, Patna, and Gaya. The valve is पङ्खा *pankha* or पङ्खी *pankhi*; also (in Patna) पखड़ी *pankhri*. In South-East Tirhut and Champāran it is गद्दी *gaddi*. The pivot on which the pair of bellows works is कोँढ़ा *konrha* north of the Ganges; also in North-West Tirhut सुरसा *sursa*. South of the Ganges, to the west, it is धूरी *dhūri*, and अँकुरा *ankura* to the east and also in Shahabad and Champāran. The pillars which support it are खम्भा *khambha* north of the Ganges and खूँटा *khūnta* south of the Ganges and in South-East Tirhut. The upper iron bar is बड़ेँड़ा *barenra* or बड़ेँड़ी *barenri* north of the Ganges, and बरेठा *baretha* in Patna and Gaya. In Shahabad it is बेँड़िया *benriya*, in South Bhagalpur डण्डा *danda*, and in South-East Tirhut डण्टा *danta*. The lever which works the bellows is छीप *chhīp* in the North Gangetic tract, and also डण्टा *danta* in Tirhut; south of the Ganges it is लाठ *lāth* or लाठा *lātha*, and in South-West Shahabad डण्डा *danda*. In South-West Shahabad a small bellows worked by both hands is मेँड़रुआ भाँथी *menrarua bhānthi*. A well-known saying about the bellows is तुलसी आह गरीब के हरि सेँ सहल न जाय, मुअला चाम का फूँक सेँ लोह भसम हो जाय *tulasi āh garīb ke hari sen sahal na jāy, muala chām kā phūnk sen loh bhasam ho jāy*,—O Tulsi! God cannot withstand the sigh of a poor man: the blowing of dead leather (in a bellows) reduces iron to ashes.

415. The बरमा *barma* is a *revolving awl* or *drill* worked with a bow, कमानी *kamāni*, with a leather string, तसमा *tasma*. Sometimes a string is used instead of a bow, and this is called दोआली *doāli* or जोती *joti*, or in South-West Shahabad जेँवर *jemwar*. The iron spike of the awl is north of the Ganges डण्डी *dandi* to the west and फल्ली *phalli* to the east. South of the Ganges we have दाँस *dāns* in Shahabad, डण्टी *danti* in Patna and Gaya, and डण्डी *dandi* again in the south-east.

416. The fixed *vice* is बाँक *bānk* or (in South Bhagalpur and South Munger) बैस *bais* (?=vice), and the hand-vice is हथ॰कल *hath-kal* or (in Patna and Gaya) हाँथ॰कल *hānthkal.* The two sides of the vice which grasp the iron are पल्ला *palla;* the screw is मुसरा *musra,* or in North-West Tirhut कब॰ला *kabla;* and the socket for the screw to work in is छुच्छी *chhuchchhi,* except in Shahabad, where it is चोंगिया *chongiya,* and South Bhagalpur and Champāran, where it is चोंगा *chonga.* The handle for turning the screw is north of the Ganges मुसरा *musra* or चलौनी *chalauni.* The latter name is also current in Shahabad, where in the south-west of the district we also have हथ॰करा *hathkara* or डण्डा *danda.* In South Bhagalpur it is हातुल *hātul* or हत्था *hattha,* and elsewhere it is हथ॰रा *hathra.* The spring is कमानी *kamāni.*

417. The *tap and die* for making screws is north of the Ganges बाँदिया *bādiya* or बद़ीया *badīya;* the latter is the usual form in North-East Tirhut. South of the Ganges, in Gaya and Shahabad, it is बड़िया *badiya,* and elsewhere बधिया *badhiya.* In South Bhagalpur it is also called डाइ *dāi* (die). Of this the female screw is कुट॰का *kutka,* the tightening screw चुट॰की *chutki,* and the nut-maker पेंच॰कस *pechkas.* ढिब॰री *dhibri,* or in Sāran कब॰ला *kabla,* is the nut of a screw.

418. The common *files* are रेती *reti,* and the round files गोलक *golak* or गोलख *golakh,* and in South Bhagalpur गोल रेती *gol reti.* The half-round file is निम॰गीरिद *nimgīrid,* and the triangular file in Sāran तिन॰फल्ला *tinphalla,* in Champāran तिर॰फाल *tirphāl,* in Shahabad तिर॰पहल *tirpahal,* in Tirhut तेफल *tephal,* in Gaya तेपहल *tepahal,* and elsewhere तिन॰पहल *tinpahal* or तिर॰पह॰ला *tirpahla.*

419. The *compasses* are पर॰काल *parkāl* or कम्पास *kampās.* The *mould* is साँचा *sāncha,* and the vessel for cooling hot iron पनिहारा *panihāra* in Champāran, West Tirhut, and Gaya; पनिहण्डा *panihanda* or पन॰हण्डा *panhanda* in Shahabad and South-East Tirhut; चाहा *chāha* (also in South Munger), लबेरी *laberi,* लाबर *lābar,* or लबेर *laber* also in South-East Tirhut; नबेर *naber* or नमेर *namer* in North-East Tirhut; and नबेरी *naberi* in Tirhut generally. In South Bhagalpur it is पन॰चाहा *panchāha.*

CHAPTER III.—THE MASON OR BRICKLAYER.

420. The mason is called राज *rāj,* also राज मिस्तिरी *rāj mistiri* north of the Ganges, and राज मजूर *rāj majūr* in South Bhagalpur and South Munger. In Sāran and Champāran he is also थवई *thawaī.*

421. He uses the बसुली *basuli,* which is a pointed *hammer* for cutting bricks. In Shahabad लोढ़ *lorh* is an iron hammer for breaking stones

422. His *trowels* are (1) करन्नी *karnī*, the largest, for mixing mortar; (2) मंझोला *manjhola* or (in South-West Shababad) अधन्ला *adhla*, a smaller one; and नहन्ला *nahla*, or in Tirhut and the west कलम *kalam* or कलन्मी *kalmi*, the smallest one, for polishing the surface of the mortar.

423. *Mortar* is मसाला *masāla* or (in North-East Tirhut) गच *gach* when made of brickdust and lime; when made of mud it is गिलावा *gilāwa*, also गर्रा *garra* (Patna, Champāran, and North-East Tirhut), गारा *gāra* (Sāran and the east), कादो *kādo* (South-West Tirhut), and लेइ *leï* (South-West Shahabad).

424. The wooden *beater* for consolidating and smoothing plaster is मुँगन्री *mungri* or थापी *thāpi*. The रोल *rol* or रौल *raul* (South Munger, Patna, Sāran, and Tirhut) is a long stick for smoothing the plaster Other names are पहन्टा *pahta* or पाटा *pāta*, पैटा *paita*, पैहन्टा *paihta* (South Munger), and फरन्मा *pharma* in Gaya. In Shahabad and South Bhagalpur चिरन्ना *chirna* is a slip of wood used for the same purpose. The *scoop* for making moulding is north of the Ganges and to the east generally गोलाकस *golākas*, and also to the east गोला *gola*. Elsewhere south of the Ganges and in Champāran it is खुरन्चुनी *khurchuni*.

425. The *plumb* is साहुल *sāhul*. The string is सूत *sūt*, and in Champāran and South-East Tirhut also डोरी *dori*; and the small pieces of wood fixed on the string are केँड़ा *kenra* or कैँड़ा *kainra* in Tirhut, Shahabad, Patna, and Gaya, पत्ती *patti* in Sāran and Champāran, फिटन्किरी *phitkiri* also in Champāran, East Tirhut, and South Munger, फिरन्की *phirki* in South-West Shahabad, and फेटन्किना *phetkina* in South Bhagalpur.

426. The *square* is गोनिया *goniya*, गुनिया *guniya*, or गुनियाँ *guniyān* to the west, also साँधन्नी *sādhni* in Patna, Gaya, and north of the Ganges generally, and रब्बिल *rabbil* in South-East Tirhut and North Bhagalpur. To the west and in Gaya it is also बटाम *batām*.

427. The *maul-stick* is मिस्तर *mistar* in Patna, the North-West, and South Tirhut. In Tirhut, Gaya, and the west it is निस्तर *nistar*. In South Bhagalpur it is चीप *chīp*.

428. The whitewashing *brush* is कूँची *kūnchi*; in South Muager it is also झरन्नी *jharni*.

429. The *ladder* is सीढ़ी *sīrhi*, and the *scaffolding* माँच *mānch* or मचान *machān* to the north of the Ganges. South of the Ganges the latter is पाढ़ *pārh* generally, or पाठ *pāth* in Shahabad. In Champāran, Patna, and Gaya it is also चाली *chāli*.

430. The तगार or तगाड़ *tagār* (also तगाड़ी *tagāri* in Tirhut) is the pot in which the mortar is mixed. The mortar-pot is नाद *nād* or नाँद *nānd.* The mortar-trough when made of clay is हाँड़ी *hānri*, also कोहा *koha* in East Tirhut, and optionally अथन्रा *athra* south of the Ganges. In South Bhagalpur it is also कड़ाह *karhāï*. When made of wood it is कठन्रा *kathra* or कठौती *kathauti.*

431. The bricks are ground into powder (सुरःखी *surkhi*) by a crusher, ढेँकी *dhenki.* or (in Champāran) लाठ *lāth.* Of this the pestle is मूसर *músar* or मुसन्रा *musra*, or (in South-East Tirhut) समाठ *samāth.* The piece of wood on which the bricks are sometimes crushed is ओखन्री *okhri* north of the Ganges; south of the Ganges it is ओखन्ला *okhla* in Gaya, उखन्ली *ukhli* in South Munger, भुरियाँ *bhuriyān* in Patna, and कँड़िया *kanriya* elsewhere. It is supported by pillars, which are खूँटा *khūnta* or खुट्टा *khutta* in East Tirhut and south of the Ganges. In the latter tract they are also called खम्भा *khambha.* In West Tirhut and Sāran and Champāran they are जङ्घा *jangha* or खामा *khāma.* The axle on which it works is called अखौता *akhauta* in Patna and Sāran, उखौता *ukhauta* in Gaya, and also अखैला *akhaila* in Patna. In Champāran and North-West Tirhut it is माँझा *mānjha,* in South-West Tirhut किल्ला *killa,* and in East Tirhut डण्टा *danta.* Sometimes a hammer is used for breaking the bricks, which is called मुँगन्रा *mungra* or (in Shahabad) हथन्कुट्टा *hathkutta*, and in Sāran थापी *thāpi.*

432. The large earthen pot for water is घैला *ghaila*, also ठिलिया *thiliya* in Gaya and गगन्री *gagri* north of the Ganges. The smaller pot is हाँड़ी *hānri* or हँड़िया *hanriya*, also कोहा *khoha* in East Tirhut. South of the Ganges the pot with a spout for pouring water on the plaster is बधन्ना *badhna*. In South Tirhut it is बधन *badhan*, and in South Bhagalpur झारी *jhāri.* North of the Ganges generally करन्वा *karwa* or कँटिया *kantiya* is used, and in East Tirhut also फुच्ची *phuchchi.*

CHAPTER IV.—THE GRAIN-PARCHER.

433. The grain-parcher is कानू *kānu* or काँदू *kāndu*, with a variant काँदून *kāndūn* in Champāran, Patna, and Gaya. In Champāran (optionally) and in South-West Shahabad he is called गोँड़ *gonr*, and north of the Ganges and to the south-east he is also known as भड़न्भूँजा *bharbhūnja.* Parched grain is भूँजा *bhūnja*, or in Shahabad भुँजन्ना *bhunjna.* When it bursts in the parching it is called लावा *lāwa* or फुटन्हा *phutha.*

BRICK-CRUSHING MACHINE *(DHENKI)*.

GRAIN-PARCHERS (KĀNDU) AT WORK.

434. His parching-house is घोनसार *ghonsār* or घोनसारी *ghonsār* to the west, and also to the west of the North Gangetic tract, भनसारी *bhansārī*. In South-West Shahabad it is भरसाँय *bharsāin*. The name कनसार *kansār* or कनिसार *kanisār* is current in East Tirhut and to the east of the South Gangetic tract, including Patna and Gaya. In Tirhut it is also कनसारी *kansāri*.

435. The *fireplace* is चूल्हा *chūlha* in Tirhut and to the east of the South Gangetic tract, including Patna and Gaya; also भार *bhār* generally, and भनसार *bhansār* north of the Ganges and in Gaya, and घोनसार. *ghonsār* in Sāran. In South-West Shahabad it is भरसाँय *bharsāin*.

436. The place in front of the stove, on which the grain falls, is परुई *paruī* in Shahabad and परुआ *paruā* in South Munger. In Patna and South-East Tirhut it is पौर *paur*; in Gaya, South Bhagalpur, and North-West Tirhut पौरी *paurī*; and in Sāran and Champāran पारी *pāri*. Another name more or less current north of the Ganges is चौतरा *chautra*.

437. The earthen pot in which the grain is parched is खापड़ *khāpar* or खपड़ा *khapra* when it is large with a wide mouth, and खपड़ी *khapri* when it is smaller. The latter is also called north of the Ganges कुण्डा *kunda* or कूँड़ा *kūnra*, to the west, and तौला *taula* to the east.

438. The iron *spoon* for taking out the hot sand is कलछुल *kalchhul* in Sāran and Champāran and South Munger, and कलछुला *kalchhula* in Patna and Gaya. In Shahabad it is कलुछ *kaluchh* or (in the south-west) कलुस *kalus*. In South-East Tirhut it is सरहिया *sarahiya*. In South-East Bihār it is called डब्बू *dabbu*. When made of earth with a bamboo handle it is called ढकनी *dhakni* north of the Ganges and in South Munger, or सरवा *sarwa* in North-East Tirhut.

439. The flat wood *stirrer* is called दबिला *dabila* to the west. In North Tirhut it is दबिया *dabiya*, and in South-East Tirhut दाब *dāb*, and in Gaya कुरूर *kurūr*. A kind of broom made of four or five reeds tied together is झारू *jhāru* (Patna and Gaya), भुँजनाठी *bhunjnāthi* or बोढ़नी *borhni* to the south-east, बढ़नी *barhni* to the east generally, लरना *larna* or लाड़नि *lārani* in North-East Tirhut, छिपनी *chhipni* in South-East Tirhut, and चलौनी *chalauni* north of the Ganges.

440. The *sieve* is चलनी *chalni* generally, but चलना *chalna* in South-West Shahabad and चालनि *chālani* in East Tirhut. To the west it is also झरना *jharna*, and also in South-East Tirhut सूप *sūp*.

441. The *poker* is खोर॰ना *khorna* or खोर॰नी *khorni* north of the Ganges and in South Bhagalpur and South Munger; elsewhere south of the Ganges it is खोड़॰ना *khorna* or खोड़॰नी *khorni.* In South-East Tirhut and Champāran it is खोर॰नाठी *khornāthi.*

442. The *basket* for the grain is north of the Ganges दौरा *daura* or दौरी *dauri.* South of the Ganges we have बट॰री *batri* in Patna, मौनी *mauni* or मौनिया *mauniya* in Gaya and South Munger, भौँकी *bhaunki* in Shahabad, and डलिया *daliya* in Champāran and South Bhagalpur. In Champāran and Gaya the सत॰घर॰वा *satgharwa*, and in South Munger the चाँड़ *chānr*, is an earthen vessel with seven or more divisions for various kinds of grain, and in South-East Tirhut a बैठ॰की *baithki* is a similar one with four divisions, and छन्ना *chhanna* one with six. कोहा *koha* or कँटिया *kantiya* in North-East and South-West Tirhut, and कर॰वा *karwa* in Champāran, are earthen pots for grain, and कठ॰रा *kathra* in Patna and Gaya, or कठौती *kathauti* elsewhere south of the Ganges, is a wooden pan.

443. The *grindstone* is जाँता *jānta* or (in South-West Shahabad) जाँत *jānt.* Its axle is किल्ला *killa* or (in South-East Tirhut) कील *kīl*, and it is made to revolve by a handle, which is हथ॰रा or हथ॰ड़ा *hathra* generally, and जूआ *jūa* to the west, also हाथर in South-East Tirhut.

444. The *wages* in grain paid to the grain-parcher is भार *bhār*, or in South Bhagalpur भारो *bhāro*, as in the proverb जौ जरि गेल, भार ला बान्हल छी *jau jari gel, bhār la bānhal chhi,*—the grain-parcher has burnt my barley and has tied me up for his fee (adding insult to injury). The quantity of grain parched at one time is घानी *ghāni.*

CHAPTER V.—THE BAKER.

445. The baker is generally नान॰बाइ *nānbāi*, with a local variant नन॰बाइ *nanbāi* in Shahabad. In Gaya he is नान॰पज *nānpaj*. He is also called रोटीवाला *rotīwāla.* He is proverbially a rude fellow, and नान॰बाइ के खिङ्गा *nanbāi ke khinga* is popularly used to mean a stout rude fellow.

446. He uses an *oven,* तनूर *tanūr* or तँदूर *tandūr.*

447. His *roasting-spit* is south of the Ganges सींख *sīnkh*, and elsewhere सीख *sīkh.* In North-East Tirhut it is also सींक *sīnk.* This is fixed on supports, which are हिच्छा *hichchha* to the west of the North Gangetic tract and in Patna, and कबाब दानी *kawāb dāni* in South-East

Tirhut, Shahabad, and South Bhagalpur. In Gaya they are चक्कस *chakkas*.

448. The *boiling-pot* is देगची or डेगची *degchi*. South of the Ganges and to the west it is also called पतीली *patīli* when made of earthenware.

449. The *cup* is रिकाबी *rikābi*, the *saucer* रिकाबी *rikābi* or कटोरा *katora*, and the *wooden spoon* डोइ *doï*, and also in East Tirhut चमच *chamach* or (to the west) चम्मच *chammach*.

450. The large wooden *stirrer* is called कफचा *kaphcha* in North Bihār, डोआ *doā* in North-East Tirhut, and डोँगा *donga* in South Tirhut. In Patna it is डाभा *dābha*, and elsewhere south of the Ganges डब्बू *dabbu* when made of iron, or कफगीर *kaphgīr* (west generally) when made of wood.

451. The *cushion* by which he places the cake on the side of the oven is रफीदा *raphīda*, or in North-East Tirhut गद्दी *gaddi*. The हश्तगना *hushtagna* is an iron *bar* hooked at the end, and the अर्रा *arra* an iron bar flattened at the end. They are used in taking cakes out of the oven. The one is held in one hand, and the other in the other. The two together are called जोड़ी *jori*, or in Champāran कन्सी *kansi*.

452. The *instrument for making ornamental marks* on pastry is north of the Ganges साँचा *sāncha*; south of the Ganges it is चोकन *chokan* in Shahabad, चोकनी *chokni* in Patna, and elsewhere चोका *choka*.

453. The खुरचनी *khurachni* is an implement for cleaning vessels.

CHAPTER VI.—THE CONFECTIONER.

454. The confectioner is हलुआइ *haluāï* in North, and हलवाइ *halwāï* in South Bihār. His *fireplace* is चूल्हा *chūlha*, and also in Champāran and South Munger भट्ठी *bhatthi*, of which the stoke-hole is मुँह *munh*, and also in Gaya and South-West Shahabad दुआर *duār*.

455. His open *cauldron* is कड़ाही *karāhi* generally, also कड़हाइ *karhāï* or तावा *tāwa* in Gaya. Of this the handles are डण्टी *danti*, कड़ा *kara*, or कन्ना *kanna*, with a variant कड़िया *kariya* in South Munger.

456. The *skimmer* is झरना *jharna* in Patna, the north-west, and East Tirhut, छनौटा *chanauta* generally north of the Ganges, पौना *pauna* in the north-west, Tirhut, and south of the Ganges. In Patna it is also पौनिया *pauniya*, in South Bhagalpur चट्टी *chatti*, and in Gaya, South Munger, and Sāran झंझरा *jhanjhra*. The *large stirrer* is कँचोचा *keoncha*, and the *small stirrer* छोलनी *chholni*. In Champāran and North Tirhut it is also खुरपी *khurpi*, and in South Bhagalpur खुरचनी *khurchani*.

457. The wooden *rolling-pin* is बेलना *belna*, which is worked on a *paste-board*. This latter is called चकला *chakla* when it is round, and चौकी *chauki* or पटरा *patra* when it is oblong. Other names are तखता *takhta* (North-East Tirhut), पिढ़िया *pirhiya* (Gaya and South Bhagalpur), and पीढ़ा *pirha* (Gaya and South Munger). The *pestle* for beating the dough is दाबा *dāba*, (South-West Shahabad) दाबी *dābi*, or (North-East Tirhut) दाब *dāb*. Other names are गुरदम *gurdam* or मुसद *musad* (Champāran), दपटन *daptan* (Patna), and मुँगरा *mungra* (South Bhagalpur).

458. The *spoon* is कलछुल *kalchhul* or in North-East Tirhut करछ *karuch*. The brass *ladle* with a wooden handle for removing the sugar from one vessel to another is डब्बू *dabbu*.

459. The wooden *platter* for sweets is गिरदा *girda* north of the Ganges and in Shahabad, खोनचा *khoncha* north of the Ganges and in Gaya and South Munger, खांचा *khāncha* in South Bhagalpur, and खाँचा *khāncha* or डगरना *dagarna* in Patna and Gaya.

460. The brass *salver* is थारी *thāri* generally, with local variants थरिया *thariya* in Shahabad and East Tirhut and थाल *thāl* in Champāran and East Tirhut. In Sāran and Tirhut it is also called छीपा *chhīpa*. The deep brass pan is परात *parāt*.

461. The sweetmeats are exposed on stands called तरौनी *tarauni*, local variants being तरौना *tarauna* in Champāran and South-East Tirhut and तरैनी *taraini* in Champāran. In South Bhagalpur they are टेखती *tekhti*.

462. He has also a wooden basin, called कठरा *kathra*, कठवत *kathwat*, or कठौती *kathauti*; a large ladle, डोहरी *dohri*; and a pair of scales, called generally तराजू *tarāju*, तरजुइ *tarjuï*, or टेकौरी *tekauri*. It is also टकौरी *takauri* in Tirhut and the west, and नरजा *narja* in Champāran.

463. हलुआइ के दोकान, दादा के फतेहा *haluāï ke dokān, dāda ke phateha*, is a well-known proverb. A *phateha* is a feast in honour of the dead, at which sweetmeats are given away for nothing. When a person wants to get a thing for nothing, which he has no right to expect, the proverb, which means 'a confectioner's shop is not my grandfather's funeral feast,' is said to him.

CHAPTER VII.—THE TOBACCO MANUFACTURER.

464. The tobacco-seller is तमाकुवाला *tamāku-wāla*, तमाकुफरोश *tamāku-phārosh*, or तमाकुलवाला *tamākul-bāla*. He uses a *crushing-lever*, ढेंकी *dhenki*, with a peg, मूसर *mūsar*, मुसरा *musra*, or समाठ *samāth*, fixed in it. It is supported on pillars, खूंटा *khūnta*, खुण्टा *khuntā*, or (in the west) जङ्घा *jangha* or जंघिया *janghiya*, by an axis-pin, किल्ला *killa* or अखौता *akhauta*. It falls on a hollow bed called ओखरी *okhri* or ओखली *okhli*, on which the tobacco is placed. When the crushed tobacco is being removed, the beam is supported by a forked stick, which is called टेकनी *tekni*, टेकानी *tekāni*, or (in Shahabad) ठेका *theka* or ठकवा *thakwa*, or in Sāran ठेकवा *thekwa*. In East Tirhut it is called ठेकनी *thekni* or अलगनी *algani*, in Champāran अरगनी *argani*, and in South Bhagalpur ठेंगना *thengna* or उचकुन *uchkun*. Sometimes a string, रस्सी *rassi*, is used for this purpose. An illustration of the similar crushing-lever used in pounding bricks will be found opposite § 431.

465. The fragments of tobacco are collected by a *broom*, झाड़ू *jhāru* or बढ़नी *barhni*, which is also called कूंची *kūnchi* or कूंचा *kūncha* towards the west and खरहरा *kharhara* in Patna. The tobacco is sprinkled with water from a *water-pot*, called पनहण्डा *panhanda*, हँड़िया *hanriya*, कड़ाही *karāhi*, पियाला *piyāla*, मटकुरी *matkuri*. In East Tirhut it is called अथरा *athrā*.

466. The *balls of manufactured tobacco* are generally पिलण्डा *pilanda* or धोंधा *dhōndha*. Other names are लोहिया *lohiya* (Champāran), गोला *gola* (Sāran and the East), लौंदा *londa* (South Munger and North-West Tirhut), लिट्टी *litti* in Patna and South Munger, and पिण्डा *pinda* in Shahabad. टिकरी *tikri* are smaller balls.

467. In a tobacco shop the broad flat metal *plates* are, north of the Ganges, सेनी *seni*, and south of it खांचा *khāncha* or खोंचा *khoncha*. The *tobacco-pots* are भाँड़ा *bhānra*, चरुआ *charua*, or चरुई *charui*. The *cloth* covering the stand for the vessels is खरुआ *kharua*, झाँप *jhāmp*, or परदा *parda*, and the board on which the tobacco is mixed is पटरा *patra* or पीढ़ा *pīrha*. When of stone it is पटिया *patiya*. Instead of पीढ़ा *pīrha*, पिढ़िया *pirhiya* or तखता *takhta* may be used.

468. Among the spices used in manufacturing tobacco are जटा मसी *jata masi*, छड़ीला *chharīla*, सुगन्द वाला *sugand wāla*, and सुगन्द कोकिला *sugand kokila*. Plain tobacco is called सादा *sādu*, that which is spiced or scented खँबीरा *khambīra* or खमीरा *khamīra*, and a mixture of the two दोरस *doras* or दोरसा *dorasa*.

CHAPTER VIII.—THE PIPE-MAKER.

469. The maker of *gurguris* (*vide post*), who is a कसेरा *kasera* or brazier, uses a kind of *lathe*, which is called खराद *kharād*. Of this खूंटा *khūnta*, or in South Bhagalpur कुन्द *kund*, is the block which holds one end of the stem as it is being turned. In it is fixed an iron spike called गूँज *gūnj*. फरन्ही *pharhi* is a piece of iron which keeps the stem in its place as it is being turned, and बघेली *bagheli*, or in South Bhagalpur बघेला *baghaila*, is a piece of wood through a hole in which the stem is passed during the operation.

470. The workman uses the *revolving awl*, बरन्मा *barma*, moved by a bow, कमानी *kamāni*, of which the string is तसन्मा *tasma*, डोरी *dori*, or जोती *joti*; a *broad chisel*, चौरन्सा *chaursa*, and a narrow *gouge*, नहरन्नी *naharni*, or in South Bhagalpur नेहनी *nehni*; an *adze*, बसुला *basula*; a small *saw*, आरी *āri*; a *knife*, छूरी *chhūri*; and *files*, रेती *reti*.

471. The maker of hubble-bubbles (नरियरन्वाला *nariyarwāla*) uses a रेती *reti* (of which the point is हूर *hūr*), आरी *āri*, बरन्मा *barma*, and गज *gaj*.

472. The pipe (हुक्का *hukka*) is of various kinds—

(1) The नरियर *nariyar* or नरियाल *nariyal*, which is the ordinary country hubble-bubble, in which the mouth is applied to the cocoanut itself. It is smoked principally by Hindus. Of this the stem bearing the bowl for burning the tobacco is बोता *bota* or गट्टा *gatta*. The short smoking-stem sometimes applied to the cocoanut, to save the hands from being blackened, is निगाली *nigāli* or नर *nar*. The bowl is चिल्लम *chillam* or चिलम *chilam*. In South Bhagalpur पोंगी *pongi* is a temporary pipe made of the leaf of a tree. In South-West Shahabad दम्मी *dammi* is a wooden pipe used by travellers, and दमन्दमाचा *damdamācha* a pipe used by women.

473. (2) The other kinds stand on the ground, and are more or less similar to each other in shape. The general name is गुड़न्गुड़ी *gurguri* when the smoking stem is joined to a tube rising from the brass bowl, and गड़न्गड़ा *gargara* when it issues directly from the brass bowl. They are generally made of metal or earth. Another name is फरन्सी *pharsi*. The tube arrangement for carrying the

A collection of pipes.

1. *Penchdār gargara.*
2. *Satak* or *penchwān.*
3. *Jilebiya kulphīdār.*
4. *Kulphīdār chaugāni.*
5. *Simple chaugāni.*
6. *Arhāī khamhā.*
7. *Simple gargara.*
8. *Phatah pench.*
9. *Hubble-bubble* or *nariyar.*
10. *Tharhiya.*
11. *Kehunidār.*
12. *Gauraiya.*

bowl is the same in principle as in the cocoanut kind. The difference is in the smoking-stems (नैचा *naicha*).

Of these there are—

(*a*) कुलफीदार *kulphīdār*, that with joints (कुलफी *kulphi*), allowing the mouth-piece to be moved in any direction. A केहनीदार कुलफी *kehanidār kulphi* is a joint like an elbow, and a जिलेबिया कुलफी *jilebiya kulphi* is a twisted joint.

(*b*) अढ़ाइ खम्हा *arhāi khamha*, that with two large bends and one small one.

(*c*) डेढ़ खम्हा *derh khamha*, that with two bends.

(*d*) ठढ़िया *tharhiya* or ठड़िया *thariya*, with a short straight stem —used only by poor Masalmāns.

(*e*) चौगानी *chaugāni*, the simplest kind—used by the poor.

(*f*) गौरैया *gauraiya*, a simple kind, made of pottery.

(*g*) लटक *latak*, which bends downwards.

(*h*) छल्लेदार *chhalledār*, ornamented with gold or silver rings (छल्ला *chhalla*).

(*i*) सटक *satak*, पेचवान *pechwān*, पेँचदार *penchdār*, or फतह पेँच *phatah pench*, are various kinds with the long, snake-like, flexible tube.

CHAPTER IX.—THE PIPE-STEM MAKER.

474. The pipe-stem maker (नैचाबन्द *naichāband* or नैचाबन *naichāban*) uses an *awl*, गज *gaj* or (in Patna) सींख *sīnkh*; a *polishing-knife*, छूरी *chhūri*; a pair of *scissors*, कैँची *kainchi* or मेकराज *mekrāj*; a *saw*, आरी *āri*; and a pair of *tweezers*, मोचना *mochna*. He also uses तरला *tarla* or reed, and चीन *chīn* (*Panicum miliaceum*), a superior kind which comes from Sylhet.

475. For making the longest snake-like stems, पेचवान *pechwān*, a *board* (तखता *takhta*), a *string* (डोरी *dori*), and a *mould* (कालिब *kālib*), are also used. The embroidered work on a pipe-stem is called in South Bhagalpur पानदार *pāndār* or मोरस्सा *morassa*. The silk work on it is सरासर *sarāsar* or भरावट *bharāwat*, the flowered silk work on it बूटी *būti*, the silver work on it अलफी *alphi*, and the ornamental cloth work, उलटी चीन *ulti chīn*.

CHAPTER X.—THE COTTON-CARDER.

476. The cotton-carder is धुनियाँ *dhuniyān*. For a description of him and his instruments, see § 334 and ff.

477. In addition may be mentioned the पटकन *patkan*, which is an instrument for teasing cotton. It is also called गज *gaj* in Tirhut, Shahabad, Gaya, and South Bhagalpur, and साटी *sāti* in Champāran and Shahabad. The फटका *phatka* or फटकी *phatki* is a simple bow used by village women for carding cotton.

478. A lion once met a cotton-carder in the forest, and seeing his carding-bow, mistook him for a hunter. To avoid being killed, the lion addressed him हाथे धनुही कान्हे बान, कहाँ चले डिल्ली सुलतान *hāthe dhanuhi kānhe bān, kahān chale Dilli Sultān*,—with bow in hand and arrow on shoulder, where is the emperor of Delhi going? The cotton-carder was equally frightened, but at length mustered courage to reply बन में रहना बन में खाना बड़े के बात बड़े पहचाना *ban men rahna, ban men khāna, bare ke bāt bare pahchāna*,—although he live and eat in the forest, only a gentleman can recognise a gentleman. These sayings have passed into proverbs, the meaning of which is obvious.

CHAPTER XI.—THE SHOE-MAKER.

479. The shoe-maker is मोची *mochi* or मोँची *monchi* in cities, and चमार *chamār* in the country. Among his tools are—

480. The thick iron *pounder* for joining the edges of two pieces of leather which have been previously smeared with paste, which is लोहिया *lohiya* north of the Ganges generally, also लहौंगा *lahaunga* to the west of that tract, and पिटना *pitna* in North-East Tirhut. In Patna, Gaya, and South-West Shahabad it is लोहङ्गा *lohanga*, and in the rest of Shahabad and in South Bhagalpur it is लेहोँगा *lehonga* or टिपना *tipna*. In South Munger it is सिँगठा *singtha*. The paste used is लेइ *leï*, or to the south-east लई *laï*. In South-East Tirhut it is खरी *khari*. लसम *lasam* is a similar paste made of pounded boiled rice.

481. The *knife* for scraping the surface of the leather is in North-West Bihār राँपी *rāmpi* or रापी *rāpi*. In Tirhut, the west, and South-East Bihār it is also खुरपी *khurpi*. In Gaya it is खुरपा *khurpa*, and in Patna रम्पा *rampa*.

482. The large *awl* is सुतारी *sutāri*, with a variant सुताली *sutāli* in Gaya. To the east it is also लोखर *lokhar*, in Champāran लाँखर

lāhkhar, and in South-East Tirhut आर *ār*. The awl with a hook at the end for sewing is कटरन्नी *katarni*. In South Bhagalpur it is टकन्ना *takna*, and in South Munger टिपुनी *tipuni*. The medium-sized awl is मँझोला *manjhola* or मँझोली *manjholi*.

483. The *horn* for grease is सिङ्गा *singa*; south of the Ganges, it is also सिङ्घ *singh*.

484. The *last* is फरन्मा *pharma* or (north of the Ganges and the South-East) कलन्बूत *kalbūt*; south of the Ganges it is also, in Gaya, कालन्बूद *kālbūd*, and कलन्बूद *kalbūd* elsewhere.

485. The *wedges* of wood or leather fastened to the last to make it fit are परन्तहा *partaha* (also in South Munger), or परन्ताहा *partāha* in Shahabad, and पच्ची *pachchi* in the south-west of the same district. In South Munger they are कपन्छेरी *kapchheri*.

486. The *chisel* for paring the edges of the sole is खुरन्पी *khurpi* The sort of wooden chisel for smoothing the surface of the leather is बेँगा *benga* to the east, बेऊँगा *beūnga* north of the Ganges, or बेओँगा *beonga* or बेओँगी *beongi* elsewhere south of it. In South Bhagalpur it is पेलन *pelan*.

487. A wooden *block* for beating the leather is हाँमर *hāmmar* in South Munger and Gaya and घामँड़ *ghāmanr* in South-West Shahabad. The *block* on which the leather is cut is पिढ़िया *pirhiya*, or in South Bhagalpur सिल्ला *silla*, and in Sāran पिरन्ही *pirhi*.

CHAPTER XII.—THE BLANKET-WEAVER.

488. The blanket-weaver is गड़ेड़ी *gareri* south of the Ganges and भँड़िहर *bhenrihar* north of the Ganges; also in East Tirhut मड़ड़ *marar*.

489. He uses a simple *loom*. The stick on which the blanket is wound as it is woven is ओखर *okhar* south of the Ganges. North of the Ganges it is सिँजोय *sinjoy*, also सिंझो *sinjo* in Tirhut and कमन्हर *kamhar* in Champāran. The supports for this beam are खुट्टी *khutti*, खूँटी *khūnti*, or (in Gaya and East Tirhut) खूँटा *khūntā*. In South-East Tirhut they are also गाली *gāli* and गल्ली *galli* or गलियारी *galiyāri* in Champāran. In Shahabad the left support is called बरन्नी *barni*, and the right hand one गाली *gāli*. In the same district the support furthest in front of him is धूरा *dhūra*, and in Champāran धूइ *dhūi*.

490. The *beam* to which the web is fastened at the opposite end rom the weaver is ओहारी *ohāri*. बेँ *ben* or बेँव *benw* is a wooden imple-

ment which is passed between the thread of the web to drive tight each thread of the woof. In South-East Tirhut it is also called हथा *hatha*.

491. The *movable sticks* placed at intervals to separate the threads of the web are तगन्धरी *tagdhari* in Tirhut and Sāran and बैलट *bailat* elsewhere, except बैलठ *bailath* in Shahabad and बरत *barat* in Champāran.

492. The *heddles*, or implement for alternately raising and depressing the threads of the web, are चपन्नी *chapni*; also in South-West Tirhut फट्ठी *phatthi*.

493. The wooden *scraper* for removing knots or excrescences from the thread is खिखोरन्ना *khikhorna* or खिखोरन्नी *khikhorni* north of the Ganges, also खिधोरन्ना *khidhorna* in Champāran. In Patna it is खिलोरन्ना *khilorna*, and elsewhere south of the Ganges खिलन्होरन्ना *khilhorna*.

494. The thick iron *needle* is सूआ *sūa*, or in South Munger सूज *sūj*. The *shuttle* is सरग्गाँ *sargān* in South Munger and north of the Ganges, and सेरङ्ग *serang* or सेरङ्गा *seranga* south of it.

495. In Sāran and South-West Tirhut the भाँड़ी *bhānri* is a thick bamboo which is placed between the two threads of the warp. In Champāran it is सासत *sāsat*, in South-East Tirhut साँसर *sānsar*, elsewhere south of the Ganges साँसत *sānsat*, and elsewhere चोँगा *chonga*.

CHAPTER XIII.—THE FANCY SILK OR FRINGE-MAKER.

496. This man is called पटवा *patwa* or पटन्हेरा *pathera*. In Sāran he is called पटन्हेरी *patheri*.

497. He uses the कतन्रा *katra* or कतन्ला *katla*, a piece of wood with four holes, in which four threads are fixed for winding.

498. The *wooden reel* furnished with a handle is बटन्नी *batni* generally. The *small wooden reel* is अट्टी *anti* or चरख *charakh*. An optional local name is गट्टी *gatti* in South-West Shahabad. गोली *goli*, or in Tirhut and South Munger पेचक *pechak*, is a ball of thread. The *winding-stick* is तीली *tili* in Patna, बेलन *belan* in Shahabad, and लटाँइ *latāïn* in North-West Bihār.

499. His *scissors* are कैँची *kainchi*. The *coarse needle* for smoothing roughnesses in thread is सलाइ *salāï*, also टकुआ *takua* in East Tirhut, and टेकुआ *tekua* in Champāran. The ivory *smoother* is मठार *mathār*,

or in Sāran मठरन्ना *matharna*. The *large darning-needle* is सूआ *sūa*. The *fine needle* is सूई *sūï*, also ननमुहिया *nanmuhiya*.

500. The iron *hook* with a ring which goes round the toe is अँकुरा or अँकुड़ा *ankura*, also अँकुसा *ankusa* and अँकुसी *ankusi* in Gaya and North-East Tirhut. This hook is supported on a stand called थूनू *thūnu* in Patna, थौना *thauna* in Gaya, थल्ला *thalla* in South-West Shahabad, धौना *dhauna* in the rest of the district, and थम *tham* to the east generally.

501. The *drum* off which the thread is wound is परेता *pareta*, परन्ता *parta*, or परन्ती *parti* in North-West Bihār. The bamboo frame on which the thread is wound is नटन्वा *natwa* or लटन्वा *latwa*. In Patna it is नटाइ *natāï*, and in Gaya and the South-East नेटन्वा *netwa*.

CHAPTER XIV.—THE EMBROIDERER.

502. The embroiderer is जरन्दोज *jardoj* or (south of the Ganges) कारन्चोबी वाला *kārchobiwāla*, and he makes embroidery (कारन्चोबी *kārchobi*) on the कारन्चोब *kārchob* or embroidery-frame, on which the work is stretched. This frame is rectangular; and of the parallel pairs of sides, one pair is called (in Patna) समन्सेर *samser* or (in Gaya and the west) समन्सेरक *samserak*, and the other तीली *tīli* in Patna, फरद *pharad* in Gaya and Sāran, and पट्टी *patti* in Shahabad.

503. The small *needle* is सूई *sūï*, and the sewing-awl सुतेमान *sutemān* north of the Ganges, सुतन्वान *sutwān* in Gaya and Shahabad, सूआ *sūa* or बड़ि सूई *bari sūï* in Patna, Gaya, and South Munger.

CHAPTER XV.—THE DYER.

504. The dyer is रँगन्रेज *rangrej*, in opposition to the रँगन्साज *rangsāj* or painter. In North-West Bihār he is called रँगन्रेजी *rangreji*.*

505. He uses a *vat* or pot sunk in the ground for his dyes. This is called north of the Ganges माट *māt*. In Patna it is माँट *mānt*, and to the east माठ *māth*. In Shahabad it is छोँड़ *chhonr*, and in the south-west of the district कुण्डा *kunda*. In Gaya and East Tirhut it is कूँड़ *kūnr*, and in South Bhagalpur and East Tirhut गोली *goli*.

---

* This word is often confounded with the word अँगन्रेजी *Angreji* 'English;' and in jest, or when speaking facetiously, the English in India are called रँगन्रेज *rangrej*, or 'dyers.'

506. His *half-round pot* is अथरा *athra* or नाद *nād* north of the Ganges, in Shahabad, and South Munger. In South-East Tirhut and South Munger it is also called कड़ाही *karāhi.* In Patna and Gaya it is हाँड़ी *hānri*, and in South Bhagalpur कड़हाइ *karhāī.*

507. The wooden *filter-frame* on which the cloth is hung like a bag with the dye inside is माँजी *mānji* or मझी *manji* generally. In South-West Tirhut it is मिरला *mirla*, in North-East Tirhut झोरी *jhori*, in Gaya माँझी *mānjhi*, and in South Bhagalpur चम्मल *chammal.* The string tied to the cloth is कसन *kasan*, and the cloth with the dye inside it in South Munger and Patna फुलगरना *phulgarna.*

508. The *stirring-stick* for mixing the dyes is डण्डी *dandi*, or in South Munger डण्टा *danta*, in South Bhagalpur टेखती *tekhti*, and in North-East Tirhut लरना *larna.*

CHAPTER XVI.—THE WOOD-PAINTER.

509. The wood-painter is रँगसाज *rangsāj*, as distinct from the रँगरेज *rangrej* or dyer. He uses two kinds of *paints*—one अस्तर *astar*, which is a paste made up with chalk and gum, and the other रोगन *rogan*, which is made up with resin and oil.

CHAPTER XVII.—THE TIN-MAN.

510. The tin-man (कलैगर *kalaigar*) uses a *bellows*, called भाथी *bhāthi* south of the Ganges and in East Tirhut; elsewhere it is called धौकनी *dhaukni.* Another name current south of the Ganges is एकहत्थू भाथी *ekhatthu bhāthi.* The two sticks used as handles are north of the Ganges and in South Munger हत्थी *hatthi* or हत्थू *hatthū*, and south of it, and also in Tirhut, डण्टा *danta.* In South-East Tirhut they are also हत्था *hattha.* The bamboo pipe is चोंगा *chonga*, also in North-West Tirhut नरौआ *naraua*, in Gaya and Shahabad नराउँ *narāūn*, and in South Bhagalpur चोंगी *chongi.*

511. The *solder* is राँगा *rānga*, and the soldering-iron कैया *kaiya.* He also uses cotton-wool, रुई *rui*, and pincers, सरसी *sarsi* or सँड़सी *sanrsi.* The ठिकड़ा *thikra* or खोरिया *khoriya* is the flat tile for melting the solder.

512. The *tin-cutter* is कैंची *kainchi*, and he also uses the small *hammer*, हथौरी *hathauri*, and the *compasses* परकाल *parkāl.* The *tin-scraper* is नेहनी *nehni* or लेहनी *lehni*; also खुरचुनी *khurchuni* in South Bhagalpur.

513. The सबरा *sabra*, सबरी *sabri*, or (in South Bhagalpur) साबल *sābal*, is a small kind of *anvil*, made of a bent piece of iron, with one end pointed and stuck in the ground.

CHAPTER XVIII.—THE JEWELLER.

514. The jeweller is सोनार *sonār*, or in Gaya सोनी *soni*. In Champāran and North-West Tirhut he is सोनगढ़ुआ सोनार *songarhua sonār*.

515. Amongst his implements are the *tongs*, which are सँड़सा *saursa* or सँड़सी *sanrsi*.

516. The *pincers* have various names. Large pincers are चिमटा *chimta* in South-West Tirhut, also सेहुना *sehuna* generally to the west; सोहना *sohna* to the east and in Gaya, and चूँटा *chūnta* in Patna. Smaller ones are चिमटी *chimti*, सेहुनी *sehuni*, सोहनी *sohni*, or चूँटी *chūnti*. Another kind is गहुआ *gahua*, which are the large pincers. Nippers are गहुई *gahuï*, or in South Bhagalpur गहुली *gahuli*. The कगमुहीँ *kagmuhīn* are nippers twisted at the head for holding the crucible in the fire. These may also be called बगसँड़सी *bagsanrsi* in North-West Bihār and बगमुहीँ *bagmuhīn* in Tirhut and Champāran.

517. The जमूरा *jamūra* or जमूरी *jamūri* are *wire drawing-pincers*, and the perforated wire plate is जन्त्री *jantri* south of the Ganges, in North-West Bihār, and East Tirhut, जैँत्री *jaintri* north of the Ganges generally, and जतरी *jatri* in Champāran and North-East Tirhut.

518. The iron needle-shaped tool for making links of chains is टेकुली *tekuli* to the north-west, टकुआ *takua* to the east and south-west, टेकुआ *tekua* in Saran, Patna, and Gaya, and टेकुरी *tekuri* in South Bhagalpur.

519. The *compasses* are परकाल *parkāl* or कम्पास *kampās*, or in South-West Shahabad चलाँकी *chalānki*.

520. The *chisel* with a round knob for embossing circular ornamentation is खलनी *khalni*, or in Tirhut खोलनी *kholni*.

521. The *cold chisel* is छेनी *chheni*, and a smaller variety is कलम *kalam* south of the Ganges.

522. The *cutters* are कैँची *kainchi*, and also to the south, except Patna, कतरनी *katarni*.

523. Amongst *hammers* हथौरा or हथौड़ा *hathaura* is the largest. The medium-sized is मरिया or मड़िया *mariya*, with a variant मरेया *mareya* in North-East Tirhut; in Gaya it is मठरनी *matharni*. The smallest

is गोलमुहाँ *golmuhān* or गोलमुहीँ *golmuhīn;* another name is खोलमरिया *kholmariya* in East Tirhut.

524. The small pointed *anvil* is समदान *samdān.* The curved anvil is एकवाइ *ekwāï*, or in East Tirhut एकाबे *ekābe.*

525. The bell-metal *anvil* sunk with several depressions for making *repoussé* work is कँसुला *kansula* in North-West Bihār, कँसला *kansla* in East Tirhut, काँसुला *kānsula* in South Tirhut, काँसला *kānsla* in South-West Bihār, and कसला *kasla* in South Bhagalpur and South Munger.

526. The square-headed *anvil* is निहाइ *nihāï*, or in Champāran and North-East Tirhut नेहाए *nehaë*, and नहाइ *nahāï* in South-East Tirhut. In South Bhagalpur it is लिहाइ *lihāï.*

527. The *anvil blocks* sunk in the ground are चाहा *chāha* in Sāran and South-West Shahabad. In Champāran and West Tirhut they are ठेहा *theha.* In Shahabad they are एकठा *ektha.* In Patna, Gaya, and Tirhut they are परकठ *parkath,* and in South-East Tirhut also पिरगिठी *piryithi.*

528. The *blow-pipe* is बकनार *baknār,* or in Sāran बकनल *baknal.*

529. The hollow *cane for blowing* up the fire is नरी *nari,* with local variants नारी *nāri* in Gaya, लारी *lāri* in North-East Tirhut and South Bhagalpur. In South-East Tirhut it is optionally फुकाठी *phukāthi.* The *fireplace* is अँगैठा *angaitha* north of the Ganges and अँगेठा *angetha* south of it. Another name for this last is बोरसी *borsi.* The *fan* for blowing up the fire is पङ्खा *pankha* or पङ्खी *pankhi;* also in South-West Shahabad it is बेनियाँ *beniyān.* In North-East Tirhut भट्टी *bhatti* is the dry powdered earth used for cooling the hot metal.

530. The small clay *crucible* is घड़िया or घरिया *ghariya.* It is made of a mixture of clay and rags called in Shahabad कँपरौट *kampraut*, and in Champāran कपरौट *kapraut.*

531. An *ingot* not beaten out is कामी *kāmi,* or in Gaya एकवाइ *ekwāï.* In Sāran it is थक्का *thakka,* in Champāran and North-West Tirhut छलकी *chhalki,* South-East Tirhut गद्दी *gaddi* or थोक *thak* (also in South Munger), in South Bhagalpur थौक *thauk,* and in Tirhut generally except the north-west छिलकी *chhilki.* A block of silver beaten out flat is चौरसा *chaursa.*

532. The iron *ingot mould* is परगहनी *pargahni* to the west and परघनी *parghani* in Patna and Gaya. In East Tirhut it is धारा *dhāra,* in Sāran कम धारा *kam dhāra,* and in South Bhagalpur नाली *nāli.*

533. The *moulds* of various sizes into which metal is beaten are कट्किरा *katkira* north of the Ganges, कठ्किरा *kathkira* south of it to the east, ठस्सा *thassa* in Sarān, and ठप्पा *thappa* in Gaya and Shahabad. In Shahabad similar moulds are बह्का *bahka*, लहेरिया *laheriya*, गोख्लू *gokhlu* (also in South Bhagalpur), and मोतिया *motiya*. To the west रहट्वार *rahatwār* is a mould in which round articles are beaten into shape, and गुंज्री *gunjri* is a similar smaller one. In the same tract पग्ड़ी ठसा *pagri thasa* are milling moulds, such as those in which the edge is given to a rupee. These last are called in South Bhagalpur खीरा बिच्ची *khīra bichchi*, बाँह *bānh*, or पग्ड़ा *pagra*.

534. *Pattern stamps* for ornaments are ठोँसा *thonsa* in Shahabad, ठासा *thāsa* in Gaya and South Bhagalpur, ठाँस *thāns* in Patna, and छापा *chhāpa* in South-West Shahabad and South Munger.

535. The कटोरी *katori* is a box or cup for holding scraps of silver. In North-East Tirhut it is called डिबिया *dibiya*, and in Tirhut and to the east सितुहा *situha* or रँगेह्री *rangehri*.

536. The *polishing-brush* is बरौँछी *baraunchhi*. In South-East Tirhut it is also called कुच्ची *kuchchi*. The polishing stone is ओप्नी *opni* or पोत *pot*.

537. The *touch-stone* is कसौटी *kasauti*. A *jeweller's wages* is गढ़ाई *garhāi*.

CHAPTER XIX.—THE LAPIDARY.

538. The lapidary is हक्काक *hakkāk*, or in South Bhagalpur मोह्ली लोहार *mohli lohār*, and he uses a revolving *grindstone* or सान *sān* or in Shahabad चकर सान *chakar sān*, made of corundum powder and lac. The bow for turning this is कमाना *kamāna* or (to the west) कमानी *kamāni*. Its props are खूँटा *khunta*, देवाली *dewāli*, or एकठा *ektha*. Its wooden axle is साँखा *sānkha* in Patna and Gaya, लट्टू *lattu* in Shahabad, and कून *kūn* to the east.

539. The agate *burnishers* are घोँटा *ghonta*, and the round ones सिल्ली *silli*; the *pincers*, चूँटी *chūnti* in Tirhut, Patna, Gaya, and the east, चिम्टा *chimta* in Sāran, and सेहुनी *sehuni* in Shahabad; the iron *graver* is सलाई *salāi*; the *cutters*, कैँची *kainchi*; the small *hammer*, हथौरी *hathauri*; the *anvil*, निहाई *nihāi*; the *pincers*, सँड़सी *sanrsi*; and the revolving *awl* जिला सान *jilā sān* or खर सान *khar sān*.

CHAPTER XX.—THE SEAL-MAKER.

540. The seal-maker is मोहरकन *moharkan*, and he uses a machine called a चरख *charakh*, of which the principal portion is a revolving awl, बरमा *barma*.

541. The **hammer** which he uses is मथनी *mathni* or मरिया *mariya;* the **stone** to which the metal to be engraved is fastened is ढेमा *dhema;* and the **diamond** pen is कलम *kalam*.

CHAPTER XXI.—THE GOLD-WASHER.

542. The gold-washer is called नियरिया *niyariya* or नियारिया *niyāriya* north of the Ganges and in Patna; elsewhere south of the Ganges he is called सनधोआ *sandhoa*, and South Bhagalpur नियार धोआ *niyār dhoa*.

543. He uses the कठरा *kathra* or **wooden pan** for washing the ashes of jewellers' shops. Another name current in Patna and Gaya is कठौती *kathauti*. The **ashes** are नियारा *niyāra* or नेआरा *neāra*, and they are collected by a scraper, खुरपा *khurpa*, and a broom, कूँची *kūnchi* or मूठा *mūtha*. South of the Ganges the पखुरी *pakhuri* is an iron instrument for collecting the ashes.

544. His **sifting-pan** is छट्टन *chhattan*, or in Patna and Gaya ढकना *dhakna*. In South Bhagalpur it is चौहट्टा *chauhatta*.

545. His **bellows** are भाथी *bhāthi;* his **blow-pipe,** बकनार *baknār*, or in Shahabad बकनल *baknal;* and the earthen pipe of the vessel which remains in the fire, सुसवा *suswa* north of the Ganges and सूँसा *sūnsa* south of it. In Sāran it is also नरौआ *naraua*.

546. His **pincers** are सँड़सी *sanrsi*, or in North-West Tirhut सनसा *sansa;* and the iron **stirrer** सींक *sīnk* north of the Ganges and सींख *sīnkh* south of it. Another name for the latter is सलाइ *salāi* in North-West Bihār.

547. The earthen crucible is घड़िया or घरिया *ghariya*, also डीब *dīb* in Patna and Gaya and अड्डा *adda* in South Bhagalpur. These crucibles are of two kinds: the first only destroys the dirt, leaving all the metals behind, and is called बगलौटी *baglauti*. The second destroys all the baser metals left by the first, and leaves only the gold and silver untouched. It is called पुनहर *punhar*.

CHAPTER XXII.—THE BRAZIER.

548. The brazier is ठठेरा *thathera,* but in Shahabad he is also called कसेरा *kasera,* which properly means a brass-founder. In North-East Tirhut he is ठठेरि *thatheri.* He is famous for his powers of swindling, as in the proverb ठठेरिं ठठेरि नहिँ बदला होय *thatheri thatheri nahiñ badla hoy,*—braziers don't traffic with each other (for if they did, it would be diamond cut diamond).

549. He uses the निहाइ *nihāï* or नेहाए *nehāë,* or *anvil.* In East Tirhut this is also called लेहाए *lehāe,* and in Patna, Gaya, and South-West Shahabad पथल *pathal.* The समदान *samdān* is the pointed anvil, which is also called in Gaya and Shahabad एकवाइ *ekwāï.* The सबरा *sabra* or, in the south-east साबर *sābar,* is an anvil round at the top. The circular anvil for shaping the mouth of a vessel is चौका *chauka* south of the Ganges and बगलभरुआ *bagalbharua* north of it. South of the Ganges the गड़िया *geriya* (Gaya) or दुगोड़ी *dugori* (west) is a sort of wooden anvil or block. The गोली सबरी *goli sabri* is a kind of anvil for pushing up any indentations. In South Bhagalpur it is called गोलसाबर *golsābar.* The खरवे *kharwe,* or in Shahabad दबठा *dabtha,* is a kind of anvil on which hollow vessels (गगरा *gagra*) are hammered out. It stands on the two-legged दुगोड़ी *dugori,* also called खराट *kharāt.*

550. The *cutters* are कैंची *kainchi,* also कात *kāt* in Gaya and North Tirhut.

551. The *stirrers* are—(*a*) for stirring solder, कैया *kaiya* south of the Ganges and सराइ *sarāï* north of it; also लोपन *lopan* in East Tirhut: (*b*) the iron stirrer for mixing up the flux, पनडेनी *pandeni* north of the Ganges and Gaya, पेनेनी *peneni* in Shahabad, and पनकाठी *pankāthi* (of wood) in South Bhagalpur.

552. The *pincers* are सनसी *sansi* or सँड़सी *sanrsi,* also गहुआ *gahua;* the *file* रेती *reti,* and the *hammers* हथौरा *hathaura* or हथौरी *hathauri,* also मठना *mathna* north of the Ganges and to the west, मरिया *mariya* in East Tirhut, and घन *ghan* in North-East Tirhut.

553. The *vessel for holding the flux,* सोहागा *sohāga* or पाएन *pāën,* is कटोरी *katori.* In South Bhagalpur it is पनवाला *panwāla.*

554. The *bellows* are भाथी *bhāthi;* the *crucible,* घड़िया or घरिया *ghariya;* the *tongs,* सनसी *sansi;* and the perforated *cover for the crucible,* ओहार *ohār* north of the Ganges, South Munger, and South-West Shahabad; also झाँप *jhāmp* in South-East Tirhut and South

Munger, झाँपन *jhāmpan* or झाँपन्ना *jhāmpna* in Patna and Gaya, छिपौना *chhipauna* elsewhere in Shahabad, and कर्‌हाइ *karhāï* or मुन्दन *mundan* to the east.

555. The *mallet* is मुंगरी *mungri*. The *scales* are तराजू *tarāju* or तर्‌जूई *tarjūï*. The *polisher* is छोलनी *chholni* or लेहनी *lehni*. In South Munger it is also नेहनी *nehni*.

CHAPTER XXIII.—THE BRASS FOUNDER.

556. He is कसेरा *kasera*, and in Gaya also तम्हेड़ा *tamhera*.

557. He uses *moulds* of various kinds, called साँचा *sāncha*, or in Shahabad कमन्धरन्ना *kamdharna*. His *lathe* is खराद *kharād*, or in Shahabad and South-East Bihār कुन्द *kund*. His large *pincers* are सँड़सा *sanrsa* or सनसा *sansā*. His *crucible* घरिया *ghariya*, of which the mouth is मुँह *munh*. His broad chisel is चौरसा *chaursa* or चौरसी *chaursi*, also लेहनी *lehni* in Shahabad and छेनी *chheni* in the south-west of the same district.

CHAPTER XXIV.—THE BRASS BANGLE-MAKER.

558. The brass (काँसा *kānsa*) bangle-maker (ठठेरी *thatheri* or ठठेरा *thatherar*) makes बाँही *bānhi*, which are brass bangles worn by the lower classes. To the east they are called बतिसी *batisi*, and in South Bhagalpur बस्ती *basti*. When a number of these are worn, those at each end are called बन *ban* or (South-East Tirhut) कचरुखी *kachrukhi* and (Sāran) कतरी *katri*. Of these the one highest up the arm is called अगुआ *agua* or अगेला *agela*, and that nearest the hand, पछुआ *pachhua* or पछेला *pachhela*.

559. He uses the following implements. Variants of the names already given in other chapters will not be repeated here:—

560. नेहाय *nehāy*, the anvil; हथौरी *hathauri*, the hammer; सँड़सी *sanrsi*, the pincers; रेती *reti*, the file; छेनी *chheni*, the cold chisel; भाथी *bhāthi*, the bellows; घड़िया *ghariya*, the crucible; and ढाड़ा *dhāra* or साँचा *sāncha*, the mould, in which कामी *kāmi* is the orifice through which the molten alloy is poured.

CHAPTER XXV.—GLASS-MAKER AND GLASS BANGLE-MAKER.

561. These are the सीसा ढरेवाला *sīsā dharewāla* or glass-manufacturer; the मनिहार *manihār*, who makes glass bangles; and the चुरिहार

or चुड़िहार *churihār* or चुड़िया *churiya*, who makes the embossed ornaments on glass bangles.

562. Their *furnace* is called भट्ठी *bhatthi*, of which the opening through which the melted glass is removed is बारा *bāra* north of the Ganges, मोहड़ा *mohra* in Shahabad, and elsewhere दरवाजा *darwāja*. This is closed by a cover called अलवारी *alwāri* north of the Ganges and in South Munger, ओलवारी *olwāri* in South-West Shahabad, ढपौना *dhapauna* in Shahabad, and elsewhere झपना *jhapna*.

563. The earthen *crucible* is ठिक्कर *thikkar* or ठिकरा *thikra* generally, also कड़ाही *karāhi* in South-East Tirhut, and डिबरा *dibra* in Patna and Shahabad.

564. The *spoon* for putting the glass into the crucible is करछुल *karchhul*. The iron *hook* for taking out the glass is अँकुरी *ankuri* or अँकुरा *ankura* in Patna and the west, अकुरा *akura* in South-East Tirhut, हथ अकुरी *hath akuri* in South Tirhut, हथ उकरी *hath ukri* in South Bhagalpur, and धरनी अकुरी *dharni akuri* in Champāran. The instrument for turning the glass in the crucible is अकुरा *akura* generally, and कलछुला *kalchhula* to the west.

565. The *stone* on which the ring is shaped is पत्थर *patthar* or पत्थल *patthal* north of the Ganges, and पथरी *pathri* south of it. The *mould* with a handle for shaping the bangle is कालबूत *kālbūt* north of the Ganges, and कलबुद *kalbud* or साँचा *sāncha* south of it. The handle of this is सरकण्डी *sarkandi*.

566. The long iron *poker* on which the glass is melted is सलाग *salāg*; the flat iron instrument for shaping the ring is माला *māla*; and the instrument for widening the ring to the required size बेधवार *bedhwār* in North-West Bihār, बधवारी *badhwāri* in Patna and South Tirhut, and बधरना *badharna* south of the Ganges. The छोटि बेधवारी *chhoti bedhwārī*, &c., or छोटि अकुरी *chhoti akuri*, is the instrument for taking the ring off the mould. In South Bhagalpur it is घरन्नी *gharanni*.

567. *Other instruments* used by the glass bangle-maker are टिखठी *tikhthi*, which are bamboo slips for holding the bangles in the fire; पन्नी *panni*, leaves of solder; फोकाठी *phokāthi* (Gaya and South Bhagalpur), फोँफी *phonphi* (West Tirhut and South-West Shahabad), or नरी *nari* (Patna, Sonth Munger, Tirhut, and rest of Shahabad), which is the pipe for blowing up the fire; the अँगेठा *angethā* or अँगेठी *angethi*, which is the fireplace; and चुँटा *chūnta* (Shahabad), चुण्टा *chunta* (Tirhut, Gaya, and South Munger), चुँटी *chūnti* (South Bhagalpur), or चिमटा *chimta* (generally), which is the pincers.

568. In Shahabad a famous maker of glass bangle ornaments was one *Samman Churiya.* It is said that when boys he and a king were pupils in the same school, and each promised that on his marriage he would show the other his wife. Samman married first, and did so. When, however, the king married, he refused to carry out the agreement and show his wife to Samman. The latter thereupon disguised himself as a female bangle-maker, and, gaining admission to the female apartments, sold some ornaments to the queen in the presence of the king, who praised the workmanship, saying the bangles were like ivory ones. Next day the king began to boast of his high character, and how *he* would never allow his wife to be seen by an outside man, when he was interrupted by Samman reciting the following verse, which showed the other how he had been made a fool of:—सम्मन चुरिया ऊ गढ़ैँ ज्यौँ हस्ती के दन्त, बाँह पकड़ि रस लेत हैँ, बैठे देखैँ कन्त *Samman Churiya ū garhen jyoñ hasti ke dant, bāṅh pakari ras let hain, baithe dekhen kant,*—Samman the bangle-embosser makes bangles like ivory. He held her by the arm, and had the pleasure (of seeing her) while her husband was sitting by.

569. The stamp for making embossed ornaments on the bangle is साँचा *sāncha* (Tirhut and the south-east), करैली कटःना *karaili katna* (Champāran), ठप्पा *thappa* (South-West Shahabad), and छापा *chhāpa* (Tirhut and elsewhere in Shahabad). In Champāran and South-West Tirhut तोगर *togar* is an instrument for embossing.

CHAPTER XXVI.—THE LAC BANGLE-MAKER.

570. The lac (लाख *lākh* or लाह *lāh*) bangle-maker is लहेरी *laheri* or लहेरा *lahera.* He uses a block of wood with a handle, on which the bangles are fitted, which is called कुन्द *kund;* a साँचा *sāncha,* which is a brass mould for embossing ornaments; and a चुभःकी *chubhki* (and also to the east चुभःती *chubhti*), which is an ivory mould for embossing. His bamboo pipe for blowing the fire is नारी *nāri* or नरि *nari,* also फुकाठी *phukāthi* or लारी *lāri* in South Bhagalpur and फुखाठी *phukhāthi* in North-East Tirhut.

571. A bangle, whether of glass or lac, is चूड़ी *chūri.* The latter variety is also called लहःठी *lahthi.* Of these the thickest, or keeper, which prevents the thinner ones slipping over the hand, is कँगःनी *kangni.* The end bangles of a set are बन्द *band,* or in South Bhagalpur लरःना *larna,* and the intermediate ones सुरःकी *surki,* and in South Bhagalpur पहःटा *pahta.*

Potter (Kumhār) at work

Lith. by Hem Chunder Ghosal Student Govt. School of Art Calcutta. Cornwallis Press Calcutta.

CHAPTER XXVII.—THE POTTER.

572. The potter is generally called कुम्हार *kumhār* or कुम्हरा *kumhra;* in the east he is also called पण्डित *pandit*, and in Patna and Gaya also परजापत *parjāpat*. In Shahabad he is कुँहार *kunhār*, and in the south-west of the district कोहार *kohār*. Concerning him there is a proverb, निचन्त सूते कुम्हरा, मटिया नऽ ले जाय चोर *nichint sūte kumhra, matiya na le jāy chor*,—the potter sleeps secure, for no one will steal clay. His wife is known as कुम्हैनि *kumhaini* or कुम्हैन *kumhaïn*, as in the proverb तेली बैल ला कुम्हैनि सत्ति *teli bail la kumhaini satti*,—for the sake of the oilman's ox, the potter's wife has become *suttee*, *i.e.*, she interests herself in other people's affairs.

573. His *wheel* is चाक *chāk*, which is turned by a stick, चकैठ *chakaith*, or in North-East Tirhut छरि *chhari*, on a peg, which is कीला *kīla* or किल्ला *killa* to the west, and खूँटी *khūnti* or खुट्टी *khutti* to the east. In South Bhagalpur it is, however, सिल्ला *silla*.

574. The implement for mixing the clay is लेहसुर *lehsur* north of the Ganges and लहसुर *lahsur* south of the Ganges generally. In Shahabad it is कटनी *katni*, and in South Bhagalpur पाट्टा *patta*.

575. The *rammer* for consolidating the clay is पीटन *pītan* when made of wood; when made of earthenware it is पींड़ *pīnr* north of the Ganges generally and in Shahabad, पिढ़ौर *pirhaur* or पिँढ़ुरी *pinrhuri* in Patna, and पिँढ़ुर *pinrhur* in Gaya. In South Bhagalpur it is पिनौरी *pinauri*. The clay is smoothed with an instrument called मिलौना *milauna* north of the Ganges and in South Munger, and also मजनी *majni* in South-East Tirhut and South Bhagalpur.

576. The *moulds* for shaping vessels are अथरी *athri* generally. Other names are कठअथरी *kathathri* in Patna and करथरी *karthari* in South Bhagalpur. The pots when ready are severed from the wheel by a string called छेवन *chhewan;* also छौनी *chhauni* in Patna and छेवनी *chhewni* to the east. In South Bhagalpur it is छेवनो *chhewno*. Another name is कमठी *kamthi* in North-West Tirhut. The सचा *sancha* or साँचा *sāncha* is a mould used in making tiles.

577. The *kiln* is आवा *āwa*.

578. The *clay-pit* has many names, viz. चुआँ *chūān* (South-West Tirhut), खँड़ार *khanrār* (Patna), मटिखान *matikhān* (West Tirhut, Gaya, and Shahabad), मटखना *matkhana* (South-West Shahabad and Tirhut), मटखभा *matkhabha* (South Bhagalpur), मटकोर *matkor* (Patna and South

Munger), and मटियार *matiyār* (South-East Tirhut). Other names are कोहँड़गर *kohanrgar* in Sāran and मटखम *matkham* in North-West Tirhut.

579. The earthen pot in which the water which the potter uses while making the vessel is kept is called चकवर *chakwar* in the north-west; also अथवानी *athwāni* in North-West Tirhut, हथवानी *hathwāni* in Gaya and South-East Tirhut, and कदैठ *kadaith* in South Munger. In South Bhagalpur it is चकोड़ी *chakori* or हथपानी *hathpāni.*

CHAPTER XXVIII.—THE FIREWORK-MAKER.

580. The firework-maker is आतसबाज *ātasbāj* or आतशबाज *atashbāj.* In Shahabad and South Bhagalpur he is रवाइसवाला *rawāiswāla.* In South Bhagalpur गोँड़ी *gonri* is the name of a caste whose employment is to make fireworks.

581. He uses a *grindstone,* which is चक्की *chakki* to the west and in South Bhagalpur, and जाँता *jānta* in Tirhut and to the east; also in East Tirhut चकरी *chakri.* In South-West Shahabad it is सिल *sil.*

582. His *ramrod* for ramming the powder is कलबुद *kalbud* generally, with a variant कलाबूत *kalābūt* in South-West Shahabad. In the rest of Shahabad it is सुम्बा *sumba,* and in South-East Tirhut optionally सुम्हा *sumha* when made of iron. In Sāran it is गज *gaj.* The wooden roller used in making a Roman candle is खोलकड़ा *kholakra,* and in South Bhagalpur also खोलनी *kholni.*

583. His *saw* is आरी *āri;* his *knife,* छूरी *chhūri.* A flat heavy one is बाँकी *bānki* in Sāran and Champāran, बाँक *bānk* in Shahabad, दाब *dāb* in Tirhut, and दबिया *dabiya* also in the north-east of the same district. His *awl* is बरमा *barma,* and his *file* is रेती *reti.*

584. His wooden *platter* is कठरा *kathra* to the west, अठरा *athra* in Tirhut, Gaya, and South-West Shahabad, कठौती *kathauti* or कठौत *kathaut* in Patna, Gaya, and East Tirhut, and कड़हाइ *karhāi* in South Bhagalpur.

585. Among the fireworks which he makes are—

(*a*) The hand *Catherine wheel,* चरखी *charkhi,* and that which is mounted on a pole, चक्कर *chakkar,* राधे चक्कर *rādhe chakkar* (South-East Tirhut), or चकरबान *chakarbān* (Shahabad).

Of these, the pipes in which the powder is placed are नाल *nāl*, or to the east लाल *lāl* or लाला *lāla*, and in South Munger नल्ला *nalla*. The pipe in which the axle works is also called नाल *nāl*, &c., as above; also पुल्ली *pulli* in South-West Shahabad, कुल्फी *kulphi* in South Bhagalpur, and in South-East Tirhut दनियाली *daniyāli*. The axle itself is मकरी *makri* or छुच्छी *chhuchchhi* north of the Ganges generally, and also फोंफी *phonphi* to the west. The spokes and rim of the wheel are ढाँचा *dhāncha* to the west or ढँचरी *dhanchri* in Sāran, ठाट *thāt* in Tirhut, मड़री *marri* in South Munger, and मेंड़रा *menrra* in South Bhagalpur.

(*b*) There are various kinds of *bombs:* amongst them are भुचम्पा *bhuchampa* or भुचप्पा *bhuchappa* (north of the Ganges) or भुइँ चम्पा *bhuīn champa* (south of it), अनार *anār* (generally), कुल्हिया *kulhiya* (north of the Ganges) or लौकी *lauki* (east generally), बमगोला *bamgola* (generally) or गोला *gola* (Champāran and North-East Tirhut), तड़াকা *tarāka* (south of the Ganges), नास पाल *nās pāl* (generally), दाँतुआ *dāntua* and तोरना *torna* (Shahabad). A long kind of bomb is north of the Ganges चहका *chahka*.

(*c*) The *balloon* is पेटारा *petāra* south of the Ganges, and पेटाड़ा *petārha* or गोबारा *gobāra* north of the Ganges, to the west. In North-East Tirhut it is उरता पेटाड़ा *urtā petārha*, and in South-East Tirhut उरन पेटाड़ा *uran petārha*.

(*d*) The *rocket* is हवाइ *hawāi* or असमान तारा *asmān tāra;* also छड़ी *chhari* in North-West Tirhut. In South-West Shahabad, Sāran, and Champāran बान *bān*, and in North-East Tirhut जङ्गी बान *jangi bān*, is a species of rocket.

(*e*) The *Roman candle* is महताबी *mahtābi* generally, also दस्ती *dasti* north of the Ganges and गल्लर *gallar* in Shahabad and East Tirhut.

(*f*) *Other fireworks* are महताब *mahtāb*, खजूर *khajūr*, किला *kilā* (a miniature fort, of which the bastions are बुरजी *burji*), गञ्ज सितारा *ganj sitāra*, कदम गाछ *kadam gāchh*, चादर पड़ाकेदार *chādar parākedār*, सादा चादर *sāda chādar*, चादर *chādar* or (East Tirhut) सौसन के टट्टी *sausan ke tatti*, चाँद चरखी *chānd charkhi*, पटेबाज *patebāj*, किरिन *kirin* or

(North-East Tirhut) किरिन चक्कर *kirin chakkar*, छुछुन्दर *chhuchhundar* (West Tirhut and South-West Shahabad), जलेबी *jalebi* (South-West Shahabad), मुरन्रा *murra* or मुरःहा *murha* (South-West Shahabad and Gaya), चन्दर कला *chandar kala* (South West Shahabad), पड़ाका *parāka* or (South-West Shahabad) पटाखा *patākha* (Chinese crackers), मूढ़ा *mūrha*, दीपक *dīpak*, जूही *jūhi*, रसन्पाल *raspāl* (Sāran and Champāran), अरन्दाना *ardāna* (East Tirhut), देब *deb* or देव *deo* (a flying monster), नटःबाज *natbāj* or लरत देब *larat deb* (fighting monsters), कैत बान *kait bān* (a round rocket), फारन्सी गोला *phārsi gola*, टट्टी लीलू फर *tatti līlu phar* (south of the Ganges), घन चक्कर *ghan chakkar* (south of the Ganges), मोर चक्कर *mor chakkar* (south of the Ganges), मोर बाज *mor bāj* (south of the Ganges), पचरन्खी *pancharkhi* (Shahabad), चौताना *chautāna* (Shahabad), हजार बीन *hajār bīn* (Shahabad), चौघड़ा *chaughara* (Shahabad), हुलुक *huluk* (Shahabad), and बतासा *batāsa* (Patna), which is also called अँगारी *angāri* in Shahabad. In South Bhagalpur लौकी *lauki* and पदुका *paduka* have been noted.

CHAPTER XXIX.—THE BOOKBINDER.

586. The bookbinder is in North-West Bihār दफन्दरी *daphdari*, and in East Tirhut दफन्तरी *daphtari*. In South-East Tirhut he is also called कागन्जी *kāgji*. South of the Ganges he is जिलन्दन्बन्द *jildband*, or in Shahabad जिलन्दन्गर *jildgar*.

587. His *screw-press* is सिकञ्जा *sikanja*. Another kind of press is मकन्री *makri*. The wooden *boards* for putting between the books in the screwpress are तखन्ता *takhta* or (in Patna and South Bhagalpur) तखन्ती *takhti*. In Shahabad and North-East Tirhut they are पटन्री *patri*; in South-East Tirhut, पिढ़िया *pirhiya*; and in South-East and North-West Tirhut, निश्न्करन्दा *nishkarda*.

588. The *paper-cutter* is कतरन्नी *katarni*, or (in Champāran) पाढ़ *pārh* or बाढ़ *bārh*. The *scissors* are कैंची *kainchi*, or in North Bihār also मेकन्राज *mekrāj*.

589. The iron *mallet* is हथौरी *hathauri* or मारन्तौल *mārtaul*, and the *awl* सूआ *sūa* north of the Ganges generally and in Shahabad and South Bhagalpur, सुराखी *surākhi* in Patna, सुलाखी *sulākhi* in Gaya,

A Native Rope Walk.

सुतारी *sutāri* north of the Ganges, and टेकुआ *tekua* optionally in South-East Tirhut. The *needle* is सूई *sūï*.

590. The *embossing-wheel*, which is an instrument with a small revolving wheel for embossing the binding, is फिरकी *phirki* in North-West Bihār and South-East Tirhut, चक्की *chakki* in Tirhut and Patna, चक्कर *chakkar* in Gaya and South Bhagalpur, and चक्का *chakka* in Shahabad. Other dies for embossing are फूल *phūl* or (optionally in Champāran and Tirhut) ठप्पा *thappa*; also झालर *jhālar*, जनजीरा *janjira*, and दोसूती *dosūti*.

591. The *cutter* for paring edges is झामा *jhāma* north of the Ganges and Patna, and सोहन *sohan* elsewhere. A file for the same purpose is रेती *reti*.

592. The wooden *tool for smoothing the binding* is सलेस *sales* (corruption of English 'slice'). It is also called तिल्ली *tilli* or तीली *tili*, and in East Tirhut कमची *kamchi*.

593. The *leather-scraper* is खुरपी *khurpi*, also north of the Ganges छिलनी *chhilni*. पत्थर *patthar* is the flat stone on which the leather is scraped.

CHAPTER XXX.—THE ROPE-TWISTER.

594. The rope-twister is कञ्जर *kanjar* in North-West Bihār and Gaya, and चाँइ *chāin* in West Tirhut. In Shahabad and Gaya he is रसबण्टा *rasbanta*. The art of rope-twisting is बटनाई *batnāï*.

595. His rope-twisting implement is called घिरनी *ghirni* or घिरनई *ghirnaī*, also घड़ी *ghari* in South-West Tirhut. Of this the भौंरकली *bhaunrkali* is a flat stone with a hook, to which the rope is fastened as it is being twisted; sometimes a peg, खूँटी *khūnti*, is used for this purpose. The board or bamboo fixed in the ground and perforated with holes, by which the strands, लर *lar*, pass is called गड़ाड़ी *garāri* north of the Ganges, गरारी *garāri* in Patna, घररी *gharri* in Gaya, and घिरनी *ghirni* in Shahabad. The strands are fixed to the ends of pegs, बेलन *belan*, which revolve in these holes.

596. The string used to move the machine is घिरना *ghirna*.

597. When cables and thick ropes are made, an instrument called (north of the Ganges) हत्था चरक *hatthā charak* and (south of the Ganges) मूठा *mūtha* is used. This is a grooved block, in the grooves of which the strands are fixed to secure uniformity in the twisting. A man holds it in his hands, and carries it forward as the strands are twisted.

598. A simpler kind of machine is called चरख *charakh* or चरखी *charkhi*. It consists of only a bent wooden handle, डंडी *dandi*, and a perforated board. The strands are fastened at one end to the handle, and the other ends are twisted by hand.

CHAPTER XXXI.—THE WEAVER'S BRUSH-MAKER.

599. The weaver's brush-maker is called कुंचबंधवा *kunchbandhwa*. The brush is called कूँची *kūnchi*, कूँच *kūnch*, &c. (See Chapter on Weaving.)

600. He uses the साँचा *sāncha*, which are two moulds for keeping the brush in order while it is being prepared. He beats the brush with a ठोकना *thokna*; and he has a flat piece of wood called पटरी *patri* for keeping the bristles in order.

CHAPTER XXXII.—THE BOW-MAKER.

601. A bow is कमान *kamān*, or in North-East Tirhut कमठा *kamtha*, and its maker is कमनगर *kamangar*. He has no special implements.

CHAPTER XXXIII.—THE WEAPON-CLEANER.

602. The सिकिलगर *sikilgar* or arms-cleaner uses a रन्दा *randa*, or in North-East Tirhut झाम *jhām*, which is a kind of plane for cleaning off rust; a गुल्ली *gulli*, a piece of hard stone for a similar purpose; कुरुन *kurun*, a kind of stone powder. He also uses a सिंघौटा *singhauta* or polishing-horn, a मसकली *maskali* or iron instrument, and गद्दी *gaddi* or thick cloth, both used for varnishing.

DIVISION II.

DOMESTIC APPLIANCES AND UTENSILS.

SUBDIVISION I.

APPLIANCES USED IN THE PREPARATION OF FOOD.

CHAPTER I.—SIEVES.

603. The winnowing-sieve is सूप *sūp* or कोल॰सूप *kolsūp.* The former is also used for sifting grains of various sizes. It is made of reeds. The latter is used for winnowing only, and is woven of bamboo slips. They are both oblong in shape, and have a low wall round three sides, called in East Tirhut मड़॰रा *marra.* Other names are कोनिया *koniya* (North-East Tirhut) and डग॰रा *dagra* (see § 47) in Gaya, Champāran, and North-West Tirhut.

604. The चल॰नी *chalni*, or (North-East Tirhut) चालनि *chālani,* is a woven sieve for sifting bran from flour, as in the proverb concerning an extravagant man, कोन पुरखक भेलहुँ गाय, चालनि लै दुहावे जाय *kon purukhak bheláhuñ gāy, chālani lai duhāwe jāy,*—of what man have I become the cow: he has brought a sieve into which to milk me. Again, चालनि टूसल सूप कैं, जनिका सहसर गोट छेद *chālani tūsal sūp keñ, janika sahasar got chhed,*—the sieve, which had a thousand holes, sneered at the winnowing-basket, *i.e.* the pot called the kettle black.

605. The चिल॰वन *chilwan*, or in Sāran, Patna, and Gaya चिलौंज *chilaunj* or चिलौंद *chilaund*, and in South Munger चिलौन *chilaun*, is a kind of sieve used for catching fish, and also (according to Crooke) in the North-Western Provinces for straining sugar-cane juice. Other names are आर॰सी *ārsi* or जङ्घा *jangha,* both used in South Bhagalpur, and the latter in North-East Tirhut and the former in Sāran.

606. The चल॰ना *chalna* is a sieve for cleaning grain. Other names are झर॰ना *jharna* south of the Ganges, तर॰छी *tarchhi* in Champāran and गुर॰चल॰ना *gurchalna* (North-East Tirhut).

607. The आँगी *āngi* or अँगिया *angiya* is a cloth-bottomed sieve for sifting fine flour. It is called हाँगी *hāngi* in Gaya and कपर॰छूर

kapardhūr optionally north of the Ganges. In Azamgarh, in the North-Western Provinces, आँघी *ānghi* is a leather sieve with very fine holes.

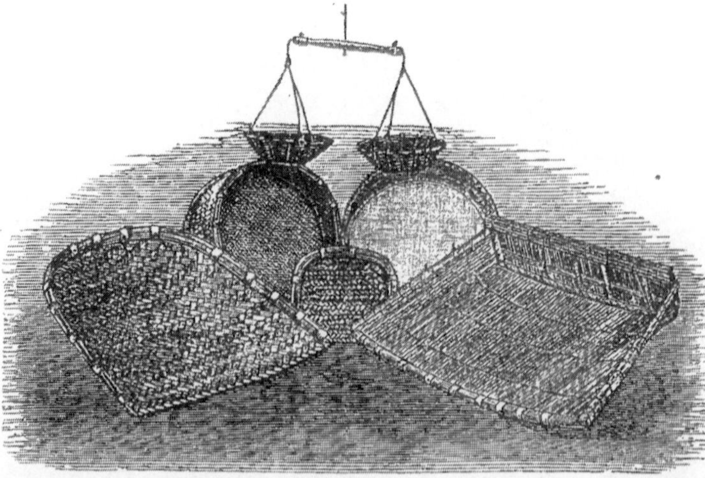

Tarāju.
Chalni. Supuli. Angi.
Kolsūp. Sūp.

CHAPTER II.—THE PEDAL FOR HUSKING GRAIN.

608. The whole apparatus, and also the movable *beam*, is called ढेँकी *dhenki* or (in Shahabad) ढेँका *dhenka* or ढेका *dheka* and (in Sāran) ढेँकुल *dhenkul*.

609. The *pillars* on which the beam rests are जङ्घा *jangha* in North and East Bihār, जाँघा *jāngha* in Shahabad, and जँघिया *janghiya* in North-West Tirhut. In Tirhut and the west they are खूँटा *khūnta*, in Patna and Gaya खुण्टा *khunta*, and in South Bhagalpur and South Munger खुट्टा *khutta*. In South-West Shahabad they are called खम्भा *khambha*.

610. The *peg* in the beam which crushes the rice is मूसर *mūsar* to the south and west, and मुसरा *musra* in Tirhut, Patna, Shahabad, and South Bhagalpur. In Sāran another name is पहरुआ *paharua*. In South Munger, Patna, and Gaya it is समाठ *samāth* or समाँठ *samānth*, and समौआ *samaua* is the iron ferule round its tip.

611. The *axle* is generally अखौत *akhaut* or अखौता *akhauta*, local names being माँझा *mānjha* in Champāran and North-East Tirhut, बेलनी *belni* in North-West Tirhut, and डण्डा *danda* also in North-East Tirhut. In Patna it is रनकी *ranki*, in South Bhagalpur असकलाइ *askalāï*, and in South-West Shahabad सारा *sāra*.

612. The *hollow wooden bed* in which the rice is crushed is ओखरी *okhri* north of the Ganges, or as a local variant ओखर *okhar* in North-East Tirhut and the north-west. ओखरी *okhri* and भुन्दो *bhundo* occur also in South Bhagalpur, and उखरी *ukhri* in South Munger. In South-West Shahabad it is काँड़ी *kānri*, in the rest of the district भुड़िया *bhuriya*, in Gaya भुइँओखरी *bhuiñokhri*, and in Patna भुँड़की *bhunrki* or घुण्डी *ghundi*. The stick used for stirring the grain while it is being pounded is in Gaya and South Bhagalpur ठेकरा *thekra*.

613. The *hand-rail* which the workman grasps is अस्थम *astham* north of the Ganges and थमनी *thamni* or अलगनी *algani* in South Bhagalpur. It is टँगनी *tangni* in Patna and South Munger, also अड़ानी *arāni* in South Munger, and हत्थी *hatthi* in Gaya. In Shahabad a rope (रस्सी *rassi*) is used.

614. The *pedal* or place where the worker rests his foot is पौदर *paudar* in Patna and Shahabad, पछहर *pachhahar* or पछाड़ *pachhār* in Sāran and Champāran, पुछड़ा *puchhra* in North-East Tirhut, पछौरा *pachhaura* in South-West Shahabad, पछुआ *pachhua* in South Munger, पुछिया *puchhiya* in South Bhagalpur, पोंछी *ponchhi* in Gaya, and लतमरा *latmara* in North-West Tirhut. The pit into which this is depressed is in Gaya गोरपौरी *gorpauri*, and in South Bhagalpur गत्तो *gatto*.

615. This implement is practically the same as the lever for breaking bricks, for an illustration of which see § 431.

CHAPTER III.—THE PESTLE AND MORTAR USED FOR HUSKING GRAIN.

616. The *mortar* is ओखरी *okhri* generally, local variants being ओखर *okhar* in North-East Tirhut and Shahabad, ओखरा *okhra* in South-West Shahabad, and ओखली *okhli* in Gaya. In Patna an optional name is कुरदन *kurdan*, and in Sāran धनकुट्टी *dhankutti*.

617. The *pestle* is मूसर *mūsar* to the west and समाठ *samāth* to the east. In Patna both words are used.

618. The iron *ferule* at the bottom of the pestle to prevent it splitting is साम *sām*, or in Patna, Gaya, and the south-east समौआ *samaua*, and in Sāran optionally समियाँ *samiyāñ*.

CHAPTER IV.—THE HAND GRINDING-MILL.

619. This is known as जाँत *jānt*, जँतन्वा *jantwa*, or जाँता *jānta*. This is worked by two women. The smaller kind, used for breaking pulses and worked by one person, is चकन्री *chakri* generally, or चक्की *chakki* to the west. North of the Ganges चकुला *chakula* is a medium-sized one.

620. The *upper stone* is उपन्रौटा *uprauta*, and the *lower stone* तरौटा *tarauta*, and also south of the Ganges तलौटा *talauta*.

621. The *handle* of the large variety is हाथड़ *hāthar* in South-East Tirhut, and elsewhere हथन्रा or हथन्ड़ा *hathra*. In Shahabad it is जूआ *jūa*. That of the smaller variety is खूँटी *khūnti*. The *axle* is किल्ला *killa* or (in South-East Tirhut) कील *kil*; and the *feeding channel*, मुँह *munh* generally; also गाली *gāli* in Shahabad, Gaya, and South Bhagalpur, गल्ली *galli* in Sāran and North-East Tirhut, गलौसी *galausi* in Champāran, खोँइछ *khoñichh* or गलियारी *galiyāri* in North-West Tirhut, गत्तो *gatto* in South Bhagalpur, and घड़िया *ghariya* in South-West Tirhut.

622. The handful of grain poured into the mill is झींक *jhīnk*, local variants being झींका *jhīnka* in Sāran, Patna, and South-East Tirhut, and झीका *jhīka* in South-East Bihār. In South Bhagalpur it is also लप्पो *lappo*.

623. The *wooden seat* on which the woman sits is पीढ़ा *pīrha*. A local variant is पीढ़ी *pirhi* or (East) पिढ़िया *pirhiya*. A similar mud seat is बैसन्नी *baisni*, or in Champāran बैठन्नी *baithni*, and in South-East Tirhut बैसन *baisan*. In South Munger it is बैसन्का *baiska*, and in South Bhagalpur बैसन्को *baisko*.

624. To roughen the stone with a chisel is north of the Ganges टाँगब *tāngab* or टूँगब *tūngab* to the west and कूटब *kūtab* to the east. South of the Ganges, to the west, it is कूटल जाइब *kūtal jāib*, and to the east कुटाएब *kutāëb* or कूटिदेब *kūtideb*. The man who does this is called जतन्कुट्टा *jantkutta*. He uses a chisel, छेनी *chheni*, and a hammer, थपुआ *thapua* or हथौरी *hathāuri*.

625. The act or profession of grinding corn is पिसान *pisān*, पिसन्वन *piswan*, or in Champāran पिसन्ना *pisna*, and in Gaya पिसाइ *pisāï*,

MILL-STONE FOR PULSES (*Chakri*) PESTLE AND MORTAR (*Okhri*). FLOUR-MILL (*Jānt*).

Lith. by Hem Chunder Ghosal, Student, Govt. School of Art Calcutta. Printed by Abdool Rahim Govt. School of Art Calcutta.

and its wages पिसाइ *pisāï*. A well-known proverb is जाइछी पटना जोड़ा एक जाँत, *jāichhi patna jora ek jānt*,—'I go to Patna for a pair of mill-stones,' something like a Newcastle-man going to London to look for coals.

CHAPTER V.—THE GRINDSTONE FOR SPICES.

626. This is सिलवट *silwat* or सिलौट *silaut*, and in Sāran सिलावट *silāwat;* also in Patna, Gaya, and South-East Tirhut सील *sil*. To the south-east it is also पाटी *pāti*.

627. The *stone roller* used with it is लोढ़ा *lorha* to the west and लोढ़ी *lorhi* to the east. In Patna another name is बट्टा *batia*.

CHAPTER VI.—THE ROLLER FOR MAKING PASTE.

628. The *rolling-pin* is बेलना *belna;* also बेलन *belan* in Patna.

629. The *pasteboard* is चौकी *chauki* to the west and चकला *chakla* to the east. In South-East Tirhut another name is चकोला *chakola*, in Gaya चौकला *chaukla*, and in North-East Tirhut चक *chak* or चाक *chāk*.

630. The dry flour sprinkled on the board to prevent the paste sticking is परथन *parthan* generally, with local variants परथनी *parthani* to the west and पलेथन *palethan* in Patna and South Munger. In South-East Tirhut it is optionally called माड़ा *māra*.

SUBDIVISION II.

DOMESTIC FURNITURE.

CHAPTER I.—STOOLS.

631. Stools made of bamboo or reeds are मोँढ़ा *monrha* when large, and मोँढ़िया *monrhiya* when small.

632. When made with a woven twine seat, a wooden frame-work, and four legs, they are called मचिया *machiya*. Another name is मचोला *machola*, current in Champāran.

633. When it has three legs, it is called तिपाइ *tipāï* north of the Ganges, and तेपाइ *tepāï* or तेपई *tepaī* south of it. In Shahabad a three-legged stool is called मेँच *mench*.

634. A wooden stool is, according to size, पीढ़ा *pīrha* (large), पीढ़ी *pīrhi* or पिढ़ि *pirhi* (smaller), and पिढ़िया *pirhiya* (smallest).

635. The wooden platform for sitting, sleeping, or bathing is, when large, तखतपोश *takhatpos*, and when small पटरा *patra*. चौकी *chauki* is used for both large and small kinds.

CHAPTER II.—THE BED AND COT.

636. A *bed* or *cot* is खाट *khāt*, खटिया *khatiya*, or पलङ्ग *palang*. When an ordinary bed, it is specially called चारपाइ *chārpāi* or चरपाइ *charpāi*, and when a cot, खटोला *khatola* or खटोली *khatoli;* also in South-East Tirhut खटुला *khatula*. Another name is पलँगिया *palangiya* or पलँगरी *palangri* in Shahabad and South Munger; another name is सजेआ *sajea* or सेजिया *sejiya*, which is used principally in poetry.

637. The *pillow* is तकिया *takiya* or तकेआ *takea*, also गेरुआ *gerua* in East Tirhut and सिढ़ानी or सिर्हानी *sirhāni* in Tirhut and the west. The *bolster* is बालीस *bālīs*, बलिस्ता *balista*, or (in South-West Shahabad) बिलस्ता *bilasta*. The side bolsters are बगली तकिया *bagli takiya*, and the heavy thick bolster for resting the back against is मसनद *masnad* or गौ तकिया *gau takiya*. The *bed clothes* are बिछाओन *bichhāon*, बिछौना *bichhauna*, or गेटम *getam*. The mattress or its equivalent is तोसक *tosak*. In Tirhut ओछाओन *ochhāön* or ओछौना *ochhauna* are the bed clothes over the body. A patchwork quilt, &c., worn by the poorer orders is गेँदड़ा *gendra*, (also in Champāran and to the east) खेँधड़ा *khendhra*, or सोजनी *sojni* in South Bhagalpur, Patna, and Gaya, खेनरा *khenra* or सुजनी *sujni* in Sāran and West Tirhut, लेँदरा *lendra* in Shahabad, and गुदड़ा *gudra* or लेवा *lewa* to the west generally. In South Bhagalpur it is भोथरा *bhothra*. See also § 731.

638. The *legs* of the bed are पौआ *paua*, पाया *pāya*, or पावा *pāwa*. The side pieces are पाटी *pāti* or पट्टी *patti* generally, also पासी *pāsi* in Tirhut and South Bhagalpur. The end pieces are चूर *chūr* or चूल *chūl*. The head of the bed is सिढ़ाना *sirhāna* or सिढ़ानी *sirhāni* north of the Ganges, also मुरथारी *murthāri* in North Tirhut and सिरमा *sirma* in North-East Tirhut. South of the Ganges it is सिरहाना *sirhāna* (Shahabad also सिरहान *sirhān*) or मुरथारी *murthāri*, also सिरवाँसी *sirwānsi* in South Bhagalpur. The foot of the bed is गोरथारी *gorthāri* or गोरथरिया *gorthariya*. In Shahabad it is गोड़तार *gortār*, and in Sāran गुनथारी *gunthāri;* also गोनतारी *gontāri* north of the Ganges generally and in South-West Shahabad, पथौनी *pathauni* in South-East and

पथाना *pathāna* in North-East Tirhut. South of the Ganges we find optionally पैताना *paitāna* in Shahabad and Patna, पौताना *pautāna* (also in South Munger) or पोथानी *pothāni* in Gaya, and पौथाना *pauthāna* in South Munger.

639. The *network* at the bottom is बिनावट *bināwat* or बिनाई *bināī*, or in East Tirhut घोराई *ghorāī*. In Patna and Gaya it is बीनन *bīnan* or बिनौट *binaut*, in Shahabad बिनाव *bināw*, and घोरन *ghoran* in South Bhagalpur and South Munger. When this is made of one string, the bed is said to be एकबधिया *ekbadhiya*; of two strings, दोबधिया *dobadhiya*; of four strings, चौबधिया *chaubadhiya* (west); and of six strings, छबधिया *chhabadhiya*. In South Bhagalpur the words एकगोटिया *ekgotiya*, दुगोटिया *dugotiya*, चरगोटिया *chargotiya*, and छगोटिया *chhagotiya* are used. In South Munger they are एकजोरिया *ekjoriya*, &c. The strings at the bottom by which the netting can be tightened at pleasure are ओरचन *orchan* or ओरदवानी *ordawāni* in Tirhut and the west. In Sāran and Patna they are ओरचन *orchan* or ओदवाइन *odwāīn*. In the east they are अराँच *arānch*. Other local names are ओनचन *onchan* in South-West Shahabad, ओदाइन *odāīn* in Gaya, अर्दवाइन *ardwāīn* to the east, ओदान *odān* in South Munger, and बाध *bādh* or गतान *gatān* in North-East Tirhut. The thick rope at the foot to which the netting is tied is सिधवानी *sidhwāni* in the north-west; also माँही *mānhi* in Champāran. In South-East Tirhut it is अजवाइन *ajwāīn*. In Patna it is माइँ *māīn*, in Gaya मेआर *meār*, in South Munger माइन *māīn*, and in South Bhagalpur बान *bān* or मैन *main*. Elsewhere it is also called ओरदवानी *ordawāni*. The string tied to the side as the netting is being made is बरुआ *barua* in the north-west and south. In Tirhut and the east generally it is ओझा *ojha*, or in South Bhagalpur also जमौआ *jamaua*. When the netting is finished this string becomes useless, and villagers believe that if it be thrown across the door of a house the members of that house will quarrel amongst themselves. The सोग *sog* or सोक *sok* are the large spaces in the netting along the frame of the bed.

CHAPTER III.—THE WEIGHING-SCALES.

640. The *large fixed scales* are रातल *rātal*, local variants being रातुल *rātul* in Shahabad and रातन *rātan* in North-East Tirhut. In South Bhagalpur they are काँटा *kānta*, which elsewhere means the small scales. Another name in the same place is मनकाँटा *mankānta*. The small scales are तराजू *tarāju*, local variants being तरजूई *tarjūi*

in the north-west, तरज्जू *tarju* in East Tirhut and South Munger, and तरज्जूआ *tarjūa* in South Bhagalpur. Other names are काँटा *kānta* and टकौरी *takauri* in the west and Patna and Gaya, and परियानी *pariyāni* in Patna and Gaya, which principally refer to goldsmith's scales. In South Bhagalpur तूल *tūl* is a weaver's scale for weighing thread or cotton.

641. The *pans* of the scale are पलरा or (in Patna and Gaya) पलड़ा *palra*. In South Bhagalpur they are also called डलनी *dalni* or पला *pulla*.

642. The *strings* of the scale are called तन्नी *tanni* (except in the east), a local variant being तानी *tāni* in Gaya. In the east they are जोती *joti* or (in South Munger) जोता *jota*. In Patna optional names are डोरी *dori* and बाधा *bādha*.

643. The *weights* are बटखरा *batkhara* or बाट *bāt*. The *make-weight* put into one scale to make the balance true is पसँघा *pasangha*, local variants being (East Tirhut) पासँघ *pāsangh* and (Patna, Gaya, and South Bhagalpur) पसँगा *pasanga*. In Patna and Gaya and South Munger it is also called धारा *dhāra*.

644. The *beam* of the scales is डण्डी *dandi*. In the south-east the beam of a jeweller's scale is नित्ती *nitti* or निक्ती *nikti*. The *indicator* is सूई *sūi*.

645. A *false balance* is नेवत *newat* or नेवता *newta* to the west and in Gaya. In East Tirhut it is लेवत *lewat*, and in Champāran नवता *nawta*. In South-West Shahabad it is जीयत *jiyat* or जीता *jita*, and so also in Gaya and South Munger. In Patna and Gaya it is झुकता *jhukta*, and in South Bhagalpur जोती *joti*.

CHAPTER IV.—NETS.

646. A small fisherman's net is जाल *jāl* or जाली *jāli*, and a महाजाल *mahājāl* is one of a larger size. North of the Ganges and in Shahabad a कुरैल *kurail* is a net fixed in the water with six sticks and worked by one man. In South Bhagalpur it is खरैल *kharail*. A similar net with three sticks is बिसारी *bisāri* north of the Ganges and in South Munger; also बिसरी *bisri* in Champāran, and बिसार *bisār* in Champāran, Gaya, and South-East Tirhut. In North-East Tirhut, however, it is called खनसारी *khansāri*, and in South Bhagalpur चौंधा *chaundha*. A casting-net is फेकैल *phekail* in Patna, Gaya, and Sāran, खेप *khep* to the west, and घुमौआ जाल *ghumaua jāl* in Tirhut and South Munger; also in North-East Tirhut खपियार *khapiyār*. In South Bhagalpur it is फेका *pheka*. The iron or earthen sink-balls attached to it are बटिवन *batiwan* and बटवन *batwan* to the west, and पौंड़ी *paunri* in North-West Tirhut. In South Bhagalpur they are भोंटिया *bhontiya*. A net attached to two poles and worked by two fishermen is डोंड़ी *donri* in Patna, Gaya, and the west, and डोंड़ *donr* in Champāran. Other fishing-nets are घनैली *ghanaili* and पसरा *pasra* to the west, and गिरगिरा *girgira*, a small variety, used in Gaya and the south-east. In the same district and in Champāran ओका *oka* is a bag dragged through the water for catching fish. In Champāran and North-East Tirhut टापी *tāpi*, in Shahabad टाप *tāp*, and in South Bhagalpur आरसी *arsi*, is a kind of bamboo fish-net, and गाँज *gānj* or गाँजी *gānji* is a horn-shaped basket for catching fish. The man who works the last is called गजवाह *gajwāh*. In this connection may be mentioned a fish-trap used in Gaya called चिलौंद *chilaund* (see, however, § 605). Fish caught in this are kept in a pit, called आपा *āpa*. A kind of pit used for catching fish is called in Gaya फरका *pharka*. A net for catching birds is घनी *ghani* north of the Ganges; also फान *phān* or फानी *phāni* in Champāran and Tirhut, and फाँदा *phānda* in Shahabad. South of the Ganges the बटियारी *batiyāri* is a net used in the daytime, and चातर *chātar* one used at night for catching birds.

647. North of the Ganges the झोला *jhola* or झोली *jholi* is a net used by cartmen for feeding bullocks. To the west it is झोरी *jhori*, and elsewhere south of the Ganges जल्ला *jalla*. जाला *jāla* is a net for carrying grass. A local variant is जल्ला *jalla* in Sāran and South Munger. In South Bhagalpur it is कपाइ *kapāi*.

648. To the west (including Patna and Gaya), and in Tirhut, सिकहर *sikhar* is a net for hanging up pots, &c., in a house. Other names are सींका *sinka* (Patna and Gaya), सीका *sika* (Sāran, Champāran, and the east generally), and सीक *sik* also in North-West and South-East Tirhut. खाँजी *khānji* in North-East Tirhut is a net for holding fruit.

649. The stick or rope for hanging up clothes is अरगेनी *argeni* in Sāran, Champāran, Patna, and North-East Tirhut, अरगनी *argani* in Shahabad and Tirhut, असगनी *asgani* in Tirhut (optionally), Shahabad, Patna, and Gaya, and रेगनी *regni* in Shahabad. Other names are टँगना *tangna* in Patna, Gaya, and South Munger, टँगनी *tangni* or दौनी *dauni* in Patna and South Bhagalpur, and जियता *jiyata* in

Shahabad. A frame used for the same purpose is ठटरी *thatri* to the west and छतरी *chhatri* in North-West Tirhut.

650. A cord net for carrying goods on the head is जलखरी *jalkhari* in West Tirhut and to the north-west, and जाली *jāli* in Shahabad, South Munger, and Tirhut. In the south-east it is जल्ला *jalla.*

651. The net used by bearers with the sling pole (बहँगी *bahangi* or, in North-East Tirhut, बहिंगा *bahinga*) is generally सिकहर *sikhar,* but सीका *sīka* in the south-east, सिक्का *sikka* in Gaya, and सीक *sīk* (optionally) in North-West and South-East Tirhut.

CHAPTER V.—THE PAD USED FOR SUPPORTING WATER-POTS &c., ON A WOMAN'S HEAD.

652. This is बिट्ठा *bittha,* बीठा *bītha,* or बीठो *bītho* to the west and in West Tirhut. In Patna, Gaya, and the south-east it is नेठो *netho* or नेठुआ *nethua.* Another name is गेँड़ुआ *genrua* to the west and in Gaya and South Munger, गेँड़ली *genruli* in Patna and Gaya, and गेँड़ुड़ी *genruri* in Tirhut. Another name (only noted north of the Ganges) is बिँड़िया *binriya* in Champāran, बिँड़ड़ी *binrri* (a small kind) in Sāran, बीँड़ो *bīnro* in East Tirhut, and बिँड़ुआ *binrua* in Tirhut generally; yet another name is लजुरी *lajuri* in South-West Shahabad.

CHAPTER VI.—THE STICK.

653. The ordinary long stick is लाठी *lāthi* (also लठ *lath* in Patna). Other names are लौर *laur* (north of the Ganges) or लाउर *lāur* to the west, and सटका *satka* north of the Ganges. The butt end of this is हूरा *hūra* north of the Ganges and in Patna, हुर्रा *hurra* in Shahabad and the south-east, हुत्था *huttha* in Gaya, and गोआ *goa* in South Munger optionally.

654. सोँटा *sonta* or सोटा *sota* is a stout short stick. It is also called डण्टा *danta,* and in Champāran डटौका *datauka.* A thin stick is छड़ी *chhari,* and to the west, including Patna and Gaya, गोजी *goji.* Other names are छाकन *chhākan* in Champāran and North-West Tirhut and छकनी *chhakni* in South Bhagalpur. A thick walking-stick is डाँग *dāng,* and also, to the west, लबदा *labda,* and a similar one, used principally by old or lame men, is ठेँघुनी *thenghuni.* This last is also called ठेगुँरी *thegunri* in Champāran and West Tirhut, ठेँग *theng* or ठेँगुनी *thenguni* in Shahabad, and ठेँगा *thenga* in the south-west of the same district. In South Bhagalpur it is ठेंगन्नी *thengni*, and elsewhere ठेंगी *thengi*. बेसाखी *besākhi* is a crutch. In Shahabad पटनकन *patkan* is a walking-stick. A piece of split bamboo used as a stick is फट्ठा *phattha*, फट्ठी *phatthi*, or फराठी *pharāthi*. It is also called बँसफट्ठा *bansphatta* or बँसफेंटा *bansphenta* in Patna and Gaya, and बत्ती *batti* in the south-east. A heavy stick is बोंग *bong*, or to the north-west बजर बोंग *bajar bong*.

655. The following Hindi lines in praise of the stick are very popular in Shahabad, a district famous for its club-men :—

लाठी ऐसी चीज है सदा राखिये सङ्ग।
नदी नार अगाह जल तहाँ बचाओ अङ्ग॥
तहाँ बचाओ अङ्ग झपट कुत्तो को मार।
दुरजन दावागीर उस को मसक झार॥
कह गिरधर कबि राय लिख भेजिये पाती।
कमर लिये तरवार हाथ में लिये लाठि॥

Lāthi aisi chīj hai sada rākhiye sang,
Nadi nār agāh jal tahān bachāo ang.
Tahān bachāo ang jhapat kutto ko mār,
Durjan dāwāgīr us ko masak jhār.
Kah Girdhar kabi rāy likh bhejiye pāti,
Kamar liye tarwār, hāth men liye lāthi.

A stick is the kind of thing you should always have with you :
If the water in a river is too deep, you can save yourself by it.
You can also at once save yourself by hitting dogs with it.
And if you meet a wicked enemy you can dust (*lit. trans.*) his head with it.
Saith Girdhar, the prince of poets, write a letter
Telling him to wear a sword in his belt, but to carry a club in his hand.

CHAPTER VII.—BOXES.

656. North of the Ganges सनुख *sanukh* or (in Sāran and South Munger) सन्दूख *sandukh* is an ordinary box. South of the Ganges it is सन्दूक *sandūk*, and in Patna and Shahabad सनूक *sanūk*. A small box is कनन्तोर *kantor* or बाकस *bākas* (box). South of the Ganges it is सँदुकन्ची *sandukchi* or सनुकन्ची *sanukchi*, the latter chiefly in Shahabad and the extreme east. पौता *pauta* or पौती *pauti*, or (in South

Bhagalpur) पौंती *paunti*, is a little box made of bamboo slips, and मोना *mona* (Champāran) or मौंनी *maunni* are similar ones made of straw or of bamboo slips.

657. पेटाढ़ा *petārha* or पेटाढ़ी *petārhi*, and also south of the Ganges पेटारा *petāra* or पेटारी *petāri*, is a light travelling box or basket for clothes, &c., carried by a man on a sling bamboo, as in the proverb थाकल बरद कें पेटार भारी *thākal barad keñ petār bhāri*,—for a tired bullock even a basket is too heavy. Other names are सखारी *sakhāri* in South-East Tirhut and झाँपी *jhāmpi* south of the Ganges and in Champāran. The sling bamboo is called बहँगी *bahangi*, or in North-East Tirhut बहिंगा *bahinga;* also सुइला *suila* in Champāran and North-West Tirhut, and सिकपटई *sikpataï* in East Tirhut.

658. The डिबिया *dibiya* is a small box for jewelry or other valuables. In Patna and Gaya it is डिब्बा *dibba*, and in Sāran also डीबा *dība*.

659. The चुनौटी *chunauti* is a box for carrying the lime (चून *chūn* or चुन्ना *chunna*) used with betel. In Champāran and North-West Tirhut it is called चुनहा *chunha.*

660. The box in two parts for holding betel, &c., is पनबट्टा *panbatta* or बेलहरा *belahra*. Local names are पनौटी *panauti* (Shahabad), पनबट्टी *panbatti* (Champāran and South-East Tirhut), बेलहरी *belahri* (Patna and Gaya), and बिरहरा *birhara* (Champāran and East Tirhut).

661. The box in which the अबटन *abtan*, or cosmetic which is rubbed on the bride at a wedding, is kept is डोकी *doki* in Shahabad, and सोगिला *sogila* or सनसोगिला *sansogila* in the south-east. Elsewhere it is माला *māla*, &c. See below.

662. The box used by women for carrying red lead is सिंधोरा *sindhora* when large, and कीया *kīya* when small. The box in which they carry the vermilion which they put on the parting of their hair is इंगरौटी *ingrauti* or कियौरी *kiyauri*. It is also हिंगोरी *hingori* in North-East Tirhut and सपरी *sapri* in South-East Tirhut.

663. A माला *māla*, मलवा *malwa*, or मलिया *maliya* is a box for holding oil. It is also called मलसी *malsi* in North-East Tirhut, तेलहण्डा *telhanda* in Patna and Gaya, and तेलभौंड़ा *telbhaura* in Shahabad.

CHAPTER VIII.—METAL VESSELS USED IN COOKING AND ORDINARY DOMESTIC PURPOSES.

664. The vessels ordinarily used by Hindus are as follow:—

तसला *tasla* or तसलवा *taslawa*, made of brass (पीतर *pītar*), a round vessel used for boiling rice. About two *sers* of rice can be cooked in it.*

665. तसली *tasli*, a similar vessel of smaller size. In Shahabad it is called तौली *tauli*.

666. बटुआ *batua* or बटू *battu*, a vessel made of alloy (फूल *phūl*, कसकुट *kaskut*, or (Gaya) भरिथ *bharith*). This is used for cooking rice, and about a *ser* of rice can be cooked in it. It is comparatively higher and narrower than the तसला *tasla*.

667. बटलोही *batlohi* or (north of the Ganges) बटुली *batuli*, a smaller similar vessel, used for cooking pulse or meat.

668. पतिली *patili* of copper (ताँबा *tāmba*) or alloy. It has a narrow flat mouth, and is used for boiling meat.

669. हण्डा *handa*, हाँड़ा *hānrha* (Patna and the south-east), खरखण्डा *kharkhanda* (Gaya), or खँखरहरा *khankhrahra* (Champāran and North Tirhut), is a very large copper vessel for boiling rice. When used by mendicants (फकीर *phakīr*) it is called by them टोकना *tokna*.

670. तामी *tāmi* or तमिया *tamiya* is south of the Ganges a large brass vessel, broad at the bottom, for cooking pulse at marriages, &c.

671. कड़ाह *karāh*. This (to the north-west and in Gaya) is a large iron pan capable of boiling as much as twenty *sers* of rice.

672. बरगुना *barguna*. This (in North-West Bihār) is a small brass vessel with an erect rim for boiling rice, pulse, &c.

673. कराही *karāhi* or कड़ाही *karāhi*, and to the east and in Champāran लोहिया *lohiya*, an iron or brass broad shallow pan with handles (करा or कड़ा *kara*), generally used for cooking vegetables.

---

* About this vessel there is a story. Once upon a time all the people of Bhojpur, in Shahabad, were robbers. When a traveller passed through one of these villages, they used to seize his cooking-pot, saying "तसला तोर की मोर *tasla tor ki mor*,"—"Is the pot mine or yours?" If the traveller replied "मोर *mor*," "mine," they would set upon him and beat him and rob him of the vessel by force. If he said "तोर *tor*," "yours," they used, on his own admission, to take it from him and let him go peaceably. Thus, in any way, they plundered him. Hence the saying तसला तोर की मोर *tasla tor ki mor* has passed into a proverb, of which the application is easy to see.

674. बहगुना *bahguna,* an iron or brass cooking-pot with straight edges and a handle.

675. तमहेड़ी *tamheri,* a round copper vessel.

676. तवा *tawa,* तावा *tāwa,* or (Patna and Gaya) ताइ *tāi,* an iron griddle plate.

677. कटोरा *katōra* to the south and north-east, कचोरा *kachora* in Sāran and Champāran, डुब्भा *dubbha* in Sāran and Champāran, बाटी *bāti* in Tirhut, and मँहिबाटी *menhibāti* in South-East Tirhut, is a vessel used for eating from, with a projection at the bottom on which it stands.

678. The तसतरी *tastari* (north of the Ganges and in Gaya, Patna, and South Munger), छिपुली *chhipuli* to the east and in Patna, जाम *jām* in Patna, Gaya, and the south-east, and कसतरी *kastari* in Shahabad, is like the कटोरा *katora,* except that it is flat-bottomed, and has no stand.

679. In the south-east the झरका *jharka* is a deep pan for eating; the कञ्चन पूरी *kanchan pūri,* a shallow one; and the अगरैल *agrail,* one with the edges straight and short.

680. The थारी *thāri* or थरिया *thariya,* also छीपा *chhipa,* and (in Patna and Gaya) खोरी *khori,* is a flat pan from which food is eaten. The मलँगिया थारी *malangiya thāri* has straight sides, and the मिरजापुरी *mirjāpuri* has curved ones.

681. परात *parāt,* a large flat pan like the थारी *thāri,* except that its sides curve gradually up to the top.

682. ठाँठी *thānthi* or टाँठी *tānthi* is a dish like the थारी *thāri,* but made of bell-metal (काँसा *kānsa*).

683. डब्बू *dabbu,* a brass or iron spoon, of which the bowl is deep and broad, principally used at marriages.

684. कलछुल *kalchhul* or करछुल *karchhul* is a spoon. कलछा *kalchha* in South-West Shahabad means an iron spoon, and कलछी *kalchhi* in Sāran, Patna, and Gaya a brass or iron one.

685. North of the Ganges and in Shahabad छनौटा *chhanauta* or झरना *jharna,* and in Patna, Gaya, and the south झँझरा *jhanjhra,* is a cullender or iron sieve with a handle. In North-West Tirhut it is also called सनौटा *sanauta,* and in North-East Tirhut झाँझ *jhānjh.*

686. पौना *pauna* or (South-East Tirhut) पौनिया *pauniya* is an iron cullender or straining-ladle.

687. The लोटा *lota* is used for drawing water and drinking.

688. The गेड़ुआ *gerua* or हथ्हर *hathhar* north of the Ganges, Patna, Gaya, and Shahabad, also सोबर्ना *sobarna* in North-East Tirhut, and झारी *jhāri* in Champāran, Patna, Gaya, and to the south-east, is a kind of *lota* with a spout (टोंटी *tonti*). It is generally made of a white alloy (फूल *phūl*). The माधब सिङ्घी *mādhab singhi* (North-East Tirhut) is a kind of drinking-vessel invented by Mādhab Singh, a former Mahāraj of Durbhanga. It is shaped like a globe surmounted by a funnel. The globe has a spout, and the whole stands on a pedestal.

689. तम्हा *tamha* north of the Ganges, and झारी *jhāri* south of it, is a similar vessel made of red alloy (कस्कुट *kaskut*). Both the last two are used for drinking.

690. अब्खोरा *abkhora* or अम्खोरा *amkhora* is a drinking-vessel, the sides of which are broader towards the mouth, and it is provided with a stand (गोड़िया *goriya*) at the bottom. It is also called खोरा *khora.* In Gaya डुब्भा *dubbha* is a large cup, and in South Bhagalpur लोट्की *lotki.*

691. गिलास *gilās* (glass), similar to the last except that the sides are straight or only slightly curved. It sometimes has no stand, and is flat-bottomed. It is, in fact, modelled closely on the lines of a European peg-tumbler, but is of metal.

692. बट्टा *batta* (Patna, Gaya, and North-East Tirhut), a kind of large metal cup. बाटी *bāti* is a small one.

693. गग्रा *gagra*, or (in Champāran and Tirhut) तम्घैल *tamghail* or तम्घैला *tamghaila*, (in Gaya) बस्नी *basni*, and (in Champāran, Patna, and to the south-east) कल्सी *kalsi*,—a copper or brass vessel used for drawing water from a well.

694. डोल *dol* or कूँड़ *kūnr*, an iron vessel for drawing water from a well.

695. लौँह्रा *lonhra* or लौँह्री *lonhri*, a small iron pan. In the south-west also used for drawing water from a well, like डोल *dol.* North of the Ganges it is also called लोहिया *lohiya.*

696. छौँढ़ *chhonrh* or मटुका *matuka*, a copper or brass vessel for storing water in.

697. The सुराही *surāhi* or सोराही *sorāhi* is used for keeping water. जल्धरी *jaldhari* (North-East Tirhut) is a water-pot.

698. अफ्ताबा *aphtāba* or अफ्ताया *aphtāya*, a water-ewer used for washing.

699. चिलिमची *chilimchi* north of the Ganges, चिलिफची *chiliphchi* in North-West Tirhut, चिलमची *chilamchi* south of the Ganges, and सिलफची *silaphchi* amongst Muhammadans, used for washing.

700. सरपोस *sarpos*, ढकना *dhakna*, or ढपना *dhapna*, a cover for other vessels.

701. मलिया *maliya* or (Gaya) मल्हिया *malhiya*, a small cup for holding oil. Sometimes it is made of wood.

702. दीयट *dīyat* or दीवट *dīwat* or चिरकदान *chirakdān* (north of the Ganges), बरदवान *baradwān* (Gaya), and चिरागदान *chirāgdān* (Shahabad and South Munger), is a lamp-stand. In North-East Tirhut it is दीअठि *diathi*, and in South Bhagalpur दिपरा *dipra* or दिपहरा *dipahra*.

703. चिमटा *chimta* or सिऊँठा *siūntha*, also चूँटा *chūnta*, a pair of small tongs used for arranging the fire or turning over cakes on the griddle.

704. सँड़सी *sanrsi*, or (to the east) बावली *bāwli*, or in South-East Tirhut बगुली *baguli*, tongs used for removing the pot (बटुली *batuli*, &c.), from the fire.

705. खोरना *khorna* or खोरनी *khorni*, also सराइ *sarāi* (North-West Tirhut), उटकन *utkan* (Patna, Gaya, and South Munger), एकठा *ektha* (Champāran), and लोपन *lopan* (East Tirhut), is an iron or wooden poker. पिहकर *pihkar* (Shahabad) is a wooden poker.

706. इमाम जिस्ता *imām jista* or (to the south-west) हावन दस्ता *hāwan dasta*, or (South-West Shahabad) निमदस्ता *nimdasta*, or (South Bhagalpur) हमाम दिस्ता *hamām dista*,—a pestle and mortar for grinding spices, &c.

707. पिकदान *piīkdān* or पिकदानी *pikdāni*, also to the west and south उगलदान *ugaldān*, (in Patna and Gaya) optionally चिरमिच्ची *chirmichchi*, and (in South Bhagalpur) पिरगदान *pirigdān*, a spittoon. To the east and in Patna it is also पिरिकदान *pirikdān*.

708. पनदान *pandān* or पनबट्टा *panbatta*,—for keeping betel.

709. लेवा *lewa*, or in Patna and Shahabad लेवन *lewan*, and in the south-west of the district लेव *leo*, is ashes plastered on the cooking-pot to save it from fire.

710. The handful of straw, &c., used for cleaning metal vessels is लूँड़ा *lūnra* or लुण्डा *lunda*. In South-East Tirhut it is optionally नूँड़ा *nūnra*. In South Bhagalpur it is नूड़ो *nūro*, and in South Munger नुण्डा *nunda*.

711. Musalmāns generally use the following vessels:—

पतीला *patīla*, a large copper vessel for cooking rice.

पतीली *patīli*, देगची *degchi*, or डेगची *degchi*, a similar vessel smaller in size.

देग *deg* or डेग *deg*, a somewhat larger pot for boiling.

बधना *badhna*, the same as the Hindu लोटा *lota*, but with a spout.

बधनी *badhni*, a similar vessel of smaller size.

कटोरा *katora*, similar to the Hindu vessel, but made of copper.

पियाली *piyāli*, a cup.

पियाला *piyāla*, similar to the last, but larger.

रिकाबी *rikābi*, a saucer.

तबाक *tabāk*, जिब्भा *jibbha* in Champāran, or तबाख *tabākh* south of the Ganges, a broad flat washing-vessel.

चिमटा *chimta*, &c., the same as used by Hindus.

सरपोस *sarpos*, ढकना *dhakna*, or ढपना *dhapna*, cover for other vessels.

चिलिमची *chilimchi*, &c., the same as for Hindus.

अफताबा *aphtāba*, the same as for Hindus.

तसत *tasat* or (when smaller) तसतरी *tastari*, a broad flat dish.

सेनी *seni* or (in South-East Tirhut) सैन *sain*, a broad shallow tray.

गगरा *gagra*, &c., as for Hindus.

लगन *lagan*, a large vessel for storing water.

कराही *karāhi*, &c., the same as for Hindus.

झरना *jharna*, छनौटा *chhanauta*, &c., as for Hindus.

पनबट्टा *panbatta*, &c., as for Hindus. The हुसुनदान *husundān* or (Gaya) कुत्ता *kutta* or कुत्ती *kutti* is similar, and contains additional compartments for lime.

खासदान *khāsdān*, for keeping *pān* or betel, with a cover.

The खिलबट्टी *khilbatti* is used for keeping ready rolled up betel leaves, with the nut and lime inside ready for use (खिल्ली *khilli*).

पिकदान *pikdān*, &c., as for Hindus.

सोराही *sorahi*, &c., as for Hindus.

Lamp-stands, viz., फतील सोज *phatīl soj*, and in Sāran also पटील सोज *patīl soj*, of brass; चिरागदान *chirāgdān*, of wood; दीवट *dīwat*, &c. (see Hindu articles) of iron; and बदवान *badwān*, of bamboo slips.

तावा *tāwa*, &c., as for Hindus.

दस्त पनाह *dast panāh* or दस पना *das pana*, tongs.

सिँखचा *sinkhcha* or सीख *sīkh;* also north of the Ganges गज *gaj*, a spit.

डब्बू *dabbu*, as amongst Hindus.

CHAPTER IX.—EARTHEN VESSELS.

712. The number of these is very large, and varies in each district. The following list does not profess to be exhaustive. It is in alphabetical order.

713. When a new earthen vessel is taken into use, it must first be used by a member of the family and not by one of the servants of the house; otherwise it is considered impure. This is considered as a dedication of the article to family use. To dedicate an article thus is उड़ाहब *urāhab*, or in South Bhagalpur उढ़ाएब *urhāëb*, and in Sāran उड़ाओल *urāöl* or अँवासल *añwāsal*.

अढ़ैया *arhaiya*, a vessel containing two and a half *sers*. In North-East Tirhut it is made of brass.

अथरा *athra*, a pan for making dough. अथरी *athri* is a smaller one used (in Gaya) for holding water, washing clothes, and roasting poppy-flower cakes.

अधकर *adhkar* (east), a vessel used in distilling.

अबखोरा *abkhora*, a drinking-vessel.

कँटिया *kantiya* or कटिया *katiya*, a little vessel with a long neck. Cows are milked into it.

कत्ती *katti* (Patna, Gaya, and Sāran), or गत्ती *gatti* (Shahabad), a round potsherd used by boys in playing.

कपटी *kapti*, a kind of cup.

करई *karaī* (South Munger), a water-vessel with a spout.

करन्ना *karna* (Sāran), an earthen vessel in which milk is boiled, also (North-West Tirhut) used for holding curds.

करन्वा *karwa* (West Bihār and South Bhagalpur), a water-vessel with a spout.

करहिया *karahiya*, for boiling milk = कराही *karāhi*.

कराही *karāhi* (north of Ganges) an earthen pan in which clarified butter (घ्यू *ghyu*) is cooked or milk boiled.

कलन्सा *kalsa*, कलन्सी *kalsi* = a घैला *ghaila*, especially when ornamented with lime and colours at weddings, &c.

कसन्तरा *kastara* (south-east), a saucer for holding curds.

कसन्तरी *kastari* (south-east) = तसन्तरी *tastari*, *q.v.*

कूँड़ *kūnr* (west and Patna), a large vessel for holding grain and food.

कूँड़ा *kūnra* (north of Ganges), an earthen vessel in which sweetmeats or balls of rice mixed with sugar (कसार *kasār*) are given to daughters when going to their father-in-law's house. In South Bhagalpur it is कुण्डा *kunda*.

कुढ़िया *kurhiya* (South Bhagalpur), a small vessel for milk.

कुण्डा *kunda* (Champāran, Shahabad, and South Bhagalpur), a large flat jar. See also कूँड़ा *kūnra*.

कोहा *koha* or पतुकी *patuki*, a small round wide-mouthed vessel for curds, or for cooking. कोहिया *kohiya* (Gaya) is a smaller variety.

खपन्ड़ा *khapra*, tiles.

खपन्ड़ी, खपन्री *khapri*, or (North-East Tirhut) खापरि *khāpari*, an earthen griddle for making bread or parching grain. When used for parching grain it is made by breaking off the top of a घैला *ghaila*, but that used as a griddle is specially made by the potter. In South Bhagalpur it is also called चढ़िया *chariya*.

खपन्रौड़ी *khaprauri* (Gaya and West Tirhut), a pot for removing the afterbirth, &c., when a child is born.

खलन्ची *khalchi* (Shahabad), a little platter.

खापरि *khāpari*. See खपन्ड़ी *khapri*.

खावा *khāwa* (South Munger), an earthen cooking-vessel.

खीखी *khīkhi* (Tirhut), a vessel for holding oil.

खूम *khūm* (Patna), a large flat jar.

खोर *khor*, खोरा *khora* (Tirhut, Patna, and the south-east), a long round earthen vessel used by saltpetre-makers (नोनिया *noniya*) for holding the mother liquor; also (to the east and in Gaya) a large jar used for various purposes.

गगरी *gagri*, a vessel used for drawing water.

गत्ती *gatti*,—see कत्ती *katti*.

गमला *gamla*, a flower-pot.

गुड़की *gurki*, a drinking-vessel, especially for drinking spirits.

घड़ा *ghara*,—see घैला *ghaila*.

घरिल *gharil*,—see घैला *ghaila*.

घरिया *ghariya* (Shahabad), a drinking-vessel.

घुच्ची *ghuchchi* (Sāran), a little dish with a narrow neck.

घुरिली *ghurili*, a little vessel with a narrow neck.

घैला *ghaila*, घैली *ghaili*, घड़ा *ghaṛa*, or घरिल *gharil*, a vessel for holding or drawing water. (See बसनी *basni*, डाबा *dāba*.)

चट्टी *chatti* (Patna and Gaya), an earthen cooking-dish.

चड़िया *chariya*,—see खपड़ी *khapri*.

चरुआ *charua*, चरुई *charui* (south of Ganges), a vessel for holding grain or for cooking = चेरुआ *cherua*.

चिकनी हाँड़ी *chikni hānri*, a vessel for cooking vegetables, pulse, &c. After using it for several months it becomes polished and durable owing to the oil and butter cooked in it.

चिराक *chirāk* (South Tirhut and the west), चिराग *chirāg*, a lamp-saucer.

चिलम *chilam*, the bowl of a pipe.

चुकड़ी *chukri* (south-east), a drinking-vessel.

चुकनी *chukni* (Gaya), a small earthen jar.

चुकड़, चुक्कर *chukkar*, a vessel with straight sides and a very short neck, used for drinking.

चुक्का *chukka*, a drinking-vessel.

चेरुआ *cherua*, चेरुई *cherui* (north of the Ganges and east), an earthen cooking-dish or for holding grain = चरुआ *charua*.

चौँपी *chaumpi* (Patna and Gaya), an earthen vessel in which milk is boiled.

छनान *chhanān* (Tirhut, Patna, and Gaya), a vessel with cloth at the top for straining toddy.

छौँढ़ *chhonrh* (to the west), a large earthen jar.

छौँढ़ी *chhonrhi* (north-west), a vessel for keeping water or grain.

जाला *jāla*, a water-jar.

झज्झर *jhajjhar*, a croft for keeping water.

झब्-भी *jhabhi*, an earthen vessel into which cows are milked.

झारी *jhāri*, a vessel with a long spout.

टरिया *tariya* (Champāran and the east), a small oil-pot.

टाड़ *tār*, टाड़ा *tāra* (Gaya), an oil-pot. A smaller variety is टाड़ी *tāri*.

टुइँया *tuñiya*, a drinking-vessel.

टूआँ *tūān*, टूईं *tuīn* (Patna and Gaya and South Munger), a drinking-vessel with a spout.

टेह्-रा *tehra* (Gaya and South Bhagalpur), a kind of pot for milk.

टोँटिया *tontiya*, a tile used as a water-spout at the eave of a house.

ठिलिया *thiliya*, a vessel used for drawing water.

डब्-री *dabri*,—see डिब्-री *dibri*.

डाबा *dāba*, a vessel used for drawing water smaller than a बस्-नी *basni* and a घैला *ghaila*. In South-East Tirhut, used for boiling milk.

डिब्-री *dibri*, and also in Shahabad डब्-री *dabri*, same as सन्-हक *sanhak*, but smaller.

ढक्-ना *dhakna* or (east) ढाकनि *dhākani*, a cover for other vessels. ढक्-नी *dhakni* is a smaller one.

ढिम्-का *dhimka* (South Bhagalpur), a saucer used as a covering for other vessels.

तर्-कट्टी *tarkatti*, the vessel in which palm-juice (ताड़ी *tāri*) is collected at the foot of the tree.

तबाक *tabāk* (Patna and Gaya), a little platter (generally of iron).

तस्-तरी *tastari*, a saucer used by Muhammadans. When made of brass, also used by Hindus. Cf. कस्-तरी *kastari*.

ताइ *tāi* (south of Ganges and Champāran), a griddle for making bread; a kind of shallow pan, with an edge for lifting it up by.

तेल्-हाँड़ी *telhānri*,, तेल्-हण्डा *telhanda*, a vessel for holding oil.

तेलाय *telāy*, an earthen vessel for cooking oil or clarified butter घ्यु (*ghyu*).

तौला *taula* (north of Ganges, Gaya, and the south-east), a large earthen dish for cooking.

थपरी *thapri* (Patna and East Tirhut), a vessel for measuring milk.

थाल *thāl*, a platter.

दबकन *dabkan* (Gaya), a saucer used as a cover for other vessels.

दवात *dawāt*, an ink-stand.

दहेँड़ी *dahenri* or (Patna and Shahabad) दहड़ी *dahri*, for holding tyre (दही *dahi*).

दियरी *diyari* (north of the Ganges and south-west), दियारी *diyāri* (North-East Tirhut), a very small lamp-saucer.

दिउरी *diuri* or दिउली *diuli*, a very small lamp-saucer.

दीप *dīp*, a lamp-saucer.

दीया *dīya*, a lamp-saucer.

दीरी *dīri* (south-east and Gaya), a very small lamp-saucer.

देग *deg*, a cauldron.

नदिया *nadiya*, for keeping tyre (दही *dahi*).

नदोइ *nadoi* (Gaya), an earthen cooking-vessel.

नरिया *nariya*, a kind of tile (खपड़ा *khapra*).

नाद *nād* or (east) लाद *lād*, a large earthen basin or bowl used as a feeding-trough and for other purposes.

पतिला *patila* (Sāran, Patna, and South Munger) or पतीला *patīla* (Sāran and Gaya), an earthen cooking-vessel.

पतुकी *patuki* (west), a small round wide-mouthed vessel for keeping tyre or for cooking.

पनचोरा *panchora* (south of Ganges), a vessel used in distilling.

परछा *parchha* (West Tirhut), a large jar for water.

पराइ *parāï* (South-West Shahabad), a saucer used as a cover for other vessels.

परिया *pariya* (Patna), a saucer used as a cover for other vessels.

पिटौआ *pitaua* (Patna), a small earthen pan.

पियाला *piyāla*, पेआला *peāla*, a drinking-cup.

फुच्ची *phuchchi* (South-East Tirhut), a vessel for measuring milk.

फूरी *phūri* (South Bihār), a saucer used by Musalmāns in feasts of the brotherhood.

बधन्ना *badhna*, a water-vessel with a spout.

बरुका *baruka* (South Tirhut), a drinking-vessel.

बसन्नी *basni*, a vessel for holding or drawing water, smaller than a घैला *ghaila* and larger than a डाबा *dāba*.

बहन्ना *bahna* (Patna and South Munger), a large flat jar.

बिथार *bithār* (Patna), a large dish.

भभन्का *bhabhka*, a vessel used in distilling.

भरुका *bharuka* or भरुकी *bharuki*, a drinking-vessel.

भाँड़ा *bhānra* or भाँड़ *bhānr*, a vessel with a neck for milk or clarified butter (घ्यु *ghyu*).

भुरन्का *bhurka*, भुरन्की *bhurki* (in Tirhut), a drinking-cup.

भोजहन्री *bhojahri* (south-east), an earthen dish used by Musalmāns at marriages.

मँगन्रा *mangra*, the tiles along the ridge of a roof.

मटन्का *matka*, and also (south of the Ganges and in Champāran) मटुका *matuka*, an earthen vessel for holding water or grain.

मटुका *matuka* = मटन्का *matka*, *q.v.*

मरन्तबान *martabān*, मरन्तवान *martawān* (south of Ganges), मिरन्तवान *mirtawān* (north of Ganges), an earthen vessel with a wide mouth ornamented with lac (लाह *lāh*).

मलन्वा *malwa* (West Tirhut, Shahabad, and South Munger) or मलिया *maliya* (North-West, West Tirhut, Patna, and South Bhagalpur), a vessel for holding oil. It is equally often of wood or metal.

माँट *mānt* (Gaya), a large flat jar.

मिरन्तवान *mirtawān* = मरन्तवान *martawān*, *q.v.*

मिटिया *mitiya* or मेटिया *metiya*, a round vessel with a short neck for water.

मेटिया *metiya* = मिटिया *mitiya*.

मेटा *meta* (South Bhagalpur and to the west) = मिटिया *mitiya*.

मेटी *meti* (South Bhagalpur), for holding tyre.

मौन *maun*, a vessel for holding date-juice.

रमकरवा *ramkarwa* (South-East Tirhut and Champāran), a drinking-vessel.

रकेबी *rakebi* = रेकाबी *rekābi, q.v.*

रमेहुक्का *ramehukka* (Patna and Gaya), a drinking-vessel.

राइस *rāis* (East Tirhut), a little vessel with a narrow neck, used for holding milk and similar purposes.

रिकाबी *rikābi*, a saucer.

रिकेबी *rikebi* = रेकाबी *rekābi, q v.*

रेकाबी *rekābi* or (Patna and Shahabad) रकेबी *rakebi*, or (south-east) रिकेबी *rikebi*, a saucer.

लबना *labna* (Patna and Champāran), a water-pot in the shape of an ellipsoid.

लबनी *labni*, the vessel in the shape of an ellipsoid, in which palm-juice (ताड़ी *tāri*) is collected from the trees.

लाद *lād* = नाद *nād, q.v.*

सनकी *sanki* (South Bhagalpur and Gaya), a saucer used by Musalmāns.

सनहक *sanhak*, सनहकी *sinhaki*, a broad flat dish used by Musalmāns for eating boiled rice.

सरबी *sarbi* (South Bhagalpur), a cup for distributing pulse, &c., from the cooking-pot. Used at marriages.

सुराही *surāhi*,—see सोराही *sorāhi.*

सेफाली *sephāli* (Patna, Gaya, and Shahabad), a flat earthen dish.

सेरहा *serha*, a vessel for drinking spirits.

सोराही *sorāhi* (north of Ganges) or सुराही *surāhi* (south of it), a water-vessel with a long narrow neck.

हँड़िया *hanriya*, diminutive of हँड़ी *hānri, q.v.*

हँड़ोला *hanrola*, diminutive of हाँड़ी *hānri, q.v.*

हथौना *hathauna*, a vessel for collecting date-juice, larger than a लबनी *labni*, used when the juice (ताड़ी *tāri*) flows freely.

हाँड़ी *hānri* or हँड़िया *hanriya* (small) or हँड़ोला *hanrola* (small), a vessel for cooking or holding milk, tyre, &c.

CHAPTER X.—WOODEN VESSELS.

714. The कठौत *kathaut* or कठौती *kathauti* is a large wooden dish for kneading flour. It is also called कठरा *kathra* south of the Ganges and to the west; तगाड़ी *tagāri* in Tirhut and Champāran. डगरा *dagra* in Champāran and Gaya is a large flat dish made of wood. The उलन्दी *uldi* in the west, कठुली *kathuli* in Shahabad and South-East Tirhut, कठोली *katholi* in North-East and South-West Tirhut, and कठली *kathli* or अढ़िया *arhiya* in Shahabad, is a small wooden dish for scraps. In Patna, Gaya, and the south-east it is पैला *paila*.

715. The कसकौल *kaskaul* (Patna), किस्ता *kista* (Gaya and the south-east), and कमण्डल *kamwandal* (generally), is a wooden cup carried by mendicants. In the north-west नरियरी *nariyari* is an oval one. तूमा *tuma*, तुम्मा *tumma*, or तुम्बा *tumba*, is the mendicant's gourd.

716. सेवती *sewti* or (North-East Tirhut) सौथी *sauthi* is a wooden platter used by sailors.

717. डोकनी *dokni* (Sāran and Champāran) and ढकना *dhakna* (North Tirhut) are small wooden dishes.

718. The डोई *doï* or (south of the Ganges) डोआ *doa*, or (South-West Shahabad) डोकी *doki* or (south-east) डोउआ *doüä*, is a wooden ladle used by Muhammadans in cooking pulse. The corresponding word amongst Hindus is, in North-East Tirhut, दाबि *dābi*, and in Champaran दाबा *dāba*. घटना *ghatna* in Gaya is a machine for stirring pottage as it is being cooked.

CHAPTER XI.—LEATHER VESSELS.

719. South of the Ganges the मलवा *malwa* is used for holding oil. In Champāran it is मलिया *maliya*. कुप्पा *kuppa* or कुप्पी *kuppi* is for holding oil or clarified butter (घ्यु *ghyu*). नदोइ *nadoï* is used in Gaya for the same purpose. In North-East Tirhut धोकड़ा *dhokra* is a sack used for the same purpose, as in the proverb गूड़क चोट धोकड़ें पुनु जान *gūrak chot dhokreñ punu jān*,—it's only the vessel that knows the pain (or weight) of the molasses, *i.e.*, only he who suffers, knows the pain. गेल्हा *gelha* is a similar smaller vessel.

गेल्हा *gelha* or (in South-East Tirhut) चमन्ड़ी *chamri* is also a vessel for carrying molasses.

720. मोट *mot* or मोटि *moti* is the large leather bucket for drawing water from a well. डोल *dol* is the smaller one. मसक *masak* is the leather water-skin borne by water-carriers. दस्ती कुप्पा *dasti kuppa* is the small leather bag used by torch-bearers (मसालची *masālchi*) for carrying oil.

CHAPTER XII.—LEAF-PLATTERS.

721. The दोना *dona* is a small round leaf-platter. In Patna, Gaya, and the north-west it is also called खोना *khona*, and in Shahabad खदोना *khadona*. The पत्तल *pattal* is a broader and flatter kind, and is also used as a kind of basket at Hindu marriages when a number of guests are to be fed. It is also called पत्तरी *patri* in Shahabad, पत्ता *patta* in South Bhagalpur, and पतरौरी *patrauri* or पनमारा *panmāra* in Champāran and North-West Tirhut.

CHAPTER XIII.—STANDS FOR VESSELS.

722. These are made of mud or brick, and known as घिरसिढ़ी *ghirsirhi* in the north-west, east, and Patna, घिसिरी *ghisiri* in Sāran, घिरसिण्डी *ghirsindi* in Patna and Gaya, घिरसिर *ghirsir* in Patna and Shahabad, and घिरसण्डी *ghirsandi* in South Munger. Other names are घैलसारी *ghailsāri* in South-East Tirhut, घलसारी *ghalsāri* in South Bhagalpur, घलथरी *ghalthari* in North-West Tirhut, घड़ौंची *gharaunchi* (South-West Shahabad), and चौतरा *chautra* or ओटा *ota* (Champāran).

SUBDIVISION III.

CLOTHES AND ORNAMENTS, &c.

CHAPTER I.—CLOTHES.

723. The general terms are कपड़ा *kapra*, चीर *chīr*, and लूगा *lūga*. The last has local variants, नूगा *nūga* (South-East Tirhut) and लुग्गा *lugga*, नुङ्गा *nunga*, or नूँगा *nūnga* south of the Ganges. Other names, current principally to the west, are पहरावा *pahrāwa*, बस्तर *bastar*, or

A Bihar Fashion Plate

CLOTHES WORN.

1. *Chit.*
2. *Kopin.*
3. *Topi khagwa.*
4. *Tahband khendhra.*
5. *Kanjhappa, dohar, dhoti.*
6. *Muretha, nimāstin, kalidār, paijāma.*
7. *Pagri, chaddar, juma, khaltedār paijāma.*
8. *Changeshiya topi, achkan, khaltedār paijāma.*
9. *Changoshiya topi, āba, churidār paijama*
10. *Babhnau topi, mirjai, dhoti.*
11. *Muretha, dhātha, kurta, chaddar, dhoti.*

कपड़ा लत्ता *kapra lutta.* A suit of clothes is called पाँचो टूक कपड़ा *pāncho tūk kapra*, and consists of a turban, loin-cloth, jacket, sheet, and bathing-cloth.

724. Amongst men's clothes are—

The turban.—पाग *pāg*, पगिया *pagiya*, पगड़ी or पगरी *pagri* is a piece of cloth woven for the purpose. The inner portion of the made-up turban (बूत के पगड़ी *būt ke pagri*) worn by the more respectable people is called फेंटा *phenta.* मुरेठा *muretha* is a piece of ordinary cloth, or even a garment, such as the गमछा *gamchha*, चद्दर *chaddar*, or दोपट्टा *dopatta*, worn round the head. चीरा *chīra* is a checked turban. A piece of cloth wound under the chin and over the head is ढाठा *dhātha ;* also गलौधी *galaudhi* in Patna and East Tirhut, गलमोछा *galmochha* in Tirhut and to the east and (optionally) south of the Ganges, and गलजिन *galjin* in North-West Tirhut and Gaya.

725. The *cap* is टोपी *topi* or ताखी *tākhi.* The round cap covering the ears worn by Brāhmans is मुण्डा *munda* in Sāran and North Tirhut, कासीवाल *kāsīwāl* in South Tirhut, ताज *tāj* in North-East Tirhut, Patna, and the west, and बभनौ *babhnau* in Shahabad and South-East Tirhut. दोपलिया *dopaliya* is a long cap made of two pieces, and the चरपलिया *charpaliya* or चौगोशिया *chaugoshiya* is round and made of four pieces. The कनटोप *kantop*, कनझप्पा *kanjhappa* (both of these also to the west and in Patna), and कानदार टोपी *kāndār topi* (all north of the Ganges), is a piece of cloth worn loose over the head. South of the Ganges it is कुल्ही *kulhi* or कनझप्पो *kanjhappo* (Patna and South Munger), कनझप्पी *kanjhappi* (Gaya), and कनझोपा *kanjhopa* (South Bhagalpur). कुल्हिया *kulhiya* in Gaya is a boy's cap. घोंघा *ghongha* in Gaya is a wide umbrella-shaped hat of *tāl* leaves, worn in rainy weather.

726. *The loin-cloth.*—This is धोती *dhoti.* North of the Ganges and in Shahabad it is also called मरदानी *mardāni*, and in Shahabad, Patna, and Gaya लुङ्गी *lungi.* The small loin-cloth is लँगोटा *langota* or लँगोटी *langoti ;* also in Patna लङ्गोट *langot.* Other names are कोपिन *kopin*, in Champāran कोपीन *kopīn*, and in the south-east नँगोट *nangot* or नँगोटा *nangota.* कप्पा *kappa* (east) is a small cloth worn round the waist by the poor. The भगवा *bhagwa*, or in Sāran भगई *bhagaī* and North-East Tirhut धरिया *dhariya*, is a small *dhoti* principally* worn by

* It is not always worn by boys. Compare the proverb चोरक भगवा डाही *chorak bhagwa dāhī*,—burn a thief's loin-cloth, *i.e.*, disgrace him as much as possible.

boys. The बिसटी *bisti*, or in Gaya बिछुटी *bichhuti*, is the scrap worn by poor boys. The small tight cloth worn by wrestlers, and also the usual cloth tightened up to allow of free play of the limbs in violent exercise, is काछा *kāchha* or कच्छा *kachchha*. Other names are चरना *charna* (Champāran, Patna, Gaya, and the east), चिट *chit* (Patna), समाली *samāli* (Gaya and the south-west), भरकछ or भड़कछ *bharkachh** (North-East Tirhut), and भड़काछ *bharkāchh* (South-East Tirhut). तहमद *tahmad*, or in Shahabad तहबन्द *tahband*, and in Champāran तही *tahi*, is a loin-cloth worn by Musalmān mendicants *(fakīrs)*. The tag of the loin-cloth tucked in behind is पिछुआ *pichhua* or पछुआ *pachhua* to the west. To the east it is ढेंका *dhenka* or ढेंकुआ *dhenkua*. The loose end which hangs down in front is खूँट *khūnt*, साँची *sānchi* (North Tirhut), and पुच्छ *puchchh* (South-East Tirhut). In South Bhagalpur it is कोंची *konchi*. The knot in the loin-cloth for holding money, &c., is फाँड़ *phānr*, फाँड़ा *phānra*, or फण्डा *phanda*. They are also called चेंट *chent* or टेंट *tent* towards the west, and पेंच *pench* in North-West Tirhut. Other local names are हरिड़ा *harira* (North-East Tirhut), ऐड़हा *airha* or मूढ़ी *mūrhi* (both South-East Tirhut).

727. *The drawers.*—These are पैजामा *paijāma*, also south of the Ganges इजार *ijār* and खिसकट *khiskat* (apparently a corruption of the Persian خشتك *khishtak*). In South Bhagalpur they are also called तमान *tamān*, and in North-West Tirhut सुरवाल *surwāl* (a corruption of the Persian شلوار *shalwār*). According to the Kānūni Islām, the *ijār* and *surwāl* are not so wide as the *paijāma*. Tight drawers are चुड़िदार *churidār*, also चुस्त *chust* to the west and in South Bhagalpur. If loose at the ankles, they are मोहरिदार *mohridār*; also खलतेदार *khaltedār* in Patna and to the west, बरकाबर *barkābar* in Gaya, and पैंचेदार *painchedār* elsewhere. If loose, with pieces let in along the thigh, they are कलिदार *kalidār*. जँघिया *janghiya* are tight-fitting short drawers, such as those worn by wrestlers.

728. *The jacket.*—This is मिरजई *mirjaī* and also खुटिया अँगरखा *khutiya angarkha*.

729. *The coat.*—This is अङ्गा *anga*, अँगरखा *angarkha*, or चपकन *chapkan*. Those worn by Hindus open on the right breast, and those by Musalmans on the left. It is tied at the neck by a string, घुण्डी

---

* Compare Manbodh's Haribans, which is a Maithil poem. कदमक तरु चढ़ि भड़कछ मारि *kadamak taru charhi bharkachh māri*,—(Krishna) mounted the *kadam*-tree and tightened his loin-cloth.

ghundi or घूँड़ी *ghūnri*, and also to the east and south भुण्डी *bhundi* or भूँड़ी *bhūnri*, and in South Bhagalpur भुण्डो *bhundo*, which runs in a hem, तुकमा *tukma*, or (in Patna and Gaya) गाली *gāli*. The अचकन *achkan* is a long loose coat buttoning right down the front. The काबा *kāba* or (south of the Ganges) कबा *kaba* is an outer coat open at the chest and sleeves. The निमास्तीन *nimāstīn* (also called नीमा *nīma* south of the Ganges) is a jacket the sleeves of which reach only to the elbows, while the शलुका *shaluka* and सदरी *sadari* leave the arms bare.

730. *The sheet.*—This is चद्दर *chaddar* or चादर *chādar*. This is of various kinds, viz. the दोहर *dohar* is a doubled sheet hemmed all round. The गिलेफ *gileph*, सलगा *salga*, or खोल *khol*, is similar, but is not hemmed all round, and is generally made of coarse cloth (मोटिया *motiya*). The एकपट्टा *ekpatta* or एकलाई *eklāi* is a sheet made of one breadth of cloth. डेढ़पट्टा *derhpatta* or डेढ़पट्टी *derhpatti* is a sheet whose whole breadth is made up by sewing together two cloths, of which the breadth of one is half that of the other. The दोपटा *dopta* or दोपट्टा *dopatta* is a sheet whose breadth is made up by sewing together two cloths of equal breadth. उतरी *utri* to the east is an outer garment. To the west it is used (*a*) for the string tied round a corpse's neck, and (*b*) for the mourning garments worn for ten days by the करता *karta*, or person who lights the funeral pyre.

731. *The stuffed quilt.*—These have various names, according to the amount of cotton-wool in them, viz. लेहाफ *lehāph* (five or six *sers*); रजाई *rajāi*, नेहाली *nehāli*, or (South Bhagalpur) लेहाली *lehāli*, all of which hold from one to three *sers*; and the दोलाई *dolāi*, सीरक *sirak*, or (in South Bhagalpur) तुराई *turāi* or सीरग *sirag*, which contain less than half a seer. The stuffing of the quilt is भरना *bharna* or (to the south) भराव *bharāw* or भराना *bharāna*. Bits of old cotton padding in a quilt are अङ्गा *anga* north of the Ganges. A similar quilt made of patchwork is गुदरा *gudra* or गुदरी *gudri*. When made of rags it is खेँधरा *khendhra*; also optionally in Tirhut, Patna, Gaya, and the east गेँदरा *gendra*, and in Shahabad लेँदरा *lendra* or लेदरा *ledra*. See also § 637.

732. The *long coat* worn by well-to-do people is आबा *āba*. The kind of court dress consisting principally of flounced petticoats is जमा *jama*.

733. The *bathing-cloth*, worn round the loins while bathing and used for drying the body afterwards, is named differently by Hindus and Musalmāns. The former call it अँगौछा *angauchha* or गमन्छा *gamchha*, a local variant being अँगोछा *angochha* to the west. A smaller kind, or *handkerchief*, is अँगौछी *angauchhi*, गमन्छी *gamchhi*, साफी *sāphi*, तौनी *tauni* (East Tirhut), or तिउनी *tiuni* (North-West Tirhut). The Muhammadans call the bathing-cloth लुङ्गी *lungi* or लूँगी *lūngi*. The हजुरिया *hajuriya* is a similar bathing-cloth worn by Hindu mendicants (बैरागी *bairāgi*).

734. *The purse.*—This is थैला *thaila*, थैली *thaili*, बट्टू *battu*, बटुआ *batua*, or बटुई *batui*. The झोरा *jhora* is a larger bag. In Gaya and to the west it is also घोघी *ghoghi* or धोकन्री *dhokri*. The बगुली *baguli* or तिलन्दानी *tildāni* is a tailor's housewife. लोखर *lokhar* is the case in which a barber carries his razors, &c. The last is also called किसन्मत *kismat* north of the Ganges and किसन्बत *kisbat* south of it. The *money-belt* is डोँड़ा *donra* or डोँड़न्हा *donrha*.

735. *The shoes.*—These are जोड़ा *jora*, जूता *jūta* (or जुत्ता *jutta*), जूती *juti*, or पनही *panahi*. जेरन्पाइ *jerpāi*, खरन्पा *kharpa*, or (south-east) चटन्का *chatka*, are usually the shoes worn by women. The wooden bathing-patten with a peg to go between the toes is खड़ाओँ *kharāon*, खड़ाउन *kharāūn*, or खड़ाँव *kharānw* (also to the east खराम *kharām* or खराओनि *kharāoni*) or चपन्टा *chapta*, and the clog held on the feet with strings or straps is बाधा *bādha* or बदन्हा *badha*. In Sāran and South-West Shahabad लतन्री *latri* are old shoes.

736. The Brahmanical cord is जनेव *janew*, जनेउ *janeu*, or (to the south-east) जनेउआ *janeüa*. The knots in the cord are परन्वर *parwar* or परन्वल *parwal*. In Tirhut and South Bhagalpur they are also परन्बल *parbal*. The सूत सिखा *sūt sikha* is the projecting part beyond the knot. The length of the cord is measured by handbreadths (चौआ *chaua*). A Brāhman's cord is 96 handbreadths long, and so also a Rajpūt's, but the knots are different.

737. *The blanket.*—This is कम्मर *kammar*, कम्मल *kammal*, or कमन्रा *kamra*. In South-West Shahabad it is also राल *rāl*. A small blanket is कमन्री *kamri* or कमरिया *kamariya*. In Champāran and the south-east धूस *dhūs* or धुस्सा *dhussa* is a thick kind of blanket. पचन्हत्थी *pachhatthi* is a large blanket five cubits long, and छहत्था *chhahattha* or छहत्थी *chha-hatthi* is six cubits long. घोघी *ghogi* is a peculiar way of tying a blanket over the head to save the wearer from rain. In South-West Shahabad it is also called घोँघी *ghonghi*, and in Patna and North-East Tirhut बुक्की *bukki*. The blanket forms the subject of many proverbs: thus ज्यों भीजे

ज्यों कम्मर भारि *jyoñ bhīje, tyoñ kammar bhāri*,—the more a blanket is allowed to become moist, the heavier it gets, *i.e.*, delays are dangerous.

738. A *patch* on the clothes is पेवन *pewan*, local variants being पेवन्द *pewand* south of the Ganges and पौना *pauna* in South-West Shahabad. It is also called पाटी *pāti* or पटिया *patiya* to the east. Another name is चेफ्ड़ी *chephri* in North-East Tirhut.

739. When cloth is doubled, the *outer piece* is अबरा *abra* or (in South Bhagalpur) पल्ला *palla*, and the *lining* अस्तर *astar* or (in Champāran and North Tirhut) तही *tahi*.

740. Among women's clothes are—

The sheet.—This is सारी or साड़ी *sāri* generally, with a variant सरिया *sariya* to the east. To the west and in Patna and Gaya it is also called खिलुआ *khilua*. It is also called लूगा *lūga*, with, in East Tirhut, a variant, नूगा *nūga*. In South Bhagalpur it is called बरहत्थी *barhatthi* (when 12 cubits long), and in South Munger खाँड़ी *khānri* or खण्डा *khanda*. An old torn sheet is लुगरी *lugri*, as in the proverb नई धोबिनियाँ आइलि, लुगरिये साबुन लाइलि *naī dhobiniyān āīli lugriye sābun lāīli*,—the new washerwoman has come and applied soap even when washing rags, *i.e.*, a new broom sweeps clean. A proverb of similar import is नया नोकर खरगोस पकड़तारे, *naya nokar khargos pakartāre*,—a new servant will catch a hare, or, as they say in Ireland, a sharp fellow won't let a hare catch him. The smaller sheet worn by poorer women is जनानी धोती *janāni dhoti* or लुगरी *lugri*. Over the साड़ी *sāri* is worn another sheet, called चद्दर *chaddar* or चादर *chādar*, or (in Gaya and South Munger) पिछौरा *pichhaura*. This may be दोपटा *dopta* or दोपट्टा *dopatta*, as in the case of a man's sheet. The small sheet worn by little girls is परखण्डा *parkhanda* to the west and in South Bhagalpur and Gaya बरकी *barki* in Patna and the south-west. It is फलिया *phaliya* in Sāran and North-West Tirhut, गाँती *gānti* in South Bhagalpur, and फरिया *phariya* in South-West Shahabad. We also find खेरुकी *kheruki* or खरुकी *kharuki*, खेरुका *kheruka* or खरुका *kharuka*, north of the Ganges, and पुतली *putli* in South Tirhut, Patna, and South Munger.

741. The hem of the sheet is generally आँचर *ānchar*, and also अँचरा *anchra* or अचरा *achra*. This is also the part which covers the bosom. The first of these words is the nominative, and the others are more properly used with postpositions. Thus ई आँचर बड़ नीमन बा *ī ānchar bar nīman bā*,—this border is very beautiful; but अचरा में बान्ह

देलीं *achra men bānh delīn*,—I tied it up in the hem of my garment. The end of the sheet gathered up and tied in front is फुफुति *phuphuti*, फुफुनी *phuphuni*, or फुफुन्दी *phuphundi* to the west, and कोँचा *koncha* or कोँची *konchi* to the east. The pocket in front formed by loosening the part tied round the waist is खोइँछा *khoinchha*, and in the extreme south-east खोएछा *khoechha* or खोँछा *khonchha*, as in the proverb बुड़बक कनेयाँ केँ नौ आना खोइँछा *burbak kaneāñ keñ nau āna khoinchha*,—it's a fool of a bride that only gets nine ānās in her pocket (for wedding presents). The loose fold on the left side is गोझनौटा *gojhnauta*. In the south-west it is पिछौरा *pichhaura*. When a woman is modest and meets a strange man, she draws her sheet or veil (see below) before her face. This action is called घोघट *ghoghat*, or in Gaya घुग्घा *ghuggha*, in South Bhagalpur घोघो *ghogho*, and to the north-west घूघ *ghūgh* or घोघ *ghogh*; and when a woman wishes to be extra modest, she pulls a great deal over her face. She is then called बड़ घोघट *bar ghoghat*.*

742. चसदार *chasdār* is a dyed cloth with a double-hemmed border worn by women in Shahabad. In the same district मसाढ़ू *masārhu* is a dyed cloth used by females of the lower orders, and झिमकी *jhimki* is a cloth printed with flower patterns. ककरेजा *kakreja* is a purple, and सालू *sālu* a red cloth, much used everywhere.

743. *The petticoat*.—This is generally लँहगा *lanhga*. A looser kind is घँघरा *ghanghra* in Gaya and to the east, घङ्घर *ghanghar* in the south-east, and घाँघर *ghānghar* in Shahabad. The घँघरी *ghanghri* is a girl's petticoat. काछा *kāchha* is a mode of tying it under the leg. The waist-band through which the string is run is नेफा *nepha*, and the string itself is इजार बन्द *ijār band*, or in the case of a bride or bridegroom नारा *nāra*. The hem is also called कमरतोइ *kamartoï*.

744. *The bodice*.—This, if it reaches to the waist, is कुरता *kurta*, झूला *jhūla*, or in North-East Tirhut कसनि *kasani*. If it is short, only covering the breasts, it is अँगिया *angiya* or चोली *choli*. A similar short bodice, worn chiefly by prostitutes, is called महरम *mahram*. This last in North-East Tirhut is called चोली *choli*.

745. The *veil* or cloth worn over the head is ओढ़नी *orhni*. When a veil or a sheet (चादर *chādar*) has a dyed border, it is called चुनरी

* As in Manbodh's Haribans, where the wife of Akrūr, although very modest, still wanted to look at Krishna when he came into the house, बड़ घोघट पुनु तकलो चाहिय *bar ghoghat punu takalo chāhia*.

chunri or चुंदरी *chundri*, and also in Sāran झिमकी *jhimki*. The border is called in North-East Tirhut पाढ़ि *pārhi* or पढ़िया *parhiya*.

746. The *drawers* are पैजामा *paijāma* or (in North-West Tirhut) सुरवाल *surwal*.

747. *Toilet requisites.*—The antimony put on the edges of the lower eyelids is सुरमा *surma*, and the lampblack applied to the eyeball is काजर *kājar*, as in the proverb ठाँव गुन काजर, कुठाँव गुन कारिख *thāmw gun kājar, kuthāmw gun kārikh*,—in the right place it is collyrium, and in the wrong place, soot. Lampblack is kept in a box called कजरौटा *kajrauta* or कजरौटी *kajrauti*. The coarser red lead put on the forehead and on the parting of the hair is सेँदुर *sendur* or सेनुर *senur*. The finer kind placed between the eyebrows is ईंगुर *ingur*. The silver spots put on the forehead are called टिकुली *tikuli*, and the round silver spot between the eyebrows is बिन्दी *bindi*. The small silver or gold spots surrounding this are, in North-East Tirhut, बेनी *beni* or बेनिया *beniya*. The comb is ककहा *kakha*, ककही *kakhi*, or कँगही *kangahi*. It is also ककवा *kakwa* in Patna, Gaya, and South Bhagalpur. The लिखगहनी *likhgahni* is a kind of comb used in Gaya. The hair-brush is ठकरी or थकरी *thakri*. To the east झरनी *jharni* is a kind of brush made of the stem of a cocoanut leaf. A tooth-brush is दतुवन *datuan*. It is made by biting one end of a sprig of wood till the fibres form a brush. Hindus use a fresh one every day, but Musalmāns keep theirs for a fortnight at a time.

748. *Washing of clothes.*—See §§ 389 and ff.

In *making clothes*, the following terms are used by the tailor or दरजी *darji*:—

पसूज *pasūj* is running, तुरपई *turpai* hemming or felling, उरमा *urma* is top-sewing, लङ्गड़ *langar* tacking or basting, and चून *chūn* gathering. बखिया *bakhiya* or बखेआ *bakhea* is stitching, चाँपा बखिया *chāmpa bakhiya* is long stitching, and डोरी दे के बखिया *dori de ke bakhiya* stitching-in piping-cord. जवा *jawa* is a long stitch and a short stitch alternately, and काँटा फोड़ी पखिया *kānta phori pakhiya* is a kind of stitching for which there is no English name. सुलतान लोढ़ी *sultān lorhi* is a mantua-maker's hem, सारजी *sārji* is herring-boning, and जाली *jāli* a kind of herring-boning for joining two cloths but not bringing their edges together. दरज *daraj* is a run-and-felled seam. When it is narrow, it is called गोल *gol*; when wide, इमलपत्ती *imalpatti*; and when very wide, चौरा *chaura*. There are false hems of various kinds. When the edges of the two pieces meet evenly, it is called पट्टी *patti;* when the edge of the added piece extends beyond the edge of the main piece, the false hem is called, if it is narrow, मगज्जी *magji,* which properly means the overlapping portion. If it is wide, it is called सञ्जाफ *sanjāph.* When the overlapping portion is very wide, the false hem is called लखनवाला सञ्जाफ *lakhnawāla sanjāph,* or in Shahabad लखनौआल सञ्जाफ *lakhnauāl sanjāph.* काज *kāj* is button-hole stitch, and हूल *hūl* eyelet-holing.

749. सिलहरा *silahra* is a kind of embroidery. Two thicknesses of muslin are sewn together. The under one has holes cut out in it which are embroidered, and are visible through the upper one. It is used as an ornamental border. बेल *bel* is similar to सिलहरा *silahra,* except that patterns of various leaves, &c., and not holes, are cut in the lower muslin. सिँघारा *singhāra* is an embroidered scolloped or vandyked edge. सोराही *sorāhi* is a piece of calico cut into an ornamental shape and *appliquéd* on to the shoulder of a coat. उलटा मुण्ढा *ulta mundha* is binding an armhole with piping-cord. कण्ठा *kantha* is a rounded collar sewn in front of the coat. A sleeve is said to be चुड़िदार *churidār* when it is gored to fit tight at the wrist. A gore is घोर *ghor.* There is no Bihāri equivalent for "dart," "pleat," or "tuck."

CHAPTER II.—CARPETS AND MATS.

750. A floor-cloth is कालीन *kālīn* south of the Ganges, north of the Ganges जाजिम *jājim,* or (to the west) फरस *pharas.* A carpet is दरी *dari,* or when larger सतरञ्जी *satranji.* A गलैचा *galaicha* or गलीचा *galīcha* is a thread mat. चट्टी *chatti* in South Bhagalpur is a canvass mat, and चाली *chāli* in Gaya is a coarse kind of mat made of bamboo slips tied together.

751. चटाइ *chatāi* or चटैनी *chataini* is a mat made of various reeds or bamboo slips. A गोनरी *gonri* or गोँदरी *gondri* is made of the *gond* reed. In Patna, Gaya, and the south-west सफ *saph* is a long *gond* mat used when a number of people are assembled at a marriage, &c. In the north-west it is ढाढ़ा *dhārha,* in South-East Tirhut चटान *chatān,* and in North-West Tirhut बरहत्था *barhattha.* A तराय *tarāy* to the east is made of palm leaves, and a तरई *tarai* in Champaran of reeds. सितलपाटी *sitalpāti* is a fine mat for sleeping on in the hot weather. When a number of Musalmāns say prayers together on one carpet, it is called जानिमाज *jānimāj,* or in South Munger जायनेमाज *jāynemāj;* and when on a mat, it is called सफ *saph.*

CHAPTER III.—JEWELRY.

752. The following are some of the varieties of jewelry commonly worn :—

a.—Worn by Men and Boys.

753. *On the ears.*—बाली *bāli* or (in Shahabad) बारी *bāri*. This is a ring. Also the कनौसी *kanausi* (Patna and Gaya, where it is worn by Hindus only). Other ear pendents are मोती *moti*, गोखुला *gokhula* (and to the west also गोरखुल *gorkhul*) (an ornamented ring), कुण्डल *kundal* (a large ring), लोर *lor* (worn principally by Goālās), and कनबाला *kanbāla*. सोना *sona* is a plain ear pendent, and अन्ती *anti* is a plain stud fixed in the lobe of the ear. फिरकी *phirki* is a double gold ring.

754. *On the arms.*—The बाँक *bānk* and चौकठा *chauktha* are worn on the right upper arm. So also the बिजावठ *bijāwath* or बिजौठा *bijautha*, which is, however, more properly a female ornament. The अनन्त *anant* and तावीज *tāwij* are various kinds of amulets.

755. *On the neck.*—The माला *māla* is the bead necklace. The उदराछ *udrāchh* is one made of the seeds of the रुद्राछ *rudrāchh* (*Eleocarpus ganitrus*). The कण्ठा *kantha* is a necklace with gold and silver ornaments or sacred relics attached to it. The मुँगवा *mungwa* is a coral (मूँगा *mūnga*) necklace, and the मोहर माला *mohar māla* or मोहन माला *mohan māla* is a long necklace of gold *mohars* and coral. The गोप *gop* is made of twisted gold wire, and it is also called घुनसी *ghunsi* in Champāran, North Tirhut, and South Munger. The सिकरी *sikri* is a long chain going round the neck.

756. *On the fingers.*—This is अँगुठी *anguthi*, ऐँठुआ *ainthua* (Gaya), or औँठी *aunthi*. The गोरख धन्हारी *gorakh dhanhāri* or गोरख धँधारी *gorakh dhandhāri* is a puzzle-ring which takes to pieces and is difficult to put together again. मुँदरी *mundri* is a ring worn on the right little finger. गोल *gol* (Shahabad) and फेरुआ *pherua* (Patna and Gaya) are kinds of rings.

757. *On the wrist.*—These are बाला *bāla* or (Patna and Gaya) बलेआ *balea*, पहुँची *pahunchi*, and also (south of the Ganges) पहुँचारी *pahunchāri*, कड़ा *kara* (south of the Ganges), बेरा *bera* in Gaya and to the west, जिग्गा *jigga* in Sāran, मठिया *mathiya* in South Bhagalpur, and तोड़ा *tora* in South-West Tirhut. These are worn principally by boys. तैँती *tainti* is a kind of amulet in South Munger, Gaya, and Shahabad.

758. *On the waist.*—The chain hung round the waist is करधन *kardhan* or करधनी *kardhani;* also हरहरा *harhara* in the east. A kind of belt is लौंगरा, and of this जावा *jāwa* or जवारी *jawāri*, लँगड़ा *langra* and जई *jai*, are portions of the clasp.

759. *On the ankles.*—A boy's anklet is गोड़ाँव *gorānw*, गोड़ाँय *gorāin*, or कड़ा *kara*. South of the Ganges we also meet गोड़हा *gorha*, घुँघुर *ghunghur*, or घुँघरू *ghunghru* (fitted with bells, used also in Tirhut), and चौरासी *chaurāsi* (when it carries 84 beads).

760. *On the toes.*—अँगुठा *angutha* is a toe-ring.

b.—Worn by Women.

761. *Ornaments for the head.*—The ornamented hair-pin is चोंटी *chonti*.

762. *Ornaments for the forehead.*—The मँगटीका *mangtika* or बन्नी *banni* is an ornament tied in the centre of the forehead by three strings, one passing round each side and the other over the top of the head. They are fastened in the hair. Of this the ornament is called चौकठा *chauktha*, and the strings सिकरी *sikri*. The spangles or wafers gummed on to the forehead are टिकुली *tikuli*. Another name in South-West Tirhut is सिसफूल *sisphūl* or चाँद *chānd*. In Shahabad सटिया *satiya* is a wafer made of embossed paper and gummed on the forehead.

763. *Nose-ornaments.*—The nose-studs fastened on to the outside of one nostril is छुच्छी *chhuchchhi*, in South Bhagalpur नकचन्दा *nakchanda*, and in Patna and to the south-west लौंग *laung*. It is not an easy thing to steal, hence the proverb कहावै ले सैयद चोरावै ले छुच्छी *kahāwai lai saiyad, chorāwai lai chhuchchhi*,—by name he is a *saiyad*, but he can steal even a nose-stud. The ring passing through the outside side of the nostril is नथ *nath*. A smaller kind is नथिया *nathiya*, and that worn by girls नथुनी *nathuni*. The बुलाक *bulāk* or बेसर *besar* is a ring hung from the centre cartilage of the nose, and the झुलनी *jhulni* is a similar one worn by women of the *Rauniyār* caste. It swings backwards and forwards, and is ornamented with beads.*

* Nose-ornaments are peculiar to females. If a mother loses a first-born son she endeavours to persuade the demon who kills children that any future boys born are only girls, and hence not worth killing. To do this, she often makes the boy wear nose-ornaments, and calls him by some nickname, as *Bulāki* (wearer of a nose-ring), &c. There are other similar customs, such as giving opprobrious names to such sons who are born after the death of a first born, which it would take too much space to mention here.

764. *Ear-ornaments.*—Ear-studs fastened to the lobe of the ear are करनफूल *karanphūl* or कनफूल *kanphūl* and खोटला *khotla*, or in East Tirhut खुटला *khutla* or खुट्टी *khutti*, to the north-west खुटली *khutli*, and in Gaya and Shahabad खुटिला *khutila*. The कनैली *kanaili* is a stud worn on the cartilage just where it leaves the head under the hair. Rings worn in the lobe of the ear are बाली *bāli*, and those worn in the upper part of the cartilage उतरना *utarna*. Broad plates worn across the ear are पात *pāt*, पत्ता *patta*, and तरकी *tarki*. A smaller kind worn in Gaya is called गोलवा *golwa*. Amongst pendents are the झूमक *jhūmak* or झुम्मक *jhummak*, which has two round pendents, and the झिमझिमिया *jhimjhimiya*, which are flat pendents. The मछरिया *machhariya* is a pendent shaped like a fish. In South Munger it is called मछलिया *machhaliya*. The लोर *lor* and कनौसी *kanausi* form a set of ear-ornaments. The first are round plates with a square cut out of the inside, forming a kind of ring with a square inside. One of these is hung in the lobe of each ear. The latter is a ring. One is hung in the upper part of the cartilage of the right ear, and two in the upper part of the cartilage of the left ear. When a hole bored in the ear for an ornament is not in use, it may be filled up with a plug, called ठेक *thek*. When the ornaments worn are too heavy for the ear to carry without tearing, a chain is fastened round the ear so as to support the heavier ornaments. This is called सिकरी *sikri*. Other ornaments for the ear are बीड़ *bīr* (Tirhut), काँप *kāmp*, and खुबिया *khubiya* in the south-east, and बिजली *bijli* in Patna and Gaya.

765. *Neck-ornaments.*—The चन्दर हार *chandar hār* is a long chain. A तावीज *tāwīj* is a similar one with an amulet attached. A set of three chains of various lengths is तेलरी *telri*, and also to the north-west तिलरी *tilri*, of five chains पचलरी *pachlari*, and of seven chains सतलरी *satlari*. The सिकरी *sikri* is a long chain, and the बद्धी *baddhi* is a long chain crossing the chest and going behind round the body. हुमेल *humel* is a necklace fitted with bells. Bosses tied to the throat are चम्पा कली *champa kali*, जुगनू *jugnu*, and ढोलना चौकी *dholna chauki*. The last is principally worn by the bride at a marriage, and is the first ornament put on before the marriage ceremony. The हँसुली *hansuli* is the solid necklet open in front which goes round the neck, and the तवक *tawak* is similar with pendents in front (worn by Muṣalmāns). सूति *sūti* in North-East Tirhut is a kind of neck-ring. जवा गोटा *jawa gota*, गलसटका

galsatka, गरदवानी *gardawāni*, and गरसी *garsi*, are various neck-ornaments used in Gaya. Other neck-ornaments are सितल्हा (South-East Tirhut), कटेसर *katesar* (Champāran, Patna, and South Bhagalpur) or कटसर *katsar* (Tirhut and South Bhagalpur), and खँभिया *khambhiya* (South Bhagalpur). हार *hār* or हरवा *harwa* is the general term for a necklace, and मोती माला *moti māla* is a pearl necklace, or one made with beads of the shape of pearls. ललरी *lalri* and दरपन *darpan* are two ornaments worn on the breast in Gaya and South Bhagalpur. A हैकल *haikal*, or in Champāran हैलक *hailak*, is a long necklace composed of flat pieces, generally nine in number. When a man marries a second wife, an ornament is made representing the first wife, which the second wife wears. On the first occasion on which the second wife applies vermilion to her hair, she first puts some on the ornament before applying it to herself. This ornament is called सौतिन *sautin*, or in South Munger सौत *saut*.

766. *On the clothes.*—मनोरी *manori* are ornaments on the veil (सारी *sāri*), and अँचरी *anchri* on the hem of the sheet.

767. *Arm-ornaments.*—The following are worn by all classes. Highest up on the arm is the बाजू *bāju*, or बाजू बन्द *bāju band*, which is a wide armlet. Below it the बिजावठ *bijāwath*, बिजाएठ *bijāeth*, or बिजौठा *bijautha*, which are five ornaments strung together; below that the बिरखी *birkhi*, which is smaller. Another name is बिरेंटी *birenti*. Below this comes the बाँक *bānk*, made of one piece. It is worn by Hindu women on the right arm, but by Musalmāns on both. Lowest down comes the बभुंटा *babhuntā*, or to the west बहुंटा *bahunta*, of five pieces and round. Arm-ornaments worn principally by Hindu women are अनन्त *anant* and तार *tār* or टरिया *tariya*. Similar to the last is also another ornament called बहुट्टा *bahutta*. सिकरी *sikri* is a chain worn on the upper part of the arm. झबिया *jhabiya* is a kind of inverted cup hanging from the arm, and to which bells (बचवा *bachwa*) are attached; and घुण्डी *ghundi* little ball pendents hanging from the बाजू *bāju* or from an अनन्त *anant*. मुन्धी *mundhi* is a clasp. बरेखी *barekhi* in South-West Shahabad is an arm-ornament worn by women of the *Goāla* caste. Arm-ornaments worn principally by Musalmān women are,—on the upper arm, जौसन *jausan*, पात *pāt* (a flat piece tied on), and बजुल्ला *bajulla*, or in Sāran बिजुलि *bijuli* (worn immediately below the बाजू *bāju*); and on the forearm नौनगा *naunaga* or (in North-East Tirhut) नवग्रह *nabgrah* of (nine stones). An ornament worn on the back between the shoulders is called by Hindus पान *pān* or पनवा *panwa*, and by Musalmāns बलमटार *balamtār*.

768. *Wrist-ornaments* are कँकना *kankna*, कँकनी *kankni*, or कँगना *kangna*, or in Champāran ककना *kakna*, कचरा *kachra* (Gaya and the south-east), कतवा *katwa* (Gaya and the south-east), कतरी *katri*, कँसौठी *kansauthi* (Gaya and the south-east), खसिया *khasiya*, गोलवा *golwa* (Gaya and the south-east), चूर *chūr*, चूरी *chūri* (bangles), छन *chhan* or छन्द *chhand*, जाल *jal*, जिग्गा *jigga*, टोड़ा *tōra*, तिनखण्डी *tinkhandi*, तिननगा *tinnaga*, तिसियौटा *tisiauta* (Gaya and the south-east), नघुरी *naghuri* or निगिहरी *nigihri*, or (in Gaya and the south-east) लघुरी *laghuri*, पचखण्डी *pachkhandi*, पछेला *pachhela* or पछेलिया *pachheliya*, पटरी *patri*, पटवा *patwa*, पहुँची *pahunchi*, बँगुरी *banguri*, बड़हड़ा *barhara*, or in Gaya बड़हर *barhar*, and in Champāran बेलहरा *belahra*, बाला *bāla*, बाँहु *bānhu*, बेरा *bera*, बौंखा *baunkha* (Gaya) (made of thread), मठिया *mathiya*, रुपौठी *rupauthi* (Gaya and the south-east), and लघुरी *laghuri* (see नघुरी *naghuri*). The समसेबन्द *samseband* is a keeper worn on the wrist to prevent the चूर *chūr* falling off.

769. *On the fingers.*—A ring is अँगुठी *anguthi.* A round solid ring is छल्ला *chhalla*. Other names are औंठी *aunthi* and ऐंठुआ *ainthua*. The गोरख धन्हारी *gorakh dhanhāri*, &c., is the same as that worn by men; so also the गोल *gol* and फेरुआ *pherua*. Other rings are तिनछलिया *tinchhaliya*, बहलोली *bahloli*, अँगुस्ताना *angustāna*, आरसी *ārsi* (which has a small mirror attached), मुंदरी *mundri*, लोभेरुआ *lobherua* (south-east), दरयाबादी *daryābādi* (*ib.*), पथरौटी *pathrauti* (*ib.*), चिरौगिया *chiraugiya* (*ib.*), अँखुआ *ankhua* (South Bhagalpur), मथानी *mathāni* (South-East Tirhut), बदामी *badāmi* (Tirhut), पोर *por* (*ib.*).

770. *On the waist.*—Waist-chains and bands are करधनी *kardhani*, कमरकस *kamarkas*, झब्बा *jhabba* or झबिया *jhabiya*, गठौरा *gathaura*, अँवरा *amwara*, कोचबन *kochban*, कमरजेब *kamarjeb*, सीपी *sīpi*, जाफरी *jāphri*. The कोथली *kothli* is a kind of pocket tied to the waist.

771. *On the feet.*—The ornament fitting on the ankle and covering and fitting on to the upper part of the foot is पाँव जेब *pānw jeb*. Like it are पावट *pāwat*, पैरी *pairi*, and पाँव सङ्कर *pānw sankar*. Over this comes the छड़ा *charra* or छड़ा *chhara*, a number of fine rings like the चूरी *chūri* on the arm; over this again the कड़ा *kara*; and at the top the चूर *chūr*. The पैंजनी *painjni* are anklets with bells; so also किँकिनि *kinkini* and घुघुरु *ghughuru* or घुँघुरु *ghunghuru* in Gaya and North-East Tirhut.

772. *On the toes*—are अँगुठा *angutha* and छल्ला *chhalla*, which are rings. An ornament fitting over all the toes is बिछिया *bichhiya*. In Gaya and the south-east बटुरी *baturi* is a toe-ring to which bells are fastened.

SUBDIVISION IV.

APPLIANCES USED IN WORSHIP.

773. The appliances of a Hindu temple are as follows:—The आंस-नी *āsni* is a sort of mat made of *kus* grass, wool, &c., for sitting on.

774. A spoon for throwing water on the *lingam* is known as आंच-मनी *āchmani*; also अच-मनी *achmani* in South-West Shahabad, अँचौना *anchauna* in Gaya, अँचौनी *anchauni* in Sāran, and कल-छी *kalchhi* in South Tirhut.

775. The जल-पातर *jalpātar* is a vessel in which water is kept, and a smaller kind is पँच-पातर *panchpātar*. The अर-घा *argha* is the saucer made of stone or metal in which the stone representing the *lingam* is placed. The पींड़ी *pīnri* or पिण्डी *pindi* is the platform on which the *lingam* is placed. Other names are सराइ *sarāi* (optional) in South-East Tirhut, चौरा *chaura* in South-West Shahabad, and जखाड़ *jakhār* in the rest of that district.

776. घण्टा *ghanta* or घड़ी *ghari*, also south of the Ganges घण्ट *ghant*, are gongs or bells, and the बिज-घण्ट *bijghant* is a kind of gong with erect edges. घण्टा *ghanta* specially means a bell; झाँझ *jhānjh* (small) or झाल *jhāl* (large) are the cymbals. सङ्ख *sankh* is the conch.

777. The idol is मूरत *mûrat*, also मुर-ती *murti* in South Bhagalpur, and पांर-खत *pārkhat* optionally in South-East Tirhut. Its throne is सिँगासन *singāsan* or (in Patna and Gaya) सिँघासन *singhāsan*.

778. होर-सा *horsa*, or in the south-east हुर-सा *hursa*, is the round stone for grinding sandal-wood (चन्दन *chandan*). Another name is चँद-रौटा *chandrauta*. The vessel in which the ground sandal-wood is plaoed is कटोरी *katori*.

779. The censer is north of the Ganges धुप-दान *dhupdān*, in Patna and Shahabad धुप-दानी *dhupdāni*, in Gaya धुपअह-रा *dhupahra*, and in the south-east धुपेड़ी *dhuperi*.

780. The दिप-दान *dipdān*, दिप-दानी *dipdāni*, is the lampstand holding only one lamp or wick. One with four or five wicks is called आर-ती *ārti*.

781. The सुमिरनी *sumirni* north of the Ganges and सुमरनी *sumarni* south of it is the rosary of nineteen beads. In Champāran and Gaya it is also सुमेर *sumer*. माला *māla*, or in Sāran and Tirhut करमाला *karmāla*, is a similar rosary of one hundred and eight beads. सुमरनी *sumarni*, &c., are also used for the large bead at the end of a माला *māla*. A जापमाला *jāpmāla* is a large rosary containing as many as a thousand beads. The अष्टोतरी *ashtotri* or अठोतरी *athotri* is a rosary which is kept in a small bag called झोरा *jhora*. Into this bag the worshipper puts his hand and turns the beads. The रुद्राछ *rudrāchh* is a rosary used by worshippers of Shiva, as in the proverb बापक गरे मुँगरी, पूतक गरे रुद्राछ *bāpak gare mungri, pūtak gare rudrāchh*,—the father has a club on his neck, and the son a rosary, *i.e.*, the father is a scoundrel and the son a devotee.

782. The तूमा *tūma*, तुम्मा *tumma*, or तुम्बा *tumba* is the hollow gourd carried by religious mendicants (साधु *sādhu* or जोगी *jogi*). It is also called कठारी *kathāri* or सागर *sāgar* in Sāran and Tirhut. The तुमड़ी *tumri* is a small gourd. The कमण्डल *kamandal* is a similar vessel used for drawing water in a temple. A दण्ड कमण्डल *dand kamandal* is a similar vessel made of metal (brass, copper, gold, &c.)

DIVISION III.

SOILS.

CHAPTER I.—CLASSIFICATION OF SOILS.

783. Soils may be classified—

(*a*) According to their distance from the village site.

(*b*) According to their constituent elements.

(*c*) According to the crops for which they are prepared, or which they usually produce.

CHAPTER II.—SOILS CLASSIFIED ACCORDING TO THEIR DISTANCE FROM THE VILLAGE SITE.

784. The concentric circles (हलका *halka*) are generally, but not always, three in number. The nomenclature and division differ according to locality.

(*a*) The belt near the homestead, which is better manured, more carefully cultivated, and adapted for superior kinds of crops. The homestead is called अबादी *abādi*, डीह *dīh*, बसन्ती *basti*; and the belt of land गोएँड़ *goënr*, गोएँड़ा *goenra*, गोँड़ा *gonrha*, or गौँड़ा *gaunrha* or बाध *bādh*; also कोरार *korār* in Patna and to the west, डिहाँस *dihāns* (Shahabad, Patna, and Gaya), घरबारी *gharbāri* in Patna and South Munger, and बाड़ी *bārī* in South Bhagalpur. The land actually in the homestead is specially called डीह *dīh*, डिहाँस *dihāns*, or (in Tirhut) भीठा *bhītha*, and in Champāran भीठ *bhīth*. डीह *dīh* is properly an old village site or mound. If there are two clusters of dwellings of the same name some distance apart, the older one will be called डीह *dīh*. अबादी *abādi* is properly settled or cultivated land. The land near the village which receives the drainage of the houses is गोहान *gohān* in Shahabad.

(*b*) The next furthest belt from the village site is बहरसी *baharsi* to the west and in Patna and South Munger. This belt is also called सरेह *sareh* to the south-west as long as crops are standing on it. It is also called ताधी *tādhi* (Champāran), बहरभूँ *baharbhūm* (Sāran and Tirhut), टाल *tāl* (South-East Tirhut), बहियार *bahiyār* (North-East Tirhut), and बैहार *baihār* (South Bhagalpur). In Hazārībāgh it is called सिङ्घा *singha*.

(*c*) The belt furthest from the village site is also called सरेह *sareh* to the west, also बहरभूँ *baharbhūm* in South Munger. So that the second and third belts are only considered as one. There are also, however, separate names for the third belt, viz. टाड़ *tār*, टाँड़ *tānr*, or टाँड़ी *tānri*, which is used to mean high extensive wastes of infertile or gravelly soil, or of hillocks and ridges such as are found in Gaya, and चौँर *chaunr*, which means low open marshy country. In South Bhagalpur भीठो *bhītho* is the land far from the village site which only produces bhadoi crops with much labour, and a still further circle is बरन *baran*, which bears no produce. In Sāran and Tirhut दीयर *diyar* are the fields situated on the further side of a river, or islands formed by rivers.

CHAPTER III.—SOILS CLASSIFIED ACCORDING TO THEIR CONSTITUENT ELEMENTS.

785. *Sandy soils.*—बाला *bāla* or बलवा *balwa*, बलथर *balthar* (North-West and in Patna and in Gaya), बलवाह *balwāh* (South Bhagalpur), and बलधूस *baldhūs* (Champāran), are soils principally composed of sand. Sandy loams are बलसुन्दर *balsundar* or बलसुंदरी *balsundri*, with local variants बलसुन *balsun* or बलसुम्ही *balsumhi* in South Tirhut, बलकसी *balkasi* in South-East Tirhut, and बलसुम *balsum* in North-East Tirhut. They are also called बलुअट *baluat* to the west, and बलिमट *balimat* in Shahabad. North of the Ganges and in South Munger बलुआ *balua* is land with sand on the surface and clay at some distance below. In Champāran and South-West Tirhut धूस *dhūs* or धूसी *dhūsi* is an arid and sterile soil consisting of an admixture of sand and clay. A loose sandy subsoil, in which a clay well will not work, is बेँगा *benga* or बेँगवा *bengwa*. In South-East Tirhut it is also

भुसनी *bhusni*. In Shahabad भीस *bhīs* is fine compact sand, and बाला *bāla* loose coarse sand.

786. *Clayey soils.*—The principal is मटियार *matiyār*, or in Gaya मटिगर *matigar*, which is a brown clay soil, well adapted for rice. It contains about 60 or 70 per cent of clay. A stronger kind, containing about 85 per cent, is called केवाल *kewāl*. This is also called करार *karār* in the south-east. केवाल *kewāl* in South Munger is of three kinds, viz. करका *karka*, which is black; गोरिअट्टा *goriatta*, which is yellowish; and चनकी *chanki* or गगरी केवाल *gagri kewāl*, which is mixed with fine gravel. This last is also called पथरटिया *pathratiya* in South Bhagalpur or (when it is of a reddish colour) गोरेँटिया पथरौटी *gorentiya pathrauti*. In South-East Tirhut केवाल *kewāl* is of two kinds, viz. गोरी केवाल *gori kewāl*, which is light-coloured, and तेलिया केवाल *teliya kewāl*, which is dark. करैल *karail* to the west is a bluish-black soil, which contains more organic matter than मटियार *matiyār*. In Shahabad it is divided into two kinds, viz. बाँगर करैल *bāngar karail*, which is apt to crack on drying, and डोमा करैल *doma karail*, which is of a more bluish colour than the other. A clay which feels greasy when rubbed in the hand is called दूधी *dūdhi* or चिक्कन मिट्टी *chikkan mitti* or चिकनी मिट्टी *chikni mitti*; and भुसुरी *bhusuri* (west) and कचौस *kachaus* (east) are clay soils which soon dry on the surface. रखौर *rakhaur* is a similar soil mixed with ashes, which is called in South Munger भसुराही *bhasurāhi*. चनकी *chanki*, or to the west सिगता *sigta*, are hard soils, which split and crack when dry. In Patna and Gaya कछुइया *kachhuiya* is a loose clay met in digging wells. ललकी मिट्टी *lalki mitti* north of the Ganges, गेरू *geru* south of it, and काबिस *kābis* in South-West Shahabad, is a red clay. नरम *naram*, and also to the east लरम *laram*, mean soft when applied to clay. North of the Ganges, to the west, and in South Munger, अकराह *akrāh* is a hard clay soil mixed with fine gravel. In South-East Tirhut it is छराही *chharāhi*. रोरियाह *roriyāh* or रोरहा *rorha* is land which goes into hard lumps the size of eggs after preparation. कुमरौटी *kumrauti*, or in Sāran कुमहौटी *kumrhauti*, and in Tirhut कारी माटी *kāri māti*, is potter's clay.

787. *Loamy soils.*—The चहल *chahal* or कदोइ *kadoi* is that which is never drier than mud, and in which crops are planted without ploughing. ढबरी *dhabri* or ढाब *dhāb* is land which is part of the year under water and part of it dry. दोरस *doras*, or (in Patna and Gaya) दोरसाही *dorsāhi*, and (in South Bhagalpur) परसोती *parsoti*, and also

पँचकटैल *panchkatail* in Tirhut, is a clayey loam; while बलसुन्दर *balsundar* (see sandy soils for other names) is a fine sandy loam. In Champāran बभनी *babhni* is a light red soil.

CHAPTER IV.—SOILS AND WATER ACTION.

788. Land thrown up by fluvial action is गङ्ग बरार *gang barār* (also spelt बड़ार *baṛār*), and that cut away गङ्ग शिकस्त *gang sikast*. छारन *chhāran* is land left by the retrocession of a river. टाँड *tānr* in South-West Shahabad, and पटपर *patpar* in South-East Bihār, is newly-formed land so situated as to receive an annual accretion of alluvial deposit; but in Sāran and South Tirhut पटपर *patpar* is barren alluviated land. In Sāran मामस *māmas* is rich alluviated land. In Tirhut, Patna, Gaya, and the south-east तरी *tari* means moist soil in hollows and at the foot of slopes. It also even means water. Thus they say, 'Are you going तरी *tari* (by water) or खुसकी *khuski* (by land)?' In Sāran तरयानी *taryāni* is similarly used. तरी *tari* is also applied to lands recovered by retrocession of a river. In Shahabad they are भागर *bhāgar*, and in the south-west of that district छिछलहिया *chhichhlahiya*. They are also called छारन *chhāran*. दीयर *dīyar* or दियारा *diyāra* is fresh land thrown up by the shifting of the course of a river. In Patna, and also in Champāran, it is called दिअरा *diara*, in South-West Shahabad डीला *dila*, in South Munger दीरा *dīra*, and in South Bhagalpur दीरा *dīra*. The alluvial deposit left by rivers while still wet is called कदई *kadaī*, कदोर *kadoī*, or पाँक *pānk* or पङ्क *pank* (see § 789). Land rendered useless by deposits of sand is called कोरा बाल *kora bāl* (in Sāran) and बलान *balān* (North-West Tirhut).

CHAPTER V.—MUDDY AND WATER-LOGGED SOILS.

789. Land in the bed of a tank is in Patna and Gaya तरी *tari*. In Shahabad it is कींच *kinch*, and to the west generally कानो किचड़ *kāno kichchar*. Marshy or muddy soils and quagmires are भास *bhās* and दलकी *dalki* to the west and in Patna, and the latter also in Gaya and South Munger. In Tirhut, Sāran, and Patna they are दलदल *daldal*, in Patna and Shahabad पँकहा *pankha*, and in the south-west of the last district खँचड़ा *khanchra*. Lands usually saturated with water are पनमार *panmār* north of the Ganges, सुगरा *sugra* in South-

West Shahabad, सिँड़ाह *siñrāh* in the rest of the district, सिड़ाहा *sirāha* in Patna and South Munger, सीड़ा *sīra* in South Bhagalpur, and सेउत *seūt* in Gaya. धसना *dhasna* is land liable to be submerged. It is called गौँची *gaunchi* in Gaya and जलकी *jalki* in South-West Shahabad; in South Munger it is गौँछी *gaunchhi*. The old dry bed of a river is छारन *chhāran* or (in North Tirhut) मरन *maran*. Other names are बाँड़ *bānr* in Patna and Shahabad and झोर *jhor* in the south-west of the last district. पाँक *pānk*, पाँकी *pānki*, or पङ्क *pank* is earth wet and soft so as to yield to the tread, adhesive and rotting. Nothing will grow in it. कादो *kādo*, कदोइ *kadoï*, or कदई *kadaī*, is mud in which crops will grow.

CHAPTER VI.—HIGHLANDS AND LOWLANDS.

790. Highlands, as contrasted with river valleys, are उपरवार *uparwār* in Patna and to the north-west, बहरभूँ *baharbhūm* in South Tirhut, and उपरार *uprār* in East Tirhut. South of the Ganges डिहाँस *dihāns* is used in Patna, टाँड़ *tānr* in Gaya and South Munger, डील *dīl* in Shahabad, and डीह *dīh* in South Bhagalpur. In Hazāribagh other names are उचास *uchās* and ढीबर *dhībar*. In South Munger गाद *gād* is the corresponding word for a lowland. झील *jhīl* or चौँर *chauñr*, or in Sāran काछ *kāchh*, is low marshy land. In Patna, Gaya, and South Munger it is जाह *jāh*. मन *man* is a large sheet of water of considerable depth, and in Tirhut जान *jān* is similar but something smaller. खाल *khāl*, खलवा *khalwa*, or in the north-west खलार *khalār* or खल्हर *khalhar*, is a hollow with or without water.

CHAPTER VII.—RAVINES AND MOUNDS, &c.

791. Land cut by ravines and broken ground is बिहड़ *bihar* or (in Gaya) बीहँड़ *bīhanr*. In South Bhagalpur it is अरियन *arian*. The elevated soil in the midst of ravines is ढूह *dhūh* or ढूही *dhūhi* in South-West Shahabad, डील *dil* in the rest of the district, टिल्हा *tilha* in Patna, Gaya, and South Munger, and टिक्कर *tikkar* in South Bhagalpur.

792. In Patna, Gaya, and South Munger टँड़ुआ *tañrua* or नाला *nāla* is a ravine. The latter word is also current to the west, and is only used when the ravine is also a water-course. In the south-east the word is डाँड़ *dānr*. डेढ़ कौआ *derh kaua* is also used in Patna. Uneven ground is उभर खाभर *ubhar khābar* to the north-west and in South-East Tirhut, and मठन्हा *matha* or डाबर *dābar* (also in Champāran) in North-East Tirhut. South of the Ganges we have ऊबर खाबर *ūbar khābar* in Patna, Gaya, and South Munger (also noted in Sāran), ऊँच खाल *ūnch khāl* in Patna and to the west, ऊखर खाबड़ *ūkhar khābar* in Shahabad, and उचल्ली *uchli* in South Bhagalpur. A high river bluff is करारा *karāra*, अर्रा *arra*, अरार *arār*, अरारि *arāri* or कछाड़ *kachhār* or कछाड़ा *kachhāra*. Other names are ढाह *dhāh* (north generally) and कँगनिया *kanganiya* (North-East Tirhut). The sloping bank of a river is in Shahabad तरसिवाइ *tarsiwāi*, and in South Munger तरि *tari*.

793. A mound generally is टिल्हा *tilha*, or in South Munger टिल्हा टाकर *tilha tākar*. In South-West Shahabad it is ढूह *dhūh*, ढूही *dhūhi* (also in Sāran), डील *dīl*, or डिल्ला *dilla*, in the rest of that district टीपुर *tīpur*, and in South Bhagalpur टिकोर *tikor* or टिक्कर *tikkar*. In South-West Shahabad पटपरी *patpari* is a hill with a flat top. The sites of ruined villages are डीह *dīh;* also भीठा *bhītha* in South Munger. The sites of old villages are often covered with potsherds, hence such sites are also called ठिकराहू *thikrāhu* in Patna, ठिकरौल *thikraul* in Sāran, ठिकरिया *thikariya* to the east, झिकटौर *jhiktaur* in Patna, Gaya, and Champāran, सिकड़ौर *sikraur* or झिकरौर *jhikraur* in Shahabad, and झिकटिया *jhiktiya* in South Bhagalpur, the words for potsherds being झिकटा *jhikta*, झिकटी *jhikti*, or ठीकर *thīkar* or ठिकड़ा *thikra*, also सिकड़ा *sikra* in Shahabad and झिकड़ा *jhikra* to the west.

CHAPTER VIII.—STONY SOILS.

794. Gravelly soils are कँकराही *kankrāhi* in Sāran and Patna, अँकरैल *ankrail* in Sāran, and अँकड़ौर *ankraur* to the west. Gravel generally is in Patna and to the west आँकड़ *ānkar*, and to the east गङ्गट *gangat;* also everywhere कङ्कड़ *kankar*. In Champāran and Tirhut it is इँकड़ी *inkri*, and in Champāran and Gaya झिकटी *jhikti* or गराँगट *garāngat*. Coarse gravel is in Shahabad अँकड़ा *ankra*, and fine अँकड़ी *ankri*. To the south-east it is गँगटा *gangta* and गँगटी *gangti*. Soil mixed with coarse gravel is गँगटियाहा *gangtiyāha* in Patna, Gaya, and South Bhagalpur, and गँगटाहा *gangtāha* in Patna and South Munger. चटान *chatān* is a hard rocky soil. Other names are डोहर *dohar* in South-West Shahabad, and पथरेहर *pathrehar* in South Munger.

CHAPTER IX.—CULTIVATED AND WASTE.

795. Classifying soils according to cultivation, we have cultivated land known as अबाद *abād* or अबादी *abādi*. It is also known in the south-east and Gaya as पह *pah*, in Patna as खील बैठाओल *khīl baithāöl*, and Shahabad as खिलमार *khilmār*.

796. An inhabited village is बसगित *basgit* or बसती *basti*, and a deserted village बे छप्पर *be chhappar* (unroofed), and also in South Munger निचिराकी *nichirāki* (without a light) and in Gaya दमका *damka*. Other names for the latter are उजड़ *ujar*, उजरल *ujral*, उजाड़ *ujār*, उजड़ा *ujra* or (optionally in Tirhut) डीह *dīh*.

797. Waste land is परीत *parīt* (Patna, Gaya, and South Munger) or परती *parti*. Land which has accidentally gone out of cultivation is specially परात *parāt* in Sāran, पराता *parāta* to the north-west, and परांँत *parānt* or परता *parta* in North Tirhut. Waste land broken up for the first time is खील *khīl*, or in the south-east खिलकट *khilkat* or खिलकट्टी *khilkatti*. In Tirhut it is also called खिलमार *khilmār*. The second year after it is broken up it is खील *khīl* to the north-west, पह *pah* in Tirhut, Shahabad, and the south-east, and पौह *pauh* in Patna and South Munger. The third year it is called खेत *khet* or (in Champāran) पही *pahi*, and North-East Tirhut पह *pah*.

CHAPTER X.—FALLOW.

798. Land left fallow for sugar-cane from the previous spring harvest till the season for sowing the cane is called मघार *maghār*, &c., see § 805. Land left uncropped in the autumn harvest and ploughed during the rains for the cereals of the spring harvest following is चौमास *chaumās*, and to the west also पलिहर *palihar*. Those lands on which a spring crop is sown without any interval after the autumn crop is cut are called नारी *nāri* in Patna and South Munger, and जरी *jari* or जरी खेत *jari khet* elsewhere south of the Ganges and in Sāran. Waste lands which are ploughed up during the rains and cold weather and sown in rice at the commencement of the next rainy season are called दोतरा चौमास *dotra chaumās* in North-West Tirhut, गजाँड़ *gajānr* in South-East Tirhut, बिड़ार *birār* in South-East Bihār, and कुलहर *kulhar* in the south-west.

799. Lands left fallow for a time to recover their strength are परती *parti* generally. Other names are परता *parta* in North Tirhut and चाँच *chānch* in South Bhagalpur. Land which never lies fallow is अबाद *abād* or अबादी *abādi.* Another name is उठन्ती *uthti* in Champāran. North of the Ganges रुल्ली *rulli* or (to the east) रुन्नी *runni* is poor-light land which requires to be left fallow for a year or two. It also means land which has lost its fertility. Other words in use are झूस *jhūs* and हलुक *haluk* to the north-west and in Patna, झूसी *jhūsi* in North-East Tirhut, कोढ़ी *korhi* in Patna, छाँछ *chhānchh* in Gayā, बँगन्राह *bangrāh* to the south-west of that district, तिलिया कोढ़ी *tiliya korhi* in South Munger, and अलग्गी *algi* in South Bhagalpur.

CHAPTER XI.—RICHNESS AND POORNESS OF SOIL.

800. बरियार *bariyār* or गहन्रा *gahra,* or in South Munger जैयद *jaiyad,* is the general term used for rich soils. Others are जीगर *jigar* (Patna) and चोखा *chokha* (North-West, Gaya, and South Munger). Poor soils are हलुक *haluk* (North-West Bihār), रुन्नी *runni* (see § 799), तपन्नाह *tapnāh* (North-East Tirhut), and ठस *thas,* अब्बर *abbar* (also in Champāran), or उसठ *usath* south of the Ganges.

CHAPTER XII.—IRRIGATED AND DRY LANDS.

801. Land artificially irrigated is पटौआ *pataua* or पटौई *pataūi* to the west. Other local names are पटौना *patauna* South-East Tirhut, and पटाओल *patāöl* North-East Tirhut and पटहुआँ *patāhuāñ* in Shahabad. In Gaya it is हथन्घिसेट *hathghiset,* and in South-West Shahabad भरैया *bharaiya.* Land irrigated from tanks or ponds is छानन *chhānan* in Sāran and Patna, फोर *phor* in South-West Shahabad, and elsewhere south of the Ganges मेलन्वानी *melwāni* or (South Bhagalpur) मेलानी *melāni.* When irrigated from wells it is मोटन्वाही *motwāhi* to the west. Unirrigated land, or land which does not require irrigation, owing to its being, or its capability of being, flooded is अपन्टा *apta.* If watered after ploughing, it is छिरिकन्नी *chhirikni* to the west, पचौआँ *pachauān* in South-West Shahabad, and पनौला *panaula* in the rest of that district. निपनियाँ *nipaniyān* are in Patna unirrigated crops. In South Munger lands which require irrigation are रूना *rūna,* and there and in Sāran those which produce crops without irrigation are हलन्ही *halhi.*

CHAPTER XIII.—LANDS WHICH RETAIN AND WHICH DO NOT RETAIN MOISTURE.

802. This is the division most common amongst natives themselves. The moisture in land is हाल *hāl.* Land which does not retain it is बाँगर *bāngar,* and that which does is भीठ *bhīth,* or in North Sāran भाठ *bhāth.* Under these divisions come other sub-divisions, such as बलुआ बाँगर *balua bāngar* (which is sandy), मटियार बाँगर *matiyār bāngar* (which is clayey), and so on, and बलुआ भीठ *balua bhīth,* मटियार भीठ *matiyār bhīth,* and so on. Crops on *bāngar* lands cannot be cultivated without irrigation, and the expense of cultivation is therefore greater, but the yield more than compensates the outlay, being a third, and sometimes double the amount of *bhīth* produce. The latter lands are sometimes irrigated and sometimes not.

CHAPTER XIV.—LANDS BEARING A SINGLE AND A DOUBLE CROP.

803. Lands which produce only one crop in the year are एकफसिला *ekphasila* or एकफसिली *ekphasili.* In Champāran they are called एकसलिया *eksaliya.* चौमास *chaumās* lands (also called पलिहर *palihar* to the west) are kept free from crop during the rains, and tilled for the cold weather crop. Lands bearing two crops in the year are दोफसिला *dophasila* or दोफसिली *dophasili,* or in Champāran दोसलिया *dosaliya.* In South Bhagalpur they are दोसाल *dosāl.* Land on which crops are grown all the year round is तिनफसिला *tinphasila.*

CHAPTER XV.—TERMS USED IN CONNECTION WITH DIFFERENT CROPS.

804. The following terms are used in connection with different crops.

805. *Sugar-cane.*—Land prepared for this crop is उखाँव *ukhāñw* or उखाव *ukhāo.* Land constantly ploughed for cane or any other crop from Asārh to Māgh are मघात *maghāt* in South-East Tirhut, मघाड़ or मघार *maghār* in Sāran, Patna, and South Munger, मघड़ा *maghra* in Gaya and the south-west, and मघुआ *maghua* in South Bhagalpur. Land under cane is उखारी *ukhāri* in Shahabad. जठहन *jathhan* in South Munger is land cropped in the previous year with cane.

806. *Cereals.*—हरजिन्सा *harjinsa* are those lands which grow all crops except transplanted rice.

807. *Garden crops.*—Land suited for growing garden crops is कोरार *korār* in Patna and to the west and कोरियार *koriyār* in Patna and Gaya. Other names are कोराँट *korānt* (South Tirhut), कैरियार *kairiyār* (Shahabad), बारी *bāri* in Tirhut, and लतिहानी *latihāni* in South Munger. These names apply rather to the use to which the land is put than to the kind of soil, most of them being connected with the word कोइरी *koïri*, which is the name of a well-known caste of garden cultivators.

808. *Cotton.*—In Shahabad the following kinds of land are suited for the various kinds of cotton:—

Cotton.	Land.
(1) रढ़िया *rarhiya*	करैल *karail.*
(2) बँड़छा *banrchha*	कोड़ार *korār.*
(3) होवन्ती *hewti*	बरियार *bariyār.*
(4) मनवाँ *manwān*	नदवाँसी *nadwāñsi.*

809. *Pulses.*—Land under gram is called चैता *chaita* in South Bhagalpur.

810. *Maizes, millets, &c.*—Land under these crops is दोतुरा *dotura* north of the Ganges. The word means properly land in which both a rainy season and a cold weather crop can be sown.

811. *Spring crops.*—Light friable soil suitable for these crops is called भीठ *bhīth* or भीठा *bhītha*, also in Gaya भिठारा *bhithāra*. See, however, § 802.

812. *Rice.*—Rice land is धनहर *dhanhar*. In Gaya it is called धन कियारी *dhan kiyāri*, and in South-West Shahabad धनखर *dhankhar*.

813. *Land under trees, brushwood, &c.*—Forests are बन *ban* or जङ्गल *jangal*. A grove is बगैचा *bagaicha* or गाछी *gāchhi*. बाग *bāg* is a garden, and बगिया *bagiya* an orchard. फुलवारी *phulwāri* is an orchard, enclosed, irrigated, and stocked with fruit-trees. A खाने बाग *khāne bāg* in Champāran and Patna or नजर बाग *najar bāg* in Gaya and Shahabad is a grove attached to a shrine or other building, and growing flowers as well as fruit.

814. A mango grove is आम के बगैचा *ām ke bagaicha*, or in Tirhut गाछी *gāchhi*; a clump of bamboos is बाँस के कोठी *bāns ke kothi* in the north-west, बँसवारी *banswāri* north of the Ganges generally, and बाँसक बीठ *bānsak bīth* in North-East Tirhut. In Patna it is बसेड़ *baser*, in South-West Shahabad बँसवार *banswār*, and elsewhere south of the Ganges बसाड़ *basār*. In South Bhagalpur it is also called बीटो *bīto*, and

in Tirhut ओध *odh*. A young grove of fruit-trees is गछुली *gachhuli* north of the Ganges, also नौराही *naurāhi* in Champāran, नरोइ *naroï* in Champāran and Tirhut, and लब गछुली *lab gachhuli* or नव गछुली *naw gachhuli* in Tirhut. Another name is नव पेड़ा *naw pera*. South of the Ganges it is लौगाछी *laugāchhi* to the south-east, केड़वारी *kerwāri* in Shahabad, नरोईं *naroïn* in Patna and South Munger, and नौकेड़ा बगैचा *naukera bagaicha* in Gaya. A belt of trees on either side of a road is पाँती *pānti* or पँतियारी *pantiyāri*, and also लखराँव *lakhrānw* to the west and पाँता *pānta* in Tirhut.

815. Land producing brushwood is झारा *jhāra* (Sāran and Patna) or बन छिहुली *ban chhihuli* (South-West Shahabad). Brushwood is झार *jhār*, झरहा *jharha*, or to the north-west and in Patna and South Munger झूर *jhūr*. Small stunted brushwood is झखुली *jhakhuli* or झखुरी *jhakhuri* north of the Ganges and in Patna, रौंजी *raunjï* in Patna, and झरकन्टी *jharkanti* in South-West Shahabad. Land producing tall thatching-grass is खढ़ौर *kharhaur* or खढ़ौल *kharhaul*, or south of the Ganges खरहूर *kharáhur*. Other names are मुजवानी *mujwāni*, कँड़वानी *kanrwāni* in the north-west, and मुँजवान *munjwān* in Shahabad. In South Munger it is खरैठा *kharaitha*. The principal of these grasses are पटेर *pater*, खर *khar* or खरई *kharaī*, रारी *rāri*, डाभी *dābhi*, इक्कर *ikkar* or इकरी *ikri*, मूँज *mūnj* or झलास *jhalās*. Of the last, मूँज *mūnj* is properly the bark used for making string, झलास *jhalās* the leaves used for making rough thatches, काँड़ा *kāñra* the stout lower part of the stalk used for roof-thatching, and सिरकी *sirki* the upper or reed part used for making sieves and mats. Reeds are नरकट *narkat*, and the land producing them is नरकान *narkān* in Champāran.

CHAPTER XVI.—LAND IMPREGNATED WITH SALT, &c.

816. Land impregnated with impure carbonate of soda रेह (*reh*) is ऊसर *ūsar* or उस्सर *ussar*. Other names are रेहाह *rehāh* or रेहाड़ *rehār* (East Tirhut) and रेहड़ा *rehra* (Pātna, Gaya, and South Munger). खारी *khāri* or (South Bhagalpur) खरवा *kharwa* is land impregnated with sulphate of soda. नोनी *noni* south of the Ganges is land impregnated with common salt. Other names are नोनियाह *noniyāh*, नोनियारी *noniyāri*, and नोनछराह *nonchharāh*. In South-West Shahabad चाँप *chāmp*, and in the rest of the district चाँदिल *chāndil*, is ऊसर *ūsar* land, in which spots of good ground are scattered.

DIVISION IV.

GENERAL AGRICULTURAL OPERATIONS.

SUBDIVISION I.

PLOUGHING AND HARROWING.

CHAPTER I.—PLOUGHING AND HARROWING.

817. To plough is हर जोतब *har jotab*, हर बहब *har bahab*, or हर चलाएब *har chalāēb*. हर नाधब *har nādhab* is properly to yoke the oxen to the plough (also called लरनी *larni* in Champāran and South-East Tirhut). Other expressions for ploughing are सिराउर के धरल *sirāur ke dharal* or सरिया के जोतल *sariya ke jotal* in Champāran, पैस धरब *pais dharab* (or पुइस धरब *puïs dharab* in North-East Tirhut) in Champāran and Tirhut, and दहिन धरेआव *dahin dhareāo* in Champāran and South-East Tirhut. One ploughing is चास *chās*, and in Gaya and to the west also बाँह *bāñh*: thus, एक बाँह *ek bāñh* the first ploughing, दो बाँह *do bāñh* the second ploughing, and so on.

818. The first ploughing is called पहिल चास *pahil chās* or फरनी *pharni.* In Gaya and Champāran it is फारन *phāran*. Lands sown after a single ploughing are भोकौआ *bhokaua* in the north-west and जोता बावग *jota bāwag* in Champāran and Tirhut. मघाड़ जोतब *maghār jotab* is north of the Ganges and in Patna and Gaya the ploughing in the month of Māgh (January–February) of lands intended to be sown at the next rainy season. In East Tirhut and Champāran this is also called चौमाँस जोतब *chaumāns jotab*. In Gaya and Champāran it is also मघड़ा चास *maghra chās*, in Shahabad मघवट *maghwat*, and in the south-west of that district कुलहर *kulhar*. In South Bhagalpur it is माघी चास *māghi chās*, and in South Munger मघाड़ *maghār*. The field which is thus ploughed is बिड़ार *birār* to the west and south and पह *pah* also south of the Ganges and in Champāran. North of the Ganges it is called चौमाँस *chaumāns*.

819. The second ploughing is दोखार or दोखाड़ *dokhār*. In Gaya and Champāran it is also called पुरन्वे *puruve*. Other names are सोमन्रा *somra* to the north-west and समार *samār* in North-East Tirhut, दोहार *dohār* in Champāran and North-West Tirhut, and दोहन्रावन *dohrāwan* in South-West Shahabad; and the same names are also applied to the field so ploughed. In the south-east the second ploughing is called चास *chās*, दोखार *dokhār* being the third ploughing.

820. The third ploughing is तेखार *tekhār* and also (in Champāran) तेखन्रा *tekhra*. To the west it is also तेहन्रावन *tehrāwan*. In the south-east it is दोखार *dokhār*. The same terms are used for the land so ploughed.

821. The fourth ploughing is in East Tirhut and Gaya चौखार *chaukhār*, and in Shahabad, Gaya, and South Bhagalpur चरन्चसी *charchasi*. Elsewhere it is चार चास *chār chās*; so also the land so ploughed.

822. The fifth ploughing is पान्न्चास *pānchās*.

823. The phrase used for successive ploughing is एक चास *ek chās*, दू चास *du chās*, and so on. Theoretically there is no limit to the number of ploughings required for some crops, as is shown in the following rhyme current in Gaya:—

सौ चास गण्डा,	*Sau chās ganda,*
पचास चास मण्डा,	*Pachās chās manda,*
तेकर आधा मोरी	*Tekar ādha mori,*
तेकर आधा तोरी	*Tekar ādha tori.*

—A hundred ploughings for cane, fifty for wheat, half that (25) for rice, and half that (12½) for oilseeds.

824. The ploughing of millets, when they are about a foot high, is बिदाह *bidāh*, a local variant being बिदहन्नी *bidahni* in Champāran, West Tirhut, Patna, and the south-east. In Gaya and Champāran it is कोड़न *koran*, and in South Munger, when hoeing is substituted for ploughing, it is कोड़न्नी *korni*. When a rice-field is flooded and then ploughed to kill the weeds, the process is called लेव *leo* in the north-west, लेवा *lewa* in Gaya, and कादो *kādo* or कद्न्वा *kadwa* to the north-west and in Tirhut. In North-West Tirhut it is called मसाह *masāh*.

825. In Sāran and Champāran ploughing with a plough of which the block is new and full-sized is नवन्ठा के जोत *nawtha ke jot*, and

with one which has a small worn block खिनौरी के जोत *khinauri ke jot*. In Tirhut and also in Champāran the corresponding words are respectively लवन्ठा के जोत *lawtha ke jot* and ठेंठा के जोत *thentha ke jot*, and in Shahabad नवहरा *nawahra* and खुँटेहरा *khuntehra*.

826. In rice cultivation, after sowing, the field is lightly reploughed to clear the weeds and cover the seed. This is called उनाह *unāh* to the north-west and in North-West Tirhut, गजर *gajar* in the North-East Tirhut, and समार *samār* in Champāran and South-East Tirhut. In Patna it is समाह *samāh*, in Gaya बिराह *birāh*, to the west and in Patna and Gaya बिदाह *bidāh*, and in Champāran and to the south-east बिदहनी *bidahni*.

827. The small pieces of the field which the plough has not touched are पैस *pais* in Champāran and South-West Tirhut and पुइस *puïs* in North-East Tirhut. In North-West and South-East Tirhut and in Champāran they are दहिना *dahina*, and in Sāran and Champāran छूटल खेत *chhūtal khet*.

828. Cross-ploughing is आरा *āra*, or in Champāran and South Bhagalpur आर *ār*, and in South-East Tirhut समार *samār*. When a field is ploughed round and round in constantly diminishing circuits, it is called चौकेठा *chauketha* or (in Patna) चौएठा *chauetha*, आरी चास *āri chās* in Gaya, चौबगली *chaubagli* in Champāran and Gaya, and चौगठिया *chaugathiya* or चौक *chauk* to the west. In Sāran and Champāran it is चौगेठ *chaugeth*, in South Munger भौँरिया *bhaunrïya*, and in North-West Tirhut चौकेर *chauker*. The centre plot in the middle, round which the bullocks have no room to turn, is called बदहार *badhār*, and this is furrowed by taking the plough across it diagonally from corner to corner. Ploughing from corner to corner is कोनिया जोत *koniya jot* or कोन *kon*, also कोनसी *konsi* in South Munger, कोनसिया *konasiya* in Champāran and South-West Tirhut, कोनी *koni* in Gaya, and कोना कोनी *kona koni* to the west. When a crookedly-shaped field has to be ploughed, it is called ऊना ड्योढ़ी जोत *ūna dyorhi jot* in Sāran and Patna and ऊनाडेढ़ी जोत *ūna derhi jot* in Champāran. When a rectangular field is ploughed straight along its length or breadth, the ploughing is called सोझौआ जोत *sojhaua jot*. Other names current are ठढ़ाईं *tharhāiṅ* in Patna and Champāran and ठढ़िया *tharhiya* to the west. Ploughing breadthways is फानी *phāni* in Sāran and North-West Tirhut, फटकी *phatki* in Champāran and the south-east, ऊना फानी *ūna phāni* in Patna, and फँदिया *phandiya* in South-West Shahabad.

829. The following rule is current in North-East Bihār as to ploughing and harrowing:—

थोर जोतिहऽ बहुत हेँगइहऽ, ऊँच कै बँधिहऽ आर ।
उपजे तऽ उपजे नाहीं तऽ घाघे दीहऽ गार ॥
Thor jotiha bahut hengaïha, ūnch ke bandhiha ār,
Upje ta upje nāhīn, ta Ghāghe dīha gār.

—Plough little, harrow much, and have your field boundaries high. If what should come does not then do so, you can abuse Ghāgh (who gives you this advice).

830. A harrow is हेँगा *henga*, &c., as described in § 30 and ff. To harrow is हेँगाएब *hengāëb*, हेँगा चलाएब *henga chalāëb*, or चौकी घुमाएब *chauki ghumāëb*. The act of harrowing is in Gaya पालट *pālat*.

831. The oxen attached to a harrow have various names. The one on the left-hand side is called पँचौट *panchaut* or कुड़दहिना *kurdahina*, and the one next to him हथौआ *hathaua*. The right-hand ox is फेरा *phera*, or in South Munger भसनी *bhasni*.

CHAPTER II.—FIELDS.

832. A field is खेत *khet*. Other names also current are टोपरी *topri* and पारी *pāri* south of the Ganges, टोपरा *topra* to the west, and डाबर *dābar* in Champāran and Gaya. In South Bhagalpur the words बारी *bāri* and बहियार *bahiyār* are used. Beds made in a field to facilitate irrigation and for other purposes are कियारी *kiyāri*, and also in Champāran घड़ारी *gharāri*, in Patna and to the south-east गँड़ारी *ganrāri*, and in Gaya गेँड़ारी *genrāri*. Similar beds in a sugar-cane field are called हाता वाला *hāta wāla* to the north-west and in Gaya and North-West Tirhut, and झोर *jhor* or झोरा *jhora* south of the Ganges. In the north-west झोरा *jhora* is a large bed, and so also are पहटा *pahta* in Gaya, Sāran, and Champāran, परिया *pariya* in South-West Tirhut, दवन *dawan* in Champāran and North-West Tirhut, and कियारा *kiyāra* or भेर *bher* in East Tirhut. The raised banks between the irrigation beds are मेँड़ *menr* in the north-west and आर *ār* in Tirhut. In Shahabad, Patna, and Gaya they are करहा *karha*, and in Patna and Gaya पँरगा *panrga*, in South Bhagalpur पलङ्गा *palanga*, and in South Munger दौग *daug*. North of the Ganges a plot marked off by a boundary is हाता वाला *hāta wāla* in the north-west and South Munger and छरकी बाला *chharki bāla* in East Tirhut. The small patch

of ground adjoining a house is कोला *kola*, कोली *koli*, or कोलवाइ *kolwāi* to the north-west, and बारी *bāri* in Champāran and Tirhut. कोला *kola* also obtains in Shahabad and the south-east. In Sāran and Patna it is खण्ड *khand* or खँड़ *khanr* (which properly means a ruined house), and in Gaya घेवारी *ghewāri*. Other optional names are गल्ली *galli* in South Bhagalpur and कोनासी *konāsi* in Shahabad. When the fields of one proprietor's share are scattered over a village, each is called तखता *takhta* or कित्ता *kitta*. The whole cultivation of such a proprietor is called खेती बारी *kheti bāri* to the west and in Tirhut; also खेत बधार *khet badhār* in Shahabad and Patna, and खेत पथार *khet pathār* in Champāran and South Munger. In Patna and Gaya खन्ध *khandh*, खन्धा *khandha*, कित्ता *kitta* or किता *kita*, is a large area of cultivated land. A division of this is खँधौट *khandhaut*, which is again divided into fields.

CHAPTER III.—BOUNDARIES.

833. The low ridge which forms the boundary of a field is everywhere आर *ār*, आरि or आरी *āri*, as in the proverb आरि जाइ तऽ कपार लाठी, बीच बङ्गा चरवाही, *āri jāi ta kapār lāthi, bīch banga charwāhi*, —if you go on a field boundary have a stick (to protect) your head, (and then) you may graze your cattle in the midst of a cotton-field. North of the Ganges it is also called डँड़ेड़ *danrer*. Other names are अहरी *ahri* (see § 919), अलङ्ग *alang*, or परांठ *parānth* in Patna, Gaya, and the south-west; पँरगा *panrga*, गँड़ारी *ganrāri*, आइल *āil*, or आल *āl* in Gaya and South Munger, and डाँड़ *dānr* in South-West Shahabad. A ditch boundary is खई *khaī*, खाइ *khāi*, खत्ता *khatta*, or खावाँ *khāwān*. Another name is खन्ता *khanta* in South Bhagalpur. In Gaya district डोभरा *dobhra* is a small ditch. An embankment used as a boundary is अहरा *ahra* (see § 919) or बाँध *bāndh*. Other names are भरबन *bharban* (Champāran), धूर *dhūr* (North Tirhut), and छरकी *chharki* (South-East Tirhut). A place where three boundaries meet is तिनकोनिया *tinkoniya*, and where four meet चौमुख *chaumukh*, चौबटिया *chaubatiya*, or चौराहा *chaurāha*. In Champāran and South-East Tirhut it is also चौपड़ *chaupar*.

834. The rural Bihari lays great stress on the importance of keeping these boundary embankments in order. Thus, there is a proverb ठारिक चुकल बानर ; आरिक चुकल किसान *thārik chukal bānar, ārik chukal kisān*,—a cultivator who neglects to look after his boundary embankments becomes like a monkey fallen from a branch. Another

proverb which may be noted here is खेत भासे, आरि कोड़ो *khet bhāse āri kori*,—the field is flooded, cut the boundary embankments, *i.e.*, passion must have its vent.

CHAPTER IV.—FURROWS.

835. A furrow is हराइ *harāi* to the west. In Champāran and Tirhut it is सिराउर *sirāur*, in Patna सिरोर *siror*, and elsewhere सिरौर *siraur*. In Gaya another name is सेवात *sewāt*. झँझिया *jhanjhiya* or धारी *dhāri* in Gaya and Sāran, and घइ *ghai* in Patna and South-East Tirhut, are the deep furrows in a field in which extra crops are grown, especially those at the edge of the field, or running from corner to corner.

836. The deep furrow used as an irrigation channel is आरा *āra* in the north-west, पैन *pain* or पैनि *paini* generally, डौंगर *daungar* in South Tirhut, Patna, and Gaya, नारी *nāri* or करहा *karha* to the west and in Patna and Gaya, भीता *bhīta* in East Tirhut, and दौग *daug* in Patna and to the south-east.

CHAPTER V.—MISCELLANEOUS TERMS USED IN CONNECTION WITH PLOUGHING.

837. To the west साँझ ले *sānjh le*, संझिया *sanjhiya*, and संझहरिया *sanjhariya* mean 'up to evening,' or 'at evening' and hence are used as adjectives with the word जोत *jot* to signify as much land as can be ploughed in a day. In Champāran and South Munger this is सगरदिना *sagardina*, and in Patna ठकहरिया *thakhariya*. The area ploughed in half a day is called दोपहरिया *dopahariya*.

838. The portion of land included in a plough circuit is आँतर *āntar*, and also to the north-west and in North-East Tirhut हट्ठा *hattha*, and to commence another circuit is दोसर आँतर धरब *dosar āntar dharab*. The place where ploughing is going on is हरवाही *harwāhi* in Patna and north of the Ganges. In Shahabad it is हरवाँही *harwānhi*. In Patna it is टोपरा *topra*, and generally हराठा *harātha*.

839. The first ploughing of the season is हरमहुतर *harmahutar* in Sāran and हरमोहतर *harmohtar* in Patna and Gaya. It is also समहुत *samhut*, and to the north सिरपँचमी *sirpanchmi* or सिरपचइ *sirpachai*, both the last two terms being derived from the festival of the *sri* *panchamī*. In South Munger it is हर महन्तर *har mahantar* or हर समत *har samat*, and in South Bhagalpur सोमाता *somāta*. Another name current in Sāran is हर॰वत *harwat*.

840. The bringing home the plough on the back of a bullock or with the share over the shoulder is हर॰खुली *harkhuli*, हर॰खोलिया *harkholiya*, or हर॰खूजल *harkhūjal*, and in South-East Tirhut (optionally) हर॰खुगानी *harkhugāni*. In South-West Shahabad it is हर॰छुटाव *harchhutāo*, and in the rest of the district and in Gaya हर॰छुट्टन *harchhuttan*. In Patna it is हर॰बिनार *harbinār* or हर॰जोआर *harjoār*, in South Munger and Champāran हर॰खोलानी *harkholāni*, and in Gaya, Champāran, and the South-East हर॰खोली *harkholi*.

841. The bullocks which draw a plough or harrow are called बरद *barad*, and to the west. also बैल *bail*. When it is wished to distinguish them specially from cart-bullocks, they are called in Champāran and Tirhut हट्ठा बरद *hattha barad*, and to the north-west and in Gaya हरेआ बैल *harea bail*. A lazy fat plough bullock, which sits down rather than work, is called कोढ़ि *korhi* or परुआ *parua*, as in the proverb कोढ़ि बरद केँ फेफरि बहुत *korhi barad keñ phephari bahut*,—it's the lazy bullock that puffs and blows.

CHAPTER VI.—PLOUGHMEN AND AGRICULTURAL LABOURERS GENERALLY.

842. A ploughman is हर॰वाहा *harwāha*, and to the west also हर॰वाह *harwāh*. In East Tirhut he is also called हरौरी *harauri*. His wages are called हर॰वाही *harwāhi*. An agricultural servant in general is मजूरा *majūra* or बनिहार *banihār*. An agricultural servant engaged for the whole year is हड़॰वर *harwar* in Sāran and भर॰सलिया *bharsaliya* in North-East Tirhut, and one for the whole day is भर॰दीना *bhardīna*. A ploughman who works for half a day is दुपहरिया *dupahariya* or दोपहरिया *dopahariya*, or in North-West Tirhut पहर॰वार *paharwār*. One who works on advances is अग॰वड़ or अग॰वढ़ जन *agwar* (or *agwarh*) *jan* to the north-west, कमाइ *kamāi* to the west, कमियई *kamiyaī* or कमियाँ *kamiyān* in Patna, Gaya, and South Munger, and लगुआ जन *lagua jan* generally. The last is usually the man who binds himself to work off a debt incurred. When a ploughman receives the use of a plough for one day in three instead of wages in cash or kind, he is called अँग॰वरिया *angwariya* or अग॰वरिया *agwariya*, and to the west अँग॰वार *angwār*. In Sāran and Champaran he is also called टेपन्टा *tepta* (so also in North-East Tirhut), or तिसन्री *tisri* or तिसरिया *tisariya*. In East Tirhut a ploughman who works without advances is called उट्ठा *uttha*, as distinguished from हरन्वाहा *harwāha* or हरौरी *harauri*, who does take them.

843. In North-East Tirhut पट *pat* or साटी पाटी *sāti pāti* is the custom of a plough-owner employing two ploughmen for each plough, each ploughman relieving the other at intervals of eight days. In Shahabad and Patna हराइ *harāï* is the custom under which every tenant lends his plough and bullocks to the landlord for two days in the year.

844. An agricultural labourer paid in kind is जन *jan*, also in Gaya and Champāran उफँगिया *uphangiya*, and in South-West Shahabad बनी *bani*. One who receives money is नोकर *nokar*, or in the north-west जाना *jāna*. One paid solely in cash is called कोरञ्जा *koranja* to the north-west. In Patna, Gaya, and South Munger the prœdial slaves who are attached to an estate, and cannot leave it, or marry, or in fact do anything without the consent of their landlords, are called नफर *naphar* or कमियाँ *kamiyān*; and food given to such is खैहन *khaihan*. A labourer who by custom works a certain number of days for nothing for Government (formerly, and for the landlord nowadays) is called बेगार *begār*. Payments made in kind to agricultural labourers are called बन *ban*, or in East Tirhut बोन *bon*. Advances to ploughmen are अगन्वड़ *agwar* in the west and अगौरी *agauri* in South-West Tirhut. Elsewhere in Tirhut and to the north-west they are called हड़ौड़ी *harauri*, and generally लगुआ *lagua*.

845. When there are spare bullocks in a field where ploughing is going on to relieve those that get tired, the boy who looks after them is called अनन्वाह *anwāh* in East Tirhut; elsewhere he is चरन्वाहा *charwāha* or गोरन्खिया *gorkhiya*.

CHAPTER VII.—RECIPROCAL ASSISTANCE IN CULTIVATION.

846. बदन्लैया *badlaiya* and पलन्टा *palta* or पलन्टी *palti* are terms for exchange of labour for labour by agriculturists. To the west it is also called पैँच *painch*, in Gaya बदन्ली *badli*, and to the south generally पाएठ *pāëth*. In East Tirhut another name is जनन्पैँचा *janpaincha*. The practice of two or more cultivators joining their ploughs and ploughing together, first the field of one and then the field of another, is called generally भाँज *bhānj*. Other names are भँजहरिया *bhanjhariya* and हर सझा *har sajjha* to the west generally भजौती *bhanjauti* in North-East Tirhut, हर भञ्जा *har bhanja* in Patna and to the north, हर पहटा *har pahta* in Champāran and Gaya, भँजेठ *bhanjeth* in South-East Bihār, and भाँजो *bhānjo* in South Bhagalpur. The cultivator in this case is भाँजा वाला *bhānjā wāla*, or in Tirhut भँजैत *bhanjait*. Another name current to the west is अँगवारा *angwāra*, though this properly refers to the custom of paying ploughmen (अँगवरिया *angwariya*, *see* last chapter) by lending them a plough and cattle one day in three.

847. The work which one cultivator does for another in this way is called to the west सापट *sāpat*.

SUBDIVISION II.

MANURING.

CHAPTER I.—KINDS OF MANURE.

848. Manure is north of the Ganges खादर *khādar*, खदौड़ *khadaur*, खद्धी *khaddhi*, or गोंदौरा *gondaura* to the west, and गोआ *goa* or करसी *karsi* to the east. South of the Ganges, to the west, it is घूर *ghūr*, and to the east (also in Sāran) गनौरा *ganaura* or गँदौरा *gandaura*. कूड़ा *kūra*, कूड़ा कुरकुट *kūra kurkut*, बहारन *bahāran*, or (in South-East Tirhut) गोनरौर *gonraur*, is rubbish or road-sweepings. Cowdung is गोबर *gobar*. When dried it is called south of the Ganges दमारा *damāra*, of which a variant in East Tirhut is दमार *damār*, also in Shahabad and Patna कण्डा *kanda*, and to the west कँड़रा *kanrra*. The latter term is also used in Sāran. In North-East Tirhut it is गौंठि *gauthi*, and in Champāran गौठी *gauthi*. In Gaya फेंटी *phenti* are pieces of dried cowdung. चोत *chot* to the west is the quantity that falls from an animal at one evacuation. Cattle urine is गौंत *gaunt* or गौत *gaut*, and to the west also मूत *mūt*. लीद *līd*, लिद्दी *liddi*, or लीदी *līdi* is the dung of horses, elephants, &c., and that of sheep or goats is भेंड़ाड़ी *bhenrāri*, भेनाड़ी *bhenāri*, or (to the west) लेंड़ी *lenri*. Other filth of various kinds is मैला *maila*, or in South Bhagalpur घिना *ghina*. The refuse of indigo after maceration used as manure is सीठ *sith*.

849. A manure heap near a house is ढेरी *dheri*, or (in East Tirhut) गोनर *gonar.** North of the Ganges generally it is also मान *mān*. A manure-pit is घूर *ghūr*, खाद *khād*, or खादर के गड़हा *khādar ke garha*. A heap of dried grass, sweepings, dung, &c., is in North-East Tirhut and Shahabad कूर *kūr*. Ashes are राख *rākh* or छाउर *chhāūr*, and in South Bhagalpur छौरो *chhauro*. In Patna and Gaya they are बानी *bāni*. An ash-heap is in North-East Tirhut छौराठ *chhaurāth*.

CHAPTER II.—MODES OF MANURING.

850. Heavily-manured land is north of the Ganges खदौड़ खेत *khadaur khet*, or it is called गोबराएल *gobrāēl*, or in South-East Tirhut भरल *bharal*. South of the Ganges it is खदौर *khadaur*, खदगौर *khadgaur*, or खरित *kharit* in Shahabad.

851. The custom of allowing cattle to stand in a field for the purpose of manuring it is called north of the Ganges भेंड़ी बैसाओल *bhenri baisāōl* or भेंड़ी हिराओल *bhenri hirāōl;* south of the Ganges it is जिवगर होए ला धूर बैसाओल *jivgar hoë la dhūr baisāōl*, and in South Munger they say खेत गोबराबे हें *khet gobrābe heñ*.

CHAPTER III.—MANURE USED AS FUEL.

852. Manure collected in the forests and grazing-grounds and dried for fuel is called north of the Ganges कँड़ड़ा *kanrra* or कड़ड़ा *karra*. South of the Ganges it is डमारा *damāra* or कण्डा *kanda*. In East Tirhut it is डमार *damār*, and to the west it is also called बिनुआ गोइठा *binua goïtha*. Another general name is बन गोइठा *ban goïtha*. When made up into cakes with chaff and other refuse, the large oblong blocks are called गोहरा *gohra* to the west and गोरहा *gorha* in Champāran and to the east. The next sized round cakes which are stuck on the wall to dry are गोंइठा *goïntha* or गोइठा *goïtha*. The smallest cakes are चिपरी *chipri*. The largest-sized slabs made with both hands are दोहथा *dohtha* or सोहथी *sohthi*. करसी *karsi*, or in Gaya and South Munger अमारी *amāri*,

---

* Compare for an example of this word the proverb गोआरक गोनर दुहु दिस चिक्कन *goārak gonar duhu dis chikkan*,—a gowāla's dunghill is neat on both sides.

are unmanufactured lumps of dry cowdung dried and stored.

853. The pile of cowdung fuel is called to the west गोहरौर *gohraur* or गोहरौरा *gohraura.* In North-East Tirhut it is गोठौर *gothaur,* in Champāran गोठौला *gothāula,* and there and in Tirhut टाल *tāl.* It is छूआ *chhūa* optionally to the west, छूहा *chhūha* or छूही *chhūhi* in Patna and Gaya छुआ छन्ना *chhua chhanna* in South Munger, and छानी *chhāni* in South Bhagalpur. The pile of the large oblong blocks is also called गोहरा *gohra* or गोरहा *gorha* as above. The house in which the fuel is stored is गोठौर *gothaur,* गोठौरा *gothaura,* or गोठौल *gothaul* generally; also गोठुल *gothul* in North-East Tirhut, गोठहुल *gothāhul* in Shahabad, and गोइठा घर *goïtha ghar* in Gaya. The operation of making the cakes is पाथब *pāthab* or पाथल *pāthal,* according to locality, or else ठोकब *thokab* or ठोकल *thokal.* The place where they are made is north of the Ganges generally पथारी *pathāri.* South of the Ganges it is पथरौर *pathraur* in the west, आड़ा *āra* in Gaya, and पाँड़र *pānrar* in Patna.

854. In selling cowdung fuel a पन *pan* equals 20, 22, or 23 गण्डा *ganda* (*i.e.* fours), according to locality. In buying the article in Patna the seller gives two cakes extra (called a पनकी *panki*) for every पन *pan* bought.

SUBDIVISION III.

SOWING AND TRANSPLANTING.

CHAPTER I.—SOWING.

855. *Sowing* is to the west बोआनी *boāni,* and to the east बावग *bāwag,* बाओग *bāög,* or बाउग *bāüg.* South of the Ganges, and also in Champāran, it is also बोआइ *boāi,* or in Patna and South Munger बोनी *boni.* In South Bhagalpur (and also in Champāran) the word is बोअनी *boani.* To sow is north of the Ganges, बोआल *boāl,* बावग करब *bāwag karab,* बूनब *būnab,* or बूनल *būnal,* according to locality. To scatter the seed is generally छिटब *chhitab* or छींटब *chhīntab.* In Patna चुलाएब *chulāëb* is also used in connection with *Bhadoï* or autumn crops.

856. *Seed* is बीया *bīya* or बीहन *bīhan.* In Gaya it is बिहनाइ *bihnāi* (also used in Champāran), बिछा *bichcha,* or गोटा *gota,* and in South Bhagalpur बिनहाइ *binhāi.* A grain of seed is दाना *dāna.*

Barren seeds are अब्बी *abbi* (or in Shahabad) अवई *awai*, and fertile seeds are सुग्गी *suggi*.

CHAPTER II.—MODES OF SOWING.

857. The following are the modes of sowing:—

(*a*) *Furrow sowing.*—धारी *dhāri* or धरिया *dhariya*. To plough in this way is धारी लगाएब *dhāri lagāëb* or धरियाएब *dhariyāëb*. South of the Ganges this method is called चुटकी *chutki*. In this method a plough goes in advance of the sower, who carries the seed in a basket. He drops it into the furrow as soon as the latter becomes visible. By this method the seed is sown deep, the stalk is stronger, and not so liable to be laid by high winds. भठाएब *bhathāëb*, दोधरिया *dodhariya*, दोहार *dohār*, or समार *samār* is the practice of filling up with soil the furrow in which the seed has been sown, by ploughing a separate furrow beside it. This is generally done in the case of *Bhadoï* crops. Sugar-cane is not covered in this way in Bihār, but by hand. The long straight lines of seed across a field are known as धारी *dhāri* or पाँती *pānti*. When the ploughing is done round a field, and not across, it is called चौकेठा *chauketha*, &c. (See § 828).

(*b*) *Sowing by drill.*—This is टार *tār*, टारी *tāri*, टोर *tor*, टोरी *tori*, often spelt टाँर, टाँड़ *tāṅr*, टोँर, टोँड़ *toṅr*, &c. To sow in this way is टारब *tārab* or टोर लगाएब *tor lagāëb*. The man who works the drill-plough is टरवाह *tarwāh* or टोरवाह *torwāh*.

(*c*) *Broadcast sowing.*—This is generally बावग *bāwag* or its variants,—*see* above. Other names are छिटा *chhitta* or छिटुआ *chhitua* north of the Ganges, and छींटा *chhīnta* south of it. Maize and similar crops are sometimes sown broadcast on land left soft after an inundation, and are then pressed into the mud by hand. This method of sowing is called डोभा *dobha*, and to sow thus is डोभब *dobhab*.

858. If the seed is sown on lands which have not been ploughed, it is called छिट्टा *chhitta*, छिट्टुआ *chhitua*, or south of the Ganges जँगल्ली बावर *jangli bāwag*, पैरा *paira* (Gaya, also in Champāran), or पाएर *pāër* or समार *samār* (Patna and South Munger). छींटा *chhīntā* or छिट्टा *chhitta* is also used to signify lands in which the seed has been scattered after a single ploughing. It is also specially used for sowing the spring (रबी *rabī*) crops on the दोफसिला *dophasila* lands, *i.e.*, those from which the autumn crop has just been cut, as contrasted with the पलिहर *palihar* or चौमास *chaumās*, which are carefully-prepared fallow lands for wheat and similar crops. The sowing of the early rice in dry lands is खरहर बावग *kharhar bāwag*. North of the Ganges it is also धुरिया बावग *dhuriya bāwag*. South of the Ganges it is in Shahabad and Patna ठर्रा *tharra*, in the rest of the district खरवाह *kharwāh*, in Gaya खरवेह *kharweh* or खरवे *kharwe*, in Patna बौघा *baugha*, and in South Munger धुरघुस्सा *dhurghussa*. In Patna and Gaya sowing in a wet field is called लेवा *lewa*. Sowing wide apart is generally पातर *pātar*. Other names are (north of the Ganges) फकाह *phakāh* or फाँफर *phānphar* to the west and छेहर *chhehar* or पेरमार *permār* generally. South of the Ganges we find पाथर *pāthar* in Gaya, पतला *patla* in South Munger, and पतील *patīl* in South Bhagalpur, the last two being also met with in Champāran. Sowing thick is generally घन *ghan*, गाढ़ *gārh*, or गाढ़ा *gārha*. North of the Ganges सजोर *sajor* is used in the same sense.

859. Grain that fails to germinate is अब्बी *abbi*, निरबीज *nirbīj*, बिजमार *bijmār*, or बीया मार *bīya mār*. In South-West Shahabad it is बरुआ *barua*. If a man wishes to say that his seeds have not come up, he says हम्मर बिहनाइ मारल गेल *hammar bihnāi māral gel*.

860. When from excess of rain followed by heat a crust is formed on the surface, which prevents the young plant from coming up, it is called to the west सपट जाइल *sapat jāīl* or सपटा जाइल *sapta jāīl*. In East Tirhut and Shahabad it is called पपरी *papri*. South of the Ganges it is तावा *tāwa* to the south-west of Shahabad, or सेवठा *sewtha* in the rest of the district and in Patna. Elsewhere it is सेवटा *sewta* or मुन्दा *munda*.

861. *Self-sown seed.*—Seed which falls on the ground in the field at harvest time, and which germinates next year, is called लमेरा *lamera* in the west, नम्हेरो *namhero* in South Bhagalpur, and नम्हेर *namher*, लम्हेर *lamher*, or लाम *lām* in South Munger.

CHAPTER III.—SEED-BEDS AND NURSERIES.

862. A nursery for rice is बिड़ार *birār* or बियार *biyār*. To the west it is also बेँगा *benga*. The young plants which are transplanted from the nursery are generally बीया *bīya* or गाछी *gāchhi*. They are also called बीहन *bīhan* or बीहनाइ *bihnāi*. South of the Ganges and to the north-west (when of rice) they are also called मोरी *mōrī*, and in Champāran जरई *jaraī*. The bundles of rice seedlings ready for transplanting are आँटी *ānti* or अँटिया *antiya*.

CHAPTER IV.—SOWING TIME.

863. The sowing season is बोआनी *boāni* north of the Ganges and बोगन्हा *bogha* south of it. It is also generally called बावग *bāwag*.

CHAPTER V.—TRANSPLANTING.

864. To transplant is रोपब *ropab*. In Gaya when a man has finished transplanting he says हमार बनुसार भेल *hammar banusār bhel*,—'I have finished transplanting,' the quantity of rice seedlings transplanted at one place being called everywhere except in the south-east बान *bān*. A bundle of seedlings is आँटी *ānti*, and the man who plants them is called डोभा *dobha* or रोपनिहार *ropnihār*. The bundles are tied in pairs and set astride over a long bamboo when carried about. This bamboo is called to the west बिहनन्ढोआ *bihandhoa* or कनाठ *kanāth*. The man who roots up the seedlings from the seed-bed is called कबरिया *kabariya*, or in Sāran कबरिहा *kabariha*. In South Munger he is also called मोरकबरा *morkabra*. Seedlings which have been re-transplanted, *i.e.*, transplanted more than once, are called north of the Ganges खारु *khāru* or खरुहन *kharuhan*.

SUBDIVISION IV.

DIGGING, HOEING, AND WEEDING.

CHAPTER I.—DIGGING.

865. To dig is कोड़ब *kōrab*. In Champāran and Tirhut it is also तामब *tāmab* or पारब *pārab*. In South-West Shahabad it is बेलज

chhejal. Digging is कोड़नी *korni,* also in Champāran and Tirhut तमनी *tamni,* in Patna, Gaya, and South Munger निकौनी *nikauni,* and in South-West Shahabad छेजनी *chhejni.* In South Bhagalpur it is कोड़न *koran* or खँड़ *khanr.* In Sāran and Champāran गोहट *gohat* is digging or hoeing the edges of fields. In Tirhut this is called आरि छाँटब *āri chhāntab.*

CHAPTER II.—HOEING.

866. Hoeing is खुरपियाना *khurpiyāna* to the north-west. In Champāran and in Tirhut generally it is केरौनी *kerauni* or कमैनी *kamaini.* South of the Ganges it is कोड़नी *korni,* or in South-West Shahabad छेजनी *chhejni.* In the month of *Asārh* (June–July) sugar-cane gets a special hoeing, which is called असाढ़ी कोर *asārhi kor,* and in Champāran and North-East Tirhut टोकब *tokab.* In Gaya it is called पासा *pāsa,* and in Patna असाढ़ी कोड़न *asārhi koran.* In Champāran and the south-east it is अदरा कोरन *adra koran,* and elsewhere it has no special name. The first hoeing of the sugar-cane crop, which generally takes place in Māgh (January–February), is called अँधेरी कोरन *andheri koran* in Patna, चालन *chālan* or उझलन *ujhlan* in Gaya and to the west, अँधेरी *andheri* or झाड़नी *jhārni* in Sarān and South Munger, and झुरनी *jhurni* in South Bhagalpur. North of the Ganges it has no special name.

CHAPTER III.—WEEDING.

867. Weeding is केरौनी *kerauni* or कमैनी *kamaini* north of the Ganges. In the west generally it is सोहनी *sohni.* Elsewhere it is generally कोड़नी *korni,* and also हरखी *harkhi* in Patna and उझलन *ujhlan* in Gaya and Shahabad. In South Bhagalpur it is optionally केलौनी *kelauni,* and केरौनी *kerauni* reappears again in South Munger. To weed deep is भर खुरपी सोहब *bhar khurpi sohab;* also कोड़ देब *kor deb* to the north-west and in North-West Tirhut, and खाभल *khābhal* in Sāran and Champāran. In Patna the operation is called बिसमादी *bismādi,* and elsewhere it has no special name. Superficial weeding is खुरपियाना *khurpiyāna* in the north-west and निकावन *nikāwan* in the south-east. In Champāran and Tirhut it is called टिपनी *tipni.* The digging up a field to clear it of weeds before ploughing is तामब *tāmab,* also in North-East Tirhut टोकब *tokab.* The operation is called तमनी *tamni,* or in North-East Tirhut टोकनी *tokni.*

Weeding by hand is चिखुरनी *chikhurni* in the north-west and उछटनी *uchhtani* in Champāran and Tirhut. In Patna, Gaya, and South Munger it is हाँथ सेँ निकाएब *hānth señ nikāëb*, and in South Bhagalpur ठकुरई *thakuraī*. In Shahabad it has no special name.

868. Weeds are घास *ghās* or घास पात *ghās pāt*. In the north-west they are also दूभ दाँदर *dūbh dāndar*, and in Tirhut धू *dhū*. When collected and burnt as manure, they are खादर *khādar* in the north-west, and गोआ *goa* there and in Tirhut. In Patna and Gaya these are अलाह *alāh* or डाही *dāhi*, हूरा *hūra* in South Munger, and छारो *chhāro* in South Bhagalpur.

869. Wages for weeding are सोहाइ *sohāi* or चिखुराइ *chikhurāi* in north-west, and in the east generally simply बन *ban*. In Patna and Gaya they are निकौनी *nikauni*, in South-West Shahabad बनी *bani*, and to the west generally बनिहारी *banihāri*.

SUBDIVISION V.

WATCHING CROPS.

870. Watching of crops is generally रखवारी *rakhwāri*, अगोरी *agori*, or अगोरिया *agoriya*. Other terms are रखवाही *rakhwāhi* or बलरक्खी *balrakkhi* in Patna, जगवारी *jagwāri* or बधवाहा *badhwāha* in Gaya, बधवार *badhwār* in East Tirhut, and जोगाएब *jogāeb* in Champāran and South Bhagalpur. In Champāran and the south-east हाँकी *hānki* is to drive crows off a field. Elsewhere it is कौआ हाँकब *kaua hānkab*, &c. A field-watchman is रखवार *rakhwār*, अगोरिया *agoriya*, or अगोरनिहार *agornihār*; also बलरक्खा *balrakkha* in Patna, अगोरा *agora* there and in Champāran and South Munger, जगवरिया *jagwariya* in Gaya, and जोगनियाँ *joganiyān* in South Bhagalpur. The बधवार *badhwār* or बधवाहा *badhwāha* is generally a man appointed to watch the fields of a number of cultivators and paid by the landlord.

871. In the north-west छेंकनिहार *chhenknihār*, and in North-East Tirhut चकलेदा *chakledār*, is a man appointed to watch on behalf of the landlord to see that none of the crops is carried away before the demand is paid. Elsewhere he is simply called पियादा *piyāda* or बराहिल *barāhil*, but to the south-east he is सिरमान *sirmān* or बलरक्खा *balrakkha*. To attach the crops thus is called रोकब *rokab*: hence the

Anglo-Indian phrase "to roke crops." The act of "roking" is called in the north-west छापा *chhāpa*.

872. When cultivators club together to watch their crops in turn, it is called north of the Ganges पारी *pāri*, भाँज *bhānj*, or भाँजा *bhānja*. It is also पलटी *palti* in Patna, Gaya, and the west; also परिहर *parihar* in Patna and Gaya, पेठी *pethi* in South-West Shahabad, and पाएठ *pāëth* in South Munger.

SUBDIVISION VI.

REAPING AND GLEANING.

CHAPTER I.—REAPING.

873. Reaping is कटनी *katni*, or to the north-west कटिया *katiya*. In South-West Shahabad it is लौनी *launi*. To reap is काटब *kātab*, or in South-West Shahabad लौनी करल *launi karal*. To cut cane is छोलल *chholal* in the north-west, गेँड़ा करल *genra karal* to the west, पारब *pārab* in Champāran and Patna and Gaya and South Munger, and घूर काटब *ghūr kātab* in South Bhagalpur.

874. The man who cuts the cane is described in section 292. A reaper is कटनिहार *katnihār* north of the Ganges and in Patna and to the south-west. He is also दिनिहर *dinihar* in Patna, Gaya, and South Munger, लेवनिहार *leonihār* or कटनियाँ *katniyān* to the west. Elsewhere he is simply जन *jan*, बनिहार *banihār*, &c. Harvest time is कटनी *katni*. The wages of harvesting are दिनौरा *dinaura* in Patna and Gaya, and दीनी *dīni* in Champāran, Gaya, and the south-east. Another name is in Gaya गुदारा *gudāra*, or in Sāran गुदार *gudār*. Elsewhere they are बन *ban*, or in South-West Shahabad बनी *bani*.

875. Cutting the ears without the stalks is बलकट *balkat* generally. Other names are टुँगनी *tungni* north of the Ganges and to the west, अगला *agla* in Champāran and Gaya, कटुइ *katuï* in South-West Shahabad, पाँगल *pāngal* to the west, and नन्हकटनी *nanhkatni* in South Munger. So also in East Tirhut it is ननकटनी *nankatni* or (also in Champāran) सिसकटनी *siskatni*, and in South-East Tirhut छिपकट्टा *chhipkatta*. It is अगड़ा *agra* in South Bhagalpur. Cutting crops at the root is जरछोरनी *jarchhorni*, (in South-East Tirhut) जरकट्टा *jarkatta*, or (in South Munger) जरछोरा *jarchhora*.

876. To shake the fruit off a tree is झरंझराएल *jhārjharāël* in the north-west. In Champāran and West Tirhut it is झरखाएब *jharkhāëb*, and in East Tirhut झकाएब *jhakāëb*. To the west it is झोरल *jhoral*, and also, generally, दोलब *dolab* or दोलाय देब *dolāy deb*. झटाहब *jhatāhab* is to knock down fruit from a tree by throwing up sticks into it (see § 41).

CHAPTER II.—CUTTING OF UNRIPE CROPS.

877. Unripe crops are sometimes cut for food. North of the Ganges this is known as गद्‌रा *gadra* or कच्चा *kachcha*. Other names are गादा *gāda* and गद्दा *gadda*. In South Munger it is गादर *gādar*, and in South Bhagalpur अँकुरी *ankuri*. The last two are also met with in Champāran. A word used to the east generally is कचरी *kachri*. In the north-west समहुत *samahut* is a little grain cut first, and this is सुमुत *sumut* in North-West Tirhut, नेवान *newān* in Saran, and नेबान *nebān* in Champāran and Tirhut. होरहा *horha* is unripe grain cut for parching. It is also called ओरहा *orha* in Tirhut and the south-east, and optionally होलहा *holha* in Champāran and South Munger. The green ears of *Eleusine coracana* (मडुआ *marua*) treated in this way are called उम्मी *ummi* or ऊमी *ūmi* to the west and in Tirhut and ऊनी *ūni* in Champāran. आलो *ālo* in Gaya is the part of the crop which is reaped by a cultivator for present eating before the whole is ripe. Sometimes unripe pulses and barley are rooted up and given as fodder to cattle. This is called in Sāran रखाँत *rakhānt*.

CHAPTER III.—GLEANING.

878. A gleaner is बिनहिहार *binnihār* or बिनियाँ *biniyān* to the west. He is also generally लोढनिहार *lorhnihār*, with variants लोढ़ताहर *lorhtāhar* in Patna, Gaya, and South Munger, and लोढ़रा *lohra* in South Bhagalpur. Gleanings left on the field for the lower orders are झरँगा *jharnga* or झारँग *jhārang* to the west, and लोढ़ी *lorhi* or लोढ़िया *lorhiya* to the east and in Champāran. Other names are झरुआ *jharua* (Patna and North-West Tirhut), झर *jhar* (South-East Tirhut), and छूटल पटल *chhūtal patal* (Champāran and Tirhut). Gleaning is called in Gaya and South Munger लोढ़ा बिच्छा *lorha bichcha*, and gleanings are लोढ़ा *lorha*.

SUBDIVISION VII.

THRESHING AND WINNOWING.

CHAPTER I.—THE THRESHING-FLOOR.

879. A threshing-floor is everywhere खरिहान *kharihān*, with an optional variant खरिहानी *kharihāni* in Patna. The shed erected on the threshing-floor is मड़ई *maraī*, खोँपड़ी *khompri*, or झोँपड़ी *jhompri*. In Patna it is मरुका *maruka* or झोँपड़ा *jhompra*, in Gaya कूड़ा *kūrha*, and in the south-east खोँपड़ा *khompra*.

CHAPTER II.—SHEAVES AND BUNDLES.

880. The cut crop is डाँठ *dānth* to the north-west, or डाँट *dānt* in North-West Tirhut. In East Tirhut it is लार *lār*. In Shahabad it is लेहनी *lehni*, in Champāran लेहन *lehan*, in Gaya पतौर *pataur*, in Patna पतौड़ी *patauri* or पतनी *patni*, in South Munger पातन *pātan*, and in South Bhagalpur पत्तन *pattan*. In Shahabad it is called पल्हारी *palhāri*, and in Sāran पथारी *pathāri*, when it is left a day in the field without being gathered.

881. In considering the nomenclature of the sheaves it will be convenient to take North and South Bihār separately.

NORTH BIHAR.

882. The smallest sheaf, about a handful, is called मूठा *mūtha*, मुट्ठा *muttha*, or पूला *pūla*; the next largest is the अँवाँसा *anwānsa* (north-west), औल्हा *aulha* (North Tirhut), and आहुल *āhul* or अहुला *ahula* (East Tirhut); the next largest is the अँटिया *antiya* or (Champāran and North-West Tirhut) पसही *pasahi*; the next largest is an armful or पाँजा *pānja*; the next largest is a बोझा *bojha*; and the largest of all, that carried on a bullock, लदना *ladna*. The relative scale of some of the above is generally as follows:—

4 मूठा *mūtha* = 1 अँवाँसा *anwānsa* or औल्हा *aulha*.
8 औल्हा *aulha* = 1 पाँजा *pānja*.
4 पाँजा *pānja* = 1 बोझा *bojha*.
16 बोझा *bojha* = 1 सोरही *sorhi*.

In East Tirhut the following scale obtains :—

4 आहुल *āhul*	=	1 केहुनी *kehuni.*
4 केहुनी *kehuni*	=	1 पाँजा *pānja.*
4 पाँजा *pānja*	=	1 बोझा *bojha.*
16 बोझा *bojha*	=	1 सोरही *sorhi.*
16 सोरही *sorhi*	=	1 सोरहा *sorha.*

883. The word सोरही *sorhi* is a common unit for measuring produce. Thus, a *raiyat* will say that such and such a field gives so many सोरही *sorhi* to the *bīgha.*

SOUTH BIHAR.

884. The proportions vary in different places, as follows :—

SOUTH-WEST SHAHABAD.

2 अँवाँसी *anwānsi*	=	1 अँटिया *antiya* or डोमड़ा *domra.*
10 ditto	=	1 पाँजा *pānja,* पूरी *pūri,* or आँटी *ānti.*
3 पाँजा *pānja,* पूरी *pūri,* or आँटी *ānti*	=	1 बोझा *bojha.*
30 ditto ditto	=	1 तिसौर *tisaur.*

SHAHABAD.

10 अँवाँसी *anwānsi*	=	1 अँटिया *antiya* or पनपिऔआ *panpiaua.*
4 अँटिया *antiya*	=	1 बोझा *bojha.*
Or 10 आँसी *ānsi*	=	1 पाँजा *pānja.*
4 पाँजा *pānja*	=	1 बोझा *bojha.*
21 बोझा *bojha*	=	1 एकैसिया *ekaisiya.*

PATNA.

4 अरपा *arpa*	=	1 आँटी *ānti.*
5 आँटी *ānti*	=	1 गाही *gāhi.*
5 गाही *gāhi*	=	1 बोझा *bojha.*
Or 5 अरपा *arpa*	=	1 पाँजा *pānja.*
5 पाँजा *pānja*	=	1 बोझा *bojha.*
21 बोझा *bojha*	=	1 एकैसी *ekaisi.*

GAYA.

	3 अर्पा *arpa*	= 1 आँटी *ānti.*
	5 आँटी *ānti*	= 1 गाही *gāhi.*
	10 गाही *gāhi*	= 1 बोझा *bojha.*
Or	9 अर्पा *arpa*	= 1 पाँजा *pānja.*
	3 पाँजा *pānja*	= 1 बोझा *bojha.*
	21 बोझा *bojha*	= 1 एकैसी *ekaisi.*

SOUTH MUNGER.

The same as Gaya, except that 4 पाँजा *pānja* = 1 बोझा *bojha.*

SOUTH BHAGALPUR.

4 गौँती *gaunti*	= 1 आँटी *ānti.*
4 आँटी *ānti*	= 1 पाँजौ *pānjau.*
16 आँटी *ānti*	= 1 बोझा *bojha.*
16 बोझा *bojha*	= 1 सोर्ही *sorhi.*

885. The word एकैसी *ekaisi* south of the Ganges is used in much the same way that सोर्ही *sorhi* is used; so also तिसौर *tisaur.* It will be seen that the above scales are not always consistent amongst themselves. This is the fact, and is due to a difference in the size of the unit according to locality. The बोझा *bojha* is about the same everywhere.

886. An अक्वार *akwār* or अँक्वार *ankwār* (optionally), or in Patna and South-East Tirhut केहुनी *kehuni,* is as much grain as can be carried between the arms, and मथःबोझा *mathbojha* is a load carried on the head. Out of each बोझा *bojha* one आँटी *ānti* is given to the labourer who cuts and carries away the crop, and the remainder is in Shahabad called गुदार *gudār.** गुण्ड *gund* in Patna or गूँड़ा *gūnra* in Gaya is a bundle of cut pulse.

CHAPTER III.—TREADING OUT GRAIN.

887. Treading out grain is दौनी *dauni* north of the Ganges. To the west and in Patna it is also दौँरी *daunri* or मिँज्नी *minjni.* The latter word is principally used when the grain is trodden out by men and not

---

*The आँटी *ānti* given to, or rather taken by, the reaper varies in size, as is witnessed by the proverb कोढ़ि कटनिहार केँ मुङ्गर सन आँटी *korhi katnihār keñ mungar san ānti,*—the lazy reaper gets a bundle as thick as a club.

by bullocks. In Shahabad it is दौरी *dauri*, and so also in the south-east. In Champāran, Patna, Gaya, and South Munger it is दवाँही *dawānhi*, and in Patna also (when trodden by men) मैंजनी *mainjni*. In South Bhagalpur सहरी *sahri* is a thorough threshing of corn. The beating out of the heads against the ground or bed to disengage any grains that remain is पीटब *pītab*, झारब *jhārab*, or झाँटब *jhāntab* north of the Ganges. It is also पेटारी *petāri* to the west, डंगौनी *dangauni* in Patna, पिटनी *pitni* in Champāran and Gaya, डेंगौनी *dengauni* in East Tirhut and South Munger, and झँटनी *jhantni* in South Bhagalpur.

888. The first treading out of the grain is called पौर *paur;* the second treading is दन्ती दाँवब *danti dānwab* north of the Ganges and in Shahabad, or तोड़ाएब *tordāēb* in North-East Tirhut. To the west it is छाँटब *chhāntab*, in Champāran and Patna it is खुरदौनी *khurdauni*, in Gaya खुरदौंती *khurdonti*, and in South-East Tirhut and South Munger खुरदाँइ *khurdāin*.

889. The stake to which the bullocks are tied in treading out the grain is मेंह *meñh*, with local variants मेंहा *meñha* (to the north-west and in South-East Tirhut), मेहटा *mehta* (Patna), and मींहों *mīñhon* (South Bhagalpur). In South-West Shahabad no centre stake is used. A bullock stands in the centre, who is called मेंहियाँ बैल *meñhiyān bail*. In other places the inner bullock next the post, which is the slowest and weakest of the team, is called मेंहियाँ *menhiyān* generally; also मेंढ़ा *menrha* in Champāran and South-East Tirhut, and मेहटा *mehta* or मेंहटा *menhta* in Gaya and South Munger. In South Munger he is also मेहा *meha*, and in South Bhagalpur मीहाँ *mīhān*. Another name for him is in Gaya कुड़दहिना *kurdahina*. The outer bullock, which is the smartest of the team, is called पाठ *pāth* or पठिया *pathiya* to the west, to the north-west and in North-West Tirhut पटिया *patiya*, and in East Tirhut पाट वाला *pāt wāla*. In South-East Tirhut it is अगदाएँ *agdāēn*, and variants of this are अगदाइँ *agdāin* in Patna and South Munger, आंगदाइन *āgdāin* or अगदैयाँ *agdainyān* in Gaya, and एगदाइँ *egdāin* in South Bhagalpur. In South-West Tirhut he is फेरा *phera*. The rope which goes round a bullock's neck is गरदाँव *gardānw* in the west and in South Munger, गरदनी *gardani* in Champāran and West Tirhut, and गरौंधा *garaundha* in Patna. The main rope to which all the bullocks are tied is मझा *manjha*, also दौंरी *daunri* to the west, दौंरड़ *daunrar* or दोगहा *dogha* in West Tirhut, and कराम *karām* in East Tirhut. In Patna, Gaya, and South Munger it is दवाँही *dawānhi*, and in South Bhagalpur दाँमर *dāmmar*. In

A threshing-floor (kharikān) *The man standing on the right of the picture holds in his right hand a threshing-rake (akhaina)*

Lith by Harilal Pal Student Govt School of Art Calcutta. Cornwallis Press Calcutta

Champāran and Gaya it is also called कांड़ *kānr* or कांड़ा *kānra*. The rope by which the main rope is tied to the stake is घूरी *ghūri* or मँहौटी *meñhauti* in Patna and Gaya, and डोंड़ा *donra* in South Bhagalpur.

CHAPTER IV.—CROPS ON THE THRESHING-FLOOR.

890. *The pile of sheaves.*—When the crop is piled in bundles on the threshing-floor it is known as गाँज *gānj*. Other names are टाल *tāl* (north of the Ganges and Shahabad), गल्ला *galla* (North-West Bihār), ढेरी *dheri* in Gaya, and कांड़ *kānr* or कांड़ा *kānra* in Champāran and to the east; also खम्हार *khamhār* in South-East Tirhut. When the cut crop is piled like a stack in England, with the grain heads inside to save them from rain, it is called कोठियौ *kothiyau* in Sāran, and पूँज *pūnj* or पुँजौर *punjaur* to the north-west and in Patna, Gaya, and the south-east. When *rahar* (*cytisus cajan*) is piled on end to ripen before threshing, it is called खड़ा टाल *khara tāl* north of the Ganges. Stacks are rarely raised on platforms in Bihār, but when it is done the platform is called मचान *machān*.

891. *The spread-out crop.*—When the crop is spread out flat on the threshing-floor, ready to be trodden out by the bullocks, it is पैर *pair* north of the Ganges and in Shahabad. Other names are पौर *paur* or पौरी *pauri* in East Tirhut, खोह *khoh* in Champāran and South East Tirhut, बड़न्होरा *barhora* in Patna and Gaya, बड़न्हरा *barhara* in South Munger, and खुआ *khūa* in South Bhagalpur.

892. *The crop after it is trodden.*—After the crop is trodden out the pile of chaff and grain ready for winnowing is सिल्ली *silli* north of the Ganges, in Patna, and the south-west. Other names are कुटाँव *kutānw* (Patna and North-West Bihār), ढेरी *dheri* in Champāran, Tirhut, and South Munger, पैर *pair* in Champāran and Gaya, and धार *dhār* in South Bhagalpur. In South-East Tirhut it is also उकाम *ukām* (also in Patna) or उकुम *ukum*, and in Shahabad उकाँव *ukānw*.

893. *The heaped grain.*—This is रास *rās* or ढेरी *dheri*, also in North-East Tirhut खोर *khor*. Over this is placed a cake of cowdung to avert the evil eye. This is बढ़ाँव *barhānw* (Patna and West Bihār) and बड़न्हावन *barhāwan* in Gaya and the west; but बढ़ाँव *barhānw* is more properly the dung deposited by the bullocks while treading. Other names for the cake are महादे *mahāde* or महादेव *mahādeb*. A piece of moist earth stamped is sometimes used in the same way, and is called चाकल *chākal* to the west and छप्पा *chhappa* generally. In South-East Tirhut a piece of wood so used is called जाक *jāk*.

894. *The heaped straw and chaff.*—Straw in bundles is पूला *pūla* in Patna and north of the Ganges, except in North-East Tirhut, where it is झटुआ *jhatua*. South of the Ganges, and optionally in Sāran, it is आँटी *ānti* or अँटिया *antiya*, except in the south-east, where it is पुल्ला *pulla* or बिँड़ा *biñra*. Loose straw that has been threshed is पुआरा *puara* (to the west) or पुआर *puār* (to the east). Local variants are पोरा *pora* (also in West Tirhut) or पोआर *poār* in Patna and South Munger. When it has not been threshed, but has been left standing in the field after the ears are cut off, and then itself cut, it is called नार *nār*, and also (to the east) लार *lār*. Its stalks are whole, and are not crushed like threshed straw. नेवारी *newāri* is straw which is cut with the ear, but is not trodden by bullocks. It is tied up in bundles, and the heads are beaten against the ground. The husks of the grains are भूसा *bhūsa* or भुस्सा *bhussa*. South of the Ganges a nasal is generally inserted—thus, भूँसा *bhūñsa*. Other names are कटुआ *katua* in Patna and Gaya, गुण्डो *gundo* in Champāran and South Bhagalpur, and खख्रा *khakhra* or ढुल्ला *dhulla* in South Munger. Bran is चोकर *chokar*, also in Patna and the west भूँसी *bhūnsi*. Other names are चलौँसी *chalaunsi* (Patna and the west), कोराइ *korāi* (Patna, Tirhut, and the west), चोँकर *chonkar* in Champāran and Patna, and चोक्रा *chokra* in South Munger. The heaped straw on the threshing-floor, or a stack of straw anywhere, is गाँज *gānj* or टाल *tāl*. सिल्ली *silli* is also specially used for the heap of straw on the floor.

895. An enclosure for stacking straw or fuel is घेरान *gherān* in West Tirhut, Sāran, and Champāran, घोरान *ghorān* in Shahabad, and घेरा *ghera* or ढाठ *dhāth* in Champāran and Tirhut, the latter specially to the east. To the west it is पुरवट *purwat*. A house for holding chaff is भुसौल घर *bhusaul ghar* in the north-west and West Tirhut, and भुसकार *bhuskār*, भुस्सभुलबा *bhussbhulba*,* or (also in Champāran) भुसखार *bhuskhār* to the east. In South-West Shahabad it is भुँसौर *bhunsaur*, and to the west generally of that district भुँसहुल *bhuñsáhul*. In Champāran and Patna it is भोँसौला

* As in the proverb छूटल घोड़ भुस्सभुलबहिँ ठाढ़ *chhūtal ghor bhussbhulbahiñ thārh*,—a horse, when he gets loose, stays in the chaff-house.

WINNOWING (OSAUNI)

Lith by Hem Chunder Ghosal, Student Govt. School of Art, Calcutta. W. Newman & Co. Limited, Calcutta-Imp.

bhoñsaula, and there and in Gaya भूसा घर *bhusa ghar*. In Champāran and South Munger it is भुसघर *bhusghar*, and in South Bhagalpur भुसकारी *bhuskāri*. खोंप *khomp* or खोंपी *khompi* north of the Ganges is a small shed for chaff. The round thatch covering a खोंप *khomp* to save it from the weather is खोंप के मथनी *khomp ke mathni*, छांवनी *chhāoni*, or टोपड़ *topar*. In South-East Tirhut चाँग *chāng* is a large basket for holding chaff equalling four टोकड़ी *tokri*. टँगौर *tangaur* in the same place is a similar one, but is rougher and made of *rahar (Cytisus cajan)*.

896. *The refuse straw and fodder.*—This is in the north-west गोथार *gothār*, to the west and in North-West Tirhut it is लथेर *lather*, in Champāran and North-East Tirhut निघास *nighās*, and South-East Tirhut निघेस *nighes*. South of the Ganges and in Champāran it is डाँटी *dānti*. The refuse straw of the *rabi* or spring-crop, and specially of the *rahar (Cytisus cajan)*, is ररेठा *raretha* generally south of the Ganges, local variants being लरेठा *laretha* in South Bhagalpur, and in Champāran रहेठा *rahetha*. In Patna it is also called खरई *kharaī*. The refuse straw of the autumn crop is डाँठ *dānth* or डँटुका *dantuka* or कुटका *kutka* north of the Ganges. It is also to the west and in Patna ढट्ठा *dhattha*, and elsewhere डाँट *dānt*, डाँटा *dānta*, or डाँटी *dānti*. In South Bhagalpur and Patna, however, it is ठठेरो *thathero*. The dry stalks of mustard (सरिसो *sariso*) are सण्ठी *santhi* in the north-west, तिलठी *tilthi* to the west and in North-West Tirhut, तोरियाठी *toriyāthi* in South-West Tirhut, तोरियठ *toriyath* in Shahabad, and तिलाठी *tilāthi* generally. The stalks of cereals without the ear are झेंगरा *jhengra* to the west and in South-West Tirhut, झेंगटा *jhegta* in Champāran, डाँट *dānt* in the rest of Tirhut, झङ्गा *jhanga* in Champāran, and झाँग *jhāng* also in South-East Tirhut.

CHAPTER V.—WINNOWING.

897. Winnowing grain is ओसौनी *osauni*. To winnow is ओसाएब *osāēb*.

898. The fine chaff which is blown away by the wind in winnowing is पम्भी *pambhi* generally; also पाँकी *pānki* or पाँभी *pāmbhi* to the west, गूँड़ी *gūnri* in Champāran and South-East Bihār, and भौंटा *bhaunta* in Patna. South of the Ganges these words are confined to the winter (*Aghani*) crop. The words for the autumn (*Bhadoï*)

crop are पुरेसी *puresi* or पुअरसी *puarsi* to the west, and पखनी *pakhni* in Patna and Gaya. In South Munger अधभरी *adhbhari* is rice not fully developed, in which the ear is only half full, the rest being all chaff.

CHAPTER VI.—MISCELLANEOUS.

899. The gathering or collecting grain at one place in the time of harvest is बटोरन *batoran* or लोढ़न *lorhan.*

900. When grain is being weighed, an extra handful is thrown in to make up for dust, &c. This is called पछुआ *pachhua* generally, but also कसर *kasar* to the west and फाव *phāo* in the south-east. It is also called लाभ *lābh* in Champāran and South Munger.

901. The grain left on the threshing-floor after removing the bulk of the crop is अगवार *agwār* generally north of the Ganges, and भाठ *bhāth* in South-East Tirhut. South of the Ganges and in Sāran it is तरी *tari.* The gleanings and refuse grain on the threshing-floor are पटपर *patpar* in the north-west and खखरा *khakhra* to the west and north. The grain which is blown away with the chaff at the time of winnowing is अगवार *agwār* or अगवारी *agwāri* to the west, अगाड़ *agār* in Champāran, Patna, and Gaya, and अगबर *agbar* in the south-east.

SUBDIVISION VIII.

DIVISION OF CROPS.

CHAPTER I.—DIVISION AND VALUATION.

902. The division of crops on the *metayer* system between landlord and tenant is called बटाइ *batāi* or बटैया *bataiya.* Local variants are बाँट *bānt* in Champāran and Gaya, बाँटी *bānti* in Champāran and South Bhagalpur, and बँटनू *bantnu* in South-West Shahabad. Land so held is called भांवली *bhāoli* or बटैया *bataiya,* as opposed to नगदी *nagdi,* of which the rent is paid in cash. In South Bhagalpur the division of the crops is called कुरताली *kurtāli.*

903. In बटाइ *batāi* a certain fixed proportion of the crop is given to the landlord as rent, as described in the following chapter. When, instead of a *proportion*, a certain fixed *quantity* of the crop per bigha is paid to the landlord, it is called मनन्खप *mankhap*, मनन्ठीका *manthika*, हुण्डा *hunda*, or मनन्हुण्डा *manhunda*. This is especially adopted in the case of जिरात *jirāt* or home-farm lands when let to a cultivator. In Patna it is called मनी बन्दोबस्त *mani bandobast*.

CHAPTER II.—THE SHARES INTO WHICH THE CROP IS DIVIDED.

904. *Half to landlord and half to tenant.*—This is called अधिया *adhiya* north of the Ganges and in the south-west, in Patna and Gaya अधन्बटैया *adhbataiya* or पह *pah*, in Champāran and the south-east अधन्बटिया *adhbatiya*. In South-West Shahabad they say दू दाना में सें एक दाना जमिदार लेहला, आउर एक दाना असामी के देहला *dū dāna meñ señ ek dāna jamidār lehala, āür ek dāna asāmi ke dehala,*—of two grains, the landlord takes one and gives one to the cultivator. The turn of the sentence which makes the landlord *give* the cultivator his share is worth noting.

905. *Seven-sixteenths to landlord and nine-sixteenths to the tenant.*—This is नौसत *nausat* or नौसत्ता *nausatta*. The practice has only been noted in the west, Patna, Gaya, and South Munger. In South-East Tirhut the custom is only observed in respect to mangoes and jack-fruit.

906. *Nine-sixteenths to the landlord and seven-sixteenths to the tenant.*—This is नौसत्ता *nausatta*. The practice has only been noted to the west and in Patna, Gaya, and South Munger; also (सेरी नौसत्ता *seri nausatta*) in West Tirhut.

907. *One-third to the landlord and two-thirds to the tenant.*—This is तेकुरी *tekuri* or तिहैया *tihaiya* in Shahabad, Patna, and Gaya, तेकुरा *tekura* in South-West Shahabad, तेखुरी *tekhuri* in South Bhagalpur, तेकुली *tekuli* in Champāran, तिसन्री *tisri* in Sāran and Champāran, and तेसन्री *tesri* in South Munger. Not noted elsewhere.

908. *Two-fifths to the landlord and three-fifths to the tenant.*—This is पचन्दू *pachdu* to the west and in West Tirhut, पच्चा दूआ *pachcha dūa* in Patna, Gaya, and the south-east, and पँचन्दू *panchdu* to the west. Not noted elsewhere.

909. *Three-fifths to the landlord and two-fifths to the tenant.*—This is पचन्दू *pachdu* to the north-west, and पाँचा दूआ *pāncha dūa* in South Munger and Tirhut. Not noted elsewhere.

910. *Landlord one-fourth, tenant three-fourths.*—This is चौथैया *chauthaiya* in Champāran and South-East Tirhut and चौठैया *chauthaiya* to the west and in Patua and Gaya. Not noted elsewhere.

911. The following remarks as to custom south of the Ganges may be of use. The division into equal shares is rare, and is confined to the cases of high-caste tenants, or where a tenant has obtained a decree of the Civil Court restricting the landlord's share to one-half. Nine-sixteenths to the landlord and seven-sixteenths to the tenant is the customary rate, the two-sixteenths in excess which are claimed by the landlord being supposed to represent the cost of collection, irrigation, and watching the crops. When the landlord takes less than a half-share of the crop, as in §§ 905, 907, 908, and 910, it is only in exceptional cases, as in time of drought, or when a jungle or waste land has to be brought under cultivation, or when land requires much labour on the part of the tenant. In these cases the settlement is always for a limited period, say one, two, or three years, and is often on a progressive scale, *i.e.*, in the first year the landlord takes one-fourth, in the second year one-third, in the third year two-fifths, and thereafter half of the gross produce. When the landlord takes three-fifths and the tenant two-fifths (§ 909), it is a case of special agreement with a landlord, who lets his private (खुद काश्त *khūd kāsht*) lands. In calculating all these shares (except in the case of division by bundles, see § 913) only the net grain produce after threshing is divided. The tenant in addition takes all the straw.

CHAPTER III.—DEDUCTIONS AND REMISSIONS.

912. A deduction of one *ser* in the maund from the amount received by the tenant is called सुपही *supahi* to the west, and also सेरही *serhi* in Shahabad. A similar deduction of 1¼ *sers* per maund is called in South Bhagalpur नेग *neg*, or perquisite. In the case of division by appraisement (see next chapter) an allowance is made for deficient produce. This is called to the west and in Tirhut छूट *chhūt*. South of the Ganges and in Champāran it is called गर्की *garki*, also नाबूद *nābūd* in Patna, छुट्टी *chhutti* in Gaya, गर्की पर्ती *garki parti* in South Munger, and मर्की गर्की *marki garki* in South Bhagalpur. A similar deduction of 1½ *sers* in the maund is called in Champāran, Patna, and Gaya डेढ़सेरी *derhseri*; and when of two *sers*, दुसेरी *duseri*. To the west दहार महार *dahār mahār* is the loss to both landlord and

tenant when the produce is deficient through inundation. A remission to a high-caste tenant is called पगड़ी *pagri* or माफी *māphi.* North of the Ganges पछुआ *pachhua* is an allowance made by the tenant for dust in the landlord's share of the grain. In Sāran and Patna अँजुरी *anjuri,* and in Shahabad आँजुर *ānjur,* is an allowance of one or two *sers* per plough taken by the tenant. खलिहानी *khalihāni* in Patna is an allowance claimed by the tenant, and so also is भाँवर *bhāmwar* in Shahabad and मँगनी *mangni* or माँगन *māngan* (½ a *ser* in the maund) in East Munger.

CHAPTER IV.—MODE OF DIVISION.

913. This may be considered under two heads,—division on the field and division on the threshing-floor.

Division on the field.—This may be done either by actual division of the bundles (बोझा *bojha*) or by appraising (कनब *kanab*) the value of the crop. When the bundles of the cut crop are divided, this is called बोझबटाई *bojhbataï* or (in Champaran and South-East Tirhut) खरबटाई *kharbatāï.* To the north-west it is जजाती बटाई *jajāti batāï.* The rough appraisement of the crops for the purpose of division is called कन *kan* or कूत *kūt,* or कनकूत *kankūt* or कनकुत्ती *kankutti.* When the valuation is done by appraisement it is called कनकुत्ती बटाई *kankutti batāī.* It is also called दानाबन्दी *dānābandi* generally, भौकट्टा *bhaukatta* in Shahabad and the south-east, दमाव *damāo* or दमकट्टी *damkatti* in Shahabad, Patna, and Gaya. When the crops are ripe for harvesting the landlord deputes an assessor (अमीन *amīn*) and an arbitrator (सालिस *sālis*) to the field. They are met there by the tenant and the village officials. The village measurer (कठाधर *kathādhar*) then measures the field with the local pole, and the arbitrator goes round it, and after a consultation with the assessor and the village officials estimates the quantity of grain in the field. If the tenant accepts the estimate, the quantity is entered in the *patwārī's* field-book (खसरा *khasra*) and the matter is at an end. If the tenant objects, his fellow tenants are called in as mediators, and if they fail to convince either party a test (परतार *partār*) takes place. On behalf of the landlord a portion of the best part of the crop is reaped, and an equal portion of the worst part is reaped on behalf of the tenant. The two portions so reaped are threshed and the grain weighed. On the quantity thus ascertained, the whole produce of the field is calculated and entered in the field-book. The tenant is then at liberty to reap the crop and take it home whenever it suits his convenience. In calculating the amount due to the landlord from the whole estimated quantity a deduction in favour of the tenant of generally two *sers* per maund, called छुटन्ती *chhutti*, &c., (see § 912), is made to allow for deficient produce and for the cost of reaping, gathering, and threshing, which in this system of division is borne by the tenant. The remainder, thus calculated, is then divided into the respective shares of the landlord and the tenant, and the latter is debited with the landlord's share in the accounts. If he pays this amount within the year, it is paid in kind ; but if he does not do so, its value in money is written against him as an arrear in next year's accounts.

914. *Division on the threshing-floor.*—This is बटाइ खरिहानी *batăi kharihāni*, अगोर बटाइ *agor batăi* (because it is watched or guarded till division), or बटाइ *batăi* simply. The man who weighs the grain is called हटन्वा *hatwa* north of the Ganges. He is also हटन्वे *hatwe* in Champāran, Patna, and Gaya, बाया *bāya* or बया *baya* to the west, सोनार *sonār* in Patna, and केआल *keāl* or बनियाँ *baniyān* in Patna and the south-east. His fees are called हटन्वाइ *hatwāi* or हटन्वई *hatwaī* north of the Ganges, and also पछुआ *pachhua* in Champāran and Tirhut. In Champāran and East Tirhut they are also मनन्पई *manpaī* or मनन्पौआ *manpaua*. To the west they are बेयाइ *beyăi* or पवही *pawahi* (¼ *ser* per maund), in Gaya and South Munger चांलन्सा *chālsa*, in Patna and Champāran धुरिया *dhuriya* (¼ *ser* per maund), and in the south-east केआली *keālī* or तौलाइ *taulăi* (one *ser* per maund). When grain is measured instead of being weighed, 16 cups (पैला *paila*) of grain make one आढ़ा *ārha*. In this system the crops are reaped under the supervision of both parties, and are gathered on a common threshing-floor (see § 879), and strictly watched by both parties. Threshing does not take place until all the crops of the village have been thus gathered. Neither party is allowed the use of the crop till the grain is threshed out, weighed, and divided. During the reaping period the tenant at the end of each day gets the gleanings of the field (लोढ़ा *loṛha*, &c., see § 878), and a fixed proportion of the gross produce (दिनौरा *dinaura*, &c., see § 874), which go as wages to the reaper. From the joint crop the village artisans and officials (carpenter, blacksmith, shoemaker, accountant, &c., see §§1193 and ff.), who have worked all the year round for both tenants and landlords, receive their perquisites. When the heap of grain is ready for division, the grain

which is blown away with the chaff (अगाड़ *agār*, *&c.*, see § 901) is not divided, but is all the property of the tenant. Out of the common heap are then set aside the dues given for religious purposes (बिसुन पिरित *bisun pirit*, *&c.*, see § 1203), and out of the grain thus left the landlord takes his share, but the refuse grain mixed with dust left after removing the bulk of the crop (तरी *tari*, *&c*, see § 901) is all taken by the tenant. In this system, too, the tenant gets all the straw, chaff, &c.

SUBDIVISION IX.

IRRIGATION.

CHAPTER I.—IRRIGATION GENERALLY.

915. To irrigate is पटाएब *patāëb*, or to the west भरल *bharal*. Irrigation is पटावन *patāwan* or पटौनी *patauni*. In South Munger it is पटान *patān*. The flooding of a field preparatory to planting rice is लेब *leb*, लेव *leo*, or लेवा *lewa*, and in South Bhagalpur अन्हाव *anhāo*. Such a flooded field is called पनियाएल *paniyāël*. A water-drawer is पनिहारा *panihāra* or पन-भरा *panbhara*. In the north-west he is also पन-भारा *panbhāra*. A man irrigating has various names. To the north-west he is पन-छन्ना *panchhanna*, and in Gaya पन-छन्दा *panchhanda*; in Sāran and Champāran he is पन-मोर-वाह *panmorwāh*; in South-West Tirhut he is खर-वाहा *kharwāha*; and in South-West Shahabad he is कम्हैया *kamhaiya*. The man who distributes the water in the field with the हत्था *hattha* or wooden shovel (see section 64) is called हथ-वाहा *hathwāha* or छिर-कना *chhirkana* to the north-west. In Shahabad he is बर-वाह *barwāh*; to the west generally पनिवाह *paniwāh*; in Patna and Gaya, खँड़-मोड़ा *khanrmora* or छिचनियाँ *chhichaniyān*; in Patna, सिँच-वाहा *sinchwāha* or खँड़-वाहा *khanrwāha*; in Champāran and South Bhagalpur, खड़-कट्टा *kharkatta*; and in South Munger, गँड़र-कट्टा *ganrarkatta*. The wages for irrigation with a lever are लठ-वाही *lathwāhi*. Sometimes cultivators combine to assist one another in irrigating. This is called जाना *jāna* in Sāran and Champāran, पैँठी *painthi* or पलटी *palti* to the west, and the latter also in Patna and Gaya, परिहर *parihar* in Patna, पटिहर *patihar* in Champāran and South Munger, and पाएट *pāët* in Champāran and South Bhagalpur.

CHAPTER II.—KINDS OF IRRIGATION.

916. There are three main kinds of irrigation :—

(*a*) *From canals.*—A canal is नहर *nahar* (which is generally used only for the Son and similar Government canals), पैन *pain*, or पैनि *paini*, and नद्दी *naddi* or (South Bhagalpur) लद्दी *laddi*. In South-West Shahabad a canal is ताल *tāl*.

(*b*) *From wells* (कूआँ *kūān*, &c.)

(*c*) *From tanks, or ponds.*—A tank is पोखर *pokhar*, पोखरा *pokhra*, or तलाव *talāo*.* A small pond is तलाइ *talāï*. In Patna, Gaya, and South Munger a reservoir of which the water is higher than the level of the surrounding country and is kept in by embankments is called खांजाना *khãjāna* or खजाना *khajāna*.

917. The embankment round all these tanks and ponds is called भींड़ *bhīnr* or भिण्डा *bhinda*. Local names are पींड़ *pīnr* in Patna and Gaya, and खाँवाँ *khānwān* or खावा *khāwa* to the west. The post erected in the centre of a tank is जाट *jāt*, जाटि *jāti*, जाठ *jāth*, or जाठि *jāthi*. In South Munger it is लाठ *lāth*.

---

* In North-East Tirhut पोखरि *pokhari* is a large tank, as is instanced by the proverbial saying—

पोखरि रजोखरि, और सभ पोखरा ।
राजा सिब सिंह, और सभ छोकरा ॥

Pokhari Rajokhari, aur sabh pokhra,
Rāja Sib Singh, aur sabh chhokra.

—"The tank at Rajokhari is indeed a tank; all the rest are puddles. Raja Sib Singh was indeed a king; all others were princelets."

Another version of this is—

ताल त भोपाल ताल, और सभ तलैया ।
राजा त सिब सिंह, और सभ रजैया ॥

Tāl ta Bhopāl tāl, aur sabh talaiya,
Rāja ta Sibai Singh, aur sabh rajaiya.

Rajokhari and Bhopāl are the names of two villages in the Darbhanga district, where there are very large tanks, said to have been dug by king Sib Singh.

CHAPTER III.—IRRIGATION FROM CANALS.

918. Flush irrigation, when the water is at a higher level than the field and the cultivator has only to cut the bank of the water channel and allow the water to flow into the field, is called अपन्टा *apta* in the north-west, and अगरपाट *agarpāt* in Champāran and North-West Tirhut. To the west it is टोड़ *tor* or मोहर *mohar*. In Patna and Gaya it is छानन *chhānan*, in South Munger मेलान *melān*, and in South Bhagalpur दुरका *dhurka*.

919. Irrigation by lift, when the water has to be raised from a lower level, is called उदह के पानी ले जाएब *udah ke pāni le jāeb* to the west, and in the south-east उखेवा *ukhewa*. A dam is sometimes built across the stream to raise the water. This is बाँध *bāndh* or बान्ह *bānh* generally; also खाँड़ *khāñr*, गड़नी *garni*, and घेरा *ghera* to the north-west, गराँड़ी *garānri* in the north-west, Patna, and Gaya, फाँड़ी *phānri* in Champāran and Patna, गरण्डी *garandi* in South Munger, and खाँड़ो *khānro* in South Bhagalpur. A gang of men employed in making such an embankment is called in Patna and Gaya गोआम *goām*. A long embankment thrown round a plain of high land in which rice is cultivated, and in which there is a flow of surface water, is डँड़ेड़ी *danreri* to the north-west and in Patna. South of the Ganges and to the north-west खजाना *khajāna*, आहर *āhar*, अहरा *ahra*, and अहरी *ahri* mean the plain itself including the embankment. The embankment as distinguished from the plain is पिण्ड *pind* or अलङ्ग *alang*. A cutting in the embankment is called in Gaya खँड़हू *khanrhu*.

CHAPTER IV.—IRRIGATION FROM WELLS.

920. Wells may be divided into three classes :—

(*a*) *Those lined with masonry.*—These are called पक्का *pakka*. In the north-west बावली *bāoli* is a large well, sometimes with a *ghāt* or flight of steps running down to the water. इनारा *ināra*, इँदारा *indāra*, इनार *inār*, or इँदरा *indra* is a large masonry well. In South Bhagalpur राहट *rāhat* is a masonry well.

(*b*) *A well without masonry lining* is called कच्चा *kachcha*; also कूआँ *kūān* or कुइयाँ *kuiyān* or कूप *kūp*. In South Bhagalpur भँड़की *bhanruki*, and generally भड़कूईं *bharkūīñ*, is a small well. In Patna and Gaya कँदरी *kandri* is a well dug on a river-bank into which the river-water filtrates and is thereby rendered pure.

(c) *Surface depressions containing water.*—These are चूईं *chūīn* north of the Ganges, चुआरी *chuāri* to the west and in Patna, and चूआँ *chūān* elsewhere. A clay well which has fallen in is called भसल *bhasal* north of the Ganges, and भरन *bharan* in Champāran and North-East Tirhut. In Champāran, Patna, and Gaya it is भट्ठा *bhattha*, and to the west भगाड़ *bhagār*. All the above are adjectives agreeing with कूआँ *kūān*. Another expression used in Shahabad is भथ्कूआँ *bhathkūān*. The space formed inside a well by the collapse of the sides is खाँखर *khānkhar* in the north-west and धोधर *dhodhar* in Champāran and South-West Tirhut. To the west it is पाल *pāl*, and in Patna and Gaya चौँर *chaunr*.

CHAPTER V.—CONSTRUCTION OF WELLS.

921. The large circular excavation made before a masonry well is built is दवड़ *dawar* to the west and in Patna and South Tirhut, and खाँखर *khānkhar* to the north. In South-West Shahabad it is गोल *gol*, and in the rest of that district गोल गाल *gol gāl*. In Gaya it is गोलम्मर *golammar* or खभार *khabhār*.

922. The spring is सोता *sota* north of the Ganges, and also in North-East Tirhut मोका *moka*. In Shahabad it is सोत *sot* or सुत्ती *sutti*, in Patna, Gaya, and South Munger सोइ *soï*, and in South Bhagalpur सोत *sot* or सँगन्रा *sangra*. The side spring in a well is तरन्सोआ *tarsoa* in north-west and in West Tirhut. Spring-water is बरियार पानी *bariyār pāni*, or in South Bhagalpur सँगन्रा *sangra*, and in South Munger जिवन्गर *jiugar*, the two latter words being adjectives. When the spring is tapped the phrase used is, north of the Ganges, तावा टूट गेल *tāwa tūt gel*, and south of it बरियार (or जिवन्गर) पानी आबि गेल *bariyār* (or *jiugar*) *pāni ābi gel*. The hole through which the water rises when the spring is reached is भूड़ *bhūnr* or भूर *bhūr*. In Patna and South Munger it is भुरन्हा *bhurha*. An optional word in South Bhagalpur is बम *bam*. When the spring is copious, it is called भुरन्फुट *bhurphut*. When the spring is not reached, the well is called सुन्न *sunn*; and a well, when the spring has risen, is पनिहा *paniha*.

923. A well supplied from a spring and not from surface drainage is सुत्तिहा *suttiha* to the west, and सोतन्ही *sothi* in the rest of that district. In Patna, Gaya, and South Munger it is सोइया *soiya*, and in South Bhagalpur जलन्धर *jaldhar*. The place where the earth begins to become moist as a well is being sunk is पनन्सेल *pansel* or पनन्सचा *pansacha* in the north-west. In the south-west it is पसोइ *pasoi*, and to the south-east पसेवा *pasewa*. In some cases there is a stratum of sand so fine that it falls in at once and chokes the well. This is known in the north-west as भास *bhās* The depth to which a well is dug is measured by the height of a man (पूरिस *pūris* or पोरन्सा *porsa*). Thus a well is said to be four, five, six, or seven पूरिस *pūris* deep.

924. The masonry cylinder of a well is खनन्जीर *khanjīr*. When a well is made up with circular hoops of kiln-burnt earthenware for sides, these hoops are called खपन्ड़ा or खपन्रा *khapra*. Other names are (north-west) नाद *nād*, (South-West Shahabad) मोखन्ड़ा *mokhra*, (Patna) गिरन्दा *girda*, (Patna and South Munger) गँडुआ *ganrua*, and पाट *pāt* in South Bhagalpur. Sometimes a coil of twigs is used for the same purpose, which is known as कोठी *kothi*, डोल *dol*, or बींड़ *bīnr* in the north-west —the last also in Patna and Shahabad, दोल *dol* in the south-east, and बिण्डी *bindi* elsewhere in the south. Wells protected in this way are कोठिला *kothila* to the west and गड़ौआँ *garauān* in Patna. Wells are sometimes lined with a wooden cylinder, and are then called कठन्कूआँ *kathkūān*. When the cylinder of a well fails to sink, a second smaller cylinder is sometimes sunk inside. This second cylinder is called परन्चूईं *parchūīn*.

925. The wooden base of the cylinder is made of *jāmun* wood, and is called जमन्वट *jamwat* or जमोट *jamot*. In South Bhagalpur it is called जमन्काठ *jamkāth*.

926. A well so large that two buckets can work it is called दोलट्ठी *dolatthi*. In Patna and the south-east it is दुजान्त *dujāt*, and in South Munger also दुजन्ता *dujanta*. One for three buckets is तिनन्लट्ठी *tinlatthi* or तेलट्ठी *telatthi*; in South Munger it is तेजत्ता *tejatta*, and in South Bhagalpur तिनन्जाँत *tinjānt*.

927. The well-dredger and well-spear are described in § 39 and ff.

CHAPTER VI.—THE LEVER USED IN RAISING WATER.

928. This is ढेंकुल *dhenkul*, ढेंकुला *dhenkula*, or ढेंकी *dhenki*. It is also called लाठ *lāth*, लट्ठा *lattha*, or लाठा *lātha* south of the Ganges, and जाँत *jānt* in South Bhagalpur.

929. The *pot* (whether earthen or of iron) is कूँड़ *kūnr*, कूँड़ी *kūnri*, or कुण्डी *kundi*. A smaller iron vessel used for drawing water by hand, and not by means of a lever, is डोल *dol*, other names being लोहँड़ा *lohanra* in Shahabad and डोल *dol* in South Bhagalpur. In North-East Tirhut, however, डोल *dol* is also used for the lever-bucket. In Gaya कठनही *kathnahi* is a wooden bucket for drawing water from a well. The stick placed across the mouth of the bucket to which the rope is fastened is किल्ली *killi* or गुल्ली *gulli*. In South Bhagalpur it is रनकिल्ली *rankilli* or पुल्ली *pulli*. The string which fastens this to the pot is कनेटी *kaneti* to the north-west and कुँड़ियाठी *kunriyāthi* generally to the north of the Ganges; also चोरकिल्ली *chorkilli* in Champāran and North-West Tirhut.

930. The *rope* of the lift is बरहा *barha*. It is also called बरह *barah* in South Munger, and हथबरही *hathbarhi* and उबहनि *ubahani* in Champāran and North-East Tirhut. The short rope joining it to the bucket by a slip-knot is पनछोर *panchhor* or छोरी *chhori*, with the following local names:—छोर *chhor* (west), जोता *jota* (Patna, Gaya, and the south-east), नाधा *nādha* (Gaya), जोती *joti* (Shahabad and South Munger), and बगहा *bagha* (South Bhagalpur).

931. The *lever-beam* is बाँस *bāns* when made of bamboo, also छीप *chhīp* in Champāran and North-East Tirhut. लाठ *lāth* or लाठा *lātha* is a shorter and stouter one. Other names are धुरही *dhurhi* (South-West Tirhut), ढेंकुल *dhenkul* (west), and डण्डा *danda* (south-east). Sometimes a thin piece of wood is spliced on to the end of the beam. This is called बँसजोर *bansjor*, and in Patna and the south-east छीप *chhīp*. The end of the beam which projects beyond the rope over the well is called अगार *agār* or अगारी *agāri*.

932. The lever-beam is weighted with a counterpoise of clods of earth, &c., fixed to the end furthest from the well. These are called लेद *led*, लेदा *leda*, and लेदी *ledi*. In East Tirhut they are लेध *ledh*, and in South-East Bihār लेधो *ledho*. Other names are पछाड़ *pachhār* (Champāran), पछेड़ *pachher* (South-East Tirhut), and चकरी *chakri* (Champāran, Patna, and Gaya). The peg with which these are

The irrigation lever (lātha), pulled down, with the bucket lowered in the well

The irrigation lever (lātha), raised, with the bucket out of the well

fastened to the beam are खूँटा *khūnta* or खूँटी *khūnti;* also गँड़मेखा *gañrmekha* (Patna and Gaya), गुल्ली *gulli* (Patna), and किल्ला *killa* (Patna and south-east).

933. The *post* on the top of which the lever swings is खम्भा *khambha;* also धोरेआ *dhorea* in Patna and Shahabad. To the west धुरई *dhuraī* is a post with two branches at the top. These posts are often made of a live tree called जीयल *jīyal* (*Odina Wodier*), which forks naturally in a convenient position, and which will grow if only a piece of it is stuck in the ground, hence its name. The forks are कान *kān*, काना *kāna*, कानी *kāni*, कन्ना *kanna*, or कन्नी *kanni*. In Champāran and the south-east they are दोकानी *dokāni* or दुकानी *dukāni*. The cross-axle is अखौता *akhauta* or अखौत *akhaut*, local variants being अखोतो *akhoto* (South Bhagalpur), अँखौता *ankhauta* (South Munger), and अखेता *akheta* or अखेद *akhed* (optional) in Gaya and Patna. Other names are माँझा *mānjha* in Champāran and Gaya, and टोना *tona* in Patna. At right angles to and underneath this cross-axle a piece of wood is tied under the lever-beam to keep the axle in its place. This is called मकड़ी *makri* in Patna, Gaya, and the west. The holes in which the cross-axle works are called खोल *khol.*

934. The wooden framework over a well on which the person who draws the water stands is called परियाठा *pariyātha* or पौठा *pautha.*

935. When a bucket or *lota* falls into a well, it is pulled up by a set of grappling-hooks, called काँटा *kānta*, कण्टा *kanta*, or झग्गार *jhaggār.*

CHAPTER VII.—THE SKIN BAG USED FOR DRAWING WATER.

936. The use of this has not been noted in East Bihār. In West Bihār it is मोटि *moti*, मोट *mot*, or मोँट *mont*. The iron ring round its neck is मेँड़ड़ा *menrra;* also कड़ाही *karāhi* and कड़ा *kara* in Sāran, and काँड़ा *kānra* in South-West Tirhut. The rope or cord which joins the bucket to this iron ring is नथियारी *nathiyāri* or सोरही *sorhi;* also नथिया *nathiya* in South-West Tirhut. The semicircular pieces of bent wood fastened to the ring to keep the mouth of the bucket open are घोरई *ghoraī* or घोरानी *ghorāni.* To these are fastened two rings of iron, which are called कड़ी *kari* or बाला *bāla.* किल्ली *killi* or गुल्ली *gulli* is a wooden peg by which the bucket is fastened to the well-rope.

CHAPTER VIII.—OTHER WELL-APPLIANCES CONNECTED WITH IRRIGATION.

937. The portion of the mouth of the well on which the bucket rests as the water is being discharged is called अड़ाँस *arāns* or अँड़ास *anrās*. Sometimes this is of wood. On this straw or rushes are placed to save the vessel and prevent splashing. In Patna and Gaya this cushion is called सीठा *sītha* or बिण्डा *binda*, and in South-West Shahabad झेंगड़ा *jhengra*. In Sāran a similar article made of leather is called छल्ला *chhalla*. When made of straw in Sāran it is called चचार *chachār*, and in Champāran चचरा *chachra*. The catch-basin into which the bucket is emptied is called तीथा *tītha* to the west. Elsewhere it is called अड़ाँस *arāns*, सीठा *sītha*, &c., as above.

938. The bullock yoke, which has two bars (see § 14), is पालो मोटहा *pālo motha* or जुआठ *juāth*. Local names are जोठ *joth* (Patna) and जूआड़ *jūar* (Champāran and Gaya). In Champāran, Patna, Gaya, and South Munger पालो *pālo* is used. The above names are also used for the upper bar, and also पल्ला *palla* in South-West Shahabad. The lower bar is तरसैल *tarsaīl* or तरसैला *tarsaila*, local names being सैला *saila* in Shahabad, गतार *gatār* in Champāran and Gaya, and जहड़ *jahar* in the south-east. The outer pins joining these two bars, and which go outside the bullock's necks, are called सईल *sail* or सैला *saila* to the west, and कनैल *kanail* to the north-west and east. The similar pins inside are समैल *samail* or (Patna and the south-east) समैला *samaila*. They are also called पचार *pachār* in Shahabad. The knob to which the rope is fastened is महादेवा *mahādewa*. In the south-east it is महदेवा *mahdewa*.

939. The wooden framework over the mouth of a well to prevent people falling in is जँगला *jangla*. The wooden beam laid over the well on which the person drawing the water stands is पावठ *pāwath* or पौठा *pautha*. Other names are लतमरा *latmara* (Patna and North-West Tirhut), गोड़पौठा *gorpautha* (South-West Tirhut), and धरना *dharna* (Champāran and South Munger). The masonry work at the mouth of a well is जगत *jagat* to the west. Other names are मुड़ेर *murer* (west), मुँड़ेरा *munrera* (also in Champāran) or निरारी *nirāri* in Patna, मुड़ेरी *mureri* in Champāran and Gaya, and मूढ़ा *mūrha* in the south-east.

940. The pulley is generally supported in the fork made by two lopped branches of the trunk of a tree erected by the well. This trunk is called धुरही *dhurhi* or खम्हा *khamha* to the north-west and in South Munger. South of the Ganges we have धुरई *dhuraī* or धोरेआ *dhorea*

The skin bag for drawing water (moti), as worked with bullocks.

(NOTE.—The photograph had necessarily to be taken from a great height, which throws the picture somewhat out of perspective. Really the bullocks are going down hill, and the receiving vat is level.)

in Shahabad. In Gaya it is जसेर *jaser* or दसेर *daser*, and in Champāran, Patna, and the south-east खम्भा *khambha* or खम्हा *khamha*. Other names are थुन्ही *thunhi* in Patna and Shahabad and दोकानी *dokāni* in the south-east. The cross beam is बँड़ेरा *banrera* in the west, and बल्ला *balla* in South-West Tirhut. In parts of Shahabad it is अराठ *arāth*, and in Patna and Gaya पाट *pāt*. The branches in which the pulley works are कन्ना *kanna* or कानी *kāni*, and the pulley axle अखौत *akhaut* or अखौता *akhauta*. Other names for this last are डण्डा *danda* in Champāran and South-West Tirhut, सर्रा *sarra* in South-West Shahabad, and टोना *tona* in Patna. The pulley itself is घड़ारी *gharāri* to the west, also गड़ारी *garāri* to the north-west and in South Munger. It is घिरनी *ghirni* in Champāran and South-West Tirhut, Patna, Gaya, and South Munger, गद्दा *gadda* in South-West Shahabad, घुरनी *ghurni* in Patna, and मकरी *makri* in Champāran and to the south-east.

CHAPTER IX.—THE PATHWAY FOR THE BULLOCKS, &c.

941. The sloping pathway for the bullocks is पौदर *paudar*, also दवर *dawar* in Shahabad, बही *bahi* in Gaya, and डगर *dagar* in Champāran, Patna, and the south-east. In South Munger it is also गोड़पौर *gorpaur*. The portion above ground is पौदर के माँथ *paudar ke mānth*, or to the west मथार *mathār*. The portion below ground is खोंइछा *khoinchha* to the west. A yoke of well-bullocks is called मोटहा जोड़ी *motha jori*. Drawing water by cattle power is मोट चलाएब *mot chalāēb*.

CHAPTER X.—THE WORKMEN EMPLOYED AT THE WELL.

942. The following labourers are employed at the well:—

The bullock-driver.—He is हँकवा *hankwa* or हँकनिहार *hanknihār*; also फेरहा *pherha* in Shahabad.

943. *The man who empties the water-bag.*—He is ढरनिहार *dharnihār* north of the Ganges, छिनवा *chhinwa* in South-West Shahabad, and मोटढरवा *motdharwa* in the rest of that district and in South Munger.

944. Both these men are called north of the Ganges मोटवाहा *motwāha*.

945. *The man who distributes water in the field* is called पनमोरा *panmora* or पनछन्ना *panchhanna* north of the Ganges. South of the Ganges he is बरवाह *barwāh* in South-West Shahabad, मोरवाह *morwāh* in the rest of that district, and खँड़ुआर *khanruār* in Gaya. He is also खरवाहा *kharwāha* in Sāran and खँड़वाहा *khanrwāha* in Patna.

946. *The man who distributes the water with a spade* has already been described in Chapter I of this subdivision.

CHAPTER XI.—THE PERSIAN WHEEL.

947. The Persian wheel is not used in Bihār. Its name, रहट *rahat*, is however known in Patna.

CHAPTER XII.—IRRIGATION FROM TANKS AND STREAMS.

948. Water is raised from these either by the swing-basket or by the spoon-lever.

949. *The swing-basket.*—The swing-basket is generally सैर *sair* to the west and चाँड़ *chānr* in Central and Eastern Bihār. In Tirhut it is also ढोस *dhos*, in South-West Shahabad दौरा *daura*, in Champāran and Gaya सर *sar*, and to the south-east सैन *sain*. The strings from which it swings are डोर *dor* or डोरी *dori*. The place where the men stand who work the basket is गोरपौर *gorpaur*, or to the west पौधा *paudha*. In South Bhagalpur it is सैनार *sainār*. The men who work it are सैरवाह *sairwāh*, चँड़िवाह *chanriwāh*, or ढोसवाह *dhoswāh* in the above-mentioned localities respectively. To work the basket is सैर (चाँड़ or ढोस) चलाएब *sair* (*chānr* or *dhos*) *chalāēb*. In South Bhagalpur it is सैन बराएब *sain barāēb*. The pit from which the water is lifted is चड़ियार *chariyār* in Gaya and South Munger.

950. *The spoon irrigation lever.*—This is a long log of wood hollowed out like a spoon. It is so balanced that the bowl end is over the water to be raised. It is depressed into the water by the foot, and, rising by its own balance, discharges the water along its stem into the higher catch-basin. It is called दोन *don* to the west, and करीन *karīn* or करींग *karing* to the east. The man who works it is called दोनवाह *donwāh* and करिनवाह *karinwāh* or करिंगवाह *karingwāh* respectively. The place where he stands is पौठा *pautha* in the west and अलतमरा *altmara* in Tirhut.

Irrigation lever (latha), showing the method of discharging water

Lith: by Choonee Lall Dass Student Govt. School of Art Calcutta. Printed by Abdool Rohim Govt. School of Art Calcutta.

Water-lifting with the swing-basket (sair or chanr).

Irrigation lever (lātha), showing the method of taking in water

CHAPTER XIII.—WATER-LIFTS AND OTHER TERMS COMMON TO IRRIGATION BY THE SWING-BASKET AND THE SPOON-LEVER.

951. The height to which the water is lifted is बोदर *bodar* in Sāran and Shahabād, अनुआ *anua* in Champāran, and गार *gār* in North-West Tirhut. South of the Ganges it is चढ़ाव *charhāo*, अनौआ *anaua* in South-West Shahabad, and एघाँव *eghānw*, &c., as follows.

952. When there are several lifts, the first reservoir is called ठेवका *thewka* in the north-west, पहला गार *pahla gār* in North-West Tirhut, and कानर *kānar* in North-East Tirhut. South of the Ganges it is खजाना *khajāna* or एघाँव *eghānw*. Of this last there are local variants एघावा *eghāwa* in Patna and एघाय *eghāy* in South Bhagalpur. The top of the lift is अड़ानी *arāni* to the west, and सीठा *sītha* in South-West Tirhut, Patna, and Gaya. The catch-basin from which the water flows into the field is तीथा *tītha* to the west. It is also परछा *parchha* in South-West Shahabad, and मेलवानी *melwāni* in Gaya.

953. When there are two or more lifts, the second from the bottom is दोघाँव *doghānw*, with a local variant दोघावा *doghāwa* in Patna. The third is तेघाँव *teghānw*, or in Patna तेघावा *teghāwa*. The fourth is चौघाँव *chaguhānw*, or in Patna चौघावा *chaughāwa*. These lifts are also called ठेउका *theūka* in South-West Shahabad. Thus दो ठेउका *do theūka*, तीन ठेउका *tin theūka*, &c. The raised bank between the two reservoirs is खाँवाँ *khānwān* in South-West Shahabad and मेँड़ *menr* in the rest of that district. In Gaya it is पीँड़ *pīnr*, and in Patna अलङ्ग *alang*. In South Munger and Patna it is आहर *āhar*, and elsewhere बाँध *bāndh* or बान्ह *bānh*.

CHAPTER XIV.—WATER-CHANNELS.

954. The channel which conveys the water into the field is generally पैन *pain* or पैनि *paini*. In Patna, Sāran, and Shahabad it is also करहा *karha*, and in South-West Shahabad बाहा *bāha*. In Tirhut it is पौठ *pauth* or दवन *dawan*, and in North-East Tirhut पौटी *pauti*. In South-East Tirhut it is बह *bah*. To the west नारी *nāri* is also used. In the south-east and Champāran we find डाँड़ *dānr*, and also (in South Bhagalpur) सिँगहा *singha*. In North-East Tirhut कनवा *kanwa*, and in Patna and Gaya कनवह *kanwah*, is a narrow branch channel leading from a पैन *pain*. A water-course generally is नदी

naddi or (in South Bhagalpur) लद्दी *laddi*, and its branches बाहा *bāha* or (north of the Ganges) बहन्ना *bahna*. In Shahabad छेर *chher* is a shallow spring of water, and its branches निगरईन *nigrain*. In Patna and Gaya भोकिला *bhokila* and टँड़ुआ *tanrua* are small water-channels. The latter is smaller than, and is a branch of, the former. A turn in a water-course is मोरानी *morāni* in Patna and the north-west, and घुमान *ghumān* in Champāran and North-East Tirhut.

DIVISION V.

AGRICULTURAL PRODUCTS AND THEIR ENEMIES.

SUBDIVISION I.

AGRICULTURAL PRODUCTS.

CHAPTER I.—WHEAT.

955. Wheat (*triticum vulgare* or *sativum*) is गेहुँ *gehuñ* north of the Ganges. In East Bihār generally, however, it is गहुम *gahum*. To the west it is also गोहुँ *gohuñ*, and elsewhere south of the Ganges and in North-East Tirhut गोहुम *gohum*. In Gaya it is also मण्डा *manda*. Cf. § 823.

956. The chief varieties are मुँड़िया *munriya*, a first-class beardless wheat. In South-West Shahabad this is मुँड़िल॰वा *munrilwa*, मुड़॰ला *murla* in Sāran and Patna, and मुड़॰ली *murli* or भुँड़िया *bhuñriya* in Gaya. दाउदी *dāudi* or दौदी *daudi* in West Bihār, or to the south-west and in Gaya दौदिया *daudiya*, is an excellent white beardless wheat. In Tirhut it is known as जमाल खानी *jamāl khāni*. A white round-bearded wheat is known as दूधी *dūdhi* or दुधिया *dudhiya* in South Tirhut, Patna, and South Munger. In South Bhagalpur it is पच॰रूखी *pachrūkhi*. लल॰का *lalka* in Shahabad and South-West Tirhut, देसी *desi* or देसिला *desila*, and हर॰ना *harna* or हँर॰रह॰वा *hañrrahwa*, in the north-west, हाड़ा *hāra* in Tirhut, हड़॰हड़ा *harhara* in South-West Tirhut, हड़॰हा *harha* (Patna), केवल॰हा *kewalha* (Gaya), and जमाली *jamāli* or जमरिया *jamariya* to the east, are a small-grained red wheat. लल॰का *lalka* also occurs in South Munger. North of the Ganges दोग॰ला *dogla* is a mixed wheat composed of जमाल खानी *jamāl khāni* and हाड़ा *hāra*. बड़॰गहुमा *bargahuma* in South-East Tirhut is a large bearded wheat. In Shahabad रैँड़ा *renra* means stunted wheat.

957. The germ of a grain of wheat is south of the Ganges पुत्ती *putti*. When a grain of wheat germinates first, the sprout is called सुइया *suïya* or सूआ *sūa;* also अँकुड़ा *ankurha* to the north-west, and

कन्नी *kanni* in Patna. In North-West Tirhut it is डेफ *deph*, and to the east डेफी *dephi*. The phrase used is सुइया गेल *suiya gail* north of the Ganges, or डेफ निकसल *deph niksal* in North-East Tirhut. To the west they say रेँड़ल बा *renral ba* or रेँड़ गेल *reñr gail*. In Gaya they say सुआल आवे है *sua āwe hai*, and in Patna कनियाएल आवत है *kaniyāēl āwa hai*. When it has further sprouted, but has not yet taken firm root, it is पुतरा *putra*. When the blade throws out shoots they are called डिब्भी *dibbhi*; also डाभी *dābhi* in South-West Shahabad, and टेँभी *tembhi* in Patna. When about six inches high it is called कौआ लुकान *kaua lukān* in Gaya, Sāran, and Shahabad, and कौआ झपान *kaua jhapān* in the south-east, both meaning sufficiently high to hide a crow. When it is cut unripe it is known as होरहा *horha*, or (Tirhut and the South-East) ओरहा *orha*, and (optionally) in South Munger as होलहा *holha*. When the ear begins to form, they say रेँड़ा भेल बा *renra bhail ba* in the north-west, गभा भेल बा *gabha bhail ba* in South-West Tirhut, and गम्हड़ा भेल अछि *gamhra bhel achhi* in the rest of Tirhut. In Shahabad they say दुधियाएल *dudhiyāēl*. In Patna and Gaya a similar phrase, or the phrase गदराएल है *gadrāēl hai*, is used, and in the south-east they say दुधैलै *dudhailai*. गदराएल *gadrāēl* is also used in Tirhut. When the grain hardens they say it is हबसाएल *habsāēl* in South-West Shahabad, कैलाएल *kailāēl* generally; in Sāran and West Tirhut also गोटाएल *gotāēl*, अधपक्कू *adhpakku* in Gaya, कैला गेल *kaila gel* in Patna, and कलाएल *kalāēl* in the south-east.

958. The beard is टूँड़ *tūnr* or टूँड़ा *tūnra* to the west, and सूँघ *sūngh* or सूँग *sūng* elsewhere. In South-West Tirhut it is सूँड़ *sūnr*. The ear itself is बाल *bāl*, except in North-West Tirhut, where it is बाली *bāli*; in South-East Tirhut, where it is सीस *sīs*; in South Bhagalpur, where it is सीसा *sīsa*; and in South Munger, where it is टुंगना *tungna*.

CHAPTER II.—MIXED CROPS.

959. Wheat and barley grown together are गोजई *gojaī*. A mixture of peas, gram, barley, or wheat, or any two or three of them, is called तेरा *terra* in South-West Shahabad, गजर मसर *gajar masar* in the rest of that district, गजर बजर *gajar bajar* in Champāran, गजा बजा *gaja baja* south of the Ganges generally, and उटरा *utra* in Patna. In the north-west it is पैरा *paira*, in West Tirhut पैर *pair*, and in East Tirhut पौर *paur* or बेझरा *bejhra*. Barley grown with the smaller pea (केराव *kerāo*) is जौ केराइ *jau kerāi*

generally, also जौ मट्रा *jau matra* to the west, जकेराइ *jakerāï* to the south-east, and जब केर्‌वा *jab kerwa* in North-East Tirhut. Other names are कुसही केराव *kusahi kerāo* in Patna and the south-east, कोसी *kosi* in South Bhagalpur, and हर्‌फोर्‌वा केराव *harphorwa kerāo* in South-West Shahabad. बेर्‌रा *berra* or बेरई *beraī* in Shahabad is barley mixed with gram, and the same is called जब बुट्टा *jab butta* north of the Ganges, and जो बट्टा *jo butta* in the south-east. जो खेस्‌रा *jo khesra* is a mixture of barley and peas (खेसारी *khesāri*) in the south-east.

960. When there is a mixture of crops, the inferior one is called तरी *tari* when compared with the other. Thus in जौ केराइ *jau kerāï* the small pea (केराव *kerāo*), being the inferior, is the तरी *tari*.

CHAPTER III.—BARLEY AND OATS.

961. Barley (*hordeum vulgare*) is जौ *jau* generally. In the north-east it is जब *jab*, and in Patna and the south-east जो *jo*. North of the Ganges जई *jaī* (also in Shahabad) or जन्तरी *jantari* are shoots of barley artificially grown and distributed by Brāhmans at the festival of the Dasahra. In Gaya they are जवारा *jawāra*, and in Patna जैंती *jainti*. The prickly hairs on the ear are टूँड़ *tūnr* in West Tirhut, Sāran, and Shahabad; टूँड़ा *tūnra* or सूँढ़ा *sūnrha* in Champāran and Tirhut; सूँड़ *sūnr* in South-West Tirhut, and also सूँघ *sūngh* or सूँग *sūng* in Patna and the east generally.

962. Oats (*avena sativa*) are called the sister of barley, and are hence named जई *jaī* or जै *jai*.

CHAPTER IV.—RICE.

963. Rice (*oryza sativum*), whether as a crop or threshed but unhusked, is called धान *dhān*. When husked it is चाउर *chāür*, but the Hindi form चावल *chāwal* has also been noted in Patna. Husked rice is of two kinds, viz. अर्‌वा *arwa*, which is not parboiled before husking and is eaten by the higher castes, and the cheaper, which is parboiled before husking and is eaten by the lower castes. This latter is called उसिना *usina*, उस्‌ना *usna*, or जोसाँदा *josānda*. Rice when partially husked is called मुह्‌चुर *muhchur* in Gaya, बोक्‌ड़ा *bokra* in Sāran, and खिजाया *khijāya* in North-East Tirhut. Rice boiled plain is भात *bhāt*, when boiled with pulses it is खिचड़ी *khichri*, and when spices are added to this it is भूनल खिचड़ी *bhūnal khichri* or कबूली *kabūli*; also in

South Bhagalpur छौँकी *chhaunki.* When rice is boiled to a mash, it is called गोलन्हथ *golhath* or गोलन्हत्थी *golhatthi.* In Gaya पनिहता *panihata* is a dish made by adding water to the rice left from last night's supper. In addition to the usual names, लार *lār,* पोआर *poār,* &c. (see § 894), the long straw of transplanted rice is called मोरी पेटारी *mori petāri,* or (in Champāran) पेटाही *petāhi* or (in Shahabad) पेटाढ़ी *petārhi.*

964. The varieties of rice grown in Bihār are very numerous, as is borne out by many proverbs, such as the following :—रजन्पूत ओ धान के ओर नाहिँ है *rajpūt o dhān ke or nāhiñ hai,*—there is no limit to the clans of Rajputs or the kinds of rice; धान बाभन कैँ एक्के हाल *dhān bābhan keñ ekke hāl,*—rice and Bābhans are one and the same (in number of kinds). Rice may be divided into two broad classes, those which are sown at once broadcast and are called बावग *bāwag,* बाओग *bāög,* (in Gaya) बोगेड़ा *bogera,* or in Patna बोगन्हा *bogha,* and those which are sown in seed-beds and transplanted, being called रोप *rop* or रोपा *ropa* or (in Gaya and Patna) रोपन्हा *ropha.* At the same time it should be noted that practice varies with locality, and that a kind of rice which is बावग *bāwag* in one place may be रोपा *ropa* in another.

A.—RICE THAT IS SOWN BROADCAST.

965. (1) साठी *sāthi.*—This is a red rice, and ripens in sixty days from sowing, as in the proverb—

साठी पाके साठ दिन,
बरन्खा होखे रात दिन.

Sāthi pāke sāth din,
Barkha hokhe rāt din.

—*Sāthi* ripens in sixty days if it rains night and day.

In the east it is also called गँभन्री *gambhri* or गम्हन्री *gamhri.* It is sown in the month of Jeth (May–June), and is cut in Sāwan (July–August).

(2) सोकन्ना *sokna* (north-west).—This is sown with the first fall of rain in Jeth (May–June), and is cut in Bhādoñ or Āsin (*i.e.,* in September). This crop is also called भदैया *bhadaiya.*

(3) The following are sown in Phāgun (February–March) and Chait (March–April), and are cut in Aghan (November–December). The names were principally

collected in *East Tirhut*, and unless the contrary is specially stated do not apply elsewhere :—

(*a*) अकाल बीर *akāl bīr*. (In Sāran अकाल गीर *akāl gīr*, and in North-East Tirhut also काला गीर *kāla gīr*.)
(*b*) उजागर *ujāgar*, or in Sāran जागर *jāgar*, which name is also current in North-East Tirhut.
(*c*) चनाबक *chanābak*.
(*d*) झलमरदन *jhalmardan*.
(*e*) दरमी *darmi* (also known in the north-west).
(*f*) देसरिया *desariya* (Tirhut and Champāran). In Sāran it is called जसरिया *jasariya*).
(*g*) पीचर *pīchar*.
(*h*) बेलौर *belaur* (also known in the north-west).
(*i*) भाँटिन *bhāntin* (Sāran).
(*j*) भैसलेट *bhaislet* (also known in the north-west).
(*k*) लाँजी *lānji* (Sāran).
(*l*) सतरिया *satariya* (Sāran).
(*m*) साहिल *sāhil* (Sāran).
(*n*) सिँगरा *singra*.
(*o*) सोबरा *sobra*.

खेड़ा *kherha* is a white bearded rice sown all over Tirhut and in Champāran. The following (also East Tirhut) are sown in Jeth (May–June). They are sometimes sown broadcast and sometimes transplanted :—

(*a*) धुसरी *dhusri* (also known in Champāran).
(*b*) बसतर *bastar*.
(*c*) राम दुलारी *rām dulāri*.

966. In *South-West Shahabad* the following kinds of rice are sown broadcast :—

(*a*) करँगा *karnga* } Two kinds with a black grain (also known
(*b*) करँगी *karngi* } in Sāran).
(*c*) करहनी *karhanni*, a small black grain (also known in Sāran).
(*d*) खाटिन *khātin*, a coarse kind.
(*e*) सहदेइया *sahdeïya*, a red kind.
(*f*) साठी *sāthi*. See above.

(g) सेहा *serha*, a small black and white grain. Like the साठी *sāthi*, it ripens in sixty days. The South-West Shahabad version of the saying already quoted is—

सेहा साठी साठ दिन, जँव देव बरसे रात दिन
Serha sāthi sāth din, jemw deb barse rāt din.

—*Serha* and *sāthi* take sixty days if it rain night and day.

In the rest of *Shahabad* the following kinds of rice are sown broadcast:—

(a) पनसारी *pansāri.*
(b) भुँइसीकर *bhuinsīkar.*
(c) मूँगा *mūnga.*
(d) राम करहनी *rām karhani.*
(e) राम दुलारी *rām dulāri.*
(f) साहिल *sāhil.*
(g) सिरहन्ट *sirhant.*

967. In *Gaya* sowing is done in the month of Akhār, in the lunar asterism of *Aradra* (June-July). About this asterism (नछत्तर *nachhattar*) and the two following ones the following rhyme is current throughout Bihār :—

अरदरा धान, पुनरबस पैया
गेल, किसान, जे बोए चिरैया
Aradra dhān, Punarbas paiya,
Gel, kisān, je boe Chiraiya.

—Paddy sown in *Aradra* turns into plenty, sown in *Punarbas* to chaff, and sown in *Chiraiya* (or *Pukh*) it turns to nothing.

The paddy is generally cut in the month of Pūs (December-January).

Amongst the kinds of paddy sown broadcast in this district are—

(a) एदली *edli.*
(b) कतिका *katika*,—cut in Kātik (October-November).
(c) कनबदा *kanbada.*
(d) करहनी *karhanni.*
(e) जोँगा *jonga.*
(f) झँरगा *jhanrga.*
(g) धुसरा *dhusra*
(h) रटवा *ratwa.*
(i) ललदेइया *laldeïya.*

(*j*) लोहन्रा *lohra.*
(*k*) सिरन्हट्टी *sirhatti.*

968. In *Patna* on the first fall of rain, which generally takes place in the asterism of *Rohni*, in the month of Jeth (May–June), the sowing is commenced. Paddy which is sown broadcast is divided into two classes—a red, which is considered superior, and is called ललन्गोँडिया *lalgondiya*, and a black, which is considered inferior, and is called कारा बोगन्हा *kāra bogha.* The former kind includes करन्हन्नी *karhanni* as the principal. The ear is black.

969. In *South Munger* the following kinds are sown broadcast:—

(*a*) अजान *ajān*, a white variety.
(*b*) कजन्री *kajri.*
(*c*) करन्हन्नी *karhanni.* See above.
(*d*) खिरन्दन्त *khirdant.*
(*e*) छगन्रा *chhagra.*
(*f*) जौगा *jauga.*
(*g*) पनन्साहा *pansāha* (a coarse red kind).
(*h*) बुढ़न्वा *burhwa.*
(*i*) राँगी *rāngi.*
(*j*) सरिहन *sarihan*, a white variety.
(*k*) सिरन्हट्टी *sirhatti.*

970. In *South Bhagalpur* the following kinds are sown broadcast:—

(*a*) कजरन्घरो *kajargharo.*
(*b*) गोहन्मा *gohma.*
(*c*) चाँग *chāng.*
(*d*) जोँगा *jonga.*
(*e*) दुदन्सर *dudsar.*

B.—RICE THAT IS TRANSPLANTED.

971. This rice is generally sown with the first rains in Jeth (May–June). It is transplanted in Sāwan (July–August). In Patna the custom is to commence transplanting on the 5th of Sāwan, after holding a festival, called नकन्पाँचो *nakpāncho*, or the "fifth of the asterism (नखत *nakhat*)." The regular harvest is held in Aghan (November–December). Before this, however, some is cut for the ceremony of बिसुन पिरित *bisun pirit* (called in Saran बिसुनटिया *bisunatiya*), at which Brāhmans are feasted on the new grain.

972. The following kinds of rice are transplanted in *Tirhut* :—

(*a*) अङ्गा *anga*, a black bearded kind.

(*b*) कनक जीर *kanak jīr* (East Tirhut).

(*c*) कमोच *kamoch*, a black kind grown in North-West.

(*d*) करम्मा *karma*, a long black kind (Tirhut).

(*e*) गऊमा *gahuma*, a red flat kind grown in North-East Tirhut.

(*f*) जगरन्नथिया *jagarnathiya*, a similar kind grown in North-West Tirhut.

(*g*) दुधन्राज *dudhrāj*, small and white.

(*h*) नन्हिया *nanhiya* (East Tirhut).

(*i*) बहरन्नी *baharni* (North-West Tirhut) or बहोरन्नी *bahorni* (North-East Tirhut), a long white variety.

(*j*) भाल सरी *bhāl sari*.

(*k*) मनसन्री *manasri*, a red variety (also known in Sāran).

(*l*) माल भोग *māl bhog*.

(*m*) रमुनी *ramuni* (also known in Sāran).

(*n*) लाल देइया *lāl deïya*, or in Sāran ललन्देइया *laldeiya*, a red variety.

(*o*) सरिहन *sarihan* (north of the Ganges generally), sown in Baisākh (April–May) and cut in Sāwan (July–August).

(*p*) सिलन्हट *silhat*, with a black husk but white grain.

973. In *South-West Shahabad* the following are transplanted :—

(*a*) जलन्होर *jalhor*, possesses a fine grain.

(*b*) झेंगी *jhengi*, a white variety.

(*c*) दुधन्काँड़र *dudhkānrar*, white.

(*d*) बांसन्मती *bāsmati*, a superior white variety.

(*e*) बैतरन्नी *baitarni*, a reddish kind.

(*f*) भेंड़न्काबर *bhenrkābar*, a coarse red kind.

(*g*) मांल देही *māl dehi*, a fine-grained variety.

(*h*) मुटुनी *mutuni*, white.

(*i*) रमन्जूआ *ramjūa*, fine.

(*j*) लौंगन्चूरा *longchūra* (a black and very fine variety).

(*k*) सिरी केवल *sirī kebal*, white.

974. In the rest of *Shahabad* the following are transplanted :—

(*a*) कनकन्जीरा *kanakjīra*.

(*b*) दुलहन्रा *dulahra*.

(*c*) दोलङ्गी *dolangi*.

975. In *Gaya* the following are transplanted :—

(a) कम-ला पर-साद *kamla parsād.*
(b) गज-पत्ता *gajpatta.*
(c) गुड-रा *gudra.*
(d) गोखुल फूल *gokhul phūl.*
(e) गोपाल भोग *gopāl bhog.*
(f) ठाकुर भोग *thākur bhog.*
(g) दुध-गिलास *dudhgilās.*
(h) धनीवा *dhanīwa.*
(i) नौ धारा *nau dhāra.*
(j) बकोइया *bakoiya.*
(k) बतास फेनी *batās pheni.*
(l) बतासा *batāsa.*
(m) ब-राँटी *brānti.*
(n) बाँस-मती *bāsmati.*
(o) माध-वा *mādhwa.*
(p) मुर-धी *murdhi.*
(q) लाल केसर *lāl kesar.*
(r) साम जीरा *sām jīra.*
(s) सूगा पङ्खी *sūga pankhi.*
(t) सेल्हा *selha.*

976. In *Patna* the following are transplanted :—

(a) बस-मतिया *basmatiya.*
(b) सफेद *saphed.*
(c) सियाह *siyāh.*
(d) सेल्हा *selha.*

977. In *South Munger* the following are transplanted :—

(a) अनार कली *anār kali.*
(b) कज-री *kajri.*
(c) कञ्चन चूर *kanchan chūr.*
(d) कारी बाँक *kāri bānk.*
(e) गज-पती *gajpati.*
(f) तुल-सी फूल *tulsi phūl.*
(g) डोल-गी *dolgi.*
(h) बाँस-मती *bāsmati.*
(i) लुप-धी *lupdhi.*
(j) सिती सार *sitī sār.*
(k) सेल्हा *selha.*

978. In *South Bhagalpur* the following are transplanted:—

(a) कनक चूर *kanak chūr.*

(b) कमोदी *kamodi* (a sweet-scented variety).

(c) गोखुल सार *gokhul sār.*

(d) दौना फूल *dauna phūl* (a sweet-scented variety).

(e) बाग नर *bāg nar.*

(f) बाँस फूल *bāns phūl.*

(g) बांसमती *bāsmati.*

(h) बासा पसिन *bāsa pasin.*

(i) मनसरा *mansara.*

(j) रमनिया *ramaniya.*

(k) राम दुलर *rām dullar.*

(l) हमचा *hamcha.*

979. Of all the above rices, the most esteemed is साम जीरा *sām jīra.* It is a fine kind, and when cooked its fragrance fills the house. The next best is बांसमती *bāsmati* or बसमतिया *basmatiya,* which is not quite so fine as the first. सेल्हा *selha* may be considered as the third best.

C.—OTHER MISCELLANEOUS KINDS OF RICE.

980. बोरो *boro* is a poor kind of rice sown in Āsin (September–October) or Katik (October–November) in the mud on the banks of streams and lakes. It is transplanted several times in Pūs and Māgh (December, January, and February). लमेरा *lamera* or (in South-East Tirhut) झर *jhar* or in (Sāran) झारन *jhāran* is rice which has fallen from the sheaves when reaping, taken root, and grown next year.

981. *Rice-lands.*—Land which has been under a rice-crop is धनहर *dhanhar,* धनखेत *dhankhet,* or धनखेती *dhankheti.* It is also धनखर *dhankhar* in Shahabad, धनकियारा *dhankiyāra* in Gaya, and धनहा *dhanha* in Patna. Fresh waste land ploughed up for rice sowing is खिलमार *khilmār;* also नवाद खेत *nawād khet* north of the Ganges, and नौखील *naukhīl* in Gaya. In the south-east it is खिलकट *khilkat* or खिलकट्टी *khil-katti.* To dig it in order to make it fit for sowing is खील कोड़ब *khīl korab* or खील तोड़ब *khīl torab.* The preparation of a rice-field is कादो (or कदवा) करब *kādo* (or *kadwa*) *karab;* also लेव करब *leo karab* in

Sāran, and मसाह करब *masāh karab* in Champāran. A man who cultivates rice is धनहा *dhanha* to the west.

982. *Seedlings.*—A nursery for rice seedlings is बिड़ार *birār* or बियार *biyār*. In South-West Shahabad it is बेँगा *benga.* The seed is बीहन *bīhan*, बिहनाइ *bihnāï*, or बीया *bīya*, and the same words are also used for the seedlings of any crop; but the seedlings of rice are specially called मोरी *mori* south of the Ganges and to the west. They are also called जरई *jaraī* in Champāran. The bundles of rice seedlings ready for transplanting are आँटी *ānti* or अँटिया *antiya* north of the Ganges and in the south-east, and the quantity transplanted at one place is everywhere except to the south-east बान *bān*. Seedlings of बोरो *boro* rice which have been transplanted once and are again transplanted are called in North-East Tirhut खारु *khāru* or खरुहान *kharuhān*. For fuller information concerning seedlings and transplanting, see 855 and ff.

CHAPTER V.—INDIAN CORN OR MAIZE.

983. Indian corn or maize (*zea mays*) is मकई *makaī* or मकैया *makaiya*. It is also called जनेरा *janera* in the west and जिनोरा *jinora* in Patna, which names ought properly to be applied to the large millet (*holcus sorghum*). The stalks are ढट्ठा *dhattha* to the west and ठठरा *thathera* to the north generally. In South Bhagalpur they are ठठेरो *thathero*, and elsewhere डाँट *dānt* or डाँटी *dānti*. The broken stalk is लथेर *lathēr* in the North-West and West Tirhut, and निघास *nighās* or निघेसा *nighesa* in East Tirhut. No special name for this has been noted south of the Ganges.

984. When the grains begin to form, but are not yet fit for eating, the ear is called सञ्चा *sancha.* The unripe ear is दुद्धा *duddha* to the west generally, and also दोधा *dodha* in Shahabad. Other names are खिच्चा *khichcha* or अजू *aju* in Tirhut, दुधघोट्टु *dudhghottu* in Gaya, दुद्धा मकई *duddha makaī* in Sāran and Patna, दुधभोरो *dudhbhoro* in South Bhagalpur, and दँतकमरा *dantkamra* in South Munger. When ripe it is भुट्टा *bhutta* or बाल *bāl.* When the seeds are ripe and hard, and not fit for eating, it is called पकठाइल *pakthāïl.* The roasted ear is होरहा *horha* generally, and also ओरहा *orha* to the east. The empty cob after the grain is beaten out is लेँढ़ा *lenrha* generally; also नेढ़ा *nerha* in East Tirhut and लेँढ़ुरी *lenruri* in Shahabad. In Patna and South-East Tirhut an optional name is बलुरी *baluri*, and South-East

Tirhut and South Munger बलरी *balri.* In South-West Shahabad the word used is खुखुड़ी *khukhuri* or खोंखरी *khonkhri,* and in South Bhagalpur हड्डी *haddi.* The grain beaten out is गोटा *gota* or गोट *got.* An ear with no grain in it is called भोराढ *bhorāh* or भोरहा *bhorha* north of the Ganges. When it contains only a few grains it is called पचगोटिया *pachgotiya.* The hair on the ear is भूआ *bhūa* to the west; also घूआ *ghūa* in South-West Shahabad. In Champāran and Gaya it is called सन *san.* In Patna it is मोंछ *monchh;* in South Munger, मोछा *mochha;* in Tirhut and South Bhagalpur, मोच *moch* or मोचा *mocha.* It is also called केसी *kesi.* The sheath of the cob is खोइया *khoïya* to the west, and बलखोइया *balkhoïya* or बोकला *bokla* generally. In Champāran another name is खलचोइया *khalchoïya,* and in South-West Tirhut बलको *balko* or कोसा *kosa.* In East Tirhut it is खोंइचा *khoincha,* in South Munger पतौरा *pataura,* and in South Bhagalpur पोचो *pocho.* The male ear is called धनबाल *dhanbāl* or धनहरा *dhanahra.*

CHAPTER VI.—THE LARGE MILLET.

985. Large millet (*holcus sorghum* or *sorghum vulgare*) जनेर *janer* or जनेरा *janera* generally. A variety of it is called मसुरिया जनेर *masuriya janer* to the west to distinguish it from maize (*zea mays,* see last chapter). So also it is called नन्हिया जनेरा *nanhiya janera* in East Munger. Local names are गेहुमा *gehuma* and जोन्हरी *jonhri* in Sāran, जिनोरा *jinora* in Patna and Gaya, and गहुमा *gahuma* in South Bhagalpur. Amongst its varieties may be mentioned a large red kind grown in Shahabad, called जोंधरी *jondhri.* This is called सिसुआ गहुमा *sisua gahuma* in South Bhagalpur. A similar red kind is called रकसा *raksa* or रकसी *raksi.* This millet is little grown south of the Ganges. The only other kind noted there is बजड़ा *bajra,* which is described as a dwarf white variety (*see* however § 987). North of the Ganges दुधिया *dudhiya,* or (in South Tirhut) लरकटिया *larkatiya* or नरकटिया *narkatiya,* is a dwarf white variety. The following also occur north of the Ganges:—झलरिया *jhalariya,* of which the head bends down, and which ripens late. जेठी *jethi* in the north-west is a kind sown for fodder. A kind with two grains in one husk is called गेंहुआँ *genhuān.*

986. The stalks cut up for fodder are ढठेरा *dhathera* or ढट्ठा *dhattha* to the west, and ठठेर *thather* or ठठेरा *thathera* to the east. When the young plant first germinates it is अँकुरा *ankura*, and the young plant is डिब्बी *dibbhi* or डीभी *dibhi*. The ears are बाल *bāl*, or in East Tirhut optionally सीस *sīs*. The large stack of the stalks cut up for fodder is गाँज *gānj* to the west and टाल *tāl* to the east. Local names are खम्हार *khamhār* or काँड़ *kānr* in South-East Tirhut.

CHAPTER VII.—THE SMALL BULRUSH MILLET.

987. This millet (*holcus spicatus* or *pencillaria spicata*) is बजड़ा *bajra* in Sāran. South of the Ganges it is sometimes incorrectly called मसुरिया जनेर (or in Patna जिनोरा) *masuriya janer* (or in Patna *jinora*), which is properly a different grain, a variety of the large millet (*holcus sorghum* ; see § 986). In South West Shahabad it is जोंधरिया *jondhariya*, and in South Bhagalpur गहुमा *gahuma*. Just as the large millet is grown principally north of the Ganges, so this millet is grown almost entirely south of it. Hence there is great confusion in their names. The following terms relate exclusively to South Bihār :—The stalk is डाँट *dānt* or डाँटी *dānti* everywhere ; also ढट्ठा *dhattha* in Shahabad and ठठेरो *thathero* in South Bhagalpur. The first shoots of the plant are अँखुआ *ankhua* or सूआ *sūa* ; also टिभिया *tibhiya* in South Munger and सुइया *suiya* in South Bhagalpur. To throw out shoots is अँखुआएब *ankhuāëb* or सुआएब *suāëb*. When the ear begins to show itself the phrase used is ललहात बा *lalhāt ba* in Shahabad, रेंड़ा भेल है *renra bhel hai* in Gaya, लहलहा रहल है *lahlaha rahal hai* in Patna, अड़ा गेल *ara gel* in South Munger, and हलहलाइछै *halhalāichai* in South Bhagalpur. When the heads are blighted and grainless, they are थुण्ठा *thuntha* in South-West Shahabad, बन्झड़ *banjhar* in the rest of that district and in West Tirhut, बाँड़ *bānr* in Gaya, ठुट्ठा *thuttha* in Patna, and मुड़िया *muriya* in the south-east. The fluffy flowers are घोंपा *ghompa* in South-West Shahabad, जावा *jāwa* in South Munger, and फुलको *phulko* in South Bhagalpur.

CHAPTER VIII.—THE SMALL MILLETS.

988. These are—

(1) *Panicum Italicum.*—This is टंगुनी *tanguni* to the south-west and in Sāran, and टाँगुन *tāngun* in Sāran and Gaya. Elsewhere it is कौनी *kauni*, or in South Munger optionally काउन *kāün*.

989. (2) *Panicum mileaceum.*—साँवाँ *sāñwāñ* or सावाँ *sāwāñ*. In Tirhut it is also सामा *sāma*, and in South Bhagalpur समा *sama*.

990. (3) *Eleusine coracana.*—This is the most important of all the millets, forming the staple food of a large portion of the population. It is मड़ुआ *marua* or मँड़ुआ *manrua*. The empty dry ears after the grain has been taken out are डाँटी *dānti* north of the Ganges; also कटुआ *katua* in North-East Tirhut, मोढ़ी *morhi* in South-East Tirhut, and पुत्ती *putti* in South-West Tirhut. In South-West Shahabad they are खोलड़ी *kholri*, and in the rest of that district भूसी *bhūsi*. In Patna and Gaya they are भूसा *bhūsa* or खलकोइया *khalkoïya*, and in the south-east they are भस्सा *bhussa*. The stalks are नेरुआ *nerua* or लेरुआ *lerua* to the west, and लार *lār* to the north-east. Another word current to the north-west is ढट्ठा *dhattha*. In Patna they are नार *nār*, in Gaya नारा *nāra*, and in the south-east लरुआ *larua* or नरुआ *narua*. In Gaya and the west डाँठ *dānth* or डाँट *dānt* or डाँटी *dānti* is also used. The green ears roasted for food are उम्मी *ummi* or ऊमी *ūmi* to the west and in Tirhut, and ऊनी *ūni* in Champāran. When cut somewhat riper, but not quite ripe, and then roasted, they are होरहा *horha* generally, and ओरहा *orha* in Tirhut and to the east. They are optionally होलहा *holha* in Champāran and South Munger. In Shahabad they are हाबुस *hābus*, and south of the Ganges generally घुँघनी *ghunghni* or घुघनी *ghughni*. This being an important food-crop, there are many popular sayings concerning it. The following may be quoted:—

जब मड़ुआ आ के गाछी भेल ।
धिया पुता सुख सुख माछी भेल ॥
जब मड़ुआ में बाल भेल ।
धिया पुता के गाल भेल ॥

Jab marua a ke gāchhi bhel,
Dhiya puta sukh sukh māchhi bhel.
Jab marua meñ bāl bhel,
Dhiya puta ke gāl bhel.

—When the *marua* began to sprout, the children dried up like flies (*i.e.*, their food had been used for seed-grain); but when the *marua* came in the ear, the children got (fat) cheeks.

मड़ुआ मीन चीन सङ्ग दही।
कोदो के भात दूध सङ्ग सही॥

Marua mīn, chīn sang dahi,
Kodo ke bhāt dūdh sang sahi.

—*Marua* should be taken with fish, *chīna* with tyre, and milk with *kodo*.

कोदो मड़ुआ अन नहिँ।
जोलहा धुनिया जन नहिँ॥

Kodo marua an nahiñ,
Jolha Dhuniya jan nahiñ.

—*Kodo* and *marua* are not really food-grains, (*i.e.* they are despised as poor men's food), just as weavers and cotton-carders can never be cultivators.

991. (4) *Panicum frumentosum.*—This is चिन्ना *chinna* or चीना *chīna*, local variants being चीन *chīn* in East Tirhut and चीन्ह *chīnh* in South-West Shahabad. It is of two kinds in Sāran,—गौरिया *gauriya* and रकसा *raksa*. The grains when boiled and then parched are called माढ़ा *mārha* or माँढ़ा *mānrha*, or in East Tirhut माड़ *mār*.

992. (5) *Paspalum frumentaceum*—This is कोदो *kodo*. In Shahabad a smaller variety is called कोदई *kodaī*.

993. *Miscellaneous.*—मकरा *makra* (*eleusine ægyptica*), a kind of grass of which the seeds are eaten. In the North-Western Provinces this name is applied to *eleusine coracana*, but not in Bihār.

CHAPTER IX.—PULSES.

994. Among the pulses are—

(1) *Cytisus Indicus* or *cajanus.*—This is रहर *rahar* or रहरी *rahri*. In North-East Tirhut it is also called रैहड़ *raihar*, राहरि *rāhari*, or राहर *rāhar*. The dry stalks are रहेठा *rahetha*

north of the Ganges, or रहाठ *rahāth* or राहठ *rāhath* in East Tirhut. South of the Ganges we have हरेठा *haretha* or ररेठा *raretha* (also used in Tirhut) in South-West Shahabad, रहरेठा *rahretha* in the rest of that district, रहरैठा *rahraitha* in Patna and Gaya, लहरैठा *lahraitha* in South Munger, and लरेठो *laretho* in South Bhagalpur. The pods are ढेंढ़ी *dhenrhi* generally, and छेमी *chhemi* also north of the Ganges and in Shahabad. To the East they are also छीमड़ि *chīmari* or छिमड़ी *chhimri*. In Gaya they are also छीमी *chhimi*, in Patna डिण्डी *dindi*, and in South Munger डींड़ी *dīnri*. The stalks used for fodder are भूस *bhūs* or भूसा *bhūsa*; also कटुआ *katua* in Patna and कटुओ *katuo* in the south-east. This and other pulses when sprouting are known as डिब्भी *dibbhi* or डीभी *dibhi*, except in the north-east, where they are गाछ *gāchh*. Bread made from this pulse, gram (बूँट *būnt*), and *phaseolus mungo* (मुङ्ग *mung*), is called लिट्टी *litti* or रोटी *roti* north of the Ganges (both these words being general terms for bread made from any grain), भभरा *bhabhra* in Patna and Gaya, and चितावा *chitāwa* in South Munger. बरी *bari* is a kind of round cake or fritters made similarly.

995. (2) *Phaseolus mungo*.—This is मुङ्ग *mung* or मूँग *mūng*. In North-East Tirhut it is also called मँहा मूँग *mañha mūng*. The pods are called the same as those of *cytisus cajanus* (रहर *rahar*). The stalks used for fodder are झेँगरा *jhengra* in Sāran, Gaya, and South-West Tirhut, झार *jhār* in Champāran and North-West Tirhut, डाँठ *dānth* in North-East Tirhut, and गाछ *gāchh*, झमड़ी *jhamri*, or झाँग *jhāng* in South-East Tirhut. South of the Ganges they are भूस *bhūs* or भूसा *bhūsa*; also कटुआ *katua* in Patna and कुटुओ *kutuo* in the south-east.

996. (3) *Phaseolus roxburghii* or *phaseolus radiatus*.—This is उरिद *urid* or (south of the Ganges optionally) उरदी *urdi*. In East Tirhut it is also called कलाइ *kalāi*, कराइ *karāi*, or मास कलाइ *mās kalāi*. There are several kinds, *e.g.*, डोमा *doma* (East Tirhut), which bears in *Pūs* and *Māgh* (January); लरही *larhi* (Sāran and South-West Tirhut), नरहू *narhu*, नरहो *narho*, लरहो *larho* or असनी *asni* (Tirhut), or अगहनुआ *aghanua* (Sāran, Cham-

pāran), which bears in *Aghan* (November–December); तेपखी *tepakhi* (Sāran and South-West Tirhut) or कतिका *katika* (elsewhere north of the Ganges), which bears in *Kātik* (October–November); and भदन्वी *bhadwi* (South Munger), which bears in *Bhādoñ* (August–September). Another division is into black and green varieties. The black varieties are डङ्गा *danga* (North-East Tirhut), कारी *kāri*, करिया *kariya* (Shahabad and the south-east), काला *kāla* in Gaya, and सियाह *siyāh* in Patna. The green kinds are तुलन्बुली *tulbulli* in North-East Tirhut, हरिअर *hariar* in Shahabad, हरन्रा *harra* in Gaya, and सबन्जी *sabji*, in Patna. The pods are ढेँढ़ी *dhenrhi*, छेमी *chhemi*, &c., as above.

997. (4) *Phaseolus aconitifolius.*—This has only been noted south of the Ganges. It is generally called मोथ *moth*. A smaller variety is मोथी *mothi*. The stalks used for fodder are भूस *bhūs*, कटुआ *katua*, &c., as above.

998. (5) *Ervum hirsutum* (one variety) or *cicer* (or *vicia*) *lens* (another variety).—This is मसूर *masūr* or मसुरी *masuri*.

999. (6) *Miscellaneous.*—कुरन्थी *kurthi* (*dolichos biflorus*), खेसारी *khesāri* (*lathyrus sativa*),* भेँट *bhent* or भेँटन्वाँस *bhent-wāns*, खेत मास *khet mās* or खेत मासु *khet māsu* (North-East Tirhut), which is apparently a variety of *phaseolus radiatus*, भिरँन्गी *bhirngi* (a kind of wild pulse eaten by the poor), and (Shahabad) लतन्री *latri*.

---

* It is unwholesome for human beings, but bullocks eat it greedily, *e.g.*, in the saying—

तुरुक तारी, बैल खेसारी,
बामन आम, कायथ काम.

Turuk tāri, bail khesāri,
Bāman ām, Kāyath kām.

—Toddy is necessary for a Musalmān's happiness, *khesāri* for a bullock's, mangos for a Brahman's, and employment for a Kāyasth's.

CHAPTER X.—PEAS.

1000. Peas (*pisum sativum*) are of various kinds. The large variety is मटर *matar*, or in South-West Shahabad मण्टर *mantar*. A smaller variety is केराव *kerāo*. This is often sown with barley, when the mixed crop is known as जौ केराइ *jau kerāï*, &c., see § 959. The principal varieties are कबिली *kabili* (north of the Ganges) or कब्ली *kabli* (south of it), which is a large white kind. It is also called घेब्ली *ghebli* in South-East Tirhut. North of the Ganges सुग्वा *sugwa* is a small green variety. Another kind is known as बज्री *bajri* in Champāran. बटुरी *baturi* in Shahabad, and कुसही *kusahi* in Patna, Gaya, and the south-east, is a small black variety. In South Bhagalpur it is called भिठ्गरा *bhithgara*. Another variety is दब्लिया *dabliya* in South-West Shahabad, डबल केराव *dabal kerāo* in the rest of that district, and ढांब्ली *dhābli* in Patna.

1001. When the plant first appears above ground, it is called डिभी *dibbhi* north of the Ganges and in Shahabad, but in the south-west of the latter district it is डाभी *dābhi*. In North-East Tirhut it is also called गाछी *gāchhi*. In Gaya and Tirhut it is अँकुरा *ankura*, in Patna and Tirhut अँखुआ *ankhua*, in South Munger कन्सी *kansi*, and in South Bhagalpur गजुर *gajur*. When the pod appears, the phrase is to the north of the Ganges पटा लागत बा *pata lāgat ba*, or a similar phrase. In South-East Tirhut they say that the plant is पटाएल *patāël* or पट्रा *patra*. In Shahabad they say it is गद्राएल *gadrāël* ; in Gaya and South-West Shahabad they say ढेँढ़ी लागल है (or बा) *dhenrhi lāgal hai* (or *ba*) ; and in Patna डिण्डी लागल है *dindi lāgal hai*. The pod when fully formed is ढेँढ़ी *dhenrhi*, छीमी *chhīmi*, छेमी *chhemi*, or छिम्ड़ी *chhimri* to the north, and डिण्डी *dindi* to the south. In South Bhagalpur it is ढेँड़ी *dhenri*. The unripe pods are गाद *gād* or गादा *gāda*, and when used to make a pottage they are called बट्कार *batkar* in South-West Shahabad. The young shoots are also used for pottage. These are called north of the Ganges साग *sāg* or भाजी *bhāji*, the latter principally to the west. When cooked to a soup it is called परेह *pareh*, and in Patna and Gaya झोर *jhor*. In South Munger they are चन्दा *chanda*, and in South Bhagalpur मट्रो साग *matro sāg*. The young shoots cooked with pulse are called दल्पैँता *dalpainta* in South-West Shahabad, and दल्सग्गा *dalsagga* in Patna, Gaya, Sāran, and the south-east.

CHAPTER XI.—GRAM.

1002. Gram (*cicer arietinum*) is बूँट *būnt* generally. It is also called चना *chana* in Saran, बेदाम *bedām* in East Tirhut, and रहिला *rahila** to the west.

1003. नोनी *noni* or खटाइ *khatāī* is the oxalic acid and acetic acid which form on the leaves. In Shahabad पीयर *pīyar* is a kind of which the grain is yellow pointed, and बूँटी *bunti*, or in Patna चनी *chani*, is a smaller variety. Another small variety is बटुरी *baturi* in Shahabad.

1004. The young shoot as it first appears above ground is said to be सुइआइल *suïāïl*. In East Tirhut they say of it सूई फेंकलन्कैक *sūi phenkalkaik*. The shoot is called दाभ *dābh* in South-West Shahabad, and डिब्भी *dibbhi* in the rest of that district. In South Munger it is टिब्भी *tibbhi*, and in South Bhagalpur गजुर *gajur* or सूआ *sūa*. The young leaves used as pot-herbs are known as साग *sāg* or भाजी *bhāji*, the latter principally in the west. The pod is ढेंढ़ी *dhenrhi* generally, also छीमी *chhīmi* north of the Ganges. Another name is छीमड़ि *chhīmari* or छिमन्ड़ी *chhimri* in East Tirhut. In Patna it is डिण्डी *dindi*, and so also in South Munger. In South Bhagalpur it is ढेंड़ी *dhenri*, and in South-East Tirhut optionally डीँरी *dīñri*. The unripe pods are कचन्रा *kachra*, and elsewhere कचन्री *kachri*. When the gram appears in the pod, the verb used is गदन्राएब *gadrāëb*. The plant is then called in South-West Shahabad पटन्की *patki*, and in the rest of that district चटन्कोहा *chatkoha*. In Gaya the phrase is चितुरा लागल है *chitura lāgal hai*,

---

* *E.g.* in the song—

एहि रहिला के पूरि कचौरी
एहि रहिला के दाल।
एहि रहिला के कैलीँ खिरवरा,
बहुत मोटैलेँ गाल ॥

Ehi rahila ke pūri kachauri,
Ehi rahila ke dāl;
Ehi rahila ke kailīñ khirawara,
Bahut motailen gāl.

—I made this gram into *pūri* (thin bread fried in clarified butter) and cakes into pottage *khirawara* (cakes of rice-flour prepared in hot water), and my cheeks got very fat.

and in Patna चट्टा धरिस है *chatta dharis hai*. The husk of the gram is बलुखा *balukha* in South-East Tirhut; elsewhere it is भुस्सा *bhussa*, भूँसा *bhūnsa*, or भूसा *bhūsa*. Gram injured by rain is मराइल *marāil*, in Sāran गलल *galal*. In Tirhut it is मारल गेल *māral gel*. South of the Ganges it is पतलग्गू *patlaggu* or पतलगुआ *patlagua*, except in South-West Shahabad, where it is उकठा *uktha*, in South Munger दहियाएल *dahiyāēl*, and in South Bhagalpur दगियाल *dagiyāl*.

CHAPTER XII.—SUGAR-CANE.

1005. Sugar-cane (*saccharum officinarum*) is known generally as ऊख *ūkh* or ऊखि *ūkhi*. In Tirhut, Patna, Gaya, and South-East Bihār a more general name is केतारी *ketāri*. In North-East Tirhut it is also known as ख़ुसियार *khusiyār*. Among the varieties are—

कुसिहार *kusihār* (south of Ganges), a dwarf hard variety.

केतार (Gaya and the south-east), केतारा *ketāra* (Patna), केवाली *kewāli* (Sāran), केवाही *kewāhi* (Shahabad), रौंदा *raunda* (South Munger), a tall thin variety. Ripens in *Kātik* (October-November).

केवाही *kewāhi*,—see केतार *ketār*.

चिनिया *chiniya* or चिनियाँ *chiniyān*, which is a soft, large, whitish cane. Good for eating in *Phāgun* or *Chait* (March). It is called पनसारी *pansāri* in Gaya and Shahabad, पनसाही *pansāhi* in Sāran, and also पनछाही *panchhāhi* or पँसहिया *pansahiya* in the south-west of that district and in West Tirhut. In South Bhagalpur it is called पौंड़ी *paunri*.

नरगोरी *nargori* (North Bihār),—see बरौंखी *baraunkhi*.

पछियारी *pachhiyāri*,—see पौंढ़ा *ponrha*.

पनछाही *panchhāhi*, पनसारी *pansāri*, पनसाही *pansāhi*,—see चिनिया *chiniya*.

पौंढ़ा *ponrha* (west), पौंड़ा *ponra* (Patna and Gaya), पछियारी *pachhiyāri* (South Bhagalpur), a tall, stout, juicy variety.

पौंड़ी *paunri*,—see चिनिया *chiniya*.

बरौंखी *baraunkhi* (Sāran), बर ऊख *bar ūkh* (South-West Tirhut), or नरगोरी *nargori* (North Bihār generally). This is thin, with a reddish bark. The juice is sweet and thick.

भुरली *bhurli* (North-West Bihār and West Tirhut), a very thick short cane, full of juice. Fit for eating in *Baisākh* (April–May).

मङ्गो *mango*,—a small, hard, red cane.

रेँवड़ा *renwra* (North-West Bihār and South-West Shahabad) or सकरचीनी *sakarchīni* (Patna and Gaya),—a yellowish kind, not good for eating.

रौँदा *raunda*,—see केतार *ketār*.

ललगोँड़ी *lalgonri*,—a tall, red variety.

सकरचीनी *sakarchīni*,—see रेँवड़ा *renwra*.

साही *sāhi* (South-West Tirhut),—a dwarf variety.

हथुनी *hathuni* (Sāran and West Tirhut),—a moderately thick variety.

1006. A cane-field is to the west उखाँव *ukhāñw* or उखारी *ukhāri*. Elsewhere it is simply ऊख (or केतारी) के खेत *ūkh* (or *ketāri*) *ke khet*. Sugarcane land requires careful cultivation, or, as the saying runs, तीन पटावन, तेरह कोड़न *tin patāwan, terah koran*,—three waterings, thirteen hoeings. Land prepared for sugar-cane is उखाँव *ukhānw* in North-West Bihār. When the land is left fallow the autumn preceding the planting, the plant is called पोढ़ा *porha* in the North-West and in South-West Tirhut, and सुँगार *sungār* in North-West Tirhut. When an autumn crop is taken the season before planting the cane, the system is known as जरी *jari* to the west, or in Sāran नारी *nāri*. In North-West Tirhut it is called दोतुरा *dotura*. South of the Ganges it is generally called चौमास *chaumās*. When cane is cultivated without irrigation, a layer of leaves, grass, &c., is thrown over the seed and acts as a sort of hotbed. This system is known as खदियाओल *khadiyaöl* to the west and in South-West Tirhut, and गोआ पटाएब *goa pataëb* in North-West Tirhut. To the west two ploughs are used in cane-planting. The first is simply called हर *har* or पहिया वाला हर *pahiya wāla har*; the second is called कान्ही के हर *kānhi ke har* in Sāran and भठौनी *bhathauni* in Champāran. The second plough has a bundle of grass tied round it, called कान्ही *kānhi* or काँनी *kānni*, to widen the furrow. The furrow is everywhere सिराउर *sirāür*, also रेह *reh* in North-East Tirhut. South of the Ganges a second plough is not used. In Āzamghar the furrow is filled up by ploughing a second furrow alongside it, but in Bihār this is usually done by hand.

1007. The first watering of the cane is गण्डा ढार *ganda dhār* in Gaya and South-West Shahabad; in the rest of Shahabad it is ढँवका

chhenucka. In Patna it is पनन्गण्डा *panganda*, and in South Bhagalpur अँधन्री पटावन *andhri patāwan*. Elsewhere it is simply पहिल पटावन *pahil patāwan*. The second watering is कोड़ा *kora* in Patna. Elsewhere it is दोसर पटावन or (पानी) *dosar patāwan* (or *pāni*), with a variant दोसन्रो पटावन *dosro patāwan* in South Bhagalpur. The third watering is आंखन्री *ākhri* in Patna; elsewhere, तेसर (or तेसन्रो in South Bhagalpur) पटावन (or पानी) *tesar* (or *tesro*) *patāwan* (or *pāni*).

1008. Cane sprouting from the roots left since the previous season is known as खूँटी *khūnti* north of the Ganges, and also खुँटिया *khuntiya* in North-East Tirhut. When sprung from fresh seed it is known as बावग *bāwag*, or (optionally) in Tirhut रोप *rop*. Cane sown after the autumn crop is cut is known as जरिया के ऊख *jariya ke ūkh* to the west, and also नारी के ऊख *nāri ke ūkh* in Sāran. In South-West Tirhut it is दोतुरा के ऊख *dotura ke ūkh*. Elsewhere it is known as चौमसिया *chaumasiya*. Cane cut up for seed is known as गँड़ा *genra* or गँड़ी *genri* to the west, and टोना *tona* or टोनी *toni* to the east. गुल्ली *gulli* is also used in Shahabad. In Patna it is also called पोँन्ह्ड़ा *ponhra*, and in South Bhagalpur बीहन *bihan*. When only the top of the cane (which sprouts quicker than the rest) is cut up for seed, the pieces are called अँगेर *anger* in Sāran, अँगेँरा *angenra* in Gaya, अगारी *agāri* in Patna, अगन्रा *agra* in South Munger, and आगा *āga* in South Bhagalpur. North of the Ganges they are called बधिया *badhiya* or (in North-West Tirhut) फुनगी *phungi*. The hole in which the cane slips are kept before planting is खाद *khād* in Sāran, खाता *khāta* in Champāran, गाड़ा *gāra* in Shahabad, गँड़न्सार *ganrsār* in Gaya, बलन्सार *balsār* in Patna, and टोनन्खाद *tonkhād* or टोनन्खावा *tonkhāwa* in the south-east.

1009. The sprouting eyes of the cane are आँखि *ānkhi* or आँख *ānkh* in Gaya and to the west generally; so also in South Munger. In North Tirhut they are अँखिया *ankhiya*, and in South-West Shahabad अँखन्वा *ankhwa*. In Patna and East Tirhut they are अँखुआ *ankhua*, and in South Bhagalpur अँखियाय *ankhiyāy*. When just sprouted, the cane is called पुआड़ी *puāri* in Champāran, पौरी *pauri* in South-West Tirhut, and गोभी *gobhi* elsewhere north of the Ganges. In Shahabad it is called पोइ *poi*, in Gaya it is said to be अँकुराएल *ankurāël*, in Patna अँखुआएल *ankhuāël*, and in Sāran सुइयाएल *suiyāël*. In South Munger it is टिब्भी *tibbhi*, and in South Bhagalpur डिफी *diphi*. The earth is hoed (कोड़ल *koral*) once after the cane has sprouted. This is called पुआरी के जोत *puāri ke jot* in Champāran, and अन्हरिया *anhariya* in North-East Tirhut. Elsewhere it has no special name. The chief hoeing is done in *Akhārh* (June–July), and is called अखाढ़ी कोड़न *akhārhi koran* or अदरा के कोड़नी *adra ke korni*. To the west it is called असाढ़ी कोड़ *asārhi kor*, and in Gaya it is पासा *pāsa*.

1010. The root is जड़ or जर *jar* to the north-east, and मूढ़ *mūrh* elsewhere north of the Ganges. In Shahabad it is जड़ खर *jar khar*, in Gaya and South Bhagalpur खूँटी *khūnti* or खुँटिया *khuntiya*, and in Patna and South Munger जड़ी *jari* or जड़िया *jariya*. When the sprouts are two or three feet high, they are called टोँटा *tonta* in Patna. Elsewhere they have no special name: the plant is simply described as भर ठेहुना *bhar thehuna*, or in some similar way. The knots on the cane are पोर *por*, and (in Shahabad) पोइ *poï*. They are also called गिरे *gire* or गिरेह *gireh*. When these become visible, the plant is called पोराना *porāna* in Champāran, Patna, Gaya, and the east generally. In West Tirhut they are गिरहाना *girhāna*, and in South-East Tirhut पोर छोड़ना *por chhorna*. In Shahabad they are called डेँड़ौका *denrauka*. When the plant is ready for cutting, it is called अगरबन्धू *agarbandhu* in Patna and अँगेरबन्धू *angerbandhu* in Gaya. In the south-east it is डाँड़ *dānr*. Elsewhere it has no special name. A sprout of cane is आँख *ānkh* north of the Ganges and in Shahabad and Gaya. In North Tirhut it is अँखिया *ankhiya*, in Patna अँखुआ *ankhua*, in South Munger कनसी *kansi*, and in South Bhagalpur गोँझी *gonjhi*. The leaves at the top and the upper part of the cane are अगेँड़ *agenr* in the west, and गेँड़ *genr* in the south-west of Shahabad. In Patna and Gaya they are अँगेरी *angeri*, and also अगरा *agra* in the latter district. In Tirhut they are पगार *pagār*, in East Tirhut छीप *chhīp*, and in the south-east पगड़ा *pagra*. The dry leaves at the top are पतैन *patain* in Sāran and South-East Tirhut, पतहर *pathar* in Champāran and North-West Tirhut, पतलो *patlo* in South-West Tirhut, and पतरस *patras* in North-East Tirhut. In Shahabad they are पतई *pataī*, in Gaya पतौरा *pataura*, in Patna पतहूल *pathūl*, in South Munger पतौरा *pataura* or पतहोल *pathol*, and in South Bhagalpur पलहोर *palhor*. Shoots coming from the knots are कनगोजर *kangojar* or कनोजर *kanojar* in South-East Tirhut.

1011. A branch springing from the bottom and injuring the plant is दोँज *donj* in Sāran and South-West Tirhut, पछखी *pachhkhi* in Champāran, फुटना *phutna* in North-West Tirhut, and गोभी *gobhi* in East Tirhut. In South-West Shahabad it is कनखी *kankhi*, and in the rest of that district गँवखा *ganwkha*. In Patna and Gaya it is जोँका *jonka*, and in the south-east पगुड़ी *paguri*. In South Bhagalpur it is also पहुँच *pahunch* or पोरनोवो *pornowo.* When a plant is attacked by insects, which are called in Sāran and Champāran सीना *sina* or ताड़ा *tāra,* it is called north of the Ganges कनाइल *kanāil* or रतड़ल *ratral,* or (in Tirhut) कनाह *kanāh.* The latter name is also current in South-West Shahabad, and variants are कनाहा *kanāha* in South Munger, कानो *kāno* in South Bhagalpur, and काना *kāna* in Patna. In Gaya it is called रताएल *ratāël,* and another term in use in Patna is रसाएल *rasāël.* North of the Ganges a plant is called मुड़ियारी मारल *muriyāri māral* when the top withers and fresh sprouts (टेनी *teni* in Sāran and दोंजी *donji* in Tirhut) come out from underneath.

1012. The green top cut for fodder is अगेंड़ *agenr* or अंगेर *anger* in Sāran, गेंड़ *genr* in Champāran and Shahabad, अंगेरी *angeri* in Patna and Gaya, and also अगड़ा *agra* in the latter district, and अगाड़ *agār* in South Munger. In Tirhut it is पगार *pagār,* and in South Bhagalpur पगड़ा *pagra.* The piece between two knots cut for eating is पोर *por.* The piece of cane chewed at one time is गुल्ला *gulla,* or (in Shahabad) optionally गुल्ली *gulli,* and the refuse thrown out of the mouth खोइया *khoiya* north of the Ganges. South of the Ganges it is generally खोहिया *khohiya* or चेपुआ *chepua,* local names being सिट्ठी *sitthi* in Shahabad and South Munger, (also used in West Tirhut) and चोपा *chopa* in South Bhagalpur. For the pieces of cane cut for the sugar-mill, see § 288.

1013. A bundle of canes is पाँजा *pānja.* A large bundle is बोझा *bojha,* which is as much as can be carried by a man.

1014. Among the *preparations of the sugar-cane* may be mentioned रस *ras,* or कचरस *kachras,* and in South Bhagalpur कांचो रस *kancho ras,* which is the juice of the cane. When boiled down and undrained, it is राब *rāb* or (in Patna and Gaya) रावा *rāwa.* When boiled down for a longer time, it becomes गुर *gur* or गूर *gūr* (often spelt गुड़, गूड़). When made up in smallish balls it is called भेली *bheli.* Other names are मिठाई *mithāi,* and, when made round and flat, चाकी *chāki* and चकरी *chakri* in Sāran, and चक्की *chakki* in Patna and Gaya. The raw sugar which remains in the bag after pressing the *rāb* is called सक्कर *sakkar,* or in Patna, Gaya, and the south-east सङ्कर *sankar.* When dried, it is called खाँड़ *khānr* or भुर्रा *bhurra* or भूरा *bhūra, i.e.* brown sugar. The molasses, or juice which runs out of the bag when the *rāb* is pressed, is called छोआ *chhoa,* or in South-West Shahabad सिरा *sira.* मिसरी *misri* is sugar-candy or loaf-sugar, and चिन्नी *chinni* or चीनी *chini* is refined brown sugar (सक्कर *sakkar* or भूरा *bhūra*). The molasses (छोआ *chhoa*) above mentioned is used in tobacco manufacture, and is then called तगार *tagār* in Gaya, गरिया *gariya* in Patna, and फाँक *phānk* in South Bhagalpur.

1015. In a sugar-refinery रस *ras* (or in the north-west सरबत *sarbat*) is the raw sugar dissolved in water. मैल *mail* is the scum taken off the boiling-pans. To the south-east this is मैला *maila*, and in North-West Tirhut and Shahabad महिया *mahiya*. The boiled juice is सीरा *sīra*, and the clear filtered juice रास के रस *rās ke ras*. To the north-west the juice after the first filtering is दोमा *doma*, and after the second थोपारी *thopāri*. When the scum is mixed with water and again boiled, it is called पसावा *pasāwa*.

CHAPTER XIII.—COTTON.

1016. The cotton-tree (*gossypium herbaceum*) is known everywhere except to the south-west as बङ्गा *banga* or बाँगा *bānga*, with a local variant बाँगो *bāngo* in South Bhagalpur. To the west it is called कपास *kapās*, which properly means the cotton in the pod. Most kinds of cotton ripen about *Baisākh* (April–May). Amongst the varieties may be noted भोगिला *bhogila* (north of the Ganges), a good kind with large pods, and of medium height; भोचरी *bhochri* (north of Ganges), a small variety, of which the cotton is apt to get blown out of the pod by the wind. फटवाल *phetwāl* is a kind grown in North-West Tirhut, and गाजर *gājar* is one grown close to the house in the बारी *bāri*, and not in the fields, in North-East Tirhut and Shahabad; रढ़िया *rarhiya* (Patna, Gaya, and the south-west), a dwarf variety; बड़ैसा *baraisa* (Patna and Gaya), a large variety; लरमा *larma* (Sāran), नरमा *narma* and हेँवती *henwti* (Shahabad), a dwarf variety. Other kinds grown in Shahabad are बँड़छा *bañrchha* or बँड़ूछा *bañrūchha*, and मनवाँ *manwān*, and in Munger we find गोला *gola* and सुफेद *suphed*. Tirhut is famous for a special kind of cotton which ripens in *Bhādoñ* (August–September), called कोकटी *kokti* or भदैया *bhadaiya*, which is of a red colour, and of which thread and cloth of extreme fineness are made. A dress of *kokti* cloth lasts a life-time.

1017. The uncleaned cotton in the pod is कपास *kapās*, also बाँगा *bānga* in East Tirhut, बाँगो *bāngo* in South Bhagalpur, and काँच रूआ *kānch rūa* in South Munger. To clean the seeds from cotton is ओटब *otab* or ओँटब *ontab*, and the operation is called

ओटनी *otni* or ओटाइ *olāi* in Sāran, and औंटाइ *auntāi* in South Bhagalpur. The last two words also mean the wages paid for cleaning. The cotton-pod is called ढेंढ़ *dhenrh* to the north-west and ढेंढ़ी *dhenrhi* in Tirhut and South Bhagalpur. In Shahabad it is ढोंढ़ी *dhonrhi*, in Gaya टेर *ter*, in Patna and South Munger डिण्डी *dindi* or डीँड़ी *dīnri*. The cotton-seed is बनौर *banaur* to the west, बँगौर *bangaur* in Tirhut, बँगौरा *bangaura* in South Munger, and बँगठी *bangthi* in South Bhagalpur. In South-West Shahabad it is बँदौर *bandaur*. A cotton-picker is लोढ़निहार *lorhnihār* (which means simply 'gatherer') in the north-west; elsewhere there is no special name. North of the Ganges he or she is paid by a share of the cotton picked. This is called पई *paī* in Sāran and South-West Tirhut, पोइ *poï* in South-East Tirhut, and बोइन *boïn* in North-East Tirhut. In North-West Tirhut the share is a fourth of the crop, and is called चौठैया *chauthaiya*.

1018. The stages of growth in the plant are as follows:—

When the first leaf shows, it is called पतियाएल *patiyāël* north of the Ganges. In South-West Shahabad it is डुब्भी *dubbhi*, in the rest of that district डिब्भी *dibbhi*, and in Patna and Gaya कनियाएल *kaniyāël*.

The next stage is दोपतिया *dopatiya* to the north-west, and also south of the Ganges generally. In Tirhut they say it is कपारी फोरल *kapāri phoral*. In Gaya it is पतिया *patiya*, in South Munger दोपत्ती *dopatti*, and in South Bhagalpur दुपतियो *dupatiyo*.

The third stage is चौपतिया *chaupatiya* or (to the north) चरपतिया *charpatiya*, and in South Bhagalpur चरपतियो *charpatiyo*.

The flower has no special name, and is simply called फूल *phūl*. To flower is फुलाएब *phulāëb*.

The pod bursting is कपास फूटब *kapās phūtab* to the west, and in East Tirhut बाँगा फूटब *bānga phūtab*. In South Bhagalpur it is बाँगो फूटब *bāngo phūtab*, and in South Munger फोटा *phota*.

1019. Raw cotton is कपास *kapās*, or बाँगा *bānga*, बाँगो *bango*, &c., as above. In East Tirhut बाँग *bāng* is also used. To the west बाँगा *bānga* means cotton stalks. From रढ़िया *rarhiya* (raw cotton) about one-sixth clean cotton is obtained; from भोचरी *bhochri* and कोकटी *kokti*, about a quarter; from भोगिला *bhogila* and हेंवती *hemcti*, about a third; and from फेटवाल *phetwāl*, about two-fifths. मिझरा *mijhra* north of the Ganges is a mixture of भोचरी *bhochri* and भोगिला *bhogila*.

1020. Cotton is the subject of many proverbs, as (for instance) South Munger proverb जेकरा बारह बिगहा बाँग, कमर मैं डोरो ना, *jekra* *bārah bigha bāṅg, kamar meñ doro na*—(here's a fine miser) he has twelve *bighas* of cotton and can't afford a string for his waist.

CHAPTER XIV.—TOBACCO.

1021. Tobacco (*nicotiana tobacum*) is तमाकू *tamāku* or तमाकुल *tamākul.* It is little grown south of the Ganges except in South-Bhagalpur and South Munger. North of the Ganges there are three main classes :—

(1) देसी *desi* or (North-East Tirhut) बड़की *barki.*

(2) बिलाएती *bilāēti* or (in Champāran and North-West Tirhut) कलकतिया *kalkatiya.*

(3) जेठुआ *jethua,* which is sown in *Māgh* (January–February) and cut in *Jeth* (May–June).

In East Bihār are found धमाकुल *dhamākul,* a broad-leafed variety, and पनडठिया *pandathiya* and खँगड़ीवा *khangriwa,* narrow-leaved varieties.

1022. In Shahabad मोरहन *morhan* are long leaves of the best kind, and छेउआ *chheua* the next quality.

1023. When manufactured, there are three main kinds :—

(*a*) *Chewing-tobacco.*—खैनी *khaini* or सुरती *surti,* or in Patna दोखता *dokhta.* Some people call this कल जुग के अमित *kal jug ke amrit,* or the ambrosia of the *kali* age.

(*b*) *Snuff,* which is नास *nās* or नस *nas.*

(*c*) *Smoking-tobacco.*—This is called पीअनि *pīani* or पीनी *pīni* generally. Among its kinds may be noticed काला *kāla* (North-West and South-East Tirhut) or पकुआ *pakua* (Tirhut), which is the coarsest kind. कन्दई *kandai* or भुसना *bhusna* in South Bhagalpur, and गूँड़ी *gūnri* in South Munger, is broken tobacco. कड़ुआ *karua* or (in South Bhagalpur) कड़ुओ *karuo* is a second-class strong kind. दोरस्सा *dorassa,* or in South Bhagalpur दोरस्सो *dorasso,* is a mixed tobacco of fair quality. Another similar kind is called मसालदार *masāldār* or महकौआ *mahkaua.* खमीरा *khamīra* is a scented kind mixed with spices, and सादा *sāda* is the plain kind in common use. मलुआ *malua* to the west is the usual kind sold in shops, and दोकानी *dokāni* is the cheap kind used by the poor.

1024. The stalks are डण्टी *danti* generally, with local variants डाँट *dānt* in South Munger and डँटकी *dantki* in South Bhagalpur. In East Tirhut they are also डाँठ *dānth*. The refuse broken leaves and stalks are झाला *jhāla* in the south-east, and in South-East Tirhut खरसान *kharsān*. When blisters come on the leaf when ripe, the verb used is चढ़ब *charhab;* also गुलठियाएब *gulthiyāeb* or चितियाएब *chitiyāeb* in Champāran. The blisters themselves are called चित्ती *chitti*. The seed-capsules are घूनी *ghūni* in Sāran, फर *phar* in Champāran, and बिच्ची *bichchi* in Tirhut generally. The nipping or cutting off of the head is पता तूरब *pata tūrab* in Sāran and South-West Tirhut, छोपनी *chhopni* in South-East Tirhut, and काटब *kātab* or कटनी *katni* elsewhere. Sometimes shoots appear after doing this, and they are called दोंजी *donji*. Other local names are पचखी *pachkhi* in Sāran and Champāran, कनोजर *kanojar* in North-East Tirhut, कनैल *kanail* or काँखी *kānkhi* in South Tirhut, and कनई *kanai* in the east generally. The first crop is called मोरहन *morhan*. A second crop raised from the roots is दोंजी *donji*, or in South Bhagalpur खुँटिया *khuntiya*. Tobacco seedlings are called पोआ *poa* in South Bhagalpur.

1025. Tobacco is the subject of many proverbs and tales. An example of the former is—

चून तमाकु सान के, बिन माँगे जे दे।
सुरपुर नरपुर नागपुर, तीनू बस कर ले॥

Chūn tamāku sān ke bin mānge je de,
Surpur narpur nāgpur, tīnu bas kar le.

—The man who mixes tobacco with lime (for chewing) and offers it without being asked, conquers (by his virtuous action) heaven, earth, and the lower regions.

1026. A folk-tale about tobacco runs that a villager who went to a distant village to visit his friends found them smoking in the morning before they had said prayers, whereupon he said—

भोर भए मनुस सभ जागे।
हुक्का चिलम बाजन लागे॥

Bhor bhae, manus sabh jāge,
Hukka chilam bājan lāge.

—At daybreak the people awoke, and immediately the *hukkas* began to gurgle.

To which one of the smoking party replied—

खैनी खाए नऽ तमाकू पीए ।
से नर बनावऽ कैसे जीए ॥
Khaini khāe, na tamāku pīe,
Se nar batāwa kaise jīe.

—Show me the man who can live without either chewing or smoking tobacco. This verse has passed into a proverb.

1027. Tobacco is often compared to the river Ganges, which has three streams,—one of which flows to heaven, another to hell, and the third to the world of mortals. So also tobacco has three branches, viz. snuff, which, by being smelt, goes upwards; smoking-tobacco, which, by being smoked, goes downwards; and chewing-tobacco, which goes neither up nor down.

CHAPTER XV.—OPIUM POPPY.

1028. Opium poppy (*papaver somniferum*) is पोस्ता *posta* or (in Patna) पोसत *posat*. The advances made to the cultivators are दाद्नी *dādni*. The average produce per *bigha* is सर्दर पर्तर *sardar partar* or पर्ता *parta* north of the Ganges and in Gaya. In Shahabad it is माल *māl*, and in Patna पैदा *paida*. The rough measurement of the field is लठाबन्दी *lathābandi* in South-West Shahabad, and elsewhere south of the Ganges नाप *nāp*. North of the Ganges it is नापी *nāpi*.

1029. The poppy petals are फूल *phūl*, and the heads ढेंढ़ी *denrhi*, or in Patna डिण्डी *dindi*. The cakes of poppy petals are फुलपता *phulpata* in Champāran, फुलपत्ती *phulpatti* in Sāran and Tirhut, and पत्तल *pattal* in Patna. Elsewhere they are रोटी *roti*.

1030. The instrument used for piercing the capsule is नहर्नी *naharni*, or in Tirhut optionally लहर्नी *laharni*. In Patna and Gaya it is नर्हन्नी *narhanni*. To lance the capsule is पाछब *pāchhab*. The milky juice which exudes is दूध *dūdh*, and the opium yield is माल *māl*. The scraper used for collecting the coagulated opium off the pod is called सितुहा *situha* or सितुआ *situa*. In South-East Tirhut sometimes a bamboo scraper is used, called पोछ्नी *pochhni*. The gathering of opium is उठाएब *uthāëb* generally. Local words are काछब *kāchhab* to the north-west and in North-West Tirhut, and पोछब *pochhab* also in North-West Tirhut. The person who lances the capsules is पछ्निहार *pachhnihār* or (*fem.*) पछ्निहारिन *pachhnihārin*, and he or she who collects the coagulated opium which has exuded from the capsule is उठौनिहार *uthaunihār* or उठौनिहारिन *uthaunihārin*. The grain of the prepared opium is दाना *dāna*, and its consistency सुखवन *sukhwan*.

1031. The grains of opium-seed are दाना *dāna*. The shell is खोइया *khoiya* north of the Ganges, and खोहिया *khohiya* in Gaya. In South-West Shahabad it is खोल्ड़ी *kholri*, in the rest of that district and in South-East Bihar बोकला *bokla*, and in Patna बकुला *bakula*. In Gaya चिटुरा *chitura* are poppy capsules which are empty and have not borne seeds. The oil-cake prepared from the seeds is पिन्ना *pinna* or पीना *pīna*.

1032. The refuse opium, consisting of the washing of the vessels, &c., is धोअन *dhoan* north of the Ganges and धोई *dhoï* south of it. In the south-east it is धोए *dhoe*. The refuse scraped from the vessels is खुरचन *khurchan*, or (Gaya, South-West Shahabad, and South Munger) खखोरन *khakhoran*. The juice which drains off the fresh opium is पसेवा *pasewa*. This is inspissated on rags, and the product is कफा *kapha*, of which काफा *kāpha* in Shahabad and कप्फा *kappha* in Sāran and South Munger are local variants. The fluid opium used in pasting the leaves on the cakes is लेवा *lewa* in Patna, and the cakes themselves are गोटी *goti*.

1033. *Preparations of opium.*—मदक *madak* is made by boiling down and inspissating the juice (अरख *arakh*) of pure opium or कफा *kapha*. This inspissated juice is known as किमाम *kimām* or (in Gaya) केमाम *kemām*. With it are mixed cut-up betel or guava leaves, known as जासू *jāsu*. The pipe used for smoking *madak* is known as महरू *mahru* or ठरिया *thariya* or ठढ़िया *tharhiya*, or to the south-east मेरू *meru*. A small piece of *madak*, known as छीटा *chhita*, is ignited in the bowl of the pipe with a spill of charcoal, called कलम *kalam* or (in South Bhagalpur) कँगड़ा *kangra*, which is held by a small pair of tongs, called चिमटा *chimta* in the north-west and चूँटी *chūnti* south of the Ganges.

1034. चण्डू *chandu* or चाँडू *chāndu* is the distilled juice of pure opium, and is smoked in an earthen bowl called चिलम *chilam* to the north-west and दवात *dawāt* south of the Ganges. This is attached to a stem called निगाली *nigāli* in Sāran, Patna, and Gaya, नरचा *narcha* in Champāran, and नर *nar* in North-West Tirhut. Another name is बम्बू *bambu* or बाँबू *bāmbu*, bamboo. It is stirred with an iron skewer, called थक *thak*.

When it is desired to make the preparation extra strong, the sediment which accumulates in the stem of the pipe is added. This is called अंची *anchi* south of the Ganges generally, इन्सी *insi* in South Munger, and इंची *inchi* in South Bhagalpur. In Patna it is also called कैंटी *kainti*, and in Champāran कैटी *kaiti*.

1035. पिनिक *pinik* is the drowsiness produced by opium intoxication, and चुसकी *chuski* the quantity of opium water drunk at one time.

CHAPTER XVI.—HEMP.

1036. The hemp plant (*cannabis sativa*) is known as गाँजा *gānja* when cultivated in Rajshahai, and भाँग *bhāng* when wild elsewhere. The leaves are known as भाँग *bhāng* or भङ्ग *bhang* (generally), सबुजी *sabuji* (north-west), or सब्जा *sabja* (Patna and Gaya). A favourite way of taking the drug is in the form of a sweetmeat, called मजूम *majūm* or माजूम *mājūm*. चरस *charas* is the resin which exudes from the flowers and leaves.

1037. The flat *gānja* is चपटा *chapta* or चिपटा *chipta*; also in Shahabad कली *kali*. The round *gānja* is गोल *gol*, also गिरगिटिया *girgitiya* in South-West Shahabad, and also पमड़ी *pamri* in the rest of that district. Broken *gānja* is रोरा *rora* or चूर *chūr*, or (in Gaya and South Munger) रई *raī*. In Shahabad बालूचर *bālūchar* and जासर *jāsar* are two kinds of imported *gānja*. *Gānja* with stalks attached is called डाढ़ी *dārhi* in Shahabad. मेदनि *medani* or मेदनी *medni* is a plant taken with *gānja*.

CHAPTER XVII.—INDIGO.

1038. Indigo (*indigofera tinctoria*) is लील *līl*. The word नील *nīl* used by Europeans is a Westernism borrowed from Ūrdu-knowing subordinates.

1039. Indigo sown before the rains and irrigated by artificial means is called पटौआ *pataua*. The first cutting is मोरहन *morhan*. The second cutting is खूँटी *khūnti* or (in South-East Tirhut) दोंजी *donji*, and the third cutting is called तेंजी *tenji* or तेलरी *telri*, or in the north-west तिराँटी *tirānti*. If the second or third cutting is allowed to grow on to the second year it is called कलम *kalam* or कलमी *kalmi*. In South Bhagalpur there are two sowings (बावग *bāwag*),—one called कतिकी

katiki (कातिक *Kātik* = October–November), and the other फल्गुनी *phalguni* (फाल्गुन *Phālgun* = February–March). In North Bihār the chief sowing is the फगुनी *phaguni* (फागुन *Phāgun* = February–March), and there is a second sowing in अखाढ़ *Akhārh* (June–July), called असाढ़ी *asārhi* or अखाढ़ी *akhārhi*. There are also sowings in कातिक *Kātik* (October–November) and बैसाख *Baisākh* (April–May).

1040. The system of obtaining the plant from cultivators on advances is called दादनी *dādni* or दादन *dādan* in the north-west, in South-West Tirhut, and in South Bhagalpur. When indigo is grown by cultivators who have entered into an agreement to do so, it is called रैयती *raiyati* or असामिवार *asāmiwār* or असामियार *asāmiyār*. Under the system called in the north-west खुश खरीद *khush kharīd*, the planter advances money to a cultivator to sow indigo. He also advances indigo-seed at a given rate, the price of which is recovered in the settlement of accounts. This is also called खुसकी *khuski* in Champāran and नविश्तखानी *nawishtakhāni* in North-West Tirhut. ठीका के लील *thīka ke līl* is when the planter takes a village in farm and cultivates the *zira'ats* (जिरात *jirāt*) and such other land as he can secure. The special cultivation carried out by the planters themselves is जिरात *jirāt*, or (in South Bhagalpur) बाड़ी *bāri*. The divisions of their estates are called जिला *jila*, each under charge of a जिलादार *jilādār*, and a subdivision is (north of the Ganges) टोक *tōk*, under charge of a टोकदार *tokdār*.

1041. अलावा *alāwa* or अलावे *alāwe* is indigo grown by the cultivator on his land after opium or other crop.

CHAPTER XVIII.—OTHER DYES.

1042. The following may be noted:—

(1) आल *āl* (*morinda citrifolia*).—This is used for dyeing red cotton cloth सालू *sālu* and the coarse red cloth खारुआँ *khāruān*. The root is divided into classes, called बाना *bāna*. The best and thinnest roots are known as फुहा *phūha*. The thickest roots are कचरी *kachri* in Shahabad and South Munger, and तोड़न *toran* or गुल्ली *gulli* in Patna and Gaya. मेल *mel* in Shahabad is a mixture of the two kinds.

1043. (2) *Safflower* (*carthamus tinctorius*).—This is कुसुम *kusum* generally north of the Ganges, and कोसुम *kosum* south of it. A local name is फूल *phūl* in Tirhut. The seed is बर्री *borri* in South Munger. It is also called to the west and in Patna and Gaya बर्रे *barre*. The following are some of the colours prepared from safflower:—

असमानी *asmāni*, light blue.
कागी *kāgi*, navy blue.
काला *kāla*, black.
काहि सबुजा *kāhi sabuja*, dark green.
केसरिया *kesariya*, saffron-yellow.
गुलाब *gulāb* or गुलाबी *gulābi*, pink.
चँपई *champaī*, orange.
नारंजी *nāranji*, orange yellow.
पैठानी *paithāni*. Made by dipping into an indigo-vat also.
फालसाही *phālsāhi*, plum-coloured.
बदामी *badāmi* or बेदामी *bedāmi*, almond-coloured.
बैंगनी *baingni*, purple.
मासी *māsi*, a very dark green.
लाल *lāl*, red.
लीला *līla*, dark blue.
सबुजा *sabuja*, green.
सुरमई *surmaī*, antimony-black.
सुरख *surukh*, red.
सोनहुला *sonáhula*, golden yellow.

Of course all the above are not made from safflower alone, but it forms the basis of all. In most of the darker colours it is used in conjunction with indigo. The following riddle shows the comprehensive range of colours embraced by safflower. At a marriage procession garments of every bright colour are worn, and the riddle is—

बाप रहल पेटे, पूत गेल बरियात.
Bāp rahal pete, pūt gel bariyāt.

—While the father was still in the womb (*i.e.*, pod), the son went to a wedding party. The father is the seed of the safflower in pod; the son is the safflower dye.

In the north-west जरुआ तेल *jarua tel* is an oil extracted by means of heat from the safflower-seeds. It is called जरठुआ तेल *jarathua tel*, and in Shahabad दढ़ुआ तेल *darhua tel*. It is used for applying to sores, and also for burning.

1044. (3) बकम *bakam* (*cæsalpina sappan*).—This is a red dye, used principally where आल *āl* is not obtainable.

CHAPTER XIX.—OILSEEDS.

1045. Oilseeds in general are चिकना *chikna*, तेलहन तीसी *telhan tisi*, or simply तेलहन *telhan*. Amongst the varieties may be noted—

(1) *Mustard* (*brassica campestris* or *sinapis dichotoma*).—This is सरिसों *sarison* or सरिसो *sariso* north of the Ganges and in the south-west; elsewhere it is सरसों *sarson*. In South Bhagalpur it is गोटो *goto*, and in North-East Tirhut also गोट *got*. Oil from this seed is called करुआ तेल *karua tel* or कड़ू तेल *karu tel*.

(2) *Mustard* (*brassica juncea* or *sinapis ramosa*).—This is लाही *lāhi* or राइ *rāi* to the west. In South Munger it is रांची *ranchi*, and in East Tirhut रैंची *rainchi*. Elsewhere it is तोरी *tori*, and so also in Champāran.

(3) *Sesamum* (*sesamum orientale* or *Indicum*).—This is तील *tīl*. In South-West Shahabad तिल्ली *tilli* is a variety with a white grain, which is sown with the autumn crop.

(4) *Linseed* (*linum usitatissimum*).—This is तीसी *tisi*. To the east it is also called चिकना *chikna*.

(5) *Safflower* (*carthamus tinctoria*).—See last chapter.

(6) *Castor-oil plant* (*ricinus communis*).—This is रेंड़ *renr* or लेंड़ *lenr*, also अँड़ड़ *anrar* in the north-west, Tirhut, and South Bhagalpur, and अण्डा *anda* in Tirhut and South Bhagalpur. The seed is लेंड़ी *leñri* or रेंड़ी *reñri* generally, also अँड़री *anrri* in the north-west, Tirhut, and South Bhagalpur, and अण्डी *andi* in Tirhut and South Bhagalpur. A plantation of this is रेंड़वारी *renrwāri* or लेंड़वारी *lenrwāri*.

(7) *Bassia latifolia*.—The tree is called मह *mahu* or महुआ *mahua*. Its clusters of buds are छत्ता *chhatta* or कोंच *konch*. The flower which falls to the ground and is used for distilling spirits is मह *mahu* or महुआ. The oilnuts which are borne by the tree are कोइन *koïn* north of the Ganges, or कोइनी *koini* in South-East Tirhut. In South-West Shahabad they are कोइन्दा *koïnda*. In South Munger the *mahua*-pickers sing a song while employed, called टोहक *toha*.

(8) *Celastrus paniculatus.*—This is मलकँगनी *malkangni* or डिठौरी *dithauri* in South-West Shahabad, मलकौनी *malkauni* in Patna and Gaya, मनकौनी *mankauni* in South-East Tirhut, कौनी *kauni* in South Munger.

(9) *Croton* (*croton tiglium*).—This is जमाल गोटा *jamāl gota* in Patna, Gaya, and the west.

(10) Two other oils may be mentioned here. One is मिमियाइ के तेल *mimiyāī ke tel*, which is supposed to be extracted from the heads of coolie emigrants to the colonies, by hanging them head downwards over a slow fire, see §1464. The other is अकोल के तेल *akol ke tel*, made from the nut of the अकोल *akol* (*aleuritis triloba*) tree, which if rubbed on a person's body makes him invisible. This is like saying that if you catch a guinea pig by the tail his eyes will drop out; for the nut is so hard that it is impossible to extract oil from it.

CHAPTER XX.—FIBRES.

1046. *Hemp*, as a drug (*cannabis sativa*).—See Chapter XVI.

1047. *Hemp*, as a fibre plant.—There are two varieties of this :—

(1) सन *san* (*crotolaria juncea*) or (North-East Tirhut) कसमिरा *kasmira* or सोन *son*.

(2) पटुआ *patua*, कुतुरम *kuturum*, or (in South Bhagalpur) कुदरुम *kudrum* (*hibiscus cannabensis*, Roxb.) This is like *san*, except that its flower is like the safflower, and that it is used only for making the coarse fibre (छन्ना *channa*). See below.

1048. The stalk is सनई *sanai* north of the Ganges generally except in North-East Tirhut, where it is सनै *sanai*. In Shahabad it is सनैठा *sanaitha*, in South Munger सनाठी *sanāthi*, and in South Bhagalpur सनसनाठी *sansanāthi*. When the bark has been removed, it is सन्ठी *santhi*, or in South Munger सनाठी *sanāthi*, and in South Bhagalpur सनसनाठी *sansanāthi*. A bundle of fibres is लरछा *larchha*, or in East Tirhut धोआ *dhoa* or थूआ *thūa*. Short stalks that remain in the fibre are called in North-East Tirhut गुदरी *gudri*, खुदर *khudar* to the west and in West Tirhut, कुदारी *kudāri* in North-East Tirhut, and गुदर *gudar* in East Tirhut. In North-East Tirhut the coarsest fibres are called चना *channa*, the next finest पटुआ *patua*, and the finest कसमिरा *kasmira*. There is no special name for the seed.

CHAPTER XXI.—BETEL.

1049. Betel (*piper betel*) is called पान *pān*, and the man who grows it बरई *baraī*. Amongst its varieties the best is कपूरी *kapūri*, which has a long leaf, mild, but slightly bitter. The next best is साँची *sānchi*. The common varieties are ककीर *kakīr* (North-East Tirhut) or ककेर *kaker* (South-East Tirhut), which has a large leaf and mild flavour; the बेलहरी *belahri* (south-west) or बेलहरी साँची *belahri sānchi* (North-East Tirhut), and the मगही *maghi*, which have a round leaf and a sweet taste; and the बँगला *bangla* or (South-West Tirhut) बँगरा *bangra*, which is small and slightly bitter. To the west there is also a kind called करारुआ *karárua*, which is small and sweet.

1050. The mound on which the plant is grown is भिण्डा *bhinda*, बरैठा *baraitha*, or पाढ़ *pārh* north of the Ganges. South of the Ganges it is भीट *bhīt*. A betel-garden is बरेव *bareo* or बरवे *barwe*. The rows in the plantation are सपुरा *sapura* in Sāran and South Tirhut, and साँपुर *sāmpur* in North-East Tirhut. In South-West Shahabad they are पास *pās*, and in the rest of that district पाँती *pānti*. The intervening spaces are आँतर *āntar* or अँतरा *antra*. They are also पाहे *pāhe* in South-East Tirhut, डौंगर *daungar* in Patna and Gaya, and डौग *daug* in the south-east. The main props down these lines are कोरो *koro* in Tirhut and कोरई *koraī* in Shahabad. In the south-east and in Sāran they are इकरी *ikri*.

1051. The spaces between these props are in North-East Tirhut कोरवास *korwās*. The supports of the plants are सरई *saraī* north of the Ganges, or in South-East Tirhut खरही *kharhi*, of which there are generally six between each main prop. In Shahabad they are called ईंकर *īnkar*, and in the south-east सरकण्डा *sarkanda*. In Shahabad ढेंपी *dhempi* are the lumps of clay in which the plants are sown. The supports of the roof are also कोरो *kōro*, except in Patna and Gaya, where they are खम्भा *khambha*, and in South Munger, where they are खाम्ही *khāmhi*. The walls are टट्टी *tatti*, or in East Tirhut टाट *tāt*, and in East Munger टाटी *tāti*. The roof is माड़ो *māro* or माँड़ो *mānro*. In South-East Tirhut it is optionally माड़ब *mārab*. In South-West Tirhut it is ठट॰रा *thatra*, and in Shahabad and East Tirhut optionally छानी *chhāni*. In South Munger it is मड़॰वा *marwa* or ठठ॰री *thathri*.

1052. The brushwood on the top is खरई *kharaī* or (in South-West Shahabad) खर॰चा *kharcha*, and in South Munger कचुआ *kachua*. The young seedlings for planting are कलम *kalam* in Patna, Gaya, and Shahabad, and बेल *bel* elsewhere. They are watered from an earthen vessel called लोटी *loti* or (in Sāran) लोट *lot*. In North-East Tirhut मटोर *mator* is a basket in which the gardener carries earth to the plant, and which he also uses for keeping the leaves. In East Tirhut भूर *bhūr*, and in South Tirhut भूरा *bhūra*, are the shoots which come out of the plant near the root in Jeth (May–June), and कन *kan* are those which come out in Bhādon (August–September).

1053. A packet of twenty leaves is called a कोरी *kori* south of the Ganges. North of the Ganges one of fifty leaves is called चौठैया *chauthaiya*, and one of a hundred leaves आधा ढोली *ādha dholi*. A ढोली *dholi* has 200 leaves.

1054. North of the Ganges and in Shahabad—

7 ढोली *dholi*	=	1 कन॰वाँ *kanwān*.
14 ditto	=	1 अध॰वा *adhwa*.
28 ditto		1 पौआ *paua* or पावा *pāwa*.
4 पौआ *paua*	=	1 लेसो *leso*.

1055. Elsewhere south of the Ganges 108 ढोली *dholi* make 1 लेसो *leso*. A leaf of betel rolled up in a cone for chewing is बीड़ा *bīra*, बिर॰वा *birwa*, or बिरिया *biriya* or खिल्ली *khilli*. It is also गिलौरी *gilauri*. सिँघारा *singhāra* are the triangular-shaped packets. Betel is kept for consumption in a wickerwork basket, called बेलहऱा *belahra* or (in East Tirhut) बिरहऱा *birahra*. In North-East Tirhut ढाकी *dhāki* is a large basket used by the betel-grower for the same purpose.

1056. The betel-nut, which is the fruit of the *areca catechu*, is called सुपारी *supāri* or सोपारी *sopāri*. Other names are कसैली *kasaili* north of the Ganges, and मुख॰सुध *mukhsudh*, मुख॰सुधि or मुख॰सुधी *mukhsudhi*, in East Tirhut. The nippers for cutting the nut are सरौता *sarauta*. A well-known proverb is मुख॰सुधि न॰ पर॰कार, तनिका अड़ियातक बड़ चमत्कार *mukhsudhi na parkār, tanika ariyātak bar chamatkār*,—he can't afford to give his guest even a bit of betel-nut, and yet he escorts him out of the house with as great pomp as if he had been actually entertaining him.

CHAPTER XXII.—GARDEN CROPS.

1057. These may be divided into—(1) edible roots, (2) gourds, (3) miscellaneous.

EDIBLE ROOTS.

(1) *Potatoes* (*solanum tuberosum* or *esculentum*).—आलू *ālu*, and in East Tirhut also आरू *āru*. Also north of the Ganges अलुआ *alua* and अलुई *aluī*. North of the Ganges ललका *lalka* or दखिनी *dackhini* is a red kind, and मलदहिया *maldahiya* or नपाली *napāli* a white one. A red variety of the last name but one is called मलदहिया कनकपुरिया *maldahiya kanakpuriya*. Seed potatoes brought from the hills are बीया के आलू *bīya ke alu*, and each eye is आँखि *ānkhi* or आँख *ānkh*. The produce of these kept for next year is called पहिला माँटी के बीया *pahila mānti ke bīya*, and the produce again of this kept for seed for the third year is दोसरा माँटी के बीया *dosra mānti ke bīya*.

1058. (2) *Yams* (*dioscorea sativa*).—These are लतार *latār* generally north of the Ganges, and also रतार *ratār* to the west. To the north-west yet another name is अतार *atār*, and to the south-west कठार *kathār*. In Patna and Gaya it is रतालू *ratālu*. In Tirhut it is also called फर *phar*, and to the east also खम्हरुआ *khamharua*.

1059. (3) *Sweet potato* (*batatas edulis*).—This is सकरकन्द *sakarkand* generally. North of the Ganges it is also called लमका अलुआ *lamka alua*, and in South-East Tirhut अल्हुआ *alhua*. In East Bihār it is अलुआ *alua*. North of the Ganges there are two varieties :—(*a*) A red one, called देसी *desi*, and also in South Tirhut ललका *lalka* ; (*b*) a white one, called बिलाएती *bilāëti*, and also करमिया *karmiya*, and in South Tirhut also उजरका *ujarka*. A large white variety, weighing from one to twenty *sers*, is called in North-East Tirhut तेकुना *tekuna*.

1060. (4) A kind of yam (*dioscorea fasciculata*).—सुथनी *suthni*.

1061. (5) *Arum colocasia*.—This is अरुई *arui* generally. Also अरबी *arabbi* in North-East Tirhut, पेकचा *pekcha* in South-East Tirhut, पेकची *pekchi* in Shahabad, पेपची *pepchi* in Gaya and Shahabad, and in South Bhagalpur

अलती *alti*. Another variety (*colocasia antiquorum*) is कचू *kachchu*. A larger variety is अरुआ *arua* or कन्दा *kanda*.

1062. (6) राम केसौर *rām kesaur* (North Tirhut), or मिसिरी कन *misiri kan* (East Tirhut), a large edible root sometimes weighing eight or nine *sers*. Considered a very cooling food.

1063. (7) आदीचक *ādīchak*, the Jerusalem artichoke (*helianthus tuberosus*).

GOURDS.

1064. (1) *The water-melon* (*cucurbit citrullus* or *citrullus vulgaris*).—These are तरबूज *tarbūj* or तरबूजा *tarbūja* or in North-East Tirhut तार्भूज *tārbhūj*. In Champāran they are also called पनिहौआ *panihaua*, and in South-West Shahabad हिनुआना *hinuāna*.

1065. (2) *The melon* (*cucumis utilatissimus* or *cucumis melo*).—खरबूजा *kharbūja*. Also लालमी *lālmi* in West Tirhut and Patna and the west, and फूँट *phūnt* (which is properly the *cucumis momordica*) to the south-east.

1066. (3) *Cucumis momordica*.—This is फूँट *phūnt* when it is ripe after bursting spontaneously. The young fruit used for cooking is डाम *dām* and (South-West Shahabad) डभको *dabhko*.

1067. (4) *The bitter gourd* (*momordica charantia*).—करैला *karaila*, also करैली *karaili* in Shahabad and South Bhagalpur and करैल *karail* in North-East Tirhut.

1068. (5) *The bottle-gourd* (*lagenaria vulgaris* or *cucurbita lagenaria*).—This is कदुआ *kadua* generally, or कद्दू *kaddu* in South Bhagalpur. Another name in Gaya, South Munger, and the west generally is लौका *lauka*, with a variant लौआ *laua* in Patna. In East Tirhut it is also called सजिवन *sajiwan*.

1069. (6) *Lagenaria acutangulus* or *cucumis acutangulus*.—This is तरोइ *taroï* generally. Other varieties are सतपुतिया *satputiya*, झिङ्गा *jhinga*, झिँगुनी *jhinguni*, or झिँगुली *jhinguli*, and नेनुआँ *nenuān*, घिउरा *ghiura*, or घेवड़ा *ghewra*.

1070. (7) *Cucumber* (*cucumis sativus*).—खीरा *khīra*. A variety is बालम खीरा *bālam khīra* in Shahabad. A large variety of cucumber is called ककड़ी *kakri* or काँकरि *kānkari* (*cucumis utilatissimus*). Natives much appreciate this vegetable, as in the proverb निकौरिया गेलाह हाट, काँकरि देखि हिया फाट *nikauriya gelāh hāt, kānkari dekhi hiya phāt*,—the man without money went to market, and his heart burst when he saw the cucumber. The great size of the plant is well illustrated by the proverb एक हाथक काँकरि, नौ हाथक बीया *ek hāthak kānkari, nau hāthak bīya*,—a cucumber only one cubit long has an offspring nine cubits long. (Cf. the parable of the grain of mustard-seed.)

1071. (8) The *sweet pumpkin* (*cucurbita pepo*).—This is कोँहड़ा *koñhra*; also in North Tirhut कोम्हड़ा *komhra*, and in East Tirhut कद्दीमा *kadīma*. Another variety, much used for making sweetmeats, is भतुआ *bhatua* to the west; also भूआ *bhūa* or भूरा *bhūra* in Gaya, सिसकोँहड़ा *siskoñhra* in Champāran, सिजकोँहड़ा *sijkoñhra* in Tirhut, सुरुजकोँहड़ा *surujkoñhra* in South-East Tirhut, and कुम्हड़ *kumhar* to the east.

1072. (9) चिचिरा *chichira* or चिचुरा *chichura* (north of the Ganges), the snake-gourd (*trichosanthes anguina*).—In East Tirhut it is कैता *kaita*, and in Sāran कैत *kait*.

MISCELLANEOUS VEGETABLES (IN ALPHABETICAL ORDER).

1073. The writer regrets that he has not been able to identify the botanical names of more than a few of the under-mentioned plants. In some cases the identification given is doubtful. He has to thank Dr. Shaw, Civil Surgeon of Darbhanga, for much assistance rendered in correcting the botanical portion of this division.

अजमोदा *ajmoda* or (Tirhut) बनजेवाइन *banjewāin*, parsley (*petroselinum sativum* or ? *apium involucratum*).—Cf. पितरसेली *pitarseli*.

अजवाइन *ajwāin*,—see जवाइन *jawāin*.

अदरख *adrakh* or अदरक *adrak*, ginger (*zingiber officinale*), also आदी *ādi* generally, आद *ād* in South-East Tirhut.

असफगोल *asaphgol*,—see सफगोल *saphgol*.

आद *ād*, आदी *ādi*,—see अदरख *adrakh*.

इमिरती *imirti*, or in Gaya रमचरना *ramcharna*, an acid curry-vegetable, the fruit of *spondia mangifera* (?).

कथ *kath*,—see खैर *khair*.

कमल पतर *kamal patr*,—see पियाज *piyāj*.

करमकला *karamkalla* or बन्धा कोबी *bandha kobi*, cabbage (*brassica olereacea*).

कलमी साग *kalmi sāg*, the tops of *convolvulus repens*, much used as a spinach.

कवाछ *kawāchh*,—see केवाँछ *kewānchh*.

कासनी *kāsni*, endive (*cichorium endivia*).

काहु *kāhu* (Patna and Gaya), a kind of lettuce (*lactuca sativa*).

कुनरी *kunri*, a creeping-plant, of which the fruit is used for curries.

केवाँछ *kewānchh* or कवाछ *kawāchh*, a plant which produces a pod like a bean (*dolichos pruriens*). In Gaya it is भूप सेम *bhūp sem*.

कैता *kaita*,—see चिचिरा *chichira*.

कोचला के साग *kochla ke sāg*, a kind of spinach.

कोबी *kobi*, the cabbage (*brassica oleracea*).

खुरफा *khurpha* or गोलावा *golāwa* (Sāran, Patna, and Gaya), purslane (*portulaca sativa*).

खुसबरी *khusbari*,—see मकोय *makoe*.

खेखसा *khekhsa*,—see चठैल *chathail*.

खैर *khair* or कथ *kath*, catechu (*acacia catechu*).

गदीना *gadīna*, a kind of pot-herb with a taste of garlic.

गजरा or गजड़ा *gajra* or (in South-West Shahabad) गाजड़ *gājar*, the carrot (*daucus carota*).

गाजड़ *gājar*,—see गजरा *gajra*.

गुलफा *gulpha*, a kind of spinach.

गेन्हरी *genhri* or (in East Tirhut) गेन्हारी *genhāri*, a pot-herb (? *amaranthus frumentaceus*).

गलहण्टा *gelhanta*, गोलभण्टा *golbhanta*,—see बैंगन *baingan*.

गोलावा *golāwa*,—see खुरफा *khurpha*.

गोल मिरिच *gol mirich* or गुलमिरिच *gulmirich*,—see मिरिच *mirich*.

घेँच *ghench* (North-East Tirhut), an aquatic tuber whose white stalk is eaten by the poor (? *aponogeton monostachyon*).

चठैल *chathail* or चटैल *chatail,* a much-appreciated curry-vegetable, a creeping-plant. In Gaya it is called खेखसा *khekhsa.*

चनसुर *chansur,* a kind of cress (*lepidum sativum*).

चितरसेली *chitarseli,*—see पितरसेली *pitarseli.*

चेंगवा *chengwa,*—see बैंगन *baingan.*

जवाइन *jawāin* (west, Patna, and South Bhagalpur), अजवाइन *ajwāin* (Gaya and South Munger), जेवाइन *jewāin* (north of the Ganges), a plant something like aniseed (*ligusticum ajowain* and *ptychotis ajowan*), खोरासानी जवाइन *khorāsāni jawāin* is *hyoscianus niger.* This plant is not the true aniseed (*anisi*).

जीरा *jīra* or (South-East Tirhut) जीर *jīr,* cummin (*cuminum cyminum*).

जेवाइन *jewāin,*—see जवाइन *jawāin.*

ठहिया *tharhiya,*—see मांरसा *mārsa.*

डिड़िया मिरचाइ *diriya mirchāi,* ढेँरिया मिरचाइ *dheñriya mirchāi,*—see मिरिच *mirich.*

तरकारी *tarkāri,*—see तीयन *tīyan.*

तरकोंका *tarkonka* (Patna), the bud of the red lotus, used for medicine.

तीयन *tīyan,* तरकारी *tarkāri,* or पतौरा *pataura,* the general term for vegetables.

धनियाँ *dhaniyān,* coriander (*coriandrum sativum*).

नेवार *newār,*—see मूली *mūli.*

पतौरा *pataura,*—see तीयन *tīyan.*

परवर *parwar,* पलवल *palwal,* परोर *paror,* परोरा *parora,* or (in South Bhagalpur) परोल *parol* (*trichosanthes dioica*), (Roxb.)

पलाँकी *palānki,*—see पालक *pālak.*

पालक *pālak,* पालकी *pālki* or (East Tirhut and Champāran) पलाँकी *palānki,* spinach (*spinacea oleracea*).

पितरसेली *pitarseli* or (Tirhut) चितरसेली *chitarseli,* parsley (*petroselinum sativum* or ? *apium involucratum*).—Cf. अजमोदा *ajmoda.*

पियाज *piyāj* or (South Bhagalpur) पेयाज *peyāj,* and north-west कमल पतर *kamal patr,* the onion (*allium cepa*).

पुदेना *pudena*,—see पोदीना *podina*.

पोदीना *podina*, पोदेना *podena*, or पुदेना *pudena*, also (Tirhut) फुदेना *phudena*, mint (*mentha sativa* or *viridis*).

फुदेना *phudena*,—see पोदीना *podina*.

फुलकोबी *phulkobi*, the cauliflower (*brassica olereacea*).

बकला *bakla*, बकुली *bakuli*, बँगला *bangla*,—see बोकला *bokla*.

बनजेवाइन *banjewäin*,—see अजमोदा *ajmoda*.

बनभुटका *banbhutka*,—see मकोय *makoë*.

बिरवाइ *birwäi* (Gaya), vegetable seedlings.

बिलाएती पटुआ *biläeti patua*, roselle (*hibiscus sabdariffa*).

बिलाएती बैँगन *biläeti baingan*, the tomato (*solanum lycopersicum*).

बैँगन *baingan*, भण्टा *bhanta* (usually confined to the round variety) or गोलभण्टा *golbhanta*, and in South Munger also गेलहण्टा *gelhanta* and चेँगवा बैँगन *chengwa baingan*. In East Tirhut it is optionally भाँटा *bhänta*; the egg-plant (*solanum melongena*). Compare the proverb काहू के भण्टा बैरी काहू के भण्टा पथ्य *kähu ke bhanta bairi, kähu ke bhanta panth*,—to some the egg-plant is an enemy, to others it is prescribed as a regimen; *i.e.*, what is one man's meat is another's poison.

बोकला *bokla* or बँगला *bangla* (north-west), बकला *bakla* (Champāran), बकुली *bakuli* (South-West Tirhut), बोकला बीन *bokla bīn* (South-East Tirhut) (?), a kind of bean (*? faba major*).

भटकुआँ *bhatküän*, भटकोँआ *bhatkoña*,—see मकोय *makoe*.

भण्टा *bhanta*,—see बैँगन *baingan*.

भिण्डी *bhindi* or राम तरोइ *rām taroï*; also to the east राम परोर *rām paror*, a long kind of fruit used for cooking (*hibiscus esculentus* or *abelmoschus esculentus*).

भुटका *bhutka*,—see मकोय *makoe*.

भूप सेम *bhūp sem*,—see केवाँछ *kewänchh*.

मकोय *makoe* (west and Tirhut), खुसबरी *khusbari* (gooseberry), or (purple variety) भटकोँआ *bhatkoña* or भटकुआँ *bhat küän*, the cape gooseberry, or *tiparee* (*physalis Peruviana*). The red variety is also भुटका *bhutka* or बनभुटका *ban bhutka* in South-East Tirhut.

मरिचा *maricha,*—see मिरिच *mirich.*

मारसा *mārsa* or ठढ़िया *tharhiya* (west), *amaranthus mangostanus.*

मिरचा *mircha,* मिरचाइ *mirchāi,*—see मिरिच *mirich.*

मिरिच *mirich* or (West Tirhut, Shahabad, and Gaya) मरिचा *maricha* and मिरचाइ *mirchāi,* (Patna) मिरचा *mircha,* (South Munger) डिढ़िया मिरचाइ *diriya mirchāi,* (Gaya) ढेँरिया मिरचाइ *dheṅriya mirchāi,* long pepper, &c. (*capsicum fastigiatum, &c.*) गोल मिरिच *gol mirich* or गुलमिरिच *gul mirich* is black pepper (*piper nigrum*). Bird's eye pepper (*capsicum baccatum*) is लौँगिया मरिचा *longiya maricha* or जैया मिरचा *jaiya mircha.*

मुनगा *munga,*—see सैयन *saiyan.*

मुरइ *muraī,* मुराइ *murāi,* मुल्ली *mulli,* मूर *mūr,* मूरो *mūro,*—see मूली *mūli.*

मूली *mūli,* मुल्ली *mulli,* or मुरइ *muraï* or (East Tirhut optionally) मूर *mūr,* (South Munger) मुराइ *murāi,* (South Bhagalpur) मूरो *mūro,* the radish (*raphanus sativus*). In Shahabad there are two kinds—(1) नेवार *newār,* which is large, and (2) लुतिया *lutiya* or देसिला *desila,* which is small.

मेथी *methi* or मेँथी *menthi,* fenugreek (*trigonella fænum Græcum*).

रमचरना *ramcharna,*—see इमिरती *imirti.*

रसून *rasūn,* रस्सुन *rassun,*—see लहसुन *lahsun.*

रहरिया सेम *rahariya sem* or राम रहर *rām rahar,* a kind of bean, not a climbing-plant, but a shrub.

राम तरोइ *rām taroï,* राम परोर *rām paror,*—see भिण्डी *bhindi.*

लहसुन *lahsun,* or to the east रसून *rasūn* or रस्सुन *rassun,* garlic (*allium sativum*). A clove of garlic is पोटी *poti* or पोट *pot.*

लुतिया *lutiya,*—see मूली *mūli.*

लौँगिया मिरिच *longiya mirich,*—see मिरिच *mirich.*

सफगोल *saphgol,* or in South-West Shahabad असफगोल *asaphgol* (*phantago isabghola*).

सलगम *salgam* and also (south of the Ganges) सलजम *saljam,* the turnip (*brassica rapa*).

सहजन *sahjan,* &c.,—see सैयन *saiyan.*

सिँघाड़ा *singhāra,* the water-caltrop (*trapa bispinosa* or *natans*).

सीम *sīm*,—see सेम *sem*.

सेम *sem* (west), सीम *sīm* (east), a bean (*phaseolus magnus*). A variety is सेमा *sema*.

सैयन *saiyan*, or (Tirhut) सोहिजन *sohijan* or सोहजन *sohjan* or सहजन *sahjan*, or (Shahabad) सँहिजन *sañhijan* or (Patna) सहजना *sahjana*, the horse-radish tree (*hyperanthera moringa*). Its fruit is called मुनगा *munga*, and is used as a vegetable, and its root (which tastes like horse-radish) is used as a condiment.

सौँफ *saumph*, ? a kind of aniseed (*peucedanum graveolens* or *anethum sowa*).

हरदी *hardi*, or in Shahabad optionally हलदी *haldi*, turmeric (*curcuma longa*).

हलदी *haldi*,—see हरदी *hardi*.

SUBDIVISION II.

INSECTS AND CAUSES OF INJURY TO CROPS.

CHAPTER I.—DESTRUCTIVE INSECTS AND DISEASES.

1074. Among these may be noted the following, which are arranged in alphabetical order:—

अँगरा *angra* (north-west), झरका *jharka* (Sāran and Tirhut), blight in cereals caused by the sharp west wind; also (Champāran) a blight in opium. See मुरका *murka*.

अरैया *araiya*,—see पोआरी *poāri*.

उकठा *uktha* (south), a sort of mildew which dries up the grain in wheat.

उकड़ा *ukrha*, उखरा *ukhra*, उकसा *uksa*,—see उखठा *ukhtha*.

उखठा *ukhtha* or उकड़ा *ukrha* (north generally), उखरा *ukhra* (Tirhut), उकसा *uksa* (north-west), withering of crops from excessive drought.

औरङ्ग *aurang* (Champāran),—see गपतू *gaptu*; also (north-west) or (in Tirhut) बभनी *babhni*, a white spot appearing in the leaf of millets, causing them to wither up.

कचोहा *kachoha* (South Bhagalpur), a disease in tobacco.

कजऽरा *kajra*,—see कजऽरी *kajri*.

कजऽरी *kajri* (generally), कजऽरा *kajra* (West Tirhut, Patna, and Gaya), कजऽला *kajla* (North-West Tirhut), मजऽरी *majri* (East Tirhut), a green grub which eats the young plants of rice, wheat, and barley when they are about six inches high.

कजऽला *kajla*,—see कजऽरी *kajri*.

कटुइ *katui*, an aquatic beetle which infests rice.

कटैया *kataiya* (South-West Shahabad), कटोई *katoï*, कटोइया *katoïya* (elsewhere south of the Ganges), a blight which attacks rice and turns the ears an orange colour and destroys them.

कटोइया *katoiya*, कटोई *katoï*,—see कटैया *kataiya*.

कतऽरी *katri* (South-West Shahabad), a disease of the rice-plant.

कनाठा *kanātha*, कान्ही *kanhi*,—see छीरी *chhīri*.

कपन्टा *kapta* (Champāran), an insect which attacks young rice.

कमुआ *kamua*,—see कम्मा *kamma*.

कम्मा *kamma* or कमुआ *kamua* (Patna), a smooth kind of caterpillar.

किरौना *kirauna*,—see गाँधी *gāndhi*.

कीरी *kīri* or (South Bhagalpur) कीरो *kīro*, a maggot.

कुकुढ़ी *kukurhi* (Sāran and Tirhut), an insect which attacks cotton.

कुकुही *kukuhi* (north-west), an insect which injures the cold-weather crops.

कुसऽवटऽना *kuswatna* (north-west), कुसियाना *kusiyāna* (Tirhut), a blight in transplanted rice.

कुसियाऽना *kusiyāna*,—see कुसऽवटऽना *kuswatna*.

केँउआँ *keñuān*,—see लरऽका *larka*.

कोइया *koiya*, a tiny black insect which does great damage in granaries.

कोइली *koili*, कोढ़िया *korhiya*, कैलिया *kailiya*, blights of various kinds in rice.

कोढ़िया *korhiya*, कैलिया *kailiya*,—see कोइली *koïli*.

खँखऽड़ी *khankhri*, a blight in cereals on account of which no grain is produced in the ear.

खपड़ोइया *khaproïya* (Champāran), गड़रा *garra* (Gaya, Sāran, and Tirhut), a small white insect which attacks rice.

खरुका *kharuka*,—see जाला *jāla*.

खैरा *khaira* (west), खैरी *khairi* (North-East Tirhut), a blight which attacks rice and turns the ears an orange colour and destroys them.

गड़रा *garra*,—see खपड़ोइया *khaproïya*.

गड़ार *garār* (north), a grub which attacks the roots of sugar-cane.

गद्ही *gadhi* (north) or (Sāran and East Tirhut) गदहिया *gadahiya*, an insect very destructive to growing pulses.

गन्धकी *gandhki* (Patna and Sāran), a small green fly, which attacks rice.

गन्धी *gandhi*,—see गाँधी *gāndhi*.

गप्तू *gaptu* or गप्तुआ *gaptua* (Patna and north), गभ्लू *gabhlu*, ठोँठियारी *thonthiyāri* (Shahabad), गप्सू *gapsu* (Sārau), and औरङ्ग *aurang* (Champāran), a disease affecting millets, sugar-cane, and Indian corn, in which the tops wither.

गभ्लू *gabhlu*,—see गप्तू *gaptu*.

गादुर *gādur* (South-West Shahabad), an insect which attacks pease and gram.

गाँधी *gāndhi* or गन्धी *gandhi*, also to the west गँधवा *gandhwa*. Other names are माँछी *mānchhi* (north generally), किरौना *kirauna* (South-West Shahabad), and भेम्रा *bhemra* (South Munger), the flying-bug,—an evil-smelling insect, which attacks principally the millets before the flowers are formed.

गेरुआ *gerua* (west), the grub which attacks the roots of sugar-cane.

गेरुई *geruī* (north and south-west), a disease of the cereal crops, in which the plant dries up and assumes a reddish colour while the ear is black. It is caused by excess of winter rains and east wind.

गोब्रौरा *gobraura* (West Tirhut and west), blight in betel.

गोभी *gobhi*, a disease produced by prevalence of severe winds, and consisting in the plant giving out little shoots, which weaken it.

गौँछी *gaunchhi* (West Tirhut, Patna, and Gaya), an aquatic beetle which destroys rice by floating from one plant to another in a boat made of a leaf.

घँघरी *ghanghri* (Shahabad),—see घोँघड़ी *ghonghri.*

घून *ghūn*, a weevil destructive to wood and grain.

घोँघड़ी *ghonghri* or (Shahabad) घँघरी *ghanghri*, a worm in the ear of millets and gram.

चतरा *chatra,*—see मुआर *muār.*

चपटवा *chapatwa* (South-West Shahabad), a small green fly which attacks rice.

छपटा *chhapta* (north-west), पचकट्टा *pachkatta* or (Tirhut) पतकट्टा *patkatta*, a green caterpillar which eats up the rice-plant.

छीरा *chhīra,*—see छीरी *chhīri.*

छीरी *chhīri* (south and west), छेँड़ी *chhenri* north-west and Tirhut), also छीरा *chhīra* in Champāran. Other names are कन्ही *kanhi* (South Munger) and कनाठा *kanātha* (South Bhagalpur), the palmer (?) worm, which attacks pulses, cotton, and tobacco.

छेँड़ी *chhenri,*—see छीरी *chhīri.*

जाला *jāla* (Tirhut, Patna, and east), पक्खन *pakkhan* (West Tirhut and Gaya), खरुका *kharuka* (South-West Shahabad), मुरका *murka* (west and West Tirhut), a blight in opium.

झरका *jharka,*—see अँगरा *angra.*

झिल्ली *jhilli* (north-west), फुलभङ्गा *phulbhanga* (Tirhut), an insect which eats the stalks of pulses and makes the leaves crumple up.

टाड़ा *tāra* or टाँड़ा *tānra* (west), a small green insect which ravages wheat and eats the roots of sugar-cane.

टाड़ा *tāra* (north-west), टाँड़ी *tānri* (North-West Tirhut), a grub which eats the young plants of wheat and barley when they are about six inches high.

टीड़ी *tīri* or (South-West Shahabad) टिर्री *tirri*, and फरिङ्गा *pharinga* (Tirhut and east), the locust.

टुनकी *tunki* (north), a disease which attacks rice.

ठोंठियारी *thonthiyāri*,—see गपटू *gaptu*.

तितिली *titili*, a butterfly.

तेलचट *telchat* (Patna and east), पटोइ *patoï* (West Tirhut, Gaya, and South Munger), a disease of the castor-oil plant.

दखिनहा *dakhinha*, (north and south-west), also दखिनाहा *dakhināha* (Gaya and south-west); also नीमा *nīma* (North Tirhut), सिरोरा *sirora* (Patna), and पीरो *pīro* (South Bhagalpur), a disease of rice, millets, and sugar-cane caused by a noxious wind from the south. A white spot appears on the leaf of millets, and they wither. In sugar-cane the tops wither.

दहिया *dahiya* (north), a disease in चीना *chīna* (*Panicum frumentosum*).

दिअँका *dianka*, दिउँका *diunka*, दियाँड़ा *diyānra*, दियार *diyār*, दिवार *diwār*,—see दीयाँ *diyān*.

दीयाँ *dīyān* or दियाँड़ा *diyānra* (Patna, Gaya, and south-east), दिउँका *diunka* (South-West Shahabad), दिअँका *dianka* or दिअका *diaka* (west generally), दियार *diyār* (Champāran and Tirhut), and दिवार *diwār* (East Tirhut), the white ant.

नीमा *nīma*,—see दखिनहा *dakhinha*.

नेढ़ा *nerha*,—see लेँढ़ा *lenhra*.

पक्खन *pakkhan*,—see जाला *jāla*.

पक्खी *pakkhi* or पखिया *pakhiya*, a small insect which attacks the *singhāra* plant or water-caltrop (*trapa natans* or *bispinosa*).

पचकट्टा *pachkatta*, पतकट्टा *patkatta*,—see छपटा *chhapta*.

पटाढ़ी *patārhi*,—see पेटाढ़ी *petārhi*.

पटोइ *patoï*,—see तेलचट *telchat*.

पिटोइ *pitoi* (Patna and South Munger), a small green insect, which ravages wheat and eats the roots of sugar-cane. = टाँड़ा *tānra*, *q.v.*

पिल्लू *pillu* or पिलुआ *pilua*, a small white maggot, which attacks cotton, safflower, and grain, whether growing or stored.

पिहिका *pihika*,—see सुखड़ा *sukhra.*

पीरो *pīro*,—see दखिनहा *dakhinha.*

पेटाढ़ी *petārhi* or पटाढ़ी *patārhi* (Tirhut), an insect which attacks stored rice only.

पेटारढ़ी *petārhi* (Shahabad), a red-coloured insect which attacks cotton, gram, and the castor-oil plant.

पैया *paiya*, a worm in the ear of grain.

पोआरी *poāri* (east) or अरैया *araiya* (South Munger), a disease of the rice-plant.

पौंछी *paunchhi* (Patna and South Munger), a branch springing from the root of sugar-cane and injuring it.

फटहा *phatha* (South Bhagalpur), फट्टा *phatta* (South Munger), a disease of the rice-plant.

फट्टा *phatta*,—see फटहा *phatha.*

फतिङ्गी *phatingi*, a kind of grasshopper which eats the leaves of sugar-cane.

फनगी *phangi* (west), a kind of grasshopper which appears in years of drought and attacks roots of wheat and gram.

फनिगा *phaniga*,—see सुरका *surka.*

फरिङ्गा *pharinga*,—see टीड़ी *tīri.*

फाटी *phāti*, a blight in the ear of rice.

फाँड़ा *phānra* (Tirhut) or फाँड़ी *phānri* (Tirhut), a weevil destructive of wood and grain.

फुलभङ्गा *phulbhanga*,—see झिल्ली *jhilli.*

बकुला *bakula*,—see बक्की *bakki.*

बकुली *bakuli* (south-west), a green caterpillar destructive to rice. Cf. कजरी *kajri.*

बकेया *bakeya*,—see बक्की *bakki.*

बक्की *bakki*, also बकेया *bakeya* or बकुला *bakula* (also in West Tirhut) in Shahabad, and बुढ़िया *burhiya* or बढ़ही *barhi* in South Bhagalpur, a small kind of caterpillar which attacks rice. A larger kind is बाँका *bānka.*

बढ़ही *barhi*,—see बक्की *bakki.*

बभनी *babhni* (Tirhut), a blight affecting rice, sugar-cane, millets, and opium. See also औरङ्ग *aurang* and मुरका *murka.*

बलुआ *balua*, बलुई *baluï*,—see बालू *bālu*.

बाँका *bānka*,—see बक्की *bakki*.

बाँकी *bānki* (Gaya), a disease which attacks the leaves of trees (especially the pepper-tree), and causes them to curl up and wither.

बाला *bāla*,—see बालू *bālu*.

बालू *bālu* or बलुआ *balua* (Patna, Gaya, and south-east), बलुई *baluï* (Shahabad), बाला *bāla* (South-West Shahabad), an insect which eats the stalks of pulses and makes the leaves crumple up.

बीझल *bījhal* (Gaya and South Munger), weevil-eaten.

बुढ़िया *burhiya*,—see बक्की *bakki*.

भङ्ख *bhankh*,—see भाँख *bhānkh*.

भरक्का *bharka* (West Tirhut and south-east), an insect injurious to rice, caused by prevalence of south winds and excess of rain.

भँवन्रा *bhañwra*,—see भेँड़ा *bhenra*.

भरक्की *bharki* (South Bhagalpur), a disease of the rice-plant.

भाँख *bhānkh* (north) and also भाँखी *bhānkhi* (north), भङ्ख *bhankh* (east), a blight which attacks the millet साँवाँ *sāñwān* (*panicum frumentaceum*).

भुइला *bhuïla*, भुइली *bhuili*, भुरन्री *bhurri*, भुरन्ली *bhurli*, भुरिला *bhurila*, भुरिली *bhurili*,—see भूआ *bhūa*.

भूआ *bhūa* (Tirhut, Patna, Gaya, and east), भुइला *bhuïla* or भुइली *bhuili* (West Tirhut and north-west), also भुरन्ली *bhurli* (Sāran), भुरिला *bhurila*, भुरिली *bhurili*, or भुरन्री *bhurri* (south-west), a hairy worm which eats the leaves of the castor-oil plant and pulses, and is fatal to cattle when eaten.

भेँड़ा *bhenra* or भेँड़न्वा *bhenrwa* (Patna and east), भँवन्रा *bhañwra* (West Tirhut and Shahabad), an insect which attacks millets and stored grain in dry weather.

भेमरा *bhemra*,—see गाँधी *gāndhi*.

मगन्रा *mangra* (South-West Shahabad), an insect which attacks the sugar-cane in the root.

मज॰री *majri*,—see कज॰री *kajri*.

मर॰हिन्ना *marhinna*, मरी *mari*,—see मुआर *muār*.

माँछी *mānchhi*,—see गाँधी *gāndhi*.

मारा *māra* (North-East Tirhut), a disease in rice which withers the plants.

मुआर *muār* (west), चत॰रा *chatra* (Patna and Gaya), मर॰हिन्ना *marhinna* (Tirhut and East), मरी *mari* (West Tirhut and South Bhagalpur), a disease in which the whole plant is burnt up.

मुर॰का *murka* (north), also अँग॰रा *angra* (Champāran), and बभ॰नी *babhni* (Tirhut), a blight in opium. See जाला *jāla*.

मुरिया *muriya*,—see सुख॰ड़ा *sukhra*.

लछ॰मिनिया *lachhminiya* (East Tirhut), a small, thin, red-coloured beetle found in granaries. It does no harm, and is reverenced by grain-merchants.

लर॰का *larka* or (Gaya) लुर॰का *lurka*, a worm which attacks gram and pease. North of the Ganges it also burrows into the ribs of the leaf of the tobacco-plant, and is then called केँउआँ *keñuān* in Tirhut.

लाही *lāhi*, plant-lice.

लेँढ़ा *lenrha* (west and West Tirhut), नेढ़ा *nerha* (Tirhut), a disease in wheat or barley in which the ears turn black.

सड़॰का *sarka*, a worm in the root of rice.

सिरुका *siruka*,—see सुर॰का *surka*.

सिरोरा *sirora*,—see दखिन॰हा *dakhinha*.

सुख॰ठा *sukhtha*,—see सुख॰ड़ा *sukhra*.

सुख॰ड़ा *sukhra* (West Tirhut and south generally), सुख॰ठा *sukhtha* (West Tirhut and west), पिहिका *pihika* (rest of Shahabad), मुरिया *muriya* (South Bhagalpur), a blight in sugar-cane.

सुंद॰री *sundri* (east), an insect which eats the leaves of the castor-oil plant.

सुण्डा *sunda*,—see सूँड़ा *sūnra*.

सुर॰का *surka* (East Tirhut and Shahabad), सिरुका *siruka* (Sāran and Patna), फनिगा *phaniga* (Tirhut and South-West Shahabad), an insect which eats the leaves of sugar-cane and destroys gram, pease, and cereals.

सूँड़ा *sūnra* or सूँड़ी *sūnri* (Tirhut and south generally), सूँढ़ *sūnrh* or सूँढ़ा *sūnrha* (Gaya), सुण्डा *sunda* (West Tirhut and south-east), a kind of weevil destructive to wood and stored grain. Cf. कीरी *kīri*.

सूँढ़ *sūnrh*,—see सूँड़ा *sūnra*.

हड्डा *hadda* a white stem growing out of the root of the tobacco-plant, and throwing it far out of the soil.

हथिया *hathiya* (North-East Tirhut and Gaya) and हथियां सुण्डा *hathiya sunda* (south-east), a small white insect which damages rice.

हर-दा *harda* (north and east), a sort of mildew which dries up the grain in cereal crops. The plant turns yellow, and the ear black.

CHAPTER II.—NOXIOUS WEEDS.

1075. These are as follows:—

अँक-टा *ankta*,—see अँक-रा *ankra*.

अँक-रा *ankra* or अँक-री *ankri* (West Tirhut and Shahabad), अँक-टा *ankta* (Tirhut and elsewhere south) (*vicia sativa*), it appears in wheat.

अगिया *agiya* (north and east), a weed which burns the rice-plant (from आग *āg*, fire).

उख-ड़ा *ukhra*,—see हड्डा *hadda*.

उर-कुस्सी *urkussi*,—see बिछौतिया *bichhautiya*.

कक-ना *kakna* (Patna, Gaya, and south-east), बन-सारी *bansāri* (Shahabad and East Tirhut), a weed which chokes crops.

कठ-रेँग-नी *kathrengni*,—see रेँग-नी *rengni*.

कन-वाँ *kanwān*, कन्ना *kanna*,—see काना *kāna*.

कन-सन *kansan*,—see काँसी *kānsi*.

काना *kāna* (Tirhut, Patna and east), कन्ना *kanna* (north-east Tirhut), कन-वाँ *kanwān* (Gaya), केना *kena* (West Tirhut and west), a weed which chokes rice (a species of *Coix*).

काँसी *kānsi* (West Tirhut, Patna, Gaya, and the south-east), कास *kās* (Shahabad and North Bihār), कन-सन *kansan* (Sāran), (*saccharum spontaneum*), a most destructive grass.

केना *kena,*— see काना *kāna.*

कोइल खो *koïl kho,* — see गोरखुल *gorkhul*

खड़ुका *kharuka,*—see खरथूआ *kharthūa.*

खरथूआ *kharthūa* (Patna and Gaya), बथुआ *bathua* (generally) खड़ुका *kharuka* (North-East Tirhut and Shahabad), मोचट्टी *mochatti* (ditto), a weed in opium.

खुरका *khurka* or मछैती *machhaiti* (north), also रुआरी *ruāri* (Sāran), a weed in opium. Cf. रुआरा *ruāra.*

गड़हर *garhar,*—see गाँड़र *gānrar.*

गढ़रो *garhro,*—see गेंड़हरुआ *gerharua.*

गड़ार *garār,*—see गाँड़र *gānrar.*

गाँड़र *gānrar* (West Tirhut and Patna), गड़ार *garār* (Tirhut and east), जमार गड़ार *jamār garār* (South Munger), गड़हर *garhar* (South-West Shahabad), a weed which injures rice (various species of *Coix*).

गेंड़हरुआ *gerharua* (north-west), गढ़रो *garhro* (North Tirhut), a weed in cereal crops.

गोखुला *gokhula,*—see गोरखुल *gorkhul.*

गोरखुल *gorkhul* (west), बाँसी *bānsi* (generally), गोखुला *gokhula* (West Tirhut, Patna, Gaya, and South Munger), कोइल खो *koïl kho,* a plant which injures rice (*tribulus terrestris*).

चपड़ा *chapra,*—see धुरपा *dhurpa.*

चिचहोर *chichhor,* चिचोर *chichor,* चिचोरी *chichori,*—see लेंड़ई *leurai.*

चौपट्टा *chaupatta,*—see पिपरा *pipra.*

जंगला *jangla,*—see झिरुआ *jhirua.*

जमार गड़ार *jamār garār,*— see गाँड़र *gānrar.*

जम्हार *jamhār,* जाम्हर *jāmhar* (Patna and South Munger), जिन्हार *jinhār* (South-West Shahabad), and डम्हरो *damharo* (South Bhagalpur), a coarse hard grass, infesting poor soils (varieties of *andropogon.*)

जाम्हर *jāmhar,*—see जम्हार *jamhār.*

जिनवाँ *jinwān,* a grass something like दूभ *dūbh, q.v.*

जिन्हार *jinhār,*—see जम्हार *jamhār.*

झर *jhar,* झरँगा *jharnga,* झार *jhār,*—see झारङ्ग *jhārang.*

झारङ्ग *jhārang* (north-west), झरँगा *jharnga* (Shahabad), झार *jhār* or झर *jhar* (Tirhut and east), a weed which injures rice

झिरुआ *jhirua* (Patna, Gaya, South Munger, and North Bihār). झिरौआ *jhiraua* (South Munger), झिर॰वा *jhirwa* (South Bhagalpur), जँग॰ला *jangla* (South-West Shahabad), झीरो *jhīro* (East Tirhut), a weed which chokes rice.

झीरो *jhīro*,—see झिरुआ *jhirua*.

ठोक॰रा *thokra*,—see बिछौतिया *bichhautiya*.

डम्हरो *damharo*,—see जम्हार *jamhār*.

डर *dar*, डेयोरा *deyora*,—see मोँथा *montha*.

डाभी *dābhi* (north) a coarse grass, injurious to crops (*xyris indica*).

तितिली *titili*,—see पिप॰रा *pipra*.

दुधिया *dudhiya*,—see हड्डा *hadda*.

दूभ *dūbh* or दूब *dūb* (north and east), also दुब्भी *dubbhi* (south), a grass which overspreads fallow fields (*cynodon dactylon*).

धुर॰पा *dhurpa* (Patna, Gaya, and South Munger), धुरुप *dhurup* (South Bhagalpur), चप॰ड़ा *chapra* (Shahabad), a tough, coarse grass spreading over uncultivated lands, which are inundated yearly (*cynodon dactylon*). It is only removed by digging.

नक॰छिक॰नी *nakchhikni*,—see रेँग॰नी *rengni*.

पिप॰रा *pipra* (Sāran, Patna, and east), पुप॰रा *pupra* (South Bhagalpur), चौपट्टा *chaupatta* (South-West Shahabad), तितिली *titili* (generally), a weed in wheat.

पुप॰रा *pupra*,—see पिप॰रा *pipra*.

बड़॰गोहुमा *bargohuma* (south and east), a weed in wheat.

बथुआ *bathua*,—see खर॰थूआ *kharthūa*.

बन॰पियजुआ *banpiyajua*, बन॰पियाज *banpiyāj*, and बन॰रस॰ना *banrasna*,—see रुआरा *ruāra*.

बन॰सारी *bansāri*,—see कक॰ना *kakna*.

बसाँढ़ी *basānrhi*,—see बसौँता *basaunta*.

बसौँता *basaunta* (West Tirhut and north-west), बसाँढ़ी *basānrhi* (Tirhut), a weed which injures the spring crops (*acalypha indica ?*)

बाँसी *bānsi*,—see गोरन्खुल *gorkhul.*

बिछौतिया *bichhautiya* or बिछन्वतिया *bichhwatiya* is a parasitic plant which injures the poppy. It is also called भरन्भाँड़ *bharbhānr* in South-West Shahabad, ठोकन्रा *thokra* in the rest of that district and north of the Ganges, and उरन्कुस्सी *urkussi* in South-East Bihār.

भँगन्रा *bhangra* (West Tirhut, Patna, Gaya, and South Munger), भँगन्रैया *bhangraiya* (Tirhut and east), भेँगरिया *bhengāriya* (North Bihār and Shahabad), भँगरिया *bhangariya* (Tirhut) (*verbesina prostrata*), a small creeping-weed with a white flower which injures rice.

भँगरिया *bhangariya*,—see भँगन्रा *bhangra.*

भरन्भाँड़ *bharbhānr*,—see बिछौतिया *bichhautiya.*

भेँगरिया *bhengariya*,—see भँगन्रा *bhangra.*

मकन्ड़ा *makra* (north and east), a rough coarse grass spreading over uncultivated lands which are inundated yearly. It is only removed by digging (*cynosurus*).

मछैती *machhaiti*,—see खुरन्का *khurka.*

मँड़ेर *mañrer* (Patna, Gaya, and east), मड़र *marar* (South Bhagalpur), मरेन *maren* (Shahabad), a weed which chokes rice.

मोचट्टी *mochatti*,—see खरन्थुआ *kharthūa.*

मोँथा *montha*, also डर *dar* and मौना *mauna* (also in West Tirhut) in the south-east, and डेयोरा *deyora* in South Munger. A coarse grass which grows in uncultivated land and injures the autumn crops (*cyperus rotundus*).

राड़ी *rāri* (north), a coarse hard grass infesting poor soils.

रुआरा *ruāra* (Patna), बनन्रसन्ना *banrasna* (Gaya and South Munger), बनन्पियाज *banpiyāj* or बनन्पियजुआ *banpiyajua* (Tirhut and Shahabad), a weed which grows in opium. Cf. खुरन्का *khurka.*

रुआरी *ruāri*,—*see* खुरन्का *khurka.* Cf. रुआरा *ruāra.*

रेँगन्नी *rengni*, the Mexican poppy (*argemone Mexicana*), a thistle-like plant, which overspreads fallow fields. It is also called नकन्छिकन्नी *nakchhikni* or (to the east) कठन्रेँगन्नी *kathrengni.* It was introduced into India in a cargo from Mexico within the last hundred years, and is now very common.

लँड़ई *leñraī* (north-west), चिचोर *chichor* (north and Gaya), चिचोरी *chichori* (Tirhut), चिचन्होर *chichhor* (east), चिचोरो *chichoro* (South Bhagalpur and Tirhut), a weed which chokes rice.

हड्डा *hadda* or उखन्ड़ा *ukhra* (West Tirhut and south), or (West Tirhut and Gaya) दुधिया *dudhiya*, a small creeping-plant injurious to crops (*euphorbia hirta*). Cf. also § 1183 for other names.

CHAPTER III.—MISCELLANEOUS.

1076. A stunted crop is बैठल हासिल *baithal hāsil* north of the Ganges. In Shahabad and West Tirhut it is सितुरियाएल *situriyāël* or ततुरियाएल *taturiyāël*, or in Sāran, सुतरियाएल *sutariyāel*. In Gaya it is ठिँगुरियाएल *thinguriyāël*, in Patna भँटन्वाँस *bhentwāns*, in West Tirhut and South Munger ठुरियाएल *thuriyāël*, and in South Bhagalpur बिरन्नियाएल *birniyāël*. A blighted ear is मराएल *marāël* north of the Ganges. In Shahabad it is अबन्दा *abda* or दगन्दार *dagdār*, in Patna and Gaya कोइल *koïl*, and in the south-east मरा *mara*. पैया *paiya* in Gaya and the west, and भोर *bhor* to the north-east, is rice in which the ears have no seed. Blighted millets are called भखियाएल *bhakhiyāël* in the north-west, and भख चटुआ *bhakh chatua* in Tirhut. In Shahabad they are खुक्खा *khukkha* or खोजन्ड़ा *khojra*, in Gaya अलन्गल *algal*, and in Patna फुलन्हर *phulhar*.

1077. Crops withered from drought are to the west and in West Tirhut मुआर *muār*; in Gaya they are मोआर *moār*, and in Patna मुअल *mual*. To the east and in Tirhut they are मरन्हेना *marhena* or मरन्हिन्ना *marhinna*, and in South Bhagalpur also मरा *mara*. An irretrievably spoilt crop is बिगन्रल हासिल *bigral hāsil* north of the Ganges. In Shahabad it is बाँकन्टा *bānkta*, and in Patna चुचुहिया *chuchuhiya*. Scarcity of rain is सुखार *sukhār*.

1078. Failure of seed is बिजन्मार *bijmār* in Gaya and the west. In South Munger it is बीया मार *biya mār*. North of the Ganges it is also निर्बिज्ज *nirbijj*, निर्बीज *nirbij*, or अबिज्ज *abijj*. Other names are बँझौरा *banjhaura* (South-West Shahabad), बाँझी *bānjhi* (rest of Shahabad), बँझौरी *banjhauri* in Patna, and दैहाएब *daihāëb* in South Bhagalpur. In North-East Tirhut there is also कौर जाएब *kaur jāëb*, and in East Tirhut भखड़ जाएब *bhakhar jāëb*.

1079. Crops trodden down by cattle are धँगाठ (also spelt धङाठ) *dhangāth* north of the Ganges, local variants being दँगाठ *dangāth* in South-East Tirhut, धँगाएल *dhangāel* in Sáran, and धँगेड़ *dhanger* in West Tirhut and Champāran. In South-West Shahabad they are लहनाएल *lahnāël*, in Gaya and South Munger खुरखून *khurkhūn*, and in South Bhagalpur खींची *khīnchi*. In East Tirhut they are also called निघेस *nighes*.

1080. Crops laid by the wind are called गिरल *giral* or खसल *khasal*. A hot dry wind which burns up crops is to the west called झोला *jhola*, and such crops are known as झोलाइल *jholāïl* or झोँकरल *jhonkral*. To the east it is ढाढ़ा *dhārha* or ढाढ़ी *dhārhi*. A frosty wind which frost-bites the crops is पाला *pāla* or (to the east) पल्ला *palla*. The same words are used for frost-bite itself, and a frost-bitten crop is पलमरुआ *palmarua*. An inundation is दहार *dahār* or बाढ़ *bārh*, also बाढ़ि *bārhi* (North-East Tirhut), धाध *dhādh* (Gaya), आफत *āphat* (Patna), and बोहा *boha* or खार *khār* in the south-east. Morning fogs are कूहा *kūha*, of which optional local variants are कुहेस *kuhes* or कुहेसा *kuhesa* to the west and कुहस्सा *kuhassa* in South Bhagalpur. कुहेस *kuhes* is also current in North-East Tirhut, and in South-East Tirhut we find कुम्हेस *kumhes*. A fog in the day-time is धून *dhūn* or धूँध *dhūndh*. Hail-stones are पत्थल *patthal*, पत्थर *patthar*, पाथर *pāthar*, or बनौरी *banauri*, a local variant of the last being बँगौरी *bangauri* or बँगौरिया *bangauriya* in West Tirhut, Patna, and the east.

DIVISION VI.

AGRICULTURAL TIMES AND SEASONS.

1081. The* Bihār agriculturist follows the Hindu year in calculating his seasons. The year is divided into twelve lunar months (मास *mās*, माँस *māñs*, महिना *mahina*, महिन्ना *mahinna*, or महीना *mahīna*) of 30 days each, and therefore consists of 360 days. Each month is further divided into a first or dark half [किसुन पख (or पच्छ) *kisun pakh* (or *pachchh*)] (commencing with the first day of the wane of the moon), and a second or light half (सुकल्ल पख *sukl pakh*). Roughly speaking, a Hindu month commences at about the 15th of an English month; but as there are thus only 360 days in a year, they begin each year somewhat earlier in the solar year than the year before, till the calendar is brought nearly right every third year by the insertion of an intercalary month (मलमास *malmās*) of 30 days every third year.

1082. Besides the above, another important division of the year must be noticed,—that into lunar asterisms (नखत *nakhat*, नछत्तर *nachhattr*, or निछत्तर *nichhattr*). There are 27 of these in each year, and consequently 2¼ in each month. Each asterism is not of equal length. The longest is हथिया *hathiya*, which is 16 lunar days. The others range from about 13 lunar days in the dry months to 15 lunar days in the wet. Every agricultural operation commences in a certain asterism, and so it is necessary to know when they occur. The accompanying table shows roughly the relative positions of the English and Hindu months and of the lunar asterisms.

---

* Part of the following will be found in Carnegy's Kachahri Technicalities, s.v. *nakhat*.

Hindu

Approximate European Month.	Name.
Part of September	
	आसिन *Āsin* or कुआर *Kuār* ...
October	
	कातिक *Kātik* ... ...
November	
	अगहन *Aghan* ... ...
December	
	पूस *Pūs* ... ...
January	
	माघ *Māgh* ... ...
February	
	फागुन *Phāgun* ... ...
March	
	चैत *Chait* ... ...
April	
	बैसाख *Baisākh* ... ...
May	
	जेठ *Jeth* ... ...
June	
	अखाढ़ *Akhārh* or असाढ़ *Asārh* ...
July	
	सावन *Sāwan* or साओन *Sāon* ...
August	
	भादों *Bhādoñ* ... ...
Part of September	

Months.

Dark half (किसुन पख *kisun pakh*) and light half (सुकल पख *sukl pakh*).	Asterisms, of which there are two and a quarter to each Hindu month.
Dark ... ... Light	¾ of उतरा फगुनी *Utra Phaguni.* हस्त *Hast* or हथिया *Hathiya.* चितरा *Chitra.*
Dark ... ... Light	स्वाती *Swāti* or सिवाती *Siwāti.* बिसाखा *Bisākha.*
Dark ... ... Light	अनुराधा *Anurādha.* जेष्ठा *Jeshtha.*
Dark ... ... Light	मूल *Mūl.* पुरबा खाढ़ *Purba Khārh.*
Dark ... ... Light	उतरा खाढ़ *Utra Khārh.* सावन *Sāwan.* धनिष्ठा *Dhanishtha.*
Dark ... ... Light	सतभीखा *Satbhīkha* पूरब भद्रपद *Pūrab Bhadrapad.*
Dark ... ... Light	उत्तर भद्रपद *Uttar Bhadrapad.* रेवती *Reoti.*
Dark ... ... Light	अश्विनी *Aswini* or असनी *Asni.* भरनी *Bharni.* कृत्तिका *Krittika.*
Dark ... ... Light	रोहनी *Rohni* or रोहिनी *Rohini.* मिरगसिरा *Mirgsira* or मिर्गिडाह *Mirgidāh.*
Dark ... ... Light	अरदरा *Aradra* or अदरा *Adra.* पुनरबस *Punarbas.*
Dark ... ... Light	पुख *Pukh* or चिरैया *Chiraiya.* असरेस *Asres* or असलेखा *Aslekha.*
Dark ... ... Light	मग्घा *Maggha.* पुरबा फगुनी *Purba Phaguni.* ¼ of उतरा फगुनी *Utra Phaguni.*

1083. The year current in Bihār is the *Fasli* year, which commences with the Hindu month of *Āsin*. The year is also popularly* divided into three seasons, viz. the hot (गरमी *garmi*), the wet (बरखा *barkha*), and the cold (जाड़ा *jāra*). The hot season commences in फागुन *Phāgun*, the wet in अखाढ़ *Akhārh*, and the cold in कातिक *Kātik*. The following rhymes, some of which will be found also in Carnegy's Kachahri Technicalities, are current over the greater part of Northern India, and show the various seasons for agricultural operations.

1084. Cultivation commences in Jeth, in the asterism of Rohni, when ploughing and sowing begin. The rain of Mirgsira is not good, and hence no sowing is done in that asterism. In Aradra sowing is recommenced and transplanting is done for the winter (*aghani*) crop. This goes on into Punarbas and Pukh if the rains are late. In Magha and Purba Phaguni the *urid*, *kurthi*, and other pulses are sown. In Hathiya rain is very important, both for the winter crops and for the sowing of the spring (*rabbi*) crops. In former days (say cultivators) the rains used to stop in Swāti, which was very good for the crops, but now they end in Hathiya. So valuable is the rain of Swāti that any drop which falls during that asterism into a pearl-oyster becomes a pearl. That is how pearls are made. The rain in Chitra, on the contrary, is very bad.

मग्घा लगावे घग्घा, सिवाती लावस टाटी ।
कहतारी हाथी रानी, हम हूँ अवात बाटी ॥

Maggha lagāwe ghaggha, siwāti lāwas tāti,
Kahtāri Hāthi rāni, ham hūñ āwat bāti.

—Maggha brings rain-storms, Swāti brings a screen (*i.e.*, rain stops), and Queen Hathiya tells (by her thunder) that she is coming.

फागु कराइ चैत चुक कित्तिक नट्ठहि तार ।
स्वाती नट्ठहि माख तिल कहि गए डाक गोआर ॥

Phāgu karāï, chait chuk, kirttik natthahi tār,
Swāti natthahi mākh til, kahi gae Dāk Goār.

---

* Astrologers and poets count six seasons, but the above is the popular division.

—If it rains in the month of Phāgun, *urid* is spoilt; if in the month of Chait, lemons;* if in the asterism of Krittika, the toddy palms; and if in that of Swāti, beans and sesamum, saith Dāk, the Gowāla.

जौँ बरसे बैसक्खा राउ ।
एक धान मैँ दोबर चाउ ॥

Jauñ barse Baisakkha rāu,
Ek dhān meñ dobar chāu.

—If King Baisākh (April–May) rain, every grain of paddy will produce two of rice.

क्रित्तिका चूए छौ ले मूए ।
जौँ रोहिनी नाहिँ कादो करे ॥

Krittika chūe chhau le mūe,
Joñ Rohini nāhiñ kādo kare.

—If it rains in Krittika, there will be no rain for the six following asterisms, provided Rohini makes no mud.

Krittika is the best asterism for sowing *chīna* (*panicum frumentosum*): hence they say in Tirhut—

जब जनिहठ खरचाक हीन ।
क्रित्तिका मैँ तूँ बोइहत चीन ॥

Jab janiha kharchāk hīn,
Krittika meñ tūñ boiha chīn.

—If you find your stock of food becoming exhausted, sow *chīna* in *Krittika.*

मिरगसिरा तबय रोहिनि लबय अरदरा जाय बदबुदाय ।
कहै डाक सुनु भिल्लरि कुत्ता भात न खाय ॥

Mirgsira tabay Rohini labay aradra jāy budbudāy
Kahai Dāk sunu Bhillari, kutta bhāt na khāy.

—If Mirgsira is hot, Rohini rains, and Aradra gives a few drops, saith Dāk, hear, O Bhillari, (rice will be so plentiful that) even dogs will turn up their noses at it.

---

* चुक *chuk* is a mess of lemons kept for fermentation, and is here applied to the fruit on the tree.

1085. The rain of Aradra (middle of June) is of considerable importance to the future crops: thus—

अदरा माँस जे बोए साठी।
दुख के मार निकालऽ लाठी॥

Adra māns je boe sāthi,
Dukh ke mār nikāla lāthi.

—If you sow sixty-day rice in Aradra, you strike distress with a club and drive it away.

आदि न बरसे अदरा हस्त न बरसे निदान।
कहहिँ डाक सुनु भिल्लरि भए किसान पिसान॥

Ādi na barse aradra, hast na barse nidān,
Kahahiñ Dāk sunu Bhillari bhae kisān pisān.

—If Aradra does not rain at the commencement, and Hathiya at its end, saith Dāk, hear, O Bhillari, the cultivator is crushed.

And—

चढ़त बरसे अरदरा उतरत बरसे हस्त।
कतेक राजा दाँड़े, रहे अनन्द गिरहस्त॥

Charhat barse aradra, utrat barse hast,
Katek rāja dānre, rahe anand girhast.

—If it rain when Aradra commences and when Hathiya is ending, no matter how much rent may be demanded, the householder is still happy.

अरदरा बरसे सभ किछु हाँ।
एक जवास पतर बिन भाँ॥

Aradra barse sabh kichhu hān
Ek jawās patr bin bhān.

—If Aradra rains everything grows (*lit.* is): only one, the *jawās* (*Hedysarum alhagi*), loses its leaves.

1086. Aradra and Punarbas are the two main asterisms of the month of Akhārh (June–July). This is the great month of the year for finishing the preparation of the fields, as the proverb says, जेकर बनल अखड़वा रे तेकर बारहो मास *jekar banal akharwa re tekar bāraho mās*, —he whose fields are ready in *Akhārh*, is ready also all the year round. If the rains are late, paddy sowing goes on as late as Punarbas or even Pukh, but this is rarely successful. These last two asterisms are usually devoted to transplanting, and not to sowing.

पुख पुनरबस बोए धान ।
मग्घा असलेखा कादो सान ॥

Pukh punarbas boe dhān,
Maggha aslekha kādo sān.

—Sow paddy in Pukh and Punarbas, and in Maggha and Aslekha mix thoroughly the mud (*i.e.* prepare the fields).

अरद्रा धान, पुनरबस पैया ।
गेल, किसान, जे बोए चिरैया ॥

Aradra dhān, punarbās paiya.
Gel, kisān, je boe chiraiya.

—Paddy sown in Aradra turns to plenty, in Punarbas it has empty ears, and sown in Pukh it turns to nothing.

1087. After Akhārh (June–July) comes Sāwan or Sāon (July–August), to which the following rhymes apply :—

साओन सुकला सप्तमी छपि कै ऊगहिं भान ।
तौं लगि मेघा बरसै जौं लगि देव उठान ॥

Sāon sukla saptami chhapi kai ūgahiñ bhān.
Tauñ lagi megha barse jauñ lagi deb uthān.

—If on the morning of the seventh day of the bright half of Sāwan the sun rises obscured by clouds, it will rain up to the festival of the *Deb Uthān* (11th of the light half of Kātik, *i.e.* early in November).

साओन सुकला सप्तमी उग के लूकहिँ सूर ।
हाँको पिया हर बरद बरखा गेल बड़ि दूर ॥

Sāon sukla saptami, ug ke lūkahiñ sūr,
Hānko piya har barad, barkha gel bari dūr.

—If on the same day as that above mentioned the sun rises (clear) and afterwards hides itself behind clouds, drive away, my dear, your plough and bullocks, for the rain is very far off.

साओन सुकला सप्तमी, उदै जौं देखे भान ।
तुम जाओ पिया मालवा हम जैबौं मुलतान ॥

Sāon sukla saptami, udai joñ dekhe bhān,
Tum jāo piya Mālwa, ham jaiboñ Multān.

—A cloudless morning on the same day (is a sure sign of drought). My dear (let us leave the country,) I am going to Multān, and you can go to Mālwa.

साओन सुकला सप्तमी रैनि होँहि मसियार।
कह भड्डर सुनु भड्डरि परबत उपजय सार॥

Sāon sukla saptami, raini hoñhi masiyār,
Kah Bhaddar sunu Bhaddari, parbat upjay sār.

—If on the same date the night is dark, saith Bhaddar, hear, O Bhaddari, excellent crops will grow even on a mountain.

साओन सुकला सप्तमी, जोँ गरजे आधी रात।
तुम जाओ पिया मालवा, हम जैबोँ गुजरात॥

Sāon sukla saptami, joñ garje ādhī rāt,
Tum jāo piya Mālwa, ham jaibon Gujrāt.

—If on the same date it thunders at midnight (there will be a drought), you must go to Mālwa and I to Gujrat.

करके भीँजै कँकरी, सिंह गरजै जाए।
कह भड्डर सुनु भड्डरि कुत्ता भात न खाए॥

Karke bhīnjai kankri, singh garjai jāe,
Kah Bhaddar sunu Bhaddari, kutta bhāt na khāe.

—"If in Cancer (Sāwan, July–August) the gravel is wet, and Leo (Bhādon, August–September) passes by with thunder," saith Bhaddar, "hear, O Bhaddari, rice will be so plentiful that even dogs will refuse it."

साओन पछवा भादब पुरवा आसिन बहे ईसान।
कातिक कन्ता सिकिओ न डोले कतय के रखबह धान॥

Sāon pachhwa, Bhādab purwa, Āsin bahe īsān,
Kātik, kanta, sikio na dole kutay ke rakhbah dhān ?

—If the west wind blow in Sāwan, the east in Bhādon, and the north-east in Āsin, and if there is so little wind in Kātik that even the reeds do not shake, where, my dear, will you have room to keep your rice? (*i.e.*, you will have a bumper crop).

साओन मास बहै पुरवैया बँचह बरद कीनह गैया।

Sāon mās bahai purwaiya, benchah barad kīnah gaiya.

—If the east wind blow in Sāwan, sell your bullocks and buy cows (it will be no use trying to plough).

साओनक पछवा दिन दुइ चारि ।
चूल्हीक पाछा उपजे सारि ॥

Sāonak pachhwa din duï chāri,
Chūlhik pāchha upje sāri.

—If the west wind blow in Sāwan for only two or three days, rice will grow even behind your hearth.

साओन पछेआ महि भरे ।
भादोँ पुरवा पथल सड़े ॥

Sāon pachhea mahi bhare,
Bhādoṅ purwa pathal sare.

—If the west wind blow in Sāwan, the land will be flooded; and if the east wind blow in Bhādoṅ, (it will rain so that) the very stones will melt.

जे न भरे असरेखा मग्घा ।
फेर भरे असरेखा मग्घा ॥

Je na bhare Asrekha Maggha,
Pher bhare Asrekha Maggha.

—That which is not filled up with water in Asres and Maggha has no chance of being filled up till they come again next year.

1088. To Bhādoṅ (August–September) the following apply:—

South Munger—

पुरवा रोपे पूर किसान ।
आधा घघरी आधा धान ॥

Purwa rope pūr kesān,
Ādha ghaghri ādha dhān.

—If a cultivator does not finish transplanting before Purwa (*i.e.* Purba Phaguni), half his crop will be paddy and half chaff.

जौँ पुरवा पुरवैया पावे । सुखले नदिया नाओ बहावे ॥

Jauṅ purwa purwaiya pāwe, sukhle nadiya nāo bahāwe.

—If the east wind blows in the asterism of Purwa (*i.e.* Purba Phaguni), there will be so much rain that ships will float in the dried-up beds of rivers.

Closely connected with this is the following :—

> पुरवा पर जौँ पछवा बहै। बिहँसि रौंड़ बात करै ॥
> एह दोनौँ के इहै बिचार। ऊ बरसै ई करै भतार ॥
>
> *Purwa par jauñ pachhwa bahai, bihañsi rāñr bāt karai,*
> *Eh donoñ ke ihai bichār ū barsai ī karai bhatār.*

—If the west wind blows during Purwa, and if a widow chats and smiles, from these facts you may judge that in the first case it will rain, and in the second case she is going to marry a second time.

With this may be compared—

> तीतिर पख मेघा ऊड़े, ओ बिधवा मुसुकाए।
> कहे डाक सुनु डाकिनि, ऊ बरसे ई जाए ॥
>
> *Titir pakh megha ūre, o bidhwa musukāė.*
> *Kahe Dāk sunu Ḍākiṇi, ū ḅarṣe ī jāë.*

—"When the clouds fly like the wings of the partridge, and when a widow smiles," saith Dāk, "hear, O Dākini, the one is going to rain and the other to marry."

> सूक करे बदरी सनीचर रहे छाए।
> ऐसन बोले भड्डरि बिन बरसे नहिँ जाए ॥
>
> *Sūk kare badri sanīchar rahe chhāe,*
> *Aisan bole Bhaddari bin barse nahiñ jāe.*

—A cloudy sky on Friday and Saturday is a sure precursor of rain.

> साओन के पुरवा, भादोँ पछिमा जोर।
> बरधा बेँचह सामी, चलह देस का ओर ॥
>
> *Sāon ke purwa, bhādoñ pachhima jor,*
> *Bardha bencha sāmi, chala des ka or.*

—My husband, let us sell our bullocks and leave the country if there is east wind in Sāon and a strong west one in Bhādoñ.

The following is current in Tirhut :—

> कुसी अमावस चौठी चान।
> अब की रोपब धान किसान ॥
>
> *Kusi amāwas chauthi chān,*
> *Ab kī ropba dhān kisān.*

—After the *Kusi Amāwas* (the festival of the 15th Bhādon, on which Brāhmans dig *kus* grass), and the *Chauk Chanda* (the moon of the 19th of Bhādoñ, O cultivator! you neede not plant out paddy.

उतरा में जनि रोपहु भैया ।
तीन धान होए तेरह पैया ॥

Utra meñ jani ropahu bhaiya,
Tīn dhān hoe terah paiya.

—Do not transplant in Utra Phaguni, for you will only get three grains to thirteen empty husks.

रातुक कागा दीनुक सियार ।
कि झरी बादर कि उपटार ॥

Rātuk kāga dinuk siyār,
Ki jhari bādar ki uptār.

—If the crow speak by night, and the jackal by day, there will be either a rain-storm or an inundation.

अौआ बौआ बहे बतास ।
तब होला बरखा के आस ॥

Aua baua bahe batās,
Tab hola barkha ke ās.

—When the wind blows from all four quarters, there is hope of rain.

1089. To Āsin (September–October) the following apply:—

हथिया बरसे तीन होत बा, सक्कर, साली, मास, ।
हथिया बरसे तीन जात बा, तील, कोदो, कपास ।

Hathiya barse tīn hot bā, sakkar, sāli, mās,
Hathiya barse tin jāt bā, tīl, kodo, kapās.

—Rain in Hathiya produces three things,—sugar-cane, rice, and pulse; and destroys three things,—sesamum, *kodo*, and cotton.

With this may be compared—

अदरा गेल तीनि गेल, सन साठी कपास ।
हाथिया गेल सभ गेल, आगिल पाछिल चास ॥

Adra gel tīni gel, san, sāthi, kapās;
Hathiya gel sabh gel, āgil pāchhil chās.

—Want of rain in Aradra destroys three crops,—hemp, sixty-day rice, and cotton. But by want of rain in Hathiya every thing is ruined, both what has been sown and what will be sown.

हथिया बरिसे, चितरा मेँड़राय।
घर बैसे धनहा रिरियाय (or अगराय)॥

Hathiya barise, chitra meñrrāy,
Ghar baise dhanha ririyāy (or *agrāy*).

—If Hathiya rains, and (the clouds of) Chitra hover about, the paddy-cultivator sits at home and utters cries of joy.

चितरा बरसे माटी मारे।
आगे भाइ गेरुई के कारे॥

Chitra barse māti māre,
Āge bhāi gerui ke kāre.

—Rain in Chitra destroys the power of the soil and is likely to produce blight.

आधा चित्रा राइ मुराइ।
आधा चित्रा जौ केराइ॥

Adha Chitra rāi murāi.
Ādha Chitra jau kerāi.

—In one-half of Chitra sow mustard and radishes, and in the other half barley and pease.

1090. To Katik (October–November), the following apply:—

एको पानि जौँ बरसे स्वाती।
कुरमिन पहिरे सोना पाती॥

Eko pāni joñ barse Swāti,
Kurmin pahire sona pāti.

—If a single shower come in Swāti it enriches people so much, that even Kurmi women get golden earrings to wear.

बेद बिदित ना होखे आन। बिना तुला नहिँ फूटे धान।
सुख सुखराती देव उठान। तकरै बरहै करह नेमान॥
तकरै बरहै खेत खरिहान। तकरै बरहै कोठिए धान॥

Bed bidit na hokhe ān, bina Tula nahiñ phūtai dhān,
Sukh sukhrāti deb uthān, takrai barhai karah nemān,
Takrai barhai khet kharihān, takrai barhai kothie dhān.

—What has been written in the Vedas cannot happen otherwise, and paddy cannot ripen before the balance (*i.e. Libra* = Kātik = October–November). From the festival of the *Sukhrāti* (*i.e.* the *Diwāli*) to the *Deb Uthān* (11th of the light half of Kātik) there will be happiness. On the twelfth day after that, hold the festival of eating the new grain; on the twelfth after that, heap up the corn on field and threshing-floor; and on the twelfth after that, put the grain in the store-house.

1091. The following are the signs of the stoppage of the rains:—

> छप के उगै तो क्या भये, निरमल्ल रैनि करन्त ।
> कीये जल देखिहठ सगरा, कामिनि कूप भरन्त ॥
>
> *Chhap ke ugai to kya bhaye, nirmal raini karant,*
> *Kīye jal dekhiha sagra, kāmini kūp bharant.*

—It matters little if the sun rises obscured by clouds, because when the nights are clear (the rains will stop). You will only find water in the sea, and women will have to go to the wells for water.

> रात निबद्दर, (or रातुक चकमक) दिन कैँ छथा ।
> कहैँ घाघ जे बरखा गया ॥
>
> *Rāt nibaddar (*or *rātuk chakmak), din keñ chhaya,*
> *Kaheñ Ghāgh je barkha gaya.*

—If you see a cloudless night and a cloudy day, be sure, says Ghāgh, that the rains are at an end.

> बोली लुखरी, फूले कास ।
> अब नाहीं बरखा के आस ॥
>
> *Boli lukhri, phūle kās,*
> *Ab nāhīñ barkha ke ās.*

—The barking of the fox and the flowering of *kās* grass are signs of the end of the rains.

> उगे अगस्त बन फूले कास ।
> अब नाहीं बरखा के आस ॥
>
> *Uge agast ban phūle kās,*
> *Ab nāhīñ barkha ke ās.*

—The appearance of the star Canopus and the flowering of the *kās* grass in the forest are signs of the end of the rains.

काँसी कूसी चौठ के चान ।
अब का रोपबऽ धान किसान ॥

Kānsi kūsi chauth ke chān,
Ab ka ropba dhān kisān.

—If the *kās* grass and the *kūs* grass flower on the fourth of the light half of Bhādon, why do you plant out, O cultivator (for the rains are stopped)?

1092. The following refer to the dry season:—

अगहन दोबर, पूस ड्योढ़ा ।
माघ सवाइ, फागुन बरसे घर हु के जाई,

Aghan dobar, Pūs dyaurha,
Māgh sawāi, Phāgun barse gharhu ke jāi.

—If it rains in Aghan, you will get double an average crop; if in Pūs, one and a half; if in Māgh, one and a quarter: but if in Phāgun, then even (the seedlings which you brought from) your house will be lost.

अगहन जे बरसे मेघ,
धन ओ राजा धन ओ देस ॥

Aghan je barse megh,
Dhan o rāja dhan o des.

—Happy are the king and people when it rains in Aghan.

पानी बरसे आधा पूस ।
आधा गेहूँ आधा भूस ॥

Pāni barse adha Pūs,
Adha gehūñ adha bhūs.

—Rain in the middle of the month of Pūs (*i.e.* early in January) will give you half wheat, half chaff.

माघ के गरमी, जेठ के जाड़, ।
पहिला पानी भर गेल ताड़ ।
घाघ कहेँ हम होबौँ जोगी ।
कूआँ कां पानी धोइहेँ धोबी ॥

Māgh ke garmi, Jeth ke jār,
Pahila pāni bhar gail tār,
Ghāgh kahen ham hobauñ jogi,
Kūān kā pāni dhoihen dhobi.

—Heat in Māgh (January–February), cold in Jeth (May–June), and the tanks filled with the first fall of rain (are signs of a drought). I'll become a beggar, says Ghāgh, and the washermen will wash with well-water.

चैत के पछेआ भादों के जल्ला ।
भादों के पछेआ माघ के पल्ला ॥
Chait ke pachhea, Bhādoñ ke jalla,
Bhadoñ ke pachhea, Māgh ke palla.

—The west wind in Chait (March–April) means rain in Bhādoñ (August–September), and the west wind in Bhādoñ means frost in Māgh (January–February).

1093. It will now be of advantage to compare the above with a native account of the behaviour of the asterisms preceding the famine of 1873-74. The poet Phatūri Lāl, in his tale of the famine, says as follows:—

June 1873.—ROHNI is the first asterism of the rainy season; but, as it came, it departed without rain.

Rainfall in Tirhut about 4 inches.

MIRGSIRA fulfilled our hopes, for it gave a few drops of rain and departed.

July.—ARADRA passed by with great majesty, thundering on every side.

Rainfall about 6½ inches, of which 4 inches were in the second week and 1½ inches in the last week.

PUNARBAS is a very holy asterism, but it was also a miser.

PUKH saved the face of the earth, but it became the end of the rains.

August.—ASRES rained upon such of the seedlings as did rise.

Rainfall about 4½ inches.

MAGHA was as poor as a beggar.

September.—PURBA PHAGUNI gave no proof of his existence by rain.

Rainfall about 4 inches.

UTRA PHAGUNI did not give even a drop to swear by.

October.—HATHIYA was like an elephant (*hāthi*) who put his trunk in his mouth.

Rainfall nil.

CHITRA was only a robber and a murderer.

November.—SWĀTI was put to public disgrace.

Rainfall nil.

DIVISION VII.

CATTLE AND OTHER DOMESTIC ANIMALS.

CHAPTER I.—CATTLE GENERALLY.

1094. Cattle generally are known as मवेशी *maweshi*, माल *māl*, or माल जाल *māl jāl*. Other names are चौआ *chaua* north of the Ganges, धूर *dhūr* in Patna and Gaya, and बरधा *bardha* in South-West Shahabad. A head of cattle is रास *rās*, and in Patna and Gaya also धूर *dhūr*. Horned cattle, exclusive of buffaloes, are गोरू *goru* or गाय गोरू *gāy goru*; also धूर डाँगर *dhūr dāngar* in Patna and Gaya. In Sāran डाँगर *dāngar* means cattle worn out from old age. In North-East Tirhut they are called लटल *latal*. A worn-out, useless cow or buffalo is said to be टुटाह *tutāh* or टूट गेल *tūt gail* north of the Ganges, or in North-West Tirhut बेहवाल *behwāl*. In Patna the term is थौंसा *thaunsa*, in Shahabad थहुसल *thahusal* or थौसल *thausal*, in Gaya नकादर *nakādar*, and in South Bhagalpur उठानो *uthāno*. Dead cattle are डाँगर *dāngar* in Shahabad and मरी *mari* in East Bihār.

CHAPTER II.—BULLS.

1095. A bull is साँढ़ *sānrh* when branded with sacrificial marks and let go, and ढाकर *dhākar* when not so branded. चौभर *chaubhar* (Patna and Gaya) or ढकरछोह *dhakarchhoh* is an imperfectly castrated bull, and बिनहामो *binhāmo* is a bull to the south-east.

CHAPTER III.—BULLOCKS.

1096. A bullock is बरध *baradh*, also in Patna, North-West Tirhut, and in Shahabad optionally बरद or बड़द *barad*. To the west it is also called बैल *bail*, and in Gaya धूर *dhūr* or पैरा *paira*. Plough-bullocks are called हराथी *harāthi* to the east. The pair are called जोड़ा *jora*. In a team of three bullocks the wheelers are called धूरी *dhūri* or धुरिया *dhuriya* to the west, and जोड़ी *jori* to the east. The leader is बीँड़ *bīnr* or बिँड़िया *binriya* to the west, and झिट्टी *jhitti* or नाटा *nāta* to the east.

1097. A yoke of well-bullocks is called मोटऽहा बरध *motha baradh*. The bullock which works blindfolded in an oil or sugar-cane press is called नाटा *nāta* or कोल्हुआ बैल *kolhua bail.* When there is ploughing going on or a cart being pulled by the aid of three bullocks, of whom only two are yoked at a time while the third one rests, the three are called तेधुरा *tedhura* or (in East Tirhut) तेधऽरी *tedhri*, or in Patna टेपऽटा *tepta*. Similarly when there are four bullocks, of whom two rest while two work, the team is called चौखर *chaukhar* or चौखरिया *chaukhariya* or चरऽबरऽधा *charbardha*, or in South-West Tirhut फेरऽवार *pherwār*. In the case of ploughing, the boy who looks after the unemployed bullocks is called in North-East Tirhut अनऽवाह *anwāh*.

1098. Bullocks are distinguished by various peculiarities, such as the following:—

A bullock unbroken to work is अदारी *adāri*, also अदार *adār* in Tirhut, in Shahabad, and in South Bhagalpur. In Patna and Gaya he is औदार *audār*, in South Munger अबोँ *aboñ*. One that sits down at work is परुआ *parua* to the west, and north of the Ganges कोढ़ि *korhi.** In South-West Shahabad he is गरिआर *gariar*, in Shahabad and Gaya गर *gar*, and in Patna मनऽकोढ़ी *mankorhi*. A vicious bullock is मरऽखाह *markhāh*, also मरऽखण्डा *markhanda* in Patna, मरऽखन्नो *markhanno* in East Bhagalpur, and मरऽखन *markhan* in Gaya. In South-West Shahabad the words मरऽकहा *markaha* and लतऽहा *latha* are used. A shying bullock is फेफऽरियाह *phephriyāh* to the north and west, and चिहुकार *chihukār* or हरऽकाह *harkāh* north of the Ganges generally. In South-West Shahabad he is बँदिया *bandiya*, in the rest of the district मझार *manjhār*, in Patna and Gaya भरऽकाहा *bharkāha*, and to the south-east हरऽकाहा *harkāha*. To butt is हुर पेटल *hur petal* in the west and मारब *mārab* in Tirhut. In Patna and the east it is धूँस मारब *dhūns mārab*, and to the south-east धूस मारब *dhūs mārab* or धूसा मारब *dhūsa mārab*. In Gaya it is धुसियाएब *dhusiyāëb*, and such a bullock is धुसमार *dhusmār* or धुसियाहा *dhusiyāha*. To break in cattle is तेवारे जोतल *tewāre jotal* to the west. In Tirhut it is पाट लगाएब or जोतब *pāt lagāëb* or *jotab*. In East Tirhut it is पाएट घुमाएब *pāët ghumāëb*, and in Gaya पीरी मेँ जोतब *pīri meñ jotab*. In Shahabad निकासल *nikāsal*, in Patna उघऽराएब

---

* Compare the proverb कोढ़ि बरद केँ फेफड़ि बहुत *korhi barad keñ phephari bahut,*— it is the lazy bullock that snorts and shies.

daghrāëb, in Gaya डह्राएब *dahrāëb*, in South Munger गोह्राएब *gohrāëb*, and in South Bhagalpur छटियाएब *chhatiyāëb*, mean to cause an animal to get up and to drive it along a village-road.

1099. A stunted bullock is ननःकिर्वा *nankirwa*, नाटा *nāta*, or नट्वा *natwa*. A dwarf bullock is गैना *gaina*.

1100. A bullock whose horns project in front is घोँचा *ghoncha* north of the Ganges and in Patna and South Bhagalpur, also घोँपा *ghompa* in East Tirhut. In Shahabad it is घोँच्वा *ghonchwa*, in Gaya घोँघर *ghonghar*, in Patna also घोँग्रा *ghongra*, and in South Munger घोँघ्रा *ghonghra*.

1101. A bullock one of whose horns is erect while the other hangs down is सरग्पताली *saragpatāli* (literally pointing to heaven and hell) or सरङ्ग्पताली *sarangpatāli*. He is also called डेब *deb* in Champāran and West Tirhut, कँसासुरी *kansāsuri* in South-West Shahabad, पताल सिङ्घी *patāl singhi* to the south-east.

1102. A bullock whose horns join in the centre is गौसिङ्घी *gausinghi* in South-West Tirhut, and सिँग्जुट्टा *singjutta* or सिँग्जूटल *singjūtal* generally.

1103. A bullock whose horns are loose and are turned down is called मैना *maina*, or in Patna and the south-east मैन *main*.

1104. A bullock whose horns are curled like a ram's is भेँड़्वा *bheñrwa*, भेँड़ *bheñr*, or मेँढ्वा *mendhwa*.

1105. A bullock one of whose horns turns to the right and the other to the left is चातर *chātar*, or चत्रा *chatra* when they are small and flat. When they are large, he is called फठाह *phathāh* or फट्हा *phatha*. In North-East Tirhut he is फरक्झाड़ा *pharakjhāra*.

1106. A bullock with stunted horns is मुठ्रा *muthra* or मुठिया *muthiya* generally, but in Shahabad it is मुठाल *muthāl* or मुठल *muthail*, and in Gaya मुठरिया *muthariya*.

1107. A bullock with no horns is मुँड़ेड़ा *munrera* in Sāran, मुण्डा *bhunda* in Champāran, भूँड़ा *bhūnra* or भुँड़्वा *bhunrwa* in Shahabad, मूँड़ा *mūnra* in North-East Tirhut, and मुण्डा *munda* in Gaya and the rest of Tirhut, मुड़्ला *murla* in South-East Tirhut, Patna, and South Munger, and मूड़ा *mūra* in South Bhagalpur. Other names are डुँड़िया *dunriya* in South-West Shahabad and ठूठा *thūtha* in South-East Bihār.

1108. A bullock with only one horn is एक-सिङ्गा *eksingha* or सिँघ-टुट्टा *singhtutta.*

1109. When a bullock has a broken tail he is called बाँड़ *bānr* or बाँड़ा *bānra* north of the Ganges and to the south-west, also नाढ़ा *nārha* in East Tirhut and the south-east. In Gaya and Champāran he is बण्डा *banda,* and in Patna लण्ढा *landha* or बण्ढा *bandha.* In South Munger he is लाँढ़ा *lānrha.* The opposite to this is पोँछ-वाला *ponchhwāla.*

1110. A bullock with its ears covered with long hair is झाबर *hābar* to the east and झब-रा *jhabhra* to the west. One with crooked eye-brows is भौँञाँ टेर *bhauñāñ ter* or भौँञाँ डेर *bhauñāñ der,* also in South Munger भाँवाँ डेरा *bhāñwāñ dera.*

1111. A bullock not used for agriculture because it has excrescences (representing Shiva) on its body, but purchased by religious mendicants, is known as जटहा *jataha* or बसहा *basaha.* Other local names are जट-हावा *jathāwa* in Shahabad and जटो *jato* in South Bhagalpur. It is the bullock ridden by Shiva.

1112. A छेरुआ *chherua* or बधिया *badhiya* is a castrated animal, as distinguished from the साँढ़ *sānrh* or entire bull devoted and let go. The sacred marks placed on this last are the तिर-सूल *tirsūl* or trident and the चक्कर *chakkar* or discus.

1113. The following rules for selecting cattle are current throughout Bihār :—

बैल बेसाहै चललह कन्त। बैल बेसहिह दू दू दन्त॥
काछ कसौटी साँचोर बान। ई छाड़ि किनिह मति आन॥
जब देखिह रूपधौर। टाका चारि दीह उपरौड़॥
जब देखिह मैना। तब एहि पार सँ करिह बैना॥
जब देखिह बैरिया गोल। उठ बैठ कै करिह मोल॥
जब देखिह करियवा कन्त। कैला गोला देखह जनु दन्त॥

Bail besāhai chalalah kant, bail besahiha dū dū dant,
Kāchh kasauti sāñor bān, ī chhāri kiniha mati ān.
Jab dekhiha rūpadhaur, tāka chāri dīha uparaur,
Jab dekhiha maina, tab ehi pār san kariha baina.
Jab dekhiha bairiya gol, uth baith kai kariha mol,
Jab dekhiha kariyawa kant, kaila gola dekhah janu dant.

—My dear, you have started to buy a bullock, be sure and buy one with only two teeth. Do not buy any which is not some shade of grey; but if you see a pure white one, you may advance your price four rupees. If you see one with loose horns, give handsel without crossing the road (to look at it more carefully, *i.e.*, it is sure to be a good one). If you see one with a red head and a light red body, don't buy till you have had a good look at it. But, my dear, if you see a black, or a yellow-grey, or a red one, don't take the trouble to look at its teeth.

The following is a warning against two kinds of bullocks:—

सरग पताली भौँआँ टेर ।
अप्पन खाय, परोसिया हेर ॥

Sarag patāli bhauṅāṅ ter,
Appan khāy parosiya her.

—A bullock with horns pointing up and down, or one with crooked eye-brows, injures its master and the neighbours as well.

CHAPTER IV.—COWS AND BREEDING.

1114. A cow is गौ *gau* or गाय *gāy*. One that has had one calf is known as a पहिलोठ or पहिलौँठ गाय *pahiloth* or *pahilaunth gāy*. Sometimes these words are spelt with ट *t* instead of with ठ *th*. A cow or buffalo within six months after calving is धेन *dhen* generally. In North-East Tirhut it is धेउन *dheün* or धेनु *dhenu*, in Patna and the south-east धेनू *dhenu*, and it is also ढेँनू *dhenu* in Patna. After this she is बकेन *baken*, or (in Shahabad and the south-east) बकेना *bakena*. A cow that calves yearly, or that never stops milking, is पुरहिया *puráhiya* north of the Ganges. A cow that breeds when five years old is पचाड़ *pachār*. In Shahabad and Patna she is धन्‌पुरही *dhanpurahi*, in Patna (also), Gaya, and South Munger बर्‌साइन *barsāïn*, and in South Bhagalpur पोरैया *poraiya*. A barren cow is बहिला *bahila* generally, also ठहरा *thahra* in South-West Shahabad.

1115. To be covered by a bull is बरधियाएब *bardhiyāëb* or परियाएब *pariyāëb*, and also south of the Ganges बरदाएब *bardāëb*. Another general term is पाल खाएब *pāl khāëb*. To copulate (of animals) is बाहब *bāhab*, also in North-East Tirhut ओहाएब *ohāëb*. In regard to buffaloes, भैँसाएब *bhainsāëb* may also be used, and of a goat छगराएब *chhagrāëb* to the west.

1116. A cow in calf is बरद्दाएल *bardāel* or गाभिन *gābhin*. In South Bhagalpur she is फरली *pharli*. The act of calving is बियान *biyān* or बियाना *biyāna*. South of the Ganges झोल देब *jhol deb* is to give birth to a number of young, *e.g.* in South-West Shahabad a man was heard saying हमार छेरी दू झोल बच्चा दिहलस हँ *hamār chheri du jhol bachcha dihlas ha*,—my goat has dropped kids on two occasions.

1117. A cow that is a good milker is दुधार *dudhār* or दुधारि *dudhāri*.* One which gives milk for one and a half years is देवढ़ *dewarh*, or in North-East Tirhut बरखु *barkhu*. A cow or buffalo that has gone five months in calf, or that has given milk for five months, is सहरोस *sahros* north of the Ganges, and also पुरहिया *purāhiya* in North-East Tirhut. One that gives little milk is चोंढ़ी *chonrhi* or चोंढ़ *chonrh*, also चोरनी *chorni*, and in Tirhut धोंछ *dhonchh*. In Shahabad it is नठहर *nathāhar*, and in South Bhagalpur चौंड़ *chaunr*. A cow that kicks at the time of milking is करकट *karkat*, or in Tirhut लथराह *lathrāh*.

CHAPTER V.—CALVES.

1118. A calf as long as it is unweaned is लेरु *leru*. A male calf is बाछा *bāchha*, बछवा *bachhwa*, or बछरू *bachhru*, and a female calf बाछी *bāchhi* or बछिया *bachhiya* when they are from 1½ to 3 years old. When a calf has two teeth, it is दोहान *dohān* north of the Ganges and in Shahabad. In the rest of Shahabad it is दुदन्त *dudant*, and elsewhere दोदन्त *dodant* or दोदन्ता *dodanta*. In West Tirhut it is दोख बैल *dokh bail*. When it has not yet got its true teeth it is called उदन्त *udant*, or to the east अदन्त *adant*. ओसर *osar*, or to the west कलोर *kalor*, is a heifer ready for the bull. In North-East Tirhut she is गौर *gaur*, in Patna फेटाइन *phetāin*, and in South Bhagalpur अँकरिया *ankariya*. In South-East Tirhut थैर *thair* is a two-year old heifer. Full-grown cattle are तैयार *taiyār*. In calculating roughly the age of pack-bullocks, the word तौल *taul*, or in Gaya पूर *pūr*, is used. Thus एक तौल *ek taul* or एक साल के तौल *ek sāl ke taul*, one year full-grown; दू तौल *du taul*, two years full-grown; and so on, the counting commencing from

---

* Cf. the proverb जाही तें किछु पाइए सहिऐ करुइ बैन ; लात खात चुचुकार तें सहत दुधारि धेन *jāhi teñ kichhu pāiai, sahiai karui bain; lāt khāt chuchukār teñ sahat dudhāri dhen*,—from whomsoever you expect to receive benefits, you must bear abusive words; even while being kicked by a milch-cow, a man will endure its actions and pat it.

the time when the bullock has eight teeth, viz. when he is four years or more old. A calf with six teeth is called छदाँत *chhadānt*. It is also called छक्कड़ *chhakkar*, छकन्ड़ा *chhakra* (male), or छकन्ड़ी *chhakri* (female). Such calves are not appreciated, as in the proverb मुइल बरन्दा छकन्ड़ी *muil barda chhakri*,—as soon as a bullock is dead (it is abused and called) a *chhakri*. A calf with seven teeth is सतन्दर *satdar* or सधन्धर *satdhar* to the west, and सत्तर *sattar* elsewhere south of the Ganges, except South Bhagalpur, where it is सतत्तर *satattar*. In West Tirhut it is सतन्दन्ता *satdanta*. A calf with eight teeth is पूरा *pūra*, *i.e.* full-grown, or अधैल *adhail*.

1119. Coaxing a cow that has lost its calf to eat grain is called तोरिया *toriya*, or in South-East Tirhut घसन्तुरिया *ghasturiya*. In South Bhagalpur it is called तोरियान *toriyān*. The same words are used for reconciling a cow or a buffalo to its newly-born calf by smearing the latter with sugar. A kind of hair string used for tickling a cow with a similar object is सेल्ह *selh* or सेल्ही *selhi*; and to do this is दाँवल *dānwal* in the north-west and सेल्हल *selhal* in South-West Tirhut. Sometimes the skin of the calf stuffed with hay is put before a cow which has lost its calf, especially at milking time. Salt is sprinkled on it and the cow licks it and lets her milk flow. The stuffed calf is called लगावन *lagāwan* north of the Ganges. In South-West Shahabad it is called खलितड़ी *khalitari*, in the rest of the district मौर *maur*, in Patna करन्ची *karchi*, and in Gaya करन्ती मूरी *karti mūri*. The kind of food given to cows when they calve is पखेव *pakheo* to the west and in Patna; also पखेवा *pakhewa* in South Munger. In North-West Tirhut it is चोहाट *chohāt* or चुहाड़ *chuhār*, and in North-East Tirhut चोहैर *chohair*. In South-East Tirhut it is महेला *mahela*, and generally मसाला *masāla*. In Gaya it is पुसन्टै *pustai*.

CHAPTER VI.—BUFFALOES.

1120. A male buffalo is भैंसा *bhainsa*, also महिसा *mahisa* in East Tirhut. A female buffalo is भैंस *bhains* or भैंसी *bhainsi*; also भइँ *bhaiñ* north of the Ganges, and महिस *mahis* or महिसी *mahisi* in East Tirhut. A buffalo calf is पड़न्रू *parru* or कड़न्रू *karru*. A male buffalo calf is पाड़ा *pāra* or काड़ा *kāra*, and a female one पाड़ी *pāri* or काड़ी *kāri*. A well-known proverb is खेत महिसी चर, पड़न्रुहिँ मार *khet mahisi char, parruhiñ mār*,—buffaloes are grazing in the fields, beat the calves, *i.e.*, in a fight the smaller men get caught, and the richer and more powerful real culprits get off. In Patna and the south-west लोचर *lochar* is a two-year old buffalo. In Gaya it is टेहान *tehān*. A buffalo with two teeth, *i.e.* three years old, is पस *pas*.

CHAPTER VII.—GOATS.

1121. A goat is छेर *chher* or बक्कर *bakkar*. A he-goat kept for breeding is generally बोका *boka*. General names for all male goats are बकरा *bakra*, खस्सी *khassi*, or खँस्सी *khañssi*. Other terms are छागर *chhāgar* or बोकड़ा *bokra* (North-East Tirhut), बोतू *botu* (Patna) or बोतो *boto* (South-East Bihār), बीयड़ *bīyar* (South-West Shahabad), and बिअहन *biahan* (rest of that district). A she-goat is बकरी *bakri* or छेरी *chheri*, also छगरी *chhagri* to the east. A castrated goat is specially खस्सी *khassi* or खँस्सी *khañssi* in Tirhut and south of the Ganges. North of the Ganges the general name is छेरुआ *chherua*.

1122. A kid is पठरू *pathru*. A male kid is पाठा *pātha* or मेमना *memna*, and a female पाठी *pāthi*, पठिया *pathiya*, or मेमनी *memni*. In South Munger it is sometimes called बकरू *bakru*. A goat kept for sacrifice is called south of the Ganges पठरू *pathru*, but when kept for other sacrifices it is called खस्सी *khassi*.

CHAPTER VIII.—SHEEP.

1123. A sheep is भेँड़ *bheñr*. A ram is भेँड़ा *bheñra* or (in South Bhagalpur) भेँड़ो *bheñro*, and a ewe भेँड़ी *bheñri*. A lamb is भेँड़िक बच्चा *bheñrik bachcha*, also पठरू *pathru* and बकरू *bakru* in Tirhut. मेमना *memna* is also used in South-East Tirhut.

1124. A flock of sheep or goats is झुण्ड *jhund* or झूँड़ *jhūnr*; also जेड़ *jer* in East Tirhut, हेड़ *her* in West Tirhut, and जेल *jel* in South Tirhut. A flock of about twenty is लँहड़ *leñhar*, and of about one hundred बाग *bāg*. गहेँड़ *gahenr* is a still larger flock of four or five बाग *bāg*. In South Bhagalpur खरुहो *kharuho*, and in South Munger सहेर *saher*, mean a flock of sheep.

CHAPTER IX.—PIGS.

1125. The general term is सूगर *sūgar* or सूअर *sūar*, also ढोका *dhoka* in North-East Tirhut. Musalmān villagers call them euphemistically

बद कौम *bad kaum*, or in North Tirhut and Patna बद खोम *bad khom* (*i.e.*, 'low caste'). Other similar names are हराम *harām* in Gaya, and बद मोहरी *bad mohri*. A young pig is पाहुर *pāhur* to the east, also (male) डहरा *dahra* north of the Ganges and in Gaya, टहरा *tahra* in Shahabad, छौना *chhauna* in Patna and the west, and छावा *chhāwa* in Gaya. Female names are डहरी *dahri* (also in Gaya) or छाई *chhāi* north of the Ganges, and कुम्भी *kumbhi* in Gaya. A full-grown boar is पट्ठा *pattha* or पठरा *pathra* in North-East Tirhut, and a full-grown sow is सोमनी *somni* in the same place. A pigsty is खोभार *khobhār*, or to the west खोभारि *khobhāri*. In South-West Shahabad it is also खोबार *khobār*, in South-East Bihār it is खभार *khabhār*, and in Patna and Gaya it is बखोर *bakhor*.

CHAPTER X.—HORSES, MULES, AND ASSES.

1126. A horse is घोड़ा or घोरा *ghora*, and a mare घोड़ी or घोरी *ghori*. A common term for both is घोड़ or घोर *ghor*. South of the Ganges and in Sāran another word for a horse or mare is चरवा *charwa*. A pony is टट्टू *tattu*, and a pony mare टटुआनी *tatuāni*, and also in Patna and Gaya मद्दियान *madiyān*. A foal is बछेड़ा *bachhera*, and a filly बछेड़ी *bachheri*.

1127. To own a horse is a great piece of display according to Bihār ideas, as in the proverb डेढ़ गोट घोड़ी, नौ गोट फौज *derh got ghori, nau got phauj* (spoken of one who makes display when he cannot afford it),—the owner of one and a half (*i.e.* two wretched) mares goes about (like a lord) with nine servants.

1128. An ass is गदहा *gadha*, a she-ass is गदही *gadhi*, and an ass's foal गदहा के बच्चा *gadha ke bachcha*, or (in East Bihār and Shahabad) छौनी *chhauni*. An ass-driver is गदहेंड़ी *gadheñri*. A mule is खच्चड़ *khachchar*.

CHAPTER XI.—ELEPHANTS.

1129. An elephant is हाथी *hāthi*, a male elephant is हत्था *hattha*, and a she-elephant हथिनी *hathini*, हथनी *hathni*, or (in East Tirhut) मेदनी *medni*, and in South-West Tirhut जोड़ी *jorhi*. A male elephant with small tusks is मकुना *makuna*. One with large tusks is पट्ठा *pattha*.

1130. Elephants are tied up with a front foot-chain, which is बेड़ी *beri* or पैकर *paikar*, and also in South-East Tirhut छनुआ *chhanua*. Its hind legs are chained with chains called डग्गी *daggi* or नङ्गर *nangar*, and also with a wooden hobble, called कठबन्धन *kathbandhan*.

CHAPTER XII.—CAMELS.

1131. A camel is ऊँट *ūnt*, also among Musalmāns शुतुर *shutur*. Its young is called बोता *bota* in North-East Tirhut. Its nose-ring is नकेल *nakel*. कठरा *kathra* or काठी *kāthi* is its wooden saddle, also called पलान *palān* in North-East Tirhut; and गदेला *gadela* or गद्दी *gaddi* is the pad.

CHAPTER XIII.—STRAYING OF CATTLE.

1132. To stray is generally हेरा जाएब *hera jāëb;* also in Saran भूला जाइल *bhūla jāïl*. Other terms are अनेर *aner* (or अनेरवा *anerwa*) जाएब *jāëb* in North-East Tirhut, बहकल *bahkal* or भोंरियाएल *bhonriyāël* in Shahabad, and बहट जाएब *bahat jāëb* in Patna and Gaya. बथान *bathān*, and also in North-East Tirhut गोआस *goās*, is a cattle enclosure. Other words are घेरा *ghera*, ढाठ *dhāth*, and ढाठा *dhātha*. लम्भब *lambhab*, लाँभब *lāmbhab*, or लाम्हब *lāmhab*, is to drive cattle into another's field to graze on the crops.

CHAPTER XIV.—COLOURS OF CATTLE.

1133. These are—

White.—This is चरक *charak* or चरका *charka*, with a variant चरको *charko* in South Bhagalpur. In Gaya it is रुपाधौ *rupādhau*, and elsewhere also रूपधर *rūpdhar* or रूपधौर *rūpdhaur*. Another word is चँवरा *chamwra* in North-West Tirhut.

1134. *Grey of various shades.*—धवर *dhawar*, धौर *dhaur*, or in Shahabad धावर *dhāwar*, is a light grey. सोकन *sokan* is a dark grey, कैल *kail* or कैला *kaila* is a yellowish grey or cream-colour, and सिलेबा *sileba* or सिलेबे *silebe*, reddish grey. साँवर *sāmwar* or सौंरा *saunra* is a black grey. कसौटी *kasauti* and काछ *kāchh* are shades of grey.

1135. *Red.*—A reddish cow is गोल *gol*, गोला *gola*, or गोलवा *golwa*. A dark red one is लाल *lāl*. A cow with a red head and the rest of the body of a lighter colour is बैरिया गोल *bairiya gol*. धुरगोलो *dhurgolo* is another shade of red in South Bhagalpur. महुगोल *mahugol* means red like the *mahua* flower (*bassia latifolia*). In Shahabad this is महुअर *mahuar*, and in South Munger महुलखा *mahulakha*.

1136. *Yellow.*—This is पीअर *piar* or पिअरा *piara*. गहुमन *gahuman* or गोहुमन *gohuman* is wheat-coloured.

1137. *Black.*—This is कारी *kāri*, करिया *kariya*, करियवा *kariyawa*, or (South Bhagalpur) करुआ *karua*.

1138. *A spotted cow* is काँस *kāns*, *a brindle one* बगछल्ला *bagchhalla* (tiger-skinned), लाल बगछल्ला *lāl bagchhalla* being a red brindle and सुफेद बगछल्ला *suphed bagchhalla* a white brindle. करकन्धा *karkandha* is *one black on the shoulders.* In Shahabad this is called करिकन्धा *karikandha*. गुलदार *guldār* is a spotted cow, and पाँच कलियान *pānch kaliyān* a piebald one, or more properly one with white stockings and a white blaze on the forehead.

CHAPTER XV.—HIDES.

1139. These are चमड़ा *chamra*, खाल *khāl*, or चरसा *charsa*. गौखा *gaukha* is raw cow's leather. It is also called गोइँटा *goita* north of the Ganges. भैंसौटा *bhainsauta* or (in South Bhagalpur) भैंसौठा *bhainsautha* is that of buffaloes. चाम *chām* is tanned cow hide. Sheep skins are खलड़ी *khalri*. A bullock's hide cut in two halves is आधा फारी *ādha phāri* or (North-East Tirhut) फाँकी *phānki*. The hides of cattle which have died a natural death are मुरदारी *murdāri* or मुरदार *murdār*, and those of killed cattle हलाली *halāli*. साबर *sābar* is tanned deer skin. A depôt for hides is चरसा के गोदाम *charsa ke godām*. In South Munger चरसा *charsa* is a cess paid by tanners to the landlord.

CHAPTER XVI.—CATTLE SLAUGHTER.

1140. A slaughter-house is लोकाना *lokāna* in Champāran, मनहर *manhar* in South-East Tirhut and Shahabad, and किलखाना *kilkhāna* in South-West Tirhut.

1141. Another name in Shahabad is गुरन्दवान *gurdawān*, and in Patna खूँट *khūnt*. Flaying and cleaning is कमौना *kamīna* or कमाना *kamāna*. A butcher is कसाइ *kasāï*, but a goat-butcher is बकरन्कसाब *bakar kasāb*, and a चिक *chik** or चीक *chīk* kills both goats and sheep. The large knife used by them is बोगन्दा *bogda*, and also north of the Ganges दबिया *dabiya*. The block is ठेहा *theha*, कुन्दा *kunda*, or कुन्दी *kundi*. In South-West Shahabad it is खोड़ *khor*, and in South Bhagalpur it is परन्कट्ठो *parkattho*. The string used for hanging up the animal to be flayed is लोकाना *lokāna*.

1142. A cultivator has many terms of abuse for his cattle. A favourite one is जाह कसैया खूँटा *jāh kasaiya khūnta*,—may you go to the butcher, or to the sacrificial stake.

CHAPTER XVII.—FEEDING CATTLE.

1143. To chew the cud is पगुरी (or पागुर) करब *paguri* (or *pāgur*) *karab* north of the Ganges and in Shahabad. South of the Ganges generally it is पघुराएब *paghurāëb* or पघुरी करब *paghuri karab*. Local names are पाज करब *pāj karab* in Tirhut, कोरी करब *kori karab* or कौरी करब *kauri karab* in Patna and Gaya, and गलठै करब *galthai karab* in South Bhagalpur.

1144. Cattle fodder, consisting of the stems of the जनेरा *janera* (*Holcus sorghum*) and similar green stuff, is cut with a chopper (see §§ 86 and ff.), and is known as कुट्टी *kutti* or कुटिया *kutiya*. In South Bhagalpur it is कुटन्री *kutri*, and in Patna कट्टा *katta*. The fodder for stall-fed cattle is गवत *gawat* north of the Ganges. Other names are लेहन्ना *lehna*—current in Shahabad, गौत *gaut* in Gaya, and गौतन्हा *gautha* in Patna. A general word for fodder is चारा *chāra*, or in North-East Tirhut चरी *chari*. गजन्रौटी *gajrauti* or (in Gaya) गजन्रौटा

* It is unlucky to touch money received from these men on an inauspicious day. Hence the proverb :—

बिप्र टहलुआ, चीक धन, ओ बेटिन्ह के बाढ़।
एहू से धन न घटे, तो करी बड़न से राड़॥

Bipra tahalua, chīk dhan, o betin ke bārh.
Ehu se dhan na gate, to kari baran se rār.

—If you cannot get rid of your wealth by having a Brāhman servant, keeping possession of money received from a butcher, or from excess of daughters, you will do it by fighting with bigger men.

gajrauta are stalks and leaves of the carrot (गाजर *gājar*) given to cattle. The chopped up sugar-cane tops (गेंड़ *genr*) given to cattle as fodder are called अगेंड़ *ageñr*, *&c.*, as described in § 1012. चाँछी *chānchhi* in North-East Tirhut is a cattle-food made of spring-crops cut before they are ripe and then dried. सानी *sāni* is the chaff and water on which bullocks are fed.

1145. To feed cattle is सानी पानी करब (or देब) *sāni pāni karab* (or *deb*). Another phrase current in Patna and Gaya is गौत देब *gaut deb.* A load of fodder is बोझा *bojha*, and also मोट *mot* in Patna, Gaya, and Shahabad. Chaff is भूसा *bhūsa,* with variants भूँसा *bhūnsa* (in Patna and Gaya) and भस्सा *bhussa*. The net full of chaff is जल्ला *jalla* or जाला *jāla* generally. In Shahabad and South Munger it is जलखर *jalkhar*, in South-West Shahabad जोरा *jora*, and in Patna कपाइ *kapāï*. The refuse grass, &c., which cattle leave behind is लथेर *lather* to the west, निघास *nighās* to the north-east, and गोथार in Patna, Gaya, and the south-east. Local names are खधेल *khadhel* in Shahabad and गोरथारो *gorthāro* in South Bhagalpur.

1146. A beast that eats little is निखोराह *nikhorāh* or निखुराह *nikhurāh*, also चिकनिया *chikaniya* or अलपजिया *alpajiya* in South-East Tirhut and गवतचोर *gawatchor* in South-West Tirhut. In Patna and Gaya it is optionally नकसोंध *naksondh*, in South Munger चिकनकौर *chikankaur*, and in South Bhagalpur चिकनजिब्भो *chikanjibbho*.

CHAPTER XVIII.—PASTURAGE.

1147. Lands set apart for pasture are generally simply परती *parti*. Special names are, however, रखात *rakhāt* north of the Ganges and रखाँत *rakhānt* (South Munger). Other names are चिरागाह *chirāgāh* in Saran, Patna, and South Munger, चराँट *charānt* or बाध *bādh* in Gaya, and अड़ार *arār* Shahabad. A cattle-yard is बथान *bathān* or बथानी *bathāni.* The field in which cows are fed is in South-West Shahabad चराइ *charāï*, in the rest of that district उबेर *uber*, and in South Munger उबेरा *ubera.* In Gaya it is बाध *bādh*, in Patna बहरसी *baharsi*, and in South Bhagalpur बहियार *bahiyār* or आर *ār*. Cattle left to graze without watch are अनेरिया *aneriya* to the west, अनेरा *anera* in West Tirhut, छुटहा *chhutha* in Gaya, उदङ्गर *udangar* in Patna, उज्झा *ujjha* in South Munger, and उजरा *ujra* in South Bhagalpur.

CHAPTER XIX.—FENCES.

1148. A fence to keep cattle out of fields is घेरान *gherān* or घेरानी *gherāni* to the north-west. In Tirhut it is बारी *bāri* or बेढ़ *berh*. South of the Ganges it is घोरान *ghorān*. Local names are घेरा *ghera* in Tirhut and छापा *chhāpa* in South Munger. In Champāran हिरांत *hirānt* is a hedge of brambles not fixed in the ground.

CHAPTER XX.—GRAZING-FEES.

1149. These are of two kinds:—

(1) Those paid to the owner of the land.

(2) Those paid to the herdsman.

1150. A cowherd is called ग्वार *gwār*, गोआर *goār*, अहीर *ahīr*, चरवाह *charwāh* or चरवाहा *charwāha*, and गोरखिया *gorkhiya* A tender of cows is in North-East Tirhut गैवाह *gaiwāh*. A shepherd is गड़ेंरी *gareñri* or भेंड़िहर *bheñrihar*. South of the Ganges the latter also takes the form भेंड़िहार *bheñrihār* or भेंड़िहारा *bheñrihāra*. A local name is भेंड़धुरै *bheñrdhurai* in South Bhagalpur.

1151. (1) The fees paid to the owner of the land are known as खरचरी *kharchari* or खरचराई *kharcharāī* north of the Ganges and in Gaya. The latter also is used in Gaya. In Shahabad the term is बरदिया *bardiya*. In Tirhut, Patna, and the east are noted कास चराई *kās charāī*, देना *dena*, भैंसोंधा *bhainsondha*, and बरदाना *bardāna*. In the south-east the word is दैना *daina*. In many places these fees are only paid for buffaloes, and not for other cattle.

1152. (2) Those paid to the herdsman are चरवाही *charwāhi* or चराई *charāī*. See also § 1205.

CHAPTER XXI.—COWHOUSES AND ENCLOSURES FOR CATTLE, CATTLE-OWNERS, &c.

1153. A cowhouse is गौसार *gausār* or गौसाला *gausāla*. To the east it is गोहाल *gohāl*. Local names are गैघरा *gaighara* in North-East Tirhut, दरखोल *darkhol* in South-West Shahabad, and दोगाह *dogāh* in Patna and Gaya. सार *sār* is also used to the west. बरघरा *barghara*, or in Gaya बहरघरा *bahargharā*, is a cattle-shed. In

Champaran a breeding-shed for cattle is called घारी *ghāri*. A place where cattle are collected is बथान *bathān*. In some places a special word is used for spots where buffaloes are collected, viz. हिरात *hirāt* in the north-west, लेँढ़ *lenrh* in North-West Tirhut, बैठार *baithār* in East Tirhut. To collect cattle is बथनियाएल *bathniyāēl*. In North-West Tirhut it is लेँढ़ियाएल *leñrhiyāēl*. A cattle enclosure is पाझा *pājha* in the north-west and पलानी *palāni* in Tirhut. In Shahabad it is अड़ार *arār*. A local name in North-East Tirhut is ढट्ठा *dhattha*, which becomes ढाठ *dhāth* in West Tirhut. A general word is बथान *bathān*. In Patna अड़ान *arān*, and in Gaya अड़ा *ara*, is an enclosure for cattle in the forest.

1154. To the west an owner of cattle is called मौआर *mauār*. The song sung by cowherds while herding is called बिरहा *birha*, or (in South Munger) महराइ *mahrāï*. Another similar song, but sung to a different air, is चाँचर *chānchar*. लोरकाइ *lorkāï* is a special cowherd's song concerning a hero called लोरिका *lorika*. In South Bhagalpur the cowherd's dance is called लोड़ियारो *loriyāro*. The man who dances is called नटुआ *natua* or नेटुआ *netua*.

1155. In Gaya चेल्हवा *chelhwa*, in West Tirhut चल्हा *chalha*, and in Sāran चाल्हा *chālha*, is a knife used by milkmen. The brand for branding cattle is साटी *sāti*.

CHAPTER XXII.—CATTLE-DEALERS.

1156. These are फेरहा *pherha* north of the Ganges, and in South Bhagalpur फेरबैक *pherbaik*. In South-West Shahabad they are हरिहा *hariha*, in Patna लेँहड़ियाला *lenhriwāla*, in South Munger गेँहड़िवाला *genhriwāla*, and elsewhere हारवाला *hārwāla*.

CHAPTER XXIII.—MILK AND ITS PREPARATIONS.

1157. *Milk* is दूध *dūdh*. Cow's milk is गव्य *gabya* or गोरस *goras*. To milk an animal is दूहब *dūhab* or लगाएब *lagāēb*. A cow that gives milk is लगहर *laghar* or लगवान *lagwān*, as opposed to नाठा *nātha* or अनाठा *anātha*, which is one that does not; one that milks plentifully is दुधारि *dudhāri*.*

* Cf. § 1117. Another proverb is दुधारि गाय के दू लातो भला *dudhāri gāy ke du lāto bhala*,—even two kicks from a good milker are to be valued.

1158. When the milk of a cow or buffalo runs dry, the word used is बिसुखब *bisukhab.* Local words are ठाँड़ होएब *thāīnth hoëb* (South-East Tirhut), बिसक्खाब *biskhāb* in Patna and South-East Tirhut, चुहटाब *chuhtāb* in Shahabad, and ठमरा *thamra* in the south-west of that district. The milk of a cow for six months after calving is धेन (or south of the Ganges ढेन) के दूध *dhen ke dūdh.* After that it is बकेन के दूध *baken ke dūdh.*

1159. The unsophisticated Bihār villager is not ignorant of the advantage which accrues to the seller by watering the milk he sells. According to popular belief the cow acts as the milkman's confederate in this, as in the proverb गाय गोआरें मिलाप, ठेहुनें पानि दुहाब, *gāy goāreñ milāp, thehuneñ pāni duhāb*—the cow and the milkman are confederates, for (without the pail leaving his) knee, she lets him milk water into it. At the same time it is but fair to add that some translate the proverb as meaning that when a cow and the milkman are friends she will let him milk her even standing in water up to her knees. Both translations are possible.

1160. *Clarified butter* is घ्यू *ghyu.* Sometimes the Hindī word घी *ghī* is used. The word is sometimes spelt घीव *ghīw.* Local names are नेउन *neun* in West Tirhut, चिक्कना *chikna* in Gaya, नैनू *nainu* or लैन *lain* in Shahabad, and नेनू *nenu* in the east. Fresh clarified butter is अहीर के घ्यू *ahīr ke ghyu,* or in South Bhagalpur गिरस्तू घ्यू *girastu ghyu;* and that stored for a time in leather vessels कुप्पी के घ्यू *kuppi ke ghyu* or गेल्हा के घ्यू *gelha ke ghyu.* South of the Ganges it is also called दखिनाहा घ्यू *dakhināha ghyu.*

1161. The sediment which settles in making clarified butter is मठियार *mathiyar,* माठ *māth,* or माठा *mātha* north of the Ganges. South of it it is लैनू *lainu* in South-West Shahabad, मठगर *mathgar* in the rest of that district, मठाहा *mathāha* in Gaya, and मठाही *mathāhi* in Patna. The refuse left in boiling it down is डाढ़ी *dārhi;* also महिया *mahiya* in North-West Tirhut, and घोर *ghor* in Tirhut generally. Other names are फाड़न *phāran* and महरन *mahran* in Shahabad, and कोरौनी *korauni,* used in the same place and in South Munger; खँखोड़ी *khankhori* in the rest of Shahabad, and खुरचनी *khurchani* in Patna.

1162. *Tyre or curdled milk* is दही or दहि *dahi.* It should be noted that this word is feminine, though grammarians say it is masculine.* Another name current in West Tirhut is सजुई *sajui*. The old curds put in to curdle milk are जोरन *joran*. Tyre is a luxury, hence the proverb घर दही, बहरो दही *ghar dahi, bahro dahi*,—only he who eats tyre at home gets it abroad.

1163. *Curdled milk* is जमाव दही *jamāo dahi* or सजाव दही *sajāo dahi*. Other names are साँची *sānchi* to the east, सजवा *sajwa* in North-East Tirhut, मिठुर *mithur* in South-East Tirhut, and जमुई *jamuï* in Gaya. The cream of this is called छाल्ही *chhālhi*, a local variant being छाली *chāli* in Patna. In South-West Shahabad it is साढ़ी *sārhi*. When this is taken off, the remainder is called कटुई दही *katuï dahi* or छलकटुई *chhalkatui*. In Shahabad it is also called छिनुई *chhinui*, and another name north of the Ganges is छिनुही *chhinuhi*. Another variety of curds, from which the whey has been expressed or boiled, is called छेना *chhena*. It is something like the dry curds from which cheese is made in England.

1164. The thick milk given by a cow just after calving, or *beesting milk*, is फेनुस *phenus* or फेनुसा *phenusa* to the west. In Tirhut and the south-east it is खिरसा *khirsa*, and in Gaya ढाकर *dhākar* means the milk of the first milking after calving, फेनुस *phenus* being that of the second. A cow that drops her milk is कामधेनुआ *kāmdhenua* or धेनुआगर *dhenuāgar* north of the Ganges, also खासर *khāsar* in East Tirhut. To allow the calf to suck the teats of a cow for an instant before milking, so as to induce the latter to let the milk flow, is फेनहाएल *phenhāël* or पेन्हाएल *penhāël*.

1165. *Cream* is मलाइ *malāï* or बलाइ *balāï*, and skim-milk पसावन *pasāwan* or (in East Tirhut) छनुआ दूध *chhanua dūdh*.

1166. *Butter* before clarification is नेउन *neün* north of the Ganges, and also नेन *nen* in North-East Tirhut. South of the Ganges it is लैनू *lainu* to the west, चिकना *chikna* and मक्खन *makkhan* in Patna and Gaya, and नेनू *nenu* there and in the south-east. Butter-milk is मट्ठा *mattha*, माठा *mātha*, or घोर *ghor*. In Gaya and the south-west it is also छाँछ *chhānchh*. A well-known proverb about butter-milk is दूधक जरेँ मट्ठा फूकि पीबे *dūdhak jareñ mattha phūki pībe*,—through having been scalded by (hot) milk, he blows on the butter-milk before he drinks it, *i.e.*, a burnt child dreads the fire.

1167. खोआ *khoä* is milk boiled down till it is thick.

---

* *E.g.*, in Manbodh's Haribans, VII, 48, एकओ दहि नहिँ लेल अधलाहि, *ekao dahi nahiñ lel adhalāhi*,—they did not take a single bad curd.

CHAPTER XXIV.—CATTLE DISEASES.

1168. Medicines are administered through a bamboo tube called ढरऽका *dharka* or काँड़ी *kānri.*

1169. The identification of the following diseases is in many cases very doubtful. The list is given rather in the hope that it may form the basis of a future identification by competent experts. Probably many of the names given as representing different diseases are merely different local names of one and the same disease.

1170. *Farcy.*—This is अगिया *agiya* or अगिनऽबाय *aginbāy.*

1171. *Diseases of the stomach.*—जोंकी *jonki* is inflammation caused by small leeches in the stomach and liver. In West Tirhut it is जोकऽटी *jokti.* पेटऽछली *petchali*, or (in Tirhut) पेटौक *petauk*, is diarrhœa; पोकब *pokab*, or in North Tirhut छींड़ी *chhīnri*, is purging. पिलऽही *pilhi* is said to be a swelling of the liver. Perhaps it is disease of the spleen.

1172. *Foot and mouth disease.*—This is खोरऽहा *khorha* in the north-west and in West Tirhut, अहऽवाह *ahwāh* also in Champaran and North-West Tirhut, खँगाहा *khangāha* in East Tirhut, खोंगऽहा *khongha* in West Tirhut, भजऽहा *bhajha* in South-East Tirhut, आभा *ābha* in Tirhut generally, and (optionally) खुरऽहा *khurha* in Patna and Gaya.

1173. *Diseases of the throat and mouth.*—आँती बढ़ब *ānti barhab*, or आँती चढ़ जाएब *ānti charh jāēb*, is swelling of the uvula. कण्ठार *kanthār* (Gaya and the north-west), भिरुखी *bhirukhi* (Tirhut), कण्ठा रोग *kantha rog* (Gaya and Tirhut), ढरऽका *dharka* (Patna), is a disease of the throat and chest, which swell and prevent the animal swallowing. ढाँसी *dhānsi* (north of the Ganges) is cough. बेंगा *benga* is inflammation of the vessels of the tongue followed by dysentery. थुकऽहा *thukha* (Patna and the south-east) is described as a disease in which saliva flows from the mouth. सुखऽभामी *sukhbhāmi* (north-west and Gaya), छेंड़ी *chheñri* (Tirhut), दँतऽनर *dantnar* (South-East Tirhut), हनुआ *hanua* (South-East Tirhut and Patna), सुकरऽवाँत *sukarwānt* (Patna, Gaya, and Shahabad), दन्त लहर *dant lahar* (South Bhagalpur), are described as diseases of the tongue. जिभी *jibbhi* (West Bihār) or जिभऽसट्टा *jibhsatta* is lampus. भुण्डी *bhundi* (Patna) is described as a throat disease. कण्ठा सारू *kantha sāru* (South-East Bihār), or in Gaya नाढ़ी कनऽवा *nādi kanwa*, is a disease in which sores form in the throat; so also in the same tract is सोना

होला *sona hola.* चोर मट-का *chor matka* (South-East Bihār) is a disease of the mouth which prevents the animal eating. मुँह-पसिजा *muñhpasija* is diarrhœa with watering at the mouth. In Gaya घर-घर-वा *ghargharwa* is a disease accompanied by rattling in the throat. घोँघ-फुल-वा *ghonghphulwa* in Gaya, and घेघुआ *gheghua* in Gaya and Shahabad, is a kind of goitre.

1174. *Diseases of the feet.*—Foot-rot is झनक-वाह *jhanakwāh* (North-West Bihār and Shahabad) and झनक *jhanak* in Tirhut. In Patna it is झनक-बाता *jhanakbāta*, and in South-West Shahabad झन-का *jhanka.* बाता *bāta* is a swelling of the knee-joint. When a bullock becomes lame through overloading, the phrase used is भर जाएब *bhar jāëb*, सरक जाएब *sarak jāëb*, or उखर जाएब *ukhar jāëb*, or in South-East Tirhut खञ्जा *khanja.* चरैया *charaiya* in the south-east is too large hoofs. खाँग *khāng* is an insect bred in the feet, which is supposed to devour the whole body. An animal affected with it is खाँगल *khāngal.*

1175. *Rinderpest.*—This is चेचक *chechak* everywhere. Other names are गोटी के निक-सारी *goti ke niksāri* and मह-माया *mahmāya,* both generally, and बर-का बेमारी *barka bemāri* in Champāran, गोसाउन *gosāün* in North-East Tirhut, अन्तर कट-वा *antar katwa* and जगद-म्मा *jagdamma* in Gaya.

1176. *Windy colic.*—This is फुल-बात *phulbāt*, पेट-फुल्ली *pet phulli* in Tirhut and Shahabad. In Patna it is बिन्धा *bindha.* A similar disease, accompanied by difficulty of breathing, is फुल-बघा *phulbagha* in Gaya and Shahabad.

1177. *Staggers.*—These are मिर-गी *mirgi* generally; other names are घुर-नी *ghurni* (Patna and the south-east), घुम-री *ghumri* in South-West Shahabad, and हतेयर-वा *hateyarwa* in the rest of that district. Perhaps टुन-की *tunki* in the South-East, which is described as a sudden death of cattle, is a variety of staggers.

1178. *Worm (or filaria) in the eye.*—This is चाँद-नी *chāndni* in Gaya, and माड़ा *māra* or माड़ा फुल्ली *māra phulli* in Shahabad.

1179. *Tumours.*—These are जहर-बाद *jaharbād*, with a variant जहर-बात *jaharbāt* in Gaya and South-West Shahabad. Another name in Shahabad is पिर-की *pirki.*

1180. *Fevers.*—अढ़ैया *arhaiya* or अढ़ेया *arheya* is a fever lasting two and a half days. In Tirhut it is called जर-खोर *jarkhor.*

1181. *Pneumonia* (?).—A disease attended with panting is called हाँफ *hāmph* in the north-west and in West Tirhut. In South-East Tirhut it is हफ॰नी *haphni*, and in North-East Tirhut बात *bāt*.

1182. कोँड़॰पक्का *konrpakka* (South Bhagalpur) is a disease in which the liver gets abscesses. खर्रा *kharra* is a kind of mange. It generally attacks young cattle.

CHAPTER XXV.—CATTLE-FODDER.

1183. The following grasses and other plants are used for cattle-fodder. Their botanical names have not been in the majority of cases identified:—

अँका॰टा *ankta*,—see अँका॰री *ankri*.

अँका॰री or अँका॰ड़ी *ankri* (west), भेख॰री *bhekhri* (north-west and Gaya), भिलोर *bhilor* (north-west), अँका॰टा *ankta* (Patna, Gaya, and south-east); also अट॰का *atka* (South Bhagalpur), *vicia sativa*.

अट॰का *atka*,—see अँका॰री *ankri*.

अँठुली *anthuli* (Gaya), आँठिल *ānthil* (South-West Shahabad and Gaya).

अन॰जान *anjān*, (Patna, Gaya, and Shahabad).

अम॰ता *amta* (West Tirhut).

अम॰रोरा *amrora* (East Tirhut, Gaya, and Champāran.)

अरैया *araiya* (generally).

आँठिल *ānthil*,—see अँठुली *anthuli*.

उन॰टा चिर॰चिरी *unta chirchiri* (East Tirhut and Gaya).

ओरी टीनी *ori tini* (Patna and Gaya).

औँकर *aunkar* (Shahabad and Gaya).

कज॰ला *kajla* (Champāran and North-East Tirhut) or कज॰री *kajri* (Shahabad).

कत॰रा *katra* (Sāran and Tirhut).

कन॰वा *kanwa*, कन्ना *kanna*,—see केना *kena*.

कर॰मी *karmi*,—see करेम *karem*.

करार *karār* (Shahabad and South Munger).

करेम *karem* (South-West Shahabad), करम्मी *karmi* or करम्मी लत *karmi lat* elsewhere, a creeping-plant with a small white flower which grows in marshes (*Convolvulus repens*).

काना *kāna*,—see केना *kena*.

कुकरौंधा *kukraundha* (north).

कुकुसा *kukusa* (South-West Shahabad).

केना *kena* (west and Gaya) or काना *kāna* (Tirhut, Patna, and South Munger); also कनन्वा *kanwa* (Gaya) and कन्ना *kanna* (South Bhagalpur and Gaya), which grows in Indian corn.

कोढ़िला *korhila* (Champāran and North Tirhut).

कौआरा *kauāra* (East Tirhut).

खगन्ड़ा *khagrā* (Shahabad).

खुखन्सा *khukhsa* (general).

खोभी *khobhi*, (South-East Tirhut, Gaya, and Champāran).

गड़न्नी *garni* (north-west).

गँड़न्हर *ganrhar* (Shahabad, Gaya, and South Munger), गड़ियार *gariyār* (west), गँड़ेर *ganrer* (Gaya), गाँड़र *gānrar* (Patna), गड़ार *garār* (south-east), गड़न्हरुआ *garharua* or गँड़ेरी *ganreri* (north).

गड़न्हरुआ *garharua*, गड़ार *garār*, गड़ियार *gariyar*, गँड़ेर *ganrer*, गँड़ेरी *ganreri*,—see गँड़न्हर *ganrhar*.

गदन्पँड़ोआ *gadpanroa*, गदन्पिड़ोड़ा *gadpirora*, गदन्पुरन्ना *gadpurna*, —see गधन्पुरन्ना *gadhpurna*.

गधन्पुरन्ना *gadhpurna* (West Tirhut and Champāran), गदन्पुरन्ना *gadpurna* (Shahabad), गदन्पँड़ोआ *gadpanroa* (Patna and Gaya), गदन्पिड़ोड़ा *gapinrora* (South Munger), पुरन्नन्वो *purnwo* (South Bhagalpur) (*Boerhaavia procumbens*).

गाँड़र *gānrar*,—see गँड़न्हर *ganrhar*.

गुँजेरा *gunjera* (South-West Shahabad).

गोधन्ना *godhna* (East Tirhut).

चकोड़ा *chakora*,—see तिनन्पतिया *tinpatiya*.

चरी *chari*,—see चोराँट *chorānt*.

चारा *chāra*, branches of trees, especially of the *pīpar* (*ficus religiosa*) or of the *bar* (*ficus Indica*) given as fodder to elephants.

चिकन्नी *chikni* (South-West Shahabad and Gaya).

चिचन्होर *chichhor*,—see चिचोरी *chichori*.

चिचोरी *chichori* (Tirhut), also चिचोर *chichor* (north and Gaya), चिचन्होर *chichhor* (east) or चिचोरो *chichoro* (South Bhagalpur and Tirhut) and लेँड़ई *lenraī* (north-west).

चिनन्वा *chinwa* (East Tirhut).

चेँच *chench* (west), गड़ौँछी *garaunchhi* (Champāran and Patna), सरौँची *saraunchi* (Gaya and South Bhagalpur), सरन्हची *sarhanchi* (Gaya and South Munger) (various species of *Achyranthus*).

चोराँट *chorānt* (Gaya and South-West Shahabad), चरी *chari* (west generally), चोराँटा *chorānta* (Patna), जुड़न्गुड़ो *jurguro* South Bhagalpur), and जुगन्ड़ा *jugra* (South Munger).

जकेराइ *jakerāi*,—see जौकेराइ *jaukerāi*.

जिनन्वाँ *jinwān* (west) or झीरो *jhīro* (East Tirhut).

जूर *jūr* (South-West Shahabad).

जुगन्ड़ा *jugra*, जुड़न्गुड़ो *jurguro*,—see चोराँट *charānt*.

जोब *job* (Tirhut, Gaya, and west generally).

जौ केराइ *jau kerāi* (generally); जकेराइ *jakerāi* (south-east). See §959.

झरुआ *jharua*,—see झार *jhār*.

झार *jhār* (Tirhut and Gaya), झरुआ *jharua* (Sāran and Patna), a kind of brushwood growing on wells, &c.

झीरो *jhīro*,—see जिनन्वाँ *jinwān*.

ठढ़िया *tharhiya* (Shahabad and East Tirhut).

डाँगर *dāngar* (Patna and Champāran), a species of Indian corn which bears no cobs.

डाभी *dābhi* (north of Ganges, Gaya, and Shahabad).

डेढ़ुआ *derhua* (South Tirhut).

तितन्ली *titli* (Gaya and west), तेतारी *tetāri* (Tirhut), तेतार *tetār* (East Tirhut).

तितोइ *titoi* (Gaya and South Munger).

तिनन्पतिया *tinpatiya* (south and west) and चकोड़ा *chakora* (Gaya south-east).

तेतार *tetār*, तेतारी *tetāri*,—see तितन्ली *titli*.

दुधिया *dudhiya*, a kind of wort. It is very poisonous.

दूब *dūb* or दूभ *dūbh*, also south of the Ganges दुब्भी *dubbhi* (*cynodon dactylon*).

धक॰रा *dhakra* (Tirhut and Champāran).

धिमोइ *dhimoï* (Gaya and west), छिमोइ *chhimoï* (South Munger).

नर॰चा *narcha* (Gaya).

नर॰जोँक *narjonk*,—see लर॰ही *larhi*.

नरुआ *narua*,—see पोआर *poār*.

नरै *narai*, नार *nār*, नेवारी *newāri*,—see लार *lār*.

पत॰लार *patlār* (Champāran).

पप॰रा *papra*,—see पिप॰रा *pipra*.

पसौँता *pasaunta*,—see बसौँता *basaunta*.

पिप॰रा *pipra* (South-East Tirhut, Patna, Gaya, and South Munger), पप॰रा *papra* (South-West Shahabad), and पुप॰रा *pupra* (Champāran and South Bhagalpur).

पुप॰रा *pupra*,—see पिप॰रा *pipra*.

पुर॰न॰वो *purnwo*,—see गध॰पुर॰ना *gadhpurna*.

पोआर *poār* (south), पोरा *pora* (West Tirhut), नरुआ *narua* (South Bhagalpur), straw which has been trampled in the threshing-floor.

फर॰का *pharka* (South-East Tirhut).

फुटिया *phutiya* (East Tirhut).

फुलेना *phulena* (north-west), शाम तुल॰सी *shām tulsi* (West Tirhut) or बन तुल॰सी *ban tulsi* (East Tirhut).

फेँफ॰ना *phephna* (East and South Tirhut).

बन तुल॰सी *ban tulsi*,—see फुलेना *phulena*.

बन पोस्ता *ban posta* (Champāran and Gaya), wild poppy.

बन केराइ *ban kerāï* (Patna, Gaya, and West).

बसौँता *basaunta* (north of the Ganges), बस॰वन्ता *baswanta* (Shahabad), or (North-East Tirhut) पसौँता *pasaunta*, which grows in Indian corn.

बिसाढ़ी *bisārhi* (East Tirhut).

बेढ़ियाँ *berhiyān*,—see बेरी *beri*.

बेल॰वन *belwan*, बेलोन्हा *belonha*, बेलौधन *belaudhan*,—see बेलौँधा *belaundha*.

बेलौँधा *belaundha*, which grows in rice and millet, found north of the Ganges, in Patna, and South Munger. In Gaya it is बेलौधन *belaudhan*, in Shahabad बेल॰वन *belwan*, and in Gaya and South Bhagalpur बेलोन्हा *belonha*.

बेरी *beri* (Gaya), बेढ़ियाँ *berhiyān* (Patna).

भिलोर *bhilor*,—see अँकरी *ankri*.

भूसी *bhūsi* (north) or भोसा *bhosa* (Tirhut), chaff.

भेखरी *bhekhri*,—see अँकरी *ankri*.

मोथा *motha* (north of Ganges, Shahabad, Gaya, and south-east) (*cyperus rotunda*).

मकई के डाँट *makaï ke dānt* (Gaya), Indian corn stalks.

मकरा *makra*, a grain (north of Ganges, South-West Shahabad, and South Munger) which grows in Indian corn. See § 993.

मण्डू के नारा *mandu ke nāra*,—see मड़ुआटी *maruāti*.

मसी *masi* (Saran).

मुटमुर *mutmur* (north of the Ganges), which grows in rice-fields.

मड़ुआटी *maruāti* (Gaya and South-West Shahabad), मण्डू के नारा *mandu ke nāra* (Gaya), *marua* straw.

मुनगा *munga*, सहजन *sahjan*, &c., (*hyperanthera moringa*), see सैयन *saiyan* in § 1074. It is very plentiful at Gaya, hence the proverb—

मुनगा, मच्छर, मोखतार, मालजादी, ई चारो सेँ साहबगञ्ज की आबादी,

Munga, machchhar, mokhtār, māljādī, ī chāro señ Sāhabganj kī ābādi.

—*Munga*, mosquitoes, attorneys, and courtezans, these four make up the population of Sāhabganj (*i.e.*, outer Gaya).

मुनमुन *munmun* (north-west).

मुरका *murka* (north), found in wheat and barley.

मुरेना *murena* (west).

रटनी *ratni* (East Tirhut).

राटन *rātan*,—see राढ़ी *rārhi*.

राड़ी *rāri* (north of Ganges).

राढ़ी *rārhi* (Shahabad, Patna, and Gaya, and South Munger), राटन *rātan* (South Bhagalpur).

लपटा *lapta* (Gaya and west.)

लरजोंका *larjonka*,—see लरही *larhi*.

लरही *larhi* (Patna), नरजोंक *narjonk* (South Munger), लरजोंका *larjonka* (South Bhagalpur).

लार *lār* or नार *nār*, also नरै *narai* (South-West Shahabad), and नेवारी *newāri* (Patna and Gaya), untrampled straw.

लेँड़ई *lenraï* (Gaya and west) or (North Tirhut) कोड़िला *korhila,* found in rice-fields. The same as चिचोरी *chichori.*

शाम तुलसी *shām tulsi,*—see फुलेना *phulena.*

साँईँ *sāñiñ* (Gaya and Shahabad) or सामी *sāmi* (North-East Tirhut).

सामा *sāma* (Tirhut),—see § 989.

सामी *sāmi,*—see साँईँ *sāñiñ.*

साँवाँ *sāñwāñ,* (Gaya, South-West Shahabad, and South Munger).

सिहोर *sihor* or सिहोड़ा *sihora* (Champāran and Tirhut).

सुअरा *suara,*—see सुरबरिया *surbariya.*

सुरबरिया *surbariya* (Patna and Gaya), सुरबार *surbār* (Gaya and Shahabad), सुअरा *suara* (Gaya and Shahabad), सुरवारी *surwāri* (north), found in millet.

सुरबार *surbār,* सुरवारी *surwāri,*—see सुरबरिया *surbariya.*

सेढ़ी *serhi* (South-West Shahabad).

हड़ा *hara,*—see हड्डा *hadda.*

हड्डा *hadda* (north of Ganges) or (East Tirhut) हड़ा *hara,* हाड़ा *hāra,* (Gaya and South-West Shahabad), which grows in millet (*euphorbia hirta*). Cf. also § 1075.

हथबै *hathbai* (East Tirhut).

हरौती *harauti* (South-East Tirhut).

हाड़ा *hāra,*—see हड्डा *hadda.*

DIVISION VIII.

LABOUR ADVANCES, WAGES, AND PERQUISITES.

CHAPTER I.—PAY AND ADVANCES TO LABOURERS.

1184. A labourer generally is मजूर *majūr,* also in Tirhut and the south-east जन *jan.* Another very general word is बनिहार *banihār.* In East Tirhut a कमरिया *kamariya* (*i.e.*, he who wears a blanket) means a labouring man generally. In Patna, Gaya, and South Munger he is also कमियाँ *kamiyān.* In Tirhut चाकर *chākar* is a paid servant, as opposed to बहिया *bahiya* and चरवाह *charwāh,* which mean an unpaid servant. A day-labourer is in South-East Tirhut रोजहा *rojha;* elsewhere he is मजूर *majūr* or जन *jan,* as above. A servant engaged by the year is नोकर *nokar* north of the Ganges, and also हरवाह *harwāh* (literally, a ploughman) in Tirhut. Forced labour is बेगारी *begāri,* and a forced labourer is बेगार *begār,* or in Gaya हाकिम हुकमी *hākim hukmi.* In East Tirhut जिरतिहा *jiratiha* is a labourer who receives land rent-free and works for his master without remuneration in the agricultural season. In the north-west the पारीवाला *pāriwāla* sometimes works for his master and sometimes for himself. In Tirhut खवास *khawās* means a male house-servant, Hindu or Musalmān. A proverb which alludes to him is चोरक सङ्ग चोर, पहरुक सङ्ग खवास, *chorak sang chor, paharuk sang khawās,*—with other thieves he is a thief, but in the presence of the watchman he is simply a servant.

1185. A labourer's pay is मजूरी *majūri,* or to the east अजूरा *ajūra.* When paid in kind it is बन *ban* or बनि *bani,* also बोनि *boni* in North-East Tirhut. When paid daily it is also called रोज *roj* or (in Patna, Gaya, and South Munger) रोजीना *rojīna.* In Champāran it is रोजबन्धी *rojbandhi.* Monthly wages is दरमाहा *darmāha,* also महिन्ना *mahinna* when it is a fixed sum, and महिनवारी *mahinwāri* when it means the average income of the month. Yearly wages is सालियाना *sāliyāna* or सालीना *sālīna.* In the north-west it is also सलीना *salīna,* and in

North-East Tirhut बरखी *barkhi.* In Sāran and North-West Tirhut मनी *mani* is an allowance of grain made to a servant in lieu of pay. In South Munger it is कोराना *korāna.*

1186. Advances of pay to labourers are फाजिल *phājil* or अगवड़ *agwar* in the north-west. In East Tirhut they are जनौर *janaur*, in West Tirhut अगौड़ी *agauri*, and in South-East Tirhut also अगाउर *agāūr*. In Shahabad they are अगवन *agwan*, in Patna अगार *agār*, in South Munger अगौरी *agauri*, and in South Bhagalpur अगड़ौर *agraur.* In Gaya they are कमियौटी *kamiyauti.* हरवर *harwar* in the west, and हरौरी *harauri* in South-West Shahabad and Tirhut (or in East Tirhut optionally हरौर *haraur*), is an advance of grain or money or a piece of land given to a ploughman when he is engaged. In the south-east it is हरवाही *harwāhi*, in Patna कमिआई *kamiai*, and in Gaya कमियौटी *kamiyauti.*

CHAPTER II.—ADVANCES TO TENANTS.

1187. Advances are generally तगावी *tagāwi* or करजा *karja.* The following special names are also used :—

1188. *Advances to buy food.*—These are खैहन *khaihan* to the west and in Patna and Gaya. In Tirhut they are called बनियौटा *baniyauta*, and when in cash करजा *karja.* In Patna and Gaya they are खरिहन *kharihan.*

1189. *Advances to buy seed.*—These are बिअहन *biahan* in East Tirhut, and बीहन *bihan* in Patna and Gaya. In Shahabad they are बीया बेंगा *biya benga* or बीया बाल *biya bāl.*

1190. *Advances for purchase of cattle and sinking wells.*—These are तगावी *tagāwi* or करजा *karja* south of the Ganges. In East Tirhut अधलावा *adhlāwa*, and in West Tirhut अधलप्पा *adhlappa*, is the advance made to a tenant for the purchase of cattle. The lender receives back the amount of the advance and half of the profit derived from the cattle.

1191. *Advances for marriage expenses.*—These are करजैन *karjain* in Patna.

1192. In Champāran दहिहक्की *dahihakki* is a remission made by the landlord to a lessee. In South-East Tirhut similar terms are छुट्टी *chhutti* (used also in Patna and Gaya) and खातिर *khātir.* In West

Tirhut and Champāran when fallow land is given to a cultivator for a quarter rent or rentfree for the first year, the custom is called खिल्ही *khilhi*. So also in South-East Tirhut it is आसा चास *āsa chās*, and in Shahabad खील मारी *khīl māri*. See also §§ 912 and 913.

CHAPTER III.—DUES PAID BY TENANTS.

1193. These are principally the cesses paid to the resident artisans and other non-cultivating residents in the village, who are known as पवनी *pawani*, पौनी *pauni*, or पौनिया *pauniya*. In East Tirhut they are पवनी पसारी *pawani pasāri*.

1194. The *carpenter* (बढ़ही *barhi*) and *blacksmith* (लोहार *lohār*), who are generally the same person, get a fee from the member of a marriage procession who gets any work done by him: This is known as बिरित *birit* in South Munger, and as बियाह दानी *biyāh dāni* in South Bhagalpur. Elsewhere it is simply इनाम *inām* or बकसिस *baksis*. His remuneration for the repairs of instruments is कठा *katha* in Sāran, जौरा *jaura* in Champāran, and पाल *pāl* in Tirhut. In Shahabad it is कमाइ *kamāï*, and so also in East Tirhut. In South-East Tirhut it is also भाँवर *bhāmwar*, and in South Munger it is कमैनी *kamaini*. When he is paid at so much paddy per plough, it is called, according to the amount, बोझा *bojha* in Sāran, Patna, Gaya, and the south-east, अँटिया *antiya* or पाँजा *pānja* in Champāran, and पँजौर *panjaur* in North-East Tirhut. Another of his perquisites received at the time of sowing is called अञ्जुर *anjur* in Shahabad and अँजुरी *anjuri* in Gaya. He receives a further remuneration for keeping the cane-mill in order. This is पचरावन *pachrāwan* or भाँवर *bhāmwar* in Shahabad, कोल्हकढ़ *kolhkarh* in Patna, कोल्हकर *kolhkar* in South Munger, and कोल्हपचरानी *kolhpachrāni* in South Bhagalpur. In Sāran he gets two rupees for each mill, and his remuneration is called खान *khān*. For repairing other implements he gets in Sāran साली *sāli*, and a similar cess in Champāran and Tirhut is known as खरिहानी *kharihāni*. In South Bhagalpur भौंरी *bhaunri* is the general term used for his perquisites. In North-West Tirhut खान *khān*, and in North-East Tirhut खन *khan* or कमाइ *kamāï* (which means wages for any work done), are the wages for making a new mill. The grain actually given is डाली *dāli*, and amounts to from 10 to 30 *sers*. The fee for repair is बिगहटी *bighati*, and is 4 annas per bigha for मोरङ्न

morhan or first cuttings, and 2 annas per bigha for खूँटी *khūnti* or second cuttings of the cane.

1195. *The weaver's perquisite.*—This is in North-West Tirhut बानी *bāni*, and elsewhere बाना *bāna*.

1196. *The shoe-maker's* (चमार *chamār*) *perquisite.*—This is भाँवर *bhāmwar* to the west. In Gaya and Shahabad, however, it is खरिहानी *kharihāni*. It is पाल *pāl* in Champāran and Tirhut, also कमाद *kamāï* and पँजौरा *panjaura* in North-East Tirhut. In the South-East it is पाँजा *pānja* or बोझा *bojha*, and in Patna and Gaya मँगनी *mangni*. बियौआ *biyaua* to the west and दत *dat* to the east is the fee given to his wife for service as a midwife.

1197. *The sweeper's* (मिहतर *mihtar*) *perquisite.*—This also is खरिहानी *kharihāni* or कमाद *kamāï* in Shahabad. In the south-east it is a sweeper's and not the shoe-maker's wife who officiates as midwife. A sweeper in the south-east is हाड़ी *hāri*, and his wife is हाड़िन *hārin*. The fee paid her for her services is दत *dat* or दत भोजनी *dut bhojni*.

1198. *The perquisites of the village accountant* (पटवारी *patwāri*) are many and various. In Patna and Gaya if the tenant's lands are नगदी *nagdi* he gets in Patna 2½ *sers* per bigha, and in Gaya 12½ *sers* per plough. This is called माँगन *māngan*, and is his recognised salary. He also gets a fee of one pice in the rupee per annum for answering a raiyat's inquiries about his rent. This is called हुजताना *hujtāna*. If the land is भांवली *bhāoli*, he gets in the same district, in addition to the above, नोँचा *noñcha* (also in Shahabad नोचिया *nochiya*) or "pluckings," which amount to ⅛th of a *ser* per maund. A similar fee is called बलकट *balkat* in Saran. In Shahabad a village accountant gets in the case of नगदी *nagdi* lands a perquisite of ½ an anna in the rupee, called टकही *takahi*. In the case of भांवली *bhāwli* rents he gets ½ a *ser* or a *ser* per maund, the first being called असेरी *aseri*, and the second सेरी *seri* or सेरही *serhi*. In the case of a general clearance of rents he gets a present of 8 annas or a rupee, called फरकतियावन *pharkatiyāwan*. In Tirhut this item is called फरकाना *pharkāna* or फरिकाना *pharikāna*. In South Munger lands are principally नगदी *nagdi*, and the village accountant is a servant of the landlord and is paid by him, and gets nothing from the tenants. His pay is as follows. In the case of नगदी *nagdi* tenures he gets a माँगन *māngan* of 5 *sers* per *bigha*. When the land is भांवली *bhāoli* he gets 2½ *sers* per maund, and his pay is called दहियक माँगन *dahiak mängan.* He also gets a फरकाना *pharkāna* of one pice per rupee in the case of a clearance of accounts. In South Bhagalpur the tenant gives the accountant a नेग *neg* of 3½ *sers* per maund. In most districts he charges a pice for every rupee for which he grants a receipt. This is called generally रसिदाना *rasidāna* or रसिदावन *rasidāwan*, also कबजाना *kabjāna* in East Tirhut. होली खेलाइ *holi kheläï* or फगुआही *phaguāhi*, दोआत पुजाइ *doāt pujäï*, and दुरगा पुजाइ *durga pujäï*, are cesses levied by the accountant on the three main *Kāyasth* festivals of the Hindu year. The above are the usual amounts of his fees, but many of them vary from village to village.

1199. *Perquisites of the weighman.*—See § 914.

1200. *The village watchman* (गोड़ैत *gorait*, कोतवाल *kotwāl*, or (when a Government servant) चौकीदार *chaukīdār*) is sometimes paid by a grant of rent-free land (जागीर *jāgīr*), and hence he is called in South Munger जागीरदार *jāgīrdār*. When otherwise paid, his remuneration is called generally south of the Ganges चौकीदारी *chaukīdāri*. In the north-west it is खरिहानी *kharihāni*, in North-East Tirhut गोड़ैतक मूठ *goraitak mūth*, and in South-East Tirhut गोड़ैती *goraiti*. In Patna and Gaya he is sometimes paid in kind, and his fee is then called फसिलाना *phasilāna*, and in Gaya also नौंचा *noncha*.

1201. *The perquisites of the landlord.*—In addition to his rent, the following customary cesses may be noted:—गोआम *goām* in Patna, Gaya, and South Munger, बन्हवैया *banhwaiya* in South-West Shahabad, and गोहार *gohār* generally, are personal services rendered to the landlord by the tenants *en masse*. हुकुमत *hukumat* or फरमाइस *pharmāïs* are occasional demands of service or produce for special purposes. This in South Munger is called मदत *madat*, and in South Bhagalpur हकमैती *hakmaiti*. His perquisite of milk from his tenants' cows is in South-West Shahabad दुहाव *duhāo*. Cesses paid on special occasions are generally called सलामी *salāmi*, but there are frequently special names. *E.g.*, when a tenant's daughter is married, the landlord gets a fee called बियाहदानी *biyāhdāni*, सादियात *sādiyāt*, सदियात *sadiyāt*, or सदियाना *sadiyāna*. In North-East Tirhut this is usually one rupee four annas at a girl's marriage, and ten annas at a boy's marriage, which is realised from every one except Brāhmans, Kāyasths, Rajputs, and Musalmāns. In South-West Shahabad it is मँड़वच्छ *mañrwanch*. In Tirhut and the east ढिंगान *dhingān* is a fee paid on the marriage of a daughter for the second time, and भोजनी *bhojni* is paid on the marriage for the first time of a boy or girl. The former cess is paid in cash, but the latter in kind; *e.g.* in rice, pulse, or clarified butter. For other cesses paid by cowherds, see § 1151. The help given by the tenant in ploughing the landlord's lands is हरी *hari* to the north and the west generally. To the east it is हरिहर *harihar*, हरिहरा *harihara*, and हरिहरी *harihari*. Local names are सँगाहा *sangāha* in North-East Tirhut, हराइ *harāī* in Shahabad and South-West Tirhut, and हराही *harāhi* in Patna and Gaya. The presents given to the landlord when he visits the village are सलामी *salāmi* or (in Shahabad) नजराना *najrāna*. His fee when a house is built or sold is चौठ *chauth* generally north of the Ganges, and also in East Tirhut जर चौठ *jar chauth*. In towns in Patna and South Munger it is चौथैया *chauthaiya*, and elsewhere simply सलामी *salāmi*. He collects cesses in the nature of a ground-rent from the resident artisans and traders in the village. These are called मोतरफा *motarpha* or मोतहरफा *motharpha* generally, कोठियारी *kothiyāri* in Champāran and Tirhut generally, and बसुढ़ी *basurhi* in East Tirhut. South of the Ganges they are दुअन्नी *duanni*, or (to the east) अबुआब *abuāb*. In Patna and Gaya the former name represents a cess of the following description. 15 *mans* of grain, or thereabouts (according to village custom) is assumed (when rent is paid in kind) as the produce of one *bigha*. For each *bigha* (or 15 *mans*) thus calculated of the tenant's share of the crop, the landlord takes a cess of 2 *ānas*. In the case of lands paying cash rates, the cess is levied at from 2 *ānas* to 9 pice on each *bigha* of land held by the tenant. पूर *pūr* is a fee of one rupee per loom paid by weavers. In South Munger चरसा *charsa* is a cess paid by tanners. In North-East Tirhut केयाली *keyāli* or कियाली *kiyāli* (also बरदाना *bardāna* in Patna) is (or was) a transit-duty levied on cartmen for every load of grain they took. Sometimes it was levied at every place where they halted for the night. In the same tract the same name is also used for a tax levied on grain-sellers' weights. This last is called कौड़ी *kauri* in the north-west, and मलिकाइ चुटकी *malikāī chutki* in South-East Tirhut. In Shahabad it is बयाइ *bayāī*. In Gaya it is किराया *kirāya*, and the corn paid is माँगनी *māngni*. In the south-east तहबजारी *tahabjāri* or तबजारी *tabjāri* is a similar tax levied on shopkeepers.

1202. Rents are generally calculated in the old *sicca* rupees of Akbar, which are converted into current coin by adding exchange rates, called बट्टा माल *batta māl* and बट्टा कम्पनी *batta kampani*. The *batta māl* is added direct to the rent in *sicca* rupees, and denotes the exchange rate between them and the Murshidābādi coin introduced in the year 1773. In 1835 the introduction of the Company's rupee, $1\frac{1}{15}$ of which equalled $\frac{15}{16}$ of the Murshidābādi rupee, led to the imposition of a further rate of exchange, called *batta kampani*, which is calculated on and added to the rent calculated in *sicca* rupees *plus* the *batta māl*. Each of these rates of exchange is generally less than one anna per rupee.

1203. *Dues given for religious purposes.*—The first fruits given to Brāhmans are बिसुन पिरित *bisun pirit*, and also (north of the Ganges) बिसुन अन्स *bisun ans*. To the west they are अँगँऊँ *angañūñ* or अँगौँआँ *angauñāñ*. On the other hand first fruits set apart for house-gods (भूमि गनेस *bhūmi ganes*) or penates are अगौँ *agaun*, or (in Shahabad) अगब्बर *agbar*, and (in Champāran) रसुअड़ *rasuar*. In South Munger three small heaps (कुद्दी *kuddi*) are put aside on the threshing-floor. One is given to the Brāhmans, and is called बिसुन पिरित *bisun pirit*; the second is given to the मुसहर *mushar* of the village, who is known as देहुरी *dehuri*, and is called सहार *sahār*; and the third, called अगौँ *agaun*, is set apart for the house-gods, and is consumed by the cultivator himself. In South-West Shahabad a small heap of grain is put aside for the village god (डिहवार *dihwār*). This is given to the village milkman (गोआर *goār*), who performs the worship of the god, and it is called पिठार *pithār*. In South Munger बहरैया *bahraiya*, and generally बेहरी *behri* or बहरिया *bahariya* (all of which mean simply a subscription), are names for the subscription for the expenses of village worship, and दहिअक *dahiak* is a similar cess of $1\frac{1}{2}$, and सवैया *sawaiya* of $1\frac{1}{4}$, seers per maund. The grain set aside for beggars (फकीर *phakīr*) are known as भिच्छा *bhichchha* or भीख *bhīkh* amongst Hindus, and रसूली *rasūli* or फकिराना *phakirāna* amongst Musalmāns. The सिब अन्स *sib ans* is the portion set aside for religious mendicants (सन्यासी *sanyāsi*).

1204. *Miscellaneous.*—पुरौंता *puraunta* is the fee paid by the members of a marriage procession to any person who does any work for them. In North-West Shahabad 10 *sers* per plough are taken each by the washerman (धोबी *dhobi*) and the blacksmith (लोहार *lohār*). This is called जौरा *jaura*. In the same place खरवन *kharwan* is an armful of crop given to each of the following:—the blacksmith, the carpenter (बढ़ई *barhi*), the barber (नौआ *naua*), and the washerman; and the केड़ा *kera* is a smaller bundle of crop given to each of the same four.

Again पूरी *pūri* is three handfuls of crop given to the same four. In West Tirhut a similar cess is called पाल पसेरी *pāl paseri.*

1205. In Shahabad, and also in South Bhagalpur, बन *ban* is an allowance of one maund in twenty-one or twenty-five of crop given to the agricultural labourer. In South-West Shahabad the cowherd receives a certain share of the milk of the cows he grazes, which is called बारा *bāra.* In South Munger this is परौँधा *paraundha,* and in South Bhagalpur परोधो *parodho.* Similarly अठवारा *athwāra* (*i.e.* paid every eighth day) in Sāran, पार *pār* in North Tirhut, भाँज *bhānj* in West Tirhut, and पारा *pāra* or दुहिया *duhiya* in South Tirhut, is the milk given to the milkman as a fee for milking cows. चरवाही *charwāhi* is a fee paid to the herdsman for herding. It is also चराइ *charāï* in Shahabad. सलामी *salāmi* or कमरखोलाइ *kamar-kholāï* is the term applied to the presents made to or demanded by a police-officer or Government peon on entering a village, and the same terms are also applied to the presents made by the local police to the menial servants of magistrates and other high Government officials when in camp in their own district. In West Tirhut they are also called इनाम *inām.*

DIVISION IX.

LAND TENURES.

CHAPTER I.—TENURES.

1206. The descriptions contained in this division do not pretend to be legal definitions of the tenures referred to. On the contrary, they are only to be taken as giving the popular ideas (always more or less indefinite) current among the villagers as to the nature of the tenures.

Land tenures may be divided into—

(1) Proprietary tenures.

(2) Tenures intermediate between proprietary and cultivating ones.

(3) Cultivating tenures.

CHAPTER II.—PROPRIETARY TENURES.

1207. (1) *Revenue-paying tenures.*—These are known everywhere as जिमिदारी *jimidāri.* A very large landlord is, however, called a तालुकादार *tālukādār*, and his tenure तालुकादारी *tālukādāri.* This is the popular distinction in Bihār between the two names. Both tenures can be held in common and can be divided. When, in popular phraseology, it is wished to name a tenure which cannot be held in severalty, but is owned by one heir, the other heirs being given villages or *parganas* on which to subsist, it is called a राज *rāj.* In a जिमिदारी *jimidāri* (or तालुकादारी *tālukādāri*) tenure the whole land is held and managed in common. The property itself is called जिमिदारी *jimidāri*, or मिलःकियत *milkiyat* if it is small, and तालुका *tāluka* if it is large. The rents with all other profits from the estate are thrown into a common stock, and after making the deductions to be noted further on the balance is divided among the proprietors according to a fixed law or share. The deductions are the Government revenue and other expenses. The Government revenue is generally मालन्गुजारी *mālgujāri* or मलन्गुजारी *malgujāri*, also लाट *lāt* and रोल *rol* in Tirhut and to the east, and खजाना *khajāna* in North-East Tirhut. In Patna and Gaya it is also known as कलटरी *kalatri.* The other expenses are known as गाईं खरच *gaīñ kharch* generally, also गाँव के खरच *gānw ge kharch* or गवैंयाँ खरच *gawaiñyāñ kharch* in Tirhut. In South-West Tirhut they are also सालीना खरच *sālīna kharch.* In Gaya (and East Tirhut optionally) they are देही खरच *dehi kharch,* in Patna एखराजात *ekhrājāt,* and in South Munger गरही खरचा *garhi kharcha.* In South Bhagalpur they are बन्हखरचा *banh-kharcha,* which properly means embankment expenses.

1208. A landlord is जिमिदार *jimidār* or मालिक *mālik;* also sometimes सरकार *sarkār.* Local names are गाँव के ठाकुर *gāñw ke thākur* in South-West Shahabad, and गौँयाँ *gauñāñ* generally in that district. When the tenure is held in joint property, the shareholders are called हिस्सेदार *hissedār,* &c., see § 1214. The Government revenue is paid in by one of the body, called लमरदार *lamardār* in Sāran and मोखतार *mokhtār* in Tirhut and Patna. In Shahabad he is लम्बरदार *lambardār.* He is also known generally as तहसिलदार *tahsildār,* कारपरदाज *kārpardāj,* or मोखतियार *mokhtiyār.* In North-East Tirhut he is also known as टिपदार *tipdār.* The inferior proprietors are known as खुरदिहा मालिक *khurdiha mālik* north of Ganges, while south of the Ganges they are खुरदिया मालिक *khurdiya mālik.* In Patna they are known as जुजवी हिस्सेदार *jujwi hissedār.*

1209. (2) *Free grants.*—These are known generally as बिरित *birit,* and the holder as बिरितिहा *biritiha* or बिरितदार *biritdār.* These are general terms, and amongst them may be mentioned the following :—

(*a*) *Granted for religious purposes.*—These are known generally as सङ्कल्प *sankalp,* and are of different varieties, such as बरमोतर *barmotar,* for the worship of Brahma; बिश्नुन प्रीत *bishun prit* or बिश्नुन अरपन *bishun arpan,* for the worship of Vishnu; सिबोतर *sibotar,* for the worship of Siva; किशन अरपन *kishan arpan,* for the worship of Krishna, and so on.

(*b*) जागीर *jāgīr,* लाखराज *lākhrāj* (rentfree), माफी *māphi,* मिनहै *minhai* (at reduced rent), or खिल्लत *khillat.* These are properly grants for warlike services. They are also (especially जागीर *jāgīr*) applied to the free grants of land for services made to the potter (कुम्हार *kumhār*), watchman (गोड़ैत *gorait*), and other village servants.

(c) A grant given to the family of a man killed in the Rāja's service in open fight. This is मरवट *marwat* in the west, and मरौटी *marauti* to the east.

(d) A बिरित *birit* may be either acquired by purchase, when it is known as खरिदगी *kharidgi*, or it may be given by favour, when it is called इनाम *inām* or इनामात *ināmāt*. Local names in such a case are खैरात *khairāt* in Shahabad, and खुसबकत *khusbakat* in South Bhagalpur.

(e) खोरिश *khorish* or मोकरी *mokri* (north of the Ganges), also पालक *pālak* (Sāran), other local names being खोराकी *khorāki* or परवसती *parwasti* (South-East Tirhut) and खानदान *khāndān* (North-East Tirhut). This is an assignment by a rāja to a younger son or brother of a certain number of villages in the estate for subsistence for himself and his descendants for ever. On failure of descendants the grant reverts to the parent estate. This occurs in the case of a rāj which cannot be divided.

CHAPTER III.—INTERMEDIATE TENURE.

1210. The principal intermediate tenure is that known as ठीकेदारी *thīkedāri*, in which the holder (ठीकेदार *thīkedār*) contracts to hold the property at a fixed rental either for a certain term of years or until a sum of money (जर समन *jar saman*) advanced on usufructuary mortgage is repaid. In the former case it is also called खुशकी ठीका *khushki thika*, and in the latter पतौतन *patautan* in Shahabad, पटौआँ *pataunān* in the North-West and Tirhut, and generally सधौआ पटौआ *sadhaua pataua*. A mortgage lease is इजारा *ijāra* or जर पेशगी ठीका *jar peshgi thīka*. See § 1487.

1211. Among other intermediate tenures may be noticed the पतनी *patni* tenures, which form the subject of special laws. They may be briefly discribed as estates created by a landlord by separating a portion of his estate and letting it in perpetuity at a fixed rent. Subdivisions of these tenures let on the same principle are called दरपतनी *darpatni*, and these last are sometimes again allotted into smaller portions, called सीपतनी *sīpatni*. The holder of *patni* lands is called a पतनीदार *patnidār*.

1212. A tenure which may be either intermediate or cultivating, and which may be noticed here, is मोकररी *mokarari*, or tenure in perpetuity at a fixed rent. In some parts of the country these are also popularly known as सिकम्मी *sikmi* tenures, which usually mean under-tenures held by a cultivating raiyat.

1213. In Champāran सिकम्मी *sikmi* tenures are described as dependent proprietory taluks paying land revenue through the landlord who is responsible for it, and not into the Government Treasury direct. Concerning सिकम्मी *sikmi* rents in Gaya, see §§ 1225, 1226.

CHAPTER IV.—SHARES AND SHARERS.

1214. A share in a village is हिस्सा *hissa* and also (in Tirhut and the west) बखरा *bakhra*. The subdivision of a village held by a proprietary body is known as पट्टी *patti* or तखता *takhta*, also थोक *thok* north of the Ganges and फाट *phāt* in Gaya. A shareholder is हिस्सेदार *hissedār* or सरिकदार *sarikdār;* also बखरदार *bakhardār* to the west, पटिदार *patidār* in Tirhut. The proprietor of a half share is called अधिया *adhiya* north of the Ganges, and आधेआध *ādheādh* in South-West Shahabad. The inferior shareholders are called खुरदिहा *khurdiha*, &c., as described in Chapter II. पट्टी *patti* is also used to mean the principal share in a village, which may contain several सिकम्मी *sikmi* or subordinate shares. The shares of a brotherhood are भैबाँट *bhaibānt* generally, or in Patna and South Munger भैया बाँट *bhaiya bānt.* In the west they are also भैवध *bhaiwadh.* A father's share is बपन्स *bapans*, also बपन्हन्स *baphans* in Sāran, बपौटी *bapauti* in North-East Tirhut, and जद्दी *jaddi* in West Tirhut. An elder brother's share (which according to popular belief was larger than the share of the younger brothers before the institution of the English law-courts) is जेठन्स *jethans,* also जेठन्हन्स *jethhans* in Sāran, and in North-East Tirhut जेठौती (not जेठौटी) *jethauti*. The Government revenue is मालगुजारी *mālgujāri*, &c., as described in Chapter II. The half-yearly instalment is known as अधखर *adhkhar* or अधकर *adhkar* north of the Ganges, also as अठनिया *athaniya* or अठन्नी *athanni* generally. In South Bhagalpur it is अधकड़ किस्त *adhkar kist.* The distribution of the revenue over the sharers in villages held by a brotherhood is in South-West Shahabad भेर *bher.* Elsewhere a periphrasis is used, such as हिस्सा पटिदारी *hissa patidāri.*

A proprietor by purchase is खरिदार *kharidār*, and also (north of the Ganges) बेदार *baidār*.

CHAPTER V.—CULTIVATING TENURES.

1215. A cultivator is known as असामी *asāmi*, रैयत *raiyat*, परजा *parja*, or कास्तकार *kāstkār*. In Patna he is also पोतेदार *potedar*. A tenant with rights of occupancy is मौरूसी *maurūsi* (*literally*, hereditary) or कदीमी *kadimi* (ancient), also देही *dehi* (resident) in Patna and Gaya, and जद्दी *jāddi* (ancestral) in Shahabad. A tenant at fixed rates is इसतमरारी *istamrāri*, but this distinction is little observed. Hardly any cultivators, and very few landlords, know the difference between a tenant at fixed rates and one with a right of occupancy. A cultivator without rights of occupancy is known as गैर मौरूसी *gair maurūsi*, also as पाही *pāhi* (*literally*, 'foreign' or 'non resident') in Patna and Gaya, and खरिदगी *kharidgi* (*literally*, acquiring by purchase) in Shahabad. In North-East Tirhut he is हाल उपारजित *hāl upārjit* (newly created). These names are interesting as showing what cultivators themselves consider to constitute a non-occupancy tenant.

1216. In Shahabad, especially along the south bank of the Ganges, there is a class of tenants called गुदशतादार *gudashtādār* or गुदस्तादार *gudastādār*. They are generally Rajpūts and Brāhmans whose ancestors conquered the country, and who, while serving under the landlords, for whom they were always ready to fight, were considered entitled to a privileged position. A गुदशता *gudashta* or गुदस्ता *gudasta* tenure is held at a rent fixed for ever,* and is alienable without the consent of the landlord. It is, in fact, a freehold subject to a rent charge. The holders seldom sublet, and are a body of peasant proprietors, very prosperous as compared with other tenants, and furnishing thousands of recruits to the army. Another similar tenure is known as गोरा *gora*. In this the rent is fixed for ever in a holding with specified boundaries, without reference to the quantity of land. The rent is not variable even if the land be found to be more or less than the quantity roughly estimated at the original settlement. It is alienable without consent of the landlord.

1217. In some estates there is a kind of head tenant, who acts as an intermediary between the proprietor and the cultivator. He collects the rents and receives in return some petty privileges and immunities. He is known generally as महतों *mahton*, and in

---

* This point of fixed rents is denied by some landlords.

Patna and Gaya as मह्तोआड़ा *mahtoāra*. In Sāran he is also known as टिप्दार *tipdār*, in North-East Tirhut as मोकदम *mokadam*, and in South Bhagalpur मँड़र *mañrar*. Generally, however, the head tenant is called जेठ्रैयत *jethraiyat*, and he usually performs the above duties. The high-caste cultivators are known as अस्राफ *asrāph*, local names being सुर्फा *surpha* in Patna, सुर्फान *surphān* in Gaya, and बड़ आद्मी *bar admi* north of the Ganges. In South Bhagalpur, the quarter of the village where such live is called बबुटोला *babutola*. The remission of rent for such high-class tenants is माफी *māphi* generally north of the Ganges, also छुट्ती *chhuti* or कम्सरे *kamsare* in East Tirhut. In South-West Shahabad and Gaya and South Munger it is रेआएत *reāet*, in the rest of Shahabad मरौअती *marauati*, in Patna कमी *kami*, इनाम *inām*, or इलाम *ilām*, and in South Bhagalpur माफ *māph*. The low-caste tenants are known as राड़ जाति *rār jāti*, नीच *nīch*, or छोट लोग *chhot log*. They are also known as रजील *rajīl* in South-West Shahabad, कमीना *kamīna* in the rest of that district, राड़ भोड़ *rār bhor* in South Bhagalpur, सोल्कन्ह *solkanh* in Tirhut, and रैयान *raiyān* in Gaya. A proverb about them is—

काएथ किछु लेलैँ देलैँ, बरह्मन खियौलैँ।
धान पान पनियौलैँ, औ राड़ जाति लतियौलैँ॥

Kāeth kichhu leleñ deleñ, Barahman khiyauleñ.
Dhān pān paniyauleñ, au rār jāti latiyauleñ.

—A Kāyasth does what you want on payment, a Brāhman on being fed, paddy and betel on being watered, but a low-caste man on being kicked.

1218. Cultivators may also be divided into resident and non-resident. The resident cultivator is छपर्बन्द *chhaparband*, also डिही *dihi* in North-East Tirhut, देही *dehi* in Patna and Gaya, and बारी बस्त *bāri bast* in the south-east. A non-resident cultivator is पाही कास्त *pāhi kāst* or पाही *pāhi* (foreign), a word frequently confounded with पाई *pāī* (*literally*, a foot; hence used to mean an under-tenant). The word पाई *pāī* has almost fallen out of use now, but it is still understood, and has led to much confusion in laws and treatises on the rent-law, rendering it possible that the rights and liabilities of the under-tenant have been transferred to the non-resident cultivator. In South Bhagalpur the non-resident cultivator is known as पैहार *paihār*. The दोहट *dohat* or दोह्टा *dohta* cultivator differs from the पाही *pāhi* cultivator in that he keeps up two establishments and cultivates in two different villages, while the पाही *pāhi* cultivator does so only in one.

1219. Below the ordinary cultivator there is sometimes an under-tenant, who is known as सिकमी *sikmi* or कुरथौली *kurthauli*, also as पेटावाला *petāwāla* in the north-west and कोलियैती असामी *koliaiti asāmi* in East Tirhut. It is said that to the south-east in the case of a कुरथौली *kurthauli* tenure the rent of the under-tenant is fixed at a money rate, but is paid in grain at the market rate of the grain at the time of payment. Elsewhere the rent of under-tenures is generally paid in kind.

CHAPTER VI.—RENTS.

1220. Rent is लगान *lagān*. North of the Ganges and in South-East Bihār it is also पोता *pota*, with an optional variant पोत *pot* in South-East Tirhut; another name current north of the Ganges is मलगुजारी *malgujāri*. Rent rates are दर *dar*, सरे *sare*, or सरह *sarah*; also दरबन्दी *darbandi* or सरहबन्दी *sarahbandi*. चुकौआ *chukaua* north of the Ganges is rent payable at a fixed rate.

1221. Rent paid in cash is known as माल *māl*, and that paid in kind as ऐन *ain*. When rents are paid in cash, the tenure is known as नगदी *nagdi*, and also in East Tirhut as खाप *khāp*. When paid in kind, it is known as मनखप *mankhap* or भावली *bhāoli*. In मनखप *mankhap* or मनठीका *manthīka*, हुण्डा *hunda* or मनहुण्डा *manhunda*, the rent is a fixed quantity of grain paid as rent, irrespective of the proportion it bears to the whole crop. This custom is current principally in Tirhut and Champāran. In Patna it is called मनी बन्दोबस्त *mani bandobast*, and a variety in which a certain number of maunds of cleaned rice per *bigha* is taken as rent is known as चौराहा *chauräha*. These tenures are principally adopted by landlords when letting their जिरात *jirāt* or home-farm lands. In भावली *bhāoli* a certain fixed proportion of the whole crop is taken by the landlord. This division is called बटाइ *batāï*, &c., and a full description will be found in §§ 902 and ff.

1222. A tenure which has been noted in Patna is the हस्तबूदी *hastbūdī*, derived from the Persian *hast*, 'is,' and *būd*, 'was,' and which means literally 'the-is-and-the-was tenure.' In this the rate of rent is fixed at so much per bigha, but rent is only charged for so much area as is actually bearing crops at the time of harvest. Thus, suppose a piece of land measuring one *bigha* is cultivated, but for some reason (such as inundation, destruction by insects, &c.) the area of land actually under crops when ready for harvest is found to be 16 *kathas*, then the rent of four *kathas* is remitted and the rent for 16 *kathas* only is demanded. It thus closely resembles the *utbandi* tenure of Bengal. Compare § 1229.

1223. हाल हासिली *hāl hāsili* tenures also exist in Patna and Gaya. In these the cash rent is determined on the spot after inspection of the existing crops on the land. A very similar tenure is known as बल्कट *balkat*. In this the landlord's men, accompanied by the tenant, inspect the crops when ready for harvest, and fix a cash rent by estimating roughly the quantity of produce and its value.

1224. A peculiar tenure, which is principally adopted in lands which are generally subject to inundation, is known as जैदादी *jaidādi*. It is also adopted where the land is extremely bad and the prospect of a crop is uncertain. The principle is that the full rent agreed upon is paid on the land in any year in which any crops whatever (however small) is grown upon it. In any year in which no crop is produced upon it, no rent is paid.

1225. The tenures* and rent system in the district of Gaya are worth noting. Four-fifths of the cultivated lands are let on the भावली *bhāoli* system, as has been described in sections 902 and following. In the lands held on the नग्दी *nagdi* system the rent conditions are somewhat peculiar. The *nagdi* tenure is of two descriptions,—सिकमी *sikmi* or शिकमी *shikmi*, and चिकठ *chikath* or चकठ *chakath*.

1226. A शिकमी *shikmi* tenure is described by Bābu Bhūp Sen Singh as that under which the landlord has not any power of enhancement, irrespective of the period for which the tenant might have been in possession. The money-rent is not fixed upon the land, but upon the crops actually grown, varying with the nature of the soil and the class of tenants, whether high caste (सुरफान *surphān*) or low caste (रैयान *raiyān*), the former having a lower rate to pay than the latter. The lands generally under this tenure are the डिहाँस *dihāns* lands, or the best land lying on the borders of the inhabited portion of the village (see § 784), and the crop grown thereon pays a higher money rent than the same crops grown on fields

* Concerning the tenures in Gaya, I have to acknowledge my indebtedness to an admirable note prepared by Bābu Bhūp Sen Singh, Government Pleader of that district.

more distant from the village site. The same *shikmi* field also pays a rent varying with the crop. Thus if a Brāhman tenant planted it with opium poppy in one year and with an ordinary spring crop next year, he would pay a higher rate of rent the first year than the second; while a low-caste tenant would have to pay for both of them a higher rent than the Brāhman. Every tenant in a village has a fixed quantity of *shikmi* land partly at the higher and partly at the lower crop rate. If the tenant grows opium poppy upon a *bhāoli* and not a *shikmi* field, he pays for one harvest *bhāoli* rent, and is liable also to pay *nagdi* rent for the poppy at the rate fixed in the village for the particular class of tenants to which he belongs for poppy grown under such circumstances. According, however, to other authorities the rate of rent of these *shikmi* tenures is unalterable, but an extra rate or cess of so much per *bigha* is put on when special crops, such as opium or sugar-cane, are grown, and is taken off again when these special crops cease to be grown. Compare § 1231.

1227. The चिकठ *chikath* or चकठ *chakath* tenure is, according to Bābu Bhūp Sen Singh, a temporary settlement of waste or uncultivated but culturable lands for limited terms of years, at nominal rents, for the purpose of reclaiming them or bringing them under cultivation. This tenure is governed by the terms of the contract between the parties. If one term be not sufficient to render the lands fit for proper cultivation, the settlement is renewed from time to time till they become capable of yielding full crops. They are then settled as *bhāoli* or *shikmi* lands, according to their quality. In *chikath* lands no right of occupancy accrues by custom, and the rent is capable of enhancement on the expiry of the term of the settlement.

1228. According to Bābu Bhūp Sen Singh when a summer or जेठुआ *jethua* crop is grown on *bhāoli* land, an additional rate of 20 annas per *bigha* is charged as rent, the local *bigha* equalling 2¼ Bengal *bighas*.

1229. In South-West Shahabad, when in rice lands, the tenant pays only for the land under rice, and not for any land which may be fallow, the phrase उठन्ती परन्ती *uthti parti* is used. Compare § 1222.

1230. A remission of rent on account of deficient produce is माफ *māph* north of the Ganges, and also छुटन्ती *chhutti* in East Tirhut. South of the Ganges it is नाबूद *nābūd*, or, when made on account of inundation, गरन्की *garki*.

1231. Special crops, such as tobacco or poppy, on which special money rents are always assessed, are known as जबद्दी *jabdi* or जपत्ती *japti*. Cf. § 1226.

1232. Of the spontaneous produce of a village, बनक्कर *bankar* is the produce from forest land, wood, gums, &c. In Shahabad it is also called बन छिचोली *ban chhioli*. जलक्कर *jalkar* is the produce derived from lakes, streams, &c.; and फलक्कर *phalkar* is the produce of fruit. शिकार माही *sikār māhi* to the west is fishing rights.

1233. Fields situated in one village and included in the area of, and belonging to the proprietors of another village, are called मोतलक्के *motalke*, or (in Nort-hEast Tirhut) तांलुका *tāluka*.

The house of a well to do cultivator on the banks of the Ganges in Patna.

DIVISION X.

THE NATIVE HOUSE.

CHAPTER I.—THE NATIVE HOUSE.

1234. A *house* is मकान *makān* or घर *ghar.* Local variants of the latter are गिरही *girhī* in Gaya and Sāran, घौर *ghaur* in South-East Tirhut, घरा *ghara* in South Munger, and ग्रिही *grihi*, घरऽ *ghara*, or घरो *gharo* in South Bhagalpūr. A name current in Shahabad is बखरी *bakhri.* An *enclosure containing several houses* is north of the Ganges हवेली *haweli* or हबेली *habeli*, and south of it हाता *hāta.* South of the Ganges and in Sāran हवेली *haweli* or हबेली *habeli* generally means the *female apartments.* A *palace* is धौरहर *dhaurahar* or धरहर *dharhar*, as in the proverb सूती खड़ तर, सपनाइ धरहर *sūti khar tar sapnāï dharhar*,—he sleeps on grass and dreams of palaces. A *hut* is झोंपड़ा *jhompra* or झोंपड़ी *jhompri*, खोंप *khomp*, खोंपड़ा *khompra*, खोंपड़ी *khompri*, or पलानी *palāni.* कूटी *kūti* or कुट्टी *kutti* is the hut of a religious mendicant (फकीर *phakīr*). Other names used north of the Ganges are मठ *math* generally, and मठिया *mathiya* to the west, अस्थल *asthal* to the north-east, and जगह *jagah* or अखड़हा *akhraha* to the south-east. मरै *marai*, मँड़ई *mañraī*, or मरई *maraī*, is a grass hut, and माँड़ो *mānro*, &c., (see section 1307) is the hut in which a marriage ceremony is conducted. A little hovel or hut is north of the Ganges गोहिया *gohiya.* South of the Ganges it is in Patna and Gaya मड़ुका *maruka* or कूड़हा *kūrha*, in Shahabad टाटी *tāti* or बरऽहौघर *barhaughar*, and in South Bhagalpur ढाको *dhāko* or मोरका *morka.* सिरकी *sirki* is a hut or tent made of reeds, as in the proverb सिरकी एक देलन्हि तानि, ताहि बेर मँ आएल पानि, सिरकी उठाबैक रहल ना बेरा, आगू नाथ न पाछू पगहा *sirki ek delanhi tāni, tāhi ber mañ āel pāni, sirki uthābaik rahal na bera, āgu nāth na pāchhu pagha*,—he pitched his hovel and it began to rain, nor could he get an opportunity for striking it; he was (like an ass) without nose-ring or tether. A ruined house or enclosure is डीह *dih* or खँड़हर *khañrhar.* A hut in the forest is north of the Ganges पाझा *pājha*, and south of it चन्चर घर *chanchar ghar* in Gaya, चाँच्वाला घर *chānch-wāla ghar* in South Bhagalpur, टट्घर *tatghar* in South Munger, and मढ़्ही *marhhi* in South Bhagalpur.

1235. Straw huts used by the poor are टटौघर *tataughar* north of the Ganges, and काही पोस *kāhi pos* south of it. In Shahabad they are also called दोच्रा *dochra*, and in South Bhagalpur खरो घर *kharo ghar*. They are also very generally known as फूस के घर *phūs ke ghar* over the whole Bihār tract. A masonry house is पक्का *pakka* or पोख्ता *pokhta*. When built of stone it is called in Shahabad चाँद्नी *chāndni*. When built partly of bricks and partly of mud, it is कच्चा पक्का *kachcha pakka* or कंचा पक्का *kancha pakka*. In Shahabad it is, however, कंचा *kancha* or काँचा *kāncha*. A house built entirely of mud is कच्चा *kachcha* ; it is also to the west खाम *khām*, and to the east भीत घर *bhīt ghar*.

1236. When a house has three openings, it is तिन्द्रा *tindara* or सेद्रा *sedra* ; with twelve openings, it is बर्दरी *bardari* or बरह्दरी *barahdari*. But these terms are not much used except south of the Ganges, from and including Patna westwards. A house provided with lattices is जाल्दार *jāldār* or जालीदार *jālidār*. A house with nine apartments is in Patna and Shahabad नौरतन *nauratan*. Rooms in a native house are generally nine cubits long by five cubits wide. Such rooms are called नौपचम *naupancham*. बासा *bāsa* or डेरा *dera* is a dwelling or lodging-house, and खिल्वत *khilwat* a house used as a private chapel by Musalmāns.

CHAPTER II.—PARTS OF A HOUSE.

1237. *The courtyard.*—This is आँगन *āngan*, अँग्नै *angnai*, or (principally in Patna and Gaya) अँग्ना *angna* ; also in South Munger एँग्ना *engna*. In South-East Tirhut it is also called डेरा *dera*. The space in front of a house is अगुआर *aguār* or अगुआरा *aguāra* ; also अग्वास *agwās* in Shahabad, अगुत्ती *agutti* in Patna and Sāran, and अगुआनी *aguāni* in Patna and the south-east. The space behind it is पिछुआर *pichhuār* or (generally in the oblique cases) पिछुआरा *pichhuāra*, or to the west पछुआर *pachhuār* or (generally in the oblique cases) पछुआरा *pachhuāra*. It is also पिछूत *pichhūt* to the west, पिछुत्ती *pichhutti* in Patna and Sāran, and पिछुआनी *pichhuāni* in Patna and the south-east.

1238. *The vestibule or outer entrance room.*—This is दुआर *duār* or दोआर *doār* generally. It is also दूरा *dūra* north of the Ganges, and दुहारी *duhāri* or दुअरिया *duariya* in Patna and Gaya. Another name current in Patna and the east is देहरी *dehri.*

1239. *The inner entrance room.*—This is the room in which the men of the family sit and meet outsiders. It is called दलान *dalān.* It is also named दोगाह *dogāh* in South-West Shahabad and दरोखा *darokha* north of the Ganges. In Patna दोगाह *dogāh* means a cattle-shed. In North-West Bihār दुमुँहाँ *dumuñhān* is a somewhat similar room, but opening both to the outer world and to the inner apartments. A sitting-room generally is बैठका *baithka.*

1240. *The upper story.*—This is कोठा *kotha,* or in the south-west पटहुआँ *patahuāñ.*

1241. *The under-ground story.*—This is तखाना *takhāna* or तह-खाना *tahkhāna.* Other optional names are भुँजबरा *bhunjabra* or तरहरा *tarahra* in Patna, Gaya, and the south-east.

1242. *The veranda.*—This is ओसारा *osāra* or ओसरा *osra,* with variants ओसारी *osāri* in South-West Shahabad, उसरा *usra* in Gaya, and ओसरो *osro* in South Bhagalpur. It is also called साएबान *sāëbān,* and in Shahabad ढाबा *dhāba.*

1243. *The sitting-platform.*—This is चौतरा *chautra* generally. Other optional names are चबुतरा *chabutra* and पिण्डा *pinda* in Patna and the south-east, and ओटा *ota* in Patna, Gaya, and Sāran.

1244. *The roof.*—The roof or ceiling is छत *chhat.* It is also छात *chhāt* south of the Ganges, छत्ता *chhatta* in Gaya, and छाता *chhāta* in South Bhagalpur. A thatched roof is छाउनि *chhāuni,* छौनी *chauni,* छान्ह *chhānh,* छान्ही *chhānhi,* or छन्हिया *chhanhiya* in North-West and South Bihār. It is also generally छप्पर *chhappar,* with an optional variant छपरी *chhapri* in the south-west. Another name current in Tirhut is चार *chār.* If it is a simple thatch without tiles, it is specially called ठाट *thāt.* A thatcher is घरामी *gharāmi* or छौनिहार *chhaunihār* north of the Ganges, and his work is छाउनी *chhāüni.* In Patna and Gaya he is सुतिहार *sutihār,* and to the south-east घर छरिया *ghar chhariya.*

1245. When a thatch is only a "lean-to" on one wall, it is known as एकपलिया *ekpaliya* to the west. In Tirhut it is एकचारी *ekchāri,* and to the south-west एकचारा *ekchāra.* In Patna, Gaya, and (optionally) the south-west it is एकछपरा *ekchhapra.* If it rests on both walls with a ridge pole in the middle, it is दोपलिया *dopaliya* to the west and दोचारा *dochāra* in Champāran and to the east. In Patna it is पलानी *palāni*, and in Gaya and (optionally) South Munger दोछपरा *dochhapra*. In Shahabad another name current is दोछरा *dochra*. A roof composed of four triangular thatches meeting in a point at the top is called चौपार *chaupār*. When there are more than one thatch in a roof, each thatch is called फरका *pharka* or पल्ला *palla*. Also in the case of two thatches the front one is called north of the Ganges अगूत के ठाट *agūt ke thāt*, and the rear one पछूत के ठाट *pachhūt ke thāt*. The thatching along the ridge is कोचानी *kochāni*, or in Gaya दोगा *doga*. A small thatch put on the top of a wall to save it from rain is परछत्ती *parchhatti* or उपरछत्ती *uparchhatti* north of the Ganges, and south of it परछत्ती *parchhatti* (with a soft *t*). Other local names are छौनी *chhauni* (North-East Tirhut), छपरी *chhapri* (Tirhut generally), and पनछत्ती *panchhatti* in Patna.

1246. To rethatch a roof is ओतब *otab* or नौठठ करब *nauthat karab*. The yearly repairs to a tiled roof are फेरौंटी *pheraunti* in the south-west, and elsewhere खपरा फेरब *khapra pherab*. The grass put on a roof to make it water-tight is फटकन *phatkan* in Saran, छाबन *chhāban* in Champāran, and छौनी *chhauni* or तरेरा *tarera* in Patna, Gaya, and the south-west. In Tirhut it is छरन *chharan*, and in the south-east छारन *chhāran*. Mud used for the same purpose is गिलावा *gilāwa*. The repairs to a tiled roof which leaks are चूअना मारब *chūana mārab* in South-West Shahabad, टोइया *toiya* in the rest of that district, टिपकारी *tipkāri* in Gaya, and टपका मारब *tapka mārab* in Patna.

1247. *The fireplace.*—This is चूल्हा *chūlha* generally, local variants being चूल्ह *chūlh* in Shahabad, चूल्ही *chūlhi* in South-East Tirhut, and चूल्हो *chhūlho* in South Bhagalpur. In East Tirhut चूल्ह *chūlh* is a fire-place with two orifices, and कौल्हा *kaulha* one with one. In South-West Tirhut this last is called एकौल्हा *ekaulha*. The mouth of the fireplace is called मुँह *muñh*, or sometimes दुआर *duār* south of the Ganges. In North-East Tirhut चिनमार *chinmār* is the raised earth platform on which the fireplace is made, and on which food is cooked, while चौका *chauka* is the similar platform smoothed for a Hindu to eat from. थौना *thauna* to the west is a raised platform on either side of the fireplace for receiving pots for straining off rice-water. When the ground is simply smoothed for eating from, it is called ठहर *thahar*, or in East Tirhut ठाँव *thānw*. आरा or आड़ा *āra* is a cupboard in the wall at a man's height from the ground, in which cooking-pots are placed at night. बोरसी *borsi* is the moveable fireplace used by jewellers and by villagers (especially females) to warm themselves in winter. In North-

East Tirhut it is बोरस *boras*. घूर *ghūr* is a hole dug in the ground filled with straw and sweepings and lighted in the evening as a fire to warm oneself at. It is also called कौर or कौड़ *kaur* in the west.* The iron or earthen moveable fireplace is अँगेठी *angaithi*. A similar one used by jewellers is अँगेठा *angaitha*. An earthen pot for holding fire is in Gaya मटप्पर *matpar*, and in Shahabad मेंटहर *mentahar* or पौड़ा *paura*.

1248. The holes on the top of the fireplace, on which the pots are placed, are called आँछी *ānchhi* or अँछिया *anchhiya;* also in South-West Shahabad ऐला *aila*. They are also called चुल्हिया *chulhiya* in East Tirhut. When there are places for four pots, it is known as a चरँछिया चूल्हा *charanchhia chūlha*, or in South-West Shahabad as a चरैला चूल्हा *charaila chulha*. The partitions between the holes are पूता *pūta*, पुत्ता *putta*, or पुत्ती *putti*. Also पुस्ती *pusti* in South-East Tirhut, and पुतिया *putiya* in South Munger. The cooking-house is amongst Musalmāns बबरची खाना *babarchi khāna;* amongst Hindus it is रसोइया घर *rasoiya ghar;* also भनसा घर *bhansa ghar* in Patna and the east. In East Tirhut it is भानस घर *bhānas ghar*. The portion of the cooking-room set apart by a partition for cooking purposes only is called चुल्हानी *chulhāni* or चुहानी *chuhāni*. The other portion is known as माँझ घर *mānjh ghar* in Sāran and South-West Tirhut, as माँह घर *mānh ghar* in Shahabad, and as खोन्ही *khonhi* in North-East Tirhut.

1249. *The door.*—A doorway is दुआर *duār*, दोआर *doār*, दुआरी *duāri*, दरवाजा *darwāja*, दरवज्जा *darwajja* or (in Patna, Gaya, and the south-east) दरौजा *darauja*. A door is केँवाड़ी *keñwāri*, or in East Tirhut केवाड़ *kewār*, केँवाँड़ी *keñwāñri*, केँवाँड़ *keñwāñr*. The main doorway is सदर दरवाजा *sadar darwāja;* also निकसार *niksār* to the west, and निकास *nikās* in East Tirhut. In South-East Bihār it is सम्मुख दरोजा *samukh daroja*. A gate is फाटक *phātak*. A side door or window with lattices is खिरकी *khirki;* also दरैंची *darainchi* in Patna and Gaya. भवाँरी *bhawānri* to the west and in West Tirhut, भँभरा *bhambhra* in East Tirhut, and to the west दरींची *darinchi*, is a hole pierced in a wall to give light and air. In South Munger it is भमरा *bhamra*, and in South Bhagalpur भोँरा *bhoñra*. In Patna and Gaya it is ताबन्दान *tābdān*. मुक्का *mukka* or मोँका *monka*, and in Champaran अँधारी *andhāri*, is an earthen pot fixed in the wall for holding pice, &c. The leaves of the door are

* Compare the proverb घर जरैन्हि, घूर बुतावु *ghar jarainhi ghūr butāw*,—when his house is on fire he puts out the *ghūr*, *i.e.* in many difficulties he grapples with the least.

पल्ला *palla*, or in Shahabad पाला *pāla*, and the strip of wood nailed on one leaf to cover the chink is बेनी *beni* or बेनियाँ *beniyān*. In South Bhagalpur this latter is बेना *bena*. The cross-pieces across the leaf of the door to hold the boards composing it together are बाता *bāta* or बत्ता *batta*. There are generally four of them.

1250. The door-frame is चौकठ *chaukath*. The top bar or lintel of this is उपरौटा *uprauta* or (in Tirhut) छात *chhāt*. The bottom bar or threshold is लतमरा *latmara*, लतमरवा *latmarwa*, or लतखोरा *latkhora*. Sometimes a second outer door-frame is added for the sake of ornament. This is called साह *sāh* or दसौढ़ी *dasaurhi*, and such a double door-frame is said to be दोहरा *dohra* or साहवाला *sāhwāla* or दसौढ़ी चौकठ *dasaurhi chaukath*. In contradistinction from this, the single doorway is सादा *sāda* or एकहरा *ekahra*. The pivot used as a hinge is चूर *chūr* or (in Patna चूल *chūl*). In South-West Shahabad it is चूढ़ *chūrh*. A similar kind of hinge is in Gaya झनकौट *jhankaut*. The wooden bar used for fastening the door is किल्ली *killī*, and also (to the extreme west) आगर *āgar*, आगल *āgal*, or अगरी *agri*. In South-West Shahabad it is डण्डा *danda*. A short bar fastened by a pin to, and revolving on, one leaf of the door, and falling on a nail fixed on the other leaf, is बिल्ली *billi* or बिलैया *bilaiya*. The nail is called मकरी *makri*. A European door-bolt is छिटकनी *chhitkani* or छिटकिनी *chhitkini*. The heavy door-bar sliding back into a recess in the wall is बेँड़ *benr* or बेँड़ा *benra*. South of the Ganges the ढेँकी *dhenki*, or in Shahabad ढेँका *dhenka*, and in the south-west of that district ठेकुरी *thekuri*, is a perpendicular bar sliding down from a recess in the top of the door-frame. घरका *gharka* (in South Munger) is a kind of bolt. The door-lock is ताला *tāla*, and the key कुञ्जी *kunji*, चाभी *chābhi*, or छोरौना *chhorauna*. The bolt of the lock is हुरका *hurka* or (in Shahabad) झार *jhār*. In South Bhagalpur हुरका *hurka* also means a piece of wood fastening the two door planks behind. When a screen or hurdle, which is टाटी *tāti* or टट्टी *tatti* or (to the west) ठटर *thatar*, is used for a door, the spar that supports it inside is बेँड़ *benr* or बेँड़ा *benra*. In Tirhut it is also बेराठी *berāthi*, बराठी *barāthi*, or (to the east) बेनाठी *benāthi*. In South-East Bihār it is बेँड़ाठी *beñrāthi* or अड़खड़ *arkhar*, and in South-West Shahabad बेँवरा *beñwra*. The straw buffers tied along the two door-posts, against which the edges of the hurdle rest, are मोख *mokh* or मोखा *mokha*.

1251. *The wall.*—A wall is दिवार *diwār* or भीत *bhīt*. Sometimes the Hindi forms दीवाल *dīwāl* or देवाल *dewāl* are used. The foundations are नेव *neo*, and also in Patna and the south-east दावा *dāwa*. The straw mixed with earth for building a mud wall is पाचर *pāchar*, or in Sāran आलन *ālan*. The lumps of damp mud used in building a wall are लोंदा *londa* or धोंधा *dhondha* in Patna, Gaya, and to the west. To the east they are गोंदी *gondi;* also चेपी *chepi* in Champaran, चक्की *chakki* in East Tirhut, and लोंदी *londi* in South-East Tirhut. In South Tirhut another name is लोइया *loïya*, and in West Tirhut चेकी *cheki*. The stages in which it is built are रद्दा *radda* or रादा *rāda*, and also optionally पींड़ *pīnr* in Sāran. In Sāran रद्दा *radda* is the piece of the stage which, being the width of the wall, is finished before commencing the next piece. The top of a wall is भीता *bhīta* north of the Ganges, and भीत *bhīt* south of it; also माँथ *mānth* in South-West Tirhut, and मथनी *mathni* in East Tirhut. The plank over the top of a doorway on which the wall is built is भराँठ *bharānth*, भरेठ *bhareth*, भरैठ *bharaith*, or भरनठ *bharnath*. In Gaya it is भरना *bharna*, and in Patna पटदेहल *patdehal*, of which a local variant in Sāran is पटदेहर *patdehar*. To the east it is also झनकट *jhankat*. If this plank is not equal in width to the wall, two or more are laid side by side. Then the plank in which the top pivot of the leaf of the door moves is गरदानक *gardānak*, or in Champāran उपरौंटा *upraunta*, and the others are called भरेठ *bhareth*, &c. An arched recess in the wall over this plank, and serving as a cupboard, is दुरौंध *duraundh* or दुरौंधा *duraundha*, or in East Tirhut छात *chhāt*. The gable-end wall of a house is पाखा *pākha*, or in Shahabad पाख *pākh*. In North-East Tirhut, however, it is चनमार *chanmār*, and in Gaya and South-East Bihār कनेटा *kaneta*.

1252. *The eaves.*—These are ओलती *olti* generally, also ओरी *ori* to the north and west. Another name current in the west is ओरियानी *oriyāni*. In Gaya and the south-east they are अगरी *agri*, and there and in the south-east ओहारी *ohāri*. The edge of the eave, which is finished off with a board or with a kind of long straw or reed wisp, is known as मोहब्बत *mohabbat;* also as पसौंड़ड़ *pasaunrar* in North-West Tirhut, पंसरौंड़ *pansraunr* in Champāran, and पनिआगर *paniāgar* in North-East Tirhut. The last three words are also used to mean the long bamboo which supports the eave along its lower edge. The pieces of wood let into the wall to support this are टेरुआ *terua* generally, and तड़क *tarak* in North-East Tirhut. In Shahabad they are also called मरुआ *marua*. The slope of the roof is तारन *tāran* to the west and गरह *garah* to the east; also गरहगर *garahgar* in North-East Tirhut and तरनगर *tarangar* in Champāran. The raised ground under the eaves is in Gaya असठी *asthi*.

1253. *The cupboard.*—This is ताखा *tākha* or ताख *tākh.* A wall-bracket for lamps is दियरख *diarakh* or दयरखा *diarkha ;* also देखर *dekhar* or देखरा *dekhra* in South-West Shahabad, धोरखा *dhorkha* in Patna and Gaya, and धरखा *dharkha* in Gaya and South Munger. In North-East Tirhut it is चक्का *chakka*, and in South-East Tirhut चिरकदान *chirakdān.* In North-East Tirhut खरिकौता *kharikauta* is a hole in the wall for keeping tooth-picks. In South-West Bihār and Gaya this is भुड़की *bhurki* or खरकोटी *kharkoti.* मुक्का *mukka*, &c. (see § 1249), is an earthen pot fixed in the wall and used for holding pice, &c.

1254. *The men's and women's quarters, &c.*—The men's quarters are मरदाना *mardāna*, and also मरदानी *mardāni.* Other terms used are दलान *dalān*, दरवजा *darwaja*, or दरौजा *darauja*, दुआर *duār*, and (south-east) बँगला *bangla.* The women's quarters are अन्दरात *andarāt*, जनाना किता *janāna kita*, or हवेली *habeli.* To the east they are also called डेरा *dera*, and (in North-East Tirhut) अँगना *angna.* The part between the two is ड्योढ़ी *deurhi* or (south-west) देवढ़ी *deurhi.* This word is often used to signify a whole house, especially that of some great person, *i.e.*, equivalent to 'palace.' The outer room is also बहर घरा *bahar ghara* or (South-East Tirhut) बन घरा *ban ghara.*

CHAPTER III.—MATERIALS USED IN THE CONSTRUCTION OF THE HOUSE.

1255. Building materials are अमला *amla* or साँगह *sāngah*, or to the south-east साँगठ *sānga.*

1256. *The posts and beams.*—The wooden pillars supporting the roof are खम्भा *khambha*, खम्भी *khambhi*, खम्भिया *khambhiya*, or खम्हिया *khamhiya.* Another name current to the west and in South Tirhut is थून्ही *thūnhi* or थून्हीं *thūnhīñ.* In North-East Tirhut another name is उचवड़ *uchwar.* In South Bhagalpur we find खम्हाँ *khamhāñ*, and in South Munger खाम्ही *khāmhi.* Sometimes to support the ridge-pole a cross-beam runs across from wall to wall, and on its centre stands a pillar, on the top of which the ridge-pole rests. This pillar is also supported by two struts running obliquely from the beam and meeting it half-way up. This beam is called धरन *dharan*, the pillar is called मनिकथम्ह *manikthamh* or मलिकथम्भ *malikthambh* or (in Shahabad) also कौरी *kauri*, and the props are called पंखी *pankhi* or in Champāran सिपवा *sipwa.* When this is found too expensive, two struts run up from opposite walls, and cross each other just under the ridge-pole, which rests on their upper angle. The struts are called भितभेड़ा *bhitbhera*, घोड़मुहाँ *ghormuhān*, or कैंची *kainchi* to the west. Other names for similar supports are हटका *hatka* and गोरिया *goriya* in Shahabad, कौअल *kaual* in Patna, Gaya, and South-East Tirhut, कहुई *kahui* in South-West Shahabad, घोड़सहा *ghorsaha* or घोड़ी *ghori* in Champāran and North-West Tirhut, कैंच *kainch* in the east generally, and गैंच *gainch* in South Bhagalpur. The टेरुआ *terua* (or in South-East Tirhut कलन्दरा *kalandara*) is a strut running out from a wall to support the eaves. पाया *pāya* is an earthen pillar for supporting the roof.

1257. The *ridge-pole* is बड़ेंर *barenr* or बड़ेंरी *bareñri*, also लरही *larhi* in Champāran and the south-west, and नरही *narhi* in North-West Tirhut. All the beams of the thatch cross each other over this the upper angle of the cross is filled in with grass, and the whole is tied up tightly. This filling in is called मँगरी *mangri*. The sloping ridge-pole down a corner where two thatches meet is called तड़क *tarak*. A beam running horizontally the length of the thatch along the centre, each end resting on the slope of a gable, is called कमरबल्ला *kamarballa*, also पाड़ *pār* in North-East Tirhut. A lean-to thatch forming the roof of a verandah is supported on a series of struts projecting from the wall, which are called टेरुआ *terua*, माला *māla*, मलुआ *malua*, मड़ुआ or मरुआ *marua*, or मँड़ुआ *mañrua*, which support a long beam or bamboo, called सरदर *sardar*, on which the thatch rests.

1258. The round *rafters* of a thatched house are बल्ला *balla*, also बाला *bāla* in Shahabad. Thick squared rafters are known as कड़ी *kari*. The rafters of whole bamboos are कोरा *kora* or कोरो *koro*. The thickest of split bamboo are बाता *bāta* or बत्ता *batta*, and the thinnest laths of bamboo are बाती *bāti* and बत्ती *batti*, also in North-East Tirhut झोंझन *jhonjhan*. निगस्ता *nigasta* is a thick rafter used in South-West Shahabad; बरगा *barga* are the thinner rafters used in supporting a flat *pakka* roof. बल्ली *balli* are rafters smaller than a बल्ला *balla*.

1259. The round poles built up inside mud walls are लेवा खाम्ही *lewa khāmhi* north of the Ganges. In Shahabad they are गोल *gol* or गोला *gola*, and so also in the south-east. In Patna they are लार *lār*, and in South Bhagalpur नार *nār*. The support of a broken wall is असथम *astham* or चाँड़ी *chānri* north of the Ganges; also चाँड़ा *chānra*, उचका *uchka*, or थमुआ *thamua* in South-East Tirhut. In Shahabad this is थून्ही *thūnhi*, in Patna and Gaya थुम्भी *thumbhi*, in South Bhagalpur

थम्हुआ *thamhua* or चाँडा *chānda*, and to the south-east ओठगनी *othgani* or ओठगन *othgan*.

1260. गोल *gol* or गोला *gola* are round beams, and चौकोर *chaukor* or चौपहल *chaupahal* squared beams. The latter are also called चौधार *chaudhār* in Shahabad. A crooked beam is said to be कूबड़ *kūbar* in Shahabad.

1261. In South West Shahabad चेँड़ा *cheñra*, in South Bhagalpur चेला *chela*, and elsewhere south of the Ganges चैला *chaila* or चैली *chaili*, are splinters of wood, a layer of which is placed between the rafters and the tiling, and is also used for fuel.

1262. *The tiles.*—These are खपड़ा *khapra* generally. Flat tiles are थपुआ *thapua*, or in Champāran पथुआ *pathua*, and in South Munger सुपतिया *supatiya*. Another name is पटरी *patri* in South-West Shahabad. Semi-circular tiles are नरिया *nariya* generally, and pointed eave-tiles are टोँटी *tonti* or (Shahabad) टोँटियारी *tontiyāri* south of the Ganges. In the north-west औँधा *aundha* is a rough mode of tiling, when only flat tiles are used. In Gaya मुँगरा *mungra*, and in Sāran मँगरा *mangra*, is a large kind of tile laid along the ridge of a roof. Bits of broken tiles are मरकन *markan* to the north-west, and झिटुकी *jhituki*, झुटका *jhutka*, or झुटकी *jhutki* to the north-east. South of the Ganges they are ठिकरी *thikri* or झिकटी *jhikti*. In Shahabad they are झिकड़ी *jhikri* or सिकड़ी *sikri*. Tiles are baked in a kiln, called आवा *āwa* or (South-West Shahabad) आँवाँ *ānwān*. The layer of loose grass on a tiled roof between the rolls of thatching-grass and the tiles are known south of the Ganges as तरेर *tarer* or तरेरा *tarera*, or (in South Bhagalpur) पटोतन *patotan*. In the north-west it is फटकन *phatkan*, and in Tirhut छरन *chharan*.

1263. *The bricks.*—These are ईंटा *īnta* generally, local variants being ईंट *īnt* or ईटा *īta* south of the Ganges, and ऐँटा *ainta* in Patna, Gaya, and South Munger. A well-known proverb is मन में आन बगल में ईंटा *man meñ ān, bagal meñ īnta*,—(pretending to have) something else in one's mind, and having really a brick under one's arm (to heave at you). Among the varieties are पक्का *pakka* or पाकल *pākal*, which are kiln-burnt (the first word is borrowed from Hindi), and कच्चा *kachcha* (also Hindi) or काँच *kānch*, which are sun-dried. Another classification is into अँगरेजी *angreji* or बड़का *barka*, which are large table-moulded bricks. These are also called गदहिया *gadahiya* in Patna and South Bhagalpur, and टाली *tāli* in South Munger. Common country bricks are देहाती *dehāti*, or in South-East Tirhut भुइलोट *bhuïlot* or पमगिल्ला

panginja. सौंदर *saundar* in Patna and the south-east is a yellow kind of country brick. The smallest-sized country bricks are लहौरी *lahauri* or लहाउरि *lahāuri* to the west, पजाइ *pajāi* in South-West Tirhut, लखौरी *lakhauri* in East Tirhut, खजवा *khajwa* in South-East Tirhut, and ठिकड़िया *thikariya* in Patna and the south-east. The bricks forming the segment of a circle, used for lining wells, are known as बकौ *bakau*, बँकौ *bankau*, बकवा *bakwa*, or बँकवा *bankwa*. In South-East Tirhut these are known as चाकैटा *chākaita* or कोठिया ईंटा *kothiya inta*. सुरुजमुखी *surujmukhi*, or in Champāran गेंडुआवा *geñruāwa*, are the bricks, narrow at one end and broad at the other, used in building the sides of wells.

1264. In the interior of Patna थवई *thawaī* is the name of the bricklayer caste. Bricks are burnt in a kiln, called पजावा *pajāwa*, पिजावा *pijāwa*, पिजवा *pijwa*, भट्ठा *bhattha*, or भाठी *bhāthi*. An over-burnt brick is झाँवाँ *jhāñwāñ* north of the Ganges, and झामा *jhāma* south of it. Local names are झाम *jhām* in East Tirhut and झामो *jhāmo* in South Bhagalpur. Half-fired bricks are पीयर *pīyar* or पियरा *pīyara*, other local names being भुसुरिया *bhusuriya* or सेवराहा *sewrāha* in Champāran, सेवर *sewar* in Shahabad, पीला *pīla* in Gaya, अवालू *awālu* in Patna, and कचकोह *kachkoh* in South Bhagalpur. Other names are भटरङ्ग *bhatrang* in North-West Tirhut and भुसरङ्गा *bhusranga* in South-East Tirhut. The outer bricks of a kiln which become half black or are partially fired are called छाल के ईंटा *chhāl ke inta*, and in South Bhagalpur also छालटी *chhālti*.

1265. *Stone.*—Stone is पत्थर *patthar* or पत्थल *patthal*. Slabs of stone are पटिया *patiya* or सिल्ली *silli*. When large they are also called चीरा *chīra* in Shahabad, and असार *asār* in Patna and Gaya. Small pieces for jambs and lintels are टोड़िया *toriya* in South-West Shahabad, टूटन *tūtan* in the rest of that district, कचरी *kachri* in Gaya, and ढोका *dhoka* in Patna.

1266. *Lime and mortar.*—The calcareous nodular limestone used for lime-making and road-metal is known generally as कङ्कड़ *kankar*, local names being आँकड़ *ānkar*, इकड़ी *ikri*, or ईंकड़ी *inkri* (also in South-East Tirhut) to the west, गङ्गट *gangat* in Patna and Gaya, and गींगट *gīngat* to the south-east. Large blocks of it are known south of the Ganges as चट्टान *chattān* or चटान *chatān*, also as लईन *laīn* in South-West Shahabad. The small pieces for road-making are अँकड़ी *ankri* or आँकड़ *ānkar* in Shahabad, कँकड़ी *kankri* in Gaya, and in Patna, Gaya, and the south-east simply लोड़ा *lora* or रोड़ा *rora*, which last may also apply to small lumps of bricks, &c., also used in road-making. छर्रा *chharra*, or in the south-east बालिस *bālis*, is coarse limestone gravel.

1267. Lime is चून *chūn*, चूना *chūna*, or चुन्ना *chunna*. It is of two varieties, viz. गिट्टी *gitti*—that made from limestone, and कली *kali*—that made from shells. In the south-east that made from gravel is also called कली *kali*. The mussel shell used for making lime is सीपी *sipi* north of the Ganges, and सितुआ *situa* or सितुहा *situha* south of it. A local name is सित्तू *sittu* in South Bhagalpur. घोंघा *ghongha*, ऐठा *aitha*, or ऐंठा *aintha* is the voluted shell of a kind of water-snail similarly used. Lime mortar is मसाला *masāla*, or in Patna दबोइ *daboï*. Plaster is लेदाल *ledāl* or नीपे *nipe*. Moistened clay used as mortar is गिलावा *gilāwa*, or in South Munger गिलेवा *gilewa*. In Patna, Gaya, and the south-east it is also called गारा *gāra*. The pounded bricks used as a substitute for sand is सुरखी *surkhi*. When a wall is whitewashed it is said to be पोचारा वाला *pochāra wāla*, चुनेटल *chunetal*, चुनवट्टल *chunwattal*, or चूना फेरल *chūna pheral*.

DIVISION XI.

FOOD.

CHAPTER I.—MEALS.

1268. The general term for a *meal* is रसोइ *rasoï;* also भानस *bhānas* in East Tirhut. The *morning meal* is नाश॰ता *nāshta.* Other names are पन॰पियाव *panpiyāo,* पन॰पियाइ *panpiyāï,* जल॰पान *jalpān,* जल॰खइ *jalkhaī,* and जल॰खावा *jalkhāwa.* Other local names are जल॰घेराव *jalgherāu* (Champāran), पन॰पियार *panpiyār* (Gaya), and दाना *dāna* or दाना दूनी *dāna dūni* in Shahabad. पन॰पियाइ *panpiyāï* is also used to mean the food eaten by the labourer in the intervals of work in the field. This in the west is also called लुकुम *lukum.*

1269. The *midday meal,* which is the main meal of the day, is called by the people कलेवा *kalewa,* कलेउ *kaleu,* or (in Tirhut) कलौ *kalau,* though according to dictionaries and pandits this is a light morning repast. Local names for this meal are खाय *khāy* in Patna, खैया *khaiya* in Gaya, खाइक *khāïk* in South Munger, and कलौआ *kalaua* in South Bhagalpur.

1270. An *evening meal* is सँझौआ *sanjhaua* in South-West Shahabad. बेआलु *beālu,* or in Champāran बेर॰हटिया *berhatiya,* is light food taken just before sleeping.

1271. A *mouthful,* or the quantity of food put into the mouth at once, is कोर *kor,* कवर *kawar,* or कौर *kaur.* In South-West Shahabad it is also नेवाला *newāla,* which, however, means in the interior of Patna the refuse food left, after eating, for servants, and which is then also called ऊलुस *ūlus.*

CHAPTER II.—KINDS OF FOOD.

1272. The following are the principal kinds of food consumed by the lower orders:—

अक॰री *akri,* एक॰री *ekri,* or एँक॰री *enkri,*—uncleaned rice.

अखरी *akhri* or (South Munger) अखरा *akhra* or (South Bhagalpur) अखरो *akhro*, also आँवट *āñwat* (North-West Bihār and South-East Tirhut),—barley ground without being first cleaned. Cf. गूरी *gūri*.

अदौरी *adauri* or (Shahabad) अदवरी *adwari*,—little round balls made of pulse.

अनाज *anāj*,—a general term for food, especially grain.

अन्न *ann*,—food generally, especially corn.

अमावट *amāwat* (west), अमोट *amot* (North-East Tirhut),—mango conserve.

अरकौँच *arkaunch*,—see रिकौँच *rikaunch*.

अरदावा *ardāwa*,—gram and barley mixed and parched. Used as a food for horses.

अमाँठी के रोटी *amānthi ke roti*,—see आँठी के रोटी *ānthi ke roti*.

आँटा *ānta* or आटा *āta*, पिसान *pisān*, कनिक *kanik* or (East Tirhut) चिकस *chikas*, and (South Bhagalpur) चिकसा *chiksa*,—flour or meal.

आँठी के रोटी *ānthi ke roti*, also किसली के रोटी *kisli ke roti* (Champāran), अमाँठी के रोटी *amānthi ke roti* (Gaya and South Munger), and गुम्मा *gumma* (South Bhagalpur),—bread made of crushed mango-stones.

आमिल *āmil* (North-East Tirhut), खटाइ *khatāī* (Sāran), and खट्टा *khatta* (South Bhagalpur),—dried chips of the mango fruit used as a conserve. It is of two kinds, दड़िमी *darimi* and खोइया *khoïya*. The first is made from small immature mangos (टिकुला *tikula* or टिकोढ़ा *tikorha*), and the second from large mangos.

आँवट *āñwat*,—see अखरा *akhra*.

ओगरा *ogra*,—see माँड़ *mānr*.

ओरहा *orha*,—see होरहा *horha*.

इमरिती *imriti*,—see जिलेबी *jilebi*.

इँगूर *ingūr* or इँगुरी *inguri* (north),—barley from which the husk has been removed by pounding.

उझिला *ujhila*,—cooked mustard-seed.

ऊमी *ūmi*,—green *marua* (*eleusine coracana*) roasted as food (see § 990).

उलवा दाल *ulwa dāl*, उलावल *ulāwal*,—see दाल *dāl*.

एकरी *ekri*, ऍकरी *enkri*,—see अकरी *akri*.

कचवनिया *kachwaniya* (Sāran, Patna, and South Munger), मोदक *modak* (Gaya and Shahabad), कसार *kasār* (South Munger),—a round sweetmeat made of rice-flour, sugar, and clarified butter.

कचरस *kachras* (north-west) or पनुआँ *panuāṅ* (South-West Shahabad),—sugar-cane juice mixed with water.

कचौड़ी *kachauri*,—cakes of flour filled with pulse, &c. The inside stuffing of pulse-flour, &c., is called पीठी *pithi* south of the Ganges.

कढ़ुआ *karhua* (south),—food saved from supper for the children.

कबूली *kabūli*,—see खिचड़ी *khichri*.

कनिक *kanik*,—see आँटा *ānta*.

कसार *kasār*,—see कचवनिया *kachwaniya*.

काँची *kānchi*,—see हलुआ *halua*.

किसली के रोटी *kisli ke roti*,—see आँठी के रोटी *ānthi ke roti*.

कुन्ती *kunti*,—see लाइ *lāï*.

कोँहरौरी *konhrauri*,—cakes made of ground pulse and pumpkin.

खजला *khajla* (north),—a sweetmeat made from wheat-flour.

खजूर *khajūr*, also (south of the Ganges) खुरमा *khurma* or (South Bhagalpur) झिलिया *jhiliya*,—a sweetmeat in the form of a date.

खटाइ *khatāi*,—see आमिल *āmil*.

खँड़ौरा *khanraura*,—see खुद्दी *khuddi*.

खबौनी *khabauni* (south),—a sweet cake of wheat.

खाजा *khāja* (north),—a sweetmeat made from wheat-flour.

खिचड़ी *khichri*,—rice boiled with pulse; also called कबूली *kabūli* or भूनल खिचड़ी *bhūnal khichri* when spices are added. This last is called छौंकी *chhaunki* (*i.e.* seasoned) in South Bhagalpur.

खिरौरा *khiraura* (South-West Shahabad),—cakes of rice-flour prepared in hot water. Sometimes spelt खिरवरा *khirawara*.

खीर *khīr*, also खीरि *khīri* in North-East Tirhut and बखीर *bakhīr* south of the Ganges,—rice boiled in milk with sugar. See also जाउर *jāür* and तसमई *tasmaī*.

खुद्दी *khuddi*, also (South-West Shahabad) खँड़ौरा *khanraura*, and South Munger मेरखुन *merkhun*,—broken pulse or rice.

खुरमा *khurma* or South Munger खोरमा *khorma*,—a sweetmeat in form of a date made of wheat-flour, sugar, and clarified butter. Cf. खजूर *khajūr*.

खुश्का *khushka*,—see भात *bhāt*.

खुस्की *khuski*,—see परथन *parthan*.

खोभिया *khobhiya*,—see लाई *lāï*.

खोइया *khoïya*,—see आमिल *āmil*.

गट्टा *gatta*,—a cheap sweetmeat made of molasses. They are sold for a *kauri* each, and are the delight of boys of the poorer classes.

गलबल *galbal*,—see डभका *dabhka*.

गुम्मा *gumma*,—see आँठी के रोटी *ānthi ke roti*.

गूरी *gūri* (Shahabad),—barley ground after being cleaned, Cf. अखरा *akhra*.

गुलगुला *gulgula*, also (Shahabad गुलौरा *gulaura*,—a pudding of wheat and sugar.

गुलदाना *guldāna* (north-west), also इलाइची दाना *ilāïchi dāna* (Sāran and South-West Tirhut), and मकुन्दी दाना *makundi dāna* (Patna),—a sweetmeat made of wheat.

गुलाब जामुन *gulāb jāmun*,—a long sweetmeat made of dry curds (छेना *chhena*).

गुल्ली *gulli*,—see लोइया *loïya*.

गुलौरा *gulaura*,—see गुलगुला *gulgula*.

गोझा *gojha* (north and south-west), also गोझिया *gojhiya*,—a kind of sweet cake. See also फरा *phara*.

घटरा *ghatra*, घटोरा *ghatora*,—see पूआ *pūa*.

घट्ठा *ghattha*,—see लपसी *lapsi*.

घटिहन *ghatihan*, घठिहन *ghathihan*,—a general term for cheap grain, such as barley, pease, &c., also (Sāran) any kind of grain which when ground absorbs much water and is not easily digested.

घटोरा *ghatora*,—see पूआ *pūa*.

घसुआ *ghasua* or घसुई रोटी *ghasuï roti*, also पोछुआ *pochhua* (Tirhut) and सोहारी *sohāri* (East Tirhut and Shahabad),—cakes fried in a little clarified butter or oil.

घाठ *ghāth*, घाठा *ghātha*, घाठो *ghātho*,—see लपसी *lapsi*.

घाठि *ghāthi*,—see बेसन *besan*.

घाँठो *ghāntho*,—see लपसी *lapsi*.

घियौड़ा *ghiyaura*, घीवर *ghiwar*, घुगुरी *ghuguri*,—see घेवर *ghewar*.

घुघनी *ghughni* (north and south-east),—a mess made of pulse, clarified butter, &c.

घेवर *ghewar* (north), घुगुरी *ghuguri* (South-West Shahabad), घियौड़ा *ghiyaura* (Patna and Shahabad), घीवर *ghīwar* (Gaya and south-east),—a sweetmeat made of wheat-flour.

घोर *ghor*, घोल *ghol*,—see मट्ठा *mattha*.

घोरजाउर *ghorjāūr*, घोरजारी *ghorjāri*,—see मठजाउर *mathjāūr*.

चक्का *chakka*.—see बजका *bajka*.

चटनी *chatni*,—"chutnee."

चबेना *chabena*, चबेनी *chabeni*, चरबन *charban*, or भूँजा *bhūnja*, also भुजना *bhujna* (Shahabad) and मूढ़ी *mūrhi* (South Bhagalpur), भूजा *bhūja* (North-East Tirhut),—parched grain.

चिकस *chikas*, चिकसा *chiksa*,—see आँटा *ānta*.

चिक्कस *chikkas* (north),—roasted barley ground up with unroasted barley.

चिउरी *chiūri* (north-west), चौरी *chauri* (South Tirhut), फरुही *pharuhi* (East Tirhut and Shahabad), फरही *pharhi* (Patna and Gaya),—unripe barley parched; but in South Bhagalyur, फरुही *pharuhi* is parched rice.

चुन्नी *chunni*,—see चून *chūn*.

चूड़ा *chūra*,—unhusked rice, parched, then moistened and pounded flat.

चून *chūn* (north-west), चुन्नी *chunni* (Patna, Gaya, and South Munger), and रई *raī* (Shahabad),—rice partially boiled, then pounded and roasted.

चोखा *chokha* or भरता *bharta*, also (East Tirhut) सना *sana*,—a mess of pounded roasted vegetables.

चोँथा *chontha* (Saran),—a dish of pulse.

चौरी *chauri*,—see चिउरी *chiuri*.

चौरेठा *chauretha*, चौरठ *chaurath*,—rice soaked in water and then dried and pounded.

छनका *chhanka*, छेवनकन *chhewkan*, छेवँकन्ना *chhewankna*, छौंकल *chhaunkal*, छौंका *chhaunka*,—see बघार *baghār*.

छेना बाड़ा *chhena bāra*,—round flat sweetmeats made of dry curds (छेना *chhena*); a Bangāli dainty adopted in Bihar.

छौंकी *chhaunki*,—see खिचड़ी *khichri*.

जवाखार *jawākhār* (south) or पाचक *pāchak* (South Bhagalpur),—ashes of burnt ears and stalks of barley, used as a cure for indigestion.

जाउर *jāūr*,—rice boiled in milk with salt. When boiled with sugar it is खीर *khīr*, *q.v.*

जाबर *jābar*,—a mess of rice, vegetables, clarified butter, &c.

जिलेबी *jilebi*,—a tubular sweetmeat in a coiled shape, made of fine wheat-flour, sugar, &c. A variety of it is known as इमरिती *imriti* or इमिरती *imirti*.

झाँझा *jhānjha* (South-West Shahabad),—a mixture of coarse sugar, hemp, clarified butter, &c.

झिलिया *jhiliya*,—see खजूर *khajūr*.

झिल्ली *jhilli*,—see लट्टा *latta*.

झोर *jhor*,—see परेह *pareh*.

टूका *tūka* (north) or (East Tirhut) टुकरी *tukri*,—the fourth part of a round cake.

टिकरी *tikri*,—a sweetmeat made of flour, fried in clarified butter or oil, and covered with sugar; also (Gaya) a small loaf or roll. In South Bhagalpur it is a round sweetmeat in the form of a cake, and made of flour, butter, and sugar. Another name for this last is टिकिया *tikiya*.

ठकुआ *thakua*,—see ठेकुआ *thekua*.

ठुर्री *thurri*,—see ठूरी *thūri*.

ठूरी *thūri*, or (Tirhut, Gaya, and South Munger) ठुर्री *thurri*, (South-West Shahabad) ठोरी *thori*, (Patna) मुर्री *murri*, and (South Bhagalpur) मूढ़ी *mūrhi*,—grain which has not burst while being parched.

ठेकुआ *thekua*, ठकुआ *thakua*,— a kind of cake pressed in a mould called अगरौटा *agarauta*.

ठोरी *thori*,—see ठूरी *thūri*.

डभका *dabhka* (north-west), गलबल *galbal* (South Tirhut), डभकल *dabhkal*,—parched unripe grain, or ripe grain soaked in water and parched.

डुप्फा *duppha*,—see महुअर *mahuar*.

तक्कर *takkar*,—a preparation of butter-milk with spices, &c. It is said to be very cooling.

तरल *taral* (North-East Tirhut),—a kind of dish consisting of vegetables cooked in clarified butter or oil. It is peculiarly a rich man's food, and is supposed to be fattening, hence the proverb तरल खाय, पुनु गरल जाय *taral khāy, punu garal jāy*,—he is a rich man, and yet he is lean.

तसमई *tasmaī*,—rice boiled in milk with sugar, usually eaten by mendicants. It differs from खीर *khīr* in that the latter may or may not have water added.

ताज खानी *tāj khāni*,—see तास खानी *tās khāni*.

तास खानी *tās khāni* (north), also (South-East Tirhut) ताज खानी *tāj khāni*,—a round sweetmeat made of rice-flour, sugar, and clarified butter.

तिलकतरी *tilkatri*,—see लाई *lāī*.

तिलकुट *tilkut*,—a sweetmeat made of sesamum and molasses, much eaten by boys in Patna.

तिलौरी *tilauri*,—small balls of *urid* or *mung* mixed with sesamum seed, dried in the sun, and then fried in clarified butter.

तिसजौरी *tisjauri* (South Tirhut) or तिसियाउर *tisiyāūr*,—linseed and rice cooked together.

दड़िमी *darimi*,—see आमिल *āmil*.

दनजाउर *danjāūr* (Sāran and South-West Tirhut),—poppy-seeds (दाना *dāna*) and rice cooked together.

दनौरी *danauri*,—the same as तिलौरी *tilauri*, poppy seeds being used instead of sesamum.

दरा *dara*, दर्रा *darra* (north),—coarse meal; but दर्रा *darra* south of the Ganges is pounded maize boiled with water and sugar.

दलपिट्ठी *dalpitthi*, दलपिठौरी *dalpithauri*,— see दाल पीठी *dāl pīthi*.

दलसग्गा *dalsagga* or (South-West Shahabad) सगपहिता *sagpahita*,—pulse boiled with vegetables.

दलही पूरी *dalhi pūri*,—see बेरही *berhi*.

दाल *dāl*,—split pease or pulse. When these are parched they are called उलावल दाल *ulāwal dāl* or उलका दाल *ulka dāl*.

दाल पीठी *dāl pīthi*, दलपिट्ठी *dalpitthi*, or (Shahabad) दलपिठौरी *dalpithauri*,—(1) balls of wheat or barley-flour stuffed with pulse inside and boiled in water; (2) balls of wheat or barley-flour cooked along with pulse. पीठा *pītha* means balls of meal boiled in water.

धुँआँर *dhuñāñr*,—see फोरन *phoran*.

धोअल दाल *dhoal dāl*, धोआँच *dhoānch*,—see धोई *dhoī*.

धोई *dhoī* (north and Shahabad), also धोआँच *dhoānch* (South-West Shahabad), elsewhere धोअल दाल *dhoal dāl*,—soaked pulse.

धोंग *dhong* (Shahabad),—a thick cake.

पकमान *pakmān* or पकवान *pakwān*,—sweetmeats.

पतौरा *pataura*,—the tops of the plant called गुम्मा *gumma* (*pharnaceum mollugo*) roasted in a castor-oil leaf.

पनुआँ *panuān*,—see कचरस *kachras*.

पपरा *papra*;—see पापर *pāpar*.

परकिया *parakiya*,—see समोसा *samosa*.

परथन *parthan*, also Gaya पलेथन *palethan*, and खुसकी *khuski*,—the dry flour rubbed on the dough as it is being made into cakes.

परमल *parmal* (Shahabad),—parched maize or grain. See also होरहा *horha*.

पराठा *parātha*,—see फराठा *pharātha*.

परेह *pareh*, रस्सा *rassa*, रासा *rāsa*, or झोर *jhor*, sauce, such as of vegetables, &c., eaten with dry food.

पलेथन *palethan*,—see परथन *parthan*.

पाग *pāg* or (south-east) रान *rān* or (South Bhagalpur) सिरा *sira*,—syrup made by melting sugar in water and boiling it down.

पाचक *pāchak*,—see जवाखार *jawākhār*.

पापर *pāpar* or पपरा *papra*,—a crisp cake of pulse flour.

पिठार *pithār* (North-East Tirhut),—rice pounded in water.

पिट्ठा *pittha* or पीठा *pītha*, also to the east बगिया *bagiya*, and in Tirhut बगेया *bageya*,—a kind of boiled pudding made of *sattu* or meal. A smaller variety is called पिट्ठी *pitthi*.

पिट्ठी *pitthi*,—see पिट्ठा *pittha*.

पिसान *pisān*,—see आँटा *ānta*.

पीच *pīch*,—see माँड़ *mānr*.

पीठा *pītha*,—see पिट्ठा *pittha*.

पीठी *pīthi*,—see कचौड़ी *kachauri*.

पूआ *pūa*, also (East Tirhut) पू *pū*, and घटोरा *ghatora* (Patna and Gaya), and घटरा *ghatra* (South Bhagalpur and Gaya),—wheat-flour and molasses mixed and cooked in clarified butter or oil. Cf. माल पूआ *māl pūa*.

पूरी *pūri*, also (north) लुचुई *luchuï*, and (Tirhut) सोहारी *sohāri* or सुहारी *suhari*,—thin cakes boiled in clarified butter. They are supposed to be as indigestible as muffins: hence the proverb about one who attempts things he cannot do, घ्यु पचे नहिँ, पूरी ला मारि *ghyu pache nahiñ pūri la māri*,—a fight for muffins, when even clarified butter won't digest.

पेठा *petha* (north), also भुआपाग *bhuāpāg* (South-East Tirhut),—candied gourd.

पेड़ा *pera*,—a sweetmeat made of sugar and milk. Those made in Mathura and Gaya are most esteemed. See also लोइया *loïya*.

फरही *pharhi*,—see चिउरी *chiuri*.

फरा *phara* (north-west), गोझा *gojha* (Shahabad), and बगिया *bagiya* (South Bhagalpur),—balls of rice steamed over a pot containing boiling water.

फराठा *pharātha* (north and south-east), पराठा *parātha* (elsewhere),—bread made like pie-crust.

फरुही *pharuhi* (South Bhagalpur), फोकना *phokna* (South Munger),—parched rice. See also चिउरी *chiuri*.

फुटपूरी *phutpūri*,—see बेरही *berhi*.

फुटहरा *phutahra*,—see लिट्टी *litti*.

फुटहा *phutha* or (South-West Shahabad) फुटहरा *phutahra*,—parched gram and pease.

फुटेहरी *phutehri*,—see लिट्टी *litti*.

फुलौरा *phulaura*,—large balls of *urid*-flour fried in clarified butter or oil, and then soaked with spices in tyre. It becomes very spongy.

फुलौरी *phulauri*,—(1) (south) a roll of coarse flour cooked by steam in a pot with some water in the bottom, and resting above on twigs; (2) (north) balls of pulse-flour boiled in clarified butter or oil.

फेनी *pheni*,—a frothy sweetmeat made of wheat-flour and sugar. See also बतास फेनी *batās pheni*.

फोकन्ना *phokna*,—see फरुही *pharuhi*.

फोरन *phoran*, also (Shahabad) धुँआँर *dhuñāñr*,—seasoning used with food.

बखीर *bakhīr* (South-West Shahabad), रसियाव *rasiyāo* (rest of Shahabad), रसिया *rasiya* (Patna, Gaya, and the south-east),—rice cooked in sugar and water. See also खीर *khīr*.

बगिया *bagiya*, बगेया *bageya*,—see पिट्ठा *pittha*.

बघार *baghār* (north-west), छेवन्कन *chhewkan* (Tirhut), छेवँकान्ना *chhewankna* (Patna), छौँकल *chhaunkal* (South Munger), छन्का *chhanka* or छौँका *chhaunka* (South Bhagalpur),—the act of seasoning food.

बचन्का *bachka*,—see बजन्का *bajka*.

बजन्का *bajka* or (Patna) बचन्का *bachka*, (north चक्का *chakka*, (North-West Tirhut) बरा *bara*, (South Bhagalpur) बारा *bāra*,—slices of gourd or vegetable covered with pulse-flour and then fried in clarified butter or oil.

बतास फेनी *batās pheni* or फेनी *pheni* (north),—a spongy sweetmeat made of sugar and flour.

बतासा *batāsa*,—a spongy sweetmeat made of sugar.

बफौरी *baphauri*,—pulse-flour cooked by steam.

बरन्जौर *barjaur*,—see बेरन्हिन *berhin*.

बरन्फी *barphi*,—a white sweetmeat made of wheat, flour, milk, and sugar.

बरा *bara* or बारा *bāra*,—cakes of *urid* pulse fried in clarified butter or oil. See also बजन्का *bajka*.

बरी *bari*,—balls of *urid*, *mūng*, or gram-flour fried in clarified butter or oil.

बलुसाही *balusāhi* or बालू साही *bālu sāhi*,—a sweetmeat made of wheat.

बसिया *basiya*,—see बासी *bāsi*.

बहुरी *bahuri*,—see होरहा *horha*.

बारा *bāra*,—see बजका *bajka* and बरा *bara*.

बालू साही *bālu sāhi*,—see बलुसाही *balusāhi*.

बासी *bāsi* or बसिया *basiya*, also (Shahabad) बासी कूसी *bāsi kūsi*,—food saved from supper for breakfast.

बीरी *biri* (Gaya), a kind of food made of leaves and flour fried in clarified butter.

बुनियाँ *buniyān*,—a small round hollow sweetmeat made of gram-*besan*, fried in clarified butter or oil and covered with sugar.

बेनिया *beniya*,—see बेरही *berhi*.

बेरहिन *berhin* or बरजौर *barjaur* (Shahabad),—pulse cakes.

बेरही *berhi*, दलही पूरी *dalhi pūri* (north), फुटपूरी *phutpūri* (South Bhagalpur), and also (Tirhut) बेनिया *beniya*, and (Shahabad) बेरहीया *berhīya*,—pulse-flour cooked inside a wheat cake.

बेसन *besan* or घाठि *ghāthi* (North-East Tirhut),—pulse-flour.

बोर *bor* or बोर बोर *bor bor* (Gaya and west), सानि *sāni* (South Bhagalpur), सोन *son* (South Munger), the act of soaking dry food, such as bread, in any liquid.

भभरी *bhabhri*,—see लिट्टी *litti*.

भात *bhāt* (amongst Hindus), खुशका *khushka* (amongst Musalmāns),—plain boiled rice.

भुआपाग *bhuāpāg*,—see पेठा *petha*.

भुजना *bhujna*, भूँजा *bhūnja*, भूजा *bhūja*,—see चबेना *chabena*.

भूनल खिचड़ी *bhūnal khichri*,—see खिचड़ी *khichri*.

मएदा *maēda* or मैदा *maida*,—fine sifted flour.

मकुनी *makuni* (1) (north),—cakes stuffed with gram-flour; (2) (south) cakes made of pease or wheat-flour. See also लिट्टी *litti*.

मटरी *matri* (north), मुठरी *muthri* (South-West Shahabad),—a sweetmeat made of wheat-flour.

मट्ठा *mattha* or माठा *mātha*, also मण्ठा *mantha* (South-West Shahabad), घोल *ghol* or घोर *ghor* (to the east), and मही *mahi* (South Tirhut),—butter-milk.

मठ्‌जाउर *mathjāūr*, also (east) घोर्‌जाउर *ghorjāūr* and (South Bhagalpur) घोर्‌जारी *ghorjāri*,—butter-milk boiled in water, with a little rice, &c., added.

मठ्‌री *mathri*,—see मट्‌री *matri*.

मड्‌सट्‌का *marsatka* (Gaya),—rice-gruel with the rice.

मण्ठा *mantha*,—see मट्ठा *mattha*.

महन भोग *mahan bhog*,—see हलुआ *halua*.

महियाउर *mahiyāūr* (north) and महेर *maher* (South-West Shahabad),—a mess of rice, &c., in butter-milk.

मह्अर *mahuar* or (South Bhagalpur) डुप्पा *duppha*,—the flowers of the *mahua* (*Bassia latifolia*), soaked over-night, crushed next morning, and made into a cake with flour, gram, pease, or linseed.

महेर *maher*,—see महियाउर *mahiyāūr*.

माठा *mātha*,—see मट्ठा *mattha*.

माँड़ *mānr* (amongst Hindus) and पीच *pīch* or ओगरा *ogra* (amongst Musalmāns),—rice-gruel.

माल पुआ *māl puā*,—wheat-flour, sugar, and milk mixed and cooked in clarified butter only, thus differing from पुआ *pūa*, *q.v.*

मीठी पूरी *mīthi pūri*,—sweet cakes.

मुर्‌री *murri*,—see ढूरी *thūri*.

मूढ़ी *mūrhi*,—see ढूरी *thūri*, चबेना *chabena*, and लाइ *lāï*.

मेर्‌खुन *merkhun*,—see खुद्दी *khuddi*.

मैदा *maida*,—see मएदा *maëda*.

मोती चूर *moti chūr*,—a sweetmeat made up of very fine बुनियाँ *buniyān* shaped like pearls.

मोदक *modak*,—see कचवनिया *kachwaniya*.

रई *raï*,—see चून *chūn*.

रस गोला *ras gola*,—round balls of dry curds (छेना *chhena*) in syrup; a Bangāli dainty adopted in Bihār.

रसिया *rasiya*, रसियाव *rasiyāo*,—see बखीर *bakhīr*.

रस्सा *rassa*, रासा *rasā*,—see परेह *pareh*.

रान *rān*,—see पाग *pāg*.

राब *rāb*,—boiled sugar-cane juice.

रिकौँच *rikaunch* or सैँदा *saindha* (north), also अरकौँच *arkaunch* (Tirhut),—a mess of pulse-flour cooked in the leaves of the अरुई *arui* (*Arum colocassia*).

लकठो *laktho*,—see सेव *seo*.

लट्टा *latta* or लाटा *lāta*, also (South Bhagalpur) झिल्ली *jhilli*,—a mess made of the flowers of the *mahua* (*Bassia latifolia*), molasses, and parched grain.

लड्डू *laddu* or लडुआ *larua*,—a sweetmeat made up of sugar and cream.

लपसी *lapsi*,—flour of any grain boiled in milk and eaten with sugar. When made with salt instead of sugar, it is called (South-West Shahabad) घाठ *ghāth*, (South-East Tirhut) घट्ठ *ghattha*, (South Munger) घाठा *ghātha*, and (South Bhagalpur) घाठो *ghātho* or घाँठो *ghāntho*.

लाई *lāī*, also (Tirhut) मूढ़ी *mūrhi*, कुन्ती *kunti* (Patna and the south-west), and तिलकतरी *tilkatri* (South Bhagalpur) and खोभिया *khobhiya*,—parched rice prepared with sugar south of the Ganges, but without it north of the Ganges.

लाटा *lāta*,—see लट्टा *latta*.

लावा *lāwa*,—maize, rice, &c., parched in hot sand.

लिट्टी *litti*, भभरी *bhabhri*, मकुनी *makuni*, or फुटेहरी *phutehri* or (south) फुटहरा *phutahra*,—various cognate kinds of cakes fried in hot ashes. The last four are generally stuffed with *sattu* and spices, while the first may or may not be so stuffed.

लुचुई *luchūī*,—see पूरी *pūri*.

लोइया *loïya* or (South Bhagalpur) गुल्ली *gulli*, the lumps of dough out of which cakes are made. In Patna, Musalmān women call them पेड़ा *pera*.

सकरपाला *sakarpāla* or (Gaya) मिरजई *mirjaī*,—a sweetmeat of wheat-flour.

सगपहिता *sagpahita*,—see दलसग्गा *dalsagga*.

सतुआ *satua*, सतुई *satui*,—see सत्तु *sattu*.

सत्तू *sattu* or सतुआ *satua*, also (Shahabad) सतुई *satui*, and (north, generally amongst mendicants) सितलबुकनी *sitalbukni*, parched gram ground into flour.

समोसा *samosa* also (Tirhut) परकिया *parakiya*,—balls of flour, with fruit, &c., inside, cooked in clarified butter.

सरबत *sarbat* (south-east),—sugar-cane juice mixed with milk; also generally *eau sucré*.

सानि *sāni*,—see बोर *bor*.

साँस *sāns*,—a sweetmeat made of बेसन *besan* and molasses, eaten by boys in Patna.

सितलबुकनी *sitalbukni*,—see सत्तू *sattu*.

सिधा *sidha* or सीधा *sīdha*,—provisions, food, as in the proverb सिधा सन्देह, गब्य गब्य करथि *sidha sandeh, gabya gabya karathi*,—it is doubtful if he should get anything at all to eat from me, and he has the impudence to ask for milk.

सिरा *sira*,—see पाग *pāg*.

सिरुआ *sirua*,—soup.

सुरका चूरा *surka chūra*,—unripe paddy parched and pounded flat.

सुहारी *suhāri* (North-East Tirhut),—see पूरी *pūri*.

सूजी *sūji*,—the flour from the centre of the wheat grain.

सेव *seo* or (Shahabad) लकठो *laktho*,—a kind of coarse macaroni, differing from सेंवई *semwai* in not being regularly coiled.

सेंवई *semwai*,—a kind of macaroni, which differs from सेव *seo* in being regularly coiled.

सैंधा *saindha*,—see रिकौंच *rikaunch*.

सोहारी *sohāri*,—see पूरी *pūri*.

सोन *son*,—see बोर *bor*.

हलुआ *halua*, also (Shahabad) काँची *kānchi*,—a sweetmeat made of flour, dried fruits, and clarified butter. Musalmāns also add eggs. A superior variety of this is known as महन भोग *mahan bhog*.

हाबुस *hābus*,—green barley roasted as food.

होरहा *horha* (west), ओरहा *orha* (east generally), also होलहा *holha* (Patna and Gaya), बहुरी *bahuri* or परमल *parmal* Shahabad),—unripe grain, roasted in the ear or pod.

होलहा *holha*,—see होरहा *horha*.

DIVISION XII.

CEREMONIES AND SUPERSTITIONS OF RURAL LIFE.

CHAPTER I.—MARRIAGE.

1273. *Marriage* is amongst Hindus बियाह *biyāh*, local optional names being सुमङ्गली *shumangali* (properly the marriage service described in § 1328) in North-West Tirhut and Champāran, and बियाह दानी *biyāh dāni* in East Tirhut. बिबाह *bibāh* is common in North-East Tirhut, and बिहा *biha* in South Bhagalpur. Amongst Musalmāns it is सादी *sādi* or शादी *shādi*, निकाह *nikāh* being the less regular form. The marriage contract is अकद *akad* amongst Musalmāns.

1274. The *husband* is everywhere (amongst Hindus) बर *bar* (properly bridegroom), भतार *bhatār*, पीया *piya* or पी *pī* (only used in poetry), पती *pati* or सामी *sāmi*. Local forms are जँवाय *jañwāy* (properly son-in-law) (South-West Shahabad) and in East Tirhut सैंएँ *saiñeñ* amongst the lower classes and स्वामी *swāmi* or सवामी *sawāmi* amongst the higher classes. भतार *bhatār* is sometimes specially used to signify a woman's second husband. Musalmāns use the word शौहर *shauhar*. The following words are used by Hindus and Musalmāns indifferently: दुलहा *dulha* (properly bridegroom), पुरुख *purukh*, मरद *marad*, खसम *khasam*, अदमी *admi* or अदिमी *adimi** (also used in South Munger to mean wife), and खाविन्द *khāwind*. South of the Ganges occur अमदी *amdi* and मरदावा *mardāwa*. A wife calls her husband मरद *marad*, or in the localities mentioned above जँवाय *jañwāy* or मरदावा *mardāwa*. In South Bhagalpur she calls him साँइँ *sāñiñ*.

1275. A *wife* is मेहरारू *mehrāru*, इस्तिरी *istiri*, माउग *māūg* or मौगी *maugi*, बहू *bahu* or बह *bah*, (also, in Champāran, बौह *bauh*) (which means literally daughter-in-law), जन्नी *janni*, बेकत *bekat* (also used to mean husband), जनाना *janāna*, जोरू *joru*, and कबिला *kabila*, the last two

* Often spelt by purists आदमी *ādami*.

being principally used by Musalmāns. जौजी *jauji* (a corruption of *zauja*) is used only by Musalmāns and Kāyasths. When talking to a respectable man about his wife, the word सवारी *sawāri* or घर के लोग *ghar ke log* or a periphrasis is used. Thus they say in Shahabad अपने के सवारी ऐली हऽ *apne ke sawāri aili ha?* 'has your wife come?'; रवाँ घर के लोग कहवाँ बाड़ीं *rawāñ ghar ke log kahwāñ bāriñ?* 'where is your wife?'; or रवाँ हवेली में कब ऐली हऽ *rawāñ habeli meñ kab āili ha?* 'when did your wife come?' *lit.* 'when did the being in your honour's inner apartments come?'

1276. When there are two wives, each is साउत *sāüt* or सौतिन *sautin* to the other, a South Ganges variety being सोतिन *sotin*, and in South Munger सैतिन *saitin*. The first wife is बियाही *biyāhi*. In Patna and Gaya बिही *bihi*, and in Shahabad मेहरी *mehri* and कबिला *kabila*, are also used in the same sense. When there are two wives, the elder is called जेठरी *jethri*, जेठकी *jethki*, or बड़की *barki*, and the younger लहुरी *lahuri* or छोटकी *chhotki*.

1277. A woman whose husband is alive is north of the Ganges एहवाती *ehwāti*, and south of the Ganges she is अहिवाती *ahiwāti* or अहियाती *ahiyāti*. A local variety is ऐहब *aihab* in South-East Tirhut. सोहागिन *sohāgin* is another word used everywhere in the same sense. Another local word in South-East Tirhut is सधवा *sadhwa*. When a married woman is living in her father's house she is a नैहरैतिन *naihraitin*, or in South Bhagalpur सवासिन *sawāsin*, and when she is living with her husband's family she is ससुरैतिन *sasuraitin*.

1278. A *widower* is रण्डा *randa* or राँड़ा *rāñra*. If he marries a second time he is दोआह *doāh* or (in East Tirhut) दुतिबर *dutibar* or दुइबियाहा *duibiyāha*, and in South Bhagalpur दोबिहा *dobiha*. If he marries a third time he is तेआह *teāh* or (in East Tirhut) त्रितिबर *tritibar*, and South Bhagalpur तेबिहा *tebiha*. In such case he is also called दोआह *doāh*.

1279. A *widow* is बेवा *bewa* or राँड़ *rāñr*. Another term is बिधवा *bidhwa*. In South-East Tirhut बैधब *baidhab* is also used. The second marriage of a Hindu widow is सगाइ *sagāi*. Optional names are सगहम *sagaham*, सम्बन्ध *sambandh* or समध *samadh*, used chiefly north of the Ganges. To the south-east चुमावन *chumāwan* or चुमौना *chumauna* is also used in this sense. Such a woman is called to the west अरधी *ardhi*, and the second husband is सगहुआ *sagáhua* or सँगहुआ *sañghua*. In Western Shahabad he is साँघुत *sānghut*, and to the west generally

अरधुआ *ardhua* or भतार *bhatār*. A child brought forth by the widow previous to the ceremony is पछलगवा *pachhlagwa* or कठबेटा *kathbeta*, or in South Bhagalpur लहबेटा *lahbeta*. The second marriage of a Musalmān widow is अकद सानी *akad sāni* or निकाह *nikāh*.

1280. A *kept-woman*, who lives with a man without marriage, is रखेलिन *rakhelin*, रखेली *rakheli*, or रखनी *rakhni*. Other names are रण्डी *randi*, उढ़री *urharhi* or उढ़री *urhari*, and ढेमनी *dhemni*. सुरैतिन *suraitin* is used in South-West Shahabad.

1281. The *bridegroom* is दुलहा *dulha*, बर *bar*, नौसे *nause* or नौशे *naushe*. Also, south of the Ganges, गभरू *gabhru*. In East Tirhut the forms बिखिया *bikhiya* and बिखेया *bikheya* are current. The bride's people call the bridegroom लरिका *larika* or बेटवा *betwa*.

1282. The *bride* is दुलहिन *dulhin* or कनेयाँ *kaneān*, also in South Bhagalpur कन्याइन *kanyāin*. The bridegroom's people call her लरिकी *lariki*, लरकिनी *larkini*, or बेटिया *betiya*.

1283. The *dowry* is जहेज *jahej* or दहेज *dahej*. In South-East Tirhut it is जैतुक *jaituk*.

1284. The *marriage settlement* amongst Musalmāns is मोहर देन *mohar den* north, and दैन महर *dain mahar* south of the Ganges.

CHAPTER II.—WEDDING CEREMONIES GENERALLY.

1285. The *proposal* for a boy in marriage by the girl's relations or *vice versâ* is amongst Hindus बरतूई *bartūi* or बरदेखी *bardekhi*, or in Shahabad बरेखि *barekhi*. In South Munger it is sometimes पनबट्टी *panbatti*. In Patna it is occasionally बभन पुछ्छी *babhan puchchhi*. Amongst Musalmāns the name for a proposal is निसबत *nisbat*.

1286. The *match-maker*, who conducts the preliminary negotiations, is everywhere अगुआ *agua*. In North and East Tirhut he is also घटक *ghatak*. The barber and Brāhman, who are messengers, and sometimes negotiators, in the matter, are called collectively नौआ ब्राह्मन *naua brāhman*. The searching for a boy in marriage is north of the Ganges, to the west, लरिका खोज *larika khōj*, in South-Tirhut बरतुहारी *bartuhāri* or सुधाबधा करब *sudhābadha karab*, while in North-East Tirhut it is कथा करब *katha karab*. South of the Ganges it is बरतुहार *bartuhār*. Most of these words, however, include the preliminary negotiations, when a suitable boy has been found. If, during the negotiations, a member of the bride's house visits the bridegroom's, or *vice versâ*, the food given him to eat is called बरतूही के भात *bartūhi ke bhāt*. The first food given to him after the marriage under similar circumstances is भथखै *bhathkhai*.

1287. The *betrothal* consists in paying the तिलक *tilak* on the occasion of the formal proposal and acceptance of the proposal of marriage. This तिलक *tilak* is a present made to the bridegroom's people by the bride's people in the bridegroom's house. Some castes pay a portion of this in advance, as a sort of retaining-fee to secure the bridegroom; and when this is done, it is called फलदान *phaldān*, छेंका *chhenka*, or बर छेंका *bar chhenka*. In Sāran and Champāran it is also called बरछा *barachchha*, in South-East Tirhut पनचढ़ी *pancharhi*, and in South Bhagalpur पनटोही *pantohi*.

1288. The man who carries the छेका *chhenka* is the छेंकहरू *chenkáhru* north of the Ganges. South of the Ganges he is छेंकहरी *chhenkáhri*, or in South Munger महतों *mahton*.

1289. The *period of marriage ceremonies* dates from the presenting of the तिलक *tilak*, and is called लगन *lagan*, or in East Tirhut सुध *sudh*.

1290. The *marriage procession* is बरियात *bariyāt*. Sometimes the Hindī form बरात *barāt* is used. When it remains at the house of the bride a day after the wedding, the halt is called मरजाद *marjād*. When a bride's father is unable through poverty to defray the expenses of the marriage, and he sends her to the bridegroom's house for the performance of the ceremony, she is called कढुई *karhui*, कढुआ *karhua*, or डोल कढुई *dol karhui*. The marriage procession is the first formal visit of the bridegroom to the bride's house.

1291. The second visit, which consists in the ceremony of going to the bride and bringing her home to her husband's house for the consummation of the marriage, is गवना *gawna*, गवन *gawan*, or गौना *gauna*. In East Tirhut it is also दुरागमन *durāgaman*, and south of the Ganges दुरागौन *durāgaun*. Another name is रोकसती *roksati*, रोकसद्दी *roksaddi*, रोसकती *roskati*, or रोसकद्दी *roskaddi* (رخصتي). Yet another is बिदागी *bidāgi*.

1292. If the bridegroom pays an intermediate visit, it is called in South-East Tirhut दुरागनघन *durāgnaghan*. Immediately before the final visit to fetch the bride, a message is sent to the bride's house with some presents, to announce the approaching of the time for the visit. The presents are called नेश्रार *neār*, and the persons who carry them नेश्ररऽधरुश्रा *neardharua*. The persons who actually fetch the bride are लौटाहर *lautāhar*, नेवऽतहर *neotahar*, लेताहर *letāhar*, or लिश्रावन *liāwan*, or in South Bhagalpur लेयारी *leyāri*.

1293. The *newly-arrived bride* is called गौनहरी *gaunahri*. In East Tirhut she is also called बहुश्रासिन *bahuāsin*. The male members of her party are लोकनाहा *loknāha*, and the females लोकनी *lokni* or लोकनिया *lokaniya*.

1294. After consummation of marriage, *the first and second visits of the bride to her parents' house* are called रोकसती *roksati*, &c., as above. The second *visit of the bride to her husband's house* is दोंगा *donga*, and her third visit is तेंगा *tenga*. Her subsequent visits to her husband's or her parents' house are called रोकसती *roksati*, बिदागी *bidāgi*, बिदागरी *bidāgri*, श्रवन गवन *awan gawan*, श्रहुरा बहुरा *ahura bahura*, श्रहोर बहोर *ahor bahor*, श्रौरा बौरा *aura baura*, or श्राइल गेल *āil gail*.

1295. A *married girl in her father's house* is called by her people दई *dai*, धी *dhi*, बबुई *babuī*, or सुश्रासिन *suāsin*. When a wife is in her father's house, and her husband wishes her to return, he sends a messenger (generally a barber by caste) to summon her, who is called पेठवनिया *pethwaniya*.

1296. Their *father-in-law's houses* are called by bride and bridegroom respectively ससुरार *sasurār*. The educated also use the Hindi word ससुराल *sasurāl*. In East Tirhut it is called सासुर *sāsur*, and in Shahabad sometimes ससुरा *sasura*.*

1297. The *wife's parents' house* is called by her in Patna and South Munger नहिरा *nahira* or मैका *maika*, and in South Bhagalpur नेहरा *nehra*. Elsewhere she calls it नैहर *naihar*.

1298. The *husband's or wife's maternal grandmother's house* is called by him or her नानीहाल *nānīhāl*, ननिहाल *nanihāl*, ननिहार *nanihār*, ननिहर *nanihar*, or ननिश्रौरा *naniaura*. Other names are ममहर *mamhar*, and (in East Tirhut) मात्रिक *mātrik*.

1299. The *husband's or wife's paternal grandmother's house* is his or her दादीहाल *dādīhāl*, ददिहाल *dadihāl*, ददिहार *dadihār*, ददिहर

* A man in his father-in-law's house is always made much of, and fed well; hence in thieves' jargon a jail is called (let us hope sarcastically) ससुरार *sasurār*.

dadihar, or ददिऔरा *dadiaura*. Another name current in East Tirhut is पैत्रिक *paitrik*, while in South Bhagalpur they say बपन्हर *baphar*.

1300. Their *maternal uncle's houses* are his or her ममन्हर *mamhar* or ममुहर *mamuhar*. So also the *paternal uncle's house* is ससुरार *sasurār*.

1301. The *paternal grandfather's house* is (north of the Ganges) अजिऔरा *ajiaura*.

1302. The *father of the bride and the father of the bridegroom* call each other समन्धी *samdhi*. Their wives call each other समन्धिन *samdhin*.

CHAPTER III.—SPECIAL WEDDING CEREMONIES AMONGST THE HINDUS.

1303. Marriage ceremonies vary somewhat according to locality and caste. The following is mainly a description of such a wedding as might take place in the house of a well-to-do goāla in Patna, see § 1353. When the marriage has been agreed upon, the father of the bridegroom visits the father of the bride, and each provides a few handfuls of paddy (धान *dhān*). These are mixed together, and then divided between the two fathers by a Brāhman, and the bridegroom's father takes his share home. This ceremony is called धनन्बट्टी *dhanbatti*. This paddy is reserved to be parched in the *chūlha* which will be subsequently mentioned.

1304. Then the females of the bride's family perform the चुमावन *chumāwan* or चुमौना *chumauna* ceremony. In this five women take rice between the thumbs and forefingers of both hands and touch in order her feet, knees, and shoulders with it. They then put it on her head. To perform this ceremony is चुमाएब *chumāeb*.

1305. On the fifth or eighth day before the expected arrival of the wedding procession, the following preparations are made in the bride's house. If they take place five days previously, they are called पच-मँगन्रा *pachmangra*; if eight days, अठ-मँगन्रा *athmangra*.

1306. *The ceremony called* मटन्कोड़न्वा *matkorwa*.—The women of the family, and their friends, go singing to a well. They level a piece of ground near the well and smooth it down with लाल माटी *lāl māti*, a kind of yellow clay which is generally found immediately over gravel. They then dig a clod up out of it, and carry it home on the head of one of them. They make a fireplace, चूल्हा *chūlha*, of this mud in the centre of the court-yard or आँगन *āngan*. In South Bhagalpur they set up a plantain-tree and a bamboo in the courtyard, under which they place the mud.

1307. The day before the expected arrival of the marriage procession, the family sets up a bamboo shed in the court-yard over the fireplace. This shed is called मड़वा *marhwa*, मँड़वा *manrwa*, or माँड़ो *mānro*, also in South Munger मड़ही *marhi*, and in South Bhagalpur मण्डप *mandap*. The same day a potter brings an earthen pot, called कलसा *kalsa*, with a four-wicked lamp, called चौमुख *chaumukh*, on its top. This is placed in the house where the family god is placed for the purposes of the marriage. This house is called कोहबर *kohbar*. According to some the pot is placed at once in the मड़वा *marhwa*.

1308. A plough-shaft (हरिस *haris*), a plough-yoke (पालो *pālo*), and some bamboo twigs (करची *karchi*), are then buried in the ground in the centre of the मड़वा *marhwa*. Then five men bring out from the कोहबर *kohbar* the कलसा *kalsa*, and place it under the मड़वा *marhwa* in front of the bamboo twigs. The father of the bride then anoints the four posts of the मड़वा *marhwa* with घ्यू *ghyu* (clarified butter), and on each the mother applies some vermilion (सेनुर *senur*). The name of this ceremony is घ्यूढारी *ghyudhāri* or ढीढारी *dhīdhāri*. In South Bhagalpur it is घिढारी *ghidhāri*. At the same time worship is offered to the progenitors of the family, which is called मन्त्रीपूजा *mantri pūja*. Then five men take turmeric (हरदी *hardi*), oil (तेल *tel*), and *dub* grass (दूबी *dūbi*), which they scatter on the bride's forehead. This is called हरदी चढ़ाएब *hardi charhāeb*. Then women anoint her body with oil and turmeric. This is called उबटन *ubtan*, &c.; see § 1342.

1309. Next day, before the arrival of the procession, the paddy saved from the धनबट्टी *dhanbatti* is parched in the fireplace under the मड़वा *marhwa*. This is prepared for the ceremony of लावा छिटाइ *lāwa chhitāi* (see § 1332), at the time of the marriage circumambulation. The fireplace is then put to one side.

1310. Next follows the ceremony of *swallowing the mango fibre*. This is called इमली घोँटाइ *imli ghontāi*. In South Bhagalpur a similar ceremony is called अमलो घोटन *amlo ghotan*. An elder male of the mother's family (usually her brother) puts into her left hand a present of money or ornaments. The barber's wife then gives him the centre fibre of one of the mango leaves hanging up in the मड़वा *marhwa*, which he presents to the mother's mouth. The mother then bites a small piece off this and deposits it in the hollow of her own right hand, into which the elder male pours a little water. The piece of fibre is called खरिका *kharika*, तिनका *tinka*—, or दन्ती *danti*. This the mother holds over her daughter's head and gulps (घोंटब *ghontab*, to gulp) it all down. The elder male then says to her, "Art thou cool (*i.e.*, pleased)? (जुड़ैलू *jurailu*)," to which she replies "I am cool (जुड़ैलौं *jurailū̃*)."

1311. Wedding wreaths of mango leaves, flowers, &c., are hung over the door, and about the मड़वा *marhwa*. These are, north of the Ganges, बन्दनेवार *bandnewār* or बनवार *banwār*. South of the Ganges they are बन्दनवार *bandanwār*, and in South Munger घेरा *ghera*. In South Bhagalpur mango branches are hung about the house, and are called पल्लो *pallo*.

1312. In the bridegroom's house, before the marriage procession starts for the marriage ceremony, very similar ceremonies are gone through; the मटकोड़वा *matkorwa* is performed. A चूल्हा *chūlha* is made in the court-yard. The plough-shaft, yoke, and bamboo twigs are buried, and the earthen pot with lights is set up. Only no मड़वा *marhwa* is built. The ceremonies of चुमौना *chumauna* and हरदी चढ़ाएब *hardi charhāeb* are performed on him, as is done to the bride.

1313. The paddy reserved from the धनबट्टी *dhanbatti* is parched in the चूल्हा *chūlha*. This parched grain is taken with the wedding procession, and mixed with that parched in the bride's house, and with it scattered at the circumambulation (§ 1332).

1314. They then cover him with cosmetic (उबटन *ubtan*, &c., see § 1342), and his nails are cut by a barber's wife, he sitting in front of his mother, and his mother wearing the *maur* (see § 1326). This, as in the bride's case, is called नहछू *nahchhu* (see § 1326). The ceremony of इमली घोंटाइ *imli ghontāi* is also observed (see § 1310).

1315. He is then bathed and anointed, and sets out with the marriage procession. A little of the water in which he was bathed is brought with him. This is called सिनेह के पानि *sineh ke pāni*. He is not allowed to bathe again until the चौथारी *chauthāri* (see § 1340). When the marriage party arrives at the bride's house, this water is given to her mother, and at the time of the girl's नहछू *nahchhu*, the barber's wife will mix it with other water, and bathe the bride with it immediately before cutting her nails.

1316. *The first scattering of rice.*—When the bridegroom arrives at the door of the bride's house, the women of her family receive him, and scatter over him uncooked rice, the dung of a heifer, balls of cooked rice, and other articles. A married woman of the family then takes a brass pan (छीपी *chhīpi* or थारी *thāri*) and a small lamp (दीया *dīya*) and gives them to the bridegroom; and then, holding two corners of her mantle (चुनरी *chunri*), touches with them the pan, then the boy's forehead, and then her own. This is called परिछावन *parichhāwan*, परिछन *parichhan*, परछावन *parchhāwan*, परछन *parchhan*, or परछौनी *parchhauni*. A similar ceremony is called in South Bhagalpur गलसेदी *galsedi*.

1317. *The ceremony of the pestle.*—The girl's mother then rubs in the palm of her hand a curry pestle (लोढ़ा *lorha*), which she applies to the cheeks of the bridegroom. This is called गाल सेंकी *gāl senki*. This custom is not known in South Bhagalpur. Instead there is performed a ceremony called धूआ *dhūa*. A man disguises himself as a woman and approaches the wedding party with a jar of water. He says he is a woman of Kāmrūp (Assam) come to give away the bride. He then sprinkles water on the bridegroom. (Compare § 1320.)

1318. *The marking of the bridegroom's forehead* with sandal paste before marriage is तिलक *tilak* or तिल्लक *tillak*. In South Bhagalpur it is चन्दन *chandan*. This is done by a man called in the west तिलकहरू *tilkahru*, and in the east तिलकदेउआ *tilakdeua* or तिलिकिया *tilikiya*. He is generally the bride's father. This *tilak* is quite distinct from the *tilak* paid at the time of proposal of marriage.

1319. These ceremonies at the door are called collectively दुआर पूजा *duār pūja*. In South Bhagalpur they are known as दुआर लगाइ *duār lagāi*. Those described above are those performed by goālas in Patna. Other castes have other customs,—the higher ones contenting themselves with giving presents to the bridegroom and scattering rice (अच्छत *achchhat*) over him.

1320. The wedding procession then proceeds to put up in a place set apart for them. This is called जनवाँसा *janwānsa* or (in North-East Tirhut) बैठकी *baithki* or बासघर *bāsghar*, and in South Bhagalpur जनमासा *janmāsa*. A male member of the bride's family (generally her sister's husband) then brings to the जनवाँसा *janwānsa* a bowl of sweet drink or *sharbat*, called धूआ *dhūa*, and covered with a red cloth. He also brings some *urid* (*dolichos pilosus*) flour mixed up with finely-powdered pepper. This is called बुकुआ *bukua*. On his arrival at the जनवाँसा *janwañsa* he scatters this in the air, causing the bridegroom's party to sneeze. He then gives all those present to drink of the *sharbat*. The whole ceremony is called बकुआ उड़ाइ *bukua urāi*. A similar ceremony is called, north of the Ganges, धुरच्छक *dhurchhak*, in which water is sent in pitchers, and a little scattered over the party with mango sprays.

1321. The barber now comes for the bridegroom's मौर *maur* or head-dress, as will be subsequently described, which he takes away to the bride's house.

1322. When all is ready the friends of the bridegroom leave the जनवाँसा *janwānsa* with great pomp, carrying with them the presents for the bride. Amongst these is a valuable cloth, called कनेआइ *kaneāi*, or in South Bhagalpur बिहौती *bihauti*, which is taken to the female apartments, and in which she is dressed. She is then brought out and made to sit in the मड़वा *marhwa*. This visit is called निरिच्छन *nirichchhan*, निरच्छन *nirachchhan*, or निरछन *nirchhan*, as the bridegroom's party see (निरेखब *nirekhab*, to see) the bride now for the first time.

1323. Then the ceremony of *making the bracelet* is performed. The bridegroom and seven other men husk paddy in a mortar. When husked, two or three grains are wrapped up in mango leaves to form a kind of bracelet. Two of these bracelets are made, and one is tied on to the bridegroom's right wrist, and the other on the bride's left wrist, by a Brāhman. These bracelets are called कङ्गन *kangan* or कङ्कन *kankan*. The ceremony is called अठोंगर *athongar*, अठौंगर *athaungar*, or (in Patna) लठौंगर *lathaungar*.

1324. Then follows the *adoration of the bride*. In this ceremony the elder brother of the bridegroom (or in default of him some elder of the bridegroom's family) offers sweetmeats, molasses (गूर *gūr*), and ornaments to the bride. He then takes some betel-leaf and tyre (दही *dahi*) in his right hand, and presses it against the bride's forehead, at the same time pressing his left hand against the back of her head.

1325. These two ceremonies are together called बन्दन *bandan*, गुरहत्थी *gurhatthi*, or गुरहत्थन *gurhatthan*, and signify that he has touched her once for all, and that if he touch her again he will be guilty of a sin. In South Bhagalpur they are performed by the bride's sister, and both bride and bridegroom are adored. There the ceremonies are called गुरौंधा *guraundha*.

1326. Then the bride's mother sits in the मड़वा *marhwa* with the bride between her knees, holding her round the waist. The ceremony that follows is the ***cutting of the nails***. This is called नहछू *nahchhu*, नहछुआ *nahchhua*, नहछुआ नहावन *nahchhua nahāwan*, नहकटिया *nahkatiya*, or (in Shahabad) नहटुङ्गी *nahtungi*. In South Munger it is नछुनाए *nachhunāē*, and in South Bhagalpur लौछुआ *lauchhua*. The bride's mother has previously sent (§ 1321) a barber (हजाम *hajām*) to the जनवाँसा *janwañsa* to ask for the head-dresses. There are two head-dresses,—one worn by the bridegroom, which is made of talipot-leaves and is called मौर *maur;* the other is worn by the bride, and is called मौरी *mauri*, or (south of the Ganges) पटवासी *patwāsi*, or पटमौरी *patmauri*. The bride's head-dress is made of date-leaves. The barber brings these two to the bride's house and puts the मौर *maur* on the mother's head and the मौरी *mauri* on the bride's head. Then the barber's wife (हजामिन *hajāmin*) cuts the finger and toe-nails of both the bride and her mother (the bridegroom's having been cut before he left home).

1327. The bridegroom's party then returns to the जनवाँसा *janwānsa*, and the bride goes inside the house and exchanges her कनेआइ *kaneāï* for her wedding dress or पिआरी *piāri* (see § 1348). The bridegroom is then sent for and is seated under the मड़वा *marhwa*, and the father or elder male relation brings the bride and seats her beside the bridegroom under the मड़वा *marhua*, to his left. Some one belonging to the bride's family then goes inside and gets the bridegroom's *maur* from the bride's mother, and brings it out, and it is put on the bridegroom's head.

1328. Then the ***marriage service*** is read by the Brāhman. This is called शुमङ्गली *shumangali* or सुमङ्गली *sumangali*. The bridegroom sits under the मड़वा *marhwa* in front of the bride. The father of the bride sits kneeling on one knee, keeping the bride sitting on his other thigh. This is the ceremouy of giving the girl in marriage, and is called कनेआँ दान *kaneāñ dān* or जाँघा (जाँघ or जँघिया) बैसाएब *jāngha* (*jāngh* or *janghiya*) *baisāëb*.

1329. It is not necessary to describe particularly the procedure carried out by the officiating Brāhman. He recites (or is supposed to recite) verses from the Vedas, and leads in various acts of worship, such as throwing incense on the fire, throwing rice (अच्छत *achchhat*) about, worshipping Gauri, and the like. At one period the Brāhman puts into the bride's father's hand a shell containing water, flower, *achchhat*, and metal, and makes him empty it round the base of the earthen pot कलसा *kalsa* on the top of which the lamp with four lights (called

चौमुख *chaumukh*) is burning. He makes him do this five or seven times. This completes the ceremony of कनेआँ दान *kaneāñ dān*.

1330. From the time of the arrival of the बरियात *bariyāt* up to the completion of the कनेआँ दान *kaneāñ dān*, the father and mother of the bride can eat nothing.

1331. Next follows the *knotting together of the clothes of the bride and bridegroom*. This is गँठ बन्धन *genth bandhan* generally. South of the Ganges it is sometimes known as गँठ जोड़ *geñth jor* or गँठजोड़न *gethjoran*, and in South Bhagalpur as जनम गँठ *janam genth*. At the same time something of small value, such as a two-āna piece or a few pice, or sometimes a piece of betel-nut, is tied in the bride's waist-band and in her breast-cloth by the Brāhman. Sometimes an ornament is tied to the bride's sheet, which is called अँचरी पालो (or पल्लो) *añchri pālo* (or *pallo*).

1332. The *circumambulation of the sacrificial fire.*—This is sometimes done by both bride and bridegroom, sometimes, *e.g.* in North-West Tirhut, by the bridegroom alone. They or he carry a winnowing sieve. The bride holds it in her hands in front of her, and the bridegroom follows her with an arm passing round her on each side, also supporting the sieve. Her brother fills the sieve as they go along with parched grain prepared in the fireplace formerly under the मड़वा *marhwa*, which the bridegroom at the same time scatters by shaking the sieve with his hands (this is called लावा छिटाइ *lāwa chhitāi* or, in Shahabad, लावा मिराइब *lāwa mirāib*). Care is taken to keep the sacrificial fire (when there is one) or the altar to the right.* It is considered unlucky for the girl to pass it to her left. This ceremony is called भाँवर *bhāñwar*, भँवरी *bhañwri*, भौँरी *bhauñri*, or सत भौँरी *sat bhauñri*. It is also called बेदि घुमाएब *bedi ghumāeb*. This circumambulation is performed five times, and is the important part of the ceremony. The couple on its conclusion are *fumigated with incense* by the officiating Brāhman. This is called आरत *ārat*, आरती *ārti*, अगती *agti*, or अगियासी *agiyāsi*. In South Bhagalpur it is called होम *hom*.

1333. When this is done, the bride's sisters and her brothers' wives amuse themselves by pushing the bridegroom about, and lifting him up by the ears. This last is supposed to be done five times, but

* The reverse rule is observed by some castes when the horoscope makes out that it is necessary.

is rarely done more than once. It will be seen that this is only done by females. Amongst the Tirhutiya Brāhmans and Kāyasths, however, it is done by the bride's brother. The ceremony is called बरक बैसाएब उठाएब *barak baisāëb uthāëb.*

1334. This is followed by the *application of vermilion.* In this the bridegroom takes a small cup containing vermilion in one hand, and applies vermilion to the parting of the bride's hair with a piece of hemp. This is called सेनुर दान *senur dān* or सिन्दुर दान *sindur dān.*

1335. *The stopping at the door.*—The couple then leave the court-yard and go into the house where the family deity is put. This house is called कोहबर *kohbar*, or in South Bhagalpur कोहबरा *kohbara.* At the door they are stopped by the sister of the bride, who requires the bridegroom to repeat certain verses, called दुरौंध *duraundh* or दुरौंधा *duraundha.* The bridegroom demands a present for doing so, and on this being given he repeats the verses. This ceremony is called दुआर छेंकाइ *duār chheñkāï* or दुआर छेंकौनी *duār chheñkauni.*

1336. *The stealing of the shoes.*—The bridegroom takes off his shoes before entering the house. If he is silent or is too nervous to speak much, the bride's sister may, as a joke, steal his shoes while he is inside, and conceal them somewhere, in order to compel him on his reappearance to speak, and say "where are my shoes?" This ceremony is called जूता चोराइ *jūta chorāï.* In South Bhagalpur they make the bridegroom bow to a pair of shoes covered with cloth, and the ceremony is called जूता गोर लगाइ *jūta gor lagāï.*

1337. The couple then kneel facing the north-east, and perform the *worship of the tutelary deity of the family,* offerings being made to him at the same time. This is called गोर लगाएब *gor lagāëb.* The clothes of the bride and bridegroom are then untied, the promised presents given to the sister of the bridegroom, and the marriage is concluded, the bridegroom returning to the जनवाँसा *janwāñsa*, and the bride remaining in the house.

1338. Shortly after the marriage, though this sometimes takes place the morning after, the bridegroom goes to his mother-in-law, who feeds him with rice-milk. After eating a little he sometimes takes the rest, dish and all, to the जनवाँसा *janwāñsa*, and finishes it there, or sometimes leaves it unfinished. This is called खीर खियाव *khīr khiyāo* or बियाही भात *biyāhi bhāt*, or (in East Tirhut) मडुअक *mahuak.*

1339. If the bride's people invite the bridegroom's people to stay over the night, it is called मरजाद राखब *marjād rākhab.* This may last for two or three days or more. On the expiry of the period of मरज्जाद *marjād*, the bride's people see the bridegroom's party off. This is called रोसकति करि देब *roskati kari dēb*, &c., as in § 1291. In South Bhagalpur it is also called लोटली *lotli*. It is managed as follows: The bride's family collects in the court-yard all the presents received from the bridegroom's party, and with the assistance of village friends assesses their value. All this time the bridegroom's party is away in the जनवाँसा *janwāṅsa*. When the value has been assessed, the bride's father collects on his side presents to the value of at least one-fourth greater value than those received, and takes them to the जनवाँसा *janwāṅsa*. These return presents constitute the dowry, and are called the दहेज *dahej*. The bride's father lays them before the bridegroom's. Then the bridegroom's father takes a new cloth (चद्दर *chaddar*) and puts it on the bride's father. The bride's father in return presents the bridegroom's father with a purse of money of the value of the *chaddar*. Then both *salām* to each other. Then the bride's father, in token of allowing the other to depart, presents him with a sum of money varying according to means, and a *lota* of water, saying "राम राम *rām rām*," to which the other replies in the same words. This ceremony is called रमरम्मी *ramrammi*, मीलन *mīlan*, मिलनी *milni*, or समधी मिलावा *samdhī milāwa*. The two fathers are now, by relation, समधी *samdhi* to each other, and in token thereof they exchange cloaks and garlands. These exchanged cloaks and garlands are called समधो *samdho*. Amongst lower castes, as the procession is about to start, the bride's father gives each member money sufficient for the way expenses and drink, called बटसारी *batsāri*, and in South Bhagalpur पाथक *pāthak*. Then the procession, bridegroom and all, goes off.

1340. *The untying of the bracelets.*—Four days after the marriage the bride and bridegroom bathe, and the bracelets on their two wrists are taken off. This ceremony is called चौथारी or चौठारी *chauthāri* or चतुरथी *chaturthi*. This is the first washing the bridegroom and bride get from the time of the arrival of the procession before the marriage. During the interval they have been anointed with cosmetics, उबटन *ubtan*, &c. ; see § 1342. Usually this is done in their respective houses, but in Patna the bridegroom sometimes goes to the bride's house to perform the ceremony. This concludes the marriage proceedings.

1341. *Miscellaneous.*—The *wedding breakfast* is (north of the Ganges) कलौ *kalau* or मझनी *majhni*. South of the Ganges, in Shahabad it is पङ्घत *panghat*, and elsewhere गोरौधा *goraudha* or गुरौधा *guraudha*.

The feast at the houses of both parties the day before the marriage procession is भतवान *bhatwān*, भतवानी *bhatwāni*, or भोज *bhoj*. Before eating the guests wash their feet, and the ceremony is called पर पखारी *pair pakhāri*, पैर पखरुआ *pair pakharua*, पाँव पखारी *pāñw pakhāri*, गोड़ धोइ *gor dhōï*, or गोड़धोआइ *gordhoāï*.

1342. The *cosmetic* of turmeric, meal, oil, &c., rubbed on the bride and bridegroom for about ten days before marriage, is north of the Ganges अबटन *abtan*, and in East Tirhut उगटन *ugtan*, कसार *kasār*, or कासा *kāsa*. South of the Ganges we find उबटन *ubtan* or (in Patna) ओबटन *obtan* very generally used; also आँवट *āñwat* and अपटन *aptan* in Shahabad, उकटन *uktan* in South Munger, and कासा *kāsa*, कसारा *kasāra*, or उटकन *utkan* in South Bhagalpur.

1343. The *horoscopes* of the boy and girl are everywhere जनम पतर *janam patr* or जनम पतरी *janam patri*. Also, very generally, टीपन *tīpan*. In West Shahabad they are also कुण्डली *kundli*. If they agree, the phrase गनना बनब *ganna banab*, or जोग मिलब *jog milab*, or रास बरग बैस गेल *rās barag bais gel*, is used. To calculate the horoscope is गिनब *ginab*, or जोग मिलाएब *jog milāëb*, or दिन गुन्नी करब *din gunni karab*, or बभन पुच्छी *babhan puchchhi*.

1344. When the auspicious day for the marriage has been fixed, an *announcing letter* is sent to the bridegroom's father. This is known as the लगन पत्री *lagan patri*, or simply as the चिट्ठी *chitthi*. The *formal invitation* to the wedding is नेँवता *neñwta* or नेवता *neota*, or (in East Tirhut) नवत *nawat*.

1345. *The feast given to the brotherhood at the wedding* is known as भइआरा *bhaïāra*, भइआरी *bhaïāri*, भइआरे *bhaïāre*, भइचारो *bhaïchāro* (Shahabad), जेवनार *jeonār*, or भोज *bhoj*.

1346. In North-East Tirhut, amongst certain castes, especially the *Bikaua* (बिकौआ) Brahmans, *caste money* is paid as follows. If the bride's father is of lower caste than the bridegroom's father, the latter pays the former a sum in compensation called कनेआँ दान *kaneāñ dān*. In South Bhagalpur this is called मैन *main*. If the bridegroom's father is of lower caste, he pays the bride's father a sum of money called बिकरी *bikri*.

1347. The *presents* given are as follows:—सनेस *sanes*, डाला *dāla*, or डाल दौरा *dāl daura*, are the presents sent by the bridegroom before the arrival of the procession. दहेज *dahej*, as already explained, is the dowry paid by the bride's father. Before the bridegroom leaves after the wedding, he goes to bid his mother-in-law good-bye. She and the other women give him presents, which are called सलामी *salāmi*. Other similar presents are in South Munger पूरन *pūran*, and in South Bhagalpur चौंक *chaunk*. निछावर *nichhāwar*, निछाउर *nichhāür*, or नेवन्छावर *neochhāwar*, are presents made to the barber and his wife. गैदान *gaidān* or गौदान *gaudān* is the present of a cow made by the girl's father to the family priest (परोहित *parohit*, or (in East Tirhut) पुरोहित *purohit* or अचार्ज *achārj*). गुरहत्थी *gurhatthi* has already been mentioned as the ceremony of giving presents to the bride by the bridegroom's elder brother (§ 1325). मोंहदेखाइ *mohdekhāi*, मुदेखौनी *mudekhauni*, or मुदेखी *mudekhi*, are the presents given to the bride by her mother-in-law or other female relatives of the bridegroom on her first coming to her husband's house.

1348. The पिअरी *piāri*, पीरी *pīri*, or (in South Bhagalpur) कनिऐती *kaniaiti*, is the bride's yellow dress, and कन्हावर *kanhāwar* or कँधावर *kandhāwar* is a red loin-cloth laid upon the bridegrom's shoulder during the ceremony.

1349. *Bringing the bride home.*—This is गौना *gauna*, &c., *vide* § 1291. The procedure is as follows :—When the bride is old enough to live with her husband, an auspicious day is fixed. Some days before the date, the bridegroom's family send a present of sweetmeats, called गौना के नेआरा *gauna ke neāra*. On the evening of the appointed day the bridegroom and his party arrive, and after feasting go off with the bride at dawn next day. The day before, a plough-shaft (हरिस *haris*), but no yoke or bamboo twigs, has been buried in the court-yards of each of the respective families. Before the bride and bridegroom start, their nails are cut. This is called नह छछाइ *nah chhachhāi* or नोह छिलाइ *noh chhilāi*. With the party the bride's people send one or more gaily-decorated earthen vessels full of sweetmeats, called कुण्डा *kunda* or महर *mahar*.

1350. When the party arrives at the bridegroom's house, the bride passes from the litter to the door, putting her feet into a basket at each step. This is called दौरा में गोर डारब *daura meñ gor dārab* or घर पैसारी *ghar paisāri*.

1351. On entering the dwelling the couple go into the house where the family god is, and worship him. This is called गोर लगाएब *gor lagāēb*.

1352. As they go into the house, another ceremony, called दुआर छेंकाइ *duār chhenkāi*, is performed. In this the bridegroom's sister demands a present, and when it is given or promised she allows them to pass.

1353. *On certain ceremonies performed by Soti Brahmans of East Tirhut.*—Different castes and different localities have various marriage customs, but the one just described may fairly be taken as a standard Hindu marriage ceremony. It describes a marriage such as would take place in a well-to-do goāla's house in the district of Patna.

1354. The Soti Brāhmans of East Tirhut have several curious marriage customs which have existed for many hundred years, some of which will now be noted. The greatest care is kept in keeping up correct genealogies of members of this clan. The genealogical registers are called पाँजी *pānji*, and they are kept up by hereditary genealogists called पँजियार *panjiyār*. Once a year or oftener there are great meetings of these Brāhmans at Saurāth, near Madhubani, and other places, where the *panjiyārs* assemble and write up the registers. They also arrange marriages after consulting their registers, and give certificates to the parents certifying that the marriage is lawful, and that the parties are not within prohibited degrees of affinity. These certificates are called अधिकार माला *adhikār māla* or असुजन पत्र *asujan patr*. The settlement of the conditions of marriage is called सिधांत *sidhānt*.

1355. When the bride is of equal or higher caste than the bridegroom, the parties meet in a distant place away from both their homes, and the conditions are proclaimed by the *panjiyārs* present. If, however, the bride is of lower caste, the following procedure is adopted:—

The bride and her family leave their house and going a little distance off erect a मड़वा *marhwa* for the marriage ceremony. On the day appointed for the wedding, the bridegroom starts from his home with his servants under the pretence that he is going out hunting. None of his relations accompany him, and although they, of course, really know for what he is starting, they pretend to be ignorant. When he arrives within a little distance of the मड़वा *marhwa*, he stops, and then the *sidhānt* is proclaimed. By this time the marriage preparations are ready, and the bride's brother comes to him and conducts him to the appointed place. On his arrival at the door the bride's female relatives, each being called for this purpose a बिधकरी *bidhkari*, catch hold of his nose with one hand, and with the other hold a sheet tied round his neck. In this condition they bring him into the मड़वा *marhwa*, and there the marriage is performed.

1356. After a time the bridegroom's friends pretend that he has been lost in his hunting expedition, and send a man called the स्रौत्र *srautra* to look for him. He returns shortly afterwards, and informs them that the bridegroom has married so and so, whereupon they all fall to and abuse him. After abusing him they change their minds and reward him.

1357. At the marriage a barber ties some paddy in a knot in the bridegroom's waist-cloth (धोती *dhoti*). This is called जनम गँठि *janam genthi.* This is not untied until the fourth day after marriage, which is by this sect called the चतुरन्थी *chaturthi.*

1358. Another ceremony is the दसौत *dasaut.* In this a professional dancer (नटुआ *natua*) comes up to the bridegroom and offers him sham sweetmeats (लड्डू *laddu*), in return for which he receives presents. After this the bride and bridegroom go into the कोहबर *kohbar* to worship the family god. On the way the bride's female relations set up shops of paltry articles, which the bridegroom is obliged to buy.

1359. Another ceremony is घसकट्टी *ghaskatti.* In this the bridegroom cuts some grass for his father-in-law, and in return the latter promises to give him a horse.

CHAPTER IV.—MARRIAGE CEREMONIES AMONGST THE MUSALMĀNS.

1360. The writer is indebted to Kāzi Sayyad Raza Husain of Patna City for the following facts :—

1361. Amongst Musalmāns there are two kinds of marriage ceremonies,—शरई (شرعي) *sharaī* and उरफी (عرفي) *urfi,* or religious and ceremonial. The more strict and educated members of the community follow the former, and the common people the latter.

1362. शरई (شرعي) *sharaī* marriages are entirely free from ceremonies of any kind. After the betrothal the marriage is performed in strict conformity with the sacred law. The amount of dowry (महर (مهر) *mahar*) is not fixed, but depends on the pecuniary circumstances of the parties. Immediately after the marriage, the wife goes to her husband and is settled for life.

1363. उरफी (عرفي) *urfi* marriages are not so frequent as they used to be. The spread of education and railways has tended to make people stricter in their religious duties, but, specially amongst the lower orders, the following ceremonies are still in vogue. In these marriages the dowry (मह्र (مهر) *mahar*) is always fixed. In the cities it is fixed at one *lākh* of rupees, and in the villages at forty-one thousand rupees and one *dīnār*. This is the amount of dowry promised by even the poorest people. It is needless to say that it is never given.

1364. *Arranging the preliminaries,* निसबत (نسبت) *nisbat.*—The parents first make themselves acquainted with one another's pecuniary circumstances, and the negotiations are carried on through a female match-maker (मुशाता (مشاطه) *mushāta*). When the preliminaries are settled, a letter of ceremony is sent by the guardian of the boy to the girl's family. This letter is written on red paper, or on white paper sprinkled with red. The carrier of the letter, on arrival at the girl's house, is given *sharbat* to drink, and detained for a day or two. The reply is written on similar paper and returned by him, and this correspondence settles the marriage question. From this time marriage presents are exchanged between the parties, the boy's guardian making the first present. If at this time any women come from the house of the bridegroom on a visit to the bride's house, the bride will not show her face to them.

1365. In some places, before the marriage is decided on the girl's guardians first see the boy. This may be done in two ways: either the girl's people send for the boy to their house, and serve him with betel-leaf, and give him rupees or gold *mohars*, or else the guardian of the bride sends some relative to the boy's house. There, on his arrival, he is given *sharbat* to drink, and the first thing given him to eat is sweetened rice (मीठा चाउर *mītha chāūr*). This relative reports concerning the boy to the girl's guardians.

1366. *Betrothal.*—This is मँगनी (منگنی) *mangni.* In this the boy's guardian, after consulting with the other party to the contract, fixes a date, on which he sends presents with considerable ceremony. Large coloured earthen pots are filled with sweetmeats and fruits, and sent with a large party. In some places a suit of clothes is also sent. The pots are carried on the heads of maid-servants, who sing songs when they start and when they approach the bride's house. As soon as they arrive they are given *sharbat* to drink, and while they drink the bride's people sing abusive and obscene songs to them. The persons that supply them with *sharbat* receive a small present. The maid-servants are also given sweetened rice to eat in a dish covered with silver leaves and pieces of fruit. Sometimes they are given sweetmeats to eat first and then dishes prepared with salt. They are detained for at least one day. When they leave the bride's house on their return journey, they are given presents in money and sometimes suits of clothes. They are also given a plain ring (छल्ला *chhalla*), a red handkerchief, and some sweetmeats as presents for the bridegroom.

1367. *The letter of promise* वादा का रुक्का (وعدہ کا رقعہ) *wāda ka rukka.*—When the time of marriage approaches, the parties, either orally or in writing, fix a date for it. Afterwards a customary letter of promise is sent, written on red paper and sprinkled over with pieces of gold or silver leaf. The letter is to the effect that such and such a day has been fixed, and that the writer hopes that it will meet with approval. Amongst poor families, the letter is sent in a bag of red cloth or velvet, together with two betel-nuts, some green grass, one or two pieces of turmeric, and a little rice. Amongst rich families, the letter is sent in a silver or golden box. The box is placed inside an embroidered bag together with the betel-nuts, &c. The whole is sent on a silver plate. The letter is always carried by a barber, who is given a handsome present, consisting of cash, clothes, and utensils by the girl's guardian. The guardian sends a reply either through the same man or through a messenger of his own. A tailor is then sent by the girl's guardian to take the measure of the boy's dress. He also gets a present from the boy's people, on going away. The marriage must take place not more than two months after this correspondence.

1368. *The going into retirement of the bride and bridegroom* मायूँ (مايون) *māyūn* or माँझा (مانجها) *mānjha.*—After the interchange of letters, the bride and bridegroom sit in *mānjha.*—The girl puts on a sheet dyed with safflower, and the women of the neighbourhood and her female relations assemble, and rub her with cosmetics (उबटन *ubtan*), singing songs as they do so. From that day the girl sits in a room, and never leaves it except for necessary purposes. She does not see the face of any man,—not even of her father or her brother. She eats only milk and fruits, and every day the barber's wife comes and applies cosmetic to her. In the meantime the boy is undergoing the same treatment. He wears similar dyed garments, is surrounded by females, and cosmetic is rubbed on his body every day. In South Munger he does not thus go into retirement.

1369. *The ceremony of the grindstone*—चक्की *chakki*—and the washing of the pulse—दाल शोई (دال شوئی) *dāl shoï* or दाल धोई *dāl dhoï*.

Two or three weeks before the marriage a grindstone is put in one of the rooms of the female apartments of both the houses, which has been previously well cleaned. The following day a number of women assemble and singing, accompany the maid-servants who carry some *mūng* (*phaseolus mungo*) to a well or river. Arrived there, they joke and sprinkle water on each other, while washing the grain. They then bring it back in the same way. It is dried in the sun, and ground into flour on the grindstone by seven women whose husbands are alive (सोहागिनि *sohāgini*). It is then made into a dish called बरी *bari* for the ceremony of कँदूरी (کندوری) *kandūri* (see § 1377).

1370. *The cutting of the clothes.*—This is called किता पारचा (قطع پارچہ) *kita pārcha*, and takes place in the bridegroom's house. Men and women are invited, songs are sung, and the tailor cuts out the marriage dress of the bride. When it is cut, all the men present congratulate the boy's guardian, and give the tailor a small present.

1371. A similar ceremony takes place in the bride's house on the day of the marriage procession. There the bridegroom's wedding garment is prepared, and when it is being despatched to him the male friends of the family assemble under a canopy in the female quarters. A few stitches purposely left unfinished in the bridegroom's drawers are then completed by the tailor, who gets some small fees from those present. This ceremony is called साज (or, in South Munger, जामा) बेओताब (ساز بیوتاب) *sāj* (or *jāma*) *beotab*.

1372. *The vigil*—रतजग्गा *ratjagga.*—This ceremony takes place in the houses of both parties. A spot in the house is washed, and a small wooden stool is placed therein. A new water-pot is placed on it, and is covered over with a new earthen cover. A red handkerchief is then tied on it. A garland of flowers is then placed round the neck of the pot, sweetmeats are cooked, and hymns sung entreating God to bless the bride and bridegroom. The women sit up the whole night near the water-pot, thereby intending to keep God awake. At dawn the sweetmeats and रिहम (رحم) *riham** and *sharbat* are offered to God. They are then distributed among the people.

1373. *The erection of the canopy*—सायाबन्दी (سایہ بندی) *sāyā-bandi* or मँड़वा *mañrhwa.*—This takes place the day after the last ceremony. A canopy with four bamboo poles is erected in the female quarters. First, brown sugar is offered to the saint named *Shakarganj*, and then garlands are tied to each pole of the canopy. When the ropes of the canopy are being tied, the sister of the bride or bridegroom,

* Rice-flour mixed with clarified butter, sugar, and milk, and made into balls.

or any near female relation of the father of either, comes in and stops the work. The persons employed are not allowed to proceed till they have promised to pay her a sum of money. When the canopy has been safely erected, a paste of sandal powder is rubbed on the faces of those present. In some places, after the erection of the canopy, a goat or a cow is sacrificed in memory of the saint Shaikh Abdul Qādir Jilāni, (شيخ عبدالقادر جلاني). The flesh of the animal sacrificed is cooked on the spot where it was killed, with rice and gram, in new earthen pots. When cooked, it is offered in the name of the saint, and then eaten.

1374. The same night another ceremony takes place. A potter is ordered to make a small water-pot. This is coloured and painted with figures of horses and elephants. It is called कलसा *kalsa.* It is placed in the courtyard and covered with an earthen cover, on which ears of rice and mango leaves are put. A four-wicked lamp (चौमुख *chaumukh*) is kept burning on it every night. This pot is neither opened nor removed till the marriage ceremony is over. When it is first deposited, the women sing a song over it, the purport of which is, "We have shut up storm, rain, serpents, scorpions, and worms herein."

1375. On the same night another ceremony, called चिहल तन (چهل تن) *chihal tan* (forty persons), takes place. A number of beggars who play the drum and fiddle are invited, and towards the end of the night a pit, four or five feet wide and two or three feet deep, is dug under the canopy. In this pit large billets of wood are burnt, while the beggars play and sing hymns in honour of the same. When the fire begins to burn brightly, they one by one fall upon it and extinguish it with their bare feet. Sometimes they carry the bridegroom in their arms while performing the ceremony. When it is over, fried gram and fried wheat mixed with sugar are offered to the forty saints.

1376. *The song of Balaimiyan.*—This is called पीर का नजा (پیر کا نیزہ) *pīr ka naija*, or बाले मीयाँ (بالے میاں) *bālai miyān.* Next day the females of the neighbourhood are invited; a spot is washed beneath the canopy, and the green branch of a mango tree with leaves on it (or sometimes simply a wooden stick 3 or 4 feet high) is erected therein. A red handkerchief dyed with safflower is spread over it. The women then sing the song of *Bālai Miyān.* At the same time an अँखिया *ankhiya** is put in a new earthen pot, offered to the saint, and then distributed to the people.

---

* A kind of cake made of wheat-flour and rice-flour and boiled in water. It is shaped like the eye, *ānkhi*: hence its name.

1377. *Offering to deceased elders.*—This is called कँदूरी (كندوري) *kandūri* or बीबी के सहनक (بيبي كي صحنك) *bībi ke sahnak*, and takes place on the same night as the last ceremony. An earthen fireplace (चूल्हा *chūlha*) is prepared at home and placed beneath the canopy. The maid-servants go singing to fetch water, carrying several water-pots covered with red cloth, and accompanied by musical instruments. They must be married women of good character; they may not be widows, or women who have married twice. In the water which they bring, rice, gram, *mūng* (*phaseolus mungo*), fruits of the egg-plant, and pumpkins, &c., are cooked. When cooked, first the rice is distributed on earthen plates, then on it the pulse, then a little tyre prepared specially for the occasion, and then the vegetables and cakes. On each plate one betel-leaf and one garland is laid. In some places only rice, curds, and sugar, are put on the plate, and this is called मीठी कँदूरी *mīthi kandūri*. These plates are prepared in great number, and have been previously kept in a room washed for the purpose Then the plates are offered, first one in the name of the prophet, then one in the name of his daughter *Bībi Fātma* (فاطمه), then one each in the names of many saints, and then one each in the names of the deceased members of the family, so far as they can be remembered. Great care is taken to make offerings in the name of all of the last. After this the females of the neighbourhood and those related to the family who have been invited assemble in a place in the courtyard (आँगन *āngan*) of the house, which has been well washed for the occasion, and sing songs in the praise of *Bībi Fātma*, and eat the offerings. No woman who has been married twice, or who is unchaste, dare eat out of these sacred plates.

1378. *The anointing.*—तेल चढ़ाएब *tel charhāēb.*—This takes place in the houses of both the bride and bridegroom the day after the last ceremony. Each is made to kneel down on a wooden bench (चौकी *chauki*), and a yellow cloth is thrown over him or her. Then seven married women (सोहागिनि *sohāgini*) tie up seven cakes (सुहाली *suhāli** and पीठा *pītha*) in a yellow handkerchief, and wave it round their heads. Then they anoint the whole body of the bride or bridegroom with oil. A small bundle is made up of mustard seeds tied up in a piece of yellow cloth, and then tied on the arm of the bride or bridegroom. This is called कँगन्ना बाँधब *kangna bāndhab*.

* A cake made of flour and turmeric and fried in clarified butter.

1379. *The marriage procession.*—This is बरियात *bariyāt*, &c., as amongst Hindus; see § 1290. When the time for the departure of the bridegroom's marriage procession draws near, the maid-servants of the bridegroom's house go out, singing songs, to fetch water. On their return they are stopped at the gate by the musicians, who refuse to let them pass till a present has been made to them. The water is placed under the canopy, where also a small stool is placed. The male members of the family assemble there, and, as songs are sung, the brother-in-law of the boy, or any near relative, digs a pit there. This is called 'digging a pond,' पोखरा खोदब *pokhra khodab*. He also gets a present for doing this. The bridegroom then bathes at this place, and puts on his wedding garments, consisting of (*a*) coloured drawers, (*b*) a kind of overcoat (जामा (جاما) *jāma*) dyed with the safflower, or made of एकरङ्गा *ekranga* or of brocade (असावरी (اساوری) *asāwari*), (*c*) a white turban covered with a red cloth, or a red turban, (*d*) a garland of flowers, and (*e*) a handkerchief carried in the hand. He then mounts on horseback, and visits first the grave of some saint, where he makes an offering of sweetmeats, and then the village *imāmbāra* (इमामबाड़ा (امام باڑا)),* where he makes a similar offering. He then starts for the bride's house, and on approaching it he pays similar visits to the tombs of saints and the *imāmbāra* there. In the meantime the bride has also bathed, put off her माँझा *mānjha* dress, and put on another which has been prepared either in her own house or in that of a relative.

1380. When the time for the arrival of the bridegroom approaches, the bride's maid-servants set out on the road on which it will come, carrying with them rice soaked in water and a newly-made ladle (डोइ *doï*), to which is tied a piece of red cloth. They stop at a well or a river, lay the ladle down on the ground, and cross over it one by one, eating the rice as they do so. They then dig up a चिरचिरा *chirchira*† shrub which they had previously noted, and carry it home, singing songs. The root of the tree is ground up and made into pills, which are administered to the bridegroom on the night of the जलवा *jalwa* (§ 1384).

1381. *The sending of presents.*—This is called साचक (ساچق) *sāchak*. Before the arrival of the marriage procession a बरी *bari* is sent

---

* An *imāmbāra* is, according to Bihār tradition, a building erected in honour of the celebrated martyr Imām Hassan, the grandson of Muhammad.

† *Achyranthus aspera*, said to be of sovereign virtue to one bitten by a venomous reptile or stung by a scorpion, &c.

to the bride's house. This word has two meanings, viz. (1) a dish of cooked pulse, and (2) that here referred to,—all the following presents taken together. It consists of :—

(1) Dresses for the bride, of from one to twenty-five suits. The first suit, or wedding dress (रीत के जोड़ा *rit ke jora*), is also called the शाहाना (شاهانه) *shāhāna* or royal suit. It is not worn after the fourth day of the ceremony. It consists of a pair of long drawers of satin cloth and a जामा *jāma* (see above) of brocade, *tasar* silk, or एकरङ्गा *ekranga*. A second suit, also of fine materials, for the fourth day is called the चौथी के जोड़ा *chauthi ke jora*; and a third suit, for the tenth day, दसहरा के जोड़ा *dasahra ke jora*. Each suit is of less value than the preceding one.

(2) The chaplet, सिहरा (سهرا) *sihra*, for the bride.

(3) Some raw thread dyed with safflower. This is called नाड़ा *nāra* or कलावा (کلاوہ) *kalāwa*, and varies in amount from one or two *chhatānks* to a maund.

(4) Some otto of spices, सोहाग के अतर (سہاگ کا عطر) *sohāg ke atar*.

(5) Sweet-scented oil.

(6) A cone-shaped basket (called सोहाग पूरा *sohāg pūra*) of bamboo, covered with red paper and containing छलछबेला *chhalchhabela*, नगर मोथा *nagar motha*, बाल छड़ *bāl chhar*, the bark of the bay-tree (तज *taj*), cardamoms, sandal-wood, grains of musk, nutmeg, mace, saffron, cassia, turmeric, &c.

(7) Sweetmeats.

(8) Fruits, viz. almonds, pistachios, grapes, dates, cocoa-nut kernel, &c.

(9) Spices for betel.

(10) Fifty-two water-pots. These are small in size and are gaily coloured. In each a little rice, some betel-nuts, and some mango-leaves, are put.

These things are carried on the heads of maid-servants in procession in trays, accompanied by torches, music, and fireworks. First comes a large tray carrying the royal robes, then small trays, on each of which is placed another suit, and then the rest. The whole is covered by a long piece of cloth called दलझकना *daljhakna*.

1382. In the meantime the bridegroom's dress is despatched from the bride's house, with a tailor, to meet the procession. The dress consists of a red जामा *jāma* (see above), long drawers of silk often worked with gold and silver flowers, a turban covered with a red handkerchief on which is laid a garland, and over this a very thin handkerchief, called मक़्नना (مقنع) *maqna* or veil, and a red handkerchief for him to carry in his hand. When the bridegroom is clothed in this by the tailor, he gives the clothes in which he has travelled so far to the barber, who follows the bridegroom, carrying an umbrella over his head. Then the ceremony of निकाह (نکاح) *nikāh* or religious marriage is performed, and dates and sweetmeats distributed to the assembled guests.

1383. After this the bridegroom goes on horseback to the bride's house with great pomp, accompanied by a large party of men with torches, fireworks, and music. When they reach the house, all the men remain standing outside, while the bridegroom enters the female quarters of the house either on foot or horseback. There he sits on a wooden stool (which is given him in dowry), and his mother-in-law (or if she be dead, some other female relation of the bride) comes to him carrying a plate containing a small lamp made of flour and a little अरवा *arwa* rice. She warms her hand at the lamp, and then touches the cheek of the bridegroom. While she is doing this, a woman comes and whispers in his ear the following Hindi verse "सोने मेँ सोहागा, सूई मेँ तागा। ओ दुलहा का मन दुलहिन से लागा॥ *sone men sohāga, sūi men tāga o dulha ka man, dulhin se lāga, i.e.*, borax* in gold, a thread in a needle, and the bridegroom fell in love with the bride." Then six married females (सोहागिनि *sohāgini*) and the mother-in-law alternately touch the cheeks of the bridegroom with the अरवा *arwa* rice. He is then given some *sharbat* to drink. This is prepared in various ways: sometimes the wet hair of the bride after she has bathed is dipped into it, sometimes a small piece of sugar is put into her hand till it becomes moist with the perspiration, and then the *sharbat* is made of it, and sometimes it is made of a piece of sugar which she has taken into her mouth and crushed between her teeth. Then the bridegroom stands on the wooden stool, and a maid-servant carries in the bride in her arms, and touches the back of the bridegroom with her feet, and takes her away: then the bridegroom returns to his own party.

* Borax is a flux for melting gold.

1384. The जलवा *jalwa.*—The day after the arrival of the procession, milk, a dish called मलीदा (مالیده) *malīda* or sweetmeats, and *sharbat*, are sent from the house of the bride to the bridegroom's party. The मलीदा *malīda* or sweetmeats are put into the milk and drunk by the bridegroom out of a cup of silver or copper, which is given to him afterwards in dowry. Then the others drink it. The same evening maid-servants come from the bride's house singing songs, and take away the procession umbrella, and under its shade seven married females grind the spices which came in the सोहाग पूरा *sohāg pūra*, and when ground, apply the powder to the hair of the bride, which they also tie with the नाड़ा *nāra* or string which came at the same time. The scented oil is also applied to her hair. Then the bride puts on the royal dress, a garland of flowers, the chaplet सिहरा (سهرا) *sihra*, and a veil, which is thrown over her face. She takes off all the ornaments of her maidenhood, and puts on new ornaments sent her by the guardians of the bridegroom. Black powder (मिस्सी *missi*) is applied to her teeth, and she is adorned in every other practicable way. During the day, it may be added, myrtle leaves have been applied to the soles of her feet to make them red. When she is ready, the bridegroom is sent for, and he comes walking, preceded by a maid-servant walking backwards, and carrying a plate on which is a burning lamp, so arranged that the smoke is thrown towards the bridegroom. When he reaches the gate of the female quarter of the house, the mother of the bride, or (if she is dead or a widow) any other married woman, meets him, and conducts him inside. The manner of doing this varies in different places. Sometimes the mother carries in her hand a plate in which lamps made of flour or silver are burning, and the wicks of which are of red cloth. A small quantity of the red thread (नाड़ा *nāra*) already mentioned is also laid on the plate. She walks backwards with her face towards him, and at every step throws down a piece of thread, and asks the bridegroom to pick it up and lay it on the plate. In this way, and at the same time touching his cheeks with her hand warmed at the lamp, she takes him into the inner yard, under the canopy. In other places the mother-in-law gives him betel to chew, which he bites and throws away.

1385. When the bridegroom comes under the canopy he sits on a wooden stool near a bed. As long as he stays there his sister (or, in her absence, a maid-servant) spreads a portion of her cloth (सारी *sāri*) over his head. Then the match-maker (मुशाता (مشاطه) *mushāta*) throws a string round his neck, and pulling it gently, refuses to let it go till she is paid something. A cloth is then hung between the bed and the stool, and the match-maker (who has also had charge of adorning the bride) makes her stand on the bed in such a way that the bridegroom can only see her face. She then places the two hands of the bride on her (the bride's) forehead, and moves the bride's head this way and that way. A coloured handkerchief, in which is tied rice and turmeric, is then given to the bridegroom, who throws it on the bride, and each time he does so he is given a betel leaf in which pieces of the root of the चिरचिरा *chirchira* shrub already mentioned are wrapped up. This moving of the head and throwing of the handkerchief is repeated seven times, and the ceremony is called जलुवा देब (جلوہ دینا) *jalwa deb.* The bridegroom then sits on the head of the bed, and the match-maker takes off the chaplet and veil from the face of the bride and shows it to the bridegroom, who for this favour gives her a present, and at the same time receives presents from the female relations of the bride. Sometimes, after this is done, a cup containing sandal-wood and a finger-ring of silver, which has a small cup made in the place where there is usually a stone, is given to the bridegroom, who, after dipping the ring into the sandal-wood, touches the forehead of the bride with it. In other places vermilion (सेनुर *senur*) is used instead of sandal-wood.

1386. Then the wife of the bride's brother, *i.e.*, the bridegroom's सरहज (سرهج) *sarhaj*, comes and sits on the bed, and throws little balls of flour at the bridegroom, who does the same to her. This ceremony is called गेँद खेलब *gend khelab.* A maid-servant then carries off the bride in her arms, followed by the bridegroom, who catches hold either of a corner of the bride's sheet (चद्दर *chaddar*) or her finger.

1387. It must be noted that throughout all these ceremonies the bride has kept her eyes shut, and never moves on foot, but is always carried in the arms of a maid-servant.

1388. The bride and bridegroom are then made to stand in an outer room (दलान *dalān*), and in the hands of both a little rice is put, but the hand of the bride is turned backwards. They are then caused to toss their hands up in the air, by a maid-servant, and thus the rice is scattered through the house, and the bride says at the same time that she is filling the house of her father and mother. The bridegroom also says that he is filling the house of his father and mother-in-law. This ceremony is called घर भरब *ghar bharab.* The bride is then carried off to a well-furnished room, where the bridegroom takes off her shoes with his own hands.

1389. The *departure of the procession.*—This is रुखसती (رخصتي) *rukhsati*, and takes place on the third day after the above-mentioned ceremony. The bridegroom is called into the female apartments, and he and the bride are given rice-milk खीर (*khīr*) to eat. He affects displeasure, and refuses to eat with her. The mother then makes him a present, and he consents to do so. Then the bride and the bridegroom sit together on a carpet, and a small piece of sugar on a betel-leaf is placed first on her head, then on her shoulder, then on the palm of her hand, then on her knees, and lastly on her feet. The bridegroom is pressed to pick up the pieces of sugar from each place with his mouth, or at least with his hands. This ceremony is called नबात चूनब *nabāt chūnab*.

1390. When the bridegroom goes off to his own house with the bride, she is carried in the arms of a maid-servant, and keeps her eyes shut till she reaches the court-yard of her husband's house. The sister of the bridegroom first meets her with a jug of water and washes her feet in a plate, which she (the sister) keeps as her perquisite. After this the ceremonies of घर भरब *ghar bharab* and नबात चूनब *nabāt chūnab* are performed again in the bridegroom's house.

1391. *The ceremony of the fourth day.*—This is चौथी *chauthi* or चौथारी *chauthāri*. It takes place on the fourth day after marriage, *i.e.* on the day after the arrival of the bride and bridegroom at the latter's house. The bridegroom takes off the thread नाड़ा *nāra* with which the hair of the bride had been tied. The women of the family then bathe the bride in the female apartments, singing songs at the same time, and the bridegroom himself bathes outside. Sometimes the bridegroom also bathes inside. The bride then puts on her dress made for this day (see § 1381), and the bridegroom also puts on the dress given him by his father-in-law. The bridegroom then enters the female apartment, and joins in the ceremony of जूआ *jūa*, or gambling. Seven spotted shells (चित्ती कौड़ी *chitti kauri*) and a necklace (चन्दन हार *chandan hār*) are thrown up in the air. A maid-servant extends the bride's hands, and the bridegroom his own, and both try to catch the falling necklace. The one who succeeds wins the game.

1392. Two or three days after the arrival of the bride in the bridegroom's house people come from her house to take her back. The bride's younger brother and other relations may form some of the party, but not elders, such as the father or uncles. They bring with them presents of sweetmeats, rice, pulse, a goat, &c., varying in quantity according to means. Two or three days afterwards they return with the bride and bridegroom.

1393. *The ten days' stay.*—This time the bridegroom stays nine or ten days in his father-in-law's house. This stay is called the दसहरा खाना *dasahra khāna*. On their arrival a room is made over to the bridegroom in the female apartments, and the bride is made to walk into this room accompanied by her female relatives and those of her husband, all singing songs. This is the first time the bride is allowed to walk since the commencement of the ceremonies. Up to this she has been always carried about. When the bride approaches the bridegroom in this room, he is expected to salute (सलाम *salām*) her. If he does not do so, showers of abuse are poured upon him.

This concludes the wedding ceremonies.

CHAPTER V.—BIRTH CUSTOMS GENERALLY.

1394. An adopted child is amongst Musalmāns मोतम्मन्ना (متبنّى) *motmanna*. Amongst Hindus he is पालक *pālak*, पोसपुत *posput*, or पोसपालक *pospālak*. Local names are पोसबेटा *posbeta* or पोसबालक *posbālak* in the south-east, and करता पुतर *karta putr* in East Tirhut. To adopt a child is पोसिया लेब *posiya leb*, गोद लेब *god leb*, or रास पर लेब *rās par leb*.

1395. When a woman cannot suckle her child, owing to pains in and hardness of the breast, she is called थनैलियाही *thanailiyāhi*. Inability to suckle on this account is थनैली *thanaili*. When a child is not well nurtured owing to the untimely death of its mother, or to her milk running dry, it is called दुधटुटुआ *dudhtutua* or दुधकटुआ *dudhkatua*. In South Bhagalpur it is कलरा *kalra*.

1396. A seven-months' child is सतवाँस *satwāns* or सतवाँसा *satwānsa* generally; also सतवाँसू *satwānsu* south of the Ganges, सतमास *satmās* in North-East Tirhut, and सतमसुआ *satmasua* in South-East Tirhut and South Bhagalpur. An eight-months' child is अठवाँस *athwāns* generally; also अठवाँसू *athwānsu* south of the Ganges, अठमास *athmās* in North-East Tirhut, and अठमसुआ *athmasua* in South Bhagalpur.

1397. An only child is एकलौता *eklauta;* also एकहुला *ekáhula* in Shahabad and एकौनियाँ *ekauniyān* in South Bhagalpur. A first-born child is पहिलौठा *pahilautha.* The youngest child, *i.e.*, the last which a woman has, is called पेटपोंछुआ *petponchhua* or कोरपोंछुआ *korponchhua.* When a girl is born after three boys (which is considered very lucky), she is called a तेतर *tetar,* and she is even often named तेतरी *tetri.* In the south-east, however, a girl born after two and not after three boys is so called. A child whose elder brother is dead is called मराछ *marāchh,* or मरछवा *marachhwa,* or (in South Bhagalpur) मरोछा *marochha,* and (in North-East Tirhut) मछई *machhaī.* Such children are treated and dressed as girls, sold to the midwife for a few cowries, and brought back again and given opprobrious names, in order to induce the demon of death to think them of small account and not worth killing.

1398. When a woman has a child every year she is बरसाइन *barsāin,* or in South Bhagalpur बरसैनो *barsaino.* A woman with only one child is एकौंज *ekaunj,* or to the east काक बन्झा *kāk banjha,* or कौआ बाँझ *kaua bānjh.* The latter name is said to be derived from the children's game of काग दुरस *kāg durus,* or "odd or even." In this game one boy guesses whether another has an odd or even number of cowries in his hand. If he guesses an odd number he says काग *kāg,* or if an even one दुरस *durus.* Hence काग *kāg* means an odd number, and specially 'one.' A barren woman is बाँझ *bānjh,* बाँझ बहिला *bānjh bahila,* or (in the south-west) बाँझिन *bānjhin.* A woman after delivery, until the purificatory ceremonies are performed, is अलवाँती *alwānti* or परसौती *parsauti.* The lying-in room is north of the Ganges सोइरी *soiri,* and to the east also सोएर *soer.* South of the Ganges it is सौर *saur,* सौरी *sauri,* or जच्चा खाना *jachcha khāna.* In this a fire is kept burning for ten days after the woman's delivery. This fire is known to the north-east as अगियासी *agiyāsi,* and in South Bhagalpur as पोड़ा *pora.* Elsewhere it is पसंघी *pásanghi,* with a variant पसँगी *pásangi* in the south-west and in South Munger.

1399. The presents given to a woman in a state of pregnancy are known as सधोर *sadhor.* In South Bhagalpur such presents are given after delivery, and are called सठोरा *sathora.* अछवानी *achhwāni* is caudle given to a lying-in woman to produce milk. It is also called सोठौर *sothaur* in the north-east and सोँठौरा *sonthaura* in Gaya and the south-west. Another name current in the north-east is

अध॰रस्सी *adhrassi*; in South Munger it is कद॰वा *kadwa*, and in South Bhagalpur आदो गूड़ *ādo gūr*. The longing of a pregnant woman is दोहद *dohad* or मन॰चलब *manchalab*. The earthen cakes which she is fond of eating when in this condition are called खप॰ड़ा *khapra*.

CHAPTER VI.—CEREMONIES PECULIAR TO THE BIRTH OF A HINDU CHILD.

1400. When the labour pains commence, the चमाइनि *chamāïni* or चमैनी *chamaini*, *i.e.* the native midwife, is sent for. She is also' called दग॰रिन or डग॰रिन *dagrin*. On her arrival she puts a finger-mark (टीका *tika*) of vermilion on the wall. This ceremony is called सोरारी *sorāri*, and is supposed to hasten the delivery of the child. As soon as the child is born, the midwife washes the forelock (लट *lat*) and feet (गोर *gor*) of the mother, which operations are called लट॰धोआइ *latdhoāï* and गोर॰धोआइ *gordhoāï* respectively. She gets a fee (नेग *neg*) for doing this. The child's navel-string (नार *nār*) is then cut. If the child is a मराछ *marāchh* (or मरछ॰वा *marachhwa*), *i.e.* if the child which was born before it from the same mother is dead, the navel-string is all thrown away. Otherwise it is buried in the floor of the lying-in room, and over it the fire (पसँघी *pásanghi*) is placed. The latter is called in South Bhagalpur पस॰नी *pasni* or घूर *ghūr*. The child's body is then rubbed with कोठ॰वार *kothwār*, which is the dust of a sun-dried granary (कोठी *kothi*), in order to take off the fœtal excretion (जावर *jāwar* or जाँवर *jāmwar*). The midwife's fee for cutting the navel-string is नार॰कटाइ *nārkatāï* or नर॰कटाइ *narkatāï*.

1401. When the child's body has been thus rubbed with dust, it is bathed in lukewarm water, and then the midwife throws it up in the air and catches it again five times. This is called लरिका लोकाएब *larika lokāëb*. At the same time another woman strikes a brass dish (थारी बजाएब *thāri bajāëb*), and the mother holds in her hand a handful (अँजुरी *anjuri*) of grain, which last is the perquisite of the midwife. The after-birth (लिझ॰ड़ी *lijhri* or नार पुरैन *nār purain*),* &c., is then thrown away in a vessel called खप॰रौर *khapraur* or (in Gaya) खप॰रौड़ी *khaprauri*, for which the midwife receives a fee called खप॰रौर फेँकाइ *khapraur phenkāï*.

1402. Two or three days after the birth, when the प॰रोहित *prohit* or family priest has fixed on a lucky day, the ceremony of नहावन

---

* The after-birth of an animal, as distinguished from that of a human being, is झर *jhar* or झार *jhār*.

nahāwan is performed. This consists in नीम *nīm* (*azadirachta Indica*) leaves being boiled in water, and both the mother and child being bathed with the decoction. Then a handful of seeds of राइ *rāi* (mustard, *sinapis racemosa*) and जेँवाँइन *jeñwāñin* (dill, *ligusticum ajowan*) is waved (निछावर करब *nichhāwar karab* or औँछब *aunchhab*) round the mother's head and thrown into an earthen cup containing fire. When the seeds are consumed, the cup is upset, and the mother breaks it with her left foot. Then she sits with grain in her hand, while the brass dish is again beaten, and the midwife again throws the child five times in the air. This all takes place in the court-yard of the house, and is done to avert the evil eye. It is the first day on which the mother comes out of the lying-in chamber. The same day this chamber is plastered over with fresh mud, amongst the rich by a maid-servant, and amongst the lower classes by the husband's sister ननद (*nanad*), who gets a fee for this, called सोइरी लिपाइ *soiri lipāï* or (south of the Ganges) सौर लिपाइ *saur lipāï*. The same day the washerman takes away the lying-in clothes (छुतका के कपड़ा *chhutka ke kapra*), and washes them. His fee for this is called छुतका *chhutka*.*

1403. The next day after bathing, the barber pares the mother's nails, which ceremony is called नोहटुङ्गी *nohtungi* or नहटुङ्गी *nahtungi*, and his fee is known as नोहटुंगाइ *nohtungāï*.

1404. On the seventh or eighth day, when the mother is first able to eat rice, the ceremony of खेँड़ी जोड़ाएब *kheñrhi jorāëb* is performed. A hole is dug in the ground, into which milk and water are poured. The mother sits close to it, and eats her first dish of cooked rice. From this day collyrium (काजर *kājar*) is put on the child's eyes. Before this, when oil was rubbed on the child's body, the child had been laid on its back during the operation, but henceforward it is laid on its face for the application. From this day, also, the mother gets a bed to sleep on. Up to this day she had been fed only on caudle and on a mixture of oil, turmeric, and molasses (हरदी गूर *hardi gūr*).

1405. On the twelfth day the ceremonies of दोँनी झाँकब *donni jhānkab* and छठी *chhathi* are performed. Sometimes the latter ceremony is omitted. In the former, five दोनी *doni* or दोना *dona*, which are a kind of platter, are prepared of leaves of the jack-tree (कटहर *kathar*). In these cakes (पूरी *pūri*), rice milk (खीर *khīr*), &c., are placed. Sometimes the leaf platters are omitted, and rice milk, &c., is simply laid

* The washerman caste is considered an unclean one because its members touch these garments.

on the ground over the cakes. Worship is then performed, and the articles eaten.

1406. The छठी *chhathi* or छट्ठी *chhatthi* ceremony is also called in Tirhut छठियार *chhathiyār* or छठि *chhathi.* As its name indicates, it should properly be performed on the sixth day after birth, but this rarely occurs now-a-days. When it is held on the twelfth day it is also called बरही *barhi.* In this ceremony a kind of square marked with diagonals and made of cowdung is fastened on the wall. At every corner and intersection cowries are fastened, and the whole is painted with vermilion, and cakes, &c., are laid before it. The child is then oiled, has collyrium applied to its eyes, is wrapped up in a cloth, and placed before it. It is then dressed in new clothes, and rings (कड़ा *kara*) are put upon its arms and feet for the first time, and some money put into its hand. On this day also the child is named, and the relatives are fed.

1407. The ceremony of purification performed on the fortieth day after birth is called छिल्ला *chhilla.* In South Munger a similar ceremony takes place on the twentieth day, and is called बसदौरी *basdauri.* The ceremony of first feeding the child with rice is called अनप्रासन *anprāsan,* also (south of the Ganges) खिरखियाइ *khirkhiyāi* and खिरचटाइ *khirchatāi.* In Gaya it is निमक चसी *nimak chasi,* and in South Munger चटावन *chatāwan.*

CHAPTER VII.—BIRTH CUSTOMS AMONGST MUSALMĀNS.

1408. The navel string (नार *nār*) is cut by a चमैनी *chamaini,* and the child is then bathed गोसल कराएब (غسل کرانا) *gosal karāeb.* Sweetmeats are then consecrated (नियाज करब (نیاز کرنا) *niyāj karab*) in the court-yard by the male members of the family, and the milk of a respectable and virtuous woman is given to the child in a shell (सितुहा *situha*). This ceremony is called दुधपिलाइ *dudhpilāi.* The people are then called to prayers by striking a brass pan (थारी *thāri*) with a stick, and this custom is called बन सलवात (بن صلوات) *ban salwāt.* In South Munger it is called बाँग सलवात *bāng salwāt.*

1409. The lying-in room, in which the mother (परसौती *parsauti*) is, is always kept warm with an अँगेठी *angethí* or moveable stove, and is called सौरी *sauri,* &c.; see § 1398. Caudle (अछवानी *achhwāni*) is given to her to produce milk, and oil mixed with turmeric and molasses is given to her to make her strong. This last mixture is called हरदी गूर *hardi* *gūr*. Until milk flows in the mother's breasts, the child is wet-nursed with the milk of the woman whose milk was given to it immediately after it was born.

1410. On the third day the mother and the child are bathed and dressed in new clothes, and the women of the neighbourhood come and sing songs, and receive oil and vermilion. Up to this the mother has had nothing to eat except the caudle and the mixture already mentioned, but now she is allowed to eat food and to sleep on a bed.

1411. On the same day the washerman takes away the lying-in garments, and the barber pares the mother's nails and shaves the child. The former operation is called नहटुङ्गी *nahtungi*, and the latter बाल तराशी (بال تراشي) *bāl tarāshi*.

1412. The fees of the midwife (चमैनी *chamaini*), of the washerman, and of the barber, are all known as परसौती के कमाई *parsauti ke kamāï*.

1413. On the same day the lying-in room is plastered over with mud plaster. This operation is known as सोएर लिपाई *soër lipāï*.

1414. On the fortieth day the consecration ceremony (नियाज (نياز) *niyāj*) is again performed, and the relations are fed.

1415. Circumcision is खतना *khatna* or सुन्नत *sunnat*. See also § 386.

CHAPTER VIII.—DISPOSAL OF THE DEAD AMONGST THE HINDUS.

1416. The burning of a corpse is दाह देब *dāh deb*, आगि देब *āgi deb*, दगध करब *dagadh karab*, or जारब *jārab*. In North-East Tirhut it is also सँस्कार देब *sanskār deb*, and in the south-east जराएब *jarāeb*. When a Hindu dies he is taken out of the house and placed on a bier. A bier is रन्थी *ranthi* generally; also टिकठी *tikthi* in South-West Shahabad, टाटी *tāti* in the east generally, ढाठ *dhāth* in North-East Tirhut, फड़की *pharki* in South-East Tirhut, and चचरी *chachri* in South Bhagalpur. Sometimes he is simply placed on a bed (चरपाई *charpāï* or खटिया *khatiya*). Four men, who are called मजिल ले जानिहार *majil le jānihār*, or in South Bhagalpur कनकठिया *kankathiya*, carry the bier on their shoulders and set it down on the ground outside the village. This is called नगर बिसराँव *nagra bisrāñw*, and is done in order that the people who are to accompany the corpse (who are called मजिलिहा *majiliha*) may collect.

1417. After the departure of the corpse from the house the walls of the latter are plastered over with fresh plaster, and outside it are placed a stoue, cowdung, iron, fire, and water for the मजिलिहा *majiliha* to touch on their return from the cremation.

1418. The four men who carried the bier take it on, when the people have collected, to the place of cremation on the bank of a river. This place is called असमसान *asmasān*, or मुरद्‌हट्टी *murdhatti* north of the Ganges. In North-East Tirhut it is समसान *samsān*. South of the Ganges it is चिरार *chirār* or चिरारी *chirāri*, or to the South-East मरघट्टी *marghatti* or मुरघटिया *murghatiya*. In East Tirhut it is also called मरघट *marghat* or मुरघट्टी *murghatti*. They then bathe the corpse (नहवाएब *nahwāëb* or असनान कराएब *asnān karāëb*). The heir or chief mourner (करता *karta*) then has his head, beard, and moustaches shaved (भदर कराएब *bhadr karāëb*), and puts on a dress of mourning (उतरी *utri* or कफनी *kaphni*). He then dresses the corpse in new clothes, viz. a waist-cloth (कच्छा *kachchha*) and a sheet, washes its mouth, and then with the assistance of the other men places it on the funeral pile. To dress a corpse in this way is कफनाएब *kaphnāëb*.

1419. A funeral pile is चिता *chita* generally, also चैती *chaiti* in Gaya and सारा *sāra* in Patna and the south-east. To prepare it a trench is dug in the form of a cross and four pointed logs (खूँटा *khūnta*) are driven into the ground at each ënd, and between them the logs of wood are piled. When the corpse is placed on the pile, the chief mourner (करता *karta*) anoints its mouth with a mixture of गुगुल *gugul* (gum of the *amyris agallocha*), barley, incense (धूप *dhūp*), water-nut (मखाना *makhāna*), honey, sesamum, and sweetmeats. He then buys fire (आगि मोल लेब *āgi mol leb*) from a डोम *Dom* (some, however, take fire from the house), and with it lights a long torch (लुका *lūka*). He then walks round the corpse five times, touches its lips each time with fire (पचकरमा *pachkarma*), and sets fire to the pile (दगध करब *dagadh karab*). When the body is nearly burnt, each of the persons present throws five sticks into the fire. These are known as पचकठिया *pachkathiya* north of the Ganges; in Gaya and the south-west they are पँचआगि *panchāgi* or पँचअगिन *panchagin*; in Patna they are पँचलकड़ी *panchlakri*; and in the south-east as पचकाठ *pachkāth* or पचकाठी *pachkāthi*. When the body is nearly all consumed, the fire is put out (पानि देब *pāni deb*) with handfuls of water, and the remaining small unburnt portion is thrown into the river for fishes and tortoises (मछकछ ला *machhkachh la*). They then wash the place where the body was burnt, and the chief mourner (करत्ता *karta*) plants a *tulsi* tree near by, and writes on the ground the words राम राम *rām rām*.

1420. They then bathe at another landing-place (घाट *ghāt*) and sit down. Then the करत्ता *karta* gets up first and walks towards home, followed by the others. When they arrive at the door of the house, they touch the stone, cowdung, iron, fire, and water already mentioned, and then their left ears, each with the little finger of his left hand. This ceremony is called कान काठी उतारब *kān kāthi utārab*. They then separate. Some castes, however, instead of performing this ceremony, simply bite a piece of bitter *nīm* leaf, and then go home.

1421. Offerings are sometimes made to the manes at the time of cremation, and these are called in South Tirhut असमसान पूजा *asmasān pūja*, or पँचपिण्डा *panchpinda*.

1422. The day after the funeral the करत्ता *karta* goes to the place of cremation, and pours on the site of the pile a little fresh milk. This is called चिता सेराएब *chita seraēb*. He then comes to the village *pīpal* tree, where he finds the barber and the family priest (पुरोहित *prohit*) waiting for him. The former has some fresh milk, and an earthen vessel (कँटिया *kantiya*) carried in a sling (सिकहर *sikhar*) of मूँज *mūnj* rope. There is a hole in the bottom of the pot, partially stopped up with a plug. The *karta* hangs this up on a branch of the tree, so that its contents will drip out through the hole on to the root. He then fills it with milk and water and covers the vessel with an earthen cup (ढकनी *dhakni*). He then goes round the tree three times, and goes home. The whole of this ceremony is called घण्ट टाँगब *ghant tāngab*. On reaching home he feeds his relatives with rice-milk and *urid* pulse, and himself eats off a potsherd (खपरी *khapri*). Before commencing to eat, each person places a small quantity of rice and milk from his platter (पत्तल *pattal*) apart on another platter. This is called रुआह काढब *ruāh kārhab*, and the whole ceremony is called दुधमुँह *dudhmuñh* or दुधमुँही *dudhmuñhi*, and also दुधी *dudhi* in South-East Tirhut.

1423. The same evening and every evening up to the tenth day (दसवाँ *dasıcān*) after the death, the करत्ता *karta* lights a lamp made of mud and placed on the top of a stick. The first day it is placed at the spot where the deceased died. The second day at a little distance from it, towards the door. The third day further off again, and so on, it being arranged that on the evening of the tenth day it reaches the spot outside the door where the five articles (stone, cowdung, iron, fire, and water) were placed.

This rite is called दीया बाती *dīya bāti*, or (in East Tirhut) सुख राति *sukh rāti*, and in Patna चिराग बत्ती *chirāg batti*. Up to the tenth day the करता *karta* every day after bathing throws into the river or the well a handful of sesamum (तिल *til*) mixed with rice and water. This is called तिलाँजुर देब *tilāñjur deb*.

1424. On the third day after the death the rite of तिराती *tirāti* is performed, and in South-East Tirhut, on the fourth day, the अथसनचन *athsanchan*. On the seventh day is performed the सतनहाएब *satnahāëb*. In this the male members of the family touch oil and oil-cake (खरी *khari*), and then bathe. When they return, the females do the same, and on their return to the house they put oil and vermilion on their heads, and a little gram soaked in water (अकुरी *akuri*) is given to each.

1425. On the tenth day is performed the rite of दसकरम *das karm*, also called दसवाँ *daswān*, and in Tirhut दसगातर *dasgātr*, and in North-West Tirhut दसाही *dasāhi*. On this occasion the male relatives shave their heads, and those who are sons of the deceased their moustaches also. Then the Brāhman who performs such obsequies, and who is called कण्टाहा *kantāha* or महाबाभन *mahābābhan*, comes, and performs the ceremony of making obsequial offerings पिण्डा पराएब *pinda parāëb*. If the deceased is a male, this Brāhman gets as a fee all the requirements of a man (clothes, bed, shoes, umbrella, fan, dishes, lota, &c.), and, if a woman, all those of a woman. On the eleventh day offerings (पिण्डा *pinda*) are again made.

1426. Brāhmans are then feasted. This is called ब्रमभोज *brambhoj*, भोज *bhoj*, or कारज *kāraj*. Amongst Brāhmans this takes place on the 13th day after the death, amongst Rajpūts on the 14th day, amongst Vaisyas and amongst some Sūdras on the 16th day, and amongst other Sūdras after the expiry of a month. The ceremony is as follows:—In the day-time, the परोहित *prohit* or family priest performs the पिण्डा *pinda* ceremony, and after it the करता *karta* sits on a square marked on the ground (चौका *chauka*). A new turban is tied round his head, and he is dressed in new clothes. This is called पगड़ी बन्हाएब *pagri banhāëb*. The relatives also put into his hand an offering of money, called नेवता *neota*. Brāhmans are then fed (ब्राह्मन जेवनार *brāhman jeonār*). Afterwards, in the evening, the caste brotherhood are fed. On this day the widow of the deceased is clothed in her widow garments, which are known as रँड़सारी *rañr sāri*, or (in Tirhut) रँड़सार *rañrsār*. Amongst the upper castes this is a white cloth, but amongst the lower ones it is a coloured one.

1427. In the case of the death of a male, पिण्डा *pinda* ceremonies are performed six months and a year after death: the first is called छमासी *chhamāsi*, and the second बरखी *barkhi.* When, however, a marriage has to be celebrated in the family, the ceremony is performed three months after death, and is called तिनपखी के पिण्डा *tinpakhi ke pinda.* On all these occasions also Brāhmans and the caste brotherhood are fed.

1428. When all the funeral ceremonies have been performed in the orthodox way, they are called किरिया करम *kiriya karm.* When the body is merely thrown into a running stream, it is called परवाह *parwāh* or जलपरवाह *jalparwāh.* On five days in the month a body must be burnt with five effigies of कुस *kus* grass (*poa cynosuroides*). These images are known as कुसपुतर *kusputr*, and the days as पचक *panchak* or पचका *pachka.* In the south-east they are पच्चक *pachchak.* The visit of the women to condole after a death is मुँह देखब *muñh dekhab*, पुछारी *puchhāri*, or पुछारो *puchhāro.*

1429. Some Hindu and semi-Hindu sects and castes bury their dead. The principal of these are *Kabirhas* (कबिरहा *kabirha*), Saiva mendicants (अतीथ *atīth* or सन्यासी *sanyāsi*), Sib Nārainis (सिब नारैनी *sib nāraini*), and *Mushars* (मुसहर *mushar*). To be buried is समाधि (or समाध) लेब *samādhi* (or *samādh*) *leb*, and to bury is मिट्टी देब *mitti deb* or समाध में बैसाएब *samādh meñ baisāëb.* The body is bathed and dressed in new clothes, the necklace (कण्ठी *kanthi*) and sectarian mark (तिलक *tilak*) are put on his neck and forehead respectively, and he is seated in the grave facing the north with the feet crossed under the buttocks (पलथी बैसब *palthi baisab*) and with cakes in his hand.

CHAPTER IX.—DISPOSAL OF THE DEAD AMONGST MUSALMĀNS.

1430. The corpse immediately after death is taken out into the verandah (साएबान *sāebān*) or court-yard (आँगन *āngan*). It is stripped and a new waist-cloth (लूँगी *lūngi* or लुङ्गी *lungi*) is put on it. It is then washed (गोसल कराएब (غسل کرانا) *gosal karāëb*). The man who washes has a kind of bag (called साफी (صافي) *sāfi*) on his hand, with which he wipes the corpse. He then performs the ceremonial ablution of the corpse (वजू कराएब (وضو کرانا) *waju karāëb*). This consists in cleaning its teeth, washing its hands, inside of the mouth, forehead, face, arms, and feet. He then dries it with a clean

साफी (صافي) *sāfī.* The waist-cloth is then taken off as unclean, and is given to the barber, who attends to call the relations, and, when they are assembled, to look after their refreshment. A fresh waist-cloth is then put upon the corpse. Amongst the *Sunnis* this washing is generally done by friends of the deceased, but amongst *Shīas* there is a special class of men who perform this work. The water with which the corpse is washed has been boiled with leaves of the बैर *bair* tree (*zizyphus jujuba*), and to this plain water is added. This washing is said to preserve the corpse from decay for a short time.

1431. A sheet is now taken, and a hole torn in the middle, through which the head of the corpse is put. The rest of the sheet hangs down before and behind. It is called झूल *jhūl* or कफनी (كفني) *kaphni.* The corpse is then laid on a bed (चारपाइ *chārpāī*), decently covered with a sheet, and taken to the grave-yard, which is known as कबरिस्तान (قبرستان) *kabristan.* The funeral itself is called जनाजा (جنازة) *janāja.* The prayers recited at the grave-yard or in the yard of a neighbouring mosque differ for men, women, and children. After their recitation the corpse is laid in the grave with the head northwards. The grave is then roofed over with bamboos or planks, over which some thatching grass (भलास *jhalās*) is laid, which is plastered over with mud. It is then filled up with dried earth, every member of the funeral procession assisting in doing so. This is called मिट्टी देब *mitti deb.* Before the party leave the grave-yard, alms (खैरात *khairāt*) are given to beggars. The man who digs the grave is a नोनियाँ *noniyān*, and his fee is known as कबर खोदाइ (قبر كهودائي) *kabr khodāī.*

1432. For four days after the death nothing is cooked in the deceased's house, and the family is supplied with food by the relatives. On the third day the brethren all assemble in an open place and 1¼ or 2½ *sers* of gram, some flowers, betel-leaf, and *sharbat*, are taken there. Each man then takes up a grain of the gram, and after reciting a benediction over it drops it on a cloth spread for the purpose. The benediction is called दरूद (درود) *darūd.* They go on doing this till all the grain is exhausted. It is then given to beggars, and the *sūra* or chapter of the Qur'ān entitled *qul huwa-l-lāhu* is read. Each one then drinks sharbat, takes betel-leaf, and the meeting separates. This ceremony is called by the educated कुल (قل) *kul*, from the first word of the title above quoted. By the ignorant it is called पान फूल *pān phūl.* It is the conclusion of the funeral ceremonies.

CHAPTER X.—CEREMONIES AT PLOUGHING AND SOWING AND TRANSPLANTING.

1433. In the south-west on the first day of ploughing the villagers scatter rice-flour over the plough and yoke. This ceremony is called समहत *samahut*. A similar ceremony is the हरमहूरत *harmahūrat* north of the Ganges, also called समहत *samahut* in Tirhut, in which a handful (मूँठ *mūnth*) of grain is thrown into the field at the north-west (भण्डार *bhandār*) corner. In South Munger the plough is worshipped. The ceremony is called हरमोतर *harmotar*, and in it a vessel of water is poured over the plough in the name of the earth-goddess धरती माइ *dharti māi*.

1434. In South-West Shahabad the मूठ पूजा *mūth pūja* is the feast at the time of commencement of sowing. The villagers give handfuls of grain to the herdsman and watchman. It is also called डिहवार पूजा *dihwār pūja*. In South Bhagalpur the मूठ पूजा *mūth pūja* consists in the cultivator feeding his labourers on rice and milk. On the last day of sowing broadcast, a small quantity of seed is brought back to the homestead and shut up in an earthen pot (कूँड़ा *kūnra*), after which food of extra quality is prepared. This is called generally कुँड़मुन्दन *kunrmundan* or कुँड़मूनन *kunrmūnan*; also हरसोधन *harsodhan* in Champāran.

1435. On the first day of transplanting rice a feast is given. This is called पहिरोप *pahirop* in Patna, and पहिरोपा *pahiropa* in the south-east. In East Tirhut it is खेत भोज *khet bhoj*, or खेत भोजनी *khet bhojni*. South of the Ganges on this occasion the cultivators face the east and plant five rice seedlings (मोरी *mori*). This is called पँचाइठ *panchāith* in Shahabad, and पचाँटी *pachānti* elsewhere. On the same occasion in South Bhagalpur wine, milk, fried grain, and oil are offered to the gods who protect the field from blights and mildews. This ceremony is called गोछी *gochhi*. In South Munger on this occasion a deity of the मुसहर *mushar* caste, named मुड़कटवा *Murkatwa*, is worshipped. The legend about him is that a cultivator once sent this man, who was his labourer, home from the fields to get some seedlings. On the labourer's return the cultivator observed a spot of vermilion (सेनुर *senur*) on his forehead, and concluded that he had been debauching his (the cultivator's) daughter, who was at home at the time, and had given the seedlings. The man was quite innocent, but the cultivator in a rage killed and hid him in the earth. He is hence worshipped as a martyr, especially by his caste-fellows.

North of the Ganges, on the first day of transplanting a feast is given to the neighbours. This is known as गवा *gawa* or गावा *gāwa*, and to give it is गवा लेब *gawa leb* or गवा लगाएब *gawa lagāeb*.

1436. The feast at the conclusion of rice transplanting is औँजली *aunjli* in South Bhagalpur, बनउसरा *banusra* or बनुसार *banusār* in Gaya, and उछाड़ी *uchhāri* or बनउखाव *banukhāo* in Patna. In Sāran, when the transplanting is over, a handful of seedlings is planted with ceremony in a corner of the field. This is called केना डेहरी *kena dehri*.

1437. In planting sugar-cane, before commencing, the direction of the wind is tested to judge of the probability of rain. This is called पवन परिच्छा *paban parichchha* in the north-west. The day on which the planting of this crop, as well as of the spring crop, is commenced, is called मूठ *mūth*, and when it has come they say मूठ लागल *mūth lāgal.* When the planting is concluded five long canes are planted in the middle of the field. This is called पँचउख *panchukh* or पँचौख *panchaukh* north of the Ganges, and पचखाँड़ *pachkhānr* south of it.

CHAPTER XI.—HARVEST CEREMONIES.

1438. When the crops are cut, some of the new grain is taken home and eaten with certain ceremonies. This feast is known as नेवान *newān* or नेवानी *newāni*, or to the south-east as नेमान *nemān*. When the grain is collected on the threshing-floor, a cake of cowdung is placed on the top of the heap to avert the evil eye (see § 839). South of the Ganges worship is also done to the village deity or डिहवार *dihwār*. A similar worship in South Bhagalpur to propitiate ghosts is called दानो पूजा *dāno pūja*.

1439. The ceremony of the first cutting of the sugar-cane takes place, south of the Ganges, on the festival of the देव उठान *deb uthān* or देवठान *deothān*. This takes place on the 11th of the bright half of Kātik (*i.e.*, early in November), and is said to be the day on which Vishnu wakes from his four months' sleep. In South-West Shahabad, on this day, the villagers tie a few canes together by the leaves, and place a neck-ring (हँसुली *hansuli*) on the top. They then pour perfumes over it, take the neck-ring away, and commence cutting. When the crushing of cane is begun a ceremony is performed, called पिठार *pithār* in South-West Shahabad, समहुत *samahut* in the rest of that district, पेतावन *petāwan* in Patna and Gaya, and पचघन *pachghan* in the south-east (see also § 299).

1440. In Shahabad, on the first day of crushing cane, the villagers take some juice home to cook with rice. This dish is called रसजाउर *rasjāür*. The ceremony at the first boiling of the juice is मिठाइ *mithāī* in the south-west, and सिरनी *sirni* in Patna and Gaya. A similar worship of a god, who is called कोइला माता *Koïla Māta*, exists in the south-east. This god exists elsewhere as a deity protecting wells.

CHAPTER XII.—MISCELLANEOUS.

1441. Among the lesser known festivals may be mentioned the following. The उरस *ūras* or चिरागा *chirāga* is, south of the Ganges, a festival held in honour of the Musalman saint मखदूम शाह *Makhdūm Shāh*. It takes place on various dates in different places, *e.g.* in Patna City it takes place in the month of *Bakrā'īd* (about December), and at other places in *Bārah wafāt* (about March). मखदुमाना *makhdumāna* is a rite performed in his honour by landlords.

1442. The छठ बरत *chhath bart* is a Hindu festival in honour of the sun held on the 6th of the light half of Kātik (early in November). The दवात पूजा *dawāt pūja* is held by men of the Kāyasth caste on the 12th of the light half of Kātik (*i.e.*, the day but one after the *diwālī*). On this day they worship their inkstands and will not touch pen and ink.

1443. In the north and east, on the 3rd Bhādoñ (August–September) occurs the तीज *tīj*, on which women fast a day and night in honour of the goddess पार्बती *Pārbati*, and eat सत्तु *sattu* (ground parched grain) next day. On the last day of Bhādoñ occurs the अनन्त *anant* or अनत *anat*, on which day both men and women fast. In the same tract the बहुरा *bahura* is a festival on which the women eat सत्तु *sattu* with sugar and clarified butter.

1444. The अखरतीज *akhartīj* in Patna, अखरतिजिया *akhartijiya* in Gaya, and अखरतीत *akhartīt* in South-West Shahabad, is the feast on the 3rd of the light half of Baisākh (early in May), on which the obligations of the spring harvest are cleared off. In South Bhagalpur it is called अछै तिरतिया *achhai tirtiya*.

1445. On the 5th of the light half of Sāon (early in August) occurs the feast of the नाग पञ्चमी *nāg panchami*, also known as लाग पञ्चमी *lāg panchmi* in North-East Tirhut, नक॰पाँचे *nakpānche* in Shahabad, नग॰पाँचे *nagpānche* in Patna and Gaya, and लग॰पाँचे *lagpānche* in the south-east. On this festival the women mark their houses with lines of cowdung, and worship सेस॰नाग *sesnāg* (the Serpent of Eternity) with milk and parched grain (लावा *lāwa*). On the गोबर पाँचे *gobar pānche*, which falls on the 5th of the dark half of the same month (late in July), the same god is often worshipped in Patna instead of on the former festival. This is called बेह॰रा पाँचे *behra pānche* in South Bhagalpur.

1446. गोधन *godhan* is a woman's rite in which they make cow-dung figures of scorpions, snakes, &c., and beat them. To the south of the Ganges, in Bhādoṅ (August–September), the women fast for twenty-four hours and make cowdung figures of Ganes and lay brambles (झाड़ झूड़ *jhār jhūr*) in the court-yard, saying the words अप्पन कर॰म भैयक धर॰म झाड़ झूड़ घुसिआवे ही *appan karm bhaiyak dharm jhār jhūr ghusiāwe hī*, an incantation which literally translated means, 'I cause my own fate and my brother's virtue to enter the bramble.' This incantation is supposed to benefit the speaker and her brother in some mysterious way. A similar ceremony is called कर॰मा धर॰मा *karma dharma* in South Bhagalpur.

1447. The जिउतिया *jiūtiya* to the west and the जितिया *jitiya* to the east is a fast and worship performed by women on the 8th of the dark half of Kātik (late in October) for the benefit of their children.

1448. In Patna the festival of the *holi* festival (full moon of Phāgun or middle of March) is distinguished by the custom called लुकारी *lukāri* or लुक॰वारी *lukwāri*. In this, at night, the village children throw lighted torches across the boundaries of the village into the neighbouring village. This is supposed to be lucky for the village which throws, and unlucky for the village which receives, and is a source of frequent fights.

1449. On the day between the 15th of Chait and the 15th of Baisakh (about the 15th of April) when the sun enters the sign of the Ram (मेख *mekh*), it is customary to feed Brāhmans with सत्तू *sattu* (ground parched barley), टिकोढ़ा *tikorha* (immature mangos), and water, and to give alms. This feast is called the सतु॰आइन *satuāin* or सतु॰आनी *satuāni*. In South Bhagalpur this festival is held on the last day of Chait, *i.e.*, the last day of the

Bangali year. On the following day there is in Tirhut a curious festival, called the जूड़ सीतल *jür sital.* The people bathe in water drawn the previous night and eat food cooked at that time, after worshipping सितला देवी *Sitla Debī*, the goddess of small-pox. Then from morning till noon all classes, rich and poor, cover themselves with mud, and shower it on all whom they meet. No one is free from this mud bath. In the afternoon the people go out with clubs and hunt jackals and hares and whatever animal they can find in the village. On their return home they boast of their valour in having killed this and that jackal, and the phrase जूड़ सीतलक सिपाही *jür sitalak sipāhi* is used like मोहरम के सिपाही *moharram ke sipāhi* to signify a braggard.

CHAPTER XIII.—ARBITRATIONS, OATHS, &c.

1450. A body of arbitrators is पँचाइत *panchāït* to the north and west. In Patna and Gaya it is पँचीत *panchīt* or पँचेता *pancheta*, and in the south-east पँचैती *panchaitī.* The head arbitrator is called सरपञ्च *sarpanch*, also south of the Ganges सरदार *sardār* or महतोँ *mahton.* In Shahabad he is also called महान *mahān*, and in South Bhagalpur मँड़ड़ *mañrar.* A caste assembly is चटाइ *chatāï* (*lit.* a mat), or पङ्गत *pangat* (*lit.* sitting in a row), and its head arbitrator परधान *pardhān* or मानजन *mānjan.* In Shahabad the man next to the chief is called the छड़ीदार *chharidār.*

1451. When one party in the case challenges the opposite party or a particular person to an oath, the phrase used is हसर करब *hasar karab*; also धारब *dhārab* in Patna, Gaya, and the south-east. The oath may be on the ammonite (सालग्राम *sālgrām* or सालिगराम *saligrām*), a copy of the Sanskrit हरिबन्स *haribans*, or on Ganges water (गङ्गा जल *ganga jal*). When Ganges water is placed in a copper vessel with some leaves of the holy basil (*Ocymum sanctum*), the oath is said to be by तुलसी ताँबा *tulsi·tamba.* Or a man may lay his hand on his son's head (बेटा का सिर पर हाँथ धै कँ *beta ka sir par hānth dhai kañ*), in which case his son is supposed to die within a year if he tells a lie, or he may touch a Brāhman's legs and swear by them (ब्राह्मन के गोर छू कँ *Brāhman ke gor chhu kañ*). In Shahabad one form of oath current is to pour forth some country liquor. This form is known as मदाइन *madāïn.* The oath taken on a cow is known as गौ किरिया *gau kiriya.* The man who swears by this oath sometimes holds the animal's tail, and sometimes simply touches it. In these cases the man before swearing bathes and puts on new clothes. North of the Ganges the गुड़ुड़ा *gurura* is a circle drawn on the ground in which the man who takes the oath stands, or from which he takes the thing claimed. The belief in these oaths is, throughout the country, very genuine, but perjury is sometimes attempted. One common trick when swearing with one's hand on one's son's head is to substitute some one else for the son. The writer remembers in the year 1879, when he was in camp in Darbhanga district, a curious incident. License-tax assessments were being held, and one well-known money-lender offered to swear on his son's head that he lent no money. The challenge was accepted, and the oath taken. Curiously enough the son was next day seized with what was said to be cholera, and the man came to the writer, and insisted on his name being written in the highest class of assessees. This was done. It is satisfactory to know that the son recovered. Bābhans are popularly supposed to have little fear of the sanction of an oath, as witness the following proverb,—सील, सुत, हरिबन्स लै, बीच गङ्गाक धार, एतेक लै बाभन, तँ ना करह इतिबार *sīl, sut, haribans lai, bīch gangāk dhār, etek lai bābhan tañ na karah itibār,* If a Bābhan swear by the ammonite, his son, the Haribans, and in the midst of the Ganges,—don't believe him.

1452. To excommunicate from caste is हुक्का (or हुक्का तमाकू) बन्द करब *hukka* (or *hukka tamāku*) *band karab.* It is also कुजात करब *kujāt karab* or पँचाइत सँ काट देब *panchāit señ kāt deb.* The headman of a caste is मुखिया *mukhiya,* चौधरी *chaudhri,* सरदार *sardār,* or मानजन *mānjan.* Amongst the Telis and Chamārs he is also called महतों *mahton,* मेहतर *mehtar,* or (in South-East Tirhut), मँड़र *mañrar.*

CHAPTER XIV.—MISCELLANEOUS SUPERSTITIONS.

1453. A wizard is ओझा *ojha* or जादूगर *jādūgar.* Other names also used are सोखा *sokha* in South-West Shahabad, गुनी *guni* in North-East Tirhut, डैया *daiya* in Patna, भगत *bhagat* in Patna, Gaya, and the south-east, and also भगतिया *bhagatiya* and चटिया *chatiya* in South Munger. His enchantments are जादू *jādu* or ओझाइ *ojhāï,* also भगताइ *bhagtāï* in South Bhagalpur. A witch is डाइन *dāïn.*

1454. An omen is सगुन *sagun,* and also north of the Ganges शगुन *shagun.* A good omen is अच्छा सगुन *achchha sagun,* or in Shahabad

सुलभ सगुन *sulabh sagun.* An evil omen is कुसगुन *kusagun*, also in the north-west बद्‌शगुन *badshagun*, and in Patna and Gaya नहस *nahas.* In East Tirhut it is असगुन *asgun.* Other names are कुसाइत *kusäit* (an unlucky time) and कुजात्रा *kujätra* (an unlucky starting).

1455. There are a vast number of village gods (ग्राम देवता *grām deota*) worshipped throughout the province. The principal amongst them will shortly be mentioned. A काली अस्थान *kāli asthān*, also called देवी अस्थान *debī asthān* or देवी थान *debi thān*, which is a mound in honour of Kāli, the wife of Shiva (सिव *Sib*), is generally erected outside each village. In Tirhut under the village *pīpal* tree there is generally a mound, decorated with clay images of the principal personages in the epic connected with him, erected in honour of the Salhes who is mentioned in the following list. This is called a सल्हेस अस्थान *salhes asthān.* The mound erected to a deceased Brahman or holy man is generally called a बरम्हम अस्थान *barham asthān.*

1456. The following is a list of the principal village deities worshipped in Bihār. The more well-known deities, such as सिव *Sib*, महादेव *Mahādeb*, बरम्हम *Barham* (*Brahma*), or क्रिश्न *Krishn*, are omitted. It will be observed that some of them are demons, who are worshipped in order to propitiate them.

अमन्ता भवानी *Amta Bhawāni* or अम्बिका भवानी *Ambika Bhawāni*, a form of Debi worshipped in Sāran.

कारू बीर *Kāru Bīr* or कारू दास *Kāru Dās* (south), also कलुआ बीर *Kalua Bīr* (Patna), worshipped by Doms and Dusādhs.

कुल देवता *Kul Deota*, the family god.

कैतुक गोसाँईं *Kaituk Gosāññi*, worshipped in South Bhagalpur by Dusādhs.

कोइला माता *Koïla Māta*, the goddess of a well spring, worshipped generally.

कोदर कट्टा *Kodar Katta*, worshipped by Doms in South Bhagalpur.

कोल *Kol*, worshipped in Gaya.

खाजे खिदर *Khāje Khidar*, the patron god of the boatman (मलाह *malāh*) caste. He is also often confused with a similar female deity गङ्गा माइ *Ganga Māï.* Musalmān women fast on every Thursday in the month of Bhādoñ (August–September) and call the fast खाजे खिदर का रोजा *khāje khidar ka roja.*

खेती भवानी *Kheti Bhawāni* (Patna and south-west), worshipped by Koïris when they plant and cut their vegetables. In Patna a Musalmān vegetable-seller (कुंजन्ड़ा *kunjra*) worships राम ठाकुर *Rām Thākur*.

गोबन्नाइ राउत *Gobnāï Rāüt* (north-west), a deified cowherd worshipped in Sāran and Champāran.

गोरैया *Goraiga* or गोरेया *Gorea*, worshipped generally south of the Ganges, especially by Doms and Dusādhs; also called गोरिया *Goriya* (Patna).

घाटों *Ghāton*, worshipped in South Bhagalpur by Dusādhs.

चतावन *Chatāwan* (Patna), worshipped by Doms and Dusādhs.

चिरन्कुटन्वा पीर *Chirkutwa Pīr*,—see डिहन्वार *Dihwār*.

चुहड़ माल *Chuhar Māl*,—see सल्हेस *Salhes*, worshipped in the south-east by Dusādhs.

चोहट *Chohat*, worshipped by Doms and Dusādhs.

जगन्दम्मा *Jagdamma*, the goddess of small-pox, worshipped in Patna and the south-east by Dusādhs.

जलासेन *Jalāsen*, the protector of bearers, worshipped in Sāran.

जौहन्री बरन्म *Jauhri Barm*, worshipped in Sāran.

झुनन्की बीर *Jhunki Bīr*, worshipped in Gaya.

डमरन्डाक *Damardāk* (south), worshipped by Doms and Dusādhs.

डाक *Dāk*, worshipped in Patna, Gaya, and South Munger.

डिहन्वार *Dihwār* (generally), also (Sāran and South Tirhut) चिरन्कुटन्वा पीर *Chirkutwa Pīr*. This is a very generally worshipped deity. There is supposed to be a separate one for each village. Every one who passes by throws a piece of cloth on his image.

ढेलन्हा पीर *Dhelha Pīr* (north) or ढेलन्वा गोसाँईं *Dhelwa Gosāññ* (south), in whose honour a heap of earth is erected on the road-side, to which every passer-by adds a clod. He protects wayfarers.

देबी *Debi*, the popular name of the goddess Durga.

धरन्मन्नाथ *Dharmnāth*, an incarnation of Sib, worshipped in Sāran.

नाएक साहेब *Nāëk Sāheb*, worshipped in Patna.

नाग *Nāg*, the snake god. Worshipped generally. In Sāon (July–August) crowds of women calling themselves his wives (नागिन *nāgin*) go out begging for 2½ days, during which period they neither sleep under a roof nor eat salt. Half the proceeds of the begging are given to Brāhmans, and the other half invested in salt and sweetmeats, which are eaten by the whole village. During the expedition several characteristic songs are sung, some of which have been published by the Asiatic Society of Bengal.

मह्न्थिन दाइ *Mahthin Dāi*, worshipped in the south-west.

पहास बर *Pahās Bar* (Patna and Gaya), worshipped by Doms and Dusādhs.

पाँचो पीर *Pāncho Pīr*, the five saints named गाजी मीयाँ *Gājī Mīyān*, हठीला *Hathīla*, परिहार *Parihār*, सहन्जा माइ *Sahja Māi*, and अजब सालार *Ajab Sālār*. They are worshipped by Musalmān drummers (डफाली *daphālī*), who during an outbreak of cholera act as village Musalmān priests. They go about, beating drums, with an iron bar wrapped in red cloth and adorned with flowers, which represents गाजी मीयाँ *Gājī Mīyān*. They are paid in kind by the people at whose doors they stop and drum. A पँचन्पिरिया *panchpiriya* is a Hindu who worships Musalmān saints. In Shahabad these five saints are worshipped conjointly with three others, as mentioned in the following verse :—

अमन्ना सती, पाँचो पीर, लँगन्ड़ा तार, सोबरन्ना तीर *Amna Sati, Pāncho Pīr, Langra Tār, Sobarna Tīr.*

Langra Tār is simply a crooked wire which is worshipped. *Sobarna Tīr* means the banks of the river *Sobarna*.

पारस नाथ *Pāras Nāth*, worshipped by bankers (महाजन *mahājan*).

फूल डाक *Phūl Dāk* (Gaya), worshipped by Doms and Dusādhs.

बखन्तौर *Bakhtaur*, a deified cowherd worshipped in South-East Tirhut.

बँदौतन्नी *Bandautni* (Gaya), worshipped by Doms and Dusādhs.

बँदौत *Bandaut* (Gaya), worshipped by Doms and Dusādhs.

बन्नी *Banni* (south-west), worshipped by Doms and Dusādhs.

बरन्दुन्वनिया *Barduaniya*, worshipped in Patna.

बरन्हम देव *Barham Deo*, worshipped in Gaya.

बसावन कुँअर *Basāwan Kuñar*, worshipped in Gaya.

बहोड़ *Bahor*, worshipped in Patna and South Munger by Dusādhs.

बिदेसी बरम्ह *Bidesi Barm*, worshipped in Sāran.

बिसहरा *Bisahra*, worshipped in North-East Tirhut.

भैरव *Bhairab* or भैरो *Bhairo*, worshipped by cultivators in the south-east.

मकार बीर *Makār Bīr* (north and east),—see § 299.

मनसा राम *Mansa Rām* (Patna), worshipped by Doms and Dusādhs.

मनानो दानो *Manāno Dāno*, worshipped by Doms in South Bhagalpur.

मनुस देव *Manus Deo* (north and west), worshipped by Doms and Dusādhs.

मलदानो *Maldāno* (south), worshipped by Doms and Dusādhs.

मसान *Masān* (Patna), worshipped by Dusādhs and Doms.

महमाया *Mahmāya*, the goddess of small-pox.

महाबीर *Mahābīr*, a form of Hanumān, the monkey-king who befriended Rām.

माता दाइ *Māta Dāi* or सितली *Sitli*, the goddess of small-pox.

मीर फजुला *Mīr Phajula*, a Musalmān saint worshipped in Sāran.

मेघू डाक *Meghu Dāk* (Patna), worshipped by Doms and Dusādhs.

मैया *Maiya* (Patna and south-east), worshipped by Mushars, Dusādhs, and Doms.

मोती राम *Moti Rām*, brother of सल्हेस *Salhes* (*q.v.*), and worshipped in the south-east by Dusādhs.

रघुनी डाक *Raghuni Dāk* (Patna), worshipped by Doms and Dusādhs.

रघू *Raghu*, worshipped in South Bhagalpur by Dusādhs.

राम ठाकुर *Rām Thākur*, worshipped in Patna and the south-east. See also खेती भवानी *Kheti Bhawāni*.

राम बीर *Rām Bīr* (Patna), or राम गोसाँइँ *Rām Gosāñiñ* (Gaya), worshipped by Dusādhs.

राह *Rāh* or (North-East Tirhut) राहु *Rāhu* is a demon worshipped by Doms and Dusādhs. The ceremonies are a kind of fire-worship, in which the devotees run along a trench filled with blazing coals.

लीला डोम *Lila Dom*, worshipped by Doms in South Bhagalpur.

सनिचरा *Sanichra* (south-west), a god worshipped by vegetable-sellers (तुरहा *turha*).

सलखो *Salkho* (south-west), worshipped by Doms and Dusādhs.

सल्हेस *Salhes* or सलेस *Sales* (south and east), worshipped by Doms and Dusādhs. He was a great hero and the first watchman. He fought a battle with चुहड़ माल *Chuhar Māl* of Mokāma, who was the first thief. A famous epic concerning him is current in Tirhut, and has been published by the Asiatic Society of Bengal.

सहजादी माइ *Sahjādi Maï*, worshipped in the south-west.

सिँगेसर *Singesar*, worshipped in North-East Tirhut.

हरिराम बरम *Harirām Barm*, worshipped in Sāran.

हरिहर नाथ *Harihar Nāth*, in Sāran, at Sonpūr.

1457. A spell or charm is गुन *gun* or मन्तर *mantr*. टोटका *totka*, टोटमा *totma*, or टोना *tona*, are spells or charms generally with an evil object. In Shahabad they were टोटरम *totram;* in Patna and Gaya they are optionally उतारा पतारा *utāra patāra*, and in South Bhagalpur निंगछा छोरी *ningchha chhori*. The जिया दान *jiya dān*, जिबदान *jib dān*, or बलिदान *balidān*, is an animal, &c., sacrified to काली *Kāli* as a kind of scapegoat. In cases of sickness various articles are exposed in a saucer at a cross-road. This custom is supposed to communicate the disease to the first person who touches it, and is called जोग *jog* or जोग टोन *jog ton*, or in South Bhagalpur ओझ टेम *ojh tem*. The contents of the saucer vary with the disease demon to be propitiated. There are generally some red ओड़ौल *orhaul* (*hibiscus*) flowers, some sand, grain, and yellow cloth. If a ghost भूत *bhūt* has to be propitiated, wine, or even a fowl, is laid there. In cases of small-pox, the cloth with which the sores were dressed is frequently put out, which often makes the superstition about communicating the disease a lamentable reality. In South-East Tirhut an oblong mound studded with flags to avert cholera is called आँसरिक *āsrik*. The खटोला *khatola* (north of the Ganges) is a miniature bedstead hung on a tree as a propitiatory offering.

1458. The following is a list of some of the various demons, ghosts, and other supernatural bogies believed in in Bihār. Those which are worshipped, and which hence have been included in the former list, are omitted.

आगि बैताल *Āgi Baitāl* or अगिया बैताल *Agiya Baitāl*, a hideous demon which lurks in trees, lives on dung beetles, and seizes wayfarers by night.

कीचिन *Kichin* (south), a kind of Lamia. She assumes the shape of a beautiful woman, and visits and seduces any man whom she may meet in a lonely place. The man dies within a few months of his yielding to the temptation. She has feet back to front, *i.e.*, toes behind and heels in front. Hence the wise may recognize her.

घोघर *Ghoghar* (north-west), a ghost invoked to frighten children.

चटुआ *Chatua* or चहऽटा *Chahta* (north-west), चटऽना *Chatna* (north-east), a vampire who drinks up the milk of cows and women. In South Bhagalpur he is called चोर मटऽका *Chor Matka*.

चुड़ैल *Churail*, also (in Shahabad) बहरिया *Bahariya*, an evil spirit which assumes the shape of a bird and sits on the roof of a house which contains a pregnant woman. This injures the child.

जिलैया *Jilaiya* or जलऽवैया *Jalwaiya* (south), or (South Bhagalpur) मरऽचिड़िया *Marchiriya*, a fiend which takes the shape of a night bird, and is able to suck the blood of any person whose name it hears. Hence women are very careful about calling their children by name in the night time. If it fly over the head of a pregnant woman, the child born will be a weakling. Such a child is called जिलऽवैया के छुअल *jalwaiya ke chhūal.*

जिन *Jin* (north), a ghost, goblin, genius, 'djin.'

डूबा *Dūba*,—see बूड़ा *būra.*

धोकर कसऽवा *Dhokar Kaswa*, a man with a bag who carries off naughty children.

नेकी बीबी *Neki Bibi* (Gaya and south-west), a ghost invoked to frighten children.

पनऽडूबी *Pandūbi*,—see बूड़ा *būra.*

बरऽम पिचास *Barm-Pichās*, a kind of ghost or goblin.

बूई *Būi* is a ghost invoked to frighten children.

बूड़ा *Būra*, डूबा *Dūba*, or पनऽडूबी *Pandūbi*, a water-demon, who drowns travellers.

बौफेर *Baupher* (north), a kind of ghost or goblin.

भाकुर *Bhākur* (north-west), a ghost invoked to frighten children.

भूत *bhūt*, a ghost or goblin generally.

भोकसन्वा *Bhokaswa* (south), a ghost invoked to frighten children.

मनुसन्देबा *Manusdeba* (north), a kind of ghost or goblin.

मरन्चिड़िया *Marchiriya*,—see जिलन्वैया *jilwaiya.*

माँञोँ *Māñoñ* (north), a ghost invoked to frighten children.

मिमियाइ के तेल *mimiyāi ke tel*, a kind of bitumen brought from Persia and elsewhere. It is said to be extracted from the heads of coolies who emigrate to the colonies, by hanging them head downwards and roasting them over a slow fire. The threat of extracting it from the head of a child is therefore an active deterrent.

राकस *Rākas*, the will o' the wisp; it breathes fire and misleads travellers, but it also lives in the fields, and where it resides grain is produced in abundance.

सुखन्ड़ा *Sukhra* (north), also सुखैनी *sukhaini* (North-East Tirhut), a vampire which sucks up children's blood.

हाउ *Hāü* (Patna), or हुम्मा *humma* (South Bhagalpur), a ghost invoked to frighten children.

1459. The उतन्सरन्ग *utsarg*, and also (in Tirhut) काननोत्सर्ग *kānanotsarg*, is the emblematical marriage of a grove to a well, without which preliminary observance it is unlawful to partake of the fruit. The बिरन्खोतन्सरन्ग *birkhotsarg*, and also (in Tirhut) the बैदिक *baidik*, is the ceremony of marriage performed in the name of a bullock let loose on the 11th day of mourning for a near relative. The जलोतन्सरन्ग *jalotsarg* is the emblematical marriage ceremony on completion of a well or tank. It is married to an image erected close by. In case of a pond it is also called तरागोतन्सरन्ग *tarāgotsarg*, and on completion of a well कुपोतन्सरन्ग *kupotsarg*. The latter is called in South Bhagalpur कूप जग *kūp jag* or कुइयाँ दान *kuïyāñ dān*. बाटोतन्सरन्ग *bātotsarg* is the ceremony on the completion of a road. No marriage is in this case performed.

1460. Water brought from a sacred river, spring, or place of pilgrimage तीरथ (*tīrath*), is much used in religious ceremonies, and is carried by men called कमरन्पन्थू *kamarpanthu*. They are also called कँवारन्थू *kamwārthu* in South-West Tirhut and कमन्रथुआ *kamrathua* in South-East Tirhut.

DIVISION XIII.

TRADE, MONEY-DEALING, AND ACCOUNTS.

CHAPTER I.—TRADE AND BAZAR ACCOUNTS.

1461. *Trade* is लेन देन *len den*, महाजनी *mahājni*, कारबार *kārbār* or कारोबार *kārobār*, बेवहार *beohār*, बेयापार *beyāpār* or बेओपार *beopār*, or बनिज *banij*. In Patna City it is also बेवहरगत *beohargat*. *Exchange* or *barter* is अदलई बदलई *adlaī badlaī*. A *money-lender* is महाजन *mahājan*, साह *sāh* or साहुकार *sāhukār*, or बेहवरिया *behwariya*. He is also called in the country बनिया *baniya*, and in South-West Shahabad साव *sāo*. In Patna City he is called कारोबारी *kārobāri* or धनी *dhani*. A *banker* is कोठीवाल *kothīwāl* or सराफ *saraph*. A *borrower* is रिनिहा *riniha*, खद्दुक *khadduk* or खदुका *khaduka*, or असामी *asāmi*. In South Munger he is also called मुजेरा *mujera*, in South Tirhut बनियौटा *baniyauta* and धारनिक *dhārnik*, and in South Bhagalpur खातब *khātab*. In Patna the words करज खौक *karj khauk* and करज खोर *karj khor* are also used.

1462. An *account-book* is बही *bahi*. A trader's account-books are called collectively बही खाता *bahi khāta*. जाकर *jākar* in Gaya is a record of cloth sales kept by cloth-merchants. Each page of the account-book is called पन्ना *panna*, and also in North-East Tirhut पत्ता *patta*.

1463. The following are the books usually kept by village money-lenders:—

(*a*) The रोजनामचा *rojnāmcha*.—This is the *day-book*. The left hand or credit side of the page is known as जमा *jama*, and the right or debit side as नाँव *nānw* or नाम *nām*.

(*b*) The रोकड़ बही *rokar bahi*.—Mr. Crooke's description of this is equally applicable to Bihār. It is exactly the same as the रोजनामचा *rojnāmcha*. There is only this difference, that it is balanced after each transaction. For example, the book shows Rs. 1,000 on the credit side; Rs. 100 are disbursed on a certain account. This is entered on the debit (बाकी *bāki* or नाँव *nānw*) side, and the book is balanced showing Rs. 900 still to credit. This is called रोकड़ बाकी *rokar bāki* or बाकी तहबील *bāki tahbīl*, and is again brought forward to credit. North of the Ganges it is called फाजिल *phājil*. A man who carries on several distinct trades keeps up a separate रोकड़ बही *rokar bahi* for each.

(*c*) The लेखा बही *lekha bahi*, the खाता *khāta*, or खाता बही *khāta bahi*.—This is the *ledger*, and is made up as time allows from the रोजनामचा बही *rojnamcha bahi*. It contains each creditor's or debtor's account separately, with a reference to the page of the day-book on which each item has been entered day by day. Some traders keep up a separate खाता बही *khāta bahi* for each of their trades or speculations, others have only one general one.

(*d*) There is also the जमाखरच *jamakharch*, which is an abstract of the day-book, and is hence also called a खतियौनी *khatiyauni*, and shows the totals of receipts and payments on each page.

1464. Small traders generally only keep up the first of these books, —the रोजनामचा *rojnāmcha* or day-book. Very small traders do not even keep this. They have a separate slip of paper containing each customer's account, and called चिट *chit*, चिट्ठा *chittha*, or चिट्ठी *chitthi*, or पुरजा *purja* or पुरजी *purji*. In South Munger it is called सरखत *sarkhat*.

1465. Large traders, such as those in the city of Patna, with whom this work has nothing to do, keep up all the above four books. For the sake of completeness, the following information, founded on that given by Elliot in his Glossary, is added. Quoting Elliot's words (with the necessary alterations to suit local variations): "The page (of an account-book) is divided into two equal parts, called in Patna रेकाना *rekāna*: each of these is again divided into two रुकन *rukan* or रुक्न *rukn*. The (first or) right-hand रेकाना *rekāna* is called the हाशो *hāsho*. The first right-hand quarter (some say half) of the left-hand रेकाना *rekāna* is called सीरा *sira*, and the remaining portion is called in Patna City

इरादा *irāda*, and elsewhere पेटा *peta* or (in North-East Tirhut) पेट *pet.* The सीरा *sīra* contains the sum finally brought to account after the necessary deductions have been made from the gross amount in the पेटा *peta* and हाशो *hāsho.*" In reading the above, it should be remembered that it refers to accounts kept in the Persian character. When kept in the *mahājni* character, the terms for right and left must be reversed.

CHAPTER II.—ACCOUNTS BETWEEN LANDLORD AND TENANT.

1466. These accounts are not usually kept in bound books, but on separate slips of paper, kept together in packets by a paper tape, called तबल्लक *tablak* or कैदक *kaidak.*

1467. A tenant's receipt for rent is known as रसीद *rasīd* or दाखिला *dākhila*, and in North-East Tirhut कबज *kabaj.*

1468. The system of accounts differs according as the rent is paid in kind or in cash. Hence two sets of accounts are kept up in a landlord's office. They are the following :—

(*a*) Accounts of rents paid in kind—

1. खसरा दानाबन्दी *khasra dānābandi.*
2. खसरा बटाई *khasra batāī.*
3. मोफरीद *mophrīd.*
4. लग्गित *laggit* and वासिल बाकी *wāsil bāki.*
5. तिरिज जिनिसवार *tirij jiniswār.*
6. सियाहा *siyāha.*
7. हिसाब बिकरी गल्ला *hisāb bikri galla.*

(*b*) Accounts of rents paid in cash—

8. खसरा *khasra.*
9. मोफरीद *mophrīd.*
10. लग्गित *laggit* and वासिल बाकी *wāsil bāki.*
11. तिरिज पटेवारी *tirij patewāri.*
12. सियाहा *siyāha.*

(*c*) In addition to the above, the following general accounts are kept, which are applicable to both kinds of rent—

13. मोलहकी *molhaki.*
14. ढड्ढा *dhaddha* or जमा वासिल बाकी *jama wāsil bāki.*

15. जमाबन्दी *jamābandi.*

16. जमाखरच *jamākharch.*

1469. The word तिरिज *tirij*, met with above, means 'abstract.' In small estates, Nos. 5, 11, and 14 are often not used.

1470. The following is a brief description of the above accounts:—

(1) The खसरा दानाबन्दी *khasra dānābandi.* This is the account paper drawn up in the field when the दाना *dāna* or estimate of the crop is being made. It contains—

(*a*) The date.

(*b*) Name of tenant.

(*c*) Quantity of land (अराजी *arāji*).

(*d*) Length (तूल *tūl*) and breadth (अरज *araj*) of the plot.

(*e*) Name of the crop (जिनिस *jinis*) thereon.

(*f*) The quantity of grain estimated.

The तिरिज तारीखवार *tirij tārīkhwār* is a daily abstract of No. 1, and shows (in the case of division by appraisement) the total area of land and the quantity of grain estimated daily. The sum of all the daily entries in this paper shows the total area of lands of which the rent is paid in kind, and the produce thereof. This account is only kept when the division of the crop is by appraisement (दानाबन्दी *dānābandi*, see § 913). Some landlords, however, also keep it in the case of actual division on the threshing-floor, as a check on No. 2.

(2) When the division is by actual division on the threshing-floor (अगोर बटाइ *agor batāi*, see § 914), a खसरा बटाइ *khasra batāi* is opened instead, containing the date, name of tenant, area, kind of crop, quantity, landlord's share, cesses, &c.

(3) The मोफरीद *mophrīd* is the bundle of papers in which separate accounts of each tenant are entered. A separate slip of paper is kept for each tenant. It is compiled from the खसरा *khasra* (No. 1). It shows the quantity of each kind of grain belonging to him which was

estimated, date by date. The area of the land under each crop at each estimate is also given. When this is abstracted out so as to show the total area and total crop for each tenant, the abstract is called तिरिज मोफ़रीद *tirij mophrīd*.

(4) The लगित *laggit* and वासिल बाकी *wāsil bāki* are written up from No. 3, a separate slip of paper being kept for each tenant. They form a kind of ledger or personal account. The heads are as follows,—the total quantity of each kind of grain and the area of land under each. The total share claimed by all the landlords (हाकिमी हिस्सा *hākimi hissa*) is then struck off. From this the shares of the other share-holders, who keep accounts separate from the landlords whose accounts we are considering, is deducted. To the remainder the cesses and other dues (अबवाब *abwāb*) are added. The total shows the quantity of grain realizable from the tenant by the landlord on whose behalf the account is prepared. This portion of the account showing the demand is called the लग्गित *laggit*. From the total demand the quantity of grain realized during the year is set off, and the balance, if any, is shown. The whole paper showing demand, realization, and balance is called the वासिल बाकी *wāsil bāki*. An abstract of the लग्गित *laggit*, showing under the head of each kind of grain separately the amount of crop of, and area of land under, that grain owned by each tenant, is called the तिरिज लग्गित *tirij laggit*. The abstract of the वासिल बाकी *wāsil bāki* is the ढड्ढा *dhaddha* (No. 14).

(5) The तिरिज जिनिसवार *tirij jiniswār* is compiled from the लग्गित *laggit* (No. 4). It shows in one entry for each tenant the total area he has under cultivation, and the amount of each kind of crop demanded from him.

(6) The सियाहा *siyāha* is the day-book of receipts and disbursements of grain. An abstract of this, called the अवारजा *awārja* or वारजा *wārja*, shows the total receipts and disbursements, date by date.

(7) The हिसाब बिकरी गल्ला *hisāb bikri galla* is the account showing the produce of the sale of the grain received as

rent. It shows the date of sale, quantity sold, rate, and price.

1471. We now come to the accounts of rent paid in cash.

(8) खसरा *khasra* is the paper in which the area (*i.e.*, तूल *tūl* or length and अरज *araj* or breadth) as ascertained by measurement of the lands held by the tenants in a village, together with the rate per bigha or class (पट्टा *patta*) of each plot, is entered. An abstract of this shows the amount measured each day, while the measurement is going on, and is called तिरिज खसरा *tirij khasra.* This खसरा *khasra* gives only the measurement of the lands held temporarily on a cash rent, and differs from the regular खसरा *khasra* or measurement papers of a village.

(9) मोफरीद *mophrīd.*—This is similar to No. 3, *mutatis mutandis.* It shows the area and different rates of rent of the various plots held by each tenant. Each tenant has a separate slip of paper, and all lands for which cash rents are paid, whether temporarily or not, are included in it. It is compiled from No. 8 and No. 10. An abstract of it, called तिरिज मोफरीद *tirij mophrīd,* shows the area of land held and total rent payable by each raiyat.

(10) लग्गित *laggit* and वासिल बाकी *wāsil bāki.*—These are similar, *mutatis mutandis,* to No. 4. They are the ledger account of each tenant. Each tenant has a page, on which is shown the area of his plots, rate of each, rent of each, total area, and total rent. From this the shares of the other shareholders are deducted, and to the remainder the cesses and dues are added, together with the value of any rent in kind (दमाव गल्ला *damāo galla*), due by the raiyat which has not been realized during the year. To this again the arrears of previous years are added, and the total shows the demand against the tenant. The paper thus far is called the लग्गित *laggit.* From the total demand is deducted the cash rent collected during the year, and the balance is struck to be carried to next year's account. The whole paper showing demand, realization, and balance is called

the वासिल बाकी *wāsil bāki*. An abstract of the लग्गित *laggit*, called the तिरिज लग्गित *tirij laggit*, shows under the head of each tenant separately the total area held and rent payable by him at each rate. The abstract of the वासिल बाकी *wāsil bāki* is the ढड्ढा *dhaddha*.

(11) The तिरिज पटेवारी *tirij patewāri* is the paper in which the name of each पट्टा *patta* or separate class of land in the village is entered, showing the total area, rate, and rent of each class. The total shows the total area of land held at various rates in the village. This paper is compiled from No. 10.

(12) The सियाहा *siyāha* is the same (*mutatis mutandis*) as No. 6. In this the daily receipts and disbursements in cash, including the price of grain sold, are entered. It is, in fact, a cash-book. An abstract of this, called the अवारजा *awārja* or वारजा *wārja*, shows the total expenditure day by day.

1472. The following accounts are applicable to both kinds of rent.

(13) The मोलहकी *molhaki* is a ledger account for each tenant, showing date by date all payments (whether in cash or kind) made by him. It is compiled from the सियाहा *siyāha*. An abstract of this, called तिरिज मोलहकी *tirij molhaki*, shows the total payments made during the year by each tenant. The totals of this should agree with the total of No. 12 (the सियाहा *siyāha*) on the receipt side. It hence serves as an abstract of the receipt side of No. 12, while the अवारजा *awārja* is the abstract of the disbursement side.

(14) The ढड्ढा *dhaddha* is also called the तिरिज वासिल बाकी *tirij wāsil bāki* or जमा वासिल बाकी *jama wāsil bāki*. It shows the name of the tenant; area of his holding at each rent; amount of rent; additions on account of cesses, unrealized grain rent and arrears of previous years; deductions on account of shares of other shareholders; deductions on account of cash rent realized; and balance. This paper is in fact an abstract of the वासिल बाकी *wāsil bāki* (Nos. 6 and 10). The latter shows the accounts of each tenant separately,

whereas the ढड्डा *dhaddha* shows all the tenants' accounts on one sheet of paper. This form of account is according to Field* said to have been invented by Udhmant Singh, of Nassipur, in the district of Murshidabad, in order to enable the zamindārs to represent the collections as they pleased to the Muhammadan Government.

(15) The जमाबन्दी *jamābandi* is the paper in which the total annual demand of the village on account of rent is entered. This paper does not usually show illegal demands from the tenants. These are generally shown only in the जमाखरच *jamakharch* (No. 16).

(16) The जमाखरच *jamākharch* is the final annual abstract of the financial condition of the village. It shows the total demand, realization, and balance of the year in more or less detail. The demand side shows the balance of previous year, the total demand according to the जमाबन्दी *jamābandi* (No. 15), and other items of demand (such as fines, illegal cesses, &c.) which do not find their way into the latter. The total is the grand total of the demand for the year. This demand is on the other side of the account again divided into money spent and balance. The money spent includes the portion of the realizations which are forwarded to head-quarters, and the portion of realizations spent on the village and on miscellaneous expenses. The balance is made up of realizations in hand, and for which the village official or the landlord's grain-merchant is responsible, and of unrealized demand, the latter of which is given in detail. Some landlords have two copies of this paper,—one for their own information, containing the illegal cesses, and the other excluding them, so as to allow of its production in court.

1473. In the appendix to this work are given translations of the various forms of account as kept by a Patna landlord.

---

* Law of Evidence, p. 670.

CHAPTER III.—INTEREST, DISCOUNT, AND COMMISSION.

1474. *Discount* and *commission* are generally सलामी *salāmi.* बट्टा *batta* is also used south of the Ganges. In Patna they are also called फिरन्ता *phiranta.* बढ़न्ती *barhti* is a *premium.* सकरई *sakraī* is a *commission* of 3 or 6 pies per cent charged by the acceptor on accepting a bill. नकरई सकरई *nakraī sakraī* is a charge at 8 ānās per cent. on a drawer of a bill when his bill is not accepted. जाबता साह जोग *jābta sāh jog* is a commission at one anna per cent. when the bill is accepted in favour of a banker. हुँडियाना *hundiyāna* or हुँडियावन *hundiyāwan* is commission on a bill-of-exchange (हुण्डी *hundi*). *Factorage*, or the commission (of one or two pice per rupee) taken by a servant on goods bought for his master is दस्तूरी *dastūri*, or, more commonly, फल *phal.* दलाली *dalāli* is *brokerage.*

1475. *Interest* is सूद *sūd.* Interest in kind, paid on seed-grain, is आघी *āghi* to the west and in South-East Tirhut. In South-West Shahabad it is अगवन *agwan*, and in Patna छाड़ा *chhāra* or कढ़ौर *karhaur.* North of the Ganges generally it is also called सवाई डेढ़ी *sawāī derhi*, in allusion to the rate at which the principal is lent. In the south-east it is बियाज *biyāj.* Elsewhere बियाज *biyāj* or बेआज *beāj* is interest on money, which in the south-east is सूद *sūd.* असल *asal* or मूर *mūr* is the capital lent out at interest; but in Shahabad it is also मूल *mūl*, and in the south-east सूदी रुपैया *sūdi rupaiya.* मोनाफा *monāpha* is profit. It is distinguished from interest (which is unlawful for them) by strict Musalmāns. Amongst others, however, the two terms are convertible. Other words for profit are बढ़ोतरी *barhotri* or नाफा *nāpha* in Shahabad, नफा *napha* or इनतिफा *intipha* to the west, इन्ताफा *intāpha* in the south-east, and बचित *bachit* in Patna, Gaya, and South Bhagalpur.

1476. पैंचा *paincha* or हथफेर *hathpher* is a loan when the exact thing is to be returned. A local variant is पैंच *painch* in South-West Shahabad. It is also called उधार *udhār*, which properly means a purchase on credit. करजा *karja* is a money loan. This is also called south of the Ganges करज *karj*, करजवाम *karjwām*, and पैंचा *paincha.* दसगरदाँ *dasgardān* or (amongst the educated) दस्तगरदाँ *dastgardān* is a temporary loan without interest. हथफेर *hathpher* or (in Shahabad) हंथ उधार *hanth udhār* is also used in this sense.

1477. A *debtor* is खदुका *khaduka* or असामी *asāmi.* Local names are खद्दुक *khadduk* in Gaya and the south-west, मुजेरा *mujera* in Patna, and खातब *khātab* in South Bhagalpur. A defaulting debtor is जमामार

jamāmār, also थनम्मार *thanmār* in Champāran and South-East Tirhut, मलम्मार *malmār* in South-West Tirhut, and थैलीमार *thailimār* in South Bhagalpur. Other names are खाऊ *khāu* in Saran, खौकार *khaukār* in South-East Tirhut, and ना देहन *na dehan* in Patna. The educated say ना देहन्द *na dehand*. *Outstandings* are लहना *lahna*. A *bad debt* is गताल खाता *gatāl khāta* in Patna and the north-west, and गयाल खाता *gayāl khāta* in Gaya and the south-west, of which गैल खाता *gail khāta* in South Munger is a variant. In South-West Shahabad it is also said to be गपताल *gaptāl*, in Tirhut they say बूड़ल भेलै *būral bhelai*, and in South Bhagalpur डूबो गेलै *dūbo gelai*. When an animal or other property is *pledged for a debt*, it is called to the north-west and in West Tirhut लावन *lāwan* or लावन झावन *lāwan jhāwan*. Elsewhere it is भरना *bharna* or गिरों *giron*.

1478. To borrow money is सूद पर रुपैया काढ़ब (or काढ़ि लेब, or काढ़ि लाएब) *sūd par rupaiya kārhab* (or *kārhi leb*, or *kārhi lāëb*).

CHAPTER IV.—RATES OF INTEREST.

1479. A rate of interest is दर *dar*. The following are the rates of interest charged. Interest at one per cent. is रुपै सैकड़ा *rupai saikra*, at two per cent., दू रुपै सैकड़ा *du rupai saikra*, and so on:—

(1) डेढ़ा *derha*, डेओढ़ा *deorha*, or in the south-east डेउढ़िया *deurhiya*. This is fifty per cent., *e.g.*, a man borrows five maunds of grain at sowing time and repays 7½ maunds at harvest, without reference to the selling price at the time of borrowing or repayment. This is confined to transactions in grain.

(2) सवाई *sawāi* or सवैया *sawaiya* is twenty-five per cent. as above.

(3) बिकरी के भाव *bikri ke bhāo* (north), or भाव के भाव *bhāo ke bhāo* (south), also असल के असल *asal ke asal* in the south-east.—In this grain is lent, and at harvest time an equivalent in grain to the real money value of the grain lent at the time of borrowing is returned.

(4) लगानी *lagāni* is giving one rupee's worth of grain and after six months receiving back one rupee two annas worth. In South Tirhut it is also called अठरहनी *athrahni*.

(5) पइसे रुपैया *paisė rupaiya* is money interest at one pice per rupee per month. So डेढ़ पैसे रुपैया *derh paise rupaiya* is one and a half pice per rupee per month.

(6) टक॰ही *takhi* is money interest at two pice or one टका *taka* per rupee per mensem. In the south-east it is also called अधअन्नी *adhanni*.

(7) गँड॰ही *gandhi* is money interest at four pice per rupee per month.

(8) चरअन्नी *charanni* is four annas per rupee per annum.

(9) पचअन्नी *pachanni* is five annas per rupee per annum.

(10) छवअन्नी *chawanni* is six annas per rupee per annum.

(11) किस्त *kist* or किस्त बन्दी *kist bandi* is when the total of principal and interest is repayed within a stated time by fixed instalments.

1480. The first money received by a shopkeeper during the day is बोह॰नी *bohni;* also बोह॰नी बट्टा *bohni batta* in Patna and Gaya, and बन॰हाइ *banhāï* in South Bhagalpur. In Patna City it is गँठौट *ganthaut* or गाँठा *gāntha*. A *pledge* or *deposit* is गिरौँ *giroñ* or बन्धिक *bandhik*. In Patna, Gaya, and South Munger it is गिर॰वीँ *girwiñ*, in Shahabad गिरइँ *giraīñ*, in the south-west of that district गिरौँ गाँठ *giroñ-gānth*, and in South Bhagalpur गिर॰मी *girmi*. पुरिया *puriya*, or in East Tirhut पुर॰जा *purja*, is a sealed or fastened-up deposit. जाकड़ *jākar* is goods which are taken away for use, if required, at a wedding, &c. The price is fixed before hand. If the goods are used, this is paid; if they are not used, they are returned, and a pice or two per rupee is paid to the shopkeeper.

CHAPTER V.—MORTGAGE.

1481. A *pawn* or *mortgage* is रेहन *rehan*, बन्धिक *bandhik*, or मक॰फूल *makphūl*. It is also गिरइँ *giraīñ* in Shahabad, and गिर॰मी *girmi* in South Bhagalpur. मक॰फूल *makphūl* is more usually applied to mortgage of land, and the other terms to pawning of moveable articles; but this distinction is not universal. A *mortgagor* is राहिन *rāhin*, and a *mortgagee* is मुर॰तहिन *murtahin*, but these words are seldom used. The villagers prefer to use words like खदुका *khaduka*, खद्दुक *khadduk*, or

असामी *asāmi* for the former, and महाजन *mahājan* for the latter. In Patna a mortgagor is मुजेरा *mujera*, and in Shahabad a mortgagee is बेवहरिया *beohariya*.

1482. A *usufructuary mortgage,* in which both the principal and interest are extinguished by being paid out of the profits of the land mortgaged for a fixed period, is पटौवा *pataua*, सटौवा पटौवा *sataua pataua*, or सधौवा पटौवा *sadhaua pataua*. सूद भरना *sūd bharna* is similar, but the usufruct is only instead of interest, the principal remaining to be paid by the mortgagor. A बै बिल वफा (بیع بالوفا) *bai bil wafa* is a mortgage of property for a fixed period, in which, if the total debt is not repaid within the period, the property becomes the mortgagee's in satisfaction of the debt. Money advanced on the security of standing crops is to the north लागी *lāgi*.

CHAPTER VI.—MISCELLANEOUS.

1483. An *invoice* or *manifest* is बीजक *bījak*, and also to the east चिट्ठा *chittha* or फिरिस्त *phirist*. *Insurance* is बीमा *bīma*, with a variant बींवा *bīñwa* in Shahabad. In the south-west of the latter district it is हुण्डा भारा *hunda bhāra*. Something additional given to a purchaser is north of the Ganges घलुआ *ghalua* or लाभ साभ *lābh sābh*. In South-East Tirhut it is also लाभ *lābh*, and in South-West Tirhut बरकत *barkat*. South of the Ganges it is generally फाव *phāo* or पिछुआ *pichhua*. A variant of the latter is पछुआ *pachhua* in the south-east. Another name is चुटकी *chutki* in Patna. जूग *jūg* is similarly used by women when making petty purchases, especially of vermilion (सेनुर *senur*) and collyrium (मिस्सी *missi*). Other names for this are मँगनी *mangni* to the west and in South Tirhut, मँगनी चँगनी *mangni changni* in Patna, लावा घोली *lāwa gholi* north of the Ganges generally, लावा दूआ *lāwa dūa* in South-West Tirhut, and डाँटी *dānti*. बेआना *beāna* or बयाना *bayāna* is a *handsel* given by the buyer to the seller to secure his purchase.

1484. गल्ला *galla* is a hole in the ground or a bag under the shop-keeper's seat in which he keeps his money. To *test coin* is बूझब *būjhab*, ठोकब *thokab*, परखब *parkhab*, जाँचब *jānchab*, बजाएब *bajāëb*, or आँकनब *anknab*. In the south-east it is परेखब *parekhab*. A *money-tester* is परखी *parkhi* or परखिया *parakhiya*, or जचवैया *jachwaiya*. In the south-east he is परेखिया *parekhiya*. In Patna he is परिख *parikh*, and in Gaya रोकरिया *rokariya*. To test the correctness of scales is साध लेब *sādh leb*. In Patna and the south-east it is धारा करब *dhāra karab*, and in Shahabad पासँघ देखल *pāsangh dekhal*. To test a weight is तारब *tārab* or साधब *sādhab*.

1485. *Capital* is पूँजी *pūnji* or पुञ्जी *punji*, and capital out at interest is बियाजू *biyāju* or बेयाजू *beāju*. It is also called सूदी रुपैया *sūdi rupaiya*. The *adjustment of accounts* is बुझारथ *bujhārath* north of the Ganges, and सफाई *saphāï* south of it. In South-West Shahabad it is बुझौता *bujhauta*. To test the entries is जाँच लेब *jānch leb* or मिला लेब *mila leb*. The testing is in Shahabad जाँच मिलान *jānch milān*. A *release in full* is फारखत्ती *phārkhatti* or फरखत्ती *pharkatti*. In the north-west they say in such a case भुभतान हो गेल *bhubhtān ho gail*, and in the east of Tirhut they say his account is राफ साफ *rāph sāph*, and in Patna that it is बेबाक भैल *bebāk bhail*. In Patna they say बही पर से नाम उतर गेल *bahī par se nām utar gel*, and in South-West Shahabad नाम घेरल गैल *nām gheral gail*, alluding to the custom of encircling the name with a line when the account is cleared off.

1486. To become *bankrupt* is दिवाला निकसब *diwāla niksab*, or दिवाला सुध हो जाएब *diwāla sudh ho jāëb*. To make a man a bankrupt is दिवाला निकासब *diwāla nikāsab*. A bankrupt is दिवालिया *diwāliya*. In Tirhut they would say of such a man साक उखड़ गेलैन्हि *sāk ukhar gelainhi*, or दिवाला उखड़ि गेलैन्हि *diwāla ukhari gelainhi*. In all the above the word may also be spelt देवाला *dewāla*. In Patna they say ओकर टाट उलटल है *okar tāt ultal hai*, in allusion to the custom amongst bankers of a bankrupt turning up one corner of his mat and sitting on it, as a notice of his condition. The action is equivalent to putting up the shutters in England. In connection with this it may be mentioned that Patna is famous for its bankrupts, as in the lines commemorating the three rascals of Bihār :—

भागलपूर के भगेलिया, कहलगाँव के ठग,
पटना के दिवालिया, तीनो नामजद,
सुने पावे छपरहिया, तीनो के तूरे रग.

Bhāgalpūr ke Bhageliya, Kahalgānw ke thag,
Patna ke diwāliya, tīno nāmjad,
Sune pāwe Chhaprahiya, tīno ke tūre rag.

—The Bhagels of Bhagalpur, the thags of Colgong, the bankrupts of Patna, are all famous (sharpers); but if a man of Chhapra hears this, he will beat them (*lit.* burst their veins) all (at their own weapons).

1487. A *bill of exchange* is हुण्डी *hundi* or हुण्डी पत्री *hundi patri*; also in Gaya and the south-west पत॰री *patri*. The duplicate of the bill is पैँठ *painth*. Also, in Patna City, पेठ *peth*. The third duplicate is पर॰पैँठ *parpainth* or पर॰पेठ *parpeth*, and the fourth जिक॰री *jikri* or जिग॰री *jigri*. This last is also a letter to a person other than the drawer for the acceptance of his endorsement by the drawer. A *letter of advice* is समाचारी चिट्ठी *samāchāri chitthi*. A *bill payable at sight* is दर॰सनी *darsani*. In Patna such bills by custom bear eleven days' date. If payable after a future date, it is मियादी *miyādi* or मुदती *mudati*. One payable five days after sight is called पहुँच पर॰मान *pahunch parmān* or (in Patna City) पहुँचे दाम *pahunche dām*. The *address* at the head of a banker's letter is जोग *jog* or सिर॰नामा *sirnāma*. A bill paid and discharged is खोखा *khokha*. In Patna it is also भुग॰तान *bhugtān*, and north of the Ganges भुभ॰तान *bhubhtān*. To *accept* a bill is सकारब *sakārab*. The date on which a bill falls due is called मित्ती *mitti*, which indeed in mercantile transactions is the general word for dates of all kinds.

1488. A *warehouse* is गोदाम *godām*. हर॰जा *harja* is *demurrage*. मह॰सूल *mahsūl* or मासूल *māsūl* is *customs, postage,* or *railway freight,* &c. A *price-current* is निरख नामा *nirakh nāma*. *Cash* or *specie* is नगद *nagad*, नग॰दा नग॰दी *nagda nagdi*, or रोक *rok*. पाव॰ना *pāwna* is a *claim*, and रसीद *rasīd* a *receipt* टक॰साल *taksāl* is a *mint*. *Merchandise* is सौदाग॰री के माल *saudāgri ke māl*. *Imports* are आम॰दनी *āmdani*, and *exports* रफ॰तनी *raphtani*.

DIVISION XIV.

WEIGHTS AND MEASURES.

CHAPTER I.—MEASURES OF LENGTH.

1489. The अङ्गुल *angul* is a finger-breadth, equal to about two-thirds of an inch. The width of the four fingers of one hand, *i.e.*, four अङ्गुल *angul*, is called a चौआ *chaua*. Instead of this, a measure is used in Shahabad called मुट्ठा *muttha*, which is the width of the closed fist. Twelve finger-breadths make one span, which is बित्ता *bitta* or बिलस्ता *bilasta*, or to the north-east बिल्हस्त *bilhast*, to the south-east बिलस्त *bilast*. South of the Ganges a still smaller scale is current. A सूत *sūt* is the thickness of thread.

3 सूत *sūt* = 1 पैन *pain*.
3 पैन *pain* = 1 finger-breadth.

1490. In Shahabad and the south-east a finger-breadth is तस्सुर *tassur*. In Shahabad and Patna in measuring wood, however, a तस्सुर *tassur* equals two finger-breadths, and fourteen of these make one गज *gaj* or हाथ *hāth* (wood measure). Twenty-four finger-breadths, or six चौआ *chaua*, or two बित्ता *bitta*, make one हाँथ *hānth* or हाथ *hāth*, which is a cubit. The हाथ *hāth* is the standard from which the others are taken, and varies from 15 to 20 inches in length, 18 inches being the average.

1491. Two cubits make one डेग *deg* or pace, and also one गज *gaj* or yard. A गिरह *girah*, गिरेह *gireh*, or गिरे *gire* is the length of the forefinger, and 16 go to a गज *gaj*. Another name for a गिरह *girah* is कन्‍वाँ *kanwān* in Patna and Gaya. Three गज *gai* or six cubits make one लग्गा *lagga* or लग्गी *laggi*, which is also called बाँस *bāns* south of the Ganges, and लट्ठा *lattha* in South-West Shahabad. Another गज *gaj* is the सिकन्दरी गज *Sikandri gaj*, also called बरा गज *bara gaj* or बड़का गज *barka gaj*, which is 2¼ cubits north of the Ganges and 48 fingers or 2 cubits south of it. It was the yard used in land measuring until Akbar's time, and properly equals 26 inches, but has become in the village mind confused with the बरा गज *bara gaj*. This is the tailor's yard, and is called by them कतई गज *kataī gaj* or कत्ती गज *katti gaj*. Akbar introduced as the standard measure of the empire the इलाही गज *ilāhi gaj*, equal to 33⅝ inches, which is still in use in the North-West Provinces.

1492. In South-East Tirhut and Patna धाप *dhāp* equals डेग *deg* or कदम *kadam*, a pace, but elsewhere north of the Ganges and in the south-east it is about half a कोस *kos;* see below. Another name of this last is मैल *mail* or मील *mīl*, a corruption of the English 'mile.' The रस्सी *rassi* or रसरी *rasri* is equal to 20 लग्गी *laggi* or 120 cubits. In South-West Shahabad 70 cubits make a रस्सी *rassi*. Generally 60 रस्सी *rassi* make one कोस *kos*, but in South-West Shahabad it is 50 रस्सी *rassi*. The कोस *kos* varies greatly in length in different districts. An ordinary कोस *kos* is however 60 रस्सी *rassi*, 1,200 लग्गी *laggi*, or 3,600 गज *gaj* or yards, or 80 yards more than two miles. The गौकोस *gaukos* is a vague measure of distance, as far as a cow's bellow can be heard. A कच्चा कोस *kachcha kos* is a short कोस *kos*, and धाप *dhāp* (see above) is generally about a mile.

1493. A cubit used in measuring earthwork and well-sinking is तरन्हा *tarha* to the north-west and खनित *khanit* (literally, digging) in the south-west. In South-West Shahabad and South-East Tirhut it is खन्ता *khanta*. In Gaya it is तरन्रा *tarra*, and to the south-east गिलन्दाजी *gilandāji* (which means simply earth-work). In digging a well the depth is measured in men's heights, called पुरिस *pūris*, &c. See § 923.

1494. The following table shows the relative value of the principal measures of length.

	Sut or thread.	*Pain* ...	*Anguli*, or finger-breadth.	*Chaua* ...	*Bitta*, or span	*Hath*, or cubit	*Gaj*, or yard...	*Laggi*, or rod...	*Rassi* ...
Sut or thread.									
Pain ...	3								
Anguli, or finger-breadth.	9	3							
Chaua ...	36	12	4						
Bitta, or span	108	36	12	3					
Hath, or cubit	216	2	24	6	2				
Gaj, or yard...	432	144	48	12	4	2			
Laggi, or rod...	1,200	432	144	36	12	6	3		
Rassi ...	25,920	8,640	2,880	720	240	120	60	20	
Kos, i.e., 2 miles 80 yards.	1,555,200	518,400	172,800	43,200	14,400	7,200	3,600	1,200	60

CHAPTER II.—SUPERFICIAL MEASURE.

1495. The पक्का बिगन्हा *pakka bigha* is fixed at 14,400 square feet, or 1,600 square yards. It is therefore a little less than ⅓ of the English acre of 4,840 square yards. The कच्चा बिगन्हा *kachcha bigha* varies in every *pargana;* it is generally smaller than, but is sometimes larger than, the standard. The foundation of the size of the *bigha* is the लग्गी *laggi* (see above, § 1491), which varies greatly in the number of cubits which it contains. A square लग्गी *laggi* is a धूर *dhūr*. Twenty धूर *dhūr* make one कट्ठा *kattha*, and 20 कट्ठा *kattha* make one बिगन्हा *bigha*. In Shahabad a कट्ठा *kattha* is called a बिसन्वा *biswa*. In East Tirhut a बिगन्हा *bigha* is also called कूरो *kūro*. North of the Ganges 4 पाइ *pāï* make one धूर *dhūr;* south of it—

9 square चौवा *chaua* make 1 sq. डेग *deg* or कदम *kadam.*
9 „ डेग 1 sq. धूर *dhūr.*

CHAPTER III.—MEASURES OF PROPORTION.

1496. Proportion is generally expressed by saying so many annas in the rupee. Thus 10 annas in the rupee = 10 : 16; 4 annas in the rupee = 1: 4; 8 annas in the rupee = 1 : 2; and so on. In calculating proportionate shares in estates, two systems are in vogue. In both the estate (मौजा *mauja* or महाल *mahāl*) is the unit. In one system the following is the scale:—

1 मौजा *mauja* or महाल *mahāl* = 16 आना *āna.*
1 आना *āna* = 20 दाम *dām.*
1 दाम *dām* = 20 कौड़ी *kauri.*
1 कौड़ी *kauri* = 20 बौड़ी *bauri.*
1 बौड़ी *bauri* = 20 फौड़ी *phauri.*
1 फौड़ी *phauri* = 20 रौड़ी *rauri.*

The other system is as follows:—

1 मौजा *mauja* or महाल *mahāl* = 16 आना *āna.*
1 आना *āna* = 12 पाइ *pāï.*
1 पाइ *pāï* = 20 कराँत *karānt.*
1 कराँत *karānt* = 20 मसाँत *masānt.*
1 मसाँत *masānt* = 20 डिसमिल *dismil* (? = *decimal*).
1 डिसमिल *dismil* = 20 बिसमिल *bismil.*

The first system is called the Hindūstāni, and the second the English system.

CHAPTER IV.—MEASURES OF WEIGHT.

1497. 25 दाम *dām* are counted to the pice (पैसा *paisa*). A दमड़ी *damri* is a nominal coin equal to 3⅛ दाम *dām*. The अद्धी *addhi* is half a दमड़ी *damri*. The टक्का *takka* or टका *taka* = 50 दाम *dām* or two pice, and the अधेला *adhela* or (in South-West Shahabad) अधेलचा *adhelcha*, is 12½ दाम *dām*, or half a pice. The दोकड़ा or दोकरा *dokra* or छदाम *chhadām* is 6¼ दाम *dām*, or ¼ of a pice. A pice is also called ढेबुआ *dhebua* or (in Gaya) कच्चा *kachcha*. The छदाम *chhadām* or sixteenth part of an *āna* is also called कनवई *kanwaī*, कनवाँ *kanwān*, or छटाँक *chhatānk*. The following table will make this clear :—

Dām.	3⅛	6¼	12½	25	50	100
	Damri.	2	4	8	16	32
		Chhadām.	2	4	8	16
			Adhela.	2	4	8
				Paisa or pice.	2	4
					Taka.	2
						Āna or anna.

1498. In weighing, the रत्ती *ratti* of 1·875 grains Troy is taken as the standard. From this the following scheme may be drawn up :—

8 रत्ती *ratti* = 1 माशा *māsa* = 15 grains Troy.

12 माशा *māsa* = 1 तोला *tola* = 7 dwt. 12 grains Troy or the weight of one rupee.

5 तोला *tola* = 1 कनन्वाँ *kanwān* or छटाँक *chhatānk* = 1oz. 17 dwt. 12 grains Troy.

16 कनन्वाँ *kanwān* or छटाँक *chhatānk* = 1 सेर *ser* = 2lb. 6 oz Troy.

40 सेर *ser* = 1 मन *man* = 100lb. Troy = 82·286lb. Avoirdupois. This is the standard मन *man* or maund, and 27·222 of these go to the English ton.

For larger weights the सेर *ser* is the standard. In local bazārs it varies greatly, not only according to locality, but according to goods sold. The bazār सेर *ser* is named as containing so many गण्डा *ganda*, a गण्डा *ganda* consisting of four तोला *tola* or sometimes four pice, and being a constant quantity.

1499. In weighing gold, jewels, &c., the standard is the red seed (*abrus precatorius*) called the करञ्जनी *karjani*, लाल *lāl*, or कच्ची रत्ती *kachchi ratti*. It is said to weigh three barleycorns (जौ *jau*).

The jeweller's scale is as follows :—

3 जौ *jau* = 1 लाल *lāl*.

4 *ditto* = 1 रत्ती *ratti*.

2 लाल *lāl* = $1\frac{1}{2}$ रत्ती *ratti*.

4 रत्ती *ratti* = 1 चौरत्ती *chauratti*.

$5\frac{1}{4}$ *ditto* = 1 अन्नी *anni*.

8 *ditto* = 1 माशा *māsa*, मस्सा *massa*, or मसिका *masika* = 15 grs. Troy.

$10\frac{1}{2}$ *ditto* = 1 दुअन्नी *duanni*.

8 दुअन्नी *duanni* or $10\frac{1}{2}$ माशा *māsa* = 1 ढक *dhak* or (in South-West Shahabad) ढाका *dhāka*, which is the weight of a rupee = 6 dwts. $6\frac{3}{4}$ grs. Troy.

12 माशा *māsa* = 1 तोला *tola* = 7 dwts. 12 grs. Troy. Here it will be seen that the jeweller's rupee is less than a tola.

1500. The following weights are common throughout Bihār :—

छटङ्की *chhatanki* = $\frac{1}{16}$ of a *ser*.

अधन्पई *adhpai*, अधन्पाऊ *adhpāū*, or अधन्पौआ *adhpaua* = $\frac{1}{8}$ of a *ser*

पाव *pāw*, पावा *pāwa*, or पौआ *paua* = $\frac{1}{4}$ of a *ser*.

अधन्सेरा *adhsera* or असेरा *asera* = $\frac{1}{2}$ a *ser*.

तिनन्पौआ *tinpaua* = $\frac{3}{4}$ of a *ser*.

सवैया *sawaiya*, properly $1\frac{1}{4}$ *ser* ; really $\frac{1}{4}$ of a पसेरी *paseri*.

डेढ़न्सेर *derhseri* = $1\frac{1}{2}$ *ser*.

अढ़ा *arha*, अढ़ैया *arhaiya*, properly $2\frac{1}{2}$ *ser* ; really $\frac{1}{2}$ of a पसेरी *paseri*.

तिनन्सेरा *tinsera* or तिनन्सेरी *tinseri* = 3 *ser*.

चरन्सेरा *charsera* or चरन्सेरी *charseri* = 4 *ser*.

पसेरी *paseri*, also (in Shahabad) पचन्सेरा *pansera*, or पचन्सेरी *panseri*. This is properly 5 *ser*, but varies greatly. It is usually said to be 7 *ser kachcha*, but is sometimes only 5 or 6. Vegetable-sellers generally call it 6 *ser*.

धारा *dhāra* = 10 *ser*. In Shahabad it sometimes means 5 *ser*.

APPENDIX.

FORMS OF ACCOUNTS USED IN A LANDLORD'S OFFICE IN PATNA.

1.

खसरा दानाबन्दी *Khasra Dānābandi.*

YEAR.—

Khasra Dānābandi of the *Crop in the Estate of*

DATE.—

Name of tenant.	Length.	Breadth.	Area of plot.	Kind of crop.	Amount of crop estimated.

1a.

तिरिज तारीखवार *Tirij Tārīkhwār.*

YEAR.—

Tirij Tārīkhwār of the Khāsra Dānābandi of Village

Date.	Total area of crop estimated.	Total amount of crop estimated.

2.

खस्रा बटाइ *Khasra Batăï.*

YEAR.—

Khasra of Division of *Crop in the Estate of*

DATE.—

Name of tenant.	Area.	Kind of crop.	Amount of grain.	Landlord's share.	*Dahiyak.**	*Pansera.*†	Total of columns 5 to 7.

2a.

Abstract of the above.

(1) Date ... ...
(2) Area ... ...
(3) Total amount of grain ... ...
(4) Landlord's share ... ...
(5) दहियक *dahiyak** ... ...
(6) पन्सेरा *pansera*† ... ...
(7) Total ... ...
(8) सोनारी *sonarī* (weighman's fees) ...
(9) गञ्ज अफ्जूद *ganj aphjud*‡ ... ...
(10) बढ़ी *barhi* § ... ...
(11) सद्धी *saddhi* || ... ...
(12) Total ... ...

In the original, the columns run across the page instead of from top to bottom.

* *Vide* foot note to form (5).

† After the division of crop, *dahiyak* is added to the landlord's share, to which again 5 seers are added, that quantity being taken from the tenant's share under the name of *pansera*.

‡ Grain found in excess at the time of second weighment on the floor after the grain has been taken over by the landlord.

§ Grain found in excess at the time of third weighment, when the grain has been carried to the landlord's granary.

|| Grain found in excess owing to swelling, &c., when the whole amount of grain stored has been sold off.

3.

मोफ्रीद *Mophrīd.*

YEAR.—

Mophrīd of the Rent in Kind for the Crop.

NAME OF TENANT.—

Black Paddy.

Date of Estimate.	Area.	Amount of Crop.

Paddy Sown Broadcast.

Date of Estimate.	Area.	Amount of Crop.

Bāsmatti Paddy.

Date of Estimate.	Area.	Amount of Crop.

and so on for every kind of grain in the tenant's holding.

Total Area.	Total Amount of Grain.

3a.

Abstract of the last.

YEAR.—

Name of Tenant.	Total Area.	Amount of Crop.

4.

लग्गित *Laggit and* वासिल बाकी *Wāsil Bāki.*

YEAR.—

Laggit of Rents Paid in Kind for the Whole Year.

NAME OF TENANT.—

Kind of grain.	Area.	Total grain.	Share of landlord.	*Dahiyak.**	Total due.	Realized.	Balance.

* *See* note to form 5.

4a.

Abstract of the last.

YEAR.—

Black Paddy.

Name of Tenant.	Area.	Amount due.

White Paddy.

Name of Tenant.	Area.	Amount due.

and so on for each kind of grain.

5.

तिरिज जिनिसवार *Tirij Jiniswār.*

YEAR.—

Tirij Jiniswār for the Village of

1. Name of tenant.
2. Area under cultivation.
3. Grain due.
4. *Dahiyak.**
5. Total.
6. Amount of maize.
7. Ditto of *marua.*
8. Ditto of *sāthi* paddy.

And so on, a separate column being allotted to each crop.

In the original, the form runs across the page in columns, and not from top to bottom.

* This is the amount the landlord receives in addition to his half share. South of the Ganges he generally realizes 5 *ser* per *man*, *i.e.* he receives 9 *ser* in every 16 *ser*, the tenant's share being 7 *ser*. This division of crop is called "नौसत्ता *nausatta*," *i.e.* 9—7 See § 906.

6.

सियाहा *Siyāha.*

YEAR.—

Day-book of Receipts and Disbursements of Grain.

DATE.—

Receipts.	Amount.	*Disbursements.*	Amount.
From so and so— *Sāthi* paddy 6 maunds, Broadcast paddy ... 2 „	7 maunds	Sent to the landlord ...	......
		Sold, viz.	......
From so and so	......	Total Mds. ...	
Total Mds. ...		Balance Mds. ...	

6a.

Abstract of above, or अवारजा *Awārja.*

Receipts.		Expenditure.	
Date.	Amount of Grain.	Date.	Amount of Grain.

7.

हिसाव विकरी गल्ला *Hisāb Bikri Galla.*

Year.—

Date.	Amount sold.	Rate.	Price realized.

8.

खसरा *Khasra.*

YEAR.—

Khasra showing the Measurements of Lands let at Cash Rates in the Village of

DATE.—

Name of Tenant.	Length.	Breadth.	Area.	Class of Land or rate per bigha.

8a.

Abstract of the above.

YEAR.—

Tirij Khasra showing the Measurements of Lands let at Cash Rates in the Village of

Date.	Area.

9.

मोफ़र्रीद *Mophrid.*

Mophrid of the Lands paying Cash Rates in the Village of

YEAR.—

NAME OF TENANT.—

At Rs. 4 per bigha.

Date of Measurement.	Area.

At Rs. 3 per bigha.

Date of Measurement.	Area.

and so on for the various rates at which the tenant holds.

9a.

Abstract of the above.

YEAR.—

Tirij Mophrid of the Lands paying Cash Rates in the Village of

Name of Tenant.	Area held by him.	Rent.

10.

लग्गित *Laggit and* वासिल-बाकी *Wāsil-bāki.*

YEAR.—

Laggit of Rents payable in Cash in the Village of

NAME OF TENANT.—

Class of land held by him.	Area.	Rate of the class.	Rent.

Total rent ... ...
Cesses... ... ...
Value of unrealized rent in kind for the year ... ...
Arrears of previous years ... ...

Total demand ... ...
Deduct realizations ... ...

Balance to be carried to next year's account ... ...

10a.

Abstract of the above.

YEAR.—

तिरिज लग्गित *Tirij Laggit of Lands paying Cash Rates in the Village of*

At Rs. 4 per bigha.

Name of Tenant.	Area.	Rent.

At Rs. 3 per bigha.

Name of Tenant.	Area.	Rent.

and so on for each rate of rent.

11.

तिरिज पटेवारी *Tirij Patewāri for the Village of*

Class of Land or Degrees of Rate.	Area.	Rate.	Rent.
1st class	......	......	......
2nd do.	......	......	......
And so on	......	......	......

12.

सियाहा *Siyāha.*

YEAR.—

Day-book of Receipts and Disbursements of Cash.

DATE.—

RECEIPTS.		EXPENDITURE.	
Name of Tenant.	Amount paid.	Description of expenditure.	Amount.

BALANCE.

12a.

Abstract of the above, or अवारजा *Awārja, showing Expenditure only.*

Amount sent to Landlord.

Date.	Amount.

Salary of Village Establishment paid.

Date.	Amount.

गिलन्दाजी *Gilandâji Expenses (Repairs to Embankments, &c.)*

Date.	Amount.

गरामन्ता *Garămta (Diet-money supplied to the* गोरैत *Gorait, who takes Money to the Landlord).*

Date.	Amount.

and so on.

13.

मौल॰हकी *Molhaki.*

YEAR.—

Molhaki of Payments in Cash and Kind for the Whole Year.

NAME OF TENANT.—

CASH PAYMENTS.		PAYMENTS IN KIND.	
Date.	Amount.	Date.	Amount of Grain.

13a.

Abstract of the above.

YEAR.—

Name of Tenant.	Total amount paid by him in cash.	Total amount paid by him in kind.

14.

ढड्डा *Dhaddha.*

(In the original, the columns run across the page, instead of from top to bottom. The various cesses, &c., named are only samples, and differ in every village.)

YEAR.—

Dhaddha Wāsilbāki for the Whole Year in the Village of

Columns.

(1) Name of tenant.
(2) Area of holding in subheads according to rate and class.
(3) Rent.
(4) दुअन्नी *duanni.**
(5) Weighman's fees (सोनारी *sonāri*).
(6) काह चराइ *kāh charāī.*†
(7) कोठी सोरा *kothi sora.*‡
(8) मोतरफा *motarpha.*§
(9) बिकरी आम *bikri am* (price of mangos).
(10) तार *tār* (rent of toddy-palms).
(11) Rent for *mahua* trees.
(12) मछली *machhli* (fishery-dues).
(13) Total of above.
(14) बट्टा माल *batta māl.*‖
(15) बट्टा कम्पनी *batta kampani.*‖
(16) Road-cess.
(17) Unrealized grain-rent.
(18) Arrears.
(19) Grand total of demand.
(20) Deduct share of other landlords.
(21) Remainder, *i.e.*, हिस्सा खास *hissa khās* (own share).
(22) Realized.
(23) Balance due.
(24) Credit, realized in excess.

---

* See § 1201.

† Dues for grazing cattle. All cattle, except buffalos, are generally exempt. Each buffalo is charged at from 2 to 4 annas a year. See § 1151.

‡ Rent of a saltpetre factory.

§ Rent of houses occupied by shopkeepers, oil-men, weavers, and other non-cultivating tenants. See § 1201.

‖ See § 1202. These are only charged on rent of land and on old settlements of other kinds. For instance, if a new settlement is made of toddy palms, it is made in Company's rupees, and no exchange rate is added to the rent. The addition of a rate of exchange, in fact, depends on whether the settlement is made in old coinage or in new; and according to custom, rent of land is generally settled, even at the present day, in the old coinage, but not so other rents.

15.

जमाबन्दी *Jamābandi.*

Jamābandi of Village *for the Whole Year* *F. S.*

Note.—The order of the items has been reversed for the sake of clearness. In the original, according to native custom, the totals are written first, and under them the subsidiary items. For a similar reason imaginary figures have been written against the various items.

	Area.			Demand.		
	B.	K.	DH.	Rs.	A.	P.
Land of 1st class, at Rs. 4 ...	200	0	0	800	0	0
Ditto 2nd ditto 3 ...	800	0	0	2,400	0	0
Ditto 3rd ditto 2-8 ...	500	0	0	1,250	0	0
Ditto 4th ditto 2 ...	500	0	0	1,000	0	0
And so on.						
Total area under cultivation ...	2,000	0	0			
Add area not under cultivation ...	100	0	0			
Total area of village ...	2,100	0	0			
Total rent-demand ...	......			5,450	0	0
Add cesses (only legal ones entered here) ...	......			300	0	0
सायर *sāyar* (*i.e.*, miscellaneous rights, *e.g.*, fishing-rights. Cf, § 1232) ...	......			250	0	0
Total demand under *jamābandi* ...	......			6,000	0	0

16.

जमाखर्च *Jamākharch.*

Jamākharch of Village *for the Whole Year* *F. S.*

Note.—The order of items has been reversed as in No. 15, from which also the imaginary figures are carried into this form.

DEMANDS.

Nature of Demands.	Rs. A. P.	Rs. A. P.
Balance of arrears of previous year's *jamakharch*—		
(*a*) Principal	300 0 0	
(*b*) Interest thereon, and fines, &c., on defaulters in respect to it	50 0 0	
Total Balance ...	......	350 0 0
Demand for present year—		
(*a*) As per *jamābandi*	6,000 0 0	
(*b*) Not in *jamābandi* (Here are entered in detail all illegal cesses, &c., which have been excluded from the *jamābandi*) Total, say	400 0 0	
Total for present year ...	......	6,400 0 0
GRAND TOTAL OF DEMAND ...	......	6,750 0 0

OUTGOINGS.

Nature of Outgoings.	Rs. A. P.	Rs. A. P.
Realized in cash and remitted to landlord ...	4,000 0 0	
Ditto in kind ditto ditto ...	500 0 0	
Total remitted to landlord ...	......	4,500 0 0
Village expenses—		
Salary of establishment	500 0 0	
गिलन्दाजी *gilandāji** expenses	247 0 0	
And so on.		
Total village expenses ...	......	747 0 0
Miscellaneous expenses—		
पनियोचा *paniyocha*†	150 0 0	
गरामता *garāmta**	3 0 0	
And so on in detail.		
Total miscellaneous expenses ...	......	153 0 0
Balance—		
With the *gumāshta* (in hand)	50 0 0	
Due from the tenants (each tenant's name in detail)	1,100 0 0	
With the grain-merchants‡	200 0 0	
Total balance ...	......	1,350 0 0
GRAND TOTAL ...	......	6,750 0 0

* See No 12*a*. | † Price of water supplied by a neighbouring landlord for irrigation. | ‡ This last balance is technically called लागी *lāgi*.

INDEX.

(The numbers refer to paragraphs.)

॥ अ *a* ॥

॥ आ *ā* ॥

॥ इ *i* ॥

॥ ई *ī* ॥

॥ उ *u* ॥

॥ ऊ *ū* ॥

॥ ए *e* ॥

॥ ए *e* ॥

॥ ऐ *ai* ॥

॥ ऐ *ai* ॥

॥ औ *o* ॥

॥ ओ *o* ॥

॥ औ *au* ॥

॥ औ *au* ॥

॥ क *k* ॥

॥ ख *kh* ॥

॥ ग *g* ॥

॥ घ *gh* ॥

॥ च *ch* ॥

॥ छ *chh* ॥

॥ ज *j* ॥

॥ झ *jh* ॥

॥ ट *t* ॥

॥ ठ *th* ॥

॥ ड *d* ॥

॥ ढ *dh* ॥

॥ त *t* ॥

॥ थ *th* ॥

॥ द *d* ॥

॥ ध *dh* ॥

॥ न *n* ॥

॥ प *p* ॥

॥ फ *ph* ॥

॥ ब *b* ॥

॥ भ *bh* ॥

॥ म *m* ॥

॥ य *y* ॥

॥ र *r* ॥

॥ ल *l* ॥

॥ व *w* ॥

॥ श *sh* ॥

॥ स *s* ॥

॥ ह *h* ॥